Humanism in Italian Renaissance
Musical Thought

Claude V. Palisca

HUMANISM IN ITALIAN RENAISSANCE MUSICAL THOUGHT

Yale University Press
New Haven and London

Published with assistance from the Louis Stern Memorial Fund.

Designed by Nancy Ovedovitz and set in Bembo type by Rainsford Type. Printed in the United States of America by Edwards Brothers, Inc., Ann Arbor, Michigan.

Library of Congress Cataloging in Publication Data

Palisca, Claude V.
  Humanism in Italian Renaissance musical thought
  Bibliography: p.
  Includes index.
  1. Music—Italy—15th century—History and criticism. 2. Music—Italy—16th century—History and criticism. 3. Renaissance—Italy. 4. Humanism. I. Title.
ML290.2.P34 1985 781.745 85–8190
ISBN 0–300–03302–8

10 9 8 7 6 5 4 3 2 1

To the memory of my mother
Gisella Fleischhacker Palisca (1895–1944)

Contents

Preface

Music historians have long been aware of a link between the revival of ancient learning and the changes in musical style and theory that occurred during the Renaissance. But the ties to antiquity have been hard to pin down, because ancient music could not be recreated as could ancient literature and architecture. Instead, the objects of revival were ancient attitudes and thoughts about music. The route by which these reached Renaissance musicians and critics has not been studied with any precision or thoroughness. Indeed, the men most responsible for the transmission of Greek thought about music have been practically ignored. Their names, some of which head chapters or sections in this book—Pietro d'Abano, Giorgio Valla, Carlo Valgulio, Antonio Gogava, Francesco Burana, Nicolò Leoniceno—are missing from even the most comprehensive accounts of the musical culture of the Renaissance.

This book aims to document the debt that Renaissance musical thought owes to ancient, particularly Greek, musical thought and to trace its path of transmission in Italy. I have had to rely almost entirely on primary sources. Because of this necessity, the previous literature on musical humanism and on music in the Renaissance has been given less attention than it truly deserves. Therefore I want to express here my debt to those who earlier explored musical humanism and lighted my way, particularly Edward E. Lowinsky, Paul O. Kristeller, Nino Pirrotta, Leo Schrade, D. P. Walker, and Edith Weber, for I have learned enormously from them.

In general the field has been dominated by the hunt for parallels between musical manifestations and those in other arts and humanities that show a strong reliance on ancient models. But even where parallels have been found, there has been little direct evidence of relationships among the composers, writers, philosophers, architects, and artists whose work is involved. I cannot claim to have discovered many such associations either, so the search must continue, for where no direct connections can be shown, the concurrent trends, like parallel lines, never meet, and we can learn little from simply contemplating the striking analogies. I have avoided drawing such parallels, limiting myself to those connections between music and ancient thought that we know existed in the minds of Renaissance men because they are recorded in writing. These considerations, too, explain why I have not allocated much space to past literature on musical humanism. As a consequence of this approach and the interdisciplinary scope of my study, the secondary literature referred to in the footnotes is restricted to those works that were specifically utilized for the material in the text, and the bibliography lists only these.

Some chapters may strike the reader as almost anthologies of extracts from Renaissance writings on music and related subjects. Since so many of the works quoted are unpublished or extremely rare, this was the only way I could let my authors speak for themselves. And since none of them wrote in English, I wanted to let the reader experience the power of their own words, with the aid of parallel translations. Whenever possible the material in the two columns corresponds line for line, consequences of which are a certain literalness and a ragged format. The translations are my own except where I have indicated otherwise.

Many organizations and individuals have generously supported my research over the years. It was begun in Florence on a Guggenheim Fellowship and completed on a second one twenty years later. In between, a Senior Fellowship of the National Endowment for the Humanities permitted a year in Paris at the remarkable collection of Renaissance books of the Bibliothèque Nationale. The Whitney Griswold Fund of Yale University aided the preparation of the manuscript. And, of course, the Yale libraries, particularly the Music Library and the Beinecke Rare Book and Manuscript Library, provided a solid home base for my investigations.

Several of my students at Yale have helped me during various stages. Joseph DiGiovanni, of the Renaissance Studies Program, transcribed parts of Leoniceno's translation of Ptolemy's *Harmonics*. Deborah Narcini, of the Medieval Studies Program, checked my translations of Pietro d'Abano's commentary on the pseudo-Aristotle *Problems*. Otto Steinmayer, of the Classics Department, reviewed most of my translations from Latin and made many essential improvements in them.

Of the many colleagues to whom I feel indebted, I should name several. Jon Solomon, of the University of Arizona, kindly made available his translation of Cleonides' *Harmonic Introduction*. Frank d'Accone, of the University of California, Los Angeles, and James Haar, of the University of North Carolina, contributed to my thinking with their learned commentaries on my first chapter when it was delivered as a lecture in honor of A. Tillman Merritt's retirement from Harvard. Thomas J. Mathiesen, of Brigham Young

University, enriched and enhanced this book in many ways, by lending me microfilms of Greek manuscripts that once belonged to Giorgio Valla, by letting me use some of the information in the catalog of Greek manuscripts of music theory he is preparing for the *Répertoire internationale des sources musicales,* by reviewing my translations of the Latin versions of Greek treatises by Burana, Leoniceno, Gogava, and Augio and offering many provident corrections and excellent suggestions, and, finally, by reading and commenting on the entire manuscript. To these scholars I, and the reader too, owe sincere thanks.

Among others who have stood behind this work, I give special thanks to Edward Tripp, Editor-in-Chief of the Yale University Press, for his encouragement and interest, to Jean van Altena for her very attentive reading and sympathetic editing, to Michael Pepper and Jay Williams for their resourceful recoding and production of the manuscript from its electronic state, to my daughter Madeline for her punctilious drafting of the index, and to my wife, Jane, for advice on many matters, big and small, and for her confidence and unfailing support.

Branford October 1984

ONE

Introduction: An Italian Renaissance in Music?

istorians generally view the Renaissance as a movement that began in Italy and spread northward. Music historians, however, have habitually begun the study of music in the Renaissance with composers associated with France and the Low Countries. Gustave Reese organized his book *Music in the Renaissance* on the premise that a central musical language arose in the fifteenth and sixteenth centuries in France, the Low Countries, and Italy, and spread to Spain, Portugal, Germany, England, and eastern Europe. In the first part of the book he defines this language in terms of the music of Dufay, Busnois, and Ockeghem, who were active principally in the north.[1]

Similarly Howard Mayer Brown takes the view that music in the Renaissance "is a northern art, or at least an art by northerners. All of the great composers of the fifteenth and early sixteenth centuries were born in what is today northern France, Belgium, and Holland."[2]

Thus, while the impetus for the Renaissance in the visual arts, literature, and philosophy is generally recognized to have come from Italy and moved across the Alps, we are confronted in music history with the thesis that music, of all artistic expressions, moved in the opposite direction. Now contrary motion may be a praiseworthy polyphonic practice, but it is disconcerting when applied to cultural historiography. If history in general has a proverbial "problem of the Renaissance," how much more acute it is in music history!

Heinrich Besseler, reflecting on his own work in Renaissance studies since

1. Gustave Reese, *Music in the Renaissance* (New York, 1954), Pt. I.
2. Howard Mayer Brown, *Music in the Renaissance* (Englewood Cliffs, 1976), p. 4. Leo Schrade, in "Renaissance: the Historical Conception of an Epoch," *Kongress-Bericht der Internationale Gesellschaft für Musikwissenschhaft, Utrecht 1952* (Amsterdam, 1953), pp. 19–32, took a similar view: "In contrast to the bonae litterae and to the visual arts as well, the rebirth of music came to pass as an achievement of northern composers . . . " (p. 30).

1

his *Die Musik des Mittelalters und der Renaissance* of 1931,[3] admitted in 1966 that he did not in that work look closely at the word or its meaning and now felt that "Renaissance" is "certainly the most problematic epoch-designation in the history of culture."[4] Besseler recalled that the word itself was not Italian but French and was first applied to historical periodization by a French historian, Jules Michelet, in 1855 in the subtitle of the seventh volume of his *Histoire de France*. In the introduction Michelet spoke of the rediscovery of the things of this world, of man.[5] Anticlerical in his leanings, Michelet celebrated what he saw as the triumph of the secular spirit. Five years later Jacob Burckhardt adopted the term in *Die Kultur der Renaissance in Italien* (Basel, 1860), which by 1919 had gone through twelve editions.

Although Besseler appreciated the book's enormous influence, he found a major fault in Burckhardt's failure to link the Renaissance with the Middle Ages. Burckhardt also failed to give sufficient credit to the religious component of the movement. Besseler reviews the corrective efforts of Henry Thode,[6] Paul Sabatier,[7] Konrad Burdach,[8] and Ernst Troeltsch.[9] August Wilhelm Ambros, Besseler notes, adopted the term "Renaissance" in the title of the third volume of his history of music.[10] Hugo Riemann used a similar designation for the period up to 1600[11] and extended the period back to the fourteenth century, incorporating a *Frührenaissance*. For Besseler, Riemann identified two points of particular significance to the Renaissance problem, that the Italian music of the trecento was "free, self-sufficient, and therefore autonomous," and that composers' names appear in such manuscripts as the Squarcialupi codex;[12] both points illustrate the individualism that Burckhardt isolated as one of the principal marks of the culture. Riemann, Besseler points out, did not know the French *ars nova*, whereas Besseler could show that Philippe de Vitry not only names himself but departs from reigning formal types. This led Besseler to annex the ars nova to the Renaissance, mocking any who disagreed, for example, Leo Schrade[13] and Friedrich Blume.[14]

3. Heinrich Besseler, *Die Musik des Mittelalters und der Renaissance* (Potsdam, 1931).

4. "Das Renaissanceproblem in der Musik," *Archiv für Musikwissenschaft* 22 (1966):1–10.

5. Jules Michelet, *Histoire de France* (Paris, 1855), VII, 1–133.

6. Henry Thode, *Franz von Assisi und die Kunst der Renaissance* (Berlin, 1885).

7. Paul Sabatier, *La vie de Saint François d'Assise* (Paris, 1893).

8. Konrad Burdach, *Von Mittelalter zur Reformation*, 11 vols. (Leipzig, 1893–1937).

9. Ernst Troeltsch, "Renaissance und Reformation," *Historische Zeitschrift* 110 (1913):519–56.

10. August Wilhelm Ambros, *Geschichte der Musik im Zeitalter der Renaissance bis zu Palestrina*, Geschichte der Musik, III (Breslau, 1868).

11. Hugo Riemann, *Das Zeitalter der Renaissance (bis 1600)*, Handbuch der Musikgeschichte, II/1 (Leipzig, 1907).

12. Besseler, "Das Renaissanceproblem," p. 4.

13. Schrade, "Renaissance."

14. Friedrich Blume, "Renaissance," in *Die Musik in Geschichte und Gegenwart*, XI (Kassel,

In seizing upon individualism as the touchstone of the Renaissance, Besseler picked the characteristic that Burckhardt had made the centerpiece of his book, in the chapter "The Development of the Individual." Whereas medieval man was conscious of himself only as part of a group, individual personality being veiled in faith, illusion, and childish prejudices, Burckhardt observed that in the Italian cities of the Renaissance individuals who had an objective view of themselves as independent spirits emerged. Dante was the prophet of this spiritual resource and independence; his *virtù* remained with him even in exile. Renaissance man needed neither family, church, nor lord. Pietro Aretino, self-exiled from Rome, could extract pensions from both Charles V and Francis I simply by promising to spare them the barbs of his pen.

Individualism was not the only characteristic brought out by Burckhardt. The patronage of the tyrants who ruled the city-states was crucial to the flourishing of the arts, and Burckhardt celebrated them in the chapter "The State as a Work of Art." The arts bolstered these uncrowned rulers through eloquent orations and dedications, portraits and motets, which conferred on them the magnificence and legitimacy that their thrones lacked. What gave the Renaissance in Italy substance and won it worldwide dominance was the "Revival of Antiquity," the subject of another chapter. Here Burckhardt considers the adoration of the ruins of Rome, the revival of the literary classics and textual criticism, led by Petrarch, the cultivation of learning in the universities and schools for patricians. In the next chapter he traces the rediscovery of the world of nature, of geographical exploration and the renewed respect for human nature in all its fullness and richness. The final chapters describe the brilliant society and its festivals, the moral decadence and fainthearted religion. All these ingredients, not only individualism, need to be considered in defining a musical Renaissance.

Since publication of Burckhardt's book, the picture painted there has been undergoing correction and completion. The canvas has been extended to the northern countries and the religious character of this phase of the movement under the leadership of Erasmus, and the reaction against the abuses and luxuries of the church in the Reformation has been fitted into the panorama.[15]

1963), 224–80; trans. M. D. Herter Norton, in Blume, *Renaissance and Baroque Music* (New York, 1967), pp. 3–80.

15. For an account of various interpretations of the Renaissance through the centuries, see W. K. Ferguson, *The Renaissance in Historical Thought, Five Centuries of Interpretation* (Boston, 1948), and for reinterpretations since Burckhardt, see Ferguson's "The Reinterpretation of the Renaissance," in *Facets of the Renaissance* (New York, 1959), pp. 1–18, also reprinted in his *Renaissance Studies* (New York, 1963), pp. 17–29. For an excellent survey of scholarship and an overview of Renaissance humanism, see William J. Bouwsma, *The Culture of Renaissance*

Particularly important in the reassessment of the period has been the effort to identify the causes of the movement and the conditions for its taking root in Italy. Ferguson suggested that the landholding agrarian economy of the feudal system was replaced in Italy by the beginning of the fourteenth century by an urban society with large scale commerce and industry and developing capitalist institutions. The massing of population in the cities, the growth of private fortunes, concentration of wealth and political power in princes and leading families encouraged the spread of lay education and lay patronage of art, learning, and letters. In the royal courts of the north, such as those of the dukes of Burgundy, a money economy also grew, as did learning, vernacular literature, and art, but they "retained the forms of feudal and chivalrous society. . . . Literary reflections of these forms had by the fifteenth century lost the vitality that had inspired the feudal literature of the twelfth and thirteenth centuries."[16]

In Italy writers and artists had to cater to the taste of men not bound by ecclesiastical traditions. Classical culture was perfectly designed to fulfill the needs of educated, urban laymen. Since there was nothing in the immediate past to satisfy them or to draw from, the classics became the natural models for artists and founts for secular knowledge, particularly in matters of human and civic interest. Hans Baron has shown that Leonardo Bruni's *laudatio*, which helped to save Florence from succumbing to Duke Giangaleazzo Visconti of Milan, was modeled on a panegyric, *Panathenaicus* (Praise of Athens), by the orator Aelius Aristides.[17]

Bruni imitated not only the rhetorical form but the general sequence of arguments, though the content, giving a portrait of the political constitution of Florence, was original and crucial to arousing the commitment of the citizenry to resist the Milanese campaign. Thus classical rhetoric could serve to defend both tyranny and republicanism. Classical models were found fruitful also on other civic occasions, such as when one wanted to construct a splendid and stout palace or to honor a statesman with a Roman-style bust or equestrian statue.

The conditions that led to the reanimation of literature, the visual arts, and learning also deeply affected music in Italy throughout the period of the Renaissance. Music historians generally have overlooked many of these manifestations because their stated objective has been a history of musical style. But style is only the audible surface of a musical culture, the essence

---

Humanism, American Historical Association, pamphlet no. 401 (The American Historical Association, 1973).

16. Ferguson, *Renaissance Studies,* p. 131.

17. Hans Baron, *The Crisis of the Early Italian Renaissance* (Princeton, 1955; revised 1966).

of which must be sought beneath. Style as a criterion is particularly mis-leading in the Italian Renaissance, because some of the most characteristic music of the period is not preserved in writing, and much of the written music exhibits style elements of undeniably transalpine origin. But this should not lead us to the conclusion that the Renaissance was a northern phenomenon. *Renaissance music,* that is, music imbued with the spirit of the Renaissance— as opposed to the *music of the Renaissance*—that is, of a par-ticular chronological period, received its first impetus in Italy just as did the other arts and literature. Every impulse of the Italian Renaissance that affected the other arts and literature can be shown to have operated also in music. The movement changed the face of European music as surely as it did other facets of thought and culture.

It has become ever more evident with recent archival work that nearly every important composer of the Renaissance, whatever his native country, benefited from the patronage of the Italian courts and princes of the church. The most sumptuous manuscripts, some containing, to be sure, chiefly French music, were produced under the same sponsorship. The best mu-sicians from everywhere were recruited to perform. There was also much music created by native musicians and poets, amateurs and professionals, a lot of it not preserved in writing. A constant demand for instruments stimulated local makers to produce them in quantity and to develop new varieties and designs. Chamber music, particularly for instrumental ensem-bles, received unprecedented impetus from the patronage of the Italian courts.[18] And to supply printed parts for all this music making, Venice became the music publishing capital of the world.

Because much of the momentum of the Renaissance was translated into performance rather than original creation, to seek its essence in a style is unproductive. There were many coexistent styles, appealing to different elements of the population and operative in different spheres, and some contained more native components than others. The Renaissance musical scene in Italy cannot adequately be characterized in stylistic terms. It is best defined in cultural terms. Renaissance music is not a set of compositional techniques but a complex of social conditions, intellectual states of mind, attitudes, aspirations, habits of performers, artistic support systems, intra-cultural communication, and many other such ingredients, which add up

---

18. Concerning these last points, see Lewis Lockwood, "Jean Mouton and Jean Michel: New Evidence on French Music and Musicians in Italy, 1505–1520," *Journal of the American Musicological Society* 32 (1979):191–246; Anne-Marie Bragard, "Les musiciens ultramontains des chapelles du pape Médicis Leon X (1513–1521), *Bulletin de l'Institut historique belge de Rome,* fasc. 50 (1980):187–215; Lawrence F. Bernstein, "Notes on the Origin of the Parisian Chanson," *Journal of Musicology* 1 (1982):275–326; Dietrich Kämper, *Studien zur instrumentalen Ensemble-musik des 16. Jahrhunderts in Italien* (Rome, 1970).

to a thriving matrix of musical energy. Eventually many of these impulses were translated into musical style, but this was a gradual process.

Perhaps the most problematic component of this scene is the revival of antiquity. It is frequently stated, and quite rightly, that Renaissance musicians had no ancient Greek or Roman exemplars to emulate, as the artists, sculptors, and architects had. Eventually some specimens of notated Greek music were discovered—and this already in the fifteenth century—but until the 1580's the notation was too much of an obstacle. It is naive, however, to be too literal (or strictly aural) about the imitation of ancient music. In the absence of the ancient sounds, composers could still imitate ancient categories and schemes, and this they did. There were countless consciously contrived imitations of odes, elegeia, epikedeia, epinikia, epithalamia, paeans, orphic songs, nomoi, and antistrophic choruses in the sixteenth century, and even some in the fifteenth and fourteenth. Many of the dramatic performances involving music, both solo and choral, were deliberately imitative of ancient practices. These are not restricted to Italy, of course, but such practices were most intensively cultivated and widespread there.

Schrade once denied that the Renaissance in music had anything to do with the imitation of antiquity. He argued that historians should recognize a Renaissance, rather, because men of the fifteenth and sixteenth centuries saw their own epoch as one of rebirth, a renewal that was independent of any revival of antiquity.[19]

It is the object of this book, however, to show that the revival of ancient learning and of certain ancient artistic and musical practices that it revealed was a potent force in the development of music in the Renaissance. Much more fundamental than any practical musical revival of antiquity was the transformation of musical thought brought about by the renewed pursuit of ancient learning.

Paul Oskar Kristeller has repeatedly emphasized that "classical humanism was, if not the only, certainly the most characteristic and pervasive intellectual current of that period."[20] As Kristeller has never tired of pointing out, the *studia humanitatis* strictly speaking were grammar, rhetoric, poetry, history, and moral philosophy, but he has recently affirmed that the renewal of learning that was first in evidence in these fields soon spread to the other branches of philosophy, to mathematics, natural science, and music.[21] Because music did not belong to the traditional humanistic studies, the earliest

19. In "Renaissance," p. 32, Schrade writes: "Renaissance means the act of rebirth effected spontaneously; in the minds of the musicians it also means an epoch well defined within the history as a whole. It does not mean the imitation of antiquity; nor does it mean the renaissance of antiquity. It means the renaissance of standards of culture in music."

20. Kristeller, *Studies in Renaissance Thought and Letters* (Rome, 1956), p. 12.

21. Kristeller, *Renaissance Thought* (New York, 1961), p. 19.

phase of humanism, in the fourteenth century, paid scant attention to it. Petrarch, Boccaccio, and Guarino Veronese, for example, give no evidence in their writings that they considered music a field ripe for any kind of humanist revival, though it should be added that the leader of the Paduan school, Pietro d'Abano, did. Music first had to be recognized as a discipline worthy of scholarly attention. The next generations of humanists were decidedly inclined toward giving music this status: Vittorino da Feltre, Ficino, Poliziano, and Giorgio Valla were all deeply interested in music, not only as a practical art but as an intellectual discipline.

An event that marks the coming of age of music as a humanistic subject is its inclusion in the curriculum of the school founded by Vittorino da Feltre at the court of Gianfrancesco Gonzaga in Mantua in 1424.[22] Vittorino's fifteenth-century biographer Bartolomeo Platina said of him, "He affirmed an education which rendered a man able, according to the time and the needs, to treat of nature, of morals, of the movements of the stars, of geometry, of harmony and music, of numbering and measuring."[23]

The core of the program at the school was Latin and Greek grammar and literature taught in these languages, but the subjects just named were not neglected. We know of musical studies at the school through Johannes [Legrense] Gallicus de Namur (c. 1415–73), who was a product of the University of Padua and a teacher in the Mantuan school. Under Vittorino, Gallicus acknowledged, he "diligently heard the Music of Boethius" and thereby "attained the true practice of this art."[24]

Gallicus recognized that the theory of Boethius was concerned not with the music of his time but with that of the ancient Greeks, and that the music of the Greeks was not subject to the modes (*tropi*) of the church but could be distinguished by octave species or by height and lowness of pitch that resulted from placing the identical constitution of notes higher or lower. Gallicus was the first Western writer to appreciate that the Greek modes and those of plainchant were different and independent systems. Thus the fresh rereading of Boethius becomes not simply a continuation of medieval Boethian studies but a vital component of the reexamination of antiquity.

Other centers of study in the fifteenth century also gave music a place.

22. Schrade and Kristeller early recognized the importance of Vittorino in the renewal of music theory. But in "Renaissance" pp. 26–27, Schrade may have gone too far in viewing him as the center of a group that included Gaffurio, Ramos de Pareja, and Spataro, as well as Gallicus and Burzio.

23. Quoted by Paul Lawrence Rose in *The Italian Renaissance of Mathematics* (Geneva, 1975), p. 16.

24. Johannes Legrense (Gallicus) de Namur, *Ritus canendi vetustissimus et novus*, I, i, in Charles-Edmond-Henri de Coussemaker, *Scriptorum de musica medii aevi* (Paris, 1864–76; Hildesheim, 1963), IV, 345a. Coussemaker dated the treatise 1458–64, ibid., IV, xiii.

From 1412, when the studio of Parma reopened, there is evidence that Giorgio Anselmi taught in the faculty of arts and medicine. Himself a product of Pavia, Anselmi completed in 1434 a set of three dialogues on music that has the character of a university textbook. It is likely that in addition to mathematics, astronomy, and medicine, Anselmi taught music as a liberal art. In 1450 Pope Nicholas V established an endowed chair in music at Bologna, to which Bartolomé Ramos de Pareja aspired when he settled there in 1472. Although he lectured publicly in Bologna for a number of years, neither he nor anyone else was ever appointed to the chair. It is likely that music was taught as part of the mathematical arts in Padua, where Prosdocimo de' Beldomandi was active from 1409.[25] From 1492 Franchino Gaffurio taught music in an academy established by Lodovico Sforza (il Moro) in Milan.[26] These facts, though meager, indicate that music early earned a place alongside the disciplines of the humanist curriculum in the main Italian centers of learning.

Music was also a subject for serious study outside formal academic circles. The best evidence is the number of treatises on musical practice and theory written and published during the fifteenth and sixteenth centuries in Italy, which by far outnumber those written and published elsewhere. Knud Jeppesen speaks of a "music-theoretical madness" that "seized Italy at the time" (the last quarter of the fifteenth century).[27]

Why should there have been such an outpouring of musical theorizing in Italy during these two centuries, both before and after the advent of printing? We cannot delve into all the causes. But certainly a principal one is the example set by the classical authors, who confided to their treatises the secrets of their art, whether architecture (Vitruvius), oratory (Cicero, Quintilian), medicine (Galen), surgery (Paulus Aeginita), education (Plu-

---

25. Prosdocimo de' Beldomandi (d. 1428), author of several treatises on music, undoubtedly included music in his teaching of mathematics from around 1409, when he received the doctorate *in artibus* at Padua.

26. A letter of 1 September 1479 from Jacopo Antiquario to Lodovico Maria Sforza, pleading for a benefice for Gaffurio, begins: "Pre[sbi]te[r] Franchino Gaffuro: quale insegna la musica qua" (Father Franchino Gaffuro, who teaches music here). In a similar application of 10 December 1493 Antiquario gives Gaffurio's qualifications for another benefice: "Pre[sbi]t[er] Franchino Gafforo Rectore qui de la chiesa de S[an] Marcellino: quale per benignita de la ex[cellen]tia V[ostra] como quella sa: lege publicamente musica in questa Inclyta Cita. . . ." (Father Franchino Gafforo, Rector here of S. Marcellino, who through the kindess of Your Excellency, as you know, lectures publicly on music in this illustrious city. . . .) Milan, Archivio di Stato, Autografi, no. 94, busta 33. For further information concerning Gaffurio's academic positions see Kristeller, "Music and Learning in the Early Italian Renaissance," *Journal of Renaissance and Baroque Music* 1 (1947):255–74.

27. ". . . der sozusagen musiktheoretischen Wut, die damals ganz Italien ergriffen hatte." From K. Jeppesen, "Eine musiktheoretische Korrespondenz des früheren Cinquecento" *Acta musicologica* 13 (1941):3.

tarch), geography (Ptolemy, Strabo), poetics (Horace, Aristotle), geometry (Euclid), or military arts (Vegetius). Not only did the treatise as a genre receive a spur through humanism, but the forms these treatises took often betrayed classical models. Some were based on Euclid's method of definitions, propositions, and corollaries (Erasmus of Höritz, Zarlino, *Dimostrationi*), but many more were in dialogue form.

The most familiar model for the didactic dialogue was Cicero's *De oratore*, in which Lucius Crassus and Marcus Antonius discuss the art of oratory in three books or discussions. Cicero himself had adopted the dialogue form in imitation of Greek authors, the most famous of whom was Plato. The format had the advantage of airing both sides of a controversial subject, and this was particularly advantageous in introducing novel methods or indirectly attacking previous authors or the opinions or deeds of the powerful. Among the early humanists, Poggio Bracciolini, writing on greed, Lorenzo Valla on pleasure, Alberti on the family, Bembo on vernacular literature, and Sadoleto and Vergerio on education, all employed the dialogue form. Among the musical treatises in dialogue are those of Anselmi, Artusi, Morley, Pontio, Zarlino (*Dimostrationi*), and several by Bottrigari.

The encouragement of patrons was an important factor in stimulating the production of treatises. Some treatises were directly commissioned by secular and religious leaders, for example, the *Liber musices* of around 1495–96 of Florentius de Faxolis by Cardinal Ascanio Maria Sforza (1455–1505).[28] Another is the *Complexus effectuum musices* of Tinctoris for Beatrice of Aragon.[29] These treatises were not printed, though they were carefully scripted and illuminated. With printing, the need for patrons was even more acute; it was too costly a process to be paid for solely by the few copies sold. Gaffurio offered beautifully illuminated manuscript copies on parchment of his *De harmonia musicorum instrumentorum opus* (1518) to four potential patrons in succession before he found one who would sponsor the printing. The shifting personnel and allegiances in the unstable political environment of Milan hindered his first three tries and caused a lag of eighteen years between completion and publication. The availability of patrons in the main centers of learning—Naples, Florence, Bologna, Rome, and Venice—greatly contributed to the boom in theoretical publications. Not only did patrons help with the expense of printing, but often they were the buyers and readers of the treatises, for noble amateurs who did not have the benefits of choir

28. Milan, Biblioteca Trivulziana, MS 2146; see Albert Seay, "The 'Liber Musices' of Florentius de Faxolis," in *Musik und Geschichte—Music and History: Leo Schrade zum sechszigsten Geburtstag* (Cologne, 1963), pp. 71–95.

29. Ed. Albert Seay, in Johannes Tinctoris, *Theoretical Works* (American Institute of Musicology, 1975) 2, 159–77.

schools or apprenticeships were eager to acquire the secrets of the musical profession.

The efflorescence of treatise writing embraced several aspects of music. That which was most obviously influenced by the classical past in content was, naturally, *musica theorica,* or speculative music. But more and more during the Renaissance, practical theory was penetrated by this influence through the desire to rationalize practice and make it conform to the precepts of musica theorica. This is especially true of the theory of composition. Least affected by classical models but still part of the vogue of treatise writing are the tutors for various instruments and singing.

Most surprising is the centrality of counterpoint theory in a nation that has been branded, at least since the late eighteenth century, as anticontrapuntal. It is habitual to think of counterpoint in the Renaissance as a Netherlandish or at least Franco-Flemish phenomenon. Yet there is no significant treatise on counterpoint, whether manuscript or printed, emanating from the Franco-Flemish or Netherlands region in the first century of the Renaissance. The authors are preponderantly Italians; a minority is made up of northerners and Spaniards who settled in Italy. Before printing became common, the principal authors include Antonio de Leno, Prosdocimo de' Beldomandi, Ugolino of Orvieto, Johannes Gallicus, John Hothby, Johannes Tinctoris, Guilelmus Monachus, and Florentius de Faxolis.[30] Among the authors of printed treatises are Ramos de Pareja, Burzio, Gaffurio, Aron, Lanfranco, Del Lago, Vanneo, Vicentino, Zarlino, Artusi, Pontio, and Tigrini. The other center of counterpoint codification was Germany, though much of the writing there derived from the Italian authors.

To reconcile these facts with the myth that counterpoint was primarily a Netherlandish phenomenon, one would need to assume that polyphonic writing was developed in the north but codified in Italy. There were two important counterpoint teachers who can be adduced as links between north and south in support of such a hypothesis: Tinctoris and Willaert.

Tinctoris wrote his counterpoint treatise in Naples in 1477 several years, perhaps five, after settling there. In the dedication to King Ferrante I, he names as composers Ockeghem, Regis, Busnois, Caron, and Faugues. He does not say they are his models; indeed, in the body of the book he is critical of some of their habits. Tinctoris learned composition in France, perhaps at Cambrai. But the motivation to write a method for the art of counterpoint must have come from his Neapolitan patron or the circle around him. The very process of devising rules would have led him to

---

30. See Klaus-Jürgen Sachs, *Der Contrapunctus im 14. und 15. Jahrhundert: Untersuchungen zum Terminus, zur Lehre und zu den Quellen* (Wiesbaden, 1974), and "Counterpoint" in *New Grove Dictionary of Music and Musicians,* ed. Stanley Sadie (London, 1980) IV, 833–45.

rationalize and purify the art of various barbarisms that he found in works then in circulation. It is inevitable that this process was affected by his reading of the many classical treatises in his prince's library, which he liberally cited in several of his works on music.

The other teacher who is thought to have transmitted northern polyphonic art to Italy, the great composer Adrian Willaert, makes an even poorer case for such transmission than Tinctoris. Although he must have gained a basic competence in counterpoint in France, particularly in his studies with Jean Mouton, latest evidence has him working for Cardinal Ippolito I d'Este at a very early age in 1515.[31] The precepts that he communicated orally to Zarlino and Vicentino must have been developed during his long experience in Ferrara, Rome, and Venice.

Through Tinctoris and Willaert and their pupils, counterpoint was progressively purged of uncontrolled dissonance, linear angularities, and other irregularities and mannerisms (particularly fauxbourdon) characteristic of the northern composers. It becomes a suave, refined, polished art that was taught essentially by the Italian and Italianized masters. The extensive correspondence among a group of northern Italian composer-teachers, including Giovanni del Lago, Spataro, Aron, Giovanni Maria Lanfranco, and others in the 1520's and 1530's, testifies to the intense theoretical activity that accompanied the forging of these rules.[32]

Other aspects of composition, besides counterpoint, figured in the revival of theoretical activity. One of the most important was modality. The theory of the modes was traditionally a part of plainchant theory; the subject rarely came up in the early treatises on counterpoint. Sebald Heyden asks: "Why is it necessary to pursue religiously the ranges of authentic and plagal tones, as they are called, and the *differentiae* added to them, when we know that they have almost no meaning in figural [that is, measured] music?"[33] Yet about this time Glarean completed his famous book celebrating the twelve modes, in which he claimed to have restored the ancient Greek system. Glarean may have been inspired partly by Gaffurio, who dedicated the first twelve chapters of Book IV of his *De harmonia* (1518) to the modes. It is this section of Glarean's own copy of Gaffurio's book that is most heavily annotated in his hand.[34] Gaffurio's treatment is pseudo-historical; he purports to be discussing the ancient modes, but he does so with almost de-

31. Lewis Lockwood, "Willaert," in *New Grove Dictionary*, XX, 421.

32. Biblioteca Apostolica Vaticana, MS Vat. lat. 5318; see Jeppesen "Eine musiktheoretische Korrespondenz,"and the forthcoming edition of the correspondence by Edward E. Lowinsky and Clement Miller.

33. Sebald Heyden, *De arte canendi* (Nuremberg, 1540), trans. Clement Miller, p. 113, quoted in Harold Powers, "Mode," in *New Grove Dictionary*, XII, 397.

34. Munich, Universitäts Bibliothek, MS 2° Art 239.

liberate ambiguity: the attributes assigned by various ancient authors to the Greek tonoi and harmoniae Gaffurio associates with a system of modes that are identifiable as those of plainchant. Without realizing it, he badly misinterpreted Ptolemy, Boethius, and Bryennius. Glarean, lacking access to the ancient authors, followed him into the same misunderstandings. Glarean also copied Gaffurio's ordering and structure of the octave species, dividing them either harmonically or arithmetically to produce the authentic and plagal forms respectively. However mistaken both Gaffurio and Glarean were about the ancient modes, their ostentatiously documented association of the modern modes with those of the Greeks and Romans enhanced the prestige and vigor of these systems in the minds of many, and consequently both composers and theorists paid more attention to them. Whereas the modes do not figure at all in Gaffurio's own eight contrapuntal rules,[35] and only one of Tinctoris's eight rules has to do with modality,[36] by contrast, Aron wrote a separate treatise on the modes in polyphony, and Zarlino dedicated all of Book IV of his *Le Istitutioni harmoniche* to them. Composers in the mid-sixteenth century likewise seem to regard them as important constructive and expressive means.

The modes were fascinating to Renaissance musicians not simply because they were a link to a noble ancient past but because they were thought to unlock the powers of music over human feelings and morals.[37] Plato in the *Republic* and *Laws,* Aristotle in the *Politics,* works previously unknown except to a very few, could now be read in printed Latin translations, and they spoke eloquently of the emotional and moral or ethical effects that could be wrought by a musician through the proper choice of mode. Gaffurio, and those who, like Glarean, followed him, by equating the modern and ancient modes, associating the effects of the latter with the former, thereby transferred these powers, theoretically at least, to the modern modes.

Gaffurio identified particular modes as appropriate to certain general feelings of the text to which melodic lines are set:

> Let the composer of a vocal piece [*cantilena*] strive to make the melody agree in sweetness with its words, so that when these are about love or a plea for death or some lament let him set and dispose mournful sounds so far as he

35. Franchino Gaffurio, *Practica musice* (Milan, 1496), III, 3.

36. Johannes Tinctoris, *Liber de arte contrapuncti* III, 5. Tinctoris did write a treatise on the modes, *Liber de natura et proprietate tonorum,* ed. Albert Seay, in Tinctoris, *Theoretical Works* I, 59–104. But apart from a few applications to polyphonic problems, it is based on medieval plainchant theory and is indebted particularly to Marchetto of Padua.

37. D. P. Walker dealt at length with the fascination with this power in his serialized article "Musical Humanism in the 16th and Early 17th Centuries," in *The Music Review* 2 (1941): 1–13, 111–21, 220–27, 288–308; 3 (1943):55–71; German translation as *Der musikalische Humanismus* (Kassel, 1949).

can, as the Venetians do. What I believe will most contribute to this is to order
the piece in the Fourth, Sixth, or even Second Tone, since these Tones are
more relaxed and are known to produce this kind of effect easily. But when
the words speak of indignation and rebuke, it is fitting to utter harsh and harder
sounds, which are ascribed most often to the Third and Seventh Tones. To
be sure, words of praise and modesty seek somehow intermediate sounds,
which are properly ascribed to the First and Eighth Tones.[38]

Although Gaffurio fails to cite a source for the correspondences between
modes and affections, a classical link is implied by his sending the reader
to the chapters in his *De harmonia,* Book IV, which are purportedly about
the Greek modes. Also, his qualification of groups of modes (*toni*) as *re-
missiores* (relaxed) and *medii* (intermediate) utilize expressions that fit the
Greek tonoi much better than the modern modes.

A layman steeped in the classics, Matteo Nardo, goes beyond the coupling
of general mood and mode to express the belief that the first thing a composer does is to consider the affection to which he wishes to move the
listener; then he chooses a suitable mode.[39] Nardo may have read Aron's
characterization of the diverse effects of the modes and of the desirability
of choosing a mode according to the feeling that the composer wants to
awaken.[40] The chapter in which Aron took up the affective nature of each
mode seems to be almost an afterthought, however, lacking integration
with the more technical descriptions. Aron was evidently not much concerned with giving instruction in composition in this book, as opposed to
determining the mode of polyphonic works already written, for he rarely
mentioned the composer's role.[41] Nardo thus articulates something Aron
left unsaid, that a choice of mode according to the affection to be expressed
is a primary step in the act of composition, that musicians, indeed, start
out with the aim of moving listeners to particular feelings.

It is common to link humanism with the increasing attention given to
the faithful rendering of the natural spoken rhythm of the text and its

38. Gaffurio,*Practica musice,* III, 15. Gaffurio refers the reader to his *De harmonia* but gives
there no affective qualities for the Hypermixolydian, if that is what he meant by the Eighth
Mode. Nicolo Burzio, in *Musices opusculum,* II, 5, fol. 36v, in describing how to compose a
polyphonic work, names the choice of mode as the third step in the process and characterizes
the modes according to their affections, but his list of qualities differs from that of Gaffurio.

39. This statement is made in a letter to a certain Hieronymo that is partly preserved in a
manuscript containing, in the same hand, an Italian translation of Carlo Valgulio's preface to
his Latin translation of pseudo-Plutarch's *De musica:* Biblioteca Apostolica Vaticana, MS Vat.
lat. 5385, fol. 57v. See ch. 5 below.

40. Pietro Aron, *Trattato della natura et cognitione di tutti gli tuoni di canto figurato* (Venice,
1525; Bologna, 1970), ch. 25, fol. e4v.

41. The composer's task is referred to in ch. 1, fol. e1v; ch. 4, fol. b1r; ch. 6, fol. c2r; ch.
21, fol. e2v; and ch. 25, fol. e4v.

affective content in musical settings. But actually it is quite difficult to find early documentary evidence for this link. The earliest that I have found invoked the famous dictum of Plato (*Republic* 3.399–400) that of the three components of song—words, rhythm, and melody—"the words are by far the most important of the three, being the very basis and foundation of the rest" is in Bishop (later Cardinal) Jacopo Sadoleto's *De pueris recte instituendis* (Venice, 1533).[42] To propose as Sadoleto did that in a song the words should dominate and rule the rest was a radical departure. It was one thing to say that the music should be suited to the text, as by the choice of mode, which would assure at most a general and consistent mood; it was quite another to suggest that the music should be subject and subservient to the text. Sadoleto introduces Plato's definition into the context of a critique of contemporary music by Jacopus, who is conversing with his son Paulus about Aristotle's *Ethics*. Jacopus complains that even when the text of a musical composition is moral and worthwhile, which in itself is rare, it is obscured by "abruptly cutting and jerking the sounds in the throat—as though music were designed not to soothe and control the spirit, but merely to afford a base pleasure to the ears, mimicking the cries of birds and beasts, which we should be sorry to resemble."[43] If he were to teach his son about music, he would say nothing of the "common and trivial harmony, which is entirely a pandering caress of the ear with sweetness and which consists of hardly anything but variation and running of notes."[44]

It was around this time that another bishop, according to his own later confession, was thinking about these matters. This was Bishop Bernardino Cirillo Franco, who did not write his thoughts down until twenty years later in 1549 in a letter to Ugolino Gualteruzzi. There he recalls that the ancients "created powerful effects that we nowadays cannot produce either

---

42. Fol. 42v, "cum constet chorus ex tribus, sententia, rhythmo (hic enim numerus nobis est) & uoce. primum quidem omnium et potissimum sententiam esse, utpote quae si sedes & fundamentum reliquorum." This passage from Plato was later quoted by Johannes Ott, *Missae tredecim*, (Nuremberg, 1539), Zarlino (*Istitutioni*, 1558, IV, 32); Giovanni Bardi, *Discorso mandato a Caccini sopra la musica e 'l cantar bene*, in Giovanni Battista Doni, *Lyra Barberina* (Florence, 1763), II, 234, 244; Giulio Caccini, in the foreword to *Le nuove musiche*, trans. in Oliver Strunk, *Source Readings in Music History* (New York, 1950), p. 378; and Giulio Cesare Monteverdi in the preface to Claudio Monteverdi's *Scherzi musicali* (Venice, 1607), trans. in Strunk, *Source Readings*, p. 407.

43. Sadoleto, *De pueris*, trans. by E. T. Campagnac and K. Forbes in *Sadoleto on Education* (London, 1916), p. 117. This passage was quoted by Galilei in *Discorso intorno all'uso delle dissonanze*, ed. Frieder Rempp in *Die Kontrapunkttraktate Vincenzo Galileis* (Cologne, 1980), fol. 194v, p. 158.

44. "Sed ego non ea dicam quae huius uulgatae, & triuialis symphoniae sint, cuius auribus tantum suauitate demulcendis omne est lenocinium, & quae in sola penè uocum flexione ac modulatione ipsa consistunt " [Sadoleto, *De pueris* (Basel, 1538 ed.), p. 130], my translation.

with rhetoric or with oratory in moving the passions and affections of the soul."[45] The only music he has heard that produces such effects is that of the pavane and galliard. He would have the music of the church "framed to the fundamental meaning of the words, in certain intervals and numbers apt to move our affections to religion and pity." Musicians should rediscover the power of the modes and the enharmonic, chromatic, and diatonic genera. Like the sculptors, painters, architects, and writers, they should seek to recover the art of the ancients, who were able with music to make the lazy active, the angry calm, the dissolute temperate, to console the afflicted and to make happy the miserable.[46]

The idea that music should move the affections, as oratory and rhetoric were intended to do, was a new goal for composers. It was different from exhorting them to imitate the divine harmony of the heavens or to propitiate the influence of a planet by synthesizing its music in man-made song. Both Sadoleto and Cirillo Franco quoted Plato, the Plato not of the *Timaeus,* but of the *Republic* and *Laws,* in which the ethical effects of music were under consideration.

Cirillo Franco's remarks point to another important source of the new ideology, the revival of rhetoric. One of the achievements of humanism was to restore the balance among the components of the old trivium. Medieval scholasticism had emphasized logic and tended to diminish the value of rhetoric, because it was through logic that the intelligence, which should govern belief and action was persuaded, whereas rhetoric held sway over the emotions. With the early humanists, and here again Petrarch led the way, this tendency began to be reversed. Disillusioned with the capacity of abstract reason to lead people to reform their lives, churchmen sought to move them by oratory, to induce an act of will through religious fervor rather than doctrinal conviction. Rhetoric was also more effective in the daily encounters of the tribunal, marketplace, and political forum, not to mention in diplomatic and personal correspondence. Artful communication that could sway people through their feelings, whether to anger at a tyrant or transgressor, sorrow for a deceased notable, joy upon victory, or enthusiasm for a cause, became a prime instrument for gaining or maintaining power. It is characteristic that Bishop Cirillo should seize upon the underutilized language of music for this purpose, a language that in the hands of

---

45. Palestrina, *Pope Marcellus Mass,* ed. and trans. by Lewis Lockwood (New York, 1975), p. 11. Franco says that he has wanted to set down these thoughts about music for twenty years. According to Oscar Mischiati the addressee of this letter really was Ugolino Guastanezzi, who was employed by Ludovico Beccadelli, secretary of Cardinal Ranuccio Farnese. See his review of Lewis Lockwood, *The Counter Reformation and the Masses of V. Ruffo,* in *Rivista italiana di musicologia* 9 (1974):304.

46. Ibid., pp. 12–13.

the ancients, or so he believed, had even greater force than verbal rhetoric. If one could unleash the powers of musical rhetoric, what wonders could be worked, particularly in the church. Thus the crusade against scholasticism has its counterpart in the campaign against abstract polyphony. Both scholasticism and polyphony were refined systems that appealed to intellectual elites—on the one hand theologians, on the other highly trained musicians—but which left the common herd of Christians and listeners unmoved and indifferent.

Such thoughts had been circulating in the Roman court for several generations. Sadoleto, with Pietro Bembo, had served as secretary to Pope Leo X. Carlo Valgulio, secretary to Cardinal Cesare Borgia (cardinal 1493–98, son of Pope Alexander VI, reigned 1492–1503) was another humanist critic of the current musical scene at the end of the fifteenth century. In an essay addressed to the musician Titus Pyrrhinus, apparently a singer, Valgulio urges him to use the translation of Plutarch's *De musica* that accompanies the essay and his own ingenuity and study to raise music to its former dignity, for music was not a science infused in the minds of ancient men by the stars but an invention of human genius, of which Titus too possesses a sufficiency for the purpose.

Valgulio pronounces the music of his time dead:

Neminem autem esse puto tam stupidum tamque plumbeum, qui cantu non moueatur. Praeclarè Theophrastus in secundo Musicae inquit naturam musicae esse animae inuecta à perturbationibus mala ab ea depellentem: quod ni musica efficeret, ut uidelicet et animum quo uellet pertraheret, naturam ipsius omnino nullam futuram. Hoc loco nostri musicam temporis lamentarer: ni iampridem complorata foret. . . . Eorum ars & scientia omnis in paucis quibusdam est syllabis, cantus nulli ferè sunt sine conspecto libro, in quo nihil est descriptum praeter certas notas & characteres: quod si uerba	I believe that there is no one in the world so insensitive, so leaden, that he is not moved by song. Theophrastus rightly said in the second book concerning music that the essence of music is the movement of the soul, driving away the evils and troubles that have invaded it. If music did not have this effect, that is, to draw the soul where it wants, it would become in essence nothing. I would lament here the music of our time, if it had not already been mourned as dead. . . . Their whole art and science consists in certain few syllables and they sing almost nothing without reading from a book. In it you see nothing written except certain notes and characters, and if sometimes

cantilenarum quandoque	they pronounce some words of
proferuntur, de medio	songs, you may say that most of
ea uulgo pleraque accepta dices.[47]	them are taken from the vernacular.

Valgulio, Sadoleto, and Cirillo are witnesses to the mounting resistance among humanists to the elaborate polyphony that dominated the repertory of the principal chapels in the first decades of the sixteenth century. The dissatisfaction must have been abundantly felt in the commission of cardinals set up to reform the church, which included Sadoleto. It found its way, as everyone knows, to the Council of Trent.[48]

Whereas on the subject of the modes and the ethical effects of music, Platonic and Aristotelian writings reinforced each other, in the matter of universal harmony, the Pythagorean-Platonic and Aristotelian spheres of influence bent the prevailing theory in opposite directions. *Harmonia est discordia concors* (Harmony is the concord wrought out of discord). This motto, which appears in a scroll over Gaffurio's head—like the bubble of a modern cartoon—in a famous woodcut in the *De harmonia,* where he is shown in a *cathedra* lecturing to students at his feet (see Figure 8.1), sums up a philosophy embraced by many musical writers up to around 1500, one that remains strong in the first decades of the sixteenth century. In the practical domain the motto symbolizes the union of diverse voices, pitches, rhythms, tempos, and instruments in polyphonic music. But of greater significance is that it epitomizes the harmony that reigns in the universe, that exists, optimally, between man and cosmos, between the faculties of the human soul and the parts of the body, and between the body and soul. Heard music is but a reflection of this harmony, which, grasped by the musician in a state of furor or enthusiasm, inspires him to give it audible form. Almost all the early Renaissance writers accepted the assumptions of this musica mundana and humana. Under the influence of humanism, the idea was transformed and elaborated and gained momentum through the Platonic revival led by Marsilio Ficino. But by the beginning of the fifteenth century a Christian mysticism had altered the concept of world harmony. Musica mundana and humana were then believed to emanate from the

47. Carlo Valgulio, *In Plutarchi Musicam, ad Titum Pyrrhinum,* in *Plutarchi Chaeronei . . . Opuscula (quae quidem extant) omnia* (Basel, 1580), fol. 244v. The Plutarch translation and preface were first published in 1507 by Angelo Britannico of Brescia.

48. We do not know whether Pietro Bembo shared Sadoleto's dissatisfaction with the current musical scene, but there is evidence that he too was interested in Greek music in his borrowing on 4 February 1518 the famous manuscript Vat. gr. 191 (return undated) containing treatises by Gaudentius, Euclid, Aristoxenus, Alypius, Ptolemy, and Cleonides. This manuscript was also borrowed by Pietro Aretino 7 July 1522 (returned 8 August), and for Cardinal Ridolfi, 25 August 1529: Maria Bertola, *I due primi registri di prestito della Biblioteca apostolica vaticana* (Vatican City, 1942), pp. 50, 55, 108.

higher harmony of celestial hosts of angels sweetly singing "Sanctus." Ugolino of Orvieto, Giorgio Anselmi, Nicolo Burzio, all unfolded with various degrees of intricacy this angelic hierarchy. The most complete and concrete picture was given by Giorgio Anselmi in the first of his dialogues on music of 1434, in which the angels of the theologians were ranged in orders to coordinate with the homocentric spheres of the astronomers. As a musician he felt some embarrassment about the prospect of nine hosts of angels all singing together without any rule of counterpoint, yet producing the fabled harmony of the spheres. Unlike his predecessors, who were content to leave the proposition literally up in the air, Anselmi sought to establish some polyphonic marching order.

Neque modo harmoniam unam	A single sphere does not in
sphera unica continuo profert,	any way continually pour forth
sed pluriformes phtongos et	one harmony but manifold tones
limmata et dieses et commata,	and limmas and dieses and commas,
ut spiritus illi felices modo	so that those happy spirits, with
cum sonitu sue sphere, modo	the sound of their spheres, now
cum eis qui proximis insident	seem to precede, then to follow,
nunc cantu precedere, nunc	now again to pursue,
sequi, nunc insequi, nunc	then to concur with
concurrere videantur atque	those situated nearby, and
mirando harmonie ludo semper	with a wonderful play of harmony
dulcius concertare credantur.[49]	are believed to concert sweetly.

Thus the spirits that dwell in the spheres sing a diversity of song; yet they make consonance: again, *in discordia concors.*

Gaffurio in his early treatises of 1480 and 1492 assimilated Anselmi's model, but in his last speculative work, *De harmonia,* he leaves behind the Christian overlay and adopts a Neoplatonic cosmology based on Ficino's *Compendium in Timaeum,* Ficino's translation of Plato's *Timaeus,* and the Latin translation by Francesco Burana of the *De musica* of Aristides Quintilianus. In his final work Gaffurio omits mention of the angels and restores the Muses as coordinators of planetary and earthly harmony. With the help of Aristides Quintilianus and Ptolemy, Gaffurio expands the conception of cosmic harmony beyond planetary to human concerns. Music or consonance controls the periodicity of the seasons, of births, and fevers. It mediates between public bodies and between individual people, making possible civic peace and well-being and personal friendship. Although Gaffurio was not able really to digest either Aristides or Ptolemy, who were even more opaque in the Latin translations of Burana and Leoniceno than they were

49. Georgius Anselmus Parmensis, *De musica,* ed. Giuseppe Massera (Florence, 1961), p. 101.

to readers of Greek, he was carried away by their ideas. He wanted to believe that the cosmos was a harmony and that this was the ultimate source of the music created by men and their enjoyment of it.

> If we believe Plato, who said that the world soul consists of musical melody, I surely do not see why it should be doubted that any other living thing possessing a soul, which, it is clear, is a gift of heaven, is also affected by and rejoices at harmonies congruent with its own nature, since it is well known that one is inclined toward something like oneself.[50]

Meanwhile Johannes Tinctoris, Gaffurio's associate for a while at the Neapolitan court, denied the existence of world harmony:

> I cannot pass over in silence the many philosophers such as Plato, Pythagoras and their successors, Cicero, Macrobius, Boethius and our own Isidore, who believe that the spheres of the stars revolve under the rules of harmonic modulation, that is by the concord of different consonances. . . . I unshakeably agree with Aristotle and his commentator, together with our more recent philosophers, who most clearly prove that there is neither real nor potential sound in the heavens. For this reason I can never be persuaded that musical consonances, which cannot be produced without sound, are made by the motion of heavenly bodies.[51]

The Florentine humanist, mathematician, astronomer, organist, and music theorist Fra Mauro—in a manuscript treatise of 1541 in which he shows that he had read Tinctoris' work—took up the question of universal harmony and denied that any audible harmony results from it.[52] But as late as Zarlino's *Istitutioni harmoniche,* 1558, the harmony of the cosmos and of the elements and body are accepted. The first published musical writer who emphatically refutes these theories is Francisco de Salinas (1577).[53] Besides the reasons given by Aristotle, which he did not repeat because they were too far afield for a music book, he argued that the creator would not have made anything so superfluous as unheard music. Moreover, the combinations of the elements

50. Gaffurio, *Practica musice* (Milan, 1496), dedication to Ludovico Maria Sforza.

51. Johannes Tinctoris, *The Art of Counterpoint,* trans. A. Seay (American Institute of Musicology, 1961), p. 13–14.

52. Fra Mauro, in *Utriusque musices epitome (Dell'una et l'altra musica),* ed. Frank A. D'Accone (Stuttgart, 1984), Prologo, p. 28, writes: "La mondana musica o vero (per dir meglio) harmonia è una debita dispositione delle parti col suo tutto, o naturali o artificiali che le sieno, considerata secondo la sostanza, quantità o qualità di qualunche cosa si vogli. Et questa è quell'armonia la quale pone il philosopho et li altri sapienti in cielo et nell'anima nostra, cioè harmonia physica et di corpi et potentie naturali, et non di suoni, come falsamente s'impone a Platone et Pythagora da questi moderni sciolti." See D'Accone, "The Florentine Fra Mauros, A Dynasty of Musical Friars," *Musica Disciplina* 33 (1979):89ff.

53. Francisco de Salinas, *De musica libri septem* (Salamanca, 1577; repr., ed. Macario Santiago Kastner, Kassel, 1958), I, 1, p. 2.

and of the parts of the soul may be based on certain ratios, but these proportions are contemplated by the reason and not the sense of hearing. Throughout his book Salinas was very scrupulous about assigning to the senses and the reason respectively what truly belongs to each of them.[54]

More important in the long run for Renaissance musical thought than the views on cosmic and human music was the changing outlook toward consonance and dissonance. The Pythagorean tradition that persisted throughout the Middle Ages and early Renaissance defined consonance in numerical terms. The intervals that were products of string-length ratios expressible by the numbers from one to four were consonances; the rest were dissonances. Eventually another category of consonance was recognized in compositional practice, the so-called imperfect consonances, but their ratios were thought to be unstable and not subject to numerical definition. Indeed, whereas there was agreement from antiquity concerning the ratios of the octave, fifth, fourth, double octave, and octave-plus-fifth, yet thirds and sixths—the imperfect consonances—were not assigned specific ratios by the authors who paid any attention to them (for example, Ptolemy) because they could come in various sizes. The first theorist to make a complete break with the Pythagorean tradition was Lodovico Fogliano in 1529. Of the musical writers he was the most learned Aristotelian. In his book he consistently follows the logic of the *Posterior Analytics* and principles drawn from Aristotle's *Metaphysics, De anima,* and *Physics*. His dual competence was unique: he read Greek well enough to contemplate an Italian translation of the works of Aristotle; at the same time he worked as a professional singer and composer. Fogliano challenged the Pythagorean position with every possible weapon—epistemology, psychology, logic, and physics. He defined consonance and dissonance not according to ratio but in terms of how they struck his ear:

Consonantia est duorum sonorum secundum acutum & graue distantium: auribus amica commixtio: . . . dissonantia contraria: est duorum sonorum secundum acutum & graue distantium auribus inimica commixto.[55]	Consonance is a mixture of two sounds distant in highness and lowness that is pleasing to the ears; dissonance, its contrary, is a mixture of two sounds distant in highness and lowness that is displeasing to the ears.

To justify these unmathematical definitions,[56] Fogliano proves by means of

---

54. The acceptance and rejection of the doctrine of the music of the spheres is surveyed in greater detail in ch. 8 below.

55. Lodovico Fogliano, *Musica theorica* (Venice, 1529; facs. ed. Giuseppe Massera, Bologna, 1970), II, 2.

56. Fogliano's definitions are actually very similar to those of Boethius in *De institutione musica* 1.8, with the difference, however, that Boethius in previous chapters, 1.5–7, limited

Aristotelian categories and logic that sound is an affective quality (*passibilis qualitas*) that exists only in the ear, and therefore the ear is the final judge of sonorous matters. Experience similarly tells us the difference between perfect and imperfect consonances. The perfect consonances leave the ear perfectly satisfied, whereas the imperfect do not fulfill the potential and desire of the ear completely.[57] Eventually Fogliano uses both numerical ratios and Euclidean geometry to define a tuning system that optimizes both perfect and imperfect consonances. He sets out a method of dividing the monochord that he describes as "a new almost materialist way, according to the sense," a method that aims to "join art and science."[58] The basic diatonic division, laid out on the C-c octave, is identical to that proposed by Zarlino thirty years later, which Zarlino identified as Ptolemy's syntonic diatonic.[59] Fogliano did not attribute it to any previous author, perhaps because he modified it by alternate solutions for some of the poorer consonances, such as Bb-D, for which he used a Euclidean construction to find the geometric mean of the 81:80 comma. (Zarlino did not credit Fogliano for his innovation either, until after Galilei pointed out his indebtedness.)

Fogliano's break with the Pythagorean tradition was a bold and important step. In treatises of musica practica, to be sure, it had been on the way for fifty years already and may be traced in Ramos de Pareja, his pupil Giovanni Spataro, and Spataro's friend Pietro Aron. But Fogliano's book is plainly entitled *Musica theorica,* and in it the author deliberately set out to establish a new scientific basis for musical theorizing. Zarlino was torn between this new approach and the attraction of Neoplatonic theories of harmonic numbers. Although Zarlino's practical theories of counterpoint and the modes had great success, his carefully erected Neoplatonic theoretical basis, truly an anachronism after Fogliano's work, was demolished by Vincenzo Galilei and other critics.[60] Galilei then proceeded to the logical next step by proclaiming that there was no natural physical difference between a consonance and a dissonance, that there was an infinity of both kinds of intervals, and that it was altogether up to practitioners to decide how to use them according to their own purposes. This emancipation of harmony from numerical theory was one of the hard fought conquests of the Renaissance. And it is one of the achievements that can be traced directly to the revival of ancient learning.

Humanism did not stop affecting the course of music history with the

---

the sphere of consonance to intervals determined by multiple and superparticular ratios using the numbers from one to four.

57. Fogliano, *Musica theorica,* II, 5.
58. Ibid., III, 1.
59. Compare the diagram in Fogliano, III, 1, with Zarlino, *Istitutioni,* II, 39, p. 122.
60. A fuller account of this controversy is given in ch. 7 below.

chronological terminus usually assigned to the Renaissance.[61] Indeed, the momentum of investigation into the ancient sources in the period between 1560 and 1580 was such that some of its effects were to be felt into the 1590's and the early years of the seventeenth century. The most obvious example is the spirit and work of the group around Giovanni Bardi known as the Camerata, most active in the 1570's. The research of Girolamo Mei into Greek music and theater fueled the practical experiments of Florentine musicians and dramaturgists for the rest of the century and beyond.

In this book I aim to show that with music, as with the other arts and letters and learning in general, the movement we call the Renaissance began in Italy, and that its chief source of inspiration was the revival of antiquity. Fundamental changes during this period in both musical thought and style issued from the ferment of ideas and activity that we celebrate as the Renaissance. The renewal of learning in Italy led to a rethinking of some fundamental issues in music theory and aesthetics that directly affected practice. Questions such as the nature of the modes, the control of dissonance, melody, and rhythm in counterpoint, the relation between text and music, and the degree to which the aural sense or mathematics should determine the rules of composition, were argued in letters, discourses, and treatises written in Italy by philosophers, humanists, musical theorists, and musicians. Their thinking was intertwined at many points with the general intellectual strands that constituted the very core of the Renaissance spirit.

61. Karl Gustav Fellerer gave an outline history of the revival of ancient learning from the late fifteenth to the eighteenth centuries in "Zur Erforschung der antiken Musik im 16.–18. Jahrhundert," *Jahrbuch der Musikbibliothek Peters für 1935* 42 (1936):84–95.

TWO

The Rediscovery of the Ancient Sources

t has often been stated that humanism reached music tardily. This is in effect true, but the lag was not as great as it has been thought. Almost the entire corpus of ancient writings on music as well as some of the notated examples had been recovered in Italy by the middle of the fifteenth century, and almost all of it had been read and commented upon by the end of that century, if not always with much understanding. There are even some isolated examples in the fourteenth century of the rediscovery of and commentary upon Greek music theory.

The momentum for a musical revival was decidedly sluggish until the end of the fifteenth century, which contrasts with the feverish activity of editing, translating, commenting, and synthesizing Greek sources that took place in the areas of literature, rhetoric, history, medicine, philosophy, and to some extent natural science. There were reasons for this lag.

Music is not preserved in verbal form, although its theory is. This it has in common with mathematics, which also lagged in the humanist movement. Because of its nonverbal nature music did not flow with the mainstream of early humanism, which was preoccupied with the study of the Greek language and Latin eloquence. If a large quantity of music in Greek notation had been found, it undoubtedly would have excited the interest of those among the early humanists who were musically inclined—and there were some—and stimulated them to try to decipher it. But this was not the case. The examples in Greek notation were few. There was a better chance of hearing vestiges of ancient Greek music in the performances of living musicians and singers in the Greek islands and surrounding territories than of ferreting them out of manuscripts. But the humanists were ill equipped to deal with oral tradition; nor would they have grasped the relationship of this music to that of ancient Greece without previously having studied the written documents.

Early humanists had a passion for old manuscripts, both Greek and Latin,

23

and for their verbal messages. The studia humanitatis were in essence studies of what is transmitted by means of written words. Petrarch, the pioneer of humanism in the fourteenth century, was attracted to the elegance of the ancient Latin prose writers, particularly Cicero; he admired Vergil and aspired to read Homer. Those who followed directly after him, some inspired by his example, as was Lorenzo Valla, were principally interested in language and eloquence. Around 1400 a new phase of humanism began in Florence, as Hans Baron and Eugenio Garin have shown,[1] with an emphasis on civic involvement and on rewriting Roman and local history from a republican viewpoint, represented particularly by Leonardo Bruni and Coluccio Salutati. Music was remote from this as it was, too, from the debates that warmed up between the antiquarians and the defenders of Dante and the *volgare lingua.*

The neglect of mathematics as a university subject in Italy hampered the advance of theoretical music, because the latter was traditionally a subdivision of mathematics within the quadrivium. There were no chairs of mathematics in Italy in the fourteenth century, though there were some private teachers attached to universities.[2] At the University of Bologna, which became the most distinguished school of mathematics in Renaissance Italy, there were already advanced chairs in astronomy in the thirteenth century, and lesser arithmetic and geometry positions beginning in 1395. Only in 1450 did Pope Nicholas V establish four chairs in the mathematical sciences, none of them destined for music. Music theory depended on the cultivation of mathematics, because the manipulation of ratios was essential to understanding the relations of intervals to each other. Of especial importance was the revived study of Euclid's *Elements,* stimulated by the publication of the translation in 1482 of Giovanni Campano da Novara, made in 1255–59 from an Arabic version, and that of Bartolomeo Zamberti in 1505, made directly from the Greek. Euclid's geometry led to new approaches to age-old problems, such as the division of superparticular intervals and the geometry of the vibrating string.

The impetus for the rediscovery of ancient musical learning came initially from the manuscript hunters. Pride of discovery and ownership and fascination with the exotic field of Greek music accounted for the concentration in a few collections of many of the principal writings on music. The earliest discoveries of unknown Greek works included some whose importance musically was incidental to their more general interest. The pseudo-Aris-

---

1. Hans Baron, *The Crisis of the Early Italian Renaissance* (Princeton, 1955); Eugenio Garin, *Der italienische Humanismus* (Bern, 1947), *L'Umanesimo italiano: Filosofia e vita civile nel Rinascimento* (Bari, 1952).

2. Paul L. Rose, *The Italian Renaissance of Mathematics,* p. 145.

totelian *Problems* on physics was such a work, practically unknown before Pietro d'Abano's commentary on it. Its nineteenth section, on music, is one of the documents most revealing of Greek musical practice and theory. Pietro apparently first encountered the work in Constantinople in the 1270's or 1280's. He worked on it at length while in Paris, completing his commentary in Padua in 1310.[3] George of Trebizon, who also translated the *Problems,* owned a copy, which Guarino Veronese purchased around 1457 from George's brother in Ferrara through Poggio Bracciolini.[4] Theodore Gaza, when he prepared his translation for Pope Nicholas V shortly after 1450 apparently had several manuscripts at his disposal.[5]

Among the writings previously unknown to the West that the eager collector Giovanni Aurispa (1376–1459) brought back from his trips to the East between 1405 and 1413 was the *Deipnosophistae* of Athenaeus.[6] Written by a Greek rhetorician and grammarian from Naucratis in Egypt, it is a rich mine of Greek musical lore. Aurispa did not study his manuscripts, of which he had 238 volumes in 1423,[7] but sold most of them. The *Deipnosophistae* was edited by the Cretan Marcus Musurus for Aldo Manuzio (Venice, 1514), based on manuscripts that disappeared shortly afterwards and that lacked the first two books, which, however, did not affect the musical content. The first Latin translation was published only in 1556.[8]

The first notice we have of the acquisition of a manuscript containing strictly musical treatises is a memorandum of Ambrogio Traversari of 1433. He tells of visiting Vittorino da Feltre in Mantua on 16 July and seeing among his books the *Music* of Aristides Quintilianus and that of Bacchius Senior.[9] In a letter to Niccolo Niccoli of 7 August 1433, he says that besides the Aristides and Bacchius Senior there was the *Musica* of Claudius Ptolemy in the same volume.[10] From the style of Ptolemy and Aristides he judged them both to be highly learned writers. In the next letter Traversari reports

3. See ch. 3 below.

4. Remigio Sabbadini, *Le scoperte dei codici latini e greci ne' secoli xiv e xv* (Florence, 1905–14), I, 45.

5. D'Abano's commentaries and the translations of Trebizon and Gaza were all eventually published. See ch. 3 below.

6. This is known through a report of Ambrogio Traversari, *Epistolae et orationes,* ed. Lorenz Mehus (Florence, 1759), II, 1028.

7. Georg Voigt, *Die Wiederbelegung des classischen Alterthums* (Berlin, 1893), I, 264.

8. By Noël dei Conti (Venice, 1556).

9. Traversari, *Hodoeporicon,* ed. Alessandro Dini-Traversari in *Ambrogio Traversari e i suoi tempi* (Florence, 1912), p. 73: "Quintiliani Musicam, & alterius senis de Musica opus . . . et quaedam alia notavimus eaque protinus Nicolao nostro per literas significavimus."

10. Traversari, *Epistolae,* Mehus ed., II, 418–19: "Offendimus *de Musica* volumina Claudii Ptolomaei, & Quintiliani cuiusdam bene eruditi, ut ex stylo animadverti & Bacchii Senis in eodem volumine."

that he also saw in Vittorino's library the *De musica* of St. Augustine and that he arranged for the Aristides and Bacchius among other works to be transcribed for Niccoli, who was the most avid collector of ancient Greek and Latin manuscripts of his time.[11] When Niccoli died on 4 February 1437, his library of more than 800 volumes was valued at 4,000 zecchini, the richest in Florence.[12] He allowed scholars free access to his books, and at the time of his death 100 were on loan. His will of 22 January 1437 stipulated that the disposition of his library should be decided by a sixteen-man commission including Cosimo and Lorenzo de' Medici, Traversari, Bruni, Poggio Bracciolini, and other scholars. Cosimo de' Medici arranged to pay all of Niccoli's considerable debts, in return for which the commission allowed Cosimo to be the sole trustee and to set up the library in the convent of San Marco, where the library was opened to the public in 1444. Giuliano Lopaccini was given the task of curator, and he noted in each book of Niccoli that it had once been his property.[13] Cosimo continued to have books purchased for the library and to pay for its maintenance.[14]

A catalog of the San Marco library prepared around 1499 includes several musical items. The Traversari manuscript containing Aristides Quintilianus is there, as well as Plutarch's *De musica,* and a codex containing writings on music, including Ptolemy's *Harmonics.*[15] Among the Latin works were Boethius on music and a collection of medieval treatises including "musica Guidonis" and "alia musica."[16]

The manuscript that Traversari saw in Vittorino's library has been identified with MS VI.10 of the Biblioteca Marciana in Venice, which is considered an optimal source for the treatises it contains, namely those of Ptolemy, Plutarch, Porphyry, Aristides, the anonymi edited by Bellermann and Najock, and Bacchius Senior, and for three anonymous hymns now attributed to Mesomedes.[17] Elegantly written by a single hand on parchment

---

11. Letter 13 August, ibid., II, 419–20.

12. Berthold L. Ullman and Philip A. Stadter, *The Public Library of Renaissance Florence: Niccolo Niccoli, Cosimo de' Medici and the Library of San Marco* (Padua, 1972), p. 9. By the time of the library's opening the number of books was down to half that (p. 16).

13. Voigt, *Die Wiederbelegung,* pp. 400–01.

14. Ullman and Stadter, *The Public Library,* p. 12.

15. The catalogue is printed in Ullman and Stadter, *The Public Library,* pp. 125ff., from a manuscript in Modena, Archivio di Stato. Aristides is Index no. 1196 (p. 263); Plutarch no. 1184 (p. 261), now Biblioteca Medicea-Laurenziana MS 80.30, from Niccoli's library, bound by Vespasiano, September 1453; Ptolemy is Index no. 1145 (p. 257): "Musicae auctores, Ptolomei musica, Nicomachi arithmetic[a], Euclidae geometria, etc."

16. Ibid., p. 201, nos. 681, 682 (Boethius); p. 210, no. 750 (Guido, etc.).

17. Giovanni Benedetto Mittarelli, *Bibliotheca codicum manuscriptorum Monasterii S. Michaelis Venetiarum prope Murianum* (Venice, 1779), col. 973: "De his Commentariis fit mentio in epistolis Ambrosii, quos ipse vidit Mantuae apud Victorinum Feltrensem, & verosimiliter est

probably in the twelfth or thirteenth century, the codex is believed to have belonged to a bishop in Thessaly. After Vittorino the manuscript somehow reached Giorgio Trivisano,[18] who sold it to the Candiani, ancestors of Francesco Barbaro, a learned humanist and procurator of San Marco in Venice. Eight manuscripts once belonging to Francesco Barbaro were at the Monastery of St. Michael in Murano when Mittarelli described that collection in 1779. Ten years later the volumes were transferred to the Marciana. There remains some doubt, however, that the manuscript Vittorino had is the same as the one later owned by Francesco Barbaro and now in the Marciana.

The inventory of books accompanying Bessarion's Act of Donation of 1468 includes among the Greek books a number of important musical items:[19]

232 Item musica Ptolomei, cum expositione Aristidis Quintiliani et Brienii in papyro [not extant]

241 Item Theonis in Platonem de mathematicis [Marc. gr. 307]

259 Item musica Ptolomei cum expositione Briennii, in papyro [Marc. gr. 321]

260 Item musica Ptolomei cum expositione Porphirii et aliorum, et a principio arithmetica cum expositione, in papyro, liber rarissimus [Marc. gr. 318]. (The inventory of 1474 describes this more fully under no. 570: Arithmetica cum expositione Asclepii, et musica cum expositione Porphyrii, Brienii, Nicomachi, et Bachii Senis, in papiro, liber optimus.)

404 Item Polideuces de elegantia, et cujusdam monachi Joseph [Rhacendyta] epithoma in rhetoricam, logicam et totam philosophiam Aristotelis, et in quattuor scientias sive mathematica, et alia quaedam, in papyro [Marc. gr. 529]

386 Item Aristotelis problemata, in pergameno [not extant]

---

idem codex, quemipse sub oculis habuit." For a description and history see Karl von Jan, *Musici scriptores graeci* (Leipzig, 1895; repr. Hildesheim, 1962), pp. XI–XIV, where it is given the siglum *V*. See Table 2 in von Jan for a facsimile. The same page, plus the following one, both containing the Mesomedes hymns, is reproduced in Egert Pöhlmann, *Denkmäler altgriechischer Musik* (Nuremberg, 1970), Abbildungen 5–6.

18. This was Georgius Trivizias, a Uniate priest from Crete, who seems to have had an interest in mathematical subjects. Concerning him see Aubrey Diller, "Three Scribes Working for Bessarion: Trivizias, Callistus, Hermonymus," *Italia medioevalia e umanistica* 10 (1967): 403–06.

19. Lotte Labowsky, *Bessarion's Library and the Biblioteca Marciana: Six Early Inventories* (Rome, 1979), pp. 166–67, 174, 185–86, 222, and, for the identification of extant manuscripts, her concordances, pp. 433ff. See also Charles Omont, "Inventaire des manuscrits grecs et latins donnés à Saint-Marc de Venise par le cardinal Bessarion (1468)," *Revue des bibliothèques* 4 (1896):149ff.

387 Item problemata Aristotelis, in papyro, et aliqua alia eiusdem [Marc. gr. 216]

Among the Latin books are two copies of the musical treatise of Boethius and one of that of St. Augustine (numbers 195, 196, and 206; Marc. lat. 333, 271, and 71) and several more Greek items:

241 Item Theonis in Platonem de mathematicis
404 Item Polideuces de elegantia, et cujusdam monachi Joseph [Rhacendyta] epitoma in rhetoricam et totam philosophiam Aristotelis, et in quattuor scientias sive mathematica et alia quaedam, in papyro

An inventory of 1474, completed after a second consignment of books arrived in Venice, contained additional musical codices, those Bessarion had kept in Rome for his own use:

84 Naucratis convivia libris octo, in pergamenis (Athenaeus, *Deipnoso-phistae*) [Marc. gr. 447]
158 Alexandri et Aristotelis problemata, in papiris [Marc. gr. 259]
545 Alexander de complexione . . . et alia pauca ex problematibus Aristotelis . . . [Marc. gr. 257]
571 Liber musicae novus in quo continentur Aristidis Quintiliani de musica libri XXXV, Manuelis Brienii de musica libri XXXV, Plutarchi de musica liber unus, Euclidis [i.e., Cleonides] introductio in musicam et eiusdem [i.e., Euclidis] partitio instrumenti, Aristoxenis de elementis musicae libri III, Alipii introductio in musicam, Gaudentii introductio in musicam, Nicomachi enchiridion in musicam, eiusdem aliud en-chiridion, Ptolemei musica in libris III, videlicet ipse textus, Porphyrii expositio in primum librum musicorum Ptolemei, et partem secundi, liber optimus, in pergameno, et difficilis inventu [Marc. gr. 322]

Thus between the Barbaro and Bessarion codices the entire corpus of specifically musical writings by Greek authors was in the Venetian area. But in 1490 Bessarion's manuscripts were still in the packing cases in which they had been sent from Rome to Venice, stacked one on top of another at the end of the Sala Novissima of the Palazzo Ducale, which was to have been a splendid reading room. A few scholars and others were granted the privilege of borrowing some of the manuscripts—and some were not re-turned—but they were not generally accessible. Two librarians were par-ticularly diligent in controlling the borrowing and restitution of books and in retrieving some that were long overdue: Andrea Navagero, from 1516 to 1524, and Pietro Bembo, from 1530 to 1543. It was during the latter's tenure in 1532 that the books were finally removed from their chests and installed in a reading room with shelves and lecterns in an upper floor of the Church of San Marco. It was not until some time between 1559 and 1565 that Bessarion's library found the kind of home the cardinal had envisioned, in the building designed by Sansovino in which it has remained until the present, except for the years 1812 and 1904, when it was in the Palazzo Ducale.[20]

Cardinal Bessarion did not deed all of his library to San Marco. He kept certain books for his own use; some of these and others he acquired in the last four years of his life were sent to Venice after his death.[21] But others were apparently sold, because Giorgio Valla in 1469 acquired a number of manuscripts from him.[22] Valla also made personal forages in Salonica and Constantinople in 1486 and eventually amassed a considerable library of 220 Greek books, of which 150 were manuscripts.[23] Among them were the following surviving musical manuscripts:

Modena, Biblioteca Estense, MS a.V.7.14 (*olim* III.E.16), containing Porphyry
Modena, Biblioteca Estense, MS a.V.7.1 (*olim* II.F.8), containing the treatises of Bryennius, Aristides, the Bellermann anonymi, Bacchius Senior, a Pseudo-Bacchius treatise, and the Mesomedes hymns
Modena, Biblioteca Estense, MS a.V.7.13 (*olim* II.E.19), containing Dio Chrysostomus, Plutarch, and excerpts from Porphyry[24]
Naples, Biblioteca Nazionale, MS III.C.2, containing Gaudentius, Theon of Smyrna, Pappus, Aristoxenus, part of Ptolemy, Cleonides, and Euclid

Valla's library passed to Alberto Pio of Carpi, who died on 8 January 1531, and it was inherited by Cardinal Rodolfo Pio of Carpi. Eventually in 1573 Duke Alfonso II d'Este bought the Greek and Oriental manuscripts. Girolamo Mei used the manuscripts when they were in the library of Cardinal Pio, and he noted concerning the Estense a.V.7.1 that "the three books of Bryennius are most diligently written, those of Aristides not perhaps so accurately, though I have not made the comparison."[25] Von Jan considered

20. See Labowsky, *Bessarion's Library*, pp. 57–100.
21. Ibid., pp. 57–100.
22. Sabbadini, *Scoperte*, I, 65.
23. Ibid., I, 65.
24. This codex is not listed by von Jan but is related to Marciana gr. VI.10 by Benedict Einarson and Phillip H. De Lacy in their edition of Plutarch (Cambridge, Mass., 1967). See Thomas J. Mathiesen, "[Response], Humanism and Music," in *International Musicological Society, Report of the Twelfth Congress, Berkeley 1977*, ed. Daniel Heartz and Bonnie Wade (Kassel, 1981), p. 879. See this discussion also for other comments concerning Valla's Greek manuscripts.
25. Letter to Vettori, 14 October 1564, London, British Library, MS Add. 10268, fol. 238v: "i tre libri di Bryennio son' diligentissimamente scrittj. gli altri d'Aristide non forse tanto. pure non hò fatto paragone. Alcune altre operette che ui son' dietro sono assaj scorette, ma le son tali in tanti essemplarj."

the Naples manuscript of particular value for the Gaudentius and the musical fragments of Ptolemy that he published in his *Scriptores*. Thomas J. Mathiesen, who has made a survey of Greek manuscripts containing musical treatises, has summed up the quality of those owned by Valla thus: "It appears that all of Valla's *codices musici* were fairly authoritative and that the Neapolitan one was of special merit."[26]

Pico della Mirandola was another assiduous collector. In 1498 his library had some 1,190 volumes, of which 157 were in Greek.[27] Pico studied music as a boy and is said to have composed in his youth. A nephew later wrote that he "accompanied his verses with song and instrumental sound."[28] Although he possessed a number of important Greek musical sources, his writings do not give evidence of his having read them. In an inventory prepared in 1498 two copies of Ptolemy's *Harmonics* are listed.[29] One of these (no. 478) reads: "Papirus Musica Ptolomei graeca et alia," which suggests that there were other musical treatises in the codex. Indeed the inventory may conceal quite a number of them, because the first item in a manuscript usually served to identify it. The other manuscript is tagged: "Musica Claudii Ptolemei." Other musical titles he owned are the treatises of Boethius and St. Augustine. The latter he loaned to Giorgio Valla, who returned it in 1492.[30] The inventory also lists "Flores musice artis impressi,"

---

26. Mathiesen, "Humanism and Music," p. 879. The inventory made for the executors of the will of Rodolfo Pio, Cardinal of Carpi on 16 May 1564, according to Johann Ludwig Heiberg, *Beiträge zur Geschichte Georg Valla's und seiner Bibliothek* (Leipzig, 1896), p. 123, listed a codex containing Bryennius, Aristides, Bacchius, together with Herodotus' *Homer,* and Julianus; another containing Porphyry, a work of Euclid, and a commentary on it by Marini, and Aristotle, *Posterior Analytics;* and a third manuscript containing the treatises of Plutarch and Ptolemy, together with five orations of Dionysius Grisostomini. The first of these matches a description of a codex given by Alberto Pio de' Carpi to the Grand Duke of Tuscany according to Latino Latini in a letter to Giovanni Vincenzo Pinelli, 17 October 1579, in Milan, Biblioteca Ambrosiana, MS D.464 inf., fol. 114r: "Il Mei ha ueduto piu exemplari de l'Isagoge di Bacchio; e tutti mal trattati, e poco integri; e per la diligentia da esso fatta; non si è trouato mai libro se non lacero, e scorretto. Sarà adesso ne la libraria de Medici il uolume grande no. 89: ch'era gia di Carpi: et in esso tutti questi insieme: Anonymi Harmonica, Bacchij Isagoge, Brienni lib. iii, Aristide Quintilianj, Ptolemaei, et Porphyri harmonica, Vita Homeri per Herod.: Data Euclid. cum Marinj Prolegom, Post: Arist: cum com: et Iuliani Caes. symp: et Antiochus. questo indice era appresso di me; che tanto mi peruenne di tutta quella libreria. La Greca tutta scritta fù donata dal s. Alberto al gran Duca: ma ne questo libro puo molto giouare à v.s. perche il Mei uidde questo ancora e lo trouò cosi diffettuoso come gli altri."

27. Paul Kibre, *The Library of Pico della Mirandola* (New York, 1936), pp. 21–23.

28. F. Calori Cesis, *Pico della Mirandola* (Mirandola, 1897), p. 151, n. 1.

29. Kibre, *The Library,* Appendix, nos. 478 and 1568.

30. Kibre, *The Library,* Appendix, no. 541: "Membranus Boetii musica et arismetrica"; no. 579: "Papirus Centiloquium et musica et alia"; Cesis, *Pico,* p. 51, no. 46: "Musica Augustini

probably *Flores musice omnis cantus gregoriani* by Hugo von Reutlingen (Venice, 1485), and a "Musica noua impressa," which may be one of Gaffurio's works published between 1480 and 1496 or perhaps Ramos de Pareja's treatise.[31] Other musical treatises were Nicolo Burzio's *Musices opusculum* and Marsilio Ficino's *De rationibus musice*.[32] Also listed are three "manuscript books of music," probably choirbooks or collections of polyphony.[33] There is ample evidence in this inventory that Pico took particular interest in music, gathering what he could of the ancient sources and even modern printed books on the subject.

Pico's library went by the terms of his will to his uncle, from whom it was purchased by Cardinal Domenico Grimani. The cardinal was a patron of Erasmus of Höritz, or Horicius, who dedicated his most important musical treatise to him around 1504–08.[34] It may be that Pico's books served Erasmus Horicius in his researches, for Erasmus shows some evidence of having studied Ptolemy's *Harmonics,* as well as the *Almagest,* which he cites specifically.[35] Cardinal Grimani in 1523 deeded his library to the Monastery of San Antonio di Castello, which he founded in Venice.[36] This library later burned, and the books salvaged after the fire were dispersed.

Among the popes Nicolas V (reigned 1447–55) made the most important contribution toward establishing the Vatican Library as a resource for scholars. It was he who, having founded it as a public library, wanted to make it the greatest since Alexandria. Poor most of his life, once pope, he surrounded himself with luxury and emulated the Medici as a patron. He spent no less than 40,000 scudi on books and before his death had amassed 5,000 volumes.[37] He hired copyists, translators, and purchasing agents.[38] His suc-

manuscripta in papiro"; Heiberg, *Beiträge,* p. 61, Pico to Valla: "Deliver to the bearer of these the following books: Augustine's *De musica...,*" trans. in Kibre, *The Library,* p. 14.

31. Cesis, *Pico,* p. 51, no. 954; p. 52, no. 583.

32. Cesis, *Pico,* p. 52, no. 564: "Musica burcij impressa"; p. 56, no 959: "Regiones varie: ordo seculorum. Marcus Phicinus de rationibus musice et alia manuscripta in papiro." The latter is published in Paul O. Kristeller, ed., *Supplementum Ficinianum,* pp. 51–56, from Florence, Biblioteca Riccardiana, MS 797, fols. 389v–93v, as *Epistola de rationibus musicae ad Dominicum Benivenium.*

33. Cesis, *Pico,* p. 51, no. 970: "Liber musica manuscriptus"; p. 52, no. 901: "Liber in musica in membrane"; p. 52, no. 863: "Liber musice manuscriptus."

34. Palisca, "The *Musica* of Erasmus of Höritz," in *Aspects of Medieval and Renaissance Music,* ed. Jan LaRue (New York, 1966), pp. 628–48.

35. Biblioteca Apostolica Vaticana, MS Reg. lat. 1245, fol. 41v.

36. Kibre, *The Library,* p. 20.

37. Voigt, *Die Wiederbelegung,* II, 196–99.

38. See Eugène Müntz and Paul Fabre, *La bibliothèque du Vaticane au xve siècle* (Paris, 1887; repr. Amsterdam, 1970).

cessor, Calistus III, however, gave away 200 Greek codices, and neither Pius II nor Paul II had any interest in antiquities. It was only with Sixtus IV (reigned 1471–84) that a librarian was appointed and the Vatican Library became a permanent institution.

Some of the most important accessions were those left to the Vatican through the will of Fulvio Orsini (1529–1600). Pope Gregory XIII in 1582 procured a pension for Orsini in exchange for his library, which formally entered the Vatican under Pope Clement VIII. In his youth Fulvio was a choirboy at St. John the Lateran and a student of Greek. In 1558 he became librarian for Ranuccio Farnese, Cardinal Sant' Angelo. He carried on a voluminous correspondence with such humanists as Vettori, Pinelli, Carlo Signoio, and Latino Latini, much of it having to do with the purchase of books for either himself or Cardinal Farnese. In the inventory appended to Orsini's will are listed 162 Greek manuscripts, 101 printed books in Greek, and 300 Latin manuscripts.[39] From the library of Angelo Colocci, A Roman humanist and collector who died in 1549, Orsini acquired what is now Vaticanus graecus 1364, a sixteenth-century codex containing Bryennius, Aristides, the anonymi, Bacchius, Dionysius, Porphyry, and the hymns.[40] From the library of Carteromachos, Orsini obtained the paper manuscript in his hand that is now Vaticanus graecus 1374, containing Plutarch's *De musica*.[41] Other codices in the Orsini inventory are the present Vaticanus graecus 1290, containing Ptolemy's *Harmonics;* Vaticanus graecus 1341, with Aristides Quintilianus and Cleonides' *Introduction;* and Vaticanus graecus 1346, with Cleonides.[42] Manuscripts of Greek treatises on music are mentioned in the earliest catalogs of the Vatican Library, starting with a list made under Pope Boniface VIII in 1294 not long after the pontifical treasure was returned to Rome from the East. The one musical item among the twenty-three codices is enigmatic: "phisica Aristotelis et de musica."[43] Whose "de musica" this may have been is uncertain, but it may have been the Aristotelian *De audibilibus*. An inventory made under Sixtus IV in 1475 listed the following items, some of which have been positively identified with present holdings, which are given in brackets:

331 Musica Ptolomei et Briennii. Ex papiro in rubeo. [Vat. gr. 176?]
334 Musica Ptolomei Nicomachi Arithmetica. Ex papiro in nigro. [Vat. gr. 186?]

39. The inventory is in the Biblioteca Apostolica Vaticana, MS Vat. lat. 7205. See Pierre de Nolhac, *La bibliothèque de Fulvio Orsini* (Paris, 1887), p. 117.

40. Nolhac, *La bibliotheque*, p. 182.

41. Ibid., p. 179.

42. Ibid., pp. 125, 179, 187, 337, 339. Vat. gr. 1290 is not listed in von Jan or Düring.

43. Robert Devreesse, *Le fonds grec de la Bibliotheque vaticane des origines à Paul V* (Vatican City, 1965), p. 3.

336 Ptolomei musica. Ex papiro in albo. [Vat. gr. 187]
347 Ptolomei musica. Nicomachi arithmetica et Euclidis geometria. Ex papiro in nigro. [Vat. gr. 196]
365 Nicomachi arithmetica et musica. Brienni musica, et Ptolomei Hermagestus. Ex papiro in rubeo. [Vat. gr. 198][44]

Another item appears in an inventory of 1481:

278 C. Claudii Ptolomaei Musica, ex papyro in gilbo. [Vat. gr. 185][45]

In 1510 appears listed "Joseph Rhacendyti summa," a work that includes an introduction to music.[46] Also in that inventory are the following musical works:

16 Enarrator anonymus in tetrabiblion Ptolomaei. . . . Claudii Ptolemaei harmonica. [Vat. gr. 1048]
141 Euclidis elementorum . . . Aristidis Quintiliani . . . Cl. Ptolemaei . . . Plutarchi de musica liber [Vat. gr. 192]
144 Tabulae astronomicae. Cl. Ptolemaei harmonicorum libri tres [Vat. gr. 188?]
163 Cleomedis . . . kyklikes . . . Nicomachi Geraseni Pythagorei arithmeticae introductionis libri duo.
171 Claudii Ptolomaei harmonicorum libri tres. [Vat. gr. 187]
175 Cl. Ptolomaei geographia . . . Manuelis Bryennii . . . Porphyrii . . . Pappi [Vat. gr. 176][47]

The present Vaticanus graecus 189 first appears in 1551 as no. 168, "Claudii Ptholomei harmonia libri tres." Also listed that year is graecus 194, "Theonis Smirnei platonici de his que in mathematicis utilia sunt ad Platonis lectionem." Vaticanus graecus 221 appears in a purchase of 1559: "Aristoxeni Armonica . . . Autor sine nomine de musica."[48]

Records of borrowings from the early years show relatively little activity in the music field. But the following items are notable. On 12 November 1494 Valgulio borrowed a paper codex of Plutarch's *Moralia* and returned it on 24 January. On 26 September 1498 Carlo Valgulio returned "quedam De musica et Arithmetica Nicomachi" (Vat. gr. 186). On 10 February 1495 Valgulio had borrowed Plutarch's *Moralia,* which was still not returned on 10 December 1518, according to an annotation by the custodian, who also

---

44. Ibid., pp. 599–60. The identifications were made by Devreesse.
45. Ibid., p. 94.
46. Ibid., p. 157.
47. Ibid., pp. 162–65. As to be expected, this inventory repeats some of the items in that of 1475.
48. Ibid., pp. 420, 422, 447.

recorded his attempts to get it back. Valgulio's translation of Plutarch's *De musica* was published in 1507.[49] On 4 February 1518 Pietro Bembo returned Vaticanus graecus 191, an anthology that contains Gaudentius, Cleonides (two copies), Euclid (two copies), Aristoxenus, Alypius, and Aristoxenus' rhythmic fragments. Pietro Paolo Aretino borrowed the same codex on 7 July 1522 for an African gentleman, who left a silver candy dish as security, and Pietro returned it on 8 August. Johannes Petrus Crassus took it out on 25 August 1529 on behalf of Cardinal Ridolfi.[50]

One of the most remarkable manuscripts in the Vatican, Barberinus graecus 265, came to it through Marcello Cervini, Cardinal of Santa Croce, elected Pope Marcellus II on 9 April 1555. Beautifully illuminated and decorated with the coat of arms of the cardinal, it unites the main musical sources: Aristoxenus, Ptolemy, Porphyry, Plutarch, Theon, Pappus, Cleonides, Euclid, Aristides, Bacchius, pseudo-Bacchius (Dionysius), Alypius, Gaudentius, and the anonymi. Purported to be written by Johannes Honorios, the codex gives variant readings for Ptolemy's *Harmonics* as well as several sets of scholiae, and it presents a text of Aristoxenus that is collated from two or more sources.[51] The Cleonides shows signs of collation with Vatican graecus 191, a chartaceous and bombycinous codex of the thirteenth or fourteenth century originating in Constantinople, and Valla's manuscript now in Naples.

A sixteenth-century library that boasted significant music holdings was that of Cardinal Nicolo Ridolfi. A humanist skilled in both Greek and Latin, Ridolfi collected a magnificent library, which he made available to scholars, notably Piero Vettori, who was promised anything he needed. After Ridolfi's death Cosimo I de' Medici considered acquiring items in it and had its inventory compared to that of his library in San Lorenzo. Among the Greek works in the Ridolfi collection that were thought to be lacking in the Laurentian library were Ptolemy's *Harmonics* and Porphyry's commentary, the treatises of Aristides and Aristoxenus, the *Problems* of Aristotle with notes upon them, and the Bryennius treatise. Simone Porzio, who made up the want list, admitted that he worked from an incomplete inventory of San Lorenzo and that if he had had a complete one, nothing or practically nothing would probably have been found lacking.[52] Cardinal

49. Brescia: Angelo Britannico.

50. Maria Bertola, *I due primi registri di prestito della Biblioteca apostolica vaticana*, pp. 57, 55, 50, 109. The records reported here are for the years 1475–1547.

51. See Düring, *Die Harmonielehre*, p. XXXVII; von Jan, *Musici scriptores graeci*, p. LXXVII; and Jon Solomon, "Vaticanus gr. 2337 and the Eisagoge Harmonike," *Philologus* 127 (1983):247–53.

52. R. Ridolfi, "La biblioteca del cardinale Nicolò Ridolfi," *La Bibliofilia* 31 (1929): 173–93.

Ridolfi's son sold the library to the Cardinal de Guise but intended it for Piero Strozzi. When Piero died, the books went to Catherine de' Medici, with whom they traveled to Paris, where they are now among the treasures of the Bibliothèque Nationale. Among the manuscripts now in Paris that must have been in Ridolfi's library are graecus 2450, a parchment codex of the fourteenth century containing Ptolemy and Theon of Smyrna; graecus 2451, a paper codex of the fifteenth century containing Ptolemy, Porphyry, and Plutarch; graecus 2532, a fifteenth-century paper manuscript with Aristides, the anonymi, Bacchius, Dionysius, and the hymns; and graecus 2549, a bombycinous codex of the fourteenth century containing Bryennius.

There was clearly an abundance of sources in Italy by the mid-sixteenth century for the study of Greek music theory. In Rome, Venice, Florence, and perhaps Urbino and Milan, it was possible for a scholar to locate at least one copy of any of the principal Greek music treatises. What he could do with such a text depended on his competence in the language and the correctness of the exemplar. Here is where obstacles were met. Few musically trained persons had even a smattering of Greek. And those few had at their disposal at most one or two copies of a work. This was not enough to resolve the very considerable textual difficulties encountered in musical texts, more corrupt than most because of the scribes' ignorance of the subject. Despite the large number of copies scattered throughout the Italian collections, the opportunities afforded an individual scholar to compare them were limited by his mobility. In effect an individual scholar like Giorgio Valla or Girolamo Mei was limited to one or two local libraries. They could cajole their correspondents to have copies made for them of distant codices, and this they did, but in the case of Greek texts, reliable copyists were scarce. Only in Rome and Venice, as Antonio Gogava was to realize, was it possible to do serious textual collation.

The State of Knowledge of Greek Theory

Before embarking on our investigation of the rediscovery of ancient learning on music, we should review the state of knowledge of Greek music theory at the dawn of the Renaissance. Then we can briefly survey what each of the freshly discovered or newly studied sources contributed to this understanding. The main links to ancient music theory known during the Middle Ages were the *De institutione musica* of Boethius,[53] the *Commentarius in Somnium Scipionis* (Commentary on the Dream of Scipio) of Macrobius,[54] the

---

53. Ed. Gottfred Friedlein in *De institutione arithmetica libri duo. De institutione musica libri quinque. Accedit geometria* (Leipzig, 1867).

54. Trans. with an introduction by William H. Stahl (New York, 1952).

De nuptiis Philologiae et Mercurii (Marriage of Philology and Mercury) by Martianus Capella,[55] and the *Institutiones divinarum et humanarum litterarum* (Institutions of Divine and Human Letters) of Cassiodorus.[56]

The musical treatise of Boethius was first printed in Venice in 1492,[57] but both before and after that it circulated widely in manuscript copies and could be found in nearly every educational institution and monastery. It was revered as having almost infallible and scriptural authority in the field of music. Written in the early years of the sixth century, when Boethius was a young man, it was a compendium of the discipline of music as studied within the framework of the quadrivium, as he named the fourfold path to knowledge that comprised music, arithmetic, geometry, and astronomy. Parallel to his *De institutione arithmetica,* which is a translation of Nicomachus' *De arithmetica,* the music treatise is partly translation, partly paraphrase, and partly commentary on Greek treatises. There is some difference of opinion between the two scholars who have recently considered the sources of Boethius as to whether Book 4 as well as the first three, derive from a major lost work on music by Nicomachus, whose extant *Manual (Encheiridion armonikēs)* is barely a compendium. Ubaldo Pizzani holds that Book 4 of Boethius is based on a variety of ancient sources: chapters 1–2 on Euclid's *Sectio canonis,* chapters 3–4 on Gaudentius in a translation by Mutianus, chapters 5–12 on an unknown source, chapter 13 on the lost work of Nicomachus, and chapters 14–18 on Ptolemy's *Harmonics.*[58] Calvin Bower has made a strong case for regarding Book 4 also as Nicomachean.[59] Book 5, on the other hand, is verifiably based on Ptolemy's *Harmonics* 1.1–14; the table of contents for this book of Boethius shows that he had planned a total of thirty chapters, which would have covered all sixteen chapters of Ptolemy's Book 1, but he finished—or at least there survive—only eighteen.

Until the Renaissance readers did not suspect that Boethius was not the author of the doctrine transmitted in the books on music. Moreover, they regarded it as universal and timeless knowledge, which, though associated with Greek music, was not limited to it in application. Up to a point this attitude was correct, for Boethius' subject is music as a mathematical science, which did not depend on Greek musical practice. Still, it was a system of

55. Trans. William H. Stahl and Richard Johnson, with E. L. Burge, as *Martianus Capella and the Seven Liberal Arts* (New York, 1977), II.

56. The music section is translated by Helen Dill Goode and Gertrude C. Drake under the title *Institutiones humanarum litterarum* (Colorado Springs, 1980).

57. *De musica libri quinque* in *Opera,* I, fols. 174–205.

58. Ubaldo Pizzani, "Studi sulle fonti del 'De Institutione Musica' di Boezio," *Sacris erudiri* 16 (1965):5–164.

59. Calvin Bower, "Boethius and Nicomachus: An Essay Concerning the Sources of *De institutione musica,*" *Vivarium* 16 (1978):1–45.

thought abstracted from Greek musical practice, and post-medieval readers who considered the matter recognized the irrelevance of much of this theory to Western music. But it remained the basis of the discipline of music theory, as opposed to musical practice, until it was partly supplanted and partly supplemented by older Greek sources discovered in the Renaissance.

Through Nicomachus and Ptolemy, Boethius absorbed elements of the two principal Greek traditions, the Pythagorean and the Aristoxenian. For Aristoxenus harmonics was a self-sufficient science of pitches as known to the ear. He was skeptical of applying numerical speculations to this realm. The Pythagoreans, on the other hand, doubted the reliability of the ear as an instrument for judging consonance or intonation. Such matters, they believed, should be referred to the reason, which measures precisely by means of number. The science of harmonics must be based on number and is consequently a branch of mathematics. It was this point of view that Boethius transmitted. Intervals, he showed, may be classified according to the ratios of string lengths of the component tones. Two genres of ratios yield consonances: the multiple (of the type xn / n) and the superparticular (of the type $n + 1 / n$). But not all ratios belonging to these genres, only those expressible by the first four numbers, are admitted to the circle of consonances. These consonances are five, of which three are formed from multiple ratios—octave (2:1), octave-plus-fifth (3:1), and double octave (4:1)–and two from superparticular—fifth (3:2) and fourth (4:3). The basis of the diatonic scale assumed by Boethius, first described by Plato,[60] utilizes the difference between the fifth and the fourth, namely a whole tone, as its building block (3:2 / 4:3 = 9:8). A fourth will contain two of these and a remainder, or *limma*: 4:3 / (9:8 × 9:8) = 256:243. When taken in descending order, two tones and a limma form the four-note module known as the tetrachord. Tetrachords are joined, either directly or through a linking whole tone, to form the heptachord, octachord, and larger scales. Boethius describes two systems that may be formed from these tetrachords, a ten-step system and a fifteen-step system. The ten-step system consists of three conjunct tetrachords (see Figure 2.1). The letter names in brackets in the left column were not known to Boethius but were assigned to the steps by medieval writers and are still used today; they do not indicate any absolute pitch. The fifteen-step system, or double diapason, consisted of two pairs of conjunct tetrachords separated by a tone of disjunction, with an added tone below the lowest tetrachord (see Figure 2.2).

Each of these systems may occur in one of the three genera, the diatonic, chromatic, and enharmonic. As described by Boethius, the diatonic module, or tetrachord, consists of the rising series: semitone, tone, tone; the chro-

60. *Timaeus* 36b.

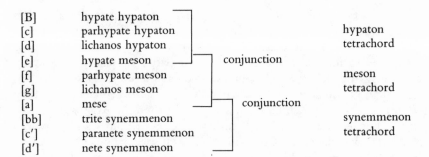

Figure 2.1:
The conjunct system

matic: semitone, semitone, and a composite of three semitones; the enharmonic: diesis, diesis, ditone. Thus the pitches of the two inner steps of the tetrachord are variable, whereas those of the boundary steps are fixed.

One of the limitations of this system discovered by the early Pythagoreans and detailed by Boethius is that a cycle of twelve fifths is larger than a cycle of seven octaves by a small interval. The first, a true cycle, and the second, really a spiral, miss coinciding in a unison by the minute amount called the comma, 524,288:531,441. Six whole tones exceed an octave by the same comma.

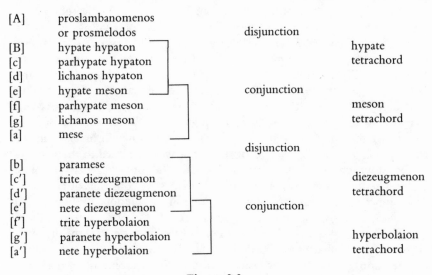

Figure 2.2:
The disjunct system

Also in the body of Boethian-Pythagorean theory was the observation that a superparticular ratio cannot be divided into two equal parts. By an equal division is meant one yielding a ratio that, multiplied by itself, equals the ratio being divided. Thus 2:1 × 2:1 is 4:1—that is, an octave added to an octave makes a double octave. Conversely, the double octave may be equally divided by extracting the square root of its ratio, 4:1, giving 2:1, the size of its component halves. But the square root of a superparticular ratio will always be a surd, for example, the equal "halves" of the interval 9:8 are each 3 / 2√2. Such irrational proportions were excluded from music by the Pythagoreans.

Whereas this doctrine of scale formation, intonation, and the limitations of the system, expounded in the first three books and the first thirteen chapters of the fourth, remained stable among the authors of Pythagorean persuasion, explanations of theoretical concepts that owe their origin to Aristoxenian theory, contained in the rest of the fourth book, are not consistent from one author to another. Boethius is particularly ambiguous on the subject of the octave species and tonoi, or *modi,* as he calls them, and their interaction.

Octave species are the most important category of consonances recognized in Greek theory. Boethius defined species as "a certain consonance-producing arrangement that has a particular form according to one of the genera and whose boundary notes are framed by a particular proportion."[61] There is always one less species than there are steps in the interval, which yields seven for the octave. For the purpose of enumerating the species of consonances, Boethius assigned letter names to the steps hypate hypaton to nete hyperbolaion.[62]

Having shown the species of octave, Boethius at the beginning of the next (fifteenth) chapter makes the startling statement: "Out of the species of consonances of the diapason arise what are called modes, which some call tropes or tonoi. Tropes are systems differing in height and lowness of pitch in their entire series of steps."[63] Medieval scholars, ignorant of Greek

61. Boethius *De institutione musica* 4.14 (Friedlein ed., p. 337): "Species autem est quaedam positio propriam habens formam secundum unumquodque genus in uniuscuiusque proportionis consonantiam faciendis terminis constituta."

62. Friedlein's edition has been emended to conform with Bower's reading of the older manuscript tradition, in "Boethius and Nicomachus," p. 29, as follows:

Friedlein: I K L   M N O
Bower: K L M N X O

63. Boethius *De institutione musica* 4.15 (Friedlein ed., p. 341): "Ex diapason igitur consonantiae speciebus existunt, qui appellantur modi, quos eosdem tropos vel tonos nominant. Sunt autem tropi constitutiones in totis vocum ordinibus vel gravitate vel acumine differentes."

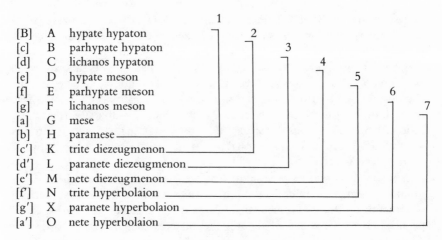

Figure 2.3:
Species of the octave

musical practice, were not in a position to interpret these statements correctly. They tended to infer that the octave species could be turned into modes, since they were familiar with a set of modes that could be formed from the same octave species as are shown in Figure 2.3, but they numbered them in the order 7 to 1 instead of 1 to 7. They also recognized an eighth mode having the same octave species as the first. The system of modi that Boethius described in chapter 16 was incompatible with this interpretation, but because he did not explain how it arose from the species, readers were thrown into confusion. What he described was a scheme in which the octave system proslambanomenos to mese was raised in pitch successively to produce eight identical species of octave on degrees separated by tone, tone, semitone, tone, tone, semitone, tone. Similar series of modi could be produced by raising the octave-plus-fifth or the double-octave systems. The eight octave-system modi produced by this process—that is, by an act of transposition— expressed with the aid of Western sharps and flats, are given in Figure 2.4. Boethius further explains that the modi thus produced were given the names Hypodorian, Hypophrygian, etc., as shown in the figure.

Each of the Boethian modes follows the same pattern: two conjunct tetrachords (rising semitone, tone, tone) with an added note below them. The octave systems can be extended to octave-plus-fifth or to double-octave systems without being considered new modes. They may be represented with our Western letter-names as in Figure 2.4.

The scheme of modes described by Boethius probably derives from Ptolemy through an intermediate source, for it is not entirely consistent with

A B c d e f g a   Hypodorian
Tone
B c♯ d e f♯ g a b   Hypophrygian
Tone
c♯ d♯ e f♯ g♯ a b c♯′   Hypolydian
Semitone
d e f g a b♭ c′ d′   Dorian
Tone
e f♯ g a b c′ d′ e′   Phrygian
Tone
f♯ g♯ a b c♯′ d′ e′ f♯′   Lydian
Semitone
g a b♭ c′ d′ e♭′ f′ g′   Mixolydian
Tone
a b c′ d′ e′ f′ g′ a′   Hypermixolydian

Figure 2.4:
The eight modes of Boethius

Ptolemy's teachings, as will be seen. It resembles the scheme described by the fourteenth-century Byzantine author Bryennius, which suggests a common or related Byzantine intermediary for the two authors. However the derivation of the scheme is not our concern here. The picture of the Greek modes given by Boethius is what the early humanists had to guide them in understanding the more general literature, such as the writings of Plato and Aristotle, which abounded with references to the powers of the Greek *harmoniai,* tonoi, or modes.

As complementary Greek sources were discovered and subsequently made available in Latin translations, the picture of the Greek tonal system given by Boethius became subject to modification. The enlightenment that fifteenth-century readers could gain from these sources was limited by their own prejudices and preconceptions. Musicians were blocked from understanding Boethius by the incorrect assumption that he described a system analogous to the eight church modes, which some medieval authors called Hypodorian, Hypophrygian, Hypolydian, etc., while others more prudently referred to them as Modes 1, 2, 3, to 8. Nonmusicians, such as the early humanists, were not handicapped in this way, but they too were usually led into the trap by the musical theorists whom they consulted. It is remarkable, in view of the confusion surrounding the modes, how faithful the earliest translators were to the texts before them when they had to render in Latin an account of the Greek tonal system.

As opposed to specialized works such as those of Boethius on arithmetic and music, the texts of Macrobius, Capella, and Cassiodorus had much more general appeal, and it is understandable that they should have survived in the Middle Ages when so many other writings were lost. Macrobius, who flourished around 400 A.D., is remembered chiefly for his commentary on Marcus Tullius Cicero, *Scipio's Dream*.[64] Macrobius' work became available in print in 1472 (Venice: Nicolaus Jenson) and by 1500 had been reprinted in Brescia and Venice five times. The first chapter of Book 2 elaborates upon the portion of Cicero's account of Scipio's dream that has to do with the harmony of the motion of the heavenly spheres. Macrobius seizes the occasion to give an account of Pythagoras' discovery of the ratios of the consonances through the hammers of the blacksmith shop, the ratios themselves, and the other intervals of the Pythagorean scale. He then goes on to show how Plato, in the *Timaeus*, applied these musical principles to fashion the world soul. These chapters are apparently based on Porphyry's *Vita Pythagorae* and his *Commentary on Plato's Timaeus*.[65]

In contrast to Boethius and Macrobius, the account of Greek music theory in *De nuptiis Philologiae et Mercurii* by Martianus Capella (early fifth century) shows little Pythagorean influence and, indeed, outlines a curriculum of the musical discipline that is derived from Aristoxenus through the eclectic late Greek author Aristides Quintilianus. It is, in fact, a compendium of Aristides' *Peri mousikēs,* or *On Music,* Book 1, sections 4 to 19.[66] Despite Martianus' dependence on this one author, he is never mentioned by name, although some other musical writers and thinkers are— for example, Theophrastus, Aristoxenus, Pythagoras, and Varro.

In this allegorical introduction to the seven liberal arts, each is represented as a bridesmaid who pronounces a discourse at the wedding of Mercury and Philology. Harmony, speaking for music, is the last, and after singing some songs and making a bow to the music of the spheres, she launches into her disquisition. Much of this has to do with the definition of technical terms and the exposition of the tonal system, which agrees in most respects with that described by Boethius, with a consideration of the principles of melodic composition, and with a survey of rhythmics. One area in which Martianus departs from Boethius is that of the modes, which he calls *tropi*.[67] Of these, he says, there are fifteen; five are principal tropes, and with each of these are associated two others. Each trope consists of five tetrachords, namely the four of the fifteen-note system, to which is added the synem-

64. Both the *Commentary* and Cicero's work are translated in Macrobius, *Commentary on the Dream of Scipio,* translated with introduction and notes by William H. Stahl (New York, 1952).

65. See ibid., pp. 34–35.

66. Aristides Quintilianus, *On Music in Three Books,* translated, with introduction, commentary, and annotations by Thomas J. Mathiesen (New Haven, 1983).

67. Martianus Capella *De nuptiis* 9.935.

menon tetrachord of the conjunct system. What Martianus says of the tropes and their relationships is quite incomprehensible outside the context of Aristides' text, which was unknown until the end of the fifteenth century. What must have impressed early Renaissance readers was that here was a system of music theory that was not Boethian, by an author who talked with reverence, not only about music theory, but about Greek musical practice as well.

Fortunately Cassiodorus was more explicit about the fifteen-mode system than Martianus. He states that the Hypodorian is the deepest-sounding mode, and that the others, separated from each other by a semitone, are in rising order Hypoiastian, Hypophrygian, Hypoaeolian, Hypolydian, Dorian, Iastian, Phrygian, Aeolian, Lydian, Hyperdorian, Hyperiastian, Hyperphrygian, Hyperaeolian, Hyperlydian. The triadic arrangement to which Martianus obliquely made reference is obvious from this complete list; each of the ethnic names appears in a hypo, simple, and hyper form, designating a low, middle, and high pitch range respectively.[68] One assumes that these modes are all identical in internal structure, but Cassiodorus neglects to say so or to say whether they are octave scales or double octaves.

Two of the Greek texts that were among the first to be translated into Latin clarified and modified the presentations of the Greek tonal system by these late classical authors. These were the *Eisagōgē harmonikē,* or *Musical Introduction,* of Cleonides and the *Harmonics* of Ptolemy.[69]

Cleonides gives a different picture of the tonoi from that of Boethius, one that bears the mark of a distinctive Aristoxenian lineage. Cleonides' treatise offered, at least potentially, a key to the interface between the Greek tonoi and the octave species, but it is doubtful that anyone without the help of Ptolemy could have connected the theory of the species with the tonoi, despite the coincidence of the ethnic names "Dorian," "Phrygian," etc., because of the mismatch in number: whereas Cleonides speaks of thirteen tonoi, he names only seven octave species, the total number possible. The system of Cleonides, which was quite transparently conveyed by Valla's translation, may be diagrammed as in Figure 2.5. I have assumed that where Cleonides gives an alternate name to the low version of a tonos, such as Hypoionian for low Hypophrygian, the higher version bears the conventional label, namely Hypophrygian. In the case of the Mixolydian, I assume that the conventional name was applied to the low version, since this pre-

68. Cassiodorus, *Institutiones,* Book II, ch. 5; Isidore of Seville, *Etymologies, Book III, ch. 15–23,* trans. Helen Dill Goode and Gertrude C. Drake, pp. 6–9.

69. The Cleonides text was translated by Giorgio Valla and pubished in Venice in 1497. See ch. 11 below. The Ptolemy treatise was first translated by Nicolò Leoniceno but was never published. See ch. 6 below.

Hypermixolydian   S
(Hyperphrygian)
    T   ⎧ high = Hyperionian
                         ⎨   S
Mixolydian   ⎩ low = Hyperdorian
    S   S
Lydian   ⎧ high
                         ⎨   S
    T   ⎩ low = Aeolian
                                                            S
Phrygian   ⎧ high
                         ⎨   S
    T   ⎩ low = Ionian
                                                            S
Dorian
    S   S
Hypolydian   ⎧ high
                         ⎨   S
    T   ⎩ low = Hypoaeolian
                                                            S
Hypophrygian   ⎧ high
                         ⎨   S
    T   ⎩ low = Hypoionian
Hypodorian   S

Figure 2.5:
The tonoi according to Cleonides, *Harmonic Introduction*, 25.4–26.15

serves the symmetry of the rising tone, tone, semitone, tone, tone, semitone, tone distances between the most familiar tonoi.

If in the system of thirteen Aristoxenian tonoi one ignores the alternately named high and low modes—namely Hyperionian, Hyperdorian, Aeolian, Ionian, Hypoaeolian, and Hypoionian—eight modes are left, separated in their ascending order by tone, tone, semitone, tone, tone, semitone, tone. This then agrees with the schemes of Bryennius[70] and Boethius (4.15), and, if the Hypermixolydian is omitted, with that of Ptolemy.[71] Moreover, if a single pitch octave is cut out of the middle of Cleonides' system, the octave

70. *Harmonics* 3.1. See ch. 6 below.
71. Ibid. 2.8–10.

species that result will be identical to those given homologous names in his list of octave species, but this is not made explicit in the treatise.[72]

The classic theory of the tonoi has been, at least for our own century, that of Ptolemy. The first Western writer to transmit this theory was Nicolò Leoniceno in his translation of Ptolemy's *Harmonics* prepared for Franchino Gaffurio and finished in 1499. Unfortunately, the translation was known to very few and had negligible influence on theoretical thought or the historiography of Greek music. Ptolemy proposed two ways of naming the steps of the double-octave system, one according to the location of the strings on a hypothetical kithara, such as proslambanomenos for the lowest string, mese for the middle string, and nete hyperbolaion for the highest. This method of naming the steps, according to their position (*thesis,*) says nothing about their relationships to each other; it only locates one higher or lower than another. A second way of naming the steps is according to their function (*dynamis*) within a system. Thus, if a tone of disjunction, an interval of a whole tone, separates two tetrachords, the lower tone of this interval is in function either a mese, a proslambanomenos, or a nete hyperbolaion. The upper boundary of this whole-tone interval functions either as a hypate hypaton or paramese. For example, a mese in function may be placed anywhere on the kithara. But always above it will be a tone of disjunction, and another tetrachord will follow. And the mese in function will always be the top note of a tetrachord.[73]

It is possible, Ptolemy shows, to leave the strings as conventionally named where they are on the kithara and to retune them so that a string that was mese, for example, becomes hypate meson by function while remaining mese by position. The purpose of this retuning is to effect modulation in one of two senses. If the entire fifteen-string instrument is retuned while preserving the original combinations of tetrachords and functions, this is a modulation that simply raises or lowers a scale or melody composed on it. It is the same structure in a new tonos, or as we would say, in a different key. If only a part of the instrument is retuned, this results in a new melodic shape, because the interval relationships are changed. Some of the original functions are preserved, while others are altered. Ptolemy explains this distinction in the sixth chapter of Book 2. If the lower two conjoined tetrachords of the original scheme, hypate hypaton to mese, with the addition of proslambanomenos below, are maintained, but a higher tetrachord is conjoined at mese, a new scale is formed, and the note above mese is no

---

72. See Jon D. Solomon, Cleonides *"Eisagōgē harmonikē:* A Critical Edition, Translation, and Commentary"* (Ph.D. diss., University of North Carolina, 1980), pp. 336–37.

73. Ptolemy *Harmonics* 2.5.

longer paramese diezeugmenon—in the diatonic a whole tone above mese—but trite synemmenon, a semitone above mese. This produces the equivalent of the synemmenon system (sometimes called lesser perfect system), which Ptolemy found superfluous, since it could be arrived at by this kind of modulation.[74] This sort of modulation, then, results in a new octave species around mese and is not simply a modulation of tonos.

The relationship of the species to the tonoi remained an enigma in Boethius and was not explicit in Cleonides, who merely hinted at a relationship by giving the same names to the octave species as to some of the tonoi. Ptolemy, however, solved the riddle. Since there were seven notes in an octave, Ptolemy argued, a mese by function could be located on each of the seven notes of the middle octave of the double octave system. This functional middle note, surrounded by the rest of its tonos, produced a different octave species for each of its locations.[75] Ptolemy did not state that the purpose of the tonoi was to produce the seven different octave species within the central octave. But he implied this, particularly when he insisted that the number of tonoi should be limited to seven, since only seven are needed to project that many different species on the middle octave.[76] Of course, not only the middle octave is affected. The entire double octave acquires seven different species or complexes of functional relationships. Because of the limited range of human voices, Ptolemy limited the theoretical gamut to the double octave of the hypothetical fifteen-string kithara, which he called the "unmodulating system" (*systema ametabolon*)—that is, proslambanomenos to nete hyperbolaion as named by position (see Figure 2.6).

We have seen that Cleonides, presumably following Aristoxenus, recognized thirteen tonoi and seven octave species, whereas Ptolemy would admit only seven of each. What of the fifteen tropes mentioned by Martianus and named by Cassiodorus? This matter was not satisfactorily clarified until Aristides Quintilianus and an obscure fragmentary treatise by a certain Alypius were given a careful reading. Martianus followed Aristides Quintilianus, who had explained that the system of fifteen tonoi resulted from "younger theorists" adding two at the top of the thirteen of Aristoxenus.[77] He described them as being, like those of Aristoxenus, a semitone apart. The Aristides treatise became known to a few scholars, notably Gaffurio, through the translation of Francesco Burana of 1494.[78] What did not become clear until the tables of Alypius were discovered was that each tonos con-

---

74. Ibid., 2.7.
75. Ibid., 2.11.
76. Ibid., 2.9.
77. Aristides Quintilianus *De musica 1.9* (Mathiesen trans., p. 86).
78. Concerning this translation see ch. 6 below.

Figure 2.6.

Ptolemy's tonol projecting the octave species on the central octave, according to
modern musicologists (brackets indicate tetrachords, M the mese by function)

tained the full fifteen-note system from proslambanomenos to nete hyperbolaion, so that the range of proslambanomenoi comprised an octave-plus-
tone and the range from the lowest proslambanomenos to the highest nete
hyperbolaion was three octaves and a whole tone. This contrasts with Ptolemy's containment of seven tonoi within a double octave range. Alypius
is assumed to have written in the third or fourth century an *Eisagōgē mousikē,*
or *Introduction to Music,* which after a few prefatory paragraphs presents a
set of tables of notation in the three genera for fifteen tonoi or tropoi (the
last six figures for the enharmonic are missing). The first scholar who studied
or transmitted any of the tables to other scholars was Girolamo Mei in
1579.[79]

79. In a letter to Vincenzo Galilei of 15 May 1579, in Palisca, *Girolamo Mei, Letters on Ancient
and Modern Music* (Rome, 1960; Stuttgart, 1977), facsimiles between pp. 164 and 165, and 172
and 173. Mei sent Galilei only the signs for eight diatonic tonoi, Hypodorian, Hypophrygian,
Hypolydian, Dorian, Phrygian, Lydian, Mixolydian, and Hypermixolydian. These are the
tables published by Galilei in his *Dialogo della musica antica et della moderna* (Florence, 1581),
pp. 92–93.

The name of Aristoxenus came up frequently in the literature about music theory, disparagingly in Boethius and Ptolemy, as a fount of archaic wisdom in Cleonides and Aristides Quintilianus; yet he remained a phantom author throughout most of the Renaissance. His *Harmonic Elements* did not attract much attention, partly because it was incomplete (three books survive), partly because it was extremely technical, but mostly because it contradicted Pythagorean doctrine. It was not available in Latin until 1562, when Antonio Gogava published it among a group of translations that included also Ptolemy's *Harmonics* and a pseudo-Aristotelian fragment on acoustics.[80] Lack of direct knowledge of Aristoxenus was partly compensated by the pervasiveness of his theoretical concepts in the writings of other Greeks. He defined harmonics as the theory of systems and tonoi, or as Henry Macran, the editor, English translator, and commentator on *The Harmonic Elements*, has put it, as of "all that relates to the theory of scales and keys."[81] He divided the field into a number of topics, which, in the version we have, are discussed in the following order: the movement of the voice in singing and speaking, intervals and their classification in general, systems or scales in general, the nature of melody, the nature and origin of scales, the genera, simple and compound intervals, the number and character of scales, species, and arrangements of intervals, and notes. Aristoxenus must have outlined a later version of this curriculum, since both Cleonides and Aristides Quintilianus clearly articulated it in seven parts, the order in Cleonides being notes, intervals, genera, systems or scales, tonoi, modulation, and melodic composition.[82] Aristides Quintilianus put scales before genera.[83]

Aristoxenus aroused the most controversy by his approach to dividing the tetrachord and the octave. An interval to him was a segment of a continuum, a discrete movement of the voice through an unbroken pitch space. The only way to measure this space was comparatively by the ear, not by assigning numbers to lengths of strings. To locate the steps within the meson tetrachord in the chromatic and enharmonic genera, for example, Aristoxenus resorted to figuring twelfths of a tone. This meant dividing the tetrachord (perfect fourth) into 30 equal units, or parts, of pitch space. He preferred this form of measurement to ratios, which he considered an inappropriate application of mathematics to sound. The small units permitted Aristoxenus to define the distances between intervals in the two genera that had a pycnon or dense region, a combination of two intervals the sum of which was less than the third remaining interval. The pycnon

---

80. *Aristoxeni . . . Harmonicorum elementorum libri iii . . . Cl. Ptolemaei Harmonicorum . . . lib. iii. Aristotelis de objecto auditus* (Venice, 1562). Concerning this translation, see ch. 7 below.

81. *The Harmonics of Aristoxenus*, ed. and trans. Henry S. Macran, (Oxford, 1902), p. 165.

82. Cleonides *Introduction* 1.

83. Aristides Quintilianus *De musica* 1.5 (Mathiesen trans., p. 77).

	ENHAR-MONIC	CHROMATIC Soft	Hemiolic	Tonic			DIATONIC Soft	Intense
mese								
	24	22	21	18			15	12
lichanos					oxypycnon	⎫		
	3	4	4½	6		⎬	9	12
parhypate					mesopycnon	pycnon		
	3	4	4½	6		⎬	6	6
hypate					barypycnon	⎭		

Figure 2.7:
Tetrachord divisions of Aristoxenus

was composed of three steps: the high limit, or oxypycnon, the middle step, or mesopycnon, and the low limit, or barypycnon. The diatonic, not having a dense region, had no pycnon, or, in other words, was apycnon. The meson tetrachord, he showed, may be divided in a large number of ways, of which he detailed several. The distances between the notes of the tetrachord in these 'shades' of tuning are indicated in Figure 2.7. These are the numbers given by Cleonides, but some authors doubled the number of units in the tetrachord to sixty in order to avoid the fraction four and a half in the hemiolic chromatic.[84] As a consequence of this method of dividing pitch space, Aristoxenians could maintain that there were six equal tones and twelve equal semitones in an octave, and that a fourth comprised exactly two and a half tones. The intense diatonic, which was adopted by Galilei, resembled an equal-tempered scale in that its tetrachords had two whole tones, each of twelve units, and a semitone of six.

Although musicians in the early Renaissance did not have available to them the text of Aristoxenus, they had access to writings of several authors imbued with his theories. Some of these authors have already been mentioned: Cleonides, Aristides Quintilianus, Alypius, and Ptolemy. Others who passed on elements of the Aristoxenian tradition were Bacchius in his *Eisagōgē mousikē (Musical Introduction),* translated probably by Francesco Burana in the mid-1490's; Gaudentius, *Harmonikē eisagōgē (Harmonic Introduction),* of which an anonymous Latin translation was prepared at an uncertain date in the sixteenth century;[85] and a collection of anonymous tracts, later known as Bellermann's anonymous, and most recently believed to be

84. Cleonides *Introduction* 7. Aristoxenus *Harmonic Elements* 1.24–27 does not specify the number of parts in each interval but compares them in twelfths of a tone, which results in the same thing. The numbers are doubled in Aristides Quintilianus *De musica* 1.9 and Ptolemy *Harmonics* 1.12.

85. See ch. 6 below.

by three different authors.[86] These anonymous writings were almost never cited because of the lack of an author's name, but they must have been known to Giorgio Valla and others, and Mei listed among the works he consulted "several fragments by diverse authors without name."[87]

Although the entire corpus of Greek music theory had been studied or translated by the end of the sixteenth century, this is not to say that these translated writings were accessible to any musician or scholar who could read Latin. Most of the translations were unpublished and in private hands. The same work was translated more than once without reference to previous translations, because these were closely guarded as privileged property rather than disseminated. Most of the knowledge garnered from the Greek writings circulated in the form of secondary literature, much of it unreliable. Citations of Greek sources were made to serve all sorts of polemic and ostentatious public displays of erudition. The fact that the ancient literature had been discovered and some of it translated—well or badly—did not mean that it was assimilated.

86. See Dietmar Najock, *Drei anonyme griechische Traktate über die Musik* (Kassel, 1972).
87. See ch. 10 below.

THREE

The Earliest Musical Humanists: Pietro d'Abano

n considering the earliest stages of the revival and revision of ancient learning, it is most fruitful to review the contributions of individual men. Once the issues begin to be identifiable later in the sixteenth century, it will be more expedient to organize our discussion topically.

Any such review of the early musical humanists must begin with a figure who, though somewhat outside the period of the Renaissance as usually defined, was imbued with the spirit of philologic humanism and a critical attitude toward medieval dogmatism. This was Pietro d'Abano (1250–1315), who gave the first impetus at the University of Padua to the scientific movement that was eventually to lead to the discoveries of Galileo.[1] He is of interest to us as the first commentator on an ancient Greek work dealing (though not exclusively) with music, the section on music of the pseudo-Aristotelian *Problems*. His commentaries enjoyed some diffusion in the fourteenth century through manuscript copies, but it was through their publication together with an older translation that they exerted a decisive influence on musical thinkers in the Renaissance. They were first published by Paulus Johannes de Puzpach in Mantua in 1475 and reprinted numerous times thereafter.[2]

During a long sojourn in Constantinople, d'Abano mastered the Greek language, which then served him for translating into Latin works of Galen,

---

1. Giuseppe Saitta, *Il pensiero italiano nell'umanesimo e nel rinascimento* (Bologna, 1949), I, 32.

2. The title of the 1475 edition in the copy of the Magliabecchiana collection of the Biblioteca Nazionale Centrale in Florence reads: *Aristotelis Grecorvm principis vtilli[ssi]ma problemata cvm expositione conciliatoris Petri de Ebano feliciter ordivntvr*. The colophon reads: "Et Impressa Mantue sub diuo Marchione Ludouico Mantue secu[n]do p[er] me Paulu[m] Joha[n]nis de puzpach. Almanu[m] Magontinensis dyocesis sub anno Jubilei M.° CCCC.° Lxx.° Cuius utilitas erit omni creature in uniuerso orbe que apponet huic operi studium su[m]ma cum diligentia."

Aristotle, Alexander of Aphrodisias, and Dioscorides. Following a brief return to Italy, d'Abano spent an extended period at the University of Paris, where he began his commentary on the *Problems,* and at the University of Montpellier. Returning to teach at Padua in 1306, d'Abano completed the work in 1310.[3] D'Abano was the first to defend the authenticity of the *Problems* as a work of Aristotle and to make them known in the West.[4] He found in them not only the method of the Peripatetic school but argued that the *Problems* are mentioned in *Metaphysics* (Book 2), in several places of the *Parva naturalia* and in *De generatione animalium.*[5] Because of the form of the work as a compilation of discussions and disputations, d'Abano recognized the need to elaborate on them through a commentary.

The translation that d'Abano presented was once thought to be by him, an assumption easily made on the basis of the explicit and Pietro's preface in both the manuscripts and printed editions.[6] The words "nullo prius interpretante" (not previously interpreted by anyone) in the explicit of the 1475 and 1482 editions would lead one to the conclusion that Pietro was the translator as well as the commentator, since the term "interpretare" was often used to mean "translate."[7] In the preface he seems to say that he found a manuscript copy of some *Problems* while he was in Constantinople and brought them back to the West and translated them, but he may have meant the *Problems* of Alexander of Aphrodisias, which he did translate. This, at least, was the opinion of Lynn Thorndike, who once thought that d'Abano was the translator but in 1955 published a paper in which he showed that the translation Pietro used is the same as one published by Rudolph Selig-sohn as that of Bartolomeo da Messina.[8] The text of the puzzling passage, with an English translation, is given below:

3. It is so dated in the explicit in Venice, Biblioteca Marciana, MS VI.127, and also in other manuscripts, e.g., Paris, Bibliothèque Nationale MS lat. 6540. See Sante Ferrari, *I tempi, la vita, le dottrine di Pietro d'Abano* (Genoa, 1900), p. 678.

4. The present-day view of the authorship of the *Problems* is that they represent at least in great part authentic Aristotelian thought probably reaching us through the medium of a disciple. This view is summarized in Gerardo Marenghi, ed., Aristotle, *Problemi musicali,* (Florence: Sansoni, [1957]), introduction.

5. Of these parallels Marenghi lists *De part. anim.* 3.15; *De anim. generat.* 2.10.3; 4.4.17; 4.7.2. Marenghi also lists others but not *Metaph.*

6. For example, Saitta, *Il pensiero,* I, 33, says that the translation is surely by him.

7. In the 1475 edition the explicit reads: "Explicit expositio succinta problematum Ar-isto[telis] qua[m] Petrus edidit Paduanus ea nullo prius interp[re]tante incepta q[u]idem Parisius & laudabiliter padue t[er]m[in]ata anno legis Chr[ist]iano[rum] 1310."

8. Thorndike, "Peter of Abano: A Medieval Scientist," *Annual Report of the American Historical Association, Year 1919,* 1: 315–26; *A History of Magic and Experimental Science* (New York, 1923–58), II, 874–947; "Peter of Abano and Another Commentary on the Problems of Aristotle," *Bulletin of the History of Medicine* 29 (1955): 517–23; Seligsohn, *Die Übersetzung der ps.-aristotelischen Problemata durch Bartholomaeus von Messina, Text und Textkritik* (Berlin, 1934).

Verumtamen extimo quod
Aristoteles problemata omnia
nundum ad nostram linguam peruenere
cum et quedam in libris de somp[nia]
et uigilia: atque
animalium semitradita
ad hunc transmissa librum in ipso
fideliter inspiciens
minime valeam
reperire
post diu huius executione
problematum aggregationem
ut discerem cum
in Constantinopoli
me transtuli
volumen aliud
problematum Aristo[telis] volui
reperire quod quidem in
linguam iam latinam transduxi.[9]

But I do not think that all the
problems of Aristotle have yet come
into our language, although certain
problems in his works on sleep and
wakefulness and [in the work] concerned with animals have been partially rendered and committed to a
book. Although I have searched
diligently for this book for a
long time, I have not been able to
find it. As for the collection I
used for this discussion, inasmuch as
I had become acquainted with it
during my stay in Constantinople,
I copied it down myself. I [also]
tried to find another volume of
the problems of Aristotle, which I
had already translated into
the Latin language.

The studies of Gerardo Marenghi have confirmed the identity of the translator as Bartolomeo da Messina, who also translated other Aristotelian and pseudo-Aristotelian works under the sponsorship of King Manfred of Sicily (reigned 1258–66).[10]

Pietro must have recognized the quality of this translation, which has the additional advantage of being based on a Greek text, now lost, that is apparently superior to any extant manuscript.[11] Although superseded by the translation of Theodore of Gaza, which is freer and more idiomatically Latin, Bartolomeo's continued to be reprinted as the *translatio vulgata, antiqua,* or *vetus.*[12] Marenghi maintains that both Gaza and George of Trebizon in their translations depended on Bartolomeo.[13]

Although Bartolomeo glossed over many textual problems noted by later scholars, his translation was adequate enough to serve musical readers and

9. From Deborah Narcini, "Pietro d'Abano's *Expositio problematum Aristotelis,* Book 19" (Paper read at Yale Renaissance Studies Seminar, 1978).

10. Gerardo Marenghi, "Un capitolo dell'Aristotele medievale: Bartolomeo da Messina traduttore dei *Problemata physica,*" *Aevum: Rassegna di scienze storiche, linguistiche, filologiche* 35 (1962): 268–83. Marenghi has edited Section 11 of the *Problems* in Aristotle, *Problemi di fonazione e di acustica* (Naples, 1963). Messina's translation is printed on pp. 105–17.

11. Marenghi, Aristotle, *Problemi,* p. 29.

12. The two were published side by side in *Problemata Ar[istotelis] cum duplici translatione, antiqua et noua T. Gaze: cum expositione Petri Aponi* (Venice: Bonetus Locatellus, 1501). Gaza's translation was printed the same year as Pietro's (Rome: Johannes Reynhardt, 1475); Mantua: Iohannes Vurster & Iohannes Baumeister, 1475 (?).

13. See the comparison of parallel passages in Marenghi, "Un capitolo," pp. 277–82.

theorists from Gaffurio to Artusi, to whom the *Problems* opened up directions of musical thought not encountered in other ancient or modern writers.
As important to these later writers as the translation of the *Problems*, were
d'Abano's commentaries, which clarified difficult passages and made musical technicalities understandable to readers not learned in Greek music
theory. They contain, in addition to elucidations, virtual little tracts on
aspects of elementary musical theory. In both Section 11, on acoustics, and
Section 19, on music, such an introduction precedes the first problem on
each of several recurring topics (the recurrences being scattered throughout
a section). Prefacing Problem 1 of Section 11 is a disquisition on the nature
of sound, referring to Aristotle's treatment of the subject in *De anima* 2.8.
At Problem 6 d'Abano considers theories of the propagation of sound; at
Problem 19, the acoustics of string instruments. Similarly in Section 19,
before the first problem there is a consideration of the definitions and classifications of music according to Isidor, Macrobius, and Boethius, making
note that so far as musica mundana was concerned Aristotle denied its
existence; also considered here are accounts of the ethical effects of music.
Ahead of Problem 3 there is a history of the Greek lyre and an exposition
of the fifteen-string system. In connection with Problem 13 d'Abano offers
a primer on the genres of proportions and the ratios of consonances, including a monochord division, with the string lengths named not in Greek
but according to the *litterae-claves* (such as a la mi re) of the solmisation
system. The commentary on Problem 15 incorporates a discussion of types
of singing used in the *nomoi,* to which the Problem is directed, and in the
theater.

   D'Abano endeavors to set the questions of the *Problems* against the history
of Greek music, which he reconstructs with the aid of Boethius, Macrobius,
Isidor, and other works of Aristotle. Although he invokes the names of
Aristoxenus and Ptolemy, he evidently did not know their work directly.
Occasionally d'Abano makes a contribution of his own toward solving a
problem posed by the Aristotelian author. As a natural scientist and medical
doctor by profession, d'Abano was attracted most to the analysis of physical
and medical problems in this Aristotelian compilation.[14] But he was also
interested and versed in music, as he had already demonstrated in the *Conciliator,* completed in 1303.[15] Here he devoted a long section, Differentia
83, to musical questions, particularly those that bore on the human pulse.
Both in Sections 11 and 19 of the *Problems* d'Abano transmitted questions

   14. The first fourteen sections deal with medical questions, others with mathematics, the
soul, philology, the nature of plants, physics, and philosophy.
   15. See Giuseppe Vecchi, "Medicina e Musica, Voci e Strumenti nel 'Conciliator' (1303)
da Pietro da Abano," *Quadrivium* 8 (1967):5–22.

and interpretations concerning acoustics that were to occupy scientists and musicians for several centuries afterwards. He interpreted the often cryptic Aristotelian problems with the help of other works of Aristotle, particularly *Politics, De anima,* and *De generatione animalium,* and sometimes of Galen, Avicenna, and an otherwise unknown author Balienus, whose *De pulsuum compendio* and *Libro de voce* he cites.[16]

D'Abano's view of the mechanics of sound is consistent with Aristotle's and is based on accurate observation. To produce sound a body must

uerberatur uehemens et uelox	vibrate vigorously and rapidly so
ut aer fortiter extendatur	that the air is forcefully stretched;
propter quod uidemus aerem	because of this we see that air,
subito et fortiter virga	when a rod is suddenly and forcefully
in ipso ducta sonum causare.[17]	moved within it, causes sound.

Applying this principle to the string, d'Abano comments in relation to Aristotle's 11.19 that a string must be thin and tense to produce a sound, and the thinner and tenser the string, the higher will be the pitch.

uidemus enim quod tacta corda	We see that a thin and stretched
subtili et tensa repercutit	string that is struck repercusses
aerem pluribus ictibus	the air with numerous impulses
antequam cesset unde tinitus	before it ceases, so that the jingle
diu remanet post tactum	persists for a long time after the
quare medium tinitu	blow, for which reason the medium
repletur. In	is filled with the jingle. With a
grossa uero corda distensa	thick and loose string, however,
non euenit illud.[18]	this does not happen.

In the commentary to 11.6 d'Abano underscores Aristotle's statement that the transmission of sound is unlike the flight of an arrow or a projectile in that the air set in motion by the sounding body is not the same air as strikes the receiving ear. The air that is first moved, d'Abano explains, is calm by the time the sound arrives at its destination. Moreover sound is diffused throughout the air around the vibrating body, an action, again, that is distinct from a projectile, which moves in a single direction. D'Abano takes pains to point out also in the same commentary that Aristotle in *De anima* disagreed with those—Plato, for example—who believed that high sounds travel faster than lower sounds. Indeed he notes that Aristotle asks in the

16. Particularly in *Conciliator* and Sec. 11.

17. D'Abano, *Problematum* 11.1. The quotations from d'Abano are from the edition of 1475, which is often faulty and therefore corrected or collated with editions of 1482 and 1520, as well as with Paris, Bibliothèque Nationale, MS lat. 6540, which is a copy of a manuscript dated 1310.

18. Ibid., 11.19, commentary.

problem why low sounds coming from afar seem higher to the receptor. In *De anima,* d'Abano points out, Aristotle had insisted that

uelox non esse accutum	the speedy is not acute (in pitch)
neque tardum graue. sed	nor the slow grave, but high pitch
accutum causatur ex uelocitate	is caused by speed of motion and
motus, graue autem ex tarditate.[19]	low by slowness.

This is further clarified in the commentary to 11.19:

in uoce accuta aer mouetur	In a high voice, the air is moved
et frangitur in partes minores.	and broken up into smaller parts.

Following Aristotle's lead in carefully observing natural phenomena, d'Abano arrived at a plausible if still vague theory of the mechanics of sound.

In the more properly musical problems of Section 19, Aristotle touches several times upon the phenomenon of sympathetic vibration. Problems 24 and 42 stimulated much discussion and some attempts at verification in the sixteenth and seventeenth centuries. Unfortunately Bartolomeo's translation of both texts is faulty, perhaps because he was reluctant to admit the possibility of sympathetic vibration, even at the octave. Problem 24 in Bartolomeo's translation asks the question:

Propter quid in tenuibus nitem	Why, in thin strings, when nete
apponere ypate	is placed alongside hypate, does
sola uidetur contrasonare.	hypate seem to sound in response?

Aristotle, on the other hand, seems clearly to ask: "Why, if nete is struck and then dampened, one seems to hear in response only hypate?" Theodore Gaza's translation, completed sometime before its publication in 1475, is faithful to Aritotle's sense: "Cur si quis netem pulsatum apprehendit: ypate sola resonare videbitur." Not realizing that the dampening of the nete string was a condition of this experience, d'Abano concentrates his commentary on the augmenting effect that the hypate string has on the nete sound. The other strings, being thinner and not as consonant with nete, are drowned out by the resonance of the hypate. By his remarks d'Abano shows that he assumes that the vibration of nete is communicated to all the strings by means of the yoke, or "throat" (*iogum*), of the instrument and that they all vibrate in response, but hypate, being longer, moves the most and dominates the others. Problem 42 states the same question slightly differently, and again Bartolomeo did not grasp the idea of stopping the string after it is struck, perhaps because he was too unfamiliar with instrumental practice. The fact that he fails to render the verb forms *psēlas* (should you pluck) and *epilabē* (should you dampen) correctly either time, strongly rules out a

---

19. Ibid., 11.6, commentary. Aristotle *De anima* 2.8.420b.

textual variant. Although the question is stated in exactly the same terms in 42 as in 24 except for the final verb (*subsonare* for *hypēchein* in 42 instead of *antisonare* for *antēchein* in 24), Bartolomeo's translation betrays a renewed search for the meaning of the question.

Propter quid siquis alteram nitem	Why, if someone strikes the other
accipiat aut ypatem accipiat	nete or the hypate, only the
ypate sola uidetur subsonare?	hypate seems to resound from under?

On the other hand d'Abano, with Bartolomeo, reads sympathetic vibration into the question of Problem 36, although later translators interpret it otherwise.[20] Bartolomeo translates the question:

Propter quid siquidem media	If the mese is moved, why do the
mouebitur et alie corde sonant:.	other strings also sound? Or, if
si autem iterum hic quidem manet.	on the other hand, this one remains
Aliarum autem quedam meueatur	still, but one of the others is
mota sola sonat.	moved, only the one moved sounds?

Supplementing Aristotle's explanation, d'Abano suggests that since the mese is consonant with all the strings, when it moves all others resound. But Aristotle's question seems to have been directed at another problem, namely, if the tuning of the mese is altered, why does the rest of the scale seem to reflect this alteration and become distorted? D'Abano is puzzled by Aristotle's answers, but his commentary shows that he appreciates the point of the problem, for he finally explains that, were the mese removed, it being the "mistress and regulator," all harmony would disappear, as the source of concordance would be missing.

The cause of the optimal consonance of two notes an octave apart is investigated in the second part of Problem 39, which seems to lack the statement of the proposition. Theodore Gaza in his translation supplied the following:

Cur sola in dyapason consonantia	Why is it customary to magadize
magadari solitum est?	only with the consonance of a
	diapason?

In clarifying this Problem, Aristotle compares the relationship that exists between the two sounds of a consonance with the relationship between the two parts of a metrical foot, such as equal to equal, or two to one, or some other. D'Abano supplies some examples. In the dactyl, a long of two tem-

---

20. Gaza again translates the question correctly: "Cur si neruus medius ex suo intentionis modo dimotus sit: ceteri quoque omnes sonos incompositos reddent: sed si integre illo manente aliquis ex ceteris sit dimotus: solus hic aberrabit: qui modo sui caruerit?"

pora is combined with two breves making up two or more tempora. The
anapest has the opposite arrangement, whereas the combination of the long
followed by a breve is illustrated in the trochee and the opposite in the
iamb. Now, Aristotle declares, two sounds of a symphony (octave) similarly
stand in a determinate relationship of motion or completion to each other.
In the other consonances, on the other hand, the endings of the second of
the two notes of the consonance are incomplete, ending on a fraction —
adds d'Abano—as does the second part of a trochaic foot. Thus, d'Abano
explains, the sound of low and youths' voices is like a spondaic foot of two
longs, while the sound of high voices is like the tribrach, consisting of three
breves. These two feet, he means to say, do not correspond in their terminations, for the tribrach ends on a fraction of the spondee. But the dactyl
and the anapest do correspond in their endings, as do the trochee and the
iamb. Thus the relationship of these two feet is analogous to the octave.

Now Aristotle becomes more specific about the relationship that exists
in the consonance of the octave. Hypate (the lower note of the octave) has
a termination (of its cycle) at the end of the period of two netes (the higher
note of the octave). "The second percussion of the air by the nete is a
hypate." Bartolomeo's translation runs as follows:

Amplius ypate accidit eundem finem	Further, hypate falls on the same
periodorum qui sunt	end of the periods which are found
in sonis habere.	in sounds generally. Indeed, the
Secunda autem neatis ictus aeris	second impulse on the air of nete
ypate est.[21]	is hypate.

In his commentary d'Abano shows that he understands by this statement
that hypate coincides in the end of its period or cycle with the ends of all
the periods existing in sounds generally, though obviously limited to the
strings of an instrument in which hypate is the lowest note:

rursus in ypate accidere quod ha-	It happens that in the hypate they
bent unum et eundum finem omnium	have one and the same end of all
periodorum siue circuitionum exis-	periods or cycles existing in sounds,
tentium in sonis in ipsam enim	so that they terminate in
tanquam in principaliorem terminan-	this the most important of them,
tur: uel melius finem periodorum,	or better, in the end of the periods,
id est, resonantium post [MS: reso-	that is, of the resonances
nantiorum] ictum remanentium diu	remaining long in the air after
in aere quod tinnitus potest dici	the blow, which may be called a ring-
et ideo	ing. Therefore it [the octave]
uocatur magistra: ipsa enim	is called the mistress, for it

21. Marenghi adds "costitutivi della scala," that is, hypate's period comprehends the periods
of all the notes in the octave scale hypate to nete.

suscipit omnes et obtundit
cum eius sit proprius
antiphonizare atque [MS: et]
organizare. sed secunda corda
correspondens ypati [1520: ipate]
per oppositum omnino est netes
siue neatis. uel nitis, id est
resonantie
siue tinnitus pretacti.
Dupliciter enim accipitur nete
42° apparens: secundo
cuius quidem ictus et sonus cantus
in aere tinit cum sono qui fuit
ab ypate: ex ambobus enim
coniungit [1520: consurgit] ut
uisum est sepius in
simphonia dyapason. et merito
quia licet non eundem sonum
reddant secundum,
se ymmo una acutum et altera
grauem tandem cum ipsarum
soni coniungantur adinuicem
contingit fieri unum et eundem
sonum omnifariam
quemadmodum accidit illis qui
sonant instrumenta sub cantu
cantantium.[22]

accepts and rounds out all;
it is thus its function to
antiphonate and
make organum. Now the second note
corresponding to an opposite hypate
is always nete
(or neate or nite), that is,
hypate is the further resonances
or ringing of nete.
Hypate, that is, accepts nete twice
as shown in Problem 42. The second
impulse and sound of the pitch
of nete rings in the air with the sound
that came from hypate, indeed
from both. As is
seen quite frequently, it joins
the symphony of the diapason; and
justly, since it is granted that they
do not both give off the same second
sound, but one is high and the other
low. Although the sounds of these
are mutually joined,
it happens that one and the same
sound is produced from all sides,
in the way that befalls those who
play instruments beneath the melody
of singers.

D'Abano here faithfully transmits and explains a conception of the physical basis of consonance that laid the foundation for later Renaissance advances in understanding its acoustical properties. Pitch is seen as originating in cycles or periods of vibration (*tinitus*) of the air set off by the plucking of a string. A string tuned to nete will move through two such cycles during the time a string an octave lower (hypate) completes one cycle, the terminations of the two cycles coinciding. This relationship holds only for the octave, which is thus the mistress of consonances. Neither d'Abano nor the author of the Problem was correct in the assertion that the termination of one period of the hypate coincides with those of all higher notes of the octave scale.

In his commentary on Problem 35, d'Abano goes beyond pseudo-Aristotle in elaborating upon the idea that the octave is the optimal consonance. As further evidence of this he cites the authority of Ptolemy's *Harmonics*: any consonance added to an octave remains a consonance. He shows in

22. D'Abano, *Problematum* 19.39, commentary.

remarks concerning Problem 41 that he would include the octave-plus-fourth as a consonance, although, having the ratio 8:3, it is not superparticular, for which reason it is excluded by the author of the *Problems,* who implies (Problem 41) that only intervals that are either superparticular or multiplex are consonances. D'Abano thus defies also the doctrine transmitted by Boethius.[23] It was Boethius who reported Ptolemy's disagreement with the Pythagoreans on this point and paraphrased Ptolemy's demonstration proving that the octave-plus-fourth is a consonance.[24] Boethius was evidently the source of d'Abano's knowledge of Ptolemy's views on this interval. D'Abano was well aware of the controversies among the followers of Pythagoras and the Aristoxenians, for he points out in his commentary on Problem 20 that whereas the Pythagoreans relied mainly on reason and Aristoxenus mainly on sensation, Ptolemy tried to find a middle road, though he too tended toward reason. Aristotle, d'Abano avers, believed that the science of music rested upon the sense of hearing and the reason equally. Nevertheless in Problem 41 Aristotle or some later author who added this Problem seems to follow the Pythagorean tradition,[25] whereas in his commentary d'Abano is partial to Ptolemy.

Beyond the questions that interested d'Abano as a natural scientist, we find him unveiling some of the vignettes of Greek musical practice that are so vividly, yet incompletely, etched in the *Problems.* Often he endeavors to reconstruct what may have been an ancient Greek listener's experience of music, which makes his comments doubly interesting.

Pietro made an honest effort to understand Greek musical practice, but, being unfamiliar with many of the technical terms and probably unfamiliar too with the musician's craft, he often went astray. His inadequacy is exposed, for example, in the two problems dealing with the *nomoi,* which he translates "leges." Although Aristotle proposes the explanation that *nomoi,* which means "laws" as well as "melodic formulas," were so called because at one time, before people could write, laws were sung,[26] d'Abano, who completely misrepresents this problem, suggests that they were called *leges* from *legendo,* as when reading divine scriptures one sings word after word without much changing the pitch.[27] Again Gaza has the correct solution:

Cur leges plereque cantilene appellentur?	Why were songs often called laws?

---

23. *De institutione musica* 2.27.
24. Ptolemy *Harmonics* 5.9.
25. Von Jan, *Musici scriptores graeci,* refers to *De sensu* 3, *Metaph.* 1.9.13 and 13.6.6 as showing that Aristotle accepted the Pythagorean theory of intervals.
26. *Problematum* 19.28.
27. Ibid., 19.15, commentary.

An quod homines priusquam litteras scirent leges cantabant: ne eas obliuioni mandarent quod etiam nostra etate Agathyrsis in morem est.	Is it because men, before they had writing, sang their laws so that they would not forget them, as the Agathyrsi are accustomed to do in our times?

Bartolomeo had missed the point:

Propter quid leges appelantur quas cantant: Aut quia prius quam sciant litteras viderunt leges: quomodo non lateant quemadmodum in agathirsis.	Why did they call what they sang laws? Is it because before they knew writing, they saw laws, so that they might not live in obscurity, just as in the case of the Agathyrsi.

Still, in Problem 15 d'Abano shows that he understands that the nomoi were not strophic (*conversivi*) like the choruses, because the actors (*agonizantes*) had to have the freedom to imitate action and extend and vary their song to suit the words. The choruses, on the other hand, being sung by amateur free men, were simple in rhythm and form and used a cyclical melody (*cantus rotatos vel conversivos*). The music for the soloist was also more melodious and full of alterations of the tune and figures (*manieres*) that could not be entrusted to the large number in a chorus. This, however, was not a very large number, because they wanted to avoid brawls.[28] D'Abano had the impression that the chorus in Greek tragedy sang in harmony and that it was thus called from *concordia,* for, when one person sang, this was *monodia,* or in Latin *unicinium,* when two it was called in Latin *bicinium,* but when many, *chorus.* When discussing the chorus in the same commentary it is not clear if he is speaking of the Greek chorus or the church choir of his own day, for he says that a chorus must have many good voices to execute the harmony and rhythm found in strophic songs or motets (*cantus conuersiui seu muteti*).

D'Abano reacted sensitively to the the revelations about instrumental accompaniment made in the *Problems.* In Problem 19.9 pseudo-Aristotle asks why we enjoy more hearing a voice accompanied by a single instrument—whether an aulos or a lyre—than by many. To the answer given by the text—that we enjoy the reinforcement if the instrument plays the same melody, but more than one aulos or lyre would make the melody less perceptible—d'Abano adds that if the instrument had one melody or dance (*cantus seu dancia*) and the voice another, this would be less pleasing because of the dissonances that would arise. He also points out that a single instrument can better follow a singer's pitch and mode (*intentionem et maneriem cantus*) than diverse instruments.

28. Ibid., 19.25, commentary.

The consonances most suitable for accompaniment are investigated in Problems 16 and 18. Bartolomeo (left below) comes closer than Gaza (right) to a correct interpretation of the question of Problem 16, though neither transmits the essential term *symphonos,* which both render vaguely as *consonus.*

Propter quid delectabilius antifonus consono: aut quia magis manifestum sit consonare aut quando ad consonare aut quando ad consonantiam cantant necesse est enim alteram consonare: quare due ad unam vocem facte destruunt alteram.	Qua de causa dissonantium copulatio quod antiphonum nominamus suauior quam consonum est? Am quod expressus ita consonantia percipi potest quam [quando?] cum voce consona addita cantatur: alteram enim vocem idem sonare necesse: est itaque duas ad unam resonare: que tertiamo offuscare facile possint.
Why is the antiphony [octave] more pleasurable than the consonance [fourth, fifth]? Either it is because making a consonance is more obvious; or because when they sing to a consonance it is necessary for yet another to be in consonance. For this reason two [consonances] made to one voice destroy the latter.	For what reason is the coupling of dissonances that we call antiphony sweeter than consonance? Is it because what is expressed by consonance can be perceived more when it is sung by an added consonant voice? It is still necessary for another voice to play the same thing, so that two sound against one, and the two may easily obscure the third.

In this and the succeeding three problems (17,[29] 18, 19), the preference for accompaniment at the octave is clearly manifested, while at the same time the alternative of a three-part texture is accepted by d'Abano as a practical possibility. If, instead of accompanying the voice at the octave, the method of consonance is adopted, then three parts are necessary, as Problem 16 implies, one of which is the principal voice, another a fourth or fifth below, and the third an octave below. The added parts, d'Abano understands, may be either voices or instruments, as, indeed, Aristotle implies. But in this texture the "symphonic" voice executing the fourth or fifth draws too much attention to itself; the principal voice is thus submerged and the melody is lost. On the other hand, antiphonal singing results virtually in a single chant, the two notes of the octave being like a single sound.

Thus, while the conclusion that the octave is the only possible interval

29. Although Bartolomeo's translation is vague, it does not completely misrepresent the proposition of Problem 17 as d'Abano does in his commentary: "Why do five or even four singers not sing in antiphony, although three or six can sing this way?" [Quare quinque cantantes vel etiam quatuor una non cantant antiphona. tres autem uel sex possunt cantare], when the question is "Why is the harmony of a fifth [or fourth] not an antiphony?" (Gaza: Cur in dyapente et dyatessaron consonantijs numquam antiphonis cantant? [1501: nun quam . . . cantatur].)

for an accompanying part—the parts "organize" with this interval, never any other, says the translation (Problem 18)—d'Abano seems ready to believe and have his readers believe that organum at the fourth or fifth and octave, both instrumental and vocal, was practiced by the Greeks. Problem 10, which raises the moot question of whether the human voice singing without words or the sound of an aulos or lyre is more pleasurable, prompts d'Abano to make an interesting reflection on the music of his time. Although we find more pleasing a voice singing words, we prefer the playing of the lyre or aulos to pure vocalizing without words, "vernare," as Bartolomeo translates *teretizontōn* (Gaza coins the word "teretare").[30] D'Abano understands by this a vocal utterance without any audible diversity of pitch or duration, like what singers in his time called *bordonizare,* "which induces very little enjoyment by itself," any more than does instrumental playing when it lacks variety of descents and ascents of pitch with proper harmonic proportions. By *bordonizare* he seems to mean the long-held notes sung by the tenor under a discant, though at another moment he describes *vernare* as a random vocalizing in which the voice passes through "proportions [intervals] that do not fall soothingly upon the ear," recalling perhaps some of the chanting he heard in the Moslem world.

D'Abano did not turn away from the difficult task of reconstructing the origin of the eight-note octave scale. With remarkable patience and perception he reconciles the often contradictory solutions offered in Problems 7, 25, 32, 33, 44, and 47. His explanation, not unlike that of more recent commentators, is that originally there was a heptachord scale made up of two conjunct tetrachords that met on the note mese, which was the true center of the scale encompassing seven notes.[31] In the commentary to Problem 44, d'Abano reconstructs this ancient seven-tone scale (see Figure 3.1). It is, he notes, equivalent to the "sinzeusim," that is, synemmenon, system. Later, in commenting upon Problem 47, d'Abano explains that Terpander added a note on top to form an octave with hypate, while at the same time removing the third note from the top, paramese, so as to preserve the same number of strings—seven—as before. D'Abano implies that Terpander retuned the paramese string to the pitch an octave above hypate (Problem 47) to get the new nete. Though d'Abano does not specifically so state, he

30. Von Jan, *Musici scriptores graeci,* p. 83, interprets this as "cum quis instrumentorum strepitum ore imitatur" (when someone imitates with the mouth the sound of instruments). Marenghi translates the word as "gorgheggii" and notes (p. 93, n. 1) that *"teretizein è voce onomatopoetica di grido d'uccello o di cicala e significa 'emettere suoni musicali senza parole, gorgheggiare su semplici vocali o sillabe' (fr. fredonner)."*

31. He cites Boethius in Problem 25 in corroboration. Against Aristotle's argument that there can be a true middle only of seven, not eight notes, d'Abano interjects (Problem 44, commentary) that eight strings too can have a middle—a geometric mean.

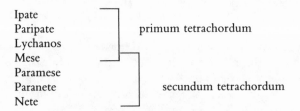

Figure 3.1:

The ancient seven-tone scale

must have assumed that the other strings remained at the same pitch as before. D'Abano also neglects to warn the reader that both he and Aristotle employed string names that may not have existed at the time of Terpander, that when they use the term *paramese* they mean "the string now called paramese." Consequently d'Abano does not take the trouble to state that when paramese became nete, the old nete or top string had to become paranete, and the old paranete became trite, after which there was a gap down to the old and undisturbed mese.

D'Abano's understanding of the transformation of the old heptachord to the post-Terpandrian one may be represented by Figure 3.2. Further evidence that Terpander respected the limitation of the number of strings to seven, says d'Abano, is that when the upper octave to hypate was added the resulting interval was not called *dyaocto*, like *dyapente* or *dyatessaron*, but *dyapason*, because there were not eight strings but seven.[32]

Another historical question raised inevitably by a reading of the Aristotelian *Problems* is that of the modes used in the tragedies and comedies. In the commentary for Problems 30 and 48 d'Abano faithfully transmits

Before Terpander	Analogous modern pitch	After Terpander
	e	nete
nete	d	[paranete]
paranete	c	[trite]
paramese	b	[omitted]
mese	a	mese
lychanos	g	lichanos
parhypate	f	parhypate
hypate	e	hypate

Figure 3.2

D'Abano's reconstruction of the ancient heptachord

32. D'Abano, *Problematum* 19.32, commentary.

the theory of the tragic and comic musical ethos. Certain harmoniai (which Bartolomeo translates "consonantiae," not far from Gaza's "concentus") are suited to the chorus, others to the actors. The chorus, representing and made up of common men, taking no part in the action, expresses a passive, such as lamenting, ethos (which Bartolomeo translates by "mos"). The actors, who, on the other hand, represent princes as heroes, require harmoniai that are magnificent, active, enthusiastic, and dionysiac (*diuina vel furiosa: aut et bachias*). Thus the Hypophrygian, which is active (*operativus*), and the Hypodorian, which is magnificent and steadfast (*magnificus et stabilis*), are suited to the actors. The least suited to the chorus is the Hypophrygian. Unfortunately, at this point there is a lacuna in all available manuscripts, and Gaza added "At vero mixolidius nimirum illa praestare potest" (but most of all the Mixolydian), probably because Aristotle in *Politics* (8.5.1340b) says that the Mixolydian is mournful. Bartolomeo, however, not recognizing the contradiction, translates literally what he finds in his manuscript (Problem 48):

Hoc autem habent alie consonantie: minus autem illis qui est ypophrygistium: diuina vel furiosa aut et bachias secundum hanc quidem patimur aliquid. passiui autem imbecilles magis fortibus sunt propter quid et ipsa conuenit choris.

[The chorus] has other harmoniai, least of which is the Hypophrygian, for it is divine or furious or also Bacchic. in accordance with this, then, we lament about something. For the weak are prone to suffer more than the strong, for which reason also these [Hypophrygian melodies] are suitable to the chorus.

In his commentary, d'Abano overlooks the contradiction in the text, yet he underscores the unsuitability to the chorus of the Hypophrygian because of its active character. It is to resolve this contradiction and because this character is traditionally attributed to the Mixolydian that Gaza added after the word *Bacchic* "but most of all the Mixolydian."

As to what these *consonantiae* named Hypodorian, Hypophrygian, etc., were, the best that d'Abano can do is to quote Boethius.

si quis totas constitutiones faciet acutiores uel in grauiores totas remittat secundam supradictas dyapason consonantie species efficiet modos septem ceu sunt ypodorius ypofrigius, ypolydius, dorius, phrygius, lydius, mysolydius

If the entire systems were made higher or lower in pitch, according to the species of consonance of the diapason mentioned earlier, the seven modes, would be produced, namely: the Hypodorian, Hypophrygian, Hypolydian, Mixolydian, Lydian,

[1475 but not 1501:	The Hypermixolydian
Ypermixolydius	accordingly doubles
duplatur] igitur uel triplat Aristo.[33]	or triples that given by Aristotle.

Without troubling to elucidate what the species of consonances were, d'Abano notes that this list of modes, or harmoniai, was not cited by Aristotle in the *Politics* (8.1340b), for there "he treats principally of the Phrygian, Dorian, and Lydian." D'Abano briefly reports the characteristics Aristotle assigned to each of them.[34] Evidently his acquaintance with the harmoniai did not go much beyond this.

D'Abano for good reasons did not press far into the complexities of Greek musical theory. If he had tried to penetrate much farther, he would have found as others did after him that more sources were needed. All that he had at this time were the works of Plato and Aristotle, and perhaps not all of those, Boethius, and a few other Latin writers. Without additional sources he could not resolve the many questions left hanging by the Aristotelian *Problems*. But in bringing the *Problems* to the attention of scholars, he added one more important authority to the few then available.

33. *De institutione musica* 4.15.9–14 (Friedlein ed., pp. 342–43). The Friedlein text does not include the name Hypermixolidius in this chapter, although it is represented in the attached table. There are other minor variants.

34. D'Abano, *Problematum* 19.38, commentary.

FOUR

The Earliest Musical Humanists: Giorgio Valla

iorgio Valla set out singlehandedly to resurrect Greek musical science in the five books on music of his encyclopedic *De expetendis et fugiendis rebus opus*. It began as a collection of translations from the Greek but grew to an encyclopedia comprehending every major field of learning. As published by his adopted son, Giampietro Cademusto Valla, in 1501, its forty-nine books constituted the largest volume ever printed by Aldo Manuzio.[1] Valla explains at the outset (I, 2) that there are three sorts of things that one strives for (*expetuntur*) and shuns (*fugiuntur*), those pertaining to the soul, to the body, and those external to both. So far as the soul is concerned, for example, there are three genres of such things: truth (*veritas*), virtue (*virtus*), and affection (*affectus*). Each of these in turn has numerous categories. Truth, for one, is divided into intelligence, reason, understanding, judgment, prudence (*consilium*), genius, and opinion. Having set forth these categories in an Aristotelian manner, Valla proceeds to distinguish science from art (I, 3). Whereas the subject of science is immutable, that of art is mutable. Philosophy concerns both; among the definitions of it he cites is that of Aristotle: "Philosophy is the art of the arts, the science of the sciences" (Philosophia est ars artium & scientiarum scientia). Valla then considers the place of mathematics in philosophy, leading up to the last ten chapters of this book, which are on mathematics.

Valla was exceptionally well qualified to write such an encyclopedia. He studied Greek with Constantin Lascaris in Milan, probably between 1462 and 1465. He apparently continued Greek studies with Matthaeus Camariotus Constantinopolitanus and Andronikos Callistos, although the places and dates are uncertain. Since Callistos left Florence for Milan in 1475, he and Valla would thus have overlapped the year 1475–76 in the Milan area.[2]

1. Carlo Dionisotti, "Aldo Manuzio umanista," *Lettere italiane* 12 (1960):375–400.
2. See Deno J. Geanakoplos, *Interaction of the "Sibling" Byzantine and Western Cultures in the Middle Ages and Italian Renaissance (300–1600)* (New Haven, 1976), p. 235.

In Pavia he pursued natural sciences, mathematics, and medicine with Giovanni Marliani. Valla's teaching career subsequently served to extend his
competence in still other directions. In Pavia he was employed to lecture
on Greek and Latin rhetoric from 1466 to 1467 and continued to teach there
until 1476 in various fields, including oratory and rhetoric. The subjects he
taught in Genoa from 1476 to 1481 are not documented. He was teaching
in Milan in 1481–82 and in Pavia 1483–84. Valla settled in Venice at the
beginning of 1485 and remained there until his death. He occupied the chair
of Latin language, but his teaching must have covered a broad area, for
before his appointment a record of a meeting of the senate in Venice describes Valla's universality of learning—"a man learned not only in humanities but also outstanding in philosophy and metaphysics."[3] From various
letters it may be ascertained that around 1492 Valla lectured on Vitruvius
and the *Elements* of Euclid, and earlier on the works of Plautus and the
oratory of Cicero.[4] In 1491 he spoke on Pliny's *Historia naturalis.*[5] There is
evidence that he lectured on the rhetoric of the *Ad Herennium* before 1490,
on the *Poetics* of Aristotle, and, just before his death, on Cicero's *Tusculan
Disputations.*[6]

Valla's activity as a translator and editor also led naturally to the encyclopedic work. Among his published writings are an introduction to medicine by Galen (1481), commentaries on Cicero's *Topica, De fato,* and *Timaeus*
(1485), a translation of the *Problems* of Alexander of Aphrodisias (1488), the
Problems of Averroes (1488), Aristotle's *Magna moralia* (1496), Cleonides'
Harmonic Introduction, Euclid's *Division of the Canon* (under Cleonides' name,
1497), and numerous items in a volume published in 1498, including, in
addition to these, Nicephorus [Blemnydas], *De arte disserendi,* his *De expedita
ratione argumentandi,* Euclid's *Elements,* Books 14–15, Nicephorus, *Astrolabi
expositio,* Proclus Diadocus, *De fabrica usuque astrolabi,* Aristarchus, *De dis-
tantia et magnitudine lunae et solis,* Timaeus Locrus, *De anima mundi,* Eusebius,
De quibusdam Theologicis ambiguitatibus, Cleomedes, *De mundo,* Athenagoras,
De resurrectione, Aristotle, *De caelo,* Psellus, *De victus ratione,* Alexander of
Aphrodisias, *De febribus,* Rhazes, *De pestilencia,*[7] and several medical tracts
of Galen.[8] Thus, aside from economics and politics, Valla had already studied, taught, or published in all of the areas included in *De expetendis.*

---

3. "Virum non solum in humanitate scientificum, sed etiam in philosophia et metaphisica
prestantem." In J. L. Heiberg, "Beiträge zur Geschichte Georg Vallas und seiner Bibliothek,"
Zentralblatt für Bibliothekswesen 16 (1896):18 (368).
   4. Ibid., p. 25 (377), Epistola 36, p. 87 (439).
   5. Ibid., Epistola 14, p. 70 (422).
   6. Ibid., p. 26; Epistola 43, p. 93 (445); p. 32 (384).
   7. Ibid., pp. 36–38 (388–90).
   8. Ibid., pp. 36–38 (388–90).

J. L. Heiberg, the only scholar who has worked extensively on Valla, observed that *De expetendis* is mainly translated directly from Greek sources. Heiberg wrote: "The entire undertaking is still half medieval and characteristic of the naive zeal for the word and excellence of Greek things, still now in the beginning of the Renaissance outside the great humanist centers. Critique and true understanding are still lacking. Thus Valla's chief work was already out of date on its appearance and had to suffer much harsh censure."[9] Heiberg has shown that the mathematical sections consist mainly of translations of the following authors:

Proclus, Introduction to Euclid: I, 14–23; X, 1–29, 110–11; XI, 1–2
Nicomachus: II, III, 1–9
Maximus Planudes: IV
Hero: X, 10–108; XIV; and XV, 1
Euclid (various works): XI, 3–7, 12–20; XII, 1–6; XIII, 1; XV, 2–3

On the other hand, some books and chapters are eclectic and represent Valla's own syntheses—for example, X, 109 and XI, 8–10—or summaries of a single author, as XII, 3, which is based on Euclid, *Elements* 8 and apparently 10. The music section will be shown to be similarly constructed (see Figure 4.1).

It cannot be denied that the work as a whole is a product of a compiler and not an original thinker. Valla was not in a position to add to the state of contemporary science through his own findings or reflections. He was hindered not only by personal limitations but also by the conservative environment of the universities in which he worked. The fount of all knowledge was thought to be Greek science and humanities, and the author's function was to choose among sources rather than to be critical of the sources chosen. Taking Valla on his own terms means to judge his choice of sources, his interpretation of them, and the organization of his exposition.

The five books on music, or harmonics,[10] were finished in December 1491, as Valla reported to Jacopo Antiquario.[11] In February he sent him a copy.[12] The nineteen books on mathematics were completed by this time, and in 1495 Valla was half done with a fair copy of the entire book, but his imprisonment by the Venetian Republic delayed publication. The case against him was based on some letters to his old friend Gian Giacomo Trivulzio, who was now in the employment of Charles VIII of France. It

9. Ibid., p. 34 (386).
10. The running head says : "Lib. V et Musicae I," whereas the incipit of the music section reads: "Liber Quintus, De Harmonia Primus."
11. Letter, Biblioteca Apostolica Vaticana, MS Vat. lat. 3537, fol. 56.
12. Letter, X Cal. Martias, 1492, in Heiberg, *Beiträge,* Epistola 11, p. 68 (420): "Quae superioribus diebus ad te nostris de musicis emisimus, gaudeo tibi grata extitisse."

was Trivulzio who led the army that eventually drove Lodovico il Moro, with whom Venice had an alliance, out of Milan. *De expetendis* was later dedicated to Trivulzio by Valla's stepson.

Valla did not follow any single Greek author in his books on music. Bryennius, to be sure, was his favorite source, but Valla did not limit himself to the curriculum established by this Byzantine author in his *Harmonics*. On the other hand, Valla leaves out of consideration questions of rhythm and meter, making the five books truly a treatise on harmonics rather than music in general. Metrics is covered in Book 38, *De poetica*. Although Valla included music in the mathematical section of the book, between arithmetic and geometry, he was well aware of its important ties to metaphysics and the verbal arts. From reading Timaeus the Locrian and the *Timaeus* of Plato, it is evident, he says, that music is involved in the causes of the universe and individual things. Many of the sages and prophets of the past were musicians, and, conversely, one untutored in music was held to be ignorant of the liberal arts. When Themistocles confessed to incompetence in music, his authority among contemporaries diminished. A grammarian should know music, because every poem consists of musical numbers, and even an oration cannot be judged without skill in music, upon which the accents of speech depend. "Therefore a knowledge of music is necessary, without a doubt, to learning the liberal arts, which are all dependent on speech."[13] This integration of music into the liberal arts as well as the mathematical sciences is a significant new departure in an encyclopedic work.

Since Valla's *De musica* is so little known and quite rare, a review of the contents of the five books and their sources should precede any attempt to judge Valla's contribution.[14] A schematic view of these sources is given in Figure 4.1. Book I opens with a chapter on the origins and early history of music, much of it drawn quite literally from pseudo-Plutarch, *De musica,* with some interpolations.[15] The sections quoted from pseudo-Plutarch review the contributions of the principal figures of Greek music, some of them legendary, such as Philammon of Delphi, Amphion, and Thamyris of Thrace, and others better documented, such as Terpander and Clonas, famous for their mastery of the kithara and aulos respectively. Plato's preference for dignified modes and his avoidance of the soft and plaintive ones, such as the Lydian, are cited, but Valla omits the sections derived from

13. Valla, *De expetendis et fugiendis rebus* (Venice, 1501), "De musica," I, 1.

14. Only eighteen copies are listed in *RISM,* and only three in the U.S., although there are probably more. The copy in Yale Beinecke Rare Book and Manuscript Library, for example, is not listed there.

15. See the edition and translation by Benedict Einarson and Phillip H. De Lacy in *Plutarch's Moralia in Fifteen Volumes,* XIV (Cambridge, Mass., 1967), 3.1131F–4.1132F;6.1133B–12.1135D;14.1135E–21.1138C; 28.1140F–30.1142B.

Plato's *Timaeus* (Plutarch 1138c–1139b) and from Aristotle (Plutarch 1139b–1140a), as well as Plutarch's own conclusions about music in education (1140a–1140f). The chapter ends with some unattributed passages from Bryennius concerning Mercury's invention of the seven-string lyre and a comparison of the strings of the tetrachord with the four elements, earth, water, air, and fire (see Figure 4.2).

In the rest of Book I Valla establishes the relationship between sounding music and the cosmos on the one hand and the human affections and the mind on the other. In taking this direction he departs from Bryennius, Ptolemy, and Aristides Quintilianus, all of whom set forth the technical parts of music first. Only Nicomachus came to cosmic music early in his work, and then for a very brief introduction to the analogies between the notes of the scale and the planets.[16]

Valla's cosmology is a composite of Ptolemy, Bryennius, and Nicomachus. From Ptolemy (3.9) he takes the analogy between the double-octave system of four tetrachords and the astrologers' four aspects of the sky. Translating Ptolemy, Valla divides the circle into two, three, four, and six parts, yielding all of the recognized consonances. From Bryennius he takes the story of the invention of the seven-string lyre by Mercury in imitation of the seven planets. The lowest string, hypate, is likened to the lowest "planet," the moon, and the other strings, sequentially, are likened to Mercury, Venus, Mars, Jupiter, and Saturn, this last and highest being compared to nete. Valla notes that Nicomachus sponsored an opposite order (in which he was followed by Boethius), pairing the moon with the highest string and Saturn with the lowest. Despite this reversal, Valla adopts Nicomachus' belief that the seven "stars" revolve around the earth, producing sounds differing in strength, speed, and pitch, according to how the mass and speed of each of them make the medium through which it revolves vibrate. He superimposes on Bryennius' diagrammatic comparison of the ancient heptachord of Hermes (Mercury) and the octochord of Pythagoras (1.1, Jonker ed., p. 66) these seven spheres of Nicomachus and adds the tone and semitone distances between planets and strings (see Figure 4.3). Thus Valla compounds what Düring called "perfectly arbitrary fantasies" in Ptolemy with elements derived from the other two authors.[17] But for Valla they were evidently not arbitrary, for he strove seriously to communicate their rationality. The chapter serves to illustrate Valla's method of interweaving a variety of chronologically and philosophically disparate sources into a continuous and integrated account.

---

16. The main sources for Valla's cosmology are probably Ptolemy *Harmonics* 3.9–13 and Bryennius *Harmonics* 1.1 (see Figure 4.1).

17. Ingemar Düring, *Ptolemaios und Porphyrios über die Musik*, p. 279.

Liber I

Cap.	1	Ps.Plut. 3.1131F–12.1135D; 14.1135E–21.1138C; 28.1140F–30.1142B; Bry. 1.1. J56.12–58.19, 54.13–34
	2	Ptol. 3.9; Bry 1.1. J60.22–62.5, 59.20–60.16; Ptol. 3.14, 16
	3	Ptol. 3.11
	4	Ptol.3.12; Bryn 1.1.; Nicom. 3.1–9
	5	Ptol. 3.13
	6	?
	7	Ptol. 3.5; AQ 3.24
	8	Ptol. 3.6
	9	Ptol. 3.7

Liber II

Cap.	1	AQ 1.4; Bacch. 1; Ptol. 1.1
	2	AQ 1.4; Bry 1.3. J86.9–88.9
	3	AQ 1.5
	4	Ptol. 1.3; Porph. 61–65, 22–23
	5	Bry. 1.2. J68.2–70.27; Bry. 1.1.J62.6–68.7
	6	Bry. 1.2. J70.28–84.13
	7	Bry. 1.4. J88.10–12; Theon 2.2–4; Bry. 1.4. 90.8–27, 92.7–98.8
	8	Bry. 1.5

Liber III

Cap.	1	Bry. 1.6
	2	Bry. 1.7
	3	Bry. 1.8
	4	Bry. 1.9
	5	Bry. 2.1
	6–48	No identifiable direct borrowings

Liber IV

Cap.	1	Bry. 2.1
	2	Bry. 2.2 (less J150.23–152.18)
	3	Bry. 2.3
	4	Bry. 2.4
	5	Bry. 2.6
	6	Bry. 2.7
	7	chapter division missing
	8	Bry. 2.8
	9	Bry. 2.9
	10	Bry. 2.10
	11	Bry. 2.11
	12	Bry. 2.12

Figure 4.1:
Greek sources of Valla, *De expetendis*, "De musica"

13		Bry. 2.13
14		Bry. 2.14
15		Bry. 2.15

Liber V		
Cap.	1	Bry. 3.1
	2	Bry. 3.2
	3	Bry. 3.3
	4	Bry. 3.4–3.5
	5	(chapter misnumbered 6) Bry. 3.5, cont.
	6	Bry. 3.6
	7	Bry. 3.7
	8	Bry. 3.8
	9	Bry. 3.9
	10	Bry. 3.10
	11	Bry. 3.11–12 (less J374.12–30)

note: AQ = Aristides Quintilianus; J = Jonker

Figure 4.1: *continued*

The second book begins the treatment of audible music as an art and science. Valla presents a number of definitions. Some say it is "the science of all instrumental precept, the expert in which is called a musician."[18] Others say it is "the theoretical and practical art of song (*inspectrix & tractatrix meli*) and of sound and all that pertains to it and instruments that tend toward melody, rhythm and meter, serving morals." The ancient authors define song (*melos*) as the practice of the broken intervallic voice suited to the pleasure of listeners. Harmonics, further, is the "preceptive science of the nature of the consonant." These definitions are not attributed to particular authors, but then Valla presents several that are so identified. Aristides' definition is reported as "the art, theoretical and practical, of perfect melos and that performed (*modulata*) by instruments."[19] Bacchius calls it "a species of song and of those things that pertain to melos."[20] Ptolemy defines harmony as "the faculty understanding the differences that exist in acute and grave sounds."[21] All of these definitions are rooted in the art of music making rather than in any metaphysical or divine conception of it, with which Valla was concerned in the first book.

The definitions are independent of the tradition that passed through the medieval writers—Boethius, Cassiodorus, Isidor—on which the "practical"

18. *De expetendis,* "De musica," II, 1, fol. f4v.
19. *De musica* 1.4.
20. *Introduction* (Meibom 1).
21. *Harmonics* 1.1.

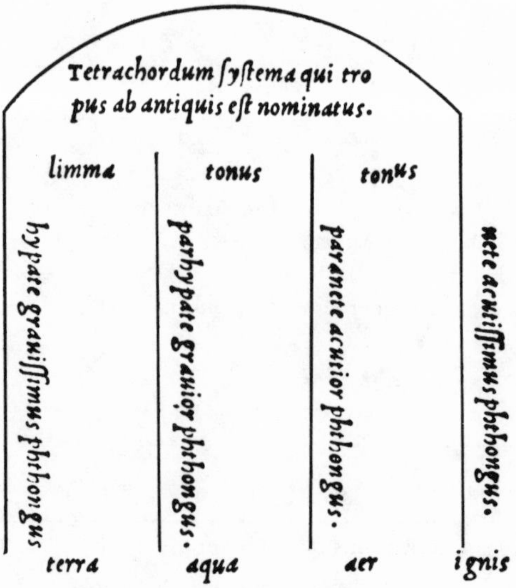

Figure 4.2:
Tetrachordal structure and the four elements,
from Valla, *De expetendis*, "De musica," I, 1.

writers on music depended. Marchettus of Padua, for example, in *Lucidarium,* divides music into "harmonica, organica and rhythmica," which is derived from Cassiodorus through Isidor.[22] Marchettus then further divides all music into plain and measured (*plana, sive mensurata*).[23] Ugolino of Orvieto qualified both speculative and practical music as a bifurcated mental discipline, one fork directing the musician toward theoretical knowledge, the other toward musical operations.[24] The most important musical writer of the second half of the fifteenth century, Johannes Tinctoris, simply repeated the triple division reported by Marchettus.[25] Only in Gaffurio's treatises do we find an eclectic approach to the definition of music similar to Valla's, but Gaffurio, before his last work, *De harmonia,* was restricted for linguistic reasons to a smaller number of sources.

22. *Etymologies* 3.19, *Lucidarium,* in Martin Gerbert, *Scriptores eccesiastici de musica sacra potissimum* (St. Blasien, 1784; reprint, Milan, 1931), I, 21a: "Ad omnem autem sonum, quae materies cantilenarum est, triformem cantibus constat. Secunda organica, quae ex flatu consistit. Tertia rhythmica, quae pulsu digitorum numeros recipit."

23. Ibid., III, 1, 15–16, p. 69a–b.

24. *Declaratio musicae disciplinae,* I, 2, ed. Albert Seay, Corpus Scriptorum de Musica 7 (Rome, 1959), I, 19. Compare with Valla's the definitions discussed in Gerhard Pietzsch, *Die Klassifikation der Musik von Boetius bis Ugolino von Orvieto* (Halle, 1929), pp. 50ff.

25. *Terminorum musicae diffinitorium,* ed. Armand Machabey (Paris, 1951), s.v. "Musica," p. 38.

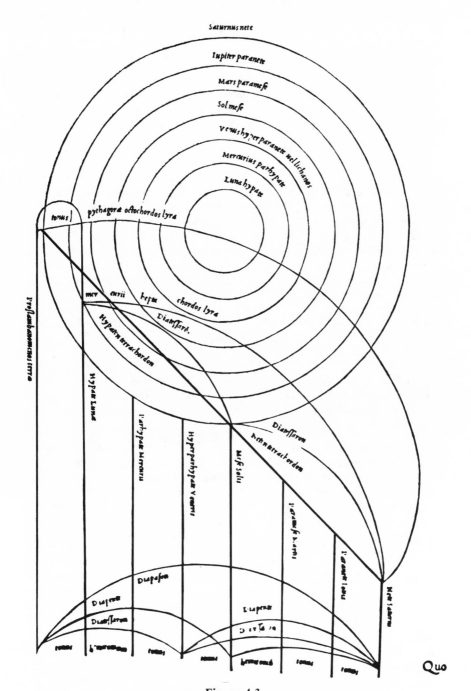

Figure 4.3:
The sounds of the octave produced by the revolving spheres,
from Valla, *De expetendis,* "De musica," I, 2.

In proceeding from general definitions and classifications of music to
more particular definitions Valla borrows significantly from Aristides Quintilianus. He translates Aristides' famous division of the movements of the
voice into three types, itself a refinement of Aristoxenus' twofold division
into continuous and intervallic, and then interpolates two glosses:

["]Continua igitur uox est, quae   "The continuous voice is that which
intensionum remissionumque obli-   is oblivious to rises and falls."
uiscitur["] quippe quae sensui   To be sure, these [rises and falls]
non comparent quod consistere   are not sensed, because [this voice]
quo ad silentium attigerit   does not seem to take up a
non uideatur propter   position by which it may
celeritatem qua   attain to silence on account of
defertur. quae vero sub   the speed with which it is proferred.
interuallum cadit tenores   Indeed, the voice that is characterized
habet manifestos & euidentes   by interval and has manifest and evi-
continuaeque contraria est   dent sustained tones is contrary to
& certe quae remissiones &   the continuous, which certainly does
intensiones apertas non habet   not have evident rises and falls,
nec his deputantur metra ambabus.[26]   nor are the sizes of either reckoned.

Although this gloss on the continuous voice is obviously dependent on
Bryennius, it introduces some new clarifications, such as the idea of silence,
and the factor of immensurability.[27] The gloss on the intervallic voice is
more truly a translation of Bryennius:

ac prorsus cum ita uox mouetur,   Further, when a voice moves in
ut auditui consistere uideatur   such a way that it appears to the ear
eam dicimus concinnam, cum autem   to hold still, we call it melodious,
stare existimatur, inde porro   since it is thought to remain steady,
locum aliquem transcendere,   then to proceed from that place to
cumque id fecerit rursus in   some other, and then again it is felt
alium tenorem prosilire idque   to leap into another sustained note
uicissim continuo facere   and to do this by turns continuously.
sentiatur huiusmodi motum   This kind of motion we call
dicimus, ut nunc hoc utar uerbo   intervallic (now to use this word),
interuallarem; caeterum sermoci-   differentiating it from the other
nalem continuum dicimus, diffe-   conversational continuous [voice],
rentibus, namque nobis ita demum   which is moved in such a way
uox per locum mouetur, ut nusquam   that it never seems to
consistere uideatur, contra autem   come to a stop. This is in contrast
habet interuallaris consistere   to the intervallic, which seems to
namque uidetur, idque qui   stand still. For this reason

26. Valla, "De Musica," II, 2.
27. Compare to Bryennius *Harmonics* 1.3, Jonker ed., pp. 87–89.

faciunt non iam loqui, sed	those who use the latter are said not
canere dicuntur qua propter	to speak but to sing.
inter differendum uocem figendam	For in the course of a conversation
non ducimus nisi	we do not draw the voice out in
ab affectu in	sustained tones unless compelled
hunc motum peruenire cogamur.	to this motion by an affection.
at in modulatu contra	In a melodizing voice we do the
facimus continuum fugimus,	opposite; we avoid the continuous
& stare studemus.	and strive to remain steady.
nam quanto magis uox una quaeque	For the more the voice stays in
consisterit, tanto magis sensui	place, the more the melos
melos uidetur examinatius.[28]	seems deliberate to the hearing.

Valla sensed the importance of the continuous–intervallic distinction and gave a very intelligent account of the Bryennius passage. An attentive and sensitive reader, he noticed that Bryennius had only two, Aristides, three, categories of voice. Valla was right to give this threefold division prominence at the beginning of the discussion.

Valla used good judgment also in adopting Aristides' famous classification of musical learning, although it is unlike him not to give credit to its author. Valla's rendering of the Greek terms is as reasonable a compromise between latinization and transliteration as we meet in later literature. The scheme may be outlined as in Figure 4.4 (the original Greek is in parentheses).[29] Valla next gives the sevenfold division of harmonics, which is also borrowed from Aristides (1.5) but is attributable to Aristoxenus: 1) *phthongi,* 2) *intervalla,* 3) *systemata,* 4) *genera,* 5) *toni,* 6) *mutationes,* 7) *melopoeia.*[30] Before embarking on these separate aspects of harmonics, Valla devotes a chapter (II, 4) to the nature of pitch. Valla's choice of sources, almost all identified with respect to authors, is again judicious. He includes much of Ptolemy 1.3, which considers different quantitative and qualitative factors in sounding bodies that influence pitch. After a brief citation from Aristotle, *De anima* 420a.28–420b.4, in which the effects of height and gravity of pitch are compared with those of color and touch, Valla translates the entire fragment from the lost musical treatise of Theophrastus preserved in Porphyry's commentary on Ptolemy.[31]

---

28. Compare to Bryennius *Harmonics* 1.3, Jonker ed., pp. 86–87.

29. "De Musica," II, 3; Aristides Quintilianus *De musica* 1.5. For an English translation of the scheme, see Aristides Quintilianus, *On Music In Three Books,* trans., with introduction, commentary, and annotations by Thomas J. Mathiesen (New Haven, 1983), p. 17, or Palisca, "Theory, theorists" in *New Grove Dictionary,* XVIII, 741.

30. Ibid., XVIII, 741.

31. Ingemar Düring, *Porphyrios Kommentar zur Harmonielehre des Ptolemaios,* 61.16–65.15. For an English translation of part of this passage, see Bengt Alexanderson, *Textual Remarks*

Musica

Inspectiva (theoretikon)		Activa (praktikon)
naturalis	artificialis	usus (christikon)
(physikon)	(technikon)	
			melopoeia (melopoeia)
arithmetica	harmonica	
(arithmetikon)	(harmonikon)	rhythmopoeia (rhythmopoeia)
	rhythmica	poesis (poesis)
	(rhythmikon)	
		enunciativa (exangeltikon)
	metrica	
	(metrikon)	organica or instrumentalis
		(organikon)
		hypocritica or histrionica
		(hypokritikon)

Figure 4.4:
Classification of the music field by Aristides Quintilianus

Theophrastus, best known for his books on plants, was Aristotle's pupil and successor as teacher in the Lyceum. In this fragment he refutes the view held by the Pythagoreans, that quantity is the basis of intervallic differences. He maintains that numbers are irrelevant to the experience of pitch and melody. For Valla to have brought the opinion of Theophrastus to the fore in the strongly Pythagorean intellectual environment of the fifteenth century was not only fair but open-minded. Valla makes this comment on the fragment:

Haec nimirum Theophrastus argute naturales perscrutatus acuminis & grauitatis differentias & prorsus quemadmodum non in phthongorum quantitate sed qualitate ac proprietate melos ponendum esse uideatur. Aristotelis preceptoris sui secutus sententiam ita statuit. Verum Archytas tarentinus dogmata secutus Pythagorica cuius scripta non modo Porphyrius sed plaerique

Theophrastus, to be sure, has thoroughly investigated the natural differences of acuity and gravity and certainly shown how not the quantity of the tones but the quality and property of the melody seem to be set. He determined the matter in this way following the conviction of Aristotle, his teacher. True, Archytas of Tarentum followed the dogmas of the Pythagoreans, whose writings not only Porphyry but

on *Ptolemy's Harmonica and Porphyry's Commentary* (Göteborg, 1969), pp. 33–34. For a summary see Edward A. Lippman, *Musical Thought in Ancient Greece* (New York, 1964), pp. 157ff.

alii suspexerunt uaehementerque comprobarunt idem quod Ptolemaeus ait in eo namque libro qui mathematices inscriptus est in ipsoque statim principio; recte inquit de mathematicis sentire nosseque mihi uisi sunt qui singula perpendere ipsas putant, hi namque bene uniuersi naturam percalluere.[32]	many others honored and vigorously confirmed, as Ptolemy asserts in that book devoted to mathematics, and right at its very beginning he rightly says concerning mathematics: those who seemed to me perceptive and knowledgeable were the ones who thought that particulars lent themselves well to mathematics, for they were quite thoroughly versed in the knowledge of the universe.

Valla then counters the Aristoxenian outlook projected by Theophrastus with a Pythagorean view as articulated by the obscure writer Panaetius (quoted by Porphyry in his commentary on Ptolemy's *Harmonics*) and by Porphyry himself.[33] The Pythagoreans defend the use of quantities in music theory, Panaetius observes, on the grounds that quantities represent relationships between notes that the ear cannot hear, this sense being less able to measure than the eye. The ear does not hear a duple relationship in an octave in that one note does not seem in any way a double of the other in magnitude; yet the underlying basis of the double octave remains the duple ratio.

The remainder of Book II describes the Greek tonal system and mainly translates Bryennius. Only the end of chapter 6, the beginning of chapter 7, and the end of chapter 8 are drawn from other authors, notably Theon, Ptolemy, and Bacchius, as shown in Figure 4.2. In chapter 7 Valla also permits himself a personal digression to enumerate different species of motion: of the soul—desire, anger, and reason; of the body—contraction, separation, commutation, alteration, diminution, augmentation, generation, corruption; of location—rectilinear, circular, continuous, discontinuous, slow, rapid, dense, rare, natural, violent. Slow and rare movements produce grave sounds, rapid and dense movements acute sounds. If a string is stretched, it sounds higher; if relaxed, lower. With a pipe or similar instrument, if someone desires to get an acute sound, he opens the upper holes and closes the lower ones, the opposite for grave sounds. Of sounds, some are straight, others round and reverberant; some rough, others flabby; some harsh, others grating; some are equal, such as unisons, others unequal, such as combinations of high and low pitch. Some are equal sounding (*aequisoni*), as are the diapason and disdiapason; others consonant, such as

32. Valla, "De Musica," II, 4, fol. f6v.
33. Düring ed., pp. 65–66.

the diapente and diatessaron. Some are melodious, such as the tone; others dissonant and hard, like the tritone; others unmelodious, such as the semiditone and ditone. There are transparent, yet not unpleasant, sounds; others are lean, like the voices of infants or sick persons; others are plump and dense, such as voices of men of warm temperament, or thin, as of boys, eunuchs, and women. Or they may be hard and bitter, harsh and violent, like thunder or hammering, or mute and raucous. Of voices some are strong and vigorous and at the same time pleasant, others broken and dissolute, weak and tremulant. The content of this digression is Aristotelian, and the passage on the qualities of sound has some parallels in pseudo-Aristotle, *De audibilibus,* which is also quoted by Porphyry, but it is neither a summary nor a paraphrase.[34]

Of Book III only the first five chapters depend on Bryennius. These have to do with the theory of intervals, genera, tonoi, modulation, the fifteen-note system, and consonances in general. Chapters 6 to 10 appear to be Valla's own quite detailed analysis of the ratios of the consonances. Chapters 11 to 15 are largely mathematical in content, dealing with the classes of ratios determining the consonances, while chapters 16 to 48 survey the ratios of dissonant intervals and a few of the compound consonant intervals. The contents of this last group of chapters parallel the less exhaustive contents of Boethius' treatises on arithmetic and music, Nicomachus' *Manual* and *Introduction to Arithmetic,* and Theon's *The Mathematical Knowledge Useful for Reading Plato.* There are no literal borrowings, however, and of these authors only Nicomachus is named.[35] Other authors cited are Philolaus, Aristoxenus, and Ptolemy. The citations of Aristoxenus in these chapters, as elsewhere in the book, do not reveal a firsthand acquaintance with this author, despite the fact that Valla owned a manuscript containing his *Harmonic Elements.*

Where Valla followed Bryennius in Book III he did so quite literally, but with some omissions. One passage in particular shows that he did not compare Bryennius to the latter's most important source, Aristides Quintilianus, even when there was good reason to suspect an error. The following instruction on how to recognize the tonos of a melody, translated literally from Bryennius (3.3, Jonker ed., 118.14–20) makes sense only if Hypodorian is emended to Dorian. Bryennius borrowed it almost literally from Aristides (1.10, Winnington-Ingram ed., 21.18–22.7), where the reading is clearly Dorian.

34. Porphyry *Commentarius,* Düring ed., pp. 67–77.
35. At III, 16, Nicomachus is cited on the comma; at 17, on the minor semitone; at 18, four times on the major semitone.

Ita igitur per cantus, aut
membra modos constituemus,
si cauum quam maxime; uel
grauissimum phthongorum syste-
matos uni assumptorum
subiiciamus,
& quae ab hoc sunt fuerimus
modulati ad grauitatem nam si
ultra conscendere non poterimus
hypodorius erit, quoniam primus,
qui audiri phthongus hypodorii
potest, proslambanomeno deputa-
tur, sin autem exaudiatur inspice
reconabimur quanto assumptum
hypodorium, hoc est grauissimam
eius excedat naturam. Ille quoque locus nobis definietur; nam
quanto assumptum excedit hypodorium, tanto & meli cauissimus
phthongus ipsius cauissimi
natura praecellit. Quod si acutissimus odae phthongus supra
hypodorium cadit per diapason
acutum existens capiemus eius
diapason ad graue, hac memorata
usi disciplina eius harmoniam
haud quaquam difficulter
admittemus.[36]

So, therefore, we establish the
modes by the song or the members,
if we substitute the deepest or
lowest note of the system of notes
for one of the added ones
[proslambanomenoi],
and from where they are,
sing down. If we cannot ascend
[recte: descend] beyond, it would
be Hypodorian, because the first
note of the Hypodorian, which is
called proslambanomenos, can be
heard. We shall try to investigate
how much the added note, of the
Hypodorian, that is its lowest,
exceeds nature. Also that locus
is defined for us by
how much the added one exceeds the
Hypodorian and by that much the
deepest note of the melody surpasses
the nature of its deepest. If the
highest note of the melody falls
above the Hypodorian, existing in a
higher diapason, we shall take its
diapason to the low range by using
the method mentioned earlier,
and we shall hear its harmony
without any difficulty.

With Book IV Valla resumes his translation of Bryennius, taking up where
he left off (at 2.1). The entire Book IV is translated from this Byzantine
author's Book 2. The exposition of the consonances and melodic intervals
is redundant because of Valla's own treatment of the same subject in the
previous book. Valla evidently felt that the extensive introduction to ratios
and intervals was necessary for understanding Book 2 of Bryennius. The
rehearsal of familiar material, however, is freshened by this author's Ptolemaic bias for superparticular ratios. Chapters 3 and 4 are important, for
they take up for the first time in Latin since Boethius the theory of the
tonoi.[37] They are presented from a Ptolemaic point of view, but, as in

---

36. Valla, "De musica," III, 3.

37. A detailed consideration of this subject is postponed until ch. 11, on the rediscovery of
the tonoi.

Boethius and Bryennius, an eighth tonos, the Hypermixolydian, is added to Ptolemy's seven. Practical solutions to problems of tuning offered in chapters 8 to 10 of this book should have been of extreme interest to musicians of the early sixteenth century. But little use of the information transmitted by Valla was made until Gaffurio in his *De harmonia* related the contents of the parallel chapters of Ptolemy, independently of Bryennius and Valla. Unlike Ptolemy, who reported the division of the tetrachord according to Aristoxenus and Archytas only to show how wrong they were, Bryennius ignored them; hence Valla presents only the "shades" that, having exclusively superparticular ratios, were approved by Ptolemy.[38] In these chapters from Bryennius, Valla sets forth, with diagrams, for the first time in the Latin language, Ptolemy's own tetrachord divisions (which, following Bryennius, he calls genera).[39] These are the diatonus homalus (*homalon*), syntonus diatonus (*syntonon*), mollis entonus (*malakos entonos*), which was equivalent to Ptolemy's diatonon toniaion, and the mollis diatonus (*diatonon malakon*). Valla continues with the chromatic tetrachords: the syntonic and the mollis. The last of the superparticular divisions is the enharmonic. By way of supplement Bryennius, like Ptolemy, gives the Pythagorean division or diatonic ditoniaion (Valla: *ditoniaeus*), because it is common, but without a stamp of approval on its ratios, since only some are superparticular. Valla reported this faithfully.

Valla's fifth book corresponds exactly in its eleven chapters with the eleven of Bryennius' Book 3, except for the truncation of the last chapter. Bryennius situates each tonos in the fifteen-string instrument, beginning with the Hypodorian and Hypermixolydian, which, he says, together fill out the system. Although he conceives each tonos as filling a double octave, he speaks at times as if they were octave scales. Only the Dorian in his view can fit all its fifteen notes into the two-octave, complete, changeless, or unmodulating, system. He has explained how the Hypermixolydian may be divided in each genus and shade. Now the method applied to it can be extended to the other tonoi.

Bryennius' third chapter presents a formidable challenge to the translator.

---

38. Bryennius does not specifically credit Ptolemy; he may have been working from an intermediate source. See Jonker ed., introduction, pp. 20ff. On the other hand, in 1.7 Bryennius described the shades briefly and there attributed them to Ptolemy. The parallel passage in Valla is IV, 2. The relation of Bryennius 1.7 to his Book 2 is not clear, since fuller treatment is not promised in 1.7, nor does the exposition of Book 2 refer back to 1.7. The terminology also differs in that in the earlier place *chroai* is used, whereas later it is *genos*. The biggest discrepancy is that in 2.8 Bryennius introduces the Hypermixolydian, the very tonos Ptolemy rejected, as a model for the division. This suggests that in Book 2 Bryennius was not working directly from Ptolemy but from an intermediate source. Boethius, whose treatment of the tonoi resembles that of Bryennius, may have had the identical or a similar source.

39. In IV, 2, where Bryennius had used the term *chroai*, Valla used *harmoniai*.

He begins by saying that he will speak of the various species of melody that composers then (in the fourteenth century) called *echoi*. The term can mean "sounds," "echos," or "ringing sounds."[40] Valla translates it "strepitus," the most common meaning of which is a crashing, rumbling, rattling sound but which is used by Horace for measured, regular—that is, musical sound.[41] To understand these echoi, Bryennius cautions, one must know the terminology for the genres of melody, both musical (vocal) and organic (instrumental). Valla gives the terms for these genres in transliterated Greek, because, he says, there are no Latin equivalents: prolepsis, eclepsis, prolemmatismos, eclematismos, melismos, procrusis, eccrusis, procrusmos, eccrusmos, compismos, teretismos, and diastole. Valla translates the definitions of each of these types of melodic motion quite adequately, although a few present particular linguistic problems.

The definitions of the terms *prolepsis, eclepsis,* and *prokrousis,* all employ an expression that has confounded translators from Valla to the present: *hyph'en esōthen* and *hyph'en exōthen,* which Jonker has rendered "hyphen on the inside" and "hyphen on the outside," in keeping with his belief that they referred to notational signs.[42] Valla defines *prolepsis* as follows:

Prolepsis igitur est ex grauiore phthongo, ad acutius iuxta musicum melos in tenore permansio nempe (ut Ciceronis utar uerbo) modificatio.[43]	Prolepsis, then (to use a word of Cicero's) is the modification with respect to musical melos in a sustained tone from a lower to a higher pitch.

Bryennius, however, had added the phrase, "some call it *hyphen on the inside,*" which Valla omitted.[44] *Eclepsis,* Valla explains, is the opposite, going from a higher to a lower tone, but this time he includes the enigmatic phrase and translates it: "hanc quidam uocant sub qua extrinsecus" (this some call somehow on the outside). In defining *prokrousis,* which is the term for rising in instrumental melody, whether by step or leap, Valla again leaves out the phrase that Jonker translates "called also by some *hyphen on the inside.*"[45] Valla may be forgiven for not knowing what to make of it.

The Byzantine echoi would appear to be alien to the ancient system of tonoi, but Bryennius found them analogous, because his Dorian octave, from lichanos hypaton to paranete diezeugmenon (like our D to d), falls

---

40. H. G. Liddell and Robert Scott, *A Greek Lexikon,* 9th ed., rev. H. Stuart Jones (Oxford, 1940).

41. Horace *Epistles* 1.2.31 and 1.14.26.

42. Jonker, ed. *The Harmonics,* p. 397.

43. Valla, "De Musica," V, 3.

44. Jonker trans., p. 309. The same phrase occurs in the first of the anonymi. See Najock, *Griechische Traktate,* Anon. I, 4, line 4, p. 70.

45. Jonker trans., p. 311.

on the same location as Echos 1; the octave from hypate meson to nete
diezeugmenon is the locus of Echos 2 and of the Phrygian; whereas the
octave from proslambanomenos to mese is the locus of the first plagal echos
and of the Hypodorian. Valla here finds it opportune to translate *echos* as
"sonitus," which, like his earlier "strepitus," also has connotations of noise
and thunder; thus we have *sonitus primus, sonitus plagius,* etc. Bryennius must
have introduced the echoi as a pedagogical device to make the ancient tonoi
more palpable to the reader. For presently (chapter 5) he drops them and
returns to melodic terminology, now introducing a new term, *analysis,*
which means transposition from a higher to a lower level of melodic succession. Valla translates this "resolutio," while the opposite, Bryennius' *pro-
sechēs* Valla renders "porrectio" (extension), which is not clearly defined.[46]
Bryennius shows how these techniques affect the use of the tonoi, which
he now calls *tropi.* Particularly interesting is Bryennius' consideration of the
role of a trope's mese in the application of the melodic devices just defined.
Analysis always begins on a mese and ends on a hypate. Prokrousis begins
on a hypate and ends on a mese. A melody that begins on the mese and,
after traversing all of the notes of the scale, ends on it, is called perfect.
Imperfect melodies are *monorrhepe* (Valla falls back on the Greek word once
again, while Jonker translates it as "monocentric") if they end on the mese
without exploiting the whole scale, and *heterorrhepe* (Jonker, "heterocen-
tric") if they modulate to the mese of another trope. The next several
chapters, because they are concerned with the mixing of genera and shades,
necessitate a discussion of the role of the pycnum, the set of two intervals
which combined is smaller than the remaining interval of the tetrachord
(chapters 7–8). The term is also used to refer to a scale that is characterized
by this density in its two lower intervals. For such a scale Valla uses the
term *densum systema.* He defines it thus:

densum siquidem est...	dense is that which...
quod ex duobus constat interuallis,	consists of two intervals
quae composita minus	which added together make a smaller
continebunt interuallum reliqui	interval than the one remaining
in diatessaron interualli.[47]	in the diatessaron.

To describe the opposite condition Valla preserves the Greek word *apycnon:*

Inspicitur autem & in huiusmodi	In this kind of genus is observed
genere concentus uocatum apycnon	also the harmony called apycnon,
hoc est non densum systema; nam	that is a nondense system [or
quae sunt ad grauissimum ipsius	scale], for it will soon be shown

46. This occurs in what should be chapter 5, but the chapter division and heading are
missing on fol. m2v, above the second line from the bottom of the page.

47. Valla, "De Musica," V, 8, fol. m4v.

phthongum interualla	that those which are at its lowest
maiora fiunt	pitch make up larger intervals than
uno quod ad acutissimam	the singe one that is at the highest
partem est, ut mox ostendetur.[48]	part, as will soon be shown.

Each of the shades previously discussed—those approved by Ptolemy—is now analyzed from this point of view, accompanied by diagrams in which the printer has placed the words "Systema densum" and "Systema non densum" rather haphazardly (chapter 8).

Valla unwarily passed on Bryennius' misleading discussion of Ptolemy's views concerning the synemmenon system. Bryennius (3.9) first shows that Ptolemy, in defiance of the Pythagoreans, demonstrated that the octave-plus-fourth is a consonance. Ptolemy did argue that it is a consonance (1.6), but his logic was different from that reported by Bryennius. Bryennius further states that Ptolemy, therefore, declared the synemmenon scale spanning that interval to be a harmonious one. Ptolemy, on the contrary, quite emphatically rejected the synemmenon system as superfluous (2.7), having shown that the same scale could be obtained by modulation (2.6). Again Valla failed to verify against Ptolemy's text, which he owned, the statements attributed to him by Bryennius.

Bryennius' discussion of *melopoeia,* or musical composition, is much fuller than parallel treatments by Aristoxenus, Aristides Quintilianus, or the Bellermann anonymi. Each melodic figure and category is carefully defined. Valla's choice of terms (IV, 10) is a mixture of translation and transliteration (see Figure 4.5).

We may now essay an estimate of Valla's transmission of ancient theory. His five books on music are a window into only a small part of the vast heritage of Greek theory contained in his manuscripts. Of the authors on harmonics, Bryennius, at once the most eclectic and thorough, obviously impressed him the most. Valla had no clue to his exact dates, but he could establish a chronological hierarchy, because Porphyry commented on Ptolemy, and Ptolemy spoke of Didymus and Aristoxenus. Bryennius in turn mentioned Ptolemy and Nicomachus but not Aristides Quintilianus. Thus Valla could surmise that Bryennius was, with Aristides, the most recent of these authors. He did not know that Bryennius wrote in the early fourteenth century, whereas Aristides flourished in the late third or early fourth.[49] What Bryennius lacked in antiquity, however, he made up in breadth, superior organization, and simpler syntax. Valla's reliance on pseudo-Plutarch for historical information is also understandable, because the theoretical authors are lean in historical matter, and Valla apparently did not

---

48. Ibid., V, 8, fol. m5r.
49. See Mathiesen trans., p. 14.

Melopoeia partes

(Bryennius)	(Valla)
lēpsis	assumptio
hypatoeidēs	hypatoides
mesoeidēs	mesoides
nētoeidēs	netoides
mixis	mixtio
chrēsis	usus
agōgē	ductus
eutheia	rectitudo
anakamptousa	reflexus
peripherēs	ambitus
plokē	complexus
petteia	lusus
tonē	firmitudo
tropoi	modi
nomikos	nomicus
dithyrambikos	dithyrambicus
tragikos	tragicus
genei	genus
enarmonios	enharmonios
chrōmatikē	chromatica
diatonos	diatonos
systēmati	systemate
nētoeidēs	netoides
mesoeidēs	mesoides
hypatoeidēs	hypatoides
tonōs	tonus
dōrios, phrygios	Dorian, Phrygian
ethos	mos
systaltikēn	systalticen
diasta[l]tikēn	diastalticen
hēsychastikon	hesychasticus

Figure 4.5:
Melopoetic terminology in Bryennius and Valla

know Athenaeus. He used Ptolemy only for the planetary aspects of music, as if an astronomer was not to be consulted on purely musical matters, and he probably supplemented this resource with Aristides Quintilianus, since manuscripts often lacked the final chapters, 14 to 16, of Ptolemy's Book 3. Nicomachus appears to be his mathematical mentor, but there are no direct citations to bear this out. Direct quotations of Aristides Quintilianus and Bacchius Senior are relatively few, and Valla seems unaware of how much Bryennius took from Aristides; he had recourse to both works and may even have thought that the debt ran in the other direction. Although one of his manuscripts, Modena, Estense a.V.7.1 (*olim* II.f.8), contained the Bellermann anonymi, Valla makes no reference to them. From Porphyry's commentary on Ptolemy, he extracted only the quotations of Theophrastus and Panaetius, and perhaps utilized the pseudo-Aristotelian *De audibilibus* quoted there. Theon is cited minimally, and Pappus even less. The often mentioned Aristoxenus is quoted indirectly.

Altogether lacking in Valla's book is any critique of his sources. True, he did not own, so far as we know, duplicate copies except for the two copies of Cleonides' *Harmonic Introduction* in Naples graecus III.C.2. Of these he used, as Mathiesen has shown, the more defective one.[50] Valla never stops to comment on difficulties in the texts or to analyze their language. If he omits passages, glosses others, or makes emendations, he does not confess to them. Although some of Valla's contemporaries were capable of philological probity, Valla was not so inclined. However, in the first two books, in which Valla's organization is not dependent on Bryennius, he shows notable skills of logical exposition. He begins with the broadest concepts of music, then proceeds to audible music and definitions of it and of its theory.

50. Thomas J. Mathiesen, "Humanism and Music," pp. 879–80.

FIVE

The Earliest Musical Humanists: Carlo Valgulio

emarkable for his independence of mind, yet the least recognized of the early musical humanists was Carlo Valgulio. His entry into musical scholarship was, as with Valla, by way of the classical authors, however not through mathematics or harmonics, but moral philosophy. Unlike Valla, he was an activist, aware of the current musical scene and committed to its improvement. He confessed that he was moved to write in defense of music and concerning its current decline by "an incredible love for music and musicians."

His principal work on music is an essay prefacing his translation into Latin of Plutarch's *De musica,* published in Brescia in 1507. The translation, with the introductory essay, was reprinted numerous times, at Basel in 1530, at Venice in 1532, in Paris in 1555, 1557, and 1566 among others. The essay is dedicated to Titus Pyrrhinus, who is described as a fine singer. Valgulio urges Pyrrhinus to follow the models of the ancients in striving to raise the level of music making and its ethical efficacy to that of former times. He addresses the essay to him, because his singing pleases whoever listens, and he wishes him to become excellent also in all the other ornaments of the best arts.[1]

Valgulio was employed as secretary to the papal treasurer Falco Sinibaldo between 1481 and 1485, and sometime after the latter's death he became secretary to Cardinal Cesare Borgia.[2] The latter was made cardinal on 21 September 1493; until then Cesare had been a student of canon law in Perugia and Pisa. Since Rodrigo Borgia did not become pope until 11 August 1492, this must have been approximately the time when Valgulio entered the

---

1. Valgulio's essay may have inspired Giovanni Bardi to address his musical reform manifesto also to a singer, Giulio Caccini. See ch. 11 below.

2. I am indebted to P.O. Kristeller's *Supplementum ficinianum* (Florence, 1937), I, 114–15, for leading me to some of the information on Valgulio.

service of Cesare. It is not known how long Valgulio remained in his service or when he died.

In the letter of dedication to Cardinal Cesare Borgia of his translation of Cleomedes, *De contemplatione orbium excelsorum,* Valgulio tells that after the death of Sinibaldo he was free of other business and devoted himself to translating two books of moral philosophy by Plutarch, which he dedicated to Pope Alexander VI. Valgulio was fluent in Greek and Latin, being a son of a student of these languages, Stefano Valgulio of Brescia. There are records of his borrowing Greek texts, evidently for the purpose of translation, from the Vatican Library in 1481, 1483, 1484, 1495, and 1498.[3] On 3 April 1497 a collection of his translations was published in Brescia, each dedicated to a different person, apparently at different times: Cleomedes, *De contemplatione orbium excelsorum disputatio,* dedicated to Cardinal Cesare Borgia:[4] Aelius Aristides, *Oratio ad Rhodienses De concordia,* preceded by a letter from Pietro Gravina to Valgulio; Dio Chrysostomus, *Oratio ad Nicomedenses, De concordia,* to Francesco Cardinal Senese; Plutarch, *De virtute morum,* to Pope Alexander VI; Plutarch, *Praecepta connubialia* to Giovanni Borgia. Of his own writings, two essays, *De sumptibus funerum* and *Contra vituperatorem musicae,* were published in Brescia in 1590.[5]

The Proem to Plutarch's *De musica*

The point of departure for the essay to Pyrrhinus is a critique of the music of his time. Valgulio recalls the ridicule heaped by the Greek old comedy on the music of that day— on its playing to the crowd by adorning itself like a woman who curls her hair with irons and wears lace; music had

3. Eugène Müntz and Paul Fabre, *La bibliothèque du vatican au xve siècle,* (Paris, 1887; repr. Amsterdam, 1970), pp. 287, 288, 292. On 11 July 1481 he borrowed some Ammonius commentaries on Aristotle (not specifically identified) and two volumes of Alexander of Aphrodisias, returning them on 27 March, 1482. On 4 May 1483 he borrowed Plutarch's *Moralia* and Cleomedes' *Meteora* and returned them on an unrecorded date. On 12 March 1484 he borrowed Ptolemy's *Almagest* and Nicomachus' *Arithmetic;* the date of return is not recorded. In addition, Maria Bertola, *I due primi registri di prestito della Biblioteca apostolica vaticana,* p. 57, gives the entry on 26 September 1498 for Vat. gr. 186: "Carolus Valgulius Brixiensis . . . restituit quedam De musica et Arithmetica Nicomachi." This manuscript contains Plutarch's *De musica,* Ptolemy's *Harmonics,* and Poprhyry's commentary on the latter. She also found that Valgulio borrowed two manuscripts of Plutarch's *Moralia* on 10 February 1495, which were not returned until 1518 (p. 57, n. 2). Musical treatises in the Vatican Library under Sixtus IV (reigned 1471– 84) included several copies each of Ptolemy's *Harmonics* and the musical treatises of Bryennius and Nicomachus: Müntz and Fabre, pp. 235–36. There was also Athenaeus' *Deipnosophistae.*

4. Letter in Edoardo Alvisi, *Cesare Borgia, Duca di Romagna, Notizie e documenti* (Imola, 1878), pp. 461–63.

5. Georg W. F. Panzer, *Annales typographici ab artis inventae origine ad annum MD* (Nuremberg, 1793–97), VI, 340, no. 21.

declined again to this condition. Yet it has great power for good or evil,
Valgulio insists. Plato compared the soul to a tetrachord, in which reason,
as the middle string, must concord with the divine, low-pitched end, rather
than with the mortal, high-pitched end of the tetrachord; only then can
music penetrate the souls of citizens and move them toward grave and
severe customs, rather than light, languid, diverse, and soft customs. Musicians have little regard for these effects, filling their books with mere play
of notes. Ignorant of grammar, they do not read the works "of Franchino
Gaffuro, an excellent musician of our age, whose books are composed with
elegance and erudition."[6]

Against what he sees as a decaying, aimless art, Valgulio sets that of the
Greek musicians, who had at their disposal a large variety of poetico-musical
genres, each suited to certain functions and for expressing particular kinds
of feelings. There were songs for praising the gods, others for honoring
the deeds of illustrious men or victors of Olympic games, nuptial songs,
lyric odes, banquet and love songs, laments, prayers to drive away the
plague, tragic and comic songs. The rhythm, rapidity of beat, melody, and
instrument were chosen to fit the matter expressed.

Valgulio displays an avid interest in the terminological and documentary
aspects of this account, as disproportionate to his rhetorical purpose as it
seems genuine to his scholarly and curious nature. Indeed, between the first
few paragraphs and the closing exhortation to Pyrrhinus, Valgulio indulges
in a dissertation on some then little-known facts about Greek music, culled
from sources that escaped those who, like Gaffurio and Valla, worked the
mainstream of the Greek music-theoretical heritage. His reason for going
to these out of the way sources is indigenous to his subject matter, which
is not theoretical so much as ethical-social. Valgulio's purpose is to show
how music was used as a moral force in Greek society, and for this pseudo-
Plutarch was a better resource than an author like Ptolemy, and even useful
were occasional remarks in plays, particularly when enlightened by marginal
scholia found in the Greek manuscripts.

The most notable such foray into theatrical texts is Valgulio's frequent
citation of the scholia that appear in some manuscripts of the comedies of
Aristophanes. He finds these particularly illuminating in dealing with poetico-musical genres. Documenting the *scolion,* a song performed by guests
at a banquet as a branch of myrtle was passed around, Valgulio cites one
by Timocreon, as quoted in a gloss to Aristophanes' *Acharnenses,* line 532,[7]
which he translates as follows: "Vtinam o caece Pluto nec terra, nec mari,

6. Fol. 244v: "Franchino Gaffuro nostri aeui praestanti musico, cuius libros & eleganter,
& eruditè compositos."
7. William G. Rutherford, ed., *Scholia Aristophanica,* II, 317–18.

nec continenti apparuisses, sed tartarum incoluisses, & Acherontem, nanque te propter cuncta mortales circumstant mala." The practice of passing around the myrtle he finds substantiated in another scholia, this time in *Nubes* of Aristophanes, line 1364.[8] In this passage Dicaearchus, author of a lost treatise *Concerning musical contests,* is quoted as saying that, based on an almost innate custom, those who recite, whether with music or not, hold something in their hand with which to direct the performance. By old established tradition those who sing at banquets do so while holding a branch of laurel or myrtle.[9] Valgulio cites the authority of Dicaearchus for a classification of song into three types, the third of which was, supposedly, that of the scolion. But only two types are defined. The first type was that sung by everyone in turn; the second was sung by those most expert and professional, but in no regular order of succession, and for this reason was called *scolion,* which means crooked, or not straight.[10] Valgulio's translation is superior to that given by Karl Müller. As Müller notes, there is a problem in the text in that the gloss mentions three categories but defines only two. He emends the text to cover three categories. Athenaeus clarifies the matter in *Deipnosophistae* 15.694, which Valgulio must not have known, although a copy of it was in the Vatican Library at the time. Otherwise he would have taken advantage of the passage:

> There are three kinds of scolia, as Artemon of Cassandreis says in the second book of his work *On the Use of Books,* comprising all the songs sung in social gatherings. Of these the first kind was that which it was customary for all to sing in chorus; the second was sung by all, to be sure, but in a regular succession, one taking it up after another; and the third kind, which came last of all in order, was that no longer sung by all the company, but by those only who enjoyed the reputation of being specially skilled at it, and in whatever part of the room they happened to be; hence because this method implied a kind of disorder, but only in comparison with the other methods, in that it was carried out neither in chorus nor in the regular order, but in whatever direction they happened to be, it was called the crooked song (*scolion*).[11]

---

8. Ibid., I, 268.

9. Also published in *Fragmenta historicorum graecorum,* ed. Carolus Mullerus II (Paris, 1848), p. 248, no. 44. Rutherford doubted that the material cited above was from Dicaearchus, whose cited text he considered lost, and he believed that the above comments are separate and not by Dicaearchus.

10. Valgulio's comment reads: "unum quod sine discrimine ab omnibus deinceps atque ordine cantabatur. Alterum quod à peritissimis ac scientissimis non deinceps, sed altero semper praeterito, & hoc Scolion ab ordine tali dicebatur" (Plutarch *Opuscula,* fol. 246r). The fragment from Dicaearchus' treatise *Concerning Musical Contests* is printed in *Fragmenta historicorum graecorum,* II, 248, no. 43, from Photius, *Lexikon.*

11. Athenaeus, trans. Charles Burton Gulick (London, 1941), VII, 217.

Valgulio clinches the argument, so far as the meaning of *scolion* is concerned, by quoting a fragment he attributes to Aristoxenus and the musician Phyllis, which he reports as follows:

In celebritatibus nuptiarum ad
unam mensam plurimis positis
sellis accubantes ramum myrteum,
laureumue tenentes manu, proximo
subinde praeterito sententias &
amatoria syntona canebant.
Periodus illa propter ordinem
non rectum canentium Scolia,
hoc est
non recta appellabatur.[12]

In celebrations of weddings,
many seats having been set for
dinner, the guests, holding a branch
of myrtle or laurel in the hand,
made toasts and sang high pitched
love songs, then frequently bypassed
the next. The circuit of those
singing the scolia was not direct
[i.e. one-to-the-next]; therefore it
was called "not straight [*scolion*]."

The significance of the term *nomos,* which Valgulio translates "lex" (law), particularly interested him. He defines it:

Lex itaque musica modus canticus
est praescriptam Harmoniam siue
concentum, & rhythmum definitum
habens.[13]

A musical law is an air for
singing having a prescribed
melody or harmony, and a defined
meter.

These airs were called "laws," because it was not lawful to change the pitches of the voice and strings, as if they were prescribed by law. Valgulio says he is aware that Aristotle doubted that songs were called laws because the ancients, not having any writing, sang their laws so that they would be memorized and remembered. (He obviously had *Problems* 19.38 in mind.) Some of the nomoi—Valgulio continues to use the term *leges*— were for wind instruments, others for strings, and others for both. He cites as an example of the force of these nomoi the Orthian nomos of Pallas, in which every element contributed to the warlike characterization: the voice, the melody of the strings, the rhythm, and the text. When Timotheus sang this nomos, Alexander of Macedonia was spurred to take up his arms and exclaimed that this was the kind of song worthy of a king. Earlier he had described the Pythic nome:

Opera precium facturum me
duxi canticum unum de
ueteribus proponendo, quod
Pythicum certamen uocabant.
Argumentum erat pugna Apollinis cum dracone Pythone.

I think I shall do something worthwhile in giving an account of one
of the songs of the ancients that
was called the Pythic contest.
The subject was the battle of Apollo
with the dragon Python. Delona

12. Plutarch *Opuscula,* fol. 246r.
13. Ibid., fol. 245r.

Delona nomen toti cantico.
Partium eius nomina, Explora-
tio, Prouocatio, Iambicum,
Spondeum, Saltatio. In prima
Apollo contemplatur an oppor-
tunus sit dimicationi locus.
In secunda prouocat draconem
in certamen. In Iambico iam
pugnatur. Haec pars continet
Odontismon uocatum, quia
draco frendens secat dentes
uulnera iam accipiens
in corpus. Quarta uictoriam
Apollinis, Quinta saltantem
ouantemque uictoriae ergò
eundem declarat. Et haec est
una de legibus tibiarum, in
qua rhythmi, & moduli eorumque
mores in canendo mutantur,
prout partes eius uarios actus
continentes postulant.[14]

was the name of the whole piece.
The names of its parts were: Exploration. Challenge, Iambic, Spondee,
Dance. In the first Apollo investi-
gates whether the place is suitable
for battle. In the second he chal-
lenges the dragon to a contest.
Now in the Iambic the battle is
fought. This part contains the
Odontismon, so called since the
dragon, gnashing his teeth, cuts
into the wounds already received on
his body. The fourth is the victory
of Apollo, and in the fifth Apollo
himself, dances and rejoices upon
his victory. This, then, is one of the
auletic nomoi, in which rhythms,
melodies, and their ethical effects
are varied while performing, according as the parts containing various actions require.

Modus and *modulus,* as well as *concentus* and *harmonia,* are used to define the Greek *melos,* which Valgulio treats as a broad concept, encompassing both melody and harmony:

De uoce Melos, quamuis uulgo
nota esse uideatur, aliquid
tamen dicendum duxi.
Melos primo significatione
membrum corporis dicitur.
Quemadmodum enim multa uaria-
que membra in uno animantis
corpore sunt uaria atque
diuersa officia praestantia,
quae tamen finem eundem uitae
conseruandae spectant, sic
quia diuersa uoces mixtae
concorditer concentum unum
conficiunt, cantum proue-
nientem inde Graeci melos,
nos modum modulumque uocamus,
aut quia melos significat quod

Although the term *melos* seems
to be commonly known, I thought
something ought to be said about it.
Melos, in the first meaning,
is defined as a member of the body.
Although there are many and diverse
members in the body of a living being
that fulfill various and diverse
functions, they all serve the single
end of preserving life.
Thus, since
diverse notes mixed
concordantly make a single consensus,
the resultant song
the Greeks called melos,
and we call it air or melody.
Or, since melos signifies what

14. Ibid., fol. 245r. Giovanni Bardi, who conceived one of the Intermedi of 1589 as a polyphonic Pythic nome, may have first learned of it through this account.

cuique curae est, quasi nihil
maiori curae homini esse debeat
quam cantus & musica, siquidem
tantopere homines atque deos
commouet melos, cantum dixere.
Nec absolute quemcunque cantum,
sed harmonia tantummodo
constantem.[15]

someone cares about, and almost
nothing ought to be of greater
concern to a man than song and music,
as it moves men and gods so much,
they called song melos.
Nor did they call absolutely any
song thus but only that consisting
of harmony.

Some problematic terms in Valgulio's definition of *lex musica* are *modus,
harmonia,* and *concentus.* The term *modus* he may have heard used for air.
Castiglione, for example, speaks of "modo o aria" as if they were synon-
ymous.[16] Valgulio employs *concentus* to define *harmonia.* Both terms, as he
uses and defines them, connote part-music. He defines *harmonia* as follows:

Est autem Harmonia ratio
compositorum corporum primo,
inde ratio mixtorum
ut uocum. Composita enim
seruant nomina
partium, ut si diceremus
corpus animantis
carnibus, ossibus, neruis,
sanguine compositum esse,
mixta uerò non seruant.
Vt mulsum neque uinum est,
neque mel, tertia quaedam
natura, quanquam est
utriusque mixtione confectum,
ita concentus neque acuta uox
est neque grauis, sed tertium
quiddam, quod neque acuta
neque grauis uox dicatur.
Harmoniarum nomina uariarum
apud ueteres usurpata haec
sunt, Doris, Ias, Aeolis,
Phrygia, Lydia, Locrica, à
Philoxeno inuenta. Harmonia
aliquot locis pro enharmonio
Plutarchus usus uidetur.
Pythagoras eam sic definiuit,

Harmony first is a proportion of
bodies that have been composed,
then a proportion of mixed things
such as pitches. Now things in composition preserve the names
of their parts, as when we say "the
living body is made up of
flesh, bones, nerves,
blood"; but mixed,
they do not keep their names.
So mead is neither wine
nor honey but a third thing,
although it is made through
the mixture of the two;
thus a consensus is neither a high
nor low note but a certain third
thing that may be said to be neither
high nor low.
The names of the various harmonies
used among the ancients are these:
Doria, Ias, Aeolia,
Phrygia, Lydia, Locrica (invented by
Philoxenus). Plutarch seems to use
"harmony" sometimes in place of
"enharmonic."
Pythagoras defined it thus:

---

15. Plutarch, *Opuscula,* fol. 245v.
16. Baldesar Castiglione, *Il Cortegiano,* II, 13.

multimixtorum & diuersa   the union of broadly mixed things
sentientium unio.[17]   which cause diverse sensations.

Up to the point where he speaks of the Dorian and other "harmonies," Valgulio's definition synthesizes what he understands by *harmonia* on the basis of diverse reading and probably lexicographical sources. It is ambiguous with regard to the perennial question as to whether harmony is a simultaneous or successive phenomenon, but Valgulio is inclined to view it as a simultaneous one. His definition of *nomos* may have been influenced by the airs for singing he heard around him, which were almost always accompanied with chords on the lute or viola da braccio. His definition of *rhythm,* on the other hand, is dependent on two authorities, Aristoxenus and Dionysius of Halicarnassus, a sophist and musician known also as Dionysius the Musician, who flourished in Rome around 30 B.C. The passage in its entirety is given below:

Rhythmus uero pater est metri   Rhythm is the father of meter,
ut interpres inquit Aristopha-   as the commentator on Aristophanes
nis, Dionysius musicus de   said. Dionysius the Musician, in
Pythagoreorum sententia in   his book concerning similarities,
libro de similitudinibus   stated concerning the opinion of the
sic de Rhythmo inquit: Pythagoreans on rhythm: "The essence
Rhythmi & cantici moduli una   of rhythm and of the melody
prope est atque eadem essentia   of song is nearly one and the same
apud eos quibus graue   according to them who view grave as
tardum, & acutum celere uidetur: slow and acute as fast.
illi autem sunt Pythagorei.   But these are Pythagoreans,
Quum autem interualla cantica   and when they establish musical
in rationibus numerorum sta-   intervals in ratios of numbers,
tuant, omnesque Rhythmi in   and all rhythms are reckoned in
aliqua una ratione numerorum   some ratio of numbers:
censeantur: alij enim sunt   (some
duplares, sesquialteri alij,   duple, others sesquialter, and
in rationeque alij alia,   others in other ratios), then
eiusdem esse naturae Modulus   melody and rhythm are seen as of
& Rhythmus uidentur. Quumque   the same nature. Moreover, when
praeterea consonantia quae   consonances which arise from
de interuallis proficiscitur   the intervals of pitches,
uocum, eorundem dogmate Diapa-   and of these the diapason is dogmati-
son in dupla statuatur, Dia-   cally established in the duple, the diapente in sesquialtera, & sic   pente in the sesquialter, and so on
de reliquis, quum item   for the others, and when the

17. Plutarch, *Opuscula,* fol. 245v.

Rhythmici pedes omnes ijsdem
rationibus distincti sint,
nam plerique,
elegantissimi quique
in Diapason ac Diapente
consonantia sunt constituti,
cognationem inter se quandam
atque familiaritatem habere
uidebuntur. Haec Dionysius.
Differunt tamen: est quidem
Rhythmus Harmoniae semper comes, ex qua modulus & cantus
oritur: caeterum modulus in
acuto & graui, Rhythmus uerò
in celeri & tardo motu spectatur.
Qui motus in oratione
consideratus, longum ac breue
dicitur, in caeteris uerò
rebus celere, ac tardum. Vt
quum pedes sublati depressi-
que alternis, apto & mediocri
nisu pulsant terram, is motus
celer, & tardus nominatur,
in metricis rhythmicisque
pedibus, qui quidem sunt apta
syllabarum compositio,
quanquam inde acceperint pedum
nomen, breuis dicitur, atque
longus. Est autem in eo discrimen atque momentum, quòd
acutum & graue qualitates
sunt, celere uerò ac tardum
quantitates, ut infra dicetur.
Aristoxenus: Rhythmorum,
inquit, ductus innumeri sunt,
quemadmodum & uocum tensiones,
tametsi semper definiti
terminatique sumuntur in
usum, ut primi, disemi,
trisemi, ac caetera temporum
nomina rhythmicorum.[18]

rhythmic feet are all
distinguished through the same ratios
(for the majority, indeed,
the most elegant are those
constituted in the consonances
of the diapason and diapente) then they
are seen to have some kinship and
familial relation among them."
This is what Dionysius said.
They [rhythm and harmony] differ,
however: rhythm is always a companion to harmony, from which arises
melody and song; melody, in addition,
is perceived in high and low [pitch];
rhythm, though, in fast and slow motion. When this motion is considered in
speech, it is called long and short;
in other things, however,
fast and slow. When
the feet, raised and lowered
alternately with apt and ordinary
step, tap the earth, this motion is
called fast or slow.
In metrical and rhythmic feet,
which are an artful
composition of syllables,
although they got their name from
feet, they are called short and
long. There is, however, both
a distinction and a point to it,
for acute and grave are qualities,
but fast and slow are
quantities, as will be explained below.
Aristoxenus says: "sequences of
rhythms are innumerable,
as are pitches of voices,
but those put to use are always finite
and determinate, such as the prime
[chronos protos], diseme,
triseme, and similarly
named rhythms."

Valgulio is not ready to accept the Pythagorean subjection of both harmony and rhythm to the same ratios. He is willing to admit that the meas-

18. Ibid., fol. 245v.

urement of time is quantitative, but the differences between pitches, he insists, are qualitative. The authority for this distinction, he says, is Panaetius "in his book concerning the ratios and intervals of geometry and music,"[19] which is quoted in Porphyry's commentary on Ptolemy's *Harmonics*. Panaetius held that consonances and intervals should be considered in terms of the quality of their components and not the quantity. Just as one cannot find the middle between hot and cold, so it is in vain to search for the middle of a consonance or of a tone. If one strikes the two notes of an octave more strongly or more lightly, thereby changing the quantity, the interval—that is, the quality—remains the same. As Zarlino later pointed out,[20] in responding to Galilei's quotation of this passage from Valgulio in an unpublished discourse of 19 July 1578, Valgulio was misleading in choosing Panaetius as the one authority for the position that pitches were qualities. Although Panaetius admits that pitches are best regarded as qualities, he goes on to say—and Valgulio does not quote this—that numerical measurement of magnitude is necessary both for objects of sight and hearing to determine their precise relationships. Valgulio's purpose would have been better served by quoting Theophrastus' more cogent proof for the qualitative position, also transcribed in Porphyry's commentary.[21]

There is no mistaking, however, Valgulio's stand on the Pythagorean-Aristoxenian debate about the quantification of sonorous qualities.

Nunc ad defensionem Aristoxeni, quem falso accusatum reprehensumque fuisse diximus, descendamus. . . . urgentque ipsum & oppugnant acriter atque importune rationibus numerorum mathematicis Pythagorei, & qui eorum sectam tuentur.[22]

Let us come now to the defense of Aristoxenus, who, as we said, was falsely accused and reproached. . . . The Pythagoreans, and those who follow their sect, press and combat him fiercely and importunely with mathematical arguments about numbers.

The opponents of Aristoxenus accuse him of doing the impossible when he divides the tone into two equal parts. They claim that the 9:8 interval cannot be so divided. If the interval is represented as 18:16, the number between the two terms, 17, does not divide the fraction equally because the interval found between smaller numbers is always larger than that found

19. Ibid., fol. 246v.

20. *Sopplimenti musicali* (Venice, 1588), p. 173.

21. For a partial English translation of Theophrastus' proof (Porphyry, 62.3 ff.), see Bengt Alexanderson, *Textual Remarks on Ptolemy's Harmonica and Porphyry's commentary*, pp. 33–39. See also the discussion of Valla, "De musica," II, 4, in ch. 4 above. For a German translation of the passage (61.16–65.15), see Düring, *Ptolemaios und Porphyrios über die Musik*, pp. 160–67.

22. Plutarch *Opuscula*, fol. 246r.

between larger numbers; therefore 17:16 is larger than 18:17. This is very
true, Valgulio says. Nevertheless, the opponents of Aristoxenus

haud tamen efficiunt quod
uolunt, nec propterea sequitur
tonum non posse in duo paria
diuidi, tametsi interiacens
unitas sesquioctauam rationem
in numeris non possit secari.
At neruus ipse, in quo tanquam
in regula alijs atque alijs
partitionibus rite factis
concentus uocum uarij forman-
tur, quoniam magnitudo per-
petua est & continua, quaecumque in parte,
quotocunque
in spacio secari potest,
ergo & aequas
in partes. Supradictum est
enim de sentencia Panaetij,
Theophrasti, Porphyrij, &
aliorum, & certè patet latis-
sime ipsa per se res, consonantias diapason, diapente,
diatessaron, tonum, & reliquas
haudquaquam ideo statui in
numerorum rationibus atque
magnitudinibus, quia ipsae
uoces uocumque interualla
sint numeri, magnitudinesue,
& respectum inter se quantum
habeant, quum manifestissime
sint qualitates, sed quia
neruus, partesque ipsius
quae uoces aedunt, habet illos
inter se respectus quantos.
Quid igitur obstat quo minus
spacium illud nerui sesquiocta-
uum, in quo statuunt tonum,
diuidi in duas aequas por-
tiones, quae semitonia paria
sint, diuidi queat, quum
quantamcunque portionem con-
tinuae quantitatis in infinita
secari posse mathematici demon-

do not accomplish what
they want, nor does it follow
that a tone cannot be divided into two
equal parts, even though the
unity that lies between the two terms
of the sesquioctave ratio cannot
be numerically divided. But since
the magnitude is unbroken and continuous, it may be cut into any kind of
part and into any number of spaces,
and therefore a string itself, in which
as in a ruler by means of partitions
duly made, now one way,
now another,
various concensus of pitches may be
formed, so it may also be cut into
equal parts. This is the opinion
of Panaetius, Theophrastus,
Porphyry, and others,
and it certainly is very self-evident
that the consonances of the
diapason, diapente,
diatessaron, tone, and others
are established, I say, in
ratios of numbers; not at all because
the pitches themselves
and the distances between the pitches
may be numbers and quantities
and have among themselves a quantitative relation (since they
are very manifestly qualities) but
because the string and its parts,
which emit the pitches, have among
themselves quantitative relations.
What, therefore, prohibits the
sesquioctave space of the string which
they assign to the tone
from being divided into portions
that would make equal semitones,
since the mathematicians demonstrate
that a portion of a continuous
quantity of whatever size may
be divided into an infinite number

strent? Mihi quoque promptum
esset in monochordo, quod
Canona Pythagorici appellant,
idem mathematicè demonstrare,
ni satis perspicuum foret
quod proposui,
falso Aristoxenum
accusari, quòd tonum censuerit
in duo semitonia aequalia
posse diuidi.[23]

of parts? Even to me it would
be easy to demonstrate the same
thing by mathematical means
on the monochord, or canon as the
Pythagoreans call it,
if what I proposed were not clear
enough already, namely, that
Aristoxenus has been falsely charged
for having judged that the tone can be
divided into two equal semitones.

For the first time since Boethius had repeated Ptolemy's condemnation of Aristoxenus' approach to the division of intervals, Aristoxenus had found a defender among musical writers. Valgulio's defense of Aristoxenus is not based on aural preference or practical expediency but on mathematical theory. Valgulio set against numerology the broader wisdom of mathematics, particularly geometry, in which continuity, infinite division, and irrationality were ubiquitous phenomena.

Valgulio understood the position of Ptolemy, but he had little sympathy for it. He explains to Titus that Ptolemy was neither a harmonist like Aristoxenus nor a canonist like Pythagoras but took a middle road. For him the judgment of the ear had to agree with that of reason. But Ptolemy was wrong, Valgulio believed, in charging Aristoxenus with ignorance of mathematics, for Aristoxenus had written volumes on the subject and was a pupil of Xenophanes the Pythagorean. Ptolemy was unjust also to the Pythagoreans for having excluded the diapason-plus-diatessaron from among the consonances. "Pythagoras, that divine man, who I believe must have been sent to earth by the providence of the divine God,"[24] had the greatest love for things simple, pure, constant, and unmixed, and banished impure and variable things. Therefore he accepted only concords that derived from multiple and superparticular proportions, leaving out such impure proportions as the superpartient, of which the octave-plus-fourth (8:3) was an example. Ptolemy ingeniously defended such proportions and divided consonances into three orders of descending perfection: homophonic, symphonic, and emmelic. Pythagoras knew that other consonances could please the ears, such as those "employed by singers of today, which they call thirds and sixths, but like the bee that picks only the most pure celestial dew, so that divine and most discriminating man admitted among his things only the most noble and simple."[25]

23. Ibid., fols. 246v–247r.
24. Ibid., fol. 247r: "Diuinus ille uir Pythagoras, quem prouidentia numinis diuini dimissum in terras fuisse puto."
25. Ibid., fol. 247r: "qualibus nostri aeui cantores, quas tertias & sextas uocant, utuntur.

The liberality that could grant the merits of both Aristoxenus and Pythagoras shines through Valgulio's recommendation to his friend Titus of
Aristotle's classification of songs into three kinds: edifying, purgative, and
recreational. Some songs were moral, others suitable for imbuing the soul
with divine spirit, and still others active. The first category is suited to
customs that are consistent with the most gentle virtue. The second class,
songs which induce ecstasy, has the capacity to purge men who are disturbed
by entering into subjects that are arousing and soft and by opening the
affections to the purgation of fear and pity, which depress and afflict men's
souls. Such melodies fill souls with a beneficial contentment. Certain modes
were suited to each of these categories. So Philoxenus, Aristotle relates,
when he tried to set some dithyrambic verses in the Dorian mode, which
is severe and grave, found himself transported into the Phrygian, more
suited to the languid and soft nature of the material. "But this illumined
and erudite knowledge has remained withered down to its roots for many
centuries already."[26] Unlike those who, following Plato, would have excluded all but the ethically efficacious music, Valgulio would have Titus
follow Aristotle's example and cultivate all kinds but choose judiciously
according to the subject matter and purpose.

A Reply to an Opponent of Music

Not long after the publication of his translation of pseudo-Plutarch, Valgulio
apparently became embroiled in a controversy with a violent opponent of
music whose identity is not known. Valgulio, himself an ardent lover of
music, could not understand how anyone of sound mind could object to
this most soothing and joyful bounty to mankind. He begins his *Contra
vituperatorem musicae,* which was published in 1509,[27] with these words:

Nihil cogitari posse arbitror	I believe that nothing can be
tam auersum a ratione: adeo	conceived so opposed to reason,

Sed diuinum ille uir, & elegantissimus, ut apis purissimum coelestem solum rorem carpit, ita
sola nobilissima & simplicissima admittebat in rebus."

26. Ibid., fol. 247v: "at haec praeclara & erudita cognitio compluribus iam ante seculis
funditus exoleuit." Aristotle *Politics* 1342a.

27. This short essay is printed with another, which concerns funeral practices, in *Caroli
Valgulii Libellus, quo demonstratur Statutum Brixianorum de sumptibus funerum optima ratione nullum
facere discrimen fortunae inter cives, nec esse honores qui vulgo putantur; eiusdem contra vituperatorem
Musicae.* Brixiae per Joannem Antonium de Gandino dictum de Caegulis. Anno MDIX. The
colophon gives the date as 10 February 1509. The only copy I know of is in London, British
Library, 662.g.13 (3). Giovanni Vincenzo Pinelli once owned a copy, which may now be in
Milan, Biblioteca Ambrosiana. See Panzer, *Annales typographici,* VI, 340, no. 21.

abhorrens a sensibus: & uniuersae	so very abhorrent to the senses, and
naturae inimicum ac	so inimical to common nature and
portentosum: quod in alicuius	ominous, that it could not be
mente hominis non reperiatur.	found in the mind of some man.
quisnam inuenire potuisse	Who would have ever thought that he
hominem unquam putasset tam	could discover a man who is
agrestem & ferum & truculentum:	so boorish, savage, and grim
aut tam stupidum & plumbeum:	or so stupid, dull,
ac luteum ut cantus musicos	and vile that he hates
seu humana uoce: seu instrumentis	musical songs, whether issuing
editos inuisos habeat:	from the human voice or instruments,
id que non modo tacitum non	who not only carries this hate around
ferat sed glorietur: ac laudi	in silence but boasts of it and consi-
sibi esse ductatur. cum nihil	ders it redounds to his praise.
in genere humano iocundius	Nothing in the human species exists
suauius gratius	that is more joyful and sweet,
nihil beatius esse constet.[28]	nothing that is more blessed.

Valgulio launches into a full-fledged *encomium musicae*. He recalls that divinities among all races of men have been propitiated by song and instrumental music, that day and night in churches men render thanks for benefits received and celebrate the glory of God with music. Songs (*cantici modis*) have been used to dispel grief, to mollify wrath, to quiet agitations, and to incite the fallen and lazy to virtue. Even birds, fish, and land animals are tamed by melody. Just as a bull is angered by the color red, so is it incited to fury and demented by melody. Plato and Aristotle and all wise philosophers have always recommended that noble youth be taught music early. Of the arguments they adduced, Valgulio proposes to set forth only the most powerful.

The human soul acquires its motion through imitation of the revolutions of the heavenly bodies. The starry sphere holds a high, simple, and constant course, but the other, lower, bodies of the cosmic globe are borne in a slower, more varied, and complex motion. These are held in check and made to agree among themselves so as to maintain the order they were given right from the beginning by the creator and almighty God through measured ratios and musical numbers and with intervals brilliantly modulated by the harmony of voices. Such is the power of music, which operates in a similar way within the human soul:

Anima quoque nostra duo genera	Our soul, too, has, in imitation of
motus imitatione motuum	celestial motions, two genres of
caelestium habet: quorum alter	motion, of which one
suapte natura simplex est: rectus	is simple by nature. The upright

28. Valgulio, *Libellus,* fol. b2v.

& uniformis eo mens uisque
animae particeps rationis
similitudinem extimi
stelliferi caelestis
globi gerens utitur.
Alter contrarius illi
uarius obliquus & multiformis: ac
tardior est animae partis
ratione uacantis
similis inferiorum
globorum caeli motibus.
At non aeque conditor noster deus
in has animae humanae
contrarias uires:
earumque diuersos motus
atque in caelestibus fecit
aeternas illas concentuum in
musicorum rationes insertauit.[29]

and unified mind and the power
of the soul which partakes of reason
and bears a likeness to the supreme
starry celestial sphere
make use of this motion. The other
[genre of motion], its opposite, is
varied, oblique, and multiformed. It
is also slower and belongs to the part
of the soul devoid of reason and
resembles the motions
of the inferior spheres of the sky.
But the creator, our God, did not deal
equally with these contrary powers of
the human soul: he created their
diverse motions even in the celestial
spheres [and in them] he inserted
those eternal
ratios of musical harmonies.

Valgulio was not accustomed to giving precise references, but here he obviously is developing the parallel between the cosmic and human soul im-
plicit in Plato's *Timaeus*. As the orbits, distances between them, and speeds
of the heavenly bodies are organized into a harmony by musical ratios, so
the parts of the soul and their motions are coordinated by the ordering and
rational force of musical harmony. Just as the lower celestial spheres are
subject to the influence of the highest sphere, that of the stars, so that part
of the mind not under control of reason, the part that resists reason's authority, must be put under its control, and this can be achieved through
music.

si huiusmodi symphonia
huiusmodique temperamento
rhythmorum musicorum aduersantes
inuicem animi partes conditor
noster consociasset: &
dissonantes concinnasset.
non tot tantasque discordias:
& pugnas dissidentium inter se
partium: non tantos aestus
insanarum cupiditatum: non tanta
incendia libidinum: non immania
studia pecuniae: nec miserandas
contentiones honorum in semetipso
quisque sentinet omnis error:

If our creator had coordinated
through this kind of symphony and
this kind of moderation of musical
rhythms the mutually
warring parts of the soul
and harmonized the dissonant parts,
each would not feel so many grave
discords and battles of dissident
parts, not the waves of
insane desires, the
flames of libido, the fierce
pursuit of money, nor the deplorable
competing honors in himself.
All error, all inconstancy,

29. Ibid., fol. b3r.

omnis inconstantia: peccatum omne: cunctaque mala a nobis procul forent: summa pace: tranquilitate: atque faelicitate frueremur.[30]	all sin, all evils would be far removed from us. We would enjoy supreme peace, tranquility, and happiness.

But this wished-for felicity is not within the reach of humanity, composed as it is of mean materials and condemned to pass its life in a lowly place. Rather the parts of our souls, in the absence of musical temperament, more often disagree among themselves. The harmony not found in human nature can, however, be achieved through the resource of music.

Verum enim uero & si musica moderatio illa: harmonicumque temperamentum animis nostris insitum a natura non fuit quod semper concordes & consonas animi diuersas appetentes partes efficeret: Attamen bonitas & prouidentia diuina consulens nobis uim potestatem facultatemque nanciscendi & comparandi ea singulari quodam munere nobis concessit: quarum opem facultatem si exciuerimus: operamque nostram & accuratam diligentiam & studium adhibuerimus musicam comparabimus: & eius suauissimis nexibus: & dulcissimis interuallis contrarios: & diuersa spectantes animorum nostrorum motus quasi fides temperare: & consonos semper interse efficere poterimus: ut qui suapte natura ratione uacant rationem semper obtemperent: eam libentes uolentesque sequantur ducem non inuiti trahantur: nec unquam eius imperium detractent. Si auxilio & opibus Musicae nostrorum motus animorum similes caelestibus conuersionibus obtinebimus:	Yet if that musical moderation and the harmonic temperament were not implanted in our souls by nature, which would have made the diverse appetitive parts of the soul concordant and consonant, nevertheless divine goodness and providence, coming to our aid, granted us by a certain special gift the power and potential for finding and comparing. If we call forth the resource of this faculty and summon our effort and careful diligence and study, and if we bring in music, with its most sweet connections and its very suave intervals, we shall be able to tune, almost like strings, the contrary and diverse motions of our souls, and we shall always be able to make them consonant among themselves so that those who are lacking in reason by nature always would obey reason. Desiring and wanting reason, not reluctantly dragged, they would follow its lead, nor would they ever despise its authority. If, with the help and resources of music, we attain a motion of our souls similar to the celestial revolutions,

30. Ibid., fol. b3r–v.

constantiam tuebimur:	we shall maintain constancy and
faelicitate beatitudineque qua	we shall enjoy happiness and an
caeleste fruemur. Nam animorum	almost heavenly grace. For the
humanorum motus aeterni sunt	motions of human souls are eternal,
& ipsi quandoquidem uim	since the souls themselves have the
principii se mouendi habent.	power of primary self-motion.
Musicam igitur omnes quicumque	Therefore anyone who loves
pacem: quietem: concordiam:	peace, tranquility, harmony, and
faelicitatem in semetipso: &	happiness in himself and within
intra domesticos parietes: &	the household walls and
in ciuitate amant habere colere	in the city must have, cultivate,
uenerari & amplecti omni ope	venerate, and embrace music with
ac studio: & ipsos quoque	all effort and zeal and with it
musicos debent.[31]	musicians too.

The Neoplatonic position receives in these words of Valgulio as eloquent and committed an expression as it was to get in the early sixteenth century.

Valgulio now turns to Aristotle's views on education. Music, in his view, should be introduced early in the training of boys, because at that age they are very apt at feigning varied customs and experiencing different manners of living. By knowing the joy of music one learns properly to love and to hate. For vocal modes contain images of gentleness, modesty, justice, and other virtues.

Valgulio closes his encomium with a review of the effects of music as recounted by various ancient authors. Even those of mediocre learning, he says, know that Terpander quieted a rebellion in the cities with lyre and song and that plagues which could not be relieved by any other means were removed by music. Even common people know that Homer tells of an army that was liberated from a severe plague by songs addressed to the heavens. By way of indicating his sources, Valgulio names a few authors of the many that anyone wishing to write about music and its virtues should read:

Plutarchi in primis Musicam:	first the *Music* of Plutarch,
Platonis de re. p. & de legibus:	the *Republic* and
Aristotelisque politicos libros.	*Laws* of Plato, and of Aristotle
Porphyrium in harmonica iuniorem:	the political books. Porphyry the
Martianum capellam: innumeros	younger on harmonics; Martianus
alios praeclaros auctores legat	Capella. Whoever would write every-
qui omnes de musica eiusque	thing concerning music and its

31. Ibid., fol. b3v.

| utilitatibus & | uses and praises should read |
| laudibus perscripsere.[32] | innumerable other excellent authors. |

This list does not exhaust the authors of whom Valgulio showed a knowledge in the introduction to his Latin translation of pseudo-Plutarch's treatise. But the absence of Ptolemy's name, when his commentator Porphyry is mentioned, is notable. Valgulio may not have had access to the *Harmonics* of Ptolemy. On the other hand, he was less interested in theoretical questions than in the lore about Greek musical practice, and for this purpose the treatise of pseudo-Plutarch deserved to be placed first. A certain pride of discovery may also have led to his assigning such a high value to the treatise. He must have come across it during his work on Plutarch's authentic moral essays, two of which he translated and published in 1497. Giorgio Valla had used and cited pseudo-Plutarch on music, but it was Valgulio's introduction and Latin translation that drew the attention of Renaissance musicographers to the work. The publication of Valgulio's translation preceded by two years the Aldine *editio princeps* of the Greek text with Plutarch's *Moralia* by Demetrius Ducas in 1509. Valgulio did not doubt that the *De musica* was authentic Plutarch. The Byzantine scholar Maximus Planudes (c. 1255–1305) had included it in his edition of Plutarch's works, and it is probably to him that we owe its survival. *De musica* is to be found in many of the Plutarchan manuscripts,[33] although, according to Einarson and De Lacy, Valgulio's source was a musical compilation, Paris, Bibliothèque Nationale, graecus 2451, a fifteenth-century manuscript stemming from Florence (including also Ptolemy and Porphyry) and belonging to the family of Vatican graecus 186, also a musical collection.[34]

It is easy to understand why the pseudo-Plutarch treatise attracted Valgulio. Not a musician himself, he was less interested in the theory or practice of music than in its social, civic, and moral uses. The possibility that music could make men better and healthier was a revelation to him. He could see a parallel between the decadence deplored by the interlocutors of the dialogue reported by pseudo-Plutarch and events in his own time. Musicians were cultivating innovations and technical virtuosity at the expense of expressivity and ethical effect. The speakers in the dialogue, although critical of most recent music, offer many examples from more ancient times that

---

32. Ibid, fol. b3v.

33. See the list in François Lasserre, *Plutarque, De la musique* (Olten, 1954), pp. 105–06.

34. See the stemma in Benedict Einarson and Phillip H. De Lacy, *Plutarch's Moralia in Fifteen Volumes*, XIV (Cambridge, Mass. 1967), p. 349. No evidence is given there for the assignment of this manuscript as the source of Valgulio's version. It is more likely that his source was Vat. gr. 186, since this was the manuscript he borrowed and then returned on 26 September 1498. Cf. n.3 above.

could be emulated by modern musicians—the lost enharmonic and chromatic genera, the power of certain modes, the majestic and simple music that developed moral character, the laudable dedication of music to worship and the praise of heroism and nobility. Valgulio responded sympathetically to this nostalgia for a once powerful, now lost, art.

The Translation of the *De musica* of Plutarch

The dialogue that Valgulio translated is perhaps the most informative concerning the ancient Greek musical culture of any of the surviving Greek writings. It preserves fragments of treatises by Heracleides Ponticus, Glaucus of Rhegium, Pratinas, Lamprocles of Athens, Aristoxenus, and various anonymi. Because of the wealth of musical lore it transmits, pseudo-Plutarch in Valgulio's translation was probably the most read of any of the Greek sources by the musical humanists of the Renaissance. For example, Galilei drew much of the information for the portions of his *Dialogo* that dwell on Greek musical practices from this translation.[35] A brief review of the contents of pseudo-Plutarch will give an idea of the treasure trove that Valgulio laid open.

The dialogue takes place during a feast on the second day of the Saturnalia. The host, Onesicrates, invites Lysias, a performer in his employ, and Soterichus of Alexandria to discuss music. Lysias begins by reporting on the invention and ancient history of music. He speaks of the oldest songs, of Terpander's kitharic nomes, and of Clonas' epic and elegiac poetry accompanied by the aulos. He recalls the names of even older musicians: Hyagnis, Marsyas, Olympus, Orpheus, Polymnestus, Sacadas, Philammon of Delphi. The ancient style of singing until the time of Phrynis was simple, and one was obliged to remain within a given harmonia and rhythm. All the music before Olympus invented the enharmonic genus had been diatonic or chromatic. It was he who came upon the enharmonic by wandering around in the diatonic, at first in the Dorian mode; later the semitone was divided also in the Lydian and Phrygian modes. These older composers used a lofty style, but some of those who followed—Crexus, Timotheus, Philoxenus—introduced a coarser idiom, full of novelties, abandoning the restriction to a few notes and the grandeur of the noble manner.

Soterichus takes over the discourse. He supplements what Lysias had said by mentioning the role of the gods, particularly Apollo, in the origin of music. He laments its recent decadence; once inspired and severe, it is now

---

35. Vincenzo Galilei, *Dialogo della musica antica et della moderna*, (Florence, 1581), pp. 79, 91, 100–03, 114–18.

effeminate and theatrical. He cites Plato's distaste for the high-pitched lamenting Lydian. The Mixolydian is also emotional and suited to tragedy. Plato preferred the Dorian for warlike and temperate men. Although he and the ancients knew also other modes, they rejected multiplicity of modes and notes, and Olympus and Terpander were able to compose with a scale of only three notes. The tragic poets avoided also the chromatic genus, which was older than the enharmonic. These limitations were a matter of choice and not ignorance. On the other hand, the ancient composers cultivated rhythmic complexity. To illustrate Plato's profound knowledge of music Soterichus explains the philosopher's construction of the soul as a harmony of intervals. In this discussion the higher pitches are given the larger numbers, as if they stood for frequency of beating rather than string length.

Recognition of the soul as a harmony led the Greeks to insist upon training the young through and in music. Educating the young, honoring the gods, and praising good men were in ancient times sufficient goals for music, and its use in the theater was unknown.

Soterichus details some of the innovations that occurred after Terpander. Archilochus developed a new rhythmic system and mixed recitation with singing as the tragic poets were also to do. Lasus of Hermione and Melanippides introduced further changes. The case of Telesias of Thebes is cited: a musician who had learned the traditional art but had then become enamored of the elaborate style of the theater; yet after memorizing many works of Philoxenus and Timotheus, he was not able to compose in this manner with success because of his earlier training. This shows the importance of habituation and education early in life. To judge music it is essential to know, however, both the sciences of harmonics and rhythmics and the moral character at which a composition aims. Soterichus now launches into a disquisition on music criticism. The host, Onesicrates, closes the dialogue by reminding his friends that even the revolutions of the universe and of the stars were believed by the ancient philosophers to depend upon music and harmony.

Valgulio's translation of pseudo-Plutarch is faithful and sympathetic in spirit as well as in the letter. The technical terms are almost always rendered appropriately, and at one point Valgulio makes clear graphically the harmonic and arithmetic divisions of the octave, which in the text are described only in prose.[36] The passage in which Heraclides (quoted by pseudo-Plutarch) compares the style of his contemporaries with that of ancient times and justifies the appellation *nomos* illustrates the felicity of Valgulio's presentation.

---

36. *De musica* 1138–39.22, in Plutarch *Opuscula,* fol. 29r.

Sed omnino citharae cantus	But Terpander's method of singing to
Terpandri ratio omni ex parte	the kithara continued generally
simplex perrexit esse usque ad	to be simple up to the time of
aetatem Phrynidis. Haud enim	Phrynis. In ancient times,
antiquitus pro libidine cuiusque,	it was not permitted, as is now
uti nunc, licebat	customary according to individual
fidibus canere, nec rhythmos	whim, to sing to the lyre, nor
concentusque transferre: In	transpose the rhythm and harmony.
ipsis nanque legibus accommodatam	For in these nomoi each observed
cuique tentionem tuebatur, cuius	the appropriate tuning. This
rei causa id nominis	is the reason why this name was
inditum erat: Leges enim sunt	given to it. They were called nomoi
uocatae, quoniam praescriptum	[laws], then, because it was ordered
quasi lege cautumque erat,	and observed almost as a law that
ne quis per quamlibet unam speciem	no one should transgress a species
formamque tentionis	and form of tuning in any one of the
transgrederetur.[37]	nomoi.

Valgulio resists here the temptation to read "mode" into the Greek *tasin,* which a translator oriented in Western music might have done.[38] When Heraclides, in the long extract from a lost work, turns to speak of the three best known tonoi, Valgulio renders the term as *toni.*

Quum itaque sint tres toni,	Since there are three tonoi, whose
autoribus Sacada	composers were Sacadas
& Polymnesto,	and Polymnestus,
Dorius, Phrygius & Lydius, in	the Dorian, Phrygian, and Lydian, in
quolibet uno Sacadam aiunt	each of which Sacadas, they say, made
fecisse stropham, & chorum canere	a strophe and taught the chorus to
docuisse, sic ut Dorium prima,	sing the first in Dorian,
Phrygium secunda, Lydium tertia	the second in Phrygian, the third
cantaret. Eamque legem propter	in Lydian. They called this nome
tripertitam mutationem triperti-	because of its tripartite mutation
lem fuisse uocatam ferunt.[39]	"Tripertile" (threefold).

The term "tripertilis," however, is not as descriptive as it might be of the Greek *trimele,* a song containing three strains.

   Probably the most important passage of the Plutarchan dialogue for the musicians of the sixteenth century was that in which the enharmonic was

   37. *De musica* 1133D.6, in Plutarch *Opuscula,* fol. 26r–v. Compare this translation with the Greek text and English translation in Einarson and de Lacy, p. 365. *De musica* 1133D.6. Cf. also the translation used by Galilei in Florence, Biblioteca Nazionale Centrale, MS Galilei 7, fol. 27r, and *Dialogo,* p. 114.
   38. For example, Lasserre (p. 135) translates this as: "On respectait pour chaque nome la tonalité qui lui était propre." He uses "tonalité" throughout for *tonos.*
   39. *De musica* 1134A.8, in Plutarch *Opuscula,* fol. 26v. Cf. MS Galilei 7, fol. 29v.

extolled as the noblest of the genera, favored by the ancients because of its majesty:

At uerò Musici nostri temporis pulcherrimum omnium, maximeque decorum genus, quod ueteres propter maiestatem grauitatemque ipsius colebant, penitus repudiarunt.[40]	The musicians of our times, though, disdained completely the most beautiful genus of all and the most fitting, which the ancients cherished for its majesty and severity.

This statement was to become the rallying cry in Vicentino's crusade for the chromatic and enharmonic genera in the 1550's.[41] Earlier in the same speech, by the interlocutor Soterichus, Aristoxenus is cited as attributing the invention of the enharmonic to Olympus, who was to become for Galilei through the influence of this translation a model for the reform of musical composition.[42] Particularly attractive to Galilei was the poverty of means that Olympus could transform into triumphs of emotional expression. It was the following passage in Valgulio's translation that particularly struck Galilei:

Iam uerò prisci omnes haud quidem quia imprudentes imperitique forent ullius concentus, & harmoniae, certis quibusdam ac definitis usi sunt, nec ignorantia autor causaque fuit eiusmodi angustiae, & fidium paucitatis. Nec sanè Olympum, nec Terpandrum, nec qui eorum sectam sunt sequuti, perpulit inscitia ad circumcidendam multitudinem fidium, uarietatemque demendam. Testantur id poëmata Olympi atque Terpandri, caeterorumque omnium eiusdem generis Musicorum ac poëtarum. Quae quum trifidia simpliciaque forent, usque adeo praestabant uarijs &	Now if all the ancients used only a few particular harmonies, it was not at all because they were unaware and inexperienced in any harmony or *harmonia,* nor was ignorance at the root and the cause of such constraint and poverty of strings. Incompetence compelled neither Olympus, nor Terpander, nor those who followed in their path to reduce the number of strings, and restrict variety. Witness the compositions of Olympus and Terpander, and of all the other musicians and poets of their sort. These compositions, although reduced to three strings and to simple means, so completely surpassed those varied

40. *De musica* 1145A.38, in Plutarch *Opuscula,* fol. 31v. Cf. MS Galilei 7, fols. 53v–54r.

41. Nicola Vicentino, *L'Antica musica ridotta alla moderna pratica* (Rome, 1555).

42. See Galilei's *Discorso intorno all'uso dell'enharmonio, et di chi fusse autore del cromatico,* ed. Frieder Rempp, in *Die Kontrapunkttraktate Vincenzo Galileis* (Cologne, 1980), pp. 165ff; and *Dubbi intorno a quanto io ho detto dell'uso dell'enharmonio, con la solutione di essi,* ibid., pp. 181ff. See also Palisca, "Vincenzo Galilei and Some Links between 'Pseudo-Monody' and Monody," *Musical Quarterly* 46 (1960): 347–48.

multifidijs, ut
nemo unus Olympi modum posset
imitari, & qui in multinerui,
multitudineque uersabantur
posteriores essent.[43]

and multistringed that
not one could rival the manner of
Olympus, and even those who worked
with many strings and multiplicity
are his inferiors.

43. *De musica* 1137A.18, in Plutarch *Opuscula,* fol. 28r. Cf. MS Galilei 7, fol. 36r–v.

SIX

The Early Translators: Burana, Leoniceno, Augio

o those who saw some of the manuscripts of Greek theoretical writings or even read lists of them it was evident that the resources in Latin were meager compared to what existed in the Greek language. The number of trained musicians who could read the treatises in their original language was very small, however. Indeed, during the entire Renaissance there were only three who figure significantly in the history of theory in Italy who could: Lodovico Fogliano, Francisco de Salinas, and Ercole Bottrigari. Others had to depend on translations. Franchino Gaffurio, Gioseffo Zarlino, and Vincenzo Galilei were among those who commissioned or stimulated translations of Greek musical treatises. Among the translators, two, though not musicians, wrote original works about music, Giorgio Valla and Carlo Valgulio. Two other humanists expert in the Greek language who wrote competently about music should be mentioned, although they too were not musicians: Girolamo Mei and Francesco Patrizi. With so few professional music theorists and musicians able to read Greek, then, translation was an essential bridge between the Greek theoretical heritage and late Renaissance musical thought.

Giovanni Francesco Burana

Of the translators who worked at the request of, or on commission from, Franchino Gaffurio, Giovanni Francesco Burana was the most productive. He completed three or four translations from the Greek: Aristides Quintilianus, *De musica,* a group of three anonymous treatises formerly known as Bellermann's anonymous, Manuel Bryennius, *Harmonics,* and probably, Bacchius Senior, *Introductio musica,* which has not survived.

Burana was born in the last quarter of the fifteenth century in Verona. The translations for Gaffurio were among his earliest works, completed between 1494 and 1497. He later studied at the university in Padua and received the doctorate in arts in 1500. He taught logic there in 1501, but there are no documents indicating a continuation of his teaching beyond 1502.[1]

Gaffurio's own compilation of Burana's translations of the three musical treatises, a paper codex that he gave to the Church of the Incoronata of Lodi in 1518, is now in the Biblioteca Capitolare of Verona, MS CCXL (201).[2] The Verona manuscript may be autograph and probably contains the treatises in the order in which they were completed. The Aristides is dated in a colophon in Gaffurio's hand 15 April 1494; the others are not dated. The contents of the manuscript are as follows:

Aristides Quintilianus, *De musica*
    Lib. 1, fol. 1r
    Lib. 2, fol. 13v
    Lib. 3, fol. 25v
Anonymi:[3]
    1, fol. 37v
    2, fol. 38r
    3, fols. 39r–44v
Bacchius Senior, compendium in Greek of his *Introductio musica,* fol. 44v
Bryennius, *Harmonics:*
    Lib. 1, fol. 48r
    Lib. 2, fol. 63v
    Lib. 3, fols. 99r–119r

The manuscript, written by one hand, is of uneven legibility; much of the Bryennius is damaged, apparently by water, so that often only a part of a page is visible. On nearly every page are marginal and some interlinear notes, in both Greek and Latin, the main purpose of which seems to be to

---

1. See G. Stabile, "Burana," in *Dizionario biografico degli Italiani,* XV (1972), 386–89. The evidence for Burana's teaching at Padua is in Elda Martellozzo Forin, ed., *Acta graduum academicorum ab anno 1501 ad annum 1525* (Padua, 1969). She reports two documents mentioning him: Item 59, I, 24, dated 6 August 1501, in which he is named witness in an examination and is designated "art[is] doctor," and Item 60, ibid., same date, where he is described as "d[ominus] mag[ister] Franciscus Burana ordinarius logice." Also attributed to Burana is a translation of Hero's *De spiraminibus* (Rome, Biblioteca Lancisiana, MS 321; see Kristeller, *Iter italicum,* II, 118).

2. For a description of the manuscript, see F. Alberto Gallo, "Le traduzioni dal Greco per Franchino Gaffurio," *Acta Musicologica* 35 (1963):172–74; and Gallo, "Musici scriptores graeci," in *Catalogus translationum et commentariorum: Mediaeval and Renaissance Translations and Commentaries,* ed. Edward Cranz and Paul O. Kristeller, III (Washington, 1976), 67–68. Of the Bryennius there is a second copy on parchment in Lodi, Biblioteca Comunale, MS XXVIII.A.8, to which Gaffurio added a colophon and date 21 January 1497.

3. These are numbered according to Najock, *Drei anonyme.*

give the reader an idea of the original Greek terminology. The manuscript was evidently tailored to Gaffurio's requirements, for although he would not have been able to translate the prose himself, he could read the Greek alphabet.

Since the translations of Burana were for the exclusive use of Gaffurio, the significance of their content for the development of musical thought is best considered in connection with Gaffurio's utilization of them in his treatises. In the present chapter I shall limit myself to general problems of translation and transmission.

Unlike Valla, Burana replaces Greek technical terms with native Latin words. For example, translating the Aristides treatise, he renders *proslambanomenos* as "assumpta" and *hypate hypaton* as "suprema supremarum." This has the double drawback of obscuring the original names familiar to readers of Boethius and other medieval authors and falsely suggesting height of pitch with the nomenclature of tetrachordal location. So *hypate hypaton* may really mean "the principal of the principals" or the "supreme of the supremes," for which *suprema supremarum* is correct, but in effect the pitch is "the lowest of the low." Less objectionable are such neologisms as "tertia coniunctae" for *trite synemmenon* or "acuta disiunctarum" for *nete diezeugmenon*" (fol. 2v). Similarly *pyknon, barypyknon, oxypyknon,* and *apyknon* become "densi," "grauis densitatis," "acutae densitatis," and "non densi" (3r). For the fixed notes of the tetrachord Burana chooses "stantes," while for the movable "ferens," cognates of the Greek *hestōtes* and *pheromenoi* (3r). Burana occasionally preserves the Greek word. Whereas in 1.8 he translates *synecheis* as "continuati," for its opposite, *hyperbaton* (gapped), he retreats to "hyperbaton." The terms for the genera are transliterated "harmonia," "diatonon," and "chroma." Of the melopoetic terms (1.12) he leaves some partly in Greek, such as *melopoeia and pettia,* others he translates, such as the three types of *agoge:* "recta," "inflexa," and "circularis." *Ploke* becomes "connexio," and *chresis* "usus." Each of these terms is defined by Aristides, so that the unfamiliar words acquire concreteness without further explanation by the translator.

One of the most difficult passages of the technical first book of Aristides Quintilianus is that describing Aristoxenus' system of tonoi (1.10; fol. 5v).[4] Aristides explains that Aristoxenus recognized thirteen tonoi, and he gives their names. To these, he says, some new theorists added two more, so that for each name there would be a low, medial, and high-pitched tonos,

---

4. I shall use the book and section designations in R. P. Winnington-Ingram's edition of the treatise, *Aristidis Quintiliani De musica libri tres* (Leipzig, 1963). An indispensable aid in studying Burana's translation has been the translation by Thomas J. Mathiesen, *Aristides Quintilianus, On Music in Three Books,* translation, with introduction, commentary, and annotations (New Haven, 1983).

producing triads of tonoi, such as Hypodoriann, Dorian, and Hyperdorian. He then describes how they were related to each other in pitch:

Quodammodo autem unusquisque grauissimi horum precedentem per acutum unumquisque per ipsorum semitonio superabit precedentem si à grauissimo initium sumam uolemus semitonio aut minor erit/ ab acutissimo inchoabimus. continent igitur ut dixi ipsorum assumpti sub diapason et tono: assumi quoque possent hac causa per symphonias, nam si coepi à grauissimo resoluero quod intendere ac rursus remittere per uarias distantias omnino unum alique ipsorum assumptum tangam. horum alij cantantur in totum/ alij non. dorius igitur totus cantatur quoad duodecim usque tonos uocem nobis suppeditat et quod eius medius assumptus sub diapason est hypodorio. Ceterorum uero qui grauiori toni sunt sub dorio consonantur/ usque ad sonus, consonantia similem limitem nete extrema hyperboleon. Sic igitur cantus uel member constituemus, si profundissimi omnium constitutionis sonorum uni assumptorum subtituimus: ac quae post hunc sequunt ad grauiorum modulemus nam si ulterius remittere non ualabimus dorius erit. per sonus primus audibilis dorij assumpto definitur: si uero audiatur consyderare certabimus quanto dorij assumpto

In a certain way every one of these will exceed every preceding one of those in height of pitch by a semitone, if we choose to begin on the lowest; or if we wish to begin on the highest, it will be smaller [lower] by a semitone. As I said, the assumed notes [proslambanomenoi] add up therefore, to a diapason-plus-tone. For this reason, they can be joined to make consonances. Now, if I choose to begin with the lowest note and raise, and then lower, the pitch through various intervals, I shall surely reach one of the other proslambanomenoi. Of these [tonoi] some are sung in their entirety, some not. Thus the entire Dorian is sung, up to as far as twelve whole tones which the voice supplies us, because its proslambanomenos is the median in the Hypodorian diapason. Of the remaining, those tones that are lower than the Dorian are sung up to the sound that is consonant with the extreme limit, nete hyperbolaeon. So now, therefore, we shall construe the song or phrase: if we substitute for the lowest of all the sounds of the constitution [i.e., scale] one of the assumed notes [proslambanomenoi] and after this direct the song toward the lower pitches, then if we do not have the capacity to descend any farther, it will be Dorian, for the first audible sound of the Dorian is defined by the proslambanomenos. If, however, it [a lower note] is heard, we shall strive to consider by how much it

tanto quanto et intus
profundissimum natura
profundissimo maior
consyderetur/
sin autem
grauissimus cantus sonus
superando dorij diapason
quae sit acutus/ assumimus
diapason ad grauitate supradicto
usi sciremus artificio/
harmoniam ipsam facile
assequeremus.[5]

exceeds the proslambanomenos of the
Dorian, as much, that is, as the
deepest note of the song is
considered greater [higher] than the
deepest by nature. But if the
lowest note of the song is
higher than the Dorian, in the upper
diapason, we assume the diapason
below. We shall know to make use
of the method stated above and
shall determine easily the harmonia
itself.

Each tonos, Burana's translation tells us, is a semitone higher or lower than the next. According to the new theorists, the proslambanomenoi, when stacked one on top of another, fill the compass of an octave-plus-tone. Proslambanomenoi may, therefore, be related to each other as consonances, for example by fourth, fifth, or octave. (This fact will be important later, when Aristides speaks of modulation.) Only one of the tonoi fits fully within the vocal range, the Dorian, because its proslambanomenos is the bottom note of the central octave of the Hypodorian, effectively the lowest note of the average male voice; let us say modern F. So in the case of the Dorian, one can sing all the way from F up to f', or from proslambanomenos to nete hyperbolaeon—in other words, the entire fifteen notes of the perfect system. But with other tonoi, which have their proslambanomenoi lower than this, the note disappears below the singable range and must be recouped in an upper octave. If we wish to determine the tonos of a song, we are told to take its lowest note and sing from it down the proslambanomenoi. If we find ourselves at the limit of the voice, we are on the Dorian's proslambanomenos, and the tonos is Dorian. If we do not reach the limit of the voice, then the tonos is higher than the Dorian by whatever interval the note reached is higher than the Dorian's proslambanomenos. However, if we need to go below this natural limit of the voice to reach the proper proslambanomenos for the given melody, then the tonos is lower than the Dorian, and the note equivalent to the "excessive" proslambanomenos will be heard in a higher octave, above the Dorian's range. For example, the proslambanomenos of the Hypophrygian (D by analogy to the modern gamut), a minor third below the natural limit, can be said to occur in the octave above the Dorian (d", a major sixth above its nete hyperbolaeon) and an octave higher than the Hypophrygian's nete hyperbolaeon (see Figure 6.1).

5. Aristides Quintilianus *De musica* 1.10, Burana trans., fol. 5v.

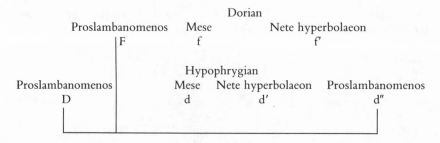

Figure 6.1:
Comparison of the locations of Dorian and Hypophrygian

Burana's translation of this passage is adequate enough; Aristides' conception and his manner of expressing it are difficult and far from transparent in any language. If Gaffurio, the destinee of this translation, failed to grasp the sense of this passage, he surely may be forgiven. On the other hand, what prevented him from understanding it were probably his preconceptions about the Greek tonal system rather than the intrinsic difficulty of Aristides' thought or Burana's translation.

In both the Aristides and the anonymous treatises Burana encountered material that was beyond the competence of a classical rhetorician, in the form of notational diagrams and tables in which there were signs that were not part of the usual Greek alphabet. Burana had no way of knowing whether his manuscript was correct and whether he was copying a sign faithfully. As a result, his transmission of the signs for pitch were full of corrupt characters. He would have had to study the exposition of the notational system in Alypius to get a grounding in the system, and then to make allowances for the disparity in dates of his various sources before he could correct one by the other. He was obviously not prepared for this task, nor did he regard it as essential to his role as translator.

A different problem is encountered in the tables, such as those of the modes in the Bryennius treatise. Many of the manuscripts, and especially the one that Burana used, labeled the modal octaves incorrectly. Burana's translation of the text and the figure itself, so far as it can be read, appear to be correct. Interestingly enough, by the time of the Bryennius translation, Burana had changed his approach to the string names and now used the more usual transliterations, such as "hypate hypaton" rather than "suprema supremarum." Gaffurio may have urged him to do this for clarity's sake. Bryennius in the chapter (2.3) in which the tonal system is described, uses the terms *hypate, mese,* and *nete* in two ways, not unlike the thetic and dynamic nomenclature of Ptolemy, but in a less precise manner. He conceives the eight tonoi as identical octaves at different pitch levels. Each of these octaves is made up of two conjunct tetrachords and a note added below, and each has a bottom (*hypate*) note, a middle (*mese*) note, a top (*nete*) note, and an added (*proslambanomenos*) note a whole tone under the hypate. The hypate note is the lowest of the lower tetrachord; the middle note is common to the two tetrachords; and the nete is the top note of the upper tetrachord. Thus the top note of the Hypodorian—its nete—is the string mese of the fifteen-string system, and it is the middle note of the Dorian octave. Similarly the mese of the Hypophrygian is the hypate of the Phrygian, and both sit on the string parhypate hypaton. The Hypodorian's nete coincides with the Hypermixolydian's proslambanomenos on the string mese. Burana's translation would have been clearer had he used Latin words, such as "gravissima," "media," "acutissima," and "assumpta" for the relative pitch positions within the tonos, confining the Greek nomenclature to the string locations.

In the next chapter (2.4) Bryennius establishes the relative pitch of the tonoi by stating how much higher or lower each one is than the others. For example, the second of the eight tonoi, the Hypophrygian, is higher than the first, the Hypodorian, by a tone, but lower than the Hypolydian by a tone, lower than the Dorian by a trihemitone, lower than the Phrygian by a fourth, and so on. The distances between the eight tonoi in rising pitch order is: tone, tone, semitone, tone, tone, semitone, tone. This too is indicated on the chart as translated by Burana, but it is missing in the chart transcribed by Jonker in his edition-translation of Bryennius (pp. 156–57).[6]

Nicolò Leoniceno

Leoniceno completed his translation of the *Harmonics* of Ptolemy in 1499 at the advanced age of seventy-two. But he was to go on to publish in subsequent years translations of eleven treatises of Galen, on which his reputation greatly rests, for he lived until the age of ninety-six. Born in Vicenza in 1428, son of a physician, Francesco, and Madalena, daughter of Antonio Loschi, humanist and secretary to Pope Alexander V, he received lessons in Latin and Greek from Ognibene de' Bonisoli and went on to study medicine and philosophy at Padua, completing the doctorate around 1453. In 1464 he was called to teach at the *studio* of Ferrara and remained there for the rest of his life except the year 1508–09, when he taught in Bologna. At Ferrara he taught mathematics, later Greek philosophy, then medicine. His most important contribution was the restoration of the teachings of Galen from the original Greek sources, as opposed to the Arabic

6. Among the manuscripts, Venice, Biblioteca Marciana, MS gr. 322 (711) has the same format as Burana, with the tonoi mislabeled and the distances indicated by *tonos* and *hemito[nos]*.

interpretations. He became involved in a controversy after questioning the dependability of Pliny on medical matters, particularly the identification of herbs. His main work in this polemic was *De Plinii, et aliorum in medicina erroribus* (Ferrara, 1482). Poliziano, Ermolao Barbaro, Pandolfo Collenuccio, and Alessandro Benedetti defended Pliny. Among Leoniceno's correspondents were Poliziano, Pico della Mirandola, Giorgio Valla, Ermolao Barbaro, and Erasmus.[7]

Leoniceno's only connection with music was his translation of Ptolemy's *Harmonics*. It was apparently done at the request of Gaffurio but with the support of Bishop Petro Barozzi of Padua. The letter of transmission of a copy of the translation presented to Barozzi, dated "K[a]l[endae]. Martii 1499," refers to two manuscripts of the Ptolemy work that he was returning to him. Gallo believes that Gaffurio, knowing that Barozzi owned some copies of Ptolemy's *Harmonics,* asked to have the work translated. Barozzi then may have gone to Leoniceno without mentioning Gaffurio's request, since, in the letter to the bishop, Leoniceno did not name Gaffurio. When Gaffurio received a copy of this translation with the letter to Barozzi, he made corrections in the letter to indicate that it was he as well as Barozzi who had requested the translation. In a copy of this manuscript in his own hand Gaffurio made further revisions of the letter and added at the end a colophon: "Claudii Ptolomei Harmonicon interprete Nicolao Leoniceno artium et medicine Ferarie professore adhortatione et opera celeberrimi viri Petri Barotii episcopi patavini ac Franchini Gafuri musicam profitentis explicit foeliciter."[8] There may have been direct contact, however, between Leoniceno and Gaffurio, for Leoniceno possessed an early draft of Gaffurio's *De harmonia,* which is now in Paris.[9]

The whereabouts of the Ptolemy manuscripts that Leoniceno used and

7. The best short biography is by Jerome J. Bylebyl, in *Dictionary of Scientific Biography* (New York, 1973), VIII, 248–50, from which most of the above facts were taken. See also Domenico Vitaliani, *Della vita e delle opere di Nicolò Leoniceno Vicentino* (Verona, 1892), and F. A. Gallo and G. Mantese, "Nuove notizie sulla famiglia e sull'opera di Nicolò Leoniceno," *Archivio veneto* 72 (1963):5–22.

8. The copy by an unknown scribe with corrections in the dedicatory letter in Gaffurio's hand is what I used for this study: Biblioteca Apostolica Vaticana, MS Vat. lat. 4570, a paper codex from the fifteenth century consisting of 58 folios. Gaffurio's copy is now in London, British Library, MS Harl. 3306, fols. 1–46. It was written by Gaffurio between 26 June and 3 August 1499. The dedicatory letter is reproduced by Gallo, "Musici scriptores graeci," III, 70–71. See R. Nares, *A Catalogue of the Harleian Mss. in the British Museum* (London, 1808), III, 15. There is a third copy, which Giovanni Giorgio Trissino, once a pupil of Leoniceno, presented to Pope Paul III in 1541: Biblioteca Apostolica Vaticana, MS Vat. lat. 3744, fols. 1–64.

9. Bibliothèque Nationale, MS lat. 7208. It contains Leoniceno's name and some annotations in Greek, but there is no dedication to him. It has an explicit signed by Gaffurio and dated 27 March 1500. See ch. 9 below.

that once belonged to Barozzi are unknown. Leoniceno in his letter to him apologizes for his lateness in delivering the translation and returning the books (codices), pleading that the first exemplar he used was full of faults, and the second only "somewhat corrected."[10]

Leoniceno had hoped for broader circulation of his translation according to Giovanni Giorgio Trissino, who in a letter to Pope Paul III stated that the translator planned to dedicate it to Pope Leo X so that it might reach scholars of music generally, because "the music of our times preserved only a third part of the force of that of the ancients," and he considered Ptolemy's treatise "the most perfect of all."[11] There is no evidence, however, that anyone besides Trissino and Gaffurio studied it. Trissino, who dedicated his *Sophonisba* to Pope Leo X in 1524, was the author of an important treatise on poetics.[12] He does not speak in it of music, which he says is not the business of the poet but should be left to singers. Nevertheless he shows in the letter that he understood the importance of Ptolemy's treatise for the theory of the tetrachords and the "shades":

Quantum autem musicae hujus nostri temporis desit, non modi tibi omnium doctissimo notum esse arbitror, sed cuivis etiam mediocris eruditionis non ignotum esse censeo. Nam praeter enharmonicam, et chromaticum, quae duo genera haec aetas non nouit, ipsum quoque diatonicum, quo solo genere utitur, non ita exquisitum et perfectum habet, ut antiqui habuere[nt].	How much is lacking in the music of our present time, I think, is known not only to you, who are the most learned of all men, but is also, I consider, not unknown to anyone of moderate erudition. For, apart from the enharmonic and chromatic—two genera that our age does not know—it does not even possess in so exquisite a form as had the ancients even the diatonic, the sole genus of which it makes use.
Boethius enim a quo Guitto aretinus, et nostri deinde omnes hanc scientiam acceperunt, cum tetrachorda, in quibus ratio totius musicae continetur, Architae, et Aristoxeni exposuisset, ac ea verbis Ptolemei	Boethius (from whom Guitto Aretinus and all our [writers] received this science), when he had set forth the tetrachords—in which the logic of all music is contained— of Archytas and Aristoxenus and rejected them with the words

---

10. "I sent you the translation of the Music of Ptolemy with the remaining books which I conveniently used to finish it rather tardily because with the first exemplar I was able to complete only a small part of what I desired to do on account of the many faults contained in it. The second exemplar, however, somewhat corrected, I received from you around the beginning of studies, in which I was so busy that I had to wait until the vacation that occurred before Lent." Latin text in Gallo, "Musici scriptores graeci," III, 70–71.

11. Ibid., III, 71.

12. Trissino, *La Poetica* (Parts I to IV: Vicenza, 1529; Parts V and VI: Venice, 1562).

reprehendisset, deinde tetrachordorum divisionem, quemadmodum Ptolemeus fieri dicat
oportere, se explicaturum polli-
cetur, quae tamen malignitate
temporum, ut ipse arbitror,
non extant. Quare necessario
ab ipso Ptolemeo, aut
Briennio, qui eadem graece a
Ptolomeo acceperat, petenda sunt:
nunc vero latini musici, et
graecorum litterarum ignari,
ea omnia cum laboribus
Leoniceni, tum consilio meo,
et benignitate
sanctitatis tuae
facile sibi poterunt comparare.[13]

of Ptolemy, promised
to explain how Ptolemy said the
division of the tetrachords ought
to be done.
But because of the ravages
of time, as I judge,
they do not survive. For this
reason, it is necessary to resort to
Ptolemy himself or to Bryennius, who
received the same in Greek from
Ptolemy. Latin musicians and those
unacquainted with Greek letters
will now be able easily to
compare all the tetrachords
for themselves through the
work of Leoniceno, with my advice
and the blessing of your Holiness.

Leoniceno faced in Ptolemy's *Harmonics* a text that was more scientific, original, and profound than those Burana had translated; it was also full of unfamiliar concepts and turns of thought. Had Leoniceno first translated Bryennius or even known Burana's translation of it, he would have been prepared for some of the complexities of Ptolemy's work, which Bryennius succeeded in simplifying, though not without sacrificing some of its logical consistency. Leoniceno hesitated to depart from the smallest detail of the original, possibly because he barely understood it. For entire pages he followed the Greek text word for word, producing a syntax that was unlike Latin and yielding no ready meaning. It is not surprising that when Gaffurio utilized passages from this translation he almost always rewrote them, departing from his normal method, which was to quote nearly verbatim. A sample of Leoniceno's translation may be taken from the crucial chapter 5 of Book 2 in which Ptolemy introduces his concepts of thetic and dynamic nomenclature of the steps of the scale. In the following English translation I have maintained as far as possible the Latin word order, with a certain loss of idiomatic quality, suggestive, I hope, of the awkwardness of Leoniceno's Latin.

Quomodo uocum appelationes et
ad situm capiuntur et ad potentiam. C[aput] 5.

How the names of the steps are
acquired according to both position and function. Chapter 5.

---

13. Letter, 13 August 1541, in Biblioteca Apostolica Vaticana, MS Vat. lat. 3744, fol. 1. This letter is printed in the appendix to the article by Gallo and Mantese, "Nuove notizie," pp. 21–22, which varies slightly in its reading in unimportant details.

Vnde igitur et diapason
et diatessaron Constitutio
coniuncta sit Consonantiae bisdiapason in sequentibus nobis
oculis subjicietur. Priora autem
perfectas et bisdiapason uoces
quindecim constituentes: quia una
communis fit: et grauiore et acu-
tiore diapason constitutis: et
media omnium: aliquando quidem
iuxta ipsum situm: et acutius
simpliciter uel grauius nominamus
mesen quidem id est
mediam, quae
dicta est inter duas diapason,
proslambanomenon autem
grauissimam
et neten hyperboleon
acutissimam: deinde
eas quae sunt post proslambanomenon ad acutum usque ad mediam
hypaten hypaton et parhypaton
et lichanon hypaton: et
hypaten meson et parhypaten meson
et lichanon meson: et
quae sunt post mesen. Similiter
usque ad neten hyperboleon
paramesen et triten diezeugmenon,
et paraneten diezeugmenon: et
neten diezeugmenon: et triten
hyperboleon et paraneten hyperboleon. Aliquando uero
et secundum potentiam
ipsam quod ad aliquid aliquomodo
se habet cui iam prius
adaptantes sitibus
eas quae secundum uocatam imper-
mutabilem constitutionem potentias
bisdiapason: deinde
communes in ipsa facientes prae-
dicationes situm et potentiarum
transumamus ipsas in alijs. alteram enim quae est in bis diapason
duorum tonorum ab ea quae est situ
media capientes: et apponentes

Whence also the constitution of
the diapason-plus-diatessaron is
connected with the consonance of
the double diapason will be put
before our eyes. But first come the
fifteen steps constituting the
perfect double diapason. Because
there is a common [step] joining
the lower and higher diapasons that
likewise is the middle of all, sometimes by its position, simply
in respect to being higher or lower,
we call it mese, that is
"middle note," so
named because it is between two
diapasons. We call proslambanomenos the lowest note
and nete hyperbolaeon the
highest. Then we name
those following the proslambanomenos up as far as the middle note:
hypate hypaton, parhypate
hypaton, and lichanos hypaton,
and hypate meson, parhypate
meson, and lichanos meson. And
those that come after mese, similarly, up to nete hyperbolaeon:
paramese, and trite diezeugmenon,
and paranete diezeugmenon,
and nete diezeugmenon, and trite
hyperbolaeon and paranete hyperbolaeon. Sometimes, however, [we
name them] according to their
function—how they behave in some
way or other towards something—
adapting to it, by their positions
the functions which [they had] according to the so called immutable system
of the double octave. Then, establishing these common terms of positions
and functions in it
we transfer them to others, that is,
taking one of the two [disjunctive]
tones lying in the double diapason
from its middle position and putting

ipsi secundum	beside it two tetrachords,
utranque partem duo tetrachorda	[one] on either side,
copulata ex quattuor	coupled together out of the four
quae sunt in toto.	that there are in all;
Deinde alterum tonum	then, assigning another tone to the
reliquo et grauissimo	remaining lowest of the
interuallorum assignantes	[disjunctive] intervals, we call
mediam quidem potentia	the middle note according to
uocamus ab ea quae tunc	function after that
erat consistentia grauissimam	which was consistently the lowest
acutioris disiunctionis	[note] of the higher disjunction
et paramesen	[i.e., mese] and "paramese" the
acutiorem.	higher [step of the disjunction];
proslambanomenon autem	"proslambanomenos" and
et neten hyperboleon grauissimam	"nete hyperbolaeon" the lowest of
grauioris disiunctionis: et	the lower disjunction, and
hypaten hypaton,	"hypate hypaton" the higher
acutiorem.[14]	[of the two disjunctive steps].

Leoniceno did not commit any inaccuracy in this passage; indeed he followed the original scrupulously. However, by adhering doggedly to the Greek word order, cases, verb forms, and other details, he has made inherently dense matter even more obscure. The participial clauses beginning or ending with "capientes," "apponentes," and "assignantes" (which have purposely been preserved in the English), more characteristic of Greek than Latin, unnecessarily complicate the train of thought.

In the foregoing passage Ptolemy explains how the middle note of the double octave acquires the name *mese* either by virtue of its position joining the two octaves or by its function of being the lower boundary in the disjunction between two tetrachords. In the latter guise it may be moved from its normal position to another, always maintaining its medial function. Similarly the other notes preserve their relative positions or functions after being transported to another location.

When Leoniceno is more at home with the content, the translation manifests some freedom, as in favoring Latin word order with the relocation of a word or two, but syntactical changes are still avoided. An example may be found below.[15]

Giovanni Battista Augio

In 1545 Giovanni Battista Augio completed a translation into Latin of Ptolemy's *Harmonics*. His Greek source must have stopped at Book 3, chapter 14,

14. Leoniceno trans., fol. 26r–v, of Ptolemy *Harmonics* 2. 5 (Düring ed., 51.17–52.10).
15. P. 291.

for that is as far as his translation goes. Another characteristic of his source must have been that it lacked chapter headings or subdivision after Book 3, chapter 9. A large number of manuscripts have these characteristics, including the early and important codex, Marciana VI.10 from the thirteenth century. However, this codex also lacks chapter headings from the second chapter of Book 2 until the end of that book,[16] whereas Augio's translation lacks a heading only for chapter 16. This it has in common with Bologna, Biblioteca Universitaria, MS graecus 2280, dated 1528, which belongs to Düring's V-branch (deriving from Vat. gr. 192) of his m-class.[17] The fact that Augio did his translation in Bologna heightens the probability that this was his source, but more positive identification must await close study of the idiosyncracies of the translation and features of other manuscripts as well as this one that would give rise to them.

Nothing is known of Augio other than what we learn from the explicit to the translation, in a hand different from the text: "Versum est opus istud Bononiae Anno 1545 Mens Augusti, Jo: Bapt.ᵃ Augio Turris brutianae calabro Interprete, Rogatu D. Nicolai Mantuani Musici et Amicorum." (This work was translated in Bologna in the year 1545, month of August, by Johannes Baptista Augius Calabrese of Brutiana Castle, Translator, at the request of Dominus Nicola Mantuanus, musician, and friends). The sole manuscript, Milan, Biblioteca Ambrosiana, P.133 sup., of the sixteenth century, cannot be autograph, as it contains errors a copyist rather than a translator would make. Besides, it is incomplete in that the tables of 2.14–15 are blocked out but the data are not filled in.

The dedicatee, Nicolo Mantovano, or Nicolo Cavallari, was maestro di canto—equivalent to director of the chapel music—of San Petronio in Bologna between 1551 and 1558 (he died on 28 November of that year). He had been a singer at San Petronio between 1527 and 1531, but his whereabouts between 1531 and 1551 are unknown; he is not mentioned in the records of that church during those years. He left no musical compositions, either printed or manuscript. Spataro said of him in a letter that he was a "homo da bene et molto perito in practica et in theoria" (a gentleman and very expert in practice and in theory).[18]

Augio's is a much more modern translation than Leoniceno's. He avoids translating terms, such as the names of the steps of the double-octave perfect

16. Düring, *Die Harmonielehre*, p. xl.

17. Ibid., p. x.

18. Gaetano Gaspari, "Memorie risguardanti la storia dell'arte musicale in Bologna al xvi secolo raccolte ed esposte dal Prof. Gaetano Gaspari," reprinted from *Atti e memorie della R. Deputazione di Storia Patria per le provincie di Romagna*, Anno 9, in *Musici e musicisti a Bologna, Ricerche, Documenti e memorie riguardanti la storia dell'arte musicale in Bologna* (Bologna, 1969), pp. 157–58; Elvidio Surian, "Bologna," in *New Grove Dictionary*, III, 3.

system, long accepted into music-theoretical Latin. He is not bound to the formal structure of his text, because he is intent upon communicating what he senses as its meaning. If that requires adding some expressions of his own, he does so. It is possible to find passages in which the Latin and Greek correspond word for word, but this is not typical. If the same two chapters that we chose to study in Leoniceno's version are inspected, it will be seen that the modernized prose does not always lead to greater illumination. Indeed, 2.11 is clearer in the Leoniceno, although one does have the feeling that Augio understood certain aspects of the theory better. In the first sentence Augio fails to get across the idea of octave species by the word "diapason," which is not a good rendering of the Greek *eidos*. Leoniceno made it quite clear that the tonoi and octave species were equal in number. In Augio's translation this fact is clouded by the use of the word "sonus" for Ptolemy's *phthongos*— a legitimate equivalent—when Ptolemy evidently meant *tonos*. The choice of "facultas," here translated "potential," for *dynamis* is weaker than Leoniceno's "potentia." Augio correctly speaks of the voice keeping to the middle octave but then shifts to strings for the point that too great tension or relaxation is required for the extreme steps of the system; this weakens Ptolemy's argument. In the last sentence of this excerpt, it is not clear whether Augio understands that *metharmogēn* means the retuning of the scale, without which the reference to the stability of some pitches is meaningless.

Quod tonos per semitonium adaugere non oporteat.	That it would not be necessary to augment the tonoi by semitone.
Cap[ut] xj.	Chapter 11.
Perspicuum est autem,	It is clear, however, that if we
quod si nos et eiusmodij	propose also a kind of
tonos subijciamus, qui sigillatim	tonos which is established step by
facultate ipsa mese	step up through a mese in function,
statuitur; peculiaris quidam ipsis	a special sound arises from these
diapason sonus exultat; cum totidem	diapasons, since there are as many
porro illi, atque huius ipsis (44r)	tonoi as there are diapasons in
enumerentur: sumpta enim Diapason	number. Taking now a diapason
consonantia penes inter	consonance having loci
medios in absoluta	in the middle of the absolute
constitutione locos, eos	system, those, that is, which
inquit, qui ab hypate meson	extend, thanks to its distinct
positione: ipsa distincta	position from the locus
ad neten diezeugmenon	of hypate meson to nete diezeug-
eius rej gratia	menon; so that the voice itself,
praetenduntur; ut vox ipsa, quae	which remains around the middle
circa medias potissimum modulandj	parts, where melodizing mainly
partes, ac raro in extremas	takes place, and rarely goes out
egreditur, iucunde admodum	to the extremes, might very happily

commutarj, ac reflecti, suumque in locum deducj possit: nervum intentionem aut remissionem subeundo, ultra modum intendj aut remitti cogatur: Porro mixolydij mese facultate ipsa deprehensa, loco paranetes diezeugmenon adaptabitur: id quod ut tonus ipse primam constituat in proposita Diapason speciem: Lydij uero mese loco trites diezeugmenon penes secundam huiusce quoque septem speciem disponetur: Phrygij itidem mese, loco ipsius parameses iuxta tertiam eiusdem speciem: at dorij mese, quippe que mediam, et quartam Diapason speciem constituit meses locum continebit; Hypolydij autem mese; lichanj meson locum, penes quintam Diapason speciem occupabit: Hypophrygij uero mese, locum parhypates meson, iuxta sextam in ordine speciem habebit: demum hypodorij mese: loco hypates meson, penes septimam illius speciem collocabitur; quo fit, ut in ipsa est constitutione; non nullos sonos obseruare ualeamus, qui quidem immobiles haereant; atque in tonorum concinnatione, structuramque magnitudinem seruent, propterea quod numquam in differentibus diuersisque tonis per similes eorum facultates sonorum locis occurrent.[19]

exchange and turn back and be led to its home, for in subjecting a string to stretching and relaxation, it is compelled [in the extremes] to to be tightened or loosened beyond measure. Further, the mese (in potential) of the Mixolydian having been removed from its place, is accommodated to the locus of the paranete diezeugmenon, that which as a tonos itself constitutes the first species of diapason. The Lydian mese, however, in the locus of the trite diezeugmenon, is arranged according to the second of the seven species. The mese of the Phrygian, in the same way is located on the paramese through the third species; but the Dorian's mese, which of course determined the middle and fourth species of diapason, will occupy the locus of the mese; the Hypolydian mese, belonging to the fifth species of diapason, will occupy the lichanus meson. The Hypophrygian mese will have the locus of the parhypate meson, through the sixth in order of the species. Finally the Hypodorian's mese will be located on the hypate meson, under its seventh species, so that in it is its constitution. We are able to observe no sounds that remain immobile, and in the adjustment of the tonoi they preserve the arrangement and pitch, because their potentials never coincide in different and diverse tonoi with their with their loci of sounds.

Returning now to the fifth chapter of Book 2, we find that Augio presents the clearer and more accurate of the two early translations. But later in the chapter, the coupling of the tetrachords around the dynamic mese to produce

19. Augio trans., fols. 43v–44r, of Ptolemy *Harmonics* 2.11.

a new tonos is obscure, as it was also in Leoniceno. Are two conjoined tetra-chords placed on one side of the mese and another pair on the other side, or are two tetrachords being arranged around it, one joined to the mese from below, the other disjoined from above? If it is the last, then how is one to account for the fact that all the tonoi besides the Dorian exceed the absolute range of the perfect system? Here is his translation:

Quo pacto sonorum denominationes partim a positione, partim a facultate ipsa capiantur. Cap[ut] 5.	In what way the appelations of the sounds may be taken partly from position, partly from the potential itself. Chapter 5.
Vnde nam igitur Diapason et diatessaron constitutio, in bis diapason adscita prodierit; ex his, quae postea dicentur perspicuum nobis evadet; uerun-tamen sonj, qui re vera bis diapa-son perfecte constituunt, quindecim eo pacto connumerantur, quod sonus unus eorum in acutiores, tum grauiores constitutarum diapason, communis exultat, ac omnium medius interiacet: equidem ab ipsa non nunquam posi-tione, et acutiorem omnino, aut grauiorem dicimus sonum, ea quae sumunt mesen apellamus uocem illam, quae in binarum, quas diximus, Diapason consonan-tiarum medio collocata est: eam uero, quae est omnium grauissima; Proslambanomenon et neten hyper-bolaeon illam, quippe quae omnes acumine antecedit; eas, deinde, quae a Proslambanomeno ad mesen usque, in acumine intenduntur, hisce nominibus apellamus: Hypatem hypaton, Par-hypaten hypaton: Lichanon hypaton: hypaten meson; Parypaten mesen; ac Lichanon et meson: At à mese ad neten hyperbolaeon: hisce quae nominibus appellamus; Mesen;	Whence, therefore it will have been shown that the constitution of the diapason-plus-diatessaron is accepted into the double diapason; this will become clear to us from things to be said later. To be sure, the sounds which completely constitute in fact the double diapason in this way are fifteen in number. For one common sound arises out of them in the higher as well as lower diapason of those constituted, and it lies in the middle of all. Sometimes we name the sound from its position itself, whether generally higher or lower, so that what they designate as mese, we call that step which is located in the middle of the consonances of the double diapason of which we spoke. That which, truly, is the lowest of all we call proslambanomenos, and that which exceeds all in height of pitch [we call] nete hyperbolaeon. Those, further, that rise in height from the proslambanomenos to the mese we call by these names: hypate hypaton, parhypate hypaton, lichanos hypaton, hypate meson, parhypate meson, and lichanos and meson [sic]. But from the mese to nete hyperbolaeon here are the names by which we call them: mese,

Paramesen; Triten diezeugmenon;
Paraneten diezeugmenon; Neten diezeugmenon; Triten hyperbolaeon,
et paraneten
hyperbolaeon: quandoque autem
ab ea ipsa facultate; qua soni
quodammodo ad aliquid referri
uidentur, eorundem quoque denomi-
nationem assumimus, ut sic exeo,
quod bis diapason uires immuta-
bilem (quam dicunt) constitutionem, plus iam positionibus
ipsis acommodare consueuimus;
ut communj facultatum, positio-
numque nomine in ea ipsa constitutione fungentes eas quoque
in aliis transferre,
atque immutare
ualeamus:
nam cum alterum ex duobus tonis,
igitur in bisdiapason includuntur,
à mese, quae ita
nimirum positione ipsa
dicitur exceperimus;
et eidem penes utramque
partem, bina Tetrachorda
coniuncta adiecerimus; ex
quattuor illis, quae in integra
bis diapason constitutione
comprehenduntur; deinde
alterum tonum ej, quod restat
grauissimosque interuallos
reddiderimus; mesen utique
facultate ab ea ipsa
constitutione, atque ordine
uocitamus grauissimam illam
acutioris disiunctionis uocem;
acutiorem uero, paramesen; at
proslambanomenon, et neten
hyperbolaeon, in grauiorj
disiunctione, grauissimam;
hypaten uero hypaton,
acutissimam;
deinde hypaten meson, uocem,
illam; quae duobus adnexis,

paramese, trite
diezeugmenon, paranete
diezeugmenon, nete diezeugmenon,
trite hyperbolaeon, and paranete
hyperbolaeon. Sometimes we assume
their denomination, though, from the
potential itself through which the
sounds seem somehow to be related
one to another, as I gather.
Because the double diapason is a
constitution possessing an immutable
quality (so they say), we were more
accustomed to suit the names to the
positions themselves so that
through the common name of the
potentials and positions in that
constitution itself we are able in
so doing to transfer them and
change them completely into
others. Now when the second of two
tones is included, therefore, in
the double diapason, from mese,
which thus we
acknowledge is named after the
position itself, and we would have
added to it on either side two
conjoined tetrachords out of the
those four that are comprehended in
the entire constitution of the
double diapason. Then we shall
have given back the second (other)
tone of those that remain the
lowest in interval. In any case we
name mese (in potential), after the
constitution itself and order, that
lowest step of the higher
disjunction; the higher step,
however [we call] paramese. But
proslambanomenos and nete
hyperbolaeon [we call] the lowest
[step] of the lower disjunction.
Then [we call] hypate hypaton the
highest [step of the disjunction],
hypate meson the step that
is common to the annexed two lower

grauioribusque Tetrachordis, a
grauiore disiunctione locatis,
communis existit: neten uero
diezeugmenon, eam dicimus uocem,
quippe quae communis exultat
coniunctis post acutiorem disiunctionem Tetrachordis: ad haec Parypaten hypaton, eam quae secundo
loco grauissimum, a grauiore
disiunctione Tetrachordum conse-
quitur; at Lichanon hypatôn,
tertiam, parypaten uero meson,
eam, quae à grauissimo sane
Tetrachordo secundum obtinuit
eius Tetrachordi locum, quod
grauissimam disiunctionem antecedit.[20]

tetrachords located at the lower
disjunction. The step that enjoys
a common conjunction after the
higher disjunction of the
tetrachord we name, of course, nete
diezeugmenon. Following this [hypate
hypaton] parhypate hypaton is named
after the lower disjunction of the
tetrachords; it is the lowest in
the second place. But [they name]
the third lichanos hypaton; but
parhypate meson, which obtained its
second place of the tetrachord,
they named after the lowest
tetrachord that is above the
lowest distinction.

With Augio's translation of Ptolemy's *Harmonics* in the Ambrosiana manuscript is the earliest Latin translation that survives of the *Harmonic Introduction* of Gaudentius. It is ascribed also to Augio but it may not be by him. It is
copied by a different scribe, who packs more lines to the page than the Ptolemy scribe and is far less legible but more accurate, though he too makes
errors that a translator would not be likely to make, such as writing in the
heading of one of the tables of notational signs "Hypoaeloci" for "Hy-
poaeoli." The Gaudentius scribe replaces the archaic *u* with the modern *v* most
of the time, but he also employs *v* for certain *u*'s. Gaudentius comes first in
the codex but may not have been completed first. The presence of a number
of chapter headings and diagrams missing from Marciana VI.10 and its prog-
eny allies this translation with the manuscript Naples graecus 260 (III.C.2),
which once belonged to Giorgio Valla.[21] In addition to the diagrams found in

20. Augio trans., fol. 36r–36v, of Ptolemy *Harmonics* 2.5.
21. See Karl von Jan, *Musici scriptores graeci,* critical apparatus. There is a copy of this
translation in Bologna, Civico Museo Bibliografico Musicale, MS B46, pp. 10–30, where it
is unattributed but in the hand of Ercole Bottrigari. A copy of the latter is in Bologna, Biblioteca
Universitaria MS 595, Busta I, no. 9. See Gallo, "Musici scriptores graeci," III, 70. Gallo
believes that the attribution to Augio is erroneous. The source of the attribution is a general
title on an unnumbered folio ahead of the Gaudentius translation that reads: "Gaudentij Philosophi Armonica Introductio Claudij Ptolomej Armonicorum Libri 3 translati a greco Bononia
anno 1545 Jo. Bapt^a Augio Turrij Brutianae Calabro Interprete." This hand appears to be of
the seventeenth century. There follows on fols. 1r–8r the Gaudentius translation in a sixteenth-
century hand. In a still different sixteenth-century hand is the Ptolemy translation. Finally, in
a fourth hand is the colophon attributing the Ptolemy translation to Augio. In view of the
scarcity of translators who could competently render into Latin the Greek of Gaudentius, I

the source, the translator may have made up some to match the text. For example, there is a table giving the stable and mobile tones which is not accounted for by von Jan, but a rubric suggests that the translator supplied it: "Videlicet infrascripti q[uid] g[au]den[tio] gradatim sunt subscriptae."[22]

The Bologna manuscript mentioned as a possible source for the Ptolemy does not contain the Gaudentius treatise. Whatever his source, the translator, appears to have had an excellent text to work with and, from samples studied, to have turned it into Latin very respectably. Among the sources that he had at his disposal was one that contained the treatise of Alypius, for at the end of the extant notational tables in Gaudentius, which break off with the Hypoaeolian diatonic, the there is the note: "The rest, which here are missing may be found in quantity in Alypius" (Reliqua quae hic desunt apud alypius copiosissima inueniet[ur]).[23] The Gaudentius treatise had been translated into Latin at least once before, by the late Latin scholar Mutianus, a friend of Cassiodorus.[24]

Of the Greek writers Gaudentius was the least known to the Renaissance. He is not cited by Gaffurio in *De harmonia,* for example. Neither Gaudentius nor his treatise has been dated with any precision. He may have flourished as early as the second century or much later. He probably read Cleonides, as there are some parallel passages,[25] and appears to draw from Aristides Quintilianus,[26] but he probably had not read Ptolemy. Gaudentius favors Aristoxenian theories; yet he incorporates Pythagorean calculations and gives one of the fullest accounts of the story of the hammers in the ancient literature. There are several original elements in the treatise. He proposes three qualities of tones (*phthongi*) in the second chapter: color (*chroia*), location (*topos*), and duration (*chronos*). By color he means not genus but qualities that make sounds of the same pitch and duration differ. By location he means height or lowness, and by duration he intends not only the length of individual tones but also the length of songs and the combination of different durations in rhythm. Another departure from other authors is the division of the octave into species of fifths and fourths. This theory may have found its way into early medieval treatises. After taking up the species of tetrachords and pentachords (in chap-

---

am inclined to accept it as the work of Augio. However, further study of the manuscripts and of the two translations in the Ambrosiana manuscript may well change this opinion.

22. Augio trans., fol. 5r.

23. Professor Thomas J. Mathiesen kindly informed me that this remark occurs in several of the Greek manuscrips of Gaudentius, so it is probably not the translator's note.

24. See Cassiodorus *Istitutiones humanarum litterarum* 2.5.1 and the translation by Helen Dill Goode and Gertrude C. Drake (Colorado Springs, 1980), p. 4.

25. See von Jan, *Musici scriptores graeci,* p. 319.

26. See ibid., p. 323.

ter 18 as numbered by von Jan) he proceeds in the next chapter to the "diapason octachord," of which he says there are twelve possible couplings of species of fourth and fifth, since there are three of the fourth and four of the fifth. But he adds that there are only seven (different) species of the octachord. Like Cleonides, he gives them the ethnic names, Mixolydian for the first, Hypodorian for the last, which he notes was also called the "common," or "Locrian," species.

One of Gaudentius' most illuminating chapters is that on the naming of the steps of the "universal system" (*hapan to systema*), as he calls it, the greater perfect system of other authors, and the application of these names to transpositions of this system. There is no parallel passage in any of the other Greek authors. This chapter, numbered 20 in the von Jan edition[27] serves as a good sample of Augio's approach to Gaudentius.

At veteres ad significandum xviij	But the ancients used names and letters
sonos nominibus vtebantur et	that are musical signs—concerning
literis quae notae musicae	which we must now speak—for
de quibus in praesentia	signifying the eighteen tones.
dicendum est	The exposition of
expositio musicarum	the musical signs
notarum ad sonos	is done for the sake
significandos effecta est,	of representing the tones.
sic nomina sigillatim	That the names of each
scriberentur atque vnica	might be written and a single
nota queat	sign fit each one and designate
aliquis abnueratur atque	the tone had been denied by some.
obsignare sonum nimirum soni	Of course, tones, each
diuersa intentione mouentem	moving at a different tension,
neque in eodem loco	do not stay in the same place
diutius persistunt.	very long.
Quare neque vna	For this reason not one
sed diuersis opus fuit	but diverse signs were necessary
in vnoquoque sonorum notis vt ex	for each tone, so as
his diuersa eique intentio	to indicate by the diverse means
denotaret in vno quoque enim modo	its tension. In any one mode
aut sono intentione diuersi omnes	or tuning, all possible tones
omnium sonj producuntur velutj	are produced, as for example
nonumquam nam grauissimum sonum	sometimes we take the lowest tone
proslambanomenon assumimus, vt	as proslambanomenos,
in hypodorio modo et mesen huic	as in the Hypodorian mode, and [we
correspondentem	name] "mese" that which responds
atque alios iuxta	to it; also the others [we name]
horum habitudinem denominamus	according to their relation to

---

27. Ibid., p. 347, line 11 to p. 349, line 1.

nonnumquam vero	these. Sometimes, though, [we
mesen ipsam quam	call upon] the mese itself, which
nunc proslambanomenon ipsi	just now answered the
	proslambanomenos
aduerso respondent loco	from the opposite place,
proslambanomenon substituentes	which is its corresponding step, to
et quae huius correspondens est	substitute for the proslambanome-
mesen subiiciendo atque alios	nos, letting the others follow the mese
insitos ex proportione	naturally according to the interval
respondentes sic vtimur	as we employ them in
vniversa constitutione	the universal system.
sepe vero et intermedium	Often, however, assuming between
proslambanomenon et meses unum	the proslambanomenos and mese a
ex hisce compositum assumentes	composite of these,
pro constitutionis principio	we avail ourselves of the proslamba-
proslambanomeno ipso vtimur	nomenos itself as the beginning
et vniuersalis	of a system, and [assume] the
constitutionis intentionem	tension of the universal system,
cum quo concinnamus.	with which we harmonize.
Necesse est autem in	It is also necessary in
vnusquisque constitutione	any system,
pluribus positis constitutionibus	several having been proposed,
vt mese se habet ad mesen vel vt	that mese be related to mese or
proslambanomenos ita et quaecumque	proslambanomenos [to another] and
eorum ipsi cognominis sutilus	any one of them [should relate], as
ad sutilum cognominem atque	cognate to cognate, stitch for stitch,
vniuersa constitutio ad istarum	and universal system to such
constitutionem. Itaque non vnica	system. Thus arises the necessity
nota in vno quoque sonorum opus	not of a single sign for any of the
extitit sed pluribus atque tot	tones, but of as many as there
adeo quot semitonijs adaugerj	are semitones to be added.
quolibet potis est sonum quot	How many tones, as indeed how many
vero semitonijs quolibet augerj	semitones, are to be added
queat sonum haud facile	to fit the tones, this cannot easily
determinarj potest nam per	be determined by
instrumentorum apparatum atque	means of instruments and
humanae vocis facultatem.[28]	the power of the human voice.

This is an excellent interpretation of a passage loaded with pitfalls. The purpose of the chapter is to explain why eighteen signs are insufficient for representing the pitches used in the various modes. It is because the eighteen steps which comprise the "major system" and the "minor system" must be able to be represented on various levels differing by a semitone. Lacking the vocabulary of "dynamic" and "thetic" of Ptolemy, Gaudentius and his

28. Augio trans., fols. 5v–6r; von Jan ed., 347.11–349.1.

translator had to make clear what this process was. Gaudentius uses the example of the Hyperphrygian tonos, although he does not give it a name or ever mention it in his exposition. He describes the process of deriving this tonos when he posits a mode in which the mese of the "universal system" becomes proslambanomenos. Thus the proslambanomenos is raised an entire octave. He shows by this, and also later in the chapter, that he accepts the Aristoxenian modal theory, for he remarks that the tonoi may be multiplied at the distance of a semitone. He thus acquiesces to the existence of a Hyperphrygian tonos, which Ptolemy did not accept.

Augio encountered in this passage two textual problems that later philologists were also to face. One was a missing word, the other a unique word. In the statement that mese should correspond with mese, meaning that the functional mese should occupy the same place in the scale as the locus mese, Gaudentius adds that, similarly, proslambanomenos should correspond to proslambanomenos, except that the second *proslambanomenos* is missing in the manuscripts. Meibom supplied "pros ton proslambanomenon" (p. 21), which von Jan accepted (348.10–11) and Ruelle incorporated in his translation.[29] Our translator fails to react to the lacuna, and his version reads: "so that mese be related to mese or as proslambanomenos," which is contrary to the sense. In the same passage, the expression *houtōs hontinaoun* (von Jan ed., 348.11) seems to have puzzled Augio. Ruelle translates the passage "le rapport... existe aussi entre une note homonyme et son homonyme,"[30] whereas Augio has "se habet... quaecumque eorum ipsi cognominem sutilus ad sutilum cognominem," inserting his own figure of speech "sutilus ad sutilum" (stitch for stitch). This drives home the idea that every step in the system must remain analogous when the "universal system" is retuned. Less successful is the use of the word "correspondens" for *antiphonos,* here translated "responds to" or "corresponds to." Actually by *antiphonos* Gaudentius means specifically the corresponding octave, as each of his examples shows. The medieval Latin verb "antiphonare" would have fit perfectly, but Augio may have been too much of a purist to resort to this.

29. Charles-Émile Ruelle, trans., *Alypius et Gaudence, Bacchius l'ancien* (Paris 1895), p. 85, n. 5.

30. Ibid., p. 85.

SEVEN

Antonio Gogava

he first Latin translation of Ptolemy's *Harmonics* to achieve publication was that of Antonio Gogava. Born in Grave in Brabant, Gogava studied classical languages and mathematics in Leiden before going to Padua for a degree in medicine. He practiced medicine in Venice for a time, then joined the court of Vespasiano Gonzaga, who took him to Madrid. Gogava died there in 1569. While still in Leiden he published in 1541 a translation of the last two books of Ptolemy's *Tetrabiblios* together with Joachimus Camerarius' translation of the first two books. This was reprinted in 1546 and 1547 under varying titles. He translated the *Harmonics* of Ptolemy while in Venice. It was published in 1562 by Vincenzio Valgrisio in a collection of translations of Greek musical writings under the title: *Aristoxeni Mvsici antiqviss. Harmonicorvm elementorvm libri iii. Cl. Ptolemaei Harmonicorum, seu de Musica lib. iii. Aristotelis de obiecto Auditus fragmentum ex Porphyrij commentarijs. Omnia nunc primum latine conscripta & edita ab Ant. Gogauino Grauiensi.*

In the preface to this collection Gogava relates that he was about to bring out the Ptolemy when Zarlino requested him to translate into Latin the *Harmonic Elements* of Aristoxenus. He apologizes for the state of the Aristoxenus, for which he had only one Greek copy and that an incomplete one. (Actually his text was as complete as any.) For the Ptolemy, he says, he compared several copies in the Marciana and Vatican libraries and consulted Danielo Barbaro on certain passages. Barbaro published both an edition and an Italian translation of Vitruvius, *De architectura,* with commentary, in which he supplemented and countered some of Vitruvius' Aristoxenian views with his own more conventional summary of Pythagorean music theory.

Ptolemy's *Harmonics*

Gogava's translation of Ptolemy's musical treatise is not as good as either Leoniceno's or Augio's; this makes the narrow dissemination of his predecessors' work all the more unfortunate. To make matters worse, the printed edition is full of errors, particularly in the diagrams; these can be easily corrected by anyone who has some notion of Greek theory, but to the novices who went to this book for enlightenment, it must have been an infuriating experience to strive to reconcile the diagrams with the text, which is usually correct concerning the points illustrated in the figures. These are particularly critical in Book 2, in which the octave species and the tonoi and the relation between them are set forth. The diagram of the species of diapason suffers from misalignments and missing and misplaced alphabetical letters.[1] Most of these errors must stem from the printer's misreading of Gogava's manuscript. On the other hand the tables of tonoi in 2.11, pp. 102–06, contain only minor faults.[2] Düring's edition lacks these tables, although they are common to most manuscripts. The tables make quite palpable what Ptolemy says in this chapter, which is adequately, if somewhat obscurely, transmitted by Gogava. By coordinating the diagram in 2.10, which shows the intervals between the tonoi, and those of 2.11, it would have been possible for a reader to arrive at the same view of Ptolemy's system as that held today. The major obstacle was that it was necessary to imagine a locus that fluctuates between its natural and sharped pitch, such as lichanos meson (let us call it g below middle c), which, when it is mese in the Hypolydian, should be moved up a semitone to g . This was no problem for the Greeks, since their system was not based on any absolute pitch, but it was to a sixteenth-century reader, as it is to us.

The most puzzling chapters are those detailing the various shades of tuning in the enharmonic, chromatic, and diatonic genera, namely, 2.13–15, and the associated tables. The errors in string lengths, ratios, and Aristoxenian parts are too frequent to even begin to list. For example, the ratios for the intervals in the enharmonic tetrachords of various authors given by Gogava may be compared with those in the critical edition by Düring (Figure 7.1). The tables to which Ptolemy refers spell out these ratios in terms of string lengths for the descending steps of two disjunct tetrachords. For each of the tunings Gogava gives a column of string lengths followed by a column of numbers that must have mystified contemporary readers. The second column, which is copied from the manuscripts, though not always accurately, gives fractions. These are notated by whole numbers that are sixtieth parts of one. For example, 77 2/15 is indicated by 77 in the

---

1. In 2.5, p. 92, the items in the second column, which should read "Speties Diapason" must each be moved down one step. The diagram for 2.6, p. 94, which demonstrates modulation of tonos, is completely unintelligible, because the octave systems represented by the letters GHKL and POMN are misplaced in relation to the perfect system. There are also many errors and omissions in detailing the alphabetical letters that represent intervals in the diagram.

2. Gogava, trans., Ptolemy *Harmonics* 2.11, pp. 102–06.

	Gogava			Düring		
Archytas	5:4	36:35	28:27	5:4	36:35	28:27
Aristoxenus	24	3	8	24	3	3
Eratosthenes	19:15	39:38	40:39	19:15	39:38	40:39
Didymus	5:4	4:3	37:36	5:4	31:30	32:31
Ptolemy	5:4	24:23	49:48	5:4	24:23	46:45

Figure 7.1:
Division of the enharmonic tetrachord in Gogava and Düring

first column and 8 in the second, signifying 77 and 8/60 (2/15).[3] Gogava's string lengths for the enharmonic of Archytas may be compared to those in the Düring edition (Figure 7.2).

Gogava's string lengths are not consistent either with the ratios that he gives or with those that should have been in the text, because the fractions have been omitted. The misrepresentation of the shades of tuning in Gogava's translation is unfortunate, because these were among the most practical and currently applicable revelations in the treatise. It is true that an attentive reader could have corrected the tables by means of Boethius and Gaffurio's De harmonia, but the state of the tables diminished the credibility of the whole translation.

The two chapters that were sampled in the Leoniceno and Augio translations may be analyzed in Gogava's version with not too disappointing results. They will reveal some of Gogava's particular solutions for Latinizing and for musical nomenclature. Systema, which is usually rendered in Latin as "constitutio" is here "complexus." Ptolemy's thesis becomes "positio," and dynamis "facultas." The fixed and movable notes of the system are "stabiles" and "mobiles" respectively. There is nothing to complain of here. Irritating, but well-meaning, are Gogava's Latin equivalents for the names of the steps of the greater perfect and lesser perfect systems. He obviously wanted to give the reader an image of the location of each step, which the Latin names do communicate. Apart from "suprema" for hypate, they are

| Gogava: | 60 | 73 | 77 2/15 | 80 | 90 | 106 1/2 | 115 43/60 | 120 |
| Düring: | 60 | 75 | 77 1/7 | 79 | 89 | 112 1/2 | 115 5/7 | 120 |

Figure 7.2:
Comparison of enharmonic string lengths in Gogava and Düring

3. The number 70 appears frequently in the second column but is an error, for Gogava mistakenly interpreted omicron, which can signify 70 as well as 0, as 70 instead of 0. This suggests that Gogava did not understand the purpose of the second column of numbers. I am indebted to Thomas J. Mathiesen for the clarification of this system of representing fractions.

no less suggestive than the parallel Greek names, but they raised an unnecessary barrier in the way of a musically trained reader, who knew by
heart the name for every step between proslambanomenos and nete hyperbolaeon yet would have had some trouble recognizing these in "assumpta" and "ultima excellentium."

In the translations below I have chosen English terms that suggest the
Latin rather than reflect the Greek original. Some are fresh coinages, such
as "penesupreme" or "paramedian," to parallel Gogava's neologisms. In
this way I hope to have given the reader some sense of Gogava's individual
interpretation. The first excerpt is of 2.5, in which Ptolemy explains the
thetic and dynamic nomenclature of the tonoi.

Quo pacto sonituum appelationes accipiantur pro eorum; tum positione, tum facultate.	How the names of the tones may be derived according to both their position and function.
Cap[ut] 5.	Chapter 5.
Vnde igitur complexionis Diapason & Diatessaron distinctio à Bis- diapason pendeat, sequentibus exponetur.	Upon what, therefore, the distinction of the complex diapason-plus-diatessaron from the double diapason depends will be set forth in the following. But now
Sed cum re uera absoluta & Bisdiapason, & quinque & decem conflata sit, eo quòd communis fiat una uox grauiori, acutiorique Diapason & omnium media, aliquando quidem propter situm in acutius simpliciter, aut grauius appellamus, mediam sanè iam dictam communem duorum Diapason, & Proslambanomenon, idest assumptam grauissimam, acutissi- mam Netem, siue ultimam excellen- tium; dein sequentes assumptam in acutius usque ad mediam Hypaten, idest, supremam supremarum & Parhypaten, idest iuxta supremam seu Penesupremam supremarum, & lichanum, idest indicem supremarum: post mediam similiter usque ad Netem, seu	in reality the double diapason is complete and made up of fifteen [steps]. By this fact a single step becomes common to the lower and higher diapason and [becomes] the middle of all [the steps]. Sometimes we name it "median" simply on account of its location in terms of higher and lower [pitch]. It is called median, to be sure, [because it is] common to two diapasons; and [we designate] "proslambanomenos," that is, the lowest added [step]; and the highest "nete," or last of the excellent. Those following upward [from] the added [step] up to the median [we name]: "hypate," that is, the supreme of the supremes, and "parhypate," that is, the next to the supreme or penesupreme of the supremes, and "lichanus," that is, the index of the supremes. Similarly after the median up to the nete or

ultimam excellentium;
Paramesen, idest paramediam,
& tertiam disiunctorum,
penultimam disiunctorum &
ultimam disiunctorum, &
tertiam excellentium, &
penultimam excellentium, &
ultimam excellentium.
Aliquando uerò propter facul-
tatem ipsam, & respectum ad aliud
accommodamus positionibus
in immutabili uocata complexione
facultates ipsas
Bisdiapason,
deinde communes in hac
facimus appellationes tum
situum, tum facultatum easque
transferimus in duas.
nam si alterum in Bisdiapason
duorum tonorum ab ea, quae
positione media est acceperimus,
& ipsi in alteram partem
apposuerimus duo tetrachorda
conjuncta, ex his quae in tota
sunt complexione tetrachordis,
deinceps tonum alterum reliquo
& grauissimo interuallorum
tribuerimus, medium profectò
facultate appellabimus à
constitutione hinc facta grauiorem acutioris disiunctonis &
Penemediam
acutiorem, assumptam
uerò & ultimam
excellentium grauiorem
grauioris disiunctionis & supremam
supremarum acitiorem [sic]: deinde
mediarum quidem supremam
communem coniunctiorum
duorum grauiorum
tetrachordorum post grauiorem
disiunctionem, ultimam uerò
disiunctorum
communem coniunctorum duorum

last of the excellent: the
"paramese", that is, paramedian,
and "third of the disjunct," the
"penultimate of the disjunct," and
the "last of the disjunct," and the
"third of the excellent," and
"penultimate of the excellent," and
"last of the excellent."
Sometimes, however, we adopt a name
rather according to function and
we suit the functions themselves
to the positions in the complex, the
double diapason, called immutable,
with respect to something else.
Then within this [double diapason]
we adopt the common names according
to location as well as function and
we carry these names along in pairs.
For if we take one of
the two tones in the double
diapason from that position which
is medial and place on one side the
two conjunct tetrachords from those
[four] tetrachords that are in the
total complex, and then assign the
other tone to the remaining and
lowest of the intervals, we shall
call "median"[4]
certainly in function,
the lower of the higher
disjunction from the constitution
here made, and "penemedian,"
the higher. We shall call "added
step", however, and "last of the
excellent," the lower [step] of the
lower disjunction, and "supreme of
the supremes," the higher. Then
"supreme of the medians" [we shall
call] the common supreme of the
conjunction of the two lower
tetrachords after the lower
disjunction. "The last of the
disjunct," though, [we shall call]
the common [step] of the two lower

4. *Medium* is probably a misprint for *mediam*.

grauiorem tetrachordorum post grauiorem disiunctionem; atque iterum Penesupremam supremarum à grauissima secundam eius, quod post grauiorem disiunctionem est tetrachordi, & indicem supremarum, eam quae tertia est, Penesupremam ueró mediarum secundam etiam grauissima eius quod grauissimam disiunctionem antecedit tetrachordi & indicem mediarum tertiam: deinde tertiam disiunctorum secundam à grauissima tetrachordi sequentis acutiorem disiunctorum tertiam, excellentium ueró tertiam à grauissima secundam antecedentis acutiorem disiunctionem tetrachordi & penultimam excellentium tertiam. Porró iuxtà has apellationes, nempe facultatum solummodo uocentur stabiles soni in generum mutationibus, assumpta & suprema supremarum, & suprema mediarum, media Penemedia, ultima disiunctorum, & ultima excellentium, quae una eademque est cum assumpta; reliqui ueró nobiles [sic], quippe transeuntibus positione facultatibus, non amplius iisdem locis quadrant stabilium mobiliumve termini. Manifestum est autem quòd primam spetiem Diapason in proposita complexione quae inimmutabilis dicitur ob dictam causam comprehendunt Penemedia, & suprema supremarum:

conjunct tetrachords after the lower[5] disjunction. Also, again, "penesupreme of the supremes" from its second lowest, because it is after the lower disjunction of the tetrachords and "index of the supremes," that which is the third; "penesupreme of the medians," however, [we shall call] its second lowest, because the lowest disjunction of the tetrachord precedes it, and "index of the medians," the third; then "third of the disjunct," the second from the lowest of the tetrachord following the higher disjunction, and "penultimate of the disjunct," the third; "third of the excellent," however, the second from the lowest of the tetrachord exceeding the higher disjunction; and "penultimate of the excellent," the third. Further, besides these names, the stable tones in the mutations of genera naturally may be named only according to the function: the added note, the supreme of the supremes, the supreme of the medians, the median, the penemedian, the last of the disjunct, the last of the excellent, which is one and the same with the added note. The remainder are movable. When the functions shift in position, the boundaries of the stable or movable no longer square with the same loci. It is evident, though, that in the complex set forth called immutable on account of the stated reason, the penemedian and the supreme of the supremes enclose the

---

5. This and the preceding "lower" (*grauiorem*) should read "higher" common to the diezeugmenon and hyperbolaeon tetrachords. This correction is permitted by the reading in Vatican gr. 176. Professor Thomas J. Mathiesen kindly pointed this out to me.

[lacuna: secundam tertia disiunctorum et penesupremam supremarum:] tertiam penultima disiunctorum, disiunctorum & index supremarum, quartam ultima disiunctarum & suprema mediarum: quintam tertia excellentium, & Penesuprema mediarum, sextam penultima excellentium, & index mediarum: septimam ultima excellentium, & assumpta, & media, ut uides annotatum in subiecta oculis hic immutabili complexione, ut in promptu sit accipere.[6]

first species of diapason; [lacuna: the third of the disjunct and the penesupreme of the supremes, the second;] the penultimate of the disjunct and the index of the supremes, the third; the last of the disjunct and the supreme of the medians, the fourth; he third of the excellent and the penesupreme of the medians, the fifth; the penultimate of the excellent and the index of the medians, the sixth; the last of the excellent and the added step, and the median, the seventh; as you see set out before your eyes here in the immutable complex, so that it may be readily grasped.

There are a number of cryptic passages in this chapter. What does Gogava mean by saying that "with respect to something else [*respectum ad aliud*] we suit the potentials themselves to the positions"? Is it that the complex is called immutable with respect to—in comparison with—something else, that is the modulating system? Another puzzling expression is "transferimus in duas." Does Gogava mean that the system may be transposed both up and down, therefore in two directions? Or is he pointing to the fact that two pairs of conjunct tetrachords will be set, one on either side of the interval of the disjunction, or, more likely, that each note will have two names? We have chosen the latter interpretation for our translation. These questions can be settled by reference to the Greek text, but it must be remembered that this was inaccessible to most of Gogava's readers. There is one lacuna, which an insightful reader could have rectified without difficulty: the steps bounding the second octave species are not named.

Chapter 11 of Book 2 is decidedly more difficult than the account of the naming of scale degrees by position and function. One of the sources of confusion is the repeated use of the word *tonos* in either one of two senses, as a key or a mode, and as a step in the scale. Gogava set out to differentiate them by capitalizing the first of these as *Tonus*. However, either he was not consistent, or, more likely, his printer did not cooperate. Those that should have been capitalized will be obvious from the translation.

Quod non oportet per Semitonium augere Tonos.

That it is not proper to increase the tonoi through the semitone.

6. Ptolemy, *Harmonics* 2.5 (Düring 51.17–53.27), trans. Gogava, pp. 90–91.

140   **Antonio Gogava**

Cap[ut] 11.
Liquet autem, quod his quoque
suppositis à nobis Tonis,
eius quae in unoquoque
facultate media est,
proprius quidam fit
Diapason sonus, quippe
totidem hi sunt, quot speties.
Nam si Diapason excipiatur
ad media quodammodo
perfectae complexionis
loca, uidelicet, à situ
Supremae mediarum ad Vltimam
diusiunctarum (eò quòd uox
lubenter [sic]conuersetur more-
turque circa medios maximè
concentus,
raro ad extrema exiliens propter
laboriosam & uiolentam, cum
immoderata fuerit, relaxationem
aut contentionem)
Mixtilidij quidem facultate
media accommodabitur loco
Penultimae disiunctarum,
ut tonus primam spetiem in
proposito faciat
Diapason:
Lydij uerò facultate media
loco Tertiae
disiunctarum,
congruens secundae
speciei: Phrygij loco
Penemediae ad
tertiam spetiem:
Dorij loco mediae
facitque quartam & mediam
spetiem ipsius Diapason:
sub Lydij uerò
loco Indicis mediarum,
faciens quintam spetiem:
sub Phrygij
loco Penesummae
mediarum congruens spetiei
sextae: Subdorij
loco mediarum

Chapter 11.
It is evident, then, that when these
tonoi have been assumed by us
(in each one of which there is
a median by function), there arises
a certain sound appropriately, of the
diapason, and, to be sure, there
are as many as there are species.
Now if a diapason is extracted from a
certain median location of the
perfect complex, for example, from
the locus of the supreme of the
medians to the last of the
disjunct (because the voice
willingly revolves and remains
mainly around the middle
harmonies,
rarely leaping out to the extremes
because of the laborious and
violent relaxation and tension,
when it would be immoderate),
the median in function of the
Mixolydian will be accommodated to
the locus of the penultimate of the
disjunct, so that the tonos would
make in the proposed [octave] the
first species of diapason. The
median in function of the Lydian,
however, in the locus of the third
of the disjunct [would make a
diapason] congruent with the second
species; the media of the Phrygian,
in the locus of the penemedian,
with the third species; the media
of the Dorian, in the median locus,
would make the fourth and middle
species of diapason; the [median]
of the Sublydian, however, in the
locus of the index of the medians,
making the fifth species; the
[median] of the Subphrygian, in the
locus of the penesupreme of the
medians agreeing with the sixth
species; [the median] of the
Subdorian, in the locus of the

supremae ad
septimam spetiem. Quare
poterunt aliqui in complexione
seruari immobiles soni
in Tonorum immutato responsu,
obseruata uocis
magnitudine,
quando in tonum differentibus
similes facultates, nunquam
in ipsorum sonorum loca incidunt.
Caeterum pluribus suppositis
tonis, ut faciunt,
qui per Semitonia excessus
eorundem accumulant, necessarium erit duorum tonorum, medias
uni soni loco penitus congruere,
ut totae moueantur complexiones,
per mutuam horum tonorum
duorum responsus mutationem,
nec amplius seruabitur communis
quaedam, quae
ab initio erat tensio,
qua uocis proprietas commen-
suratur. Nam Hypodorij,
uerbi gratia, facultate media
connexa ei, quae est
situ mediarum suprema,
Hypophrygij ueró
Penesupremae
mediarum
intercep[er]unt ab hisce tonum,
qui uocatur ab ipsis
Hypophrygius,
ad differentiam illius acutioris,
oportebit suam ipsius
mediam, aut apud supremam
habere mediarum, quemadmodum
& Hypodorius, aut apud Penemediam,
[*recte:* Penesupremam
mediarum], ut acutior quoque
Hypophrygius: quod ei
eueniat postquam inter seinuicem
commutauerimus, eos
qui communem sonum nacti sunt
tonos, mouebitur quidem hic

supreme of the medians, with the
seventh species. For this reason
some tones in the complexes may be
preserved as immovable,
as the correspondence of the tonoi
changed, if the limits of the voice
are observed, inasmuch as when
tonoi differ, the
same functions never fall in the
locus of the same tones. On the
other hand, if more tonoi were
assumed, as they do who pile them
up by increments of semitones, it
would be necessary for the medians
of two tonoi completely to
coincide on the locus of one tone,
so that entire complexes would
be moved by mutual mutation of the
correspondence of these two tonoi;
some commonality will no longer be
preserved which was the pitch from
the beginning and by
which the proper range of the voice
is measured. For the median in
function of the Hypodorian, for
example, coincides with that which
is by location the supreme of the
medians, the [median] of the
Hypophrygian, however, with the
penesupreme of the medians, but if
they took away from these the tonos
that is called by these [Aristo-
xenians: Düring] Hypophrygian to
differentiate it from the high one,
it will be necessary for its own
median to fall on the supreme of
the medians; likewise the
Hypodorian, on the penemedian
[*recte:* penesupreme of the
medians], as also the higher
Hypophrygian, for this would
happen after we
transpose among themselves those
tonoi which have obtained a common
tone: the tension here would be

contentus, aut relaxatus semitonio, ad hoc uero quod eadem
in utroque tono facultas sit,
uidelicet ea, quae mediae est,
sequentur & reliquorum omnium
tonorum intensiones aut remissiones, eò quòd conseruent
rationes ad mediam easdem, quae
erant & ante mutationem, iuxta
commune amborum tonorum genus
acceptae: quare neutiquam
alius uidebitur spetie tonus
à priore, sed Hypodorius
iterum, aut idem
Hypophrygius acutius sonans
grauiusque duntaxat. Quòd
igitur rectè sufficienterque
septem habeantur toni, hactenus
explicitum sit.[7]

raised or relaxed by a semitone to
a point where it would be the same
function in each of the tonoi,
that is, the one that is median,
and a retuning of all remaining
tones up and down would follow,
because they preserve the same
relationships to the median that
existed before the mutation, with
respect to the genus common to
both tonoi. For this reason the
tonos does not at all seem to be
other than it was before, but
again the Hypodorian, or the same
Hypophrygian merely sounding higher
and lower. That there are
correctly seven tonoi, then, has
been sufficiently explained.

Before proceeding to show how the number of tonoi must be based on
the number of octave species, Ptolemy selects the octave that is the most
comfortable for the voice for the location of the mesai. This is the octave
hypate meson to nete diezeugmenon. If the mesai are placed in this range
as described, and the tetrachords are formed around them to fit within the
prescribed octave, the seven octave species enumerated will result. This is
rendered clearly enough. What is not plain is how some notes remain "immovable" when the functions fall on different steps in each of the seven
tonoi. If Gogava meant that certain strings need not be retuned, he is correct,
but the thought is poorly expressed.

Ptolemy's argument for the limitation to seven tonoi emerges in the next
few sentences. By thus limiting the number of tonoi, enough stable tones
are held in common by a few tonoi that modulation from one to another
becomes possible through common stable tones. If, on the other hand, a
tonos is allowed on every semitone, a large number would be incompatible
because of the distant relationships engendered by the semitone shift. Besides, some tonoi will be duplicated with regard to octave species, because
only seven are possible. This reasoning is transparent in Gogava's translation. I have translated *interceperunt* literally as "they took away," but, surely,
the Greek *lambanomenon* suggests the admission of intermediate tonoi between the regular ones rather than a subtraction.

---

7. Ptolemy *Harmonics* 2.11, Gogava, p. 100.

Pseudo-Aristotle's *De audibilibus*

The choice of Aristoxenus for inclusion in Gogava's collection was due to Zarlino, as we saw. The addition of the pseudo-Aristotelian *De audibilibus*[8] and Porphyry's *De decem praedicamentis* is not justified in the preface. As a medical scientist Gogava may have been attracted to the Aristotelian fragment because it applied physiological method to the study of the singing voice. Porphyry's commentary on Aristotle's categories may have simply served as a filler to round out the gathering of four folios of which each register in the book is formed. It has no immediate connection with music, although Porphyry in his commentary makes frequent use of the theory of categories, particularly with reference to sensible qualities.

At the time of Gogava's writing, the *De audibilibus* was thought to be a genuine work of Aristotle. As the only work attributed to him dealing exclusively with music, even though fragmentary, it was a natural choice for early translation. It is one of several important fragments by various early authors on acoustics embedded in Porphyry's commentary on Ptolemy's *Harmonics*. Two others were noted by Valgulio, as we have seen, namely, excerpts from musical treatises by Theophrastus and Panaetius. Porphyry introduces the essay Gogava translated as a work of Aristotle.[9] Porphyry notes, however, that because of its length he has abbreviated it.

Since the mid-nineteenth century the essay has been considered spurious.[10] Among the authors to whom it has been assigned are: Heracleides Ponticus, by von Jan,[11] and Strato by Brandis, Diels, Capelle, and Düring;[12] others, including Zeller, Susemihl, Regenbogen, and Wehrli, have declined to attribute it securely to anyone.[13] Gottschalk has made a convincing case for rejecting Heracleides and giving it to Strato.[14]

The theory of sound presented in *De audibilibus* is distinctly Aristotelian. It agrees on many points with his *De anima*, the commentary on it by Themistius, and the pseudo-Aristotelian *Problems*. Some elements of the theory are more clearly expressed here than in any other ancient source. It is not surprising that the work was frequently quoted in the Renaissance,

8. Gogava's title is "Aristotelis Peri Akoustōn, Idest de Obiecto Auditus, siue Audibilibus," p. 151.

9. Düring ed. 69.24 to 77.18; Wallis ed., *Harmonicorum libri tres* (Oxford, 1682), pp. 246–54. It is edited with an English translation by W. S. Hett in Aristotle, *Minor Works* (Cambridge, Mass., 1936), pp. 49–79.

10. See H. B. Gottschalk, "The De audibilibus and Peripatetic Acoustics," *Hermes* 96 (1968):435–60.

11. *Musici scriptores graeci,* pp. 55, 137.

12. See Gottschalk, "The De audibilibus," p. 435, for bibliography.

13. Ibid., pp. 435–36.

14. Ibid., pp. 435–36.

particularly after Gogava's translation appeared. Gogava seems to have been more at home in this work than in Ptolemy, and his vocabulary is adequate to the demands made by this scientific treatise. The mechanics of sound is concisely explained in the opening paragraph:

Voces omnes & soni, uel corpo- rum, uel aeris ad corpora impulsum sequuntur, non quòd aer figu- retur, ut nonnulli putant: sed quia mouetur conformiter contractus ipse & extensus atque interceptis, complodiens etiam feriensque ob spiritus & chordarum qui fiunt ictus. Cum enim spiritu aer, qui deinceps est, uerberatur, hic sane ui mouetur unaque contiguum sibi aerem impellit ut quoquo uersum extendatur uox similiter, quatenus per aeris motionem licet.[15]	All voices and sounds result from the impulse of bodies or of air on bodies, not because air is shaped, as some believe, but because it is moved in conformance with what is contracted and expanded, and by the passing, striking together, and knocking of breath and strings, which cause the impact. For when air, which in turn is struck by the breath, is moved with force, it similarly impels any air that is next to it, so that the sound extends in every direction as far motion of the air allows.

The author denies that sounds result from the shape of the air, as Theophrastus believed.[16] Sounds result rather from the impact of bodies or of air against bodies, and air moves in response to contractions and expansions of air originally struck. As the breath moves against an object or two objects are struck together or a string is set in motion against the air, a movement is initiated that travels in every direction from the source. This movement is transmitted by air that is set in motion by the air reverberating around the sounding object.

The quality of the sounds, whether harsh or mellow, loud or soft, depends on the characteristics of the material vibrating and the violence of the motion:

Ac si chordas manibus durius contrectes, minimeque molliter, necesse est responsum quoque eas reddere ualidiorem: quae uero minus contortae fuerint & cornua, quae crudiora sint, uoces praese ferunt molliores: ut & longiora organa; quippe aeris ictus grauio- res mollioresque fiunt, ob longitudinem locorum: contra,	And if you touch strings harder and not at all softly with the hands, it is necessary that the response also will return more vigorously. Strings less stretched and horns that are more raw will make softer tones, as also longer instruments. Of course, the blows of the air are made lower and softer on account of the length of the spaces. On the

15. *De audibilibus* 800a.1–11, Gogava, p. 152.
16. Gottschalk, ibid., p. 449, adduces this point against Theophrastus' authorship.

quae breuiora sunt, sonant ob chordarum contractionem. Id etiam ex hoc addiscas, quod eiusdem organi duriores contingit esse uoces, ubi quis non in medio chordas pulset, eo quod prope iugum, & quod Chordotonum uocant, ab intendendis chordis, magis hae tendantur.[17]	contrary, those which are shorter sound harder owing to the contraction of the strings. This you learn from the fact that on the same instrument the tones tend to be harsher when one plucks not in the middle of the string, rather near the yoke and what they call the chordotonos—where the strings are stretched— because there they are under greater tension.

This passage preserves in the Latin the ambiguities of the original. The author reflects on both the softer and lower sounds made by instruments of greater length and the harsher sound made by tighter and shorter strings. This harshness is particularly noticed when a string is plucked near the yoke or bridge (*chordotonos*). A later passage is clearer in elaborating the mechanics of strings and the perception of sound as continuous rather than interrupted movement:

qualia enim impulsi aeris momenta fuerint, tales etiam oportet effici penes auditum uoces, puta raras, aut densas, mollesve, aut duras, tenues, aut crasses. semper enim alius aer alium mouens similiter, uocem edit similiter omnem, quemadmodum se res habet etiam in acumine & grauitate: enimuero & celeritates percussionis aliae aliis succedentes, conseruant uoces principiis suis congruas: ictus uero ferunt aeris à chordis plurimi & separati, sed ob exiguitatem intercedentis temporis nequeunte auditu discernere interualla, uidetur nobis una continuaque uox effici: non secus ac in coloribus quoque:	Whatever kind may be the motions of the impulses of air, such, necessarily, will be the corresponding tones that affect the hearing, for example, sparse or dense, soft or hard, thin or thick. As some air moves other air similarly, it always yields a whole sound that is similar to its source just as in height or lowness. And as the rapidity of percussion succeeds from one part to the next, it preserves tones that are congruent with their beginnings. The blows made on the air by strings are several and separate, but because of the shortness of time intervening, and the hearing not being able to discern the intervals [of time], it seems to us that a single and continuous tone is sounded, not unlike what happens with colors,

17. *De audibilibus* 803a.33, Gogava p. 158.

etenim & hi cum saepenumero
distent, uidentur nobis se mutuo
contingere, cum uelociter mouentur.
Idem uero accidit in consonantiis;
praeterea enim quod comprehendan-
tur alij soni ab aliis
unaque requiescant, fugiunt
nos interiectae identidem uoces.
Saepius enim in omnibus conso-
nantiis, licet ab acutoribus
sonis, primo fiant ueris
ictus ob motus celeritatem:
postremus tamen sonus una
nobis ad auditum peruenit,
etiam à grauiore chorda editus,
eo quod auditus sentire nequit,
quemadmodum ductum est,
interiectas uoces,
unde uidemur nobis simul
continuoque ambos exaudire
sonos.[18]

for even when these are separated,
they seem to us to blend into each
when they are moving rapidly. The
same happens in consonances. Since
some sounds are embraced by others,
should they cease at the same
time, the intervening tones
escape our notice. For in all
consonances, it is granted that
with higher sounds the blows on the
air are, first of all, made more frequently because of the rapidity of the
motion; nevertheless afterwards the
sound reaches our hearing at the same
time as that which came from the
lower string, because it is so
communicated that the hearing is
not able to sense the intervening
tones; for this reason we seem to
hear both sounds as simultaneous
and continuous.

In this passage Gogava transmits a conception of sound that is not limited to the quality that exclusively interested the Pythagoreans, namely pitch, but includes more elusive characteristics, such as thinness and thickness, softness and hardness. All of these qualities, the author proposes, are communicated in the movement of the air, just as pitch is. How these other qualities are conserved by the air motion is not explained. But for pitch it is obviously the rapidity of motion, which is the same at the point of the blow as it is later when the sound reaches the ear. The ear senses not a series of blows but a continuous sound. This is because of the shortness of time between blows, which the hearing is not able to detect. The sight similarly reacts to colors in motion, which appear to blend into each other. Here Gogava understood the comparison better than the modern English translator who rendered the passage: "and the sound seems to us as one and continuous, just as occurs in the case of colours; for often sounds which are really separate seem to us to dovetail into each other, when they are travelling rapidly."[19] Gogava appreciated that the colors are traveling, not the sounds.

18. *De audibilibus* 803b.27–804a.8, Gogava, p. 159.
19. *De audibilibus* 803b.37–40, Hett, trans., Aristotle, *Minor Works,* p. 73. Wallis also rendered the passage correctly, p. 252: "una continuaque nobis vox apparet; pariter atque in coloribus. Nam & colores distantes, saepe nobis videntur se mutuo contingere, quando celeriter moventur."

The statement concerning consonances is also interpreted more narrowly by Gogava than the English translator, who has for 803b.41: "Exactly the same thing occurs in harmonies."[20] The key term is *tas symphonias,* which could either mean specifically fifths and fourths or consonances in general, but it does not necessarily imply simultaneous "harmonies." Indeed, it probably did not. Rather, the author seems to suggest that when tones that are consonant, such as those that are an octave, fourth, or fifth apart, are heard in succession, one is not aware of the individual sounds coming to an end, because they blend while still sounding. The idea that one tone is comprehended in another vaguely suggests simultaneous harmony, such as a triad or tetrad, and this interpretation is conveyed by the English translator. But did the Aristotelian author mean this? Probably not. It is tempting to think that by one sound comprehended in another he referred to the phenomenon, also noted in the Aristotelian *Problems* of a sounding tone seeming to contain one an octave higher.[21] Because of this confusion of a sound with its octave, or even fifth, one is not aware of the "interiectae voces" (*metaxy phonai*), tones intermediate between the highest and lowest. This sensation is not the main point of the passage, however, but only serves as an example of the way that the ear glosses over the reality of discrete phenomena by hearing them as one. Thus a series of blows of the string upon the air is heard as a continuous sound. What the author meant in the last sentence by the statement that "the hearing is not able to sense the intervening tones" is not clear. But Gogava has represented the thought faithfully. The author may simply have meant that we hear the attack of the pitch and its demise but are not aware of intervening blows or tones, that is, we cannot count them and therefore cannot say that there were more in the high sound than in the low. The passage contains one further important revelation, that lower sounds reach the ear at the same time as higher sounds. Plato had said that higher sounds travel faster.[22]

Gogava's readers would not have found the theory of sound expressed in *De audibilibus* entirely new. Boethius had made several of the same points,[23] which he evidently received from Nicomachus, and Gaffurio had repeated them. Boethius associates high pitches with rapid and frequent motion and tension, low with slow infrequent motion and relaxation. He likewise notes that sound consists of repeated striking of the air, but that an uninterrupted sound is heard. His image of the revolving top, in which a vertical red stripe seems to tint the entire surface a single color, reminds one of the

20. Hett trans., p. 73.
21. Aristotle *Problems* 19.8, 14, 24, 42.
22. Plato *Timaeus* 80a.
23. Boethius *De institutione musica* 1.3.

comparison made by the Aristotelian author. Also the idea that the movement of the air is transmitted in all directions is present in Boethius, who compares the action of a sounding object on the air with a pebble thrown into a puddle, which makes a circular wave that expands in all directions until it hits an obstacle or dies away. Similarly, he says, the air that is struck by the instrument "starts a circular wave in the air" (rotundum fluctum aeris ciet), but at a distance this "wave of impelled air" (pulsi aëris unda) is weaker.[24] Many other points, however, would have struck the Renaissance reader as new. This is particularly true of the many insights into the character of sounds produced by various sources, both animal and artificial. The author attempts to account for the diverse character of sound obtained from various instruments and the materials from which they are manufactured. Gogava translates the terms for instruments in the conventional way: the aulos becomes "tibia," and the *salpinx* (trumpet) "tuba." Kithara remains "cithara," *kerata* (horns) are "cornua," and the general word for instrument is "organum." In all it was a very serviceable translation of a work of prime importance.

Aristoxenus' *Harmonic Elements*

Gogava has been remembered by the philologists chiefly for his translation of Aristoxenus' *Harmonic Elements,* concerning which none of them, from Girolamo Mei[25] and Marcus Meibom[26] to Rosetta da Rios,[27] has had a kind word. Meibom's judgment of it is utterly damning. The translation displays, he says, no knowledge of music and is the work of one little steeped in the Greek language. It would be excusable, Meibom concedes, if Gogava erred only in obscure and corrupt places, but when he distorts and entangles those that are plain, it makes Meibom wonder how Gogava could have had the courage to submit it to the judgment of posterity. He would have won more praise if he had simply given to a printer his emended Greek codex, which he finds akin to the Scaligerianus in Leiden that he himself used. This is what Johannes van Meurs did, and for this he deserves praise, although he allowed many errors of transcription to be perpetuated.[28]

Henry S. Macran, who first translated Aristoxenus into English, calls Gogava's translation—which he dates incorrectly 1542—"a worthless work

---

24. Ibid., 1.14.
25. See Palisca, *Girolamo Mei,* p. 108.
26. Marcus Meibom, *Antiquae musicae auctores septem,* (Amsterdam, 1652), I, 87.
27. Rosetta da Rios, ed., *Aristoxeni Elementa harmonica* (Rome, 1954), pp. x–xii.
28. The work in question is *Aristoxenus, Nicomachus, Alypius, auctores musices antiquissimi, hactenus non editi Ioannes Meursius nunc primus vulgavit, et notas addidit* (Leiden, 1616), ed. J. Lamius in Meursius, *Opera omnia* (Florence, 1741–63).

crowded with errors."[29] He is equally severe with van Meurs, who, he says, "displays gross ignorance of the general theory of Greek music, and of the doctrine of Aristoxenus in particular."[30] Rosetta da Rios, the editor of the most recent critical text of the *Harmonic Elements* finds few merits in Gogava's work, complaining that it abounds in serious errors.[31]

Da Rios renders a useful service, however, in identifying Gogava's probable source: Venice, Marciana graecus 322, a manuscript once belonging to Cardinal Bessarion. She finds numerous places where words or phrases omitted in it are also omitted in Gogava's translation and errors in the text that are reflected in the translation. This corroborates Meibom's impression that Gogava based his translation on Scaliger's manuscript, for from her stemma it appears that the Scaliger codex is derived directly from the Bessarion manuscript.[32]

Gogava's translation cannot be defended in terms of modern or even seventeenth-century philological criteria. He gives no account of his emendations, of suspected lacunae, of the places where he had to take liberties to ensure a coherent sentence. There are no annotations, whether of a critical or explanatory nature. But these shortcomings are not unique to Gogava's volume; they were the norm for the mid-sixteenth century, although some translations then being prepared had both critical and explanatory notes.[33] Meibom and modern editors have not been interested in evaluating Gogava's work in terms of the state of scholarship in his time or of its usefulness to its intended readers. They asked themselves what Gogava contributed to establishing a reliable text and a translation into Latin that would stand the test of time and sophisticated scholarship on Greek music. Gogava's book could not pass such a test.

More appropriate questions to ask about the book are: Did it make an important work accessible to readers of Latin who could use its evidence critically to reconstruct the theory of Greek music? Was the translation reliable on most substantive points, granted that no work had been done up to that time on collation of disparate readings? Does Gogava give the impression that he understood his author and that he was capable of expressing this in coherent Latin? Although Meibom might have given negative answers to these questions also, it is well to address them now.

We may begin consideration of the adequacy of Gogava's interpretation

---

29. Henry S. Macran, ed. and trans., *The Harmonics of Aristoxenus* (Oxford, 1902), p. 92.
30. Ibid., p. 92.
31. Rosetta da Rios, ed., pp. x–xii.
32. Ibid., p. cvi.
33. For example, *Petri Victorii Commentarii in primum librum Aristotelis de arte poetarum* (Florence, 1560), Piero Vettori's edition and commentary on the first book (actually all that is extant) of Aristotle's *Poetics,* has both.

and translation of Aristoxenus by reviewing a few of Meibom's criticisms of specific passages. In the notes to his translation Meibom frequently compares his own version to Gogava's. Often he admits that the passage is difficult and prints Gogava's translation simply as a parallel, albeit inferior, interpretation or to show that Gogava too was compelled to assume some missing word or to correct his source. More often, though, Meibom quotes passages from Gogava to expose their silliness, ineptness, thick-headedness, and inadequacy in Greek. For example, Meibom characterized Aristoxenus' definition of "tone" (*phthongos*) (1.15) as rendered "stupidly" (*inscite*) by Gogava.[34] The translations of Gogava, Meibom, Macran, and Da Rios may be compared:

Gogava:

ac ut compendio dicatur uocis
casus in unam sensionem [*sic*]
est sonus. Etenim uidetur
sonus existere
cadente uoce in statum cantui
congruum, dum ibi in una
tensione cessat.

And, to be brief, a tone is the
incidence of the voice on one
tension [pitch]. For a tone seems
to exist when the voice
falls on a fixed point suitable
for song, providing it delays
there in one tension.

Meibom:

Sonus est vocis casus, in unam
tensionem. Tunc enim sonus
ejusmodi esse videtur,
ut in cantum
modulatè constitutum collocari
possit, cum vox in una tensione
stare videtur.

A tone is an incidence of the voice
on one tension. A tone
of such sort seems
to be that which may be placed in
a song melodiously when the
voice seems to stay on a single
tension [pitch].

Macran:

Briefly it [a note] is the incidence of the voice upon one point of pitch. Whenever the voice is heard to remain stationary on one pitch, we have a note qualified to take a place in a melody.

Da Rios:

Per dirla in breve, *la nota è la caduta della voce su di un grado,* poichè allora sembra che il fermarsi su un grado produca un suono tale da poter esser ordinato nella melodia armonizzata. Questa è la nota.

The four translations convey essentially the same thought. Both Gogava's and Meibom's are wordier than the two modern translations. The idea of placing the note in a song is missing in Gogava, probably because the verb

34. Meibom, I, 87.

tattesthai, added by van Meurs,[35] was missing in his source. Macran improves on both his predecessors by substituting "is heard" for "seems," the literal meaning of *phainetai,* which da Rios restores (da Rios, 20.1). She has also glossed the "placing" of the tone with the implication of "harmonic" assignment within the melody, which is probably not called for. Gogava does not suffer much from this comparison.

Another passage criticized by Meibom is one that he found very difficult (*severa dificilis.*)[36] He charges that Gogava did not understand the verb *lambanein* or *eklambanein*—it is the latter word that occurs in the passage, and Gogava has rendered it correctly as "accipere," to understand. Meibom also complains that Gogava did not take note of the word *akounta* (those who listen). This Gogava seems to have replaced with "animadvertere" (to observe). What is worse, though, Gogava missed the point of the passage:

Verum enimuero oportet unumquodque horum recte accipere accurateque
animaduertere, ne
redditam de
singulis rationem praetereamus,
siue exacta, sit siue crassior
planiorque ac ubi in eam addi-
scendum incubuimus, tunc paratos
nos ad reliqua intelligenda
docilesque fore
putemus.[37]

It is necessary correctly to understand and accurately to observe
everyone of these [definitions],
lest we overlook the account given
about individual cases,
whether it be exact or rather approximate and plain; and where in it
we took care to learn and thus
consider ourselves ready to understand the rest and to be easily
taught.

Both Meibom and Macran express the thought correctly, and I give Macran's translation, which is somewhat freer:

Here we would ask our hearers to receive these definitions in the right spirit, not with jealous scrutiny of the degree of their exactness. We would ask him to aid us with his intelligent sympathy, and to consider our definition sufficiently instructive when it puts him in the way of understanding the thing defined[38]

The discussion of the difference between the "continuous" movement of the voice in speech and the intervallic steps of melody is faithfully rendered in Gogava's translation until a passage that is singled out by Meibom as put "stupidly and confusedly" (*inscite et confuse*). But these epithets are surely too severe, even if Gogava failed to realize that Aristoxenus was still speaking of the difference between melody and speech as well as of a third kind

35. Da Rios, p. 20, n.
36. Meibom, I, 87.
37. Gogava, p. 14.
38. Macran, p. 176.

of motion. Again a comparison of Gogava (above) and Meibom (below) is revealing:

Iamque ferè liquet à melo de industria confecto interuallo uocis motu differre musicum melos, ab incondito autem & erroneo pro compositionis differentia interuallorum simplicium.[39]	It is quite clear that musical melody differs from melody of practice made up of intervallic motion of the voice and from the disorderly and faulty melody with respect to the difference of composition of simple intervals.
Et certe utcunque patet, Musicum cantum ab illo, qui naturali aptitudine exercetur, distinctum esse eo, quod interuallo utatur & alio vocis motu: à non modulato verò rudiori; incompositorum interuallorum compositionis differentiā.[40]	And certainly it is clear how musical melody is distinct from that practiced through natural aptitude, for it makes use of interval and the other motion of the voice; and from that which is not modulated and is rougher, but is different in the composition of incomposite intervals.

Meibom does not make it altogether clear that the three types of pitch motion being compared are musical melody, the melody of speech, and unharmonious melody, and that the use of intervals distinguishes musical melody from speech, but that true melody differs from unharmoniously composed melody in the way that the incomposite intervals are placed. Gogava's "incondito autem & erroneo" comes closer to the intended sense than Meibom's "non modulato vero & rudiori," but Gogava leaves the pitch motion of speech out of the comparison.

These have been minor matters. It is important to determine if Gogava's translation was able to communicate the particular philosophy of music theory that Aristoxenus promulgated. A key section of the treatise from this standpoint is that in Book 2 in which he proclaims the principle that auditory experience and not numbers determine the laws of harmonics. Below is the kernel of that discussion:

quarum rerum demonstrationes dicere aggrediamur apparentibus confessas: non, ut qui nos praecessere, qui uel aliud agentes & sensum	We would undertake to present demonstrations of these matters that acknowledge appearances, not as those who preceded us, who either pursued something other than the

39. Gogava, p. 15.
40. Meibom, I, 18.29.

declinantes
tanquam minus exactum
intelligibiles tantum causas
astruxerunt, atque (aiunt) rationes quasdam esse numerorum &
celeritates erga se mutuo, in
quibus acumen grauitasque
consistat: omnium absurdissima
maximeque his,
quae apparent
contraria sententia, uel tanquam
oracula sine ratione aut de-
monstratione proferunt omnia: ac
ne ipsa quidem, quae apparent,
rectè enumerant. Nos uero tum
principia conemur accipere ea
tantum, quae experientibus in re
Musica uiris uisa sunt, tum ex
iis euenientia demonstrare. Est
autem nobis, ut in summa dicatur,
contemplatio de Melo omni musico
quod tam uoce quàm
instrumentis conficitur; ac
reducitur totum negotium ad duo,
ad auditum, scilicet & cogitationem
enim illo iudicamus interuallorum
magnitudines hac facultates eorum
contemplamur.[41]

[task at hand] and, rejecting
the sense as less accurate, built
up merely intellectual reasons, and
proposed some ratios of numbers and
velocities in relation to each other
in which height and lowness of pitch
might consist, which is the
most absurd of all their opinions
and most contrary to things
as they appear. Or they
proclaim everything as if oracles
without reason or demonstration, and
those things which are apparent they
do not even enumerate correctly. We,
however, strive to seize upon the
principles that are evident to men
experienced in musical matters
and then demonstrate
their consequences. It is for us,
if it may be stated generally,
to investigate all musical melody
produced by the voice as well as
instruments, and this entire task is
limited to two [faculties],
the hearing and reflection.
For with the first we judge the sizes
of intervals, with the second we
contemplate their functions.

Gogava expressed the argument forcefully, but the translation into Latin results in a loss of the concept of phenomena, which is rendered through active verb forms, such as "quae apparent," for which I have found English equivalents rather than reverting to the Greek-derived *phenomena*. The statement of principles is epistemologically less striking as a result, but there is no mistaking the preference acknowledged for sense perception as the primary source of knowledge concerning musical matters.

As professional musicians and cultivated amateurs became aware that ancient music theory promised solutions to problems that current theory did not solve or even face, demand arose for vernacular translations. For Zarlino it was sufficient to have Ptolemy and Aristoxenus translated into Latin, but for someone like Vincenzo Galilei, a lutanist who lacked the rigorous Latin training of the ecclesiastical schools, this language barred access to the ancient treatises as much as Greek. Writings originally in Latin,

41. Gogava, pp. 22–23 (Meibom, I, 32–33; Da Rios, 41.17–42.13).

such as the music treatise of Boethius, and those originally in Greek and now available in Latin translations, such as those by Valla, Valgulio, and Gogava, were natural candidates for translation into Italian.

Galilei's papers show that he may have attempted to translate Valgulio's Latin version of pseudo-Plutarch's *De musica* but that he eventually gave up and had someone more expert in classics do the job for him.[42] The Italian translation of Aristoxenus that survives among his papers is also probably not by Galilei himself.[43] It is utterly dependent on the Latin version of Gogava, showing no sign that a Greek text was consulted, even to remedy obviously faulty passages. The translator seems not to have been a musician, as he sometimes renders musical terms that he does not understand in a technically meaningless way, when the reference would have been obvious to a musician. For example, whereas usually he translates *incompositum* (incomposite) as "semplice," on one occasion it becomes "non elegante."[44] Another time he splits the name *penesuprema* (parhypate) into two words and separates them (fol. 14r): "Il luogo tonico adunque del Indice si sottomette, ma quasi alla minima suprema del Diesis" for Gogava's (p. 18) "Indicis ergo locus toniaeus subiicitur, at pene supremae diesios minimae" (da Rios 30.9). Instead of restoring such names as *parhypate,* which a musician would have done, the translator finds for Gogava's neologisms Italian equivalents such as "penesuprema." Indeed, Galilei in the margin often noted the normal names, such as *lichanos* for "Indice" (Gogava's "Index"). The translator's total dependence on Gogava is demonstrated not only by terminology and syntax but also by the lacunae and misreadings, which are retained in this translation. The following passage (Gogava left; Galilei, right) contains an easily remedied lacuna (the missing words are in brackets) that a musical theorist would have recognized:

Interuallorum uero id quod est	ma degl'interuallo certo si canta
Supremae & Penesupremae canitur	eguale et ineguale al istesso Pene-

---

42. Florence, Biblioteca Nazionale Centrale, MSS Galilei 7, fols. 19r–22v, containing a part of the Plutarch work in Italian, has the appearance of a draft, but on fol. 23r begins a fair copy by another hand of the entire treatise in Italian, with some marginal notes by Galilei. The second translation seems less dependent on Valgulio and may have been done by someone who consulted the Greek text.

43. Florence, Biblioteca Nazionale Centrale, MS Galilei 8, fols. 3r–38r. The treatise begins with the title "Il Primo libro d'Aristossene de gl'Elementi Harmonici" and the text incipit, "Essendo la scienza del canto in uarie parti, et in molte spetie diuisa," and continues with "Il secondo lib. d'Aristossene de gl'Elementi Harmonicj," fol. 18r; "Il Terzo Lib. de gl'Elem. Harmo:—d'Aristosseno," fol. 31r; and the explicit, "Ma che non interuenga che à piu modi ne le parti del Diatessaron si collochi, che quali noi hauiamo detto, è ageuol' cosa conoscerlo," fol. 38r. Thus the treatise is as complete as it is in the modern editions of Macran and da Rios.

44. On fol. 31v (da Rios 75.11): "Ma è interuallo non elegante" for Gogava's (p. 37) "Incompositum uero est interuallum."

aequale & inaequale ipsi Penesupremae & Indici, ac Penesupremae & Indicis [& Indicis] &
Mediae tam aequale quam inaequale ambobus. In causa est,
quod communes sunt Penesupremae
utrique generi.[45]

suprema et al Indice, ma a tutte e
due tanto eguale, quanto ineguale
della Penesuprema, e del Indice
[, e Indice] e della media:
l'importanza è perche
le penesupreme son communi
al'uno et laltro genere.

That is:

> Of the intervals that which is between the hypate and parhypate is sung equal
> and unequal to that between the same parhypate and the lichanos, that between
> the parhypate and the lichanos and that between the lichanos and the mese are
> both equal and unequal. The reason is that the parhypates are common to the
> two genres [chromatic and diatonic].

Here the intervals between pairs of notes are being compared. One of the
notes, the "Media" obviously needs a pair, which is the "Index," a scribal
omission resulting from the duplication of this word in the phrase. This is
not the kind of mistake Galilei would have been likely to make, though a
scribe copying his autograph might have done it.

The translation can be dated roughly from the watermarks on the copy
in the Galilei papers. The single watermark that runs throughout the codex
is similar to Zonghi numbers 1681, dated 1567, and 1679, dated 1573. The
translation probably belongs to the period in the early 1570's when Galilei
was deeply involved in research on Greek music, just before and during his
first contacts with Girolamo Mei, which began in 1572.[46]

Despite the awkward nomenclature and the compounding of Gogava's
errors and those of his text, the translation was serviceable and certainly
gave Galilei firsthand contact with the thought of the author of the *Harmonic
Elements*. The following sample from Book 2, the same passage translated
into English from Gogava above (p. 152), shows both the pitfalls and the
often surprising fidelity of this twice-removed version of Aristoxenus:

> . . . delle quali cose mettiamoci a dire le dimostrationi: confessate per quelle
> che appariscano, non come quelle che ci sono andati auanti i quali ò attendendo
> ad altro, o declinando il senso come imperfetto, affermorono solamente le
> cause, le quali si possano intendere, e dicano che sono certe ragioni di numeri,
> e le uelocità, scambieuolmente uerso di loro; nelle quali consiste l'acutezza, e
> la grauità. Prolungano tutte le cose più sconueneuoli che l'altre, et massime a
> q[uell]e che appariscano contrarie per parere, o come sentenze senza ragione ò
> dimostratione e quelle che appariscano non le numeran bene. Ma noi ci sfor-

---

45. Gogava, p. 19 (Meibom, I, 27); Galilei MS, fol. 15v.
46. The Plutarch translation in the same collection is written on paper whose watermarks
match those on letters by Giorgio Bartoli dated 1572 to 1574.

zeremo pigliar solamente quei principij iquali son pari a quelli huomini, iquali hanno fatto fatto [sic] proua nelle cose della Musica, et mostrar quelli, che acca[de]uano [the *de* is hidden in the binding] per quelli. Ma noi lasciamo (per dirla insomma) contemplarne d'ogni melodia Musicale, ilche tale si fà co la uoce quanto co gli istrumenti, e tutto il negotio si riduce a due al udito, et al pensiero massimamente, impero giudichiamo per quello le grandezze de gl'interualli e per questo contempliamo le facultà di quelli.[47]

The first sentence may be translated into English: "Of these matters let us begin by setting forth the demonstrations, confessed to be what they appear." This is quite far from Gogava's "demonstrationes . . . apparentibus confessas" (demonstrations . . . that acknowledge appearances) and even farther from Aristoxenus' sense, which is "demonstrations that are in accord with the phenomena."

Aristoxenus' rejection of the numerical ratios pierces the mist momentarily, but then we are befogged again by the sentence that begins "Prolungano," which may be translated: "They drag out the most inappropriate things and particularly those that appear contrary by opinion, or as statements without reason or demonstration, and those that appear they do not enumerate well." The sense of the passage is: "Their proclamations about all things are like oracles, without rational defense or demonstration, and they do not enumerate the phenomena correctly." The rest of the passage, though garbled, manages to convey the author's message to a reader who has not by then lost all patience.

This translation undoubtedly contributed to the frustration about Greek music theory that led Galilei to initiate the correspondence with Mei. He must have asked Mei's opinion concerning some obscure places in the Gogava translations, because in his long letter of 8 May 1572 Mei replies:

> In Ptolemy there are, truly, as you say, many obscure places, and when I say this I mean the Greek text, because about the Latin I would not know how to give any account, not having read it diligently nor at length. I am inclined to believe that part of the obscurity may arise from the incorrectness of the copy, for of eight written texts that I have gotten my hands on, five at least were so marred that it is a wonder, and perhaps one similar to these may have been the text of the translator.[48]

Later in the same letter he responded to a hint of Galilei that the Latin translation needed correction:

> Correcting the Latin text of Ptolemy, if there are places that require it, is not something in which I can oblige, because there is no time and it is a project

47. Book 2, fol. 19r (Gogava, p. 22   Meibom, I, 32).
48. Italian text in Palisca, *Girolamo Mei: Letters on Ancient and Modern Music to Vincenzo Galilei and Giovanni Bardi* (Stuttgart, 1977), p. 108.

for a young person or at least men who willingly busy themselves in everything to become known and to demonstrate their adequacy, and not for the likes of me, old and unhealthy and entirely devoid of such fancies and thoughts.[49]

The Aristoxenus translation in particular Mei appears not to have looked at, because he says: "Of Aristoxenus there are not found more than two books and a half or slightly more, which you say are translated."[50]

Despite the condition of the Gogava translations, Galilei became in many respects a confirmed Aristoxenian. He embraced the idea of separating musical practice from scientific investigation of ratios and velocities, and he adopted a pragmatic approach to tuning, eventually championing the equal division of the octave sponsored by Aristoxenus.

Bottrigari's Corrections

A much more critical and studious reader of Gogava's Aristoxenus in the sixteenth century was Ercole Bottrigari. Indeed, he claimed to have translated the *Harmonic Elements* into Italian, along with numerous other Greek and Latin musical treatises: those of Euclid (including Cleonides), Ptolemy, Alypius, Psellus, Gaudentius, and musical sections from Martianus Capella, Censorinus, Cassiodorus, and other Latin authors, and from the *Problems* of Aristotle. He makes this statement in a preface to his translation of the five books on music by Boethius dated 1597.[51] Further, a translation by Bottrigari of Aristotle, *De audibilibus,* survives.[52] There is, moreover, ample evidence of his penetration into Gogava's translations of Aristoxenus and Ptolemy in a copy that Bottrigari owned that is now in Bologna in the Civico Museo Bibliografico Musicale.[53]

Copious marginal and interlinear notes and calculations, pasted inserts,

49. Ibid., p. 109.
50. Ibid., p. 109.
51. See Gaspari, *Catalogo della Biblioteca musicale G. B. Martini di Bologna* (Bologna, 1890; repr. Bologna, 1961), I, 197–98. Of most of these there is no trace; some translations are found in his hand, but they are not attributable to him: a volume containing anonymous Latin translations of Gaudentius and Alypius, together with a Latin translation of Plutarch's *De musica* by Hermannus Cruserius, is also in Bologna, Civico Museo Bibliografico Musicale, MS B46, of which a copy is also in Bologna, Biblioteca Universitaria, MS 595, Busta 50, no. 9, both transcribed by Bottrigari between 1596 and 1598.
52. Bologna, Biblioteca Universitaria, MS lat. 326, no. 6: "Dell'oggetto dell'vdito overo delle cose udibili, Libbro Frammentato di Aristotile tradutto in Lingua Italiana Dal Molto Illustre Signore Cavaliere Hercole Bottrigari," dated 14 January 1606. It is preceded in the codex by Francesco Patrizi's Latin translation of the same work, on which Bottrigari's must have been based: "De iis, qvae sub auditv cadunt sive de audibilibvs Aristotelis libri Fragmentum Francisco Patricio Interprete."
53. MS A/1.

and underscoring testify to Bottrigari's close study of Gogava's translations. There are some corrections of the prose texts, certain words struck out and replaced by others, such as *complexio*—almost everywhere changed to "constitutio"—and *rationes* to "proportiones," but most of the corrections are applied to tables and diagrams, some of which are redrawn on added sheets, others corrected and supplemented. Bottrigari found less fault with the Aristoxenus translation than with the Ptolemy. For the most part his marginalia for the Aristoxenus consist of catchwords and summaries of the contents of the text, and the underscorings are those typical of a student flagging important passages. He notes many *loci paralleli* in Ptolemy and Cleonides (which he calls Euclid, *Isagoge*). He adds occasional musical examples, such as conjunct and disjunct tetrachords (p. 36) and string lengths (p. 32). He notes alternate terminology—"species" for Gogava's *figurae*, "rhythmus" for his *rhythmos* (p. 23).

In the Ptolemy, however, Bottrigari embarked on a thoroughgoing revision and eventually advertised his editorial role on Gogava's internal title page (p. 47). To Gogava's title, which reads: "CL. PTOLEMAEI *PELV-SIENSIS* / *Harmonicorum, siue de Musica libri tres,* / *nunc primum editi:* / Ant. Gogauino Grauiensi Interprete," Bottrigari added the following tag: "et nunc demum / summo studio, intensique labore, ac vigiliis / AB HERCULE BVTTRIGARIO EQU[ES]. S. L. R. RVR. / mendis innumerabilibus; quibus scatent, / et penitus ferè deformat circumferuntur, / expurgati ad legitimam formam / sunt restituti."

Here, perhaps partly in jest, he refers to his intense labor and wakeful nights spent expurgating the work of the many faults that deformed it and restoring it to its legitimate form. That the recast title page was not intended for publication is betrayed by the vulgar play with the syllables of the translator's name in the right margin: GO-GA-VINO.

Bottrigari's emendations and glosses are of several kinds. There are corrections to the Latin text, from individual words to entire sentences. These are not numerous and are certainly far fewer than Gogava's translation demands. For *magades* (movable bridges) on p. 64 he suggests "ponticuli hemisphaeri" and later on the same page for the same device "scabella circularia," but even these may have been intended as glosses rather than corrections. The lacuna in 2.5 (Gogava, p. 91), where Ptolemy describes the octave species, Bottrigari correctly fills: "Hinc secundam tertia disiunctarum, et penesuprema supremarum." In 2.11 (Gogava, p. 101) he changes all uses of "Tonus" for *tonos* to "modus." He correctly inserts "grauior" (line 18) before "Hypophrygius" to indicate low Hypophrygian, correctly emends *penemediam* to "penesupremam" (line 21), and corrects *concentus* to "intensus" (lines 23–24). In effect, Bottrigari identified and correctly emended the most essential textual errors in these two chapters

| Bottrigari (and Düring): | 60 | 76 | 78 | 80 | 90 | 114 | 117 | | 120 |
| Gogava | 60 | 74 | 77 | 80 | 90 | 114 | 117 1/2 | | 120 |

Figure 7.3:

Comparison of string lengths in Bottrigari and Gogava

in Ptolemy that we have been using to test the accuracy of the various translations.[54]

Numbers in both the text and translation are corrected; again Bottrigari did not spot every error, but he found a good many. Some of geometric diagrams are redrawn. The bulk of Bottrigari's contribution is in the revision of the tables of the shades of tuning in the three genera. For this purpose Bottrigari consulted a Greek source. In one place (p. 76) he writes in the margin: "Ex codice graeco tamen emendato sic" above a revised table. Under Gogava's text for 2.14 he writes a Latin translation of the remainder of this chapter as found in certain manuscripts.

Gogava's source must have ended at Düring 71.7; Bottrigari's goes on to 74.3, including all of the material Düring puts in small type and attributes to the fourteenth-century Byzantine Isaac Argyros, the editor of Vatican graecus 176.[55] Bottrigari, therefore, must have had at his disposal a manuscript deriving from this original. Only two copies of this manuscript survive, one in Nuremberg, the other in Paris. The text of the supplementary passage spells out the ratios for the various tunings, and even without an emended version Bottrigari would have been able to correct the tables once he had these ratios. Calculations scribbled on these pages show that Bottrigari checked all the string lengths by means of them. Thus for the enharmonic of Eratosthenes, for example, he gives the following string lengths, which are compared in Figure 7.3 with the values in Gogava. Not all of Bottrigari's values are equally correct, however, probably because he was content with approximations.

Bottrigari's work marks the application of a text-critical method to the task of arriving at a Latin version of the fundamental texts of Aristoxenus and Ptolemy. His object may have been to use the emended Latin of Gogava as the basis for a set of Italian translations. In Italy, at least, the vernacular had replaced Latin as the language of music theory, and if the ancient authors were to serve modern readers, they would have to be turned into the vernacular.

Two translations into Italian besides those in the Galilei manuscripts may

54. See above, p. 139.

55. Düring, *Die Harmonielehre*, p. LXVI: "Was die Redaktion des Argyros sofort von allen anderen Hss. der Harmonielehre unterscheidet, ist die vollständigen Ergänzung des Kap. II/14."

be connected with Bardi's circle. These are Lorenzo Giacomini's translation of pseudo-Aristotle's *Problems* and Giorgio Bartoli's translation of Boethius' *De institutione musica*. Giacomini left several unpublished translations from the Greek: an incomplete one of pseudo-Aristotle's *Oeconomica,* one of the Epistle to Philip, and one of the *Nicomachean Ethics.* Some of these are extant in copies made by Giorgio Bartoli, who served as Giacomini's amanuensis.[56] The translation of the *Problems,* also in the hand of Bartoli, probably dates from around 1582.[57] It was Bartoli who copied the letters to Galilei and Bardi from Girolamo Mei that survive in the Biblioteca Apostolica Vaticana, MS Regina latinus 2021. These cover the period from May 1572 to around September 1581. The emendations in Problem 48 (numbered 49 in the older sources) made by Mei in the translation he sent to Galilei around September 1581 are adopted by Giacomini.[58] Indeed, the translations are identical. Giacomini may have had Mei's assistance also on other points in the *Problems,* which abound with linguistic and technical difficulties. Giacomini's translation is done with scholarly acumen and sensitivity to what was known of Greek musical practice and would merit greater attention than can be given to it here.

Giorgio Bartoli's translation of Boethius is dated 17 March 1579 and survives in Bartoli's autograph.[59] It is on the whole an excellent translation, in fluent and proper Tuscan,[60] yet scrupulously faithful to the original. The choice of technical vocabulary is particularly cognizant of the nuances of Boethius' Latin and reveals a scholar who must have been trained in music theory. Bartoli's translation, were it published with suitable annotation, could benefit Italian-speaking readers today.

56. Florence, Biblioteca Riccardiana, MSS 1599 and 1612. See Bernard Weinberg, "Nuove attribuzioni di manoscritti di critica letteraria del cinquecento," *Rinascimento* 3 (1952):245–59. However, not all the writing in MS 1599 identified by Weinberg as in Bartoli's hand was copied by him, in my judgment.

57. Biblioteca Riccardiana, MS 1612, fols. 86r–100r. The single watermark that runs throughout this codex is identical to that in letters from Bartoli to Giacomini of 4 March and 23 September 1582 in Biblioteca Riccardiana, MS 2438.

58. See Palisca, *Girolamo Mei,* pp. 178–79 and (2d ed.), Appendix, p. 207. The copy of selected letters by Mei in the Regina manuscript may have been made for Giacomini, who is known to have owned at least one letter of Mei. See ibid., p. 208.

59. Florence, Biblioteca Nazionale Centrale, MS Magl. XIX.75. On fol. 1r appears in Bartoli's hand the title: "De la musica di Boethio libro primo." The translation ends on fol. 156v with Book V, chapter 18, and the annotation "Finito à di 17 di Marzo 1579."

60. Bartoli is best known for his treatise *Degli elementi del parlar toscano* (Florence: Ne le case de' Giunti, 1584).

EIGHT

Harmonies and Disharmonies of the Spheres

armonia est discordia concors. So is inscribed the scroll placed beside the figure of the author in the illuminated manuscripts of Gaffurio's *De harmonia,* as he sits in his cathedra lecturing to the students at his feet (see Figure 8.1).[1] At his right are three organ pipes, measuring three, four, and six lengths, on the left three strings with the same measurements, and beside them a pair of dividers. Thus the octave is divided through the harmonic mean with the fifth below and the fourth above. Also on his desk is an hour glass, perhaps to remind this preceptor that if he does not keep an eye on it, however important his message, the bright looks on his pupils' faces will soon fade.

"Harmony is concord [wrought] out of discord"—a fitting motto for Gaffurio's book, indeed for his time. Harmony in practical terms was a union created out of diversity—of voices, of pitches, of rhythms, of tempos, of instruments. But harmony was also thought to prevail in the universe, between man and universe, among the faculties of the human soul, among the parts of the body, and between the body and soul. The scroll says nothing about music, because Gaffurio's timely lesson is that harmony is universal, and audible music is only one of its manifestations.

Is this something Gaffurio believed, or is it, like so much of the treatise, ancient erudition addressed to Greekless musicians? Is the harmony of the universe and man a nice allegory, or is it a doctrine that underlies an aesthetic position? Is universal and human harmony relevant to musical practice and creativity in the early Renaissance? The answers to these questions are by no means easily arrived at.

The tradition of musica mundana and humana goes back to the ancient Pythagoreans and to Plato. Partly rejected by Aristotle, it was revived by

---

1. The same figure occurs as a vignette on the title page of the printed edition of 1518.

Figure 8.1.
The first page of text of Gaffurio's *De harmonia musicorum instrumentorum opus,* in the manuscript Vienna, Österreichische Nationalbibliothek, MS Ser. nov. 12745, fol. 4r. Gaffurio is shown in a *cathedra* lecturing to his disciples: "Harmony is concord [wrought] out of discord." In the border is inscribed "Franchino Gaffurio of Lodi carefully wrote three books concerning music: the theory, the practice, and the harmony of instruments." Courtesy of Bild-Archiv der Österreichischen Nationalbibliothek, Vienna.

Cicero and his commentators, by Nicomachus and Boethius, and elaborated by a number of medieval authors.[2]

Boethius presented two contrasting versions of the cosmic harmony. One was based on Nicomachus, and is in the image of a lyre in which hypate meson is Saturn, parhypate meson Jupiter, lichanos meson Mars, mese the sun, trite synemmenon Venus, paranete synemmenon Mercury, and nete synemmenon the moon.[3] Boethius' other version is that of Cicero as revealed in Scipio's dream, to which we may go for the classic account of the celestial order:

> "What is this large and agreeable sound that fills my ears?" "That is produced," he replied, "by the onward rush and motion of the spheres themselves; the intervals between them, though unequal, being exactly arranged in a fixed proportion; by an agreeable blending of high and low tones various harmonies are produced; for such mighty motions cannot be carried on so swiftly in silence; and Nature has provided that one extreme shall produce low tones while the other gives forth high. Therefore this uppermost sphere of heaven, which bears the stars, as it revolves more rapidly, produces a high, shrill tone, whereas the lowest revolving sphere, that of the moon, gives forth the lowest tone; for the earthly sphere, the ninth, remains ever motionless and stationary in its position in the centre of the universe. But the other eight spheres, two of which move with the same velocity, produce seven different sounds—a number which is the key of almost everything."[4]

Ugolino of Orvieto

As with every other sphere of thought, ideas about cosmic and human harmony were transformed by humanism. This process will be evident if we consider the status of the concept at the beginning of the fifteenth century. The ancient idea of world harmony was permeated at this time with Christian mysticism and beatitude. Ugolino of Orvieto (c. 1380–1457) provides a sample in his *Declaratio musicae disciplinae,* probably completed in Ferrara between 1430 and 1435.[5] Instead of being itself the font of all harmony, musica mundana is seen as an offshoot of a higher harmony, the

2. See the concise survey in Giuseppe Massera, *Severino Boezio e la scienza armonica tra l'antichità e il medio evo* (Parma, 1976), pp. 27–50. For a detailed history, see James Haar, *"Musica mundana:* Variations on a Pythagorean Theme," (Ph.D. diss., Harvard University, 1960).

3. Boethius *De institutione musica* 1.27; Nicomachus *Manual of Harmony* 3. The text of Nicomachus may be faulty, because Mercury is placed between Venus and the sun instead of between Venus and the moon.

4. Cicero *De Re Publica* 6.8, trans. Clinton Walker Keyes.

5. Albert Seay, "Ugolino of Orvieto," in *New Grove Dictionary,* XIX, 320.

ineffably sweet song of the celestial hierarchy of angels proclaiming without end, "Sanctus, Sanctus, Sanctus." This, says Ugolino, is the beginning and origin of all cosmic, human, and instrumental music; from it flows the proportion of all melodies, the conjunction of all consonances, the concord of all notes, the smooth and uniform mixture of all grave and acute sounds, that agreeable union (*coaptatio*) in which there is no discord or asperity, no break in smoothness, no disproportion or awkward distance. All this harmony, moreover, imitates the celestial music that exists to praise the creator.[6] Human music harmonizes the parts of the soul, the sense's capacity to feel with the intellect's to perceive, and bridges the infinite gulf between the material and mortal body and the immaterial and immortal soul. It also permits the elements and parts of the body to be harmonized within itself.

Giorgio Anselmi

Giorgio Anselmi (before 1386–c.1440–43) is much more concrete in spiritualizing the music of the spheres in a treatise of 1434, consisting of three dialogues: on *harmonia celestis, harmonia instrumentalis,* and *harmonia cantabilis*. Aside from the apparent originality of his approach, Anselmi's treatment of the topic is important because of Gaffurio's absorption of parts of his doctrine in his early works. Those spirits that Socrates in Plato's *Republic* (10.617b) called sirens are regarded by "our theologians"[7] as angels ranged in nine orders. Anselmi seems to invoke here a system of concentric spheres, or orbs, for he uses the terms *sphera* and *orbus* as well as *ordines*. His naming of Socrates recalls the myth of Er, related by Socrates in the tenth book of the *Republic*. Here Necessity, helped by the three Fates—Lachesis, Clotho, and Atropos—turns the cosmic spindle around which whirl the planets and stars, each in its own rim. Each rim holds a siren, who sings her particular note. The earth is imagined to be in the center, and the whirling mass around it a cylinder. In place of the sirens, Anselmi has assigned to each sphere angels of various ranks, who sing forth not from rims but spheres, in keeping with the geocentric universe of concentric globes that was then the accepted view. An outer sphere, or shell, of stars contained the spheres of the planets, the sun, the moon, and, at the center, the earth.

On the innermost sphere, the earth, Anselmi places the Angels who proclaim to humanity the divine will. In the second or lunar orb are the special messengers, the Archangels; in the third, that of Mercury, are the

---

6. Ugolino of Orvieto, *Declaratio musicae disciplinae,* ed. Albert Seay, I, 1, pp. 15–16.

7. Giorgio Anselmi, *De musica,* ed. Giuseppe Massera (Florence, 1961), p. 103. Anselmi does not say who these "theologians" were, and his modern editor has not supplied the information. However, see n. 9 below.

angels called the Virtues, through whom God reveals great miracles and portents; on the fourth, that of Venus, are the Powers (*Potestates*), who restrain the malignant spirits that threaten man and are capable of injuring him. The fifth, the sphere of the sun, holds the Principalities (*Principatus*), who serve God in governing his kingdom. The sixth, of Mars, hosts the Dominations (*Dominationes*), the army of militant angels, defenders of the righteous and opponents of the unjust on earth. The seventh is the order of the Thrones (*Throni*), who have their seat in the orb of Jove, and whose function is to transmit the decrees and laws of God. The eighth order, the Cherubim, reside in the sphere of Saturn, and, because of their proximity to the Supreme Wisdom, interpret it for the masses. The ninth host of angels are in the sphere of Uranus; they, the Seraphim, excel all others in wisdom, authority, and happiness and participate most intensely in the divine flame and love of God.

Gaffurio repeated this exposition of the angel hosts almost verbatim in his *Theorica musice*,[8] citing Anselmi and probably not realizing there was a venerable tradition behind him.[9] In the introduction to his edition of Anselmi, Massera shows that Gaffurio cannot have come into possession of Anselmi's treatise before 1484; in fact the citations of Anselmi are not found in the 1480 *Theoricum opus,* only in the *Theorica musice* of 1492 and later works. The passages taken from Anselmi are among the insertions made in the 1480 text. In his edition of Anselmi, Massera has identified Gaffurio's borrowings in notes to the text.

Anselmi was not content to leave the concept of cosmic harmony in the mystic realm. He sought to explain how the diversity of motions could produce a music sweet and satisfying to the ear. There was, after all, a

---

8. Gaffurio, *Theorica musice,* I, 1, fol. a4r–v.

9. Anselmi, *De musica,* pp. 103–06. The hierarchy of the angels that Anselmi describes goes back to an ancient tradition; in a Jewish-Christian document transmitted in Arabic and Ethiopian, the *Adam Apocalypse,* it is stated that the first day God created heaven and earth, water, air, and fire, and the angels—namely the Thrones, Dominations, Principalities, Powers, Cherubim, and Seraphim; on the second day he created the lower heaven, called the firmament. See Kathi Meyer-Baer, *Music of the Spheres and the Dance of Death* (Princeton, 1970), pp. 23–26. The Greek tract *The Celestial Hierarchy,* attributed to the first-century church father Dionysius the Areopagite, but actually a fifth- or sixth-century forgery—a fact not known to the Renaissance—divided the nine angel hosts into three groups of three each: the Counsellors—Seraphim, Cherubim, and Thrones; the Rulers—Dominations, Virtues, and Powers; and the Servants—Principalities, Archangels, and Angels. The work was known in the Middle Ages in the Latin translations of John Scotus Erigena (c.810–880) and Robert Grosseteste (c.1168–1253) and through commentaries by Jean Gerson. See Meyer-Baer, *Music of the Spheres,* p. 38. Also see L. D. Reynolds and N. G. Wilson, *Scribes and Scholars, A Guide to the Transmission of Greek & Latin Literature,* 2d ed. (Oxford, 1974), p. 105; and Jacques Handschin, "Ein mittelalterlichen Beitrag zur Lehre von Sphärenharmonie," *Zeitschrift für Musikwissenschaft* 9 (1927):193–208.

harmony in the sounds produced by the several kinds of motion. The diurnal
motion, by which one assumes Anselmi meant the rotation of the outer
sphere of fixed stars around the earth in twenty-four hours, emits a very
high pitch, while, consonant with it, the self-moved sphere (the empyreum
of Aristotle's prime mover?) produces a very low sound. In between, the
seven errant spheres, in which the planets, sun, and moon move independently and in complex patterns against the stars, make sounds of intermediate pitch. The epicycles produce semitones. Here Anselmi seems to
refer to the Ptolemaic model in which a planet revolved in a small circle
the center of which was on the sphere of that planet. As these epicycles run
through the stars the collisions produce dieses and commas. The movement
of the heavens gives rise to three genera of music: diatonic, chromatic, and
enharmonic. The revolution of the spheres themselves, that is their velocities, produce diatonic sounds. Between Saturn and Jupiter there is a diapason-plus-diapente, for, whereas the former takes nearly thirty years to
make its circuit, Jupiter takes approximately twelve. (The ratio 30:12, or
5:2, fits the octave-plus-fifth, 3:1, only approximately.) Jupiter to Mars is
a double diapason; between Mars and the sun, the sun and Venus, and
Venus and Mercury are a diapason-plus-diapente. (The period, in each case,
which Anselmi does not mention, is considered to be one year. The ratio
1:1, however, does not yield an octave-plus-fifth.)[10]

Anselmi is torn between the Christian model of angels perched on their
spheres singing "Sanctus" and the traditional explanation of spheres emit-
ting musical sounds because of their rapid movement. He adds to these a
third source of music, the collisions, or rubbing, of planets in their epicycles
against the fixed stars. There is no rigor, of course, in all this, as Gaffurio
must have realized, for he selected carefully what he borrowed from Anselmi.

Franchino Gaffurio

Unlike Anselmi, Gaffurio does not project an unadulterated Christian vision
of celestial harmony. Anselmi's description of the angelic choirs summarized
above is inserted into a discussion of various myths about music in the
opening chapter of *Theorica musice,* which is a vastly expanded *laus musicae*
drawn from the parallel chapter of *Theoricum opus.* Musica mundana proper
is discussed in the second chapter, but Gaffurio does not lose sight of
Anselmi's sweeping view of celestial harmony, for he inserts several more
passages from his treatise in the midst of classical sources to remind us that
one should subordinate the classical writers to Christian theology. At least

10. See Simeon K. Heninger, Jr., *Touches of Sweet Harmony: Pythagorean Cosmology and
Renaissance Poetics* (San Marino, California, 1974), p. 123.

1480 ed Lines	1492 ed. Lines	Source
1–9	1–7	Gaffurio
——	7–13	Anselmi 100.148
9–16	13–17	Boethius 1.2.187.26–29
16–17	18	Aristotle *De coelo* 2
18–26	19–23	Boethius 1.2.187.29–188.6
——	23–32	Anselmi 101.149–150
26–35	35–37	Cicero *Somnium Scipionis* 5.1
——	38–50	Anselmi 97.134–98.138; Ambrose *Exameron* 2
——	50–51	Gaffurio
35–55	51–64	Boethius 1.2.188.7–25
56–71	64–73	Macrobius, *Somnium* 2.3.12–15
71–79	73–78	Censorinus 13.2
79–99	78–90	Censorinus 13; Pliny *Hist. nat.* 2.22
——	90–92	Gaffurio
——	92–94	Anselmi 102.153
99–102	94–96	
——	96–97	Stravo *Geographia* 10
102–11	97–103	Censorinus 13.5

Figure 8.2:
Sources for Book I, chapter 2

that seems to be the message, but, given Gaffurio's patchwork method, one is never sure. The borrowings in the chapter are shown in Figure 8.2, which also displays a concordance between the *Theoricum opus,* 1480, and *Theorica musice,* 1492.

Despite the disparity of sources and the Christian-pagan synthesis, Gaffurio manages to project a coherent defense of the theory of cosmic music. He begins by relating that the Pythagoreans believe that the world is in constant motion and that the various celestial bodies and elements are mixed in such a way that their revolutions and collisions produce sounds and consonances. The supreme maker would not have perfected such a splendid machine only to leave it immobile and uselessly silent (Anselmi). Therefore philosophers believe that as the heavens turn, the troops of celestial spirits and human souls that have withdrawn to that region sing harmonic chants in admiration of his work (Anselmi). How could such a swift massive machine, in which the orbits of the stars are coordinated so perfectly, move silently and without harmony? (Boethius). Yet Aristotle denied that the spheres made any sound. God governs the heavens not casually but with order, so that the soul of the world is joined to bodies by means of proportions, such as sesquialtera, sesquitertia, and sesquioctava (Anselmi). A harmony similarly unites the opposing forces of the four elements and the four seasons of the year (Boethius). Thus, according to Macrobius,[11] a certain number of *stadia,* or stades (a measurement based on the length of the Italian stadium, 625 Roman feet), separate the earth from the moon, the moon from Mercury, Mercury from Venus, Venus from the sun, the sun from Mars, Mars from Jupiter, Jupiter from Saturn, and Saturn from the sphere of the stars, and these distances are related as simple ratios. Pythagoras measured the distance from the moon to Mercury as a major semitone,[12] from earth to the moon as a tone, from Mercury to Venus a minor semitone, Venus to the sun a tone-plus-minor-semitone, from the sun to the earth a diapente, from the sun to Mars a tone, from Mars to Jupiter a minor semitone, from Jupiter to Saturn a major semitone, from there to the summit of the sky, the zodiac, a minor semitone,[13] and from the top of the sky to the sun a diatessaron. Thus, from the earth to the summit of the sky is five tones and two minor semitones, or a diapason. In this way Plato, and before him the Pythagoreans, concluded that the entire universe is made up of musical ratios and comprises a harmony. And Dorilaus said for this reason that the universe is the organ of God, on which he plays melodies that, because of the magnitude of the sounds and the limitations of our ears, are inaudible to us.[14]

In his last work, *De harmonia,* Gaffurio leaves behind the Christian overlay and adopts a Neoplatonic cosmology. The major sources for this revised view are Ficino's translation of Plato's *Timaeus,* Ficino's *Compendium in Timaeum,* and the Latin translation of Aristides Quintilianus. Gaffurio had purchased a copy of the *Opera* of Plato in the translation of Ficino already in 1489. This contained the *Timaeus,* including Ficino's introductory *Compendium,* the *Critias,* the *Laws,* the *Epinomis,* and the letters.[15]

---

11. *Somnium* 2.3.13; see also Censorinus *De die natali* 13.

12. Gaffurio's passage concerning the interval distances between the spheres is copied verbatim from Censorinus, except that Gaffurio has qualified the value of the semitones by "major" or "minor." The eventual source of the theory is Pliny *Natural History* 2.30, who also does not specify the size of the semitone.

13. Pliny *Natural History* 2.30 has *sescuplum,* a tone and a half.

14. Gaffurio, *Theorica* I, 2; Macrobius *Somnium* 2.4.14; Censorinus *De die natali* 13.1.

15. Otto Kinkeldey, "Franchino Gafori and Marsilio Ficino," *Harvard Library Bulletin,* 1 (1947):379–82. Below the colophon, which gives no date of publication, Gaffurio wrote: "Franchini Gaffori musicis professoris est hic liber / die vi maii 1489 emptus." The first edition of the *Opera* was by Laurentius de Alopa, Florence, 1484–85. Gaffurio must have owned the complete Plato, as among the books he donated to the Incoronata of Lodi was "Opera Platonis duplicat. in duobus voluminibus," according to Emilio Motta, "I libri della chiesa dell'Incoronata di Lodi nel 1518," *Il libro e la stampa* 1 (1907):105–12. At the time Kinkeldey saw the volume it was in the Houghton Library of Harvard University, on loan from its owner. It is no longer there, and the library does not know its whereabouts.

Ficino, by making the *Timaeus* accessible through his translation and commentary, gave the speculation about cosmic harmony a fresh and fruitful new direction. Cosmic harmony ceased to be a representation of the world in eternal balance; it became a play of forces that had moral consequences, that could influence and be influenced by men and demons. This was made possible by Plato's notion of a world soul that was in a number of ways analogous to the planetary system. Through the world soul the individual human soul could aspire to participate in cosmic harmony and absolute virtue.

Ficino asks why Plato made the soul a musical consonance. Although Plato had in mind the soul of the universe, Ficino applies this by analogy to the human soul:

> Musical consonance occurs in the element which is the mean of all [i.e., air], and reaches the ears through motion, spherical motion: so that it is not surprising that it should be fitting to the soul, which is both the mean of things, and the origin of circular motion. In addition, musical sound, more than anything else perceived by the senses, conveys, as if animated, the emotions and thoughts of the singer's or player's soul to the listeners' souls; thus it preeminently corresponds with the soul. Moreover, as regards sight, although visual impressions are in a way pure, yet they lack the effectiveness of motion, and are usually perceived only as an image, without reality; normally therefore, they move the soul only slightly. Smell, taste, and touch are entirely material, and rather titillate the sense organs than penetrate the depths of the soul. But musical sound by the movement of the air moves the body: by purified air it excites the aerial spirit which is the bond of body and soul: by emotion it affects the senses and at the same time the soul: by meaning it works on the mind; finally, by the very movement of the subtle air it penetrates strongly: by its contemperation it flows smoothly: by the conformity of its quality it floods us with a wonderful pleasure: by its nature, both spiritual and material, it at once seizes, and claims as its own, man in his entirety.[16]

Ficino had previously commented on the passage (32b) in which Plato explained that the four elements of the body of the universe were fire, air, water, and earth, and that the extremes—fire and earth—had two means; as in a geometrical proportion, fire is to air as air is to water, and air to water, and water to earth.[17] Now Ficino addresses himself to one of these means between earth and fire, namely air. It is through this medium that musical sounds reach the ears, and through them the aerial spirit that is the bond between the soul and the body. This gives music a more direct route to the feelings than, say, savors or touch. At the same time music is a link

---

16. Ficino, *Commentaria in Timaeum*, ch. 29, in *Opera omnia*, p. 1453, trans. in D. P. Walker, *Spiritual and Demonic Magic from Ficino to Campanella* (London, 1958), pp. 8–9.

17. *Commentaria*, ch. 23.

beween a higher order of things and the human soul. The soul and the
"celestial kithara" both vibrate to the same ratios. Just as a celestial melody
is made of high and low pitch, and the atmosphere is composed of gravity
and lightness, cold and heat, and humidity and dryness, so in human minds
there are united gentleness and magnanimity, temperance and fortitude.
Also, out of the two there can be a union, as of low and high voices. But
here, it must be said, Ficino seems to introduce a concept of simultaneous
consonance foreign to Plato's thought. The soul is able to judge and appreciate harmony because it is caused by a harmony that is higher than
itself. "Our soul contains all the same proportions as the soul of the world.
None of these ratios is mathematical; rather, they have a natural force. They
are not to be thought of as solely mathematical ratios but as machinating
and generating."[18]

Ficino's thought and the *Timaeus* itself are reflected in Gaffurio's treatment
of cosmic harmony. One important component of ancient cosmology restored by Gaffurio is the role given to the Muses in planetary and earthly
harmony. We shall see that Gaffurio quoted from Ficino's translation of the
Timaeus the passage in which music, both harmony and rhythm, is said to
have been given to intelligent men by the Muses to harmonize the inner
discord in the revolutions of their souls.[19] In *De harmonia* the Muses take
over from the angel choirs the role of producers and controllers of the
cosmic music. This idea is not derived from Plato, who in recounting the
myth of Er in the *Republic* assigned to individual sirens the singing of the
tones of the musical scale, each on her proper sphere as she rotated around
the spindle of Necessity. There were nine sirens, as there are Muses. Gaffurio, after reporting numerous theories about the Muses, drawn from a
variety of authors, settles for the belief that the Muses are associated with
particular spheres, modes, and degrees of the scale.

Ad haec Nos musas ipsas Astris modulisque (quod Plerique consentiunt) ita conuenire putamus; ut	We think that to these Muses certain stars and modes are fitting (and about this many agree), so that we

---

18. Ficino *Commmentaria*, ch. 29, p. 1453: "Constat enim anima nostra ex omnibus pro-
portionibus quibus anima mundi. Qua quidem sicut nec in illa, ita nec in nostra rationes
quaedam mathematicae sunt, sed potius naturales uim habentes, ad proportiones mathematicas
non iudicandas solum, sed machinandas etiam atque generandas." In the edition possessed by
Gaffurio the commentary was probably entitled "Compendium in Timaeum," as it is in the
Opera of Plato (Basel, 1561), where it is reprinted as a preface to Ianus Carnarius' Latin
translation. In the *Opera* of Ficino (Basel, 1576), reprinted by Bottega d'Erasmo, Turin, 1959,
it is printed under the rubric of "Commentaria." In fact, it is neither a compendium nor a
commentary but an introduction. Its contents only partly parallel those of the *Timaeus*, and
Ficino introduces ideas quite foreign to Plato.

19. *Theorica*, I, 1, fol. a5r; Plato *Timaeus* 46d. See ch. 9 below.

eas solis chordis ipsis: quibus modulorum exordia conferuntur ascribiamus: singula singulis conferendo.[20]	shall assign particular notes [of the scale] on which modes begin to each of them.

With this remark Gaffurio introduces the famous figure in which a triple-headed dog, Cerberus, wagging a serpent's tail, is stretched over the strings of the octave canon (see Figure 8.3).[21] Gaffurio failed to name his sources for the analogies in the figure, James Haar believes, because his main source is a modern one, the music theorist Bartolomé Ramos de Pareja, with whom Gaffurio had had a disagreement. Gaffurio had borrowed a copy of Ramos' *Musica practica* from Giovanni Spataro, returning it to him full of marginal annotations,[22] much to Spataro's disgust. Ramos does have a figure that parallels Gaffurio's in the pairing of Muses, planets, scale-degree names, and modes.[23] Ramos, in addition, has circles delimiting the eight modal octaves, and for this reason, at least, encompasses two octaves in his diagram. Ramos adds a note below proslambanomenos, which he calls *Coruph*, and a note above nete hyperbolaeon, called *Crisis*. He also labels the scale degrees of the double octave Gamma to a, another feature missing in Gaffurio. Ramos' figure, though, lacks the pictorial representations and any mention of Apollo, the three Graces, Cerberus, or the three elements. Thus Gaffurio's figure appears to be at once an expurgation and embellishment of that of Ramos.

Gaffurio devised his figure before he knew the work of Aristides Quintilianus, so it is not surprising that the correspondences of Muses and modes do not agree with those of this ancient author.[24] The figure, indeed, was published as the frontispiece of *Practica musice* in 1496 without commentary. The sources that Ramos admits he used and which in fact yield the correspondences in the figure were Macrobius' commentary on Cicero's *Dream of Scipio* and Martianus Capella's *De nuptiis,* both of which were known to

---

20. *De harmonia,* V, 12, fol. 93v. In the translation below, *chorda* is rendered "note" rather than the usual "string," because in this context a *chorda* is a step of a theoretical gamut, not a string of a polychordal instrument.

21. There have been several exhaustive commentaries on this figure and its sources. They are listed in James Haar, "The Frontispiece of Gafori's *Practica musicae* (1496)," *Renaissance Quarterly* 27 (1974):7–22, which is the best of these studies.

22. These are given in footnotes to the edition by Johannes Wolf in Publikationen der internationalen Musikgesellschaft, II (Leipzig, 1901).

23. See Haar, "The Frontispiece," p. 19; Wolf ed., p. 61.

24. Gaffurio is forced to admit this at the end of his verbal description of the diagram: "Aristides autem quintilianus in calcae secundi musicae suae: quasi quodammodo huic contrariam musarum & modulorum conuenientiam pernotauit" (Aristides Quintilianus at the end of the second [book] of his Musica presented a correspondence of Muses to modes quite contrary to this).

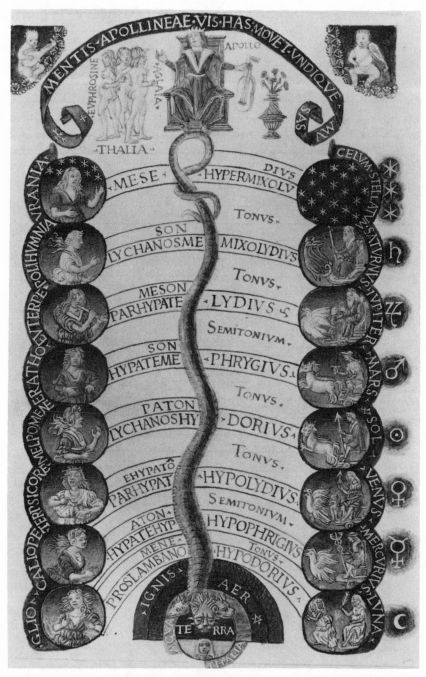

Figure 8.3.
The harmonious union of the Muses, strings, modes, and planets, in Vienna,
Österreichische Nationalbibliothek, MS Ser. nov. 12745, fol. 64v.
Courtesy of Bild-Archiv der Österreichischen Nationalbibliothek, Vienna.

Gaffurio. The correspondence in the figure between scale degrees and planets is also reported by Boethius,[25] who ascribed it to Cicero, but he reports it as an alternate system to the one (that of Nicomachus) he seems to prefer. But these were not sources Gaffurio much favored, once he had access to Bryennius, Aristides, and Ptolemy.

In terms of the development of Gaffurio as a humanist, then, the figure marks an early stage; yet it is interesting to dwell upon it. The figure obviously represents the agreement of cosmic and instrumental harmony. As such it is highly appropriate as a frontispiece or illustration for *De harmonia,* and it is not altogether inappropriate for the *Practica,* though certainly less relevant. It is significant that the hierarchies of angels are not anywhere represented; here is a thoroughly pagan and classically inspired system. The use of the Hypermixolydian as the highest mode, which has puzzled some commentators, is consistent with this, as it follows a Hellenistic tradition, supported by Boethius and Bryennius. The placement of the Hypodorian on proslambanomenos, with the other modes following on the succeeding steps, is also consistent with Boethius; any resemblance to the plainchant modes is incidental.

The general layout of the figure has the appearance of a highly embellished monochord, or *chordotonus* as Gaffurio called it, whereas the version in Ramos has a more characteristic monochord design. On the musical monochord has been superimposed, as it were, the monochord of the cosmos, with medallions doubling as spheres, showing in the manner of the emblematic artwork of the time the attributes of the Muses and of the several gods and goddesses after whom the planets are named. The signs of the zodiac are also given, as is usual when the planetary system is represented. Apollo, as Musagetes, or leader of the Muses, is at the top of the diagram, holding an instrument that is a cross between a lira da braccio and a lute.

The function of the very prominent serpent has never been adequately explained. Meyer-Baer suggested that it shows the "Pythicos" side of Apollo, that of vanquisher of the serpent, on which he plants his feet. But Gaffurio identifies the serpent as Cerberus, a three-headed dog with hair of snakes that watches over the entrance to the lower world. Musically the hybrid animal functions as the string of the monochord. Apollo serves as a yoke for the string, the yoke, in turn, supported by the scroll, in the manner of ancient kitharas. The representation of the harmony of the four elements at the bottom completes the cosmic picture. Thalia is placed below the earth, because, according to Martianus Capella, after the eight spheres were assigned to eight of the Muses, one Muse was left, and she was assigned to Earth; Thalia was the appropriate choice, since she was the Muse of

25. *De institutione musica* 1.27.

agriculture, plant growth, and seed. The Graces (*Charites*), one of whom is Thalia, dancing at Apollo's right, associated with Apollo in Macrobius' *Saturnalia,* are not integrated in any clear way into the cosmic scheme. Gaffurio may have confused them with the three Fates who in the myth of Er help turn the spindle of Necessity around which the spheres revolve.

The figure comes at the end of a group of twelve chapters on the ancient modes in which Gaffurio drew on sources he worked upon in the early 1490's. It may have capped the end of an earlier version of Book IV, a version finished as early as 1496, since the *De harmonia* is repeatedly mentioned in the *Practica,* several times each in three of the four books,[26] suggesting that much of it was by then already drafted. Thus the figure of the serpent monochord may have been designed for *De harmonia.* The figure marks a dividing point in Book IV; after it Gaffurio exploits two sources available to him only in the late 1490's, namely Aristides and Ptolemy.

These two authors, as we saw in my first chapter, offer Gaffurio the means to expand the conception of cosmic harmony beyond the planetary and the one to one correspondences with music characteristic of the earlier chapters. Music or consonance controls the periodicity of the moon, the seasons, of births and fevers. It mediates between public bodies and between individual people to make possible civic peace and well-being and friendship. Thus the fifteen notes of the double-octave system correspond to the fifteen days of the waxing of the moon.[27] In the perfect, unmodulating system the hypaton tetrachord corresponds to earth, the meson to water, the synemmenon to air, the diezeugmenon to fire, and the hyperbolaeon to the summit of the sky.[28] The elements in turn are ascribed to certain seasons of the year and to numbers that form consonant ratios: spring and air to the number 8 (mild), summer and fire to 4 (hot), autumn and earth to 6 (dry), and winter and water to 12 (wet).[29]

These final chapters demonstrate a fascination with the ramifications of cosmic harmony, if not a well-digested reading of Aristides and Ptolemy. Indeed, Gaffurio barely scratched the surface. To be sure, the theorizing of these authors is rarely transparent, and in the translations of Burana and Leoniceno, it was positively opaque. The temptation to regard these chapters as a vain display of erudition is strong. Yet a genuine enthusiasm breaks through Gaffurio's feverish copying. He is carried away by the ideas he transmits. The depth of conviction is tempered at times by such feeble

26. *Practica,* I, 2; I, 4; I, 6; I, 7; II, 1; III, 1; III, 3; III, 13; III, 15; IV, 1; IV, 5.

27. Gaffurio, *De harmonia,* IV, 19; Aristides Quintilianus *De musica* 3.13.

28. Gaffurio, *De harmonia,* IV, 19; Aristides Quintilianus *De musica* 3.14, Burana trans., fol. 31r.

29. Gaffurio, *De harmonia* IV, 19; Aristides Quintilianus *De musica* 3.19; Burana trans., fol. 32v.

avowals as: "We do not consider it incongruous to agree with the Pythagoreans and Plato," concerning the existence, that is, of discrete pitches in the cosmic music.[30] Usually the doctrines presented are attributed to an authority by such phrases as "posuit Aristides" (Aristides laid down),[31] "Plato in Timaeum docuit" (Plato taught in the *Timaeus*),[32] "diuidunt animam nostram Philosophi" (Philosophers partition our soul).[33] In these virtual disclaimers, Gaffurio defensively puts a distance between himself and the authorities, as he coolly reports their opinions without committing himself.

Yet what Gaffurio wants to believe he shows as much by what he fails to quote as by his citations. For example, he draws one sentence of Themistius' paraphrase of Aristotle's *De anima* (407b), which introduces the idea that the artist can create harmony out of wood and stone.[34] "When we receive something in sounds that is aptly and suitably put together, if it is intermingled and suitably in agreement with us, we take delight in it, recognizing it to be constructed in similitude with ourselves."[35] But the point of the passage in both Aristotle and Themistius—not evident in Gaffurio's selective quotation—is that the soul cannot be a harmony. Aristotle's and Themistius' arguments against the proposition are ignored. Gaffurio wants to believe and to persuade the reader to believe in the harmony of the soul.

In his treatment of musica humana likewise Gaffurio progressed from the 1480 version and the sources known to his predecessors—Boethius, Macrobius, and Censorinus— through the 1492 version, with its inclusion of Themistius, to an attachment to Aristides and Ptolemy, and a greater penetration of Plato through Ficino's translation and commentary in the *De harmonia*. The idea that the immortal soul is united to the body and the elements of the body are joined together by musical ratios, Gaffurio attributes at the outset to "the Pythagoreans and Platonists."[36] But it is obvious from his borrowing that the source is Boethius,[37] who states—and Gaffurio paraphrases—that a kind of consonance, like that of high and low voices, mixes the incorporeal vitality of reason with the body, joins the parts of

---

30. Gaffurio, *De harmonia,* IV, 14.
31. Ibid., IV, 13.
32. Ibid., IV, 15.
33. Ibid., IV, 17.
34. Themistius *Paraphrases* on the *De anima* of Aristotle, trans. Ermolao Barbaro (Paris, 1535), I, 23; Heinze ed., p. 25; 1554 ed., p. 74. For a fuller account of these editions, see ch. 9, n. 37.
35. *Theorica musice,* I, 3.
36. *Theoricum opus,* I, 3.
37. *De institutione musica* 1.2.

the soul, which Aristotle called rational and irrational, and intermixes the elements of the body. Consonance in sound is the mixture of low and high pitch striking the ears sweetly and uniformly. Such consonance can manifest itself in the suitability of the components of a composite structure or of successive things to each other. From Macrobius Gaffurio derives the idea that the body and soul are combined by means of numbers.[38] He concludes: "And so, just as the soul itself is joined to the body by numbers, so they are confirmed by musical harmonies made out of the same numbers, and we do not doubt that not only is the soul mixed with the body but [their] elements and movements are determined by, as it were, a natural disposition and fitting agreement."[39] Pythagoras and the Platonists believed that the soul is a harmony, Gaffurio adds. Theophrastus recognized musical harmony not only in the voice, like Socrates, or in movements of bodies, like Aristoxenus, but in both of these and in the motion of the soul.[40] Indeed, Pythagoras, according to Censorinus, believed that human birth depended on harmonic numbers.[41] The doctrine that Censorinus reports is based on the numbers 6, 8, 9, and 12, the numbers of days the lacteus humor, then blood, then flesh, and finally the body take to form. The total multiplied by 6 gives the length of a "minor" birth; multiplied by 7 the length of a "major" birth.

In *De harmonia* Gaffurio does not penetrate any deeper into musica humana, but he uses sources that are more ancient: Aristides Quintilianus and Ptolemy. The numerology of birth is reported according to Aristides. Healthy births and stillbirths result from consonant and discordant periods or days respectively. A healthy human birth requires 270 days, and this results from a harmony of numbers, those that represent the stable notes of the octave bounding the tetrachords: 6, 8, 9, and 12. These are added to make 35; then to this is added the sum of the numbers representing the consonances, 1, 2, 3, and 4—that is, 10—making 45. This number, multiplied by 6—the first sign of generation—produces 270.[42]

In both Aristides and Ptolemy, Gaffurio found further substantiation for the proposition that harmony, whether cosmic or sonic, could move the soul and body to certain virtues, states of mind, and sensations. The tetrachords, for example, promote the virtues: the hypaton and meson tetrachords temperance, the diezeugmenon fortitude, and the hyperbolaion

---

38. Macrobius *Somnium* 1.6.

39. *Theorica musice,* I, 3.

40. Censorinus *De die natali* 12.

41. Ibid., 11. Gaffurio expands the brief mention of this in the 1480 book to a lengthy disquisition in the 1492 version, drawn almost verbatim from Censorinus.

42. Gaffurio, *De harmonia,* IV, 18; Aristides Quintilianus *De musica* 2.18; Burana trans., fol. 32r.

prudence.[43] Such influences are possible because the human soul is organized according to musical ratios. The intellective part corresponds to the octave, the sensitive to the fifth, and the habitual to the fourth. The species of fourth are analogous to the motions of the habitual soul—increase, stasis, and decrease; the species of fifth, to the powers of the sensitive soul—sight, hearing, smell, and taste; the species of octave, to the functions of the intellective soul—imagination, intellect (Burana: *intellectus*), thought (*conceptus*), reflection (*mens*), opinion (*opinio*), reason (*ratio*), and knowledge (*scientia*),[44]

To Gaffurio the musician, cosmic and human harmony were more than abstractions; they were the very basis of music's power and purpose. In the dedication of the *Practica musice* to Duke of Milan Lodovico Maria Sforza, Gaffurio several times recalls music's power and its metaphysical status. After extolling its potential for soothing the cares of people of every condition, he speaks of its force over inanimate things. Finally he invokes musica mundana and humana.

Et enim si Platoni credimus qui	If we believe Plato, who said
Mundi animam Musica modulatione	that the world soul consists
constare dixit: non video	of musical melody, I surely do
profecto cur dubitari possit	not see why it should be doubted
caetera quoque qualicunque	that any other living thing
anima degentia: quam eis coelitus	possessing a soul, which, it is
datam liquet: non affici	clear, is a gift of heaven, is
laetarique	also affected by and rejoices in
nature suae congruentia:	harmonies congruent with its own
cum similitudinem sibi amicam	nature, since it is well known that
esse iam palam	one is inclined toward something
constet.[45]	like oneself.

All souls, then, are imbued with harmony, and they derive pleasure from music because it answers to the harmony within themselves.

In the first chapter of the *Practica* Gaffurio cites those who recommended the practice of singing and playing for the education of youth: the Pythagoreans, Platonists, and Peripatetics, and he singles out Aristoxenus, who, as reported by Cicero

ipsius corporis intensionem	maintained that a certain tuning
quandam velut in cantu & fidi-	pitch exists in one's body like that
bus: quae harmonia dicitur:	of the voice and instruments called

---

43. Gaffurio, *De harmonia,* IV, 20; Aristides Quintilianus *De musica* 3.16; Burana trans., fol. 31v.

44. Gaffurio, *De harmonia,* IV, 17; Ptolemy *Harmonics* 3.5; Leoniceno trans., fol. 51r–v.

45. Gaffurio, *Practica musice,* dedication.

sic ex totius corporis	harmony; just as sounds are made
natura & figura varios modos	in singing, so out of the nature
fieri [recte: motus cieri] tanque	and form of the whole body issue
in cantu sonos affirmauerit.[46]	various vibrations.

Gioseffo Zarlino

After Gaffurio comparatively little interest is shown by Italian music theorists in cosmic or human music until Zarlino. Pietro Aron, for example, gives only a perfunctory review of the subject.[47] Zarlino dedicated a chapter to each kind of music, more out of an academic desire for completeness than because cosmic and human music suited his purpose. Indeed, at the end of the chapter on musica humana he admits: "Because these things belong more to philosophical discussions than to those about music, I shall leave speaking any more about it, content to have said these few words and demonstrated the variety of animistic music, of which I shall make no further mention, since it little suits my purpose, or not at all."[48]

What interested him more than the conventional theories was the power that music had on the passions and the means by which it could be activated, and to these matters he devoted two chapters in Book II.[49] If Zarlino considered the Boethian categories at all, it was because he wanted to make a classification of music that departed from the conventional one, although starting from it. He wanted to define each class of music "so as not to stray from the good order maintained by the ancients, who desired that every discussion of anything that is done rationally must begin with a definition, in order that the subject of the discussion be understood."[50] He therefore divides all music into animistic (*animastica*) and organic (*organica*), the first containing musica *mondana* and humana, the second divided into harmonic, or natural—that is, vocal music—and artificial, or instrumental, music.

For Zarlino musica mondana bonds things seen and known in the heavens, joins the elements, and controls the seasons. With respect to the heavens, harmony reigns over the revolutions, distances, and parts of the celestial spheres, and it determines the aspects, nature, and locations of the seven planets. Although he concedes that Aristotle rejected celestial music, Zarlino

---

46. *Tusculan Disputations* 1.9.19–20: "proxime autem Aristoxenus, musicus idemque philosophus, ipsius corporis intentionem quandam, velut in cantu et fidibus quae harmonia dicitur, sic ex corpori totius natura et figura varios motus cieri tamquam in cantu sonos."

47. *Toscanello in musica* (Venice, 1523), 1529 ed., I, 4. The authors he mentions are Plato, Cicero, and Boethius, but he probably knew them only through Gaffurio.

48. *Le Istitutioni harmoniche*, I, 18.

49. Ibid., II, 7, 8.

50. Ibid., I, 5, p. 10.

pleads that it was nevertheless favored by Cicero and many ancient philosophers, particularly Pythagoras. Zarlino defends with some persuasion the idea of celestial harmony, if not its audible or inaudible music.

> But every reason persuades us to believe at least that the world is composed with harmony, both because its soul is a harmony (as Plato believed), and because the heavens are turned around their intelligences with harmony, as may be gathered from their revolutions, which are proportionate to each other in velocity. This harmony is known also from the distances of the celestial spheres, for these distances (as some believe) are related in harmonic proportion, which, although not measured by the sense, is measured by the reason.[51]

Zarlino attributes to Pliny the intervallic distances between the planets as measured by the Pythagoreans, but the doctrine he transmits, taken from Gaffurio, is based not on Pliny but on Censorinus. For a correlation between the parts of the sky and consonances, Zarlino refers the reader to Ptolemy. There is further correspondence between the longitudes and the diatonic, chromatic, and enharmonic genres, and between the latitudes and the modes. The faces of the moon are coordinated with the conjunctions of the tetrachords. As for the aspects of the planets, there is such a variety "that it is impossible to explain it."[52] Astrologers, however, believe that certain aspects are malignant, others benificent. For example, when Jupiter is found between Saturn and Mars, it tempers their ill effects. The elements and their associated qualities of hot-cold, dry-humid, are also mediated and harmonized by numerical proportions. Thus fire and water are twice mediated by air through the sesquialter proportion; heat mediates fire and air, and humidity mediates air and water. Other proportions govern the transmutation of one element into another, as water into air. A similar harmony is found in the four seasons. Therefore, when Mercury discovered the lyre or kithara, according to Boethius and Macrobius, he gave it four strings, after the four elements and four seasons, while Terpander gave it seven strings, in imitation of the seven planets.

Zarlino displays no deep commitment to this ancient lore, but he does not try to refute it. He omits any mention of angels, although he does say that "many were of the opinion that in this life every soul is won by music, and, although the soul is imprisoned by the body, it still remembers and is conscious of the music of the heavens, forgetting every hard and annoying labor."[53]

Zarlino is more decisive about musica humana, which, he asserts, every-

---

51. Ibid., I, 6, pp. 12–13.
52. Ibid., I, 6, p. 13.
53. Ibid., I, 6, p. 12.

Ptolemy 3.5	Gaffurio IV, 17	Gogava III, 4	Zarlino I, 7
phantasia	phantasia	imaginatio	imaginatione
nous	intellectus	mens	mente
ennoia	conceptus	memoria	memoria
dianoia	mens	inquisitio	cogitatione
doxa	opinio	opinio	opinione
logos	ratio	ratio	ragione
epistēmē	scientia	scientia	scienza

Figure 8.4.
Terminology in Ptolemy, Gaffurio, Gogava, and Zarlino

one can contemplate in himself. This harmony "mixes with the body the incorporeal animation of reason" and unifies the rational and irrational parts of the soul.[54] Zarlino's schedule for the development of the human embryo departs from that of Censorinus—the numbers are 6, 9, 12, and 18, at the end of which cumulative period of 45 days human generation is completed, and the body receives from God the intellective soul. Although the numbers combine to form fifths, fourths, and octaves, Zarlino would not call this musica humana. Rather, true human music is that which welds the parts of the body together and similarly those of the soul, and the two together. Zarlino, like Gaffurio, draws from Ptolemy the analogies between the consonances and the three parts of the soul and between the species of consonances and the intellective, sensitive, and habitual functions.[55] Zarlino's terminology is not unlike Gaffurio's, but this can be attributed to the coincidence of Gogava's and Leoniceno's solutions for the Latinization of the Greek terms. In the cases where Gaffurio and Gogava differ widely, Zarlino follows Gogava. For example, in the faculties of the intellective soul, which are compared to the seven species of diapason, Leoniceno-Gaffurio, Gogava, and Zarlino offer the mostly parallel solutions to Ptolemy's terminology shown in Figure 8.4.

Where Gogava and Gaffurio differ, namely, in the pairs *imaginatio-phantasia, memoria-conceptus, inquisitio-mens,* Zarlino followed Gogava. Zarlino chose *memoria* despite the fact that it is an incorrect translation of the Greek word, showing that he did not have the Greek before him. Another clue to the independence of Zarlino from Gaffurio in this chapter is the clinching statement that Anger, Reason, and Virtue harmonized could produce Justice or Fortitude. Gaffurio omitted discussion of this difficult passage in Ptolemy, which was adequately translated by Gogava but badly contracted by Zarlino.

54. Ibid., I, 7, p. 16.
55. Ptolemy *Harmonics* 3.5.

Another important kind of harmony is that joining the soul and body. The two are linked, Zarlino notes, by the spirit, a concept he attributes to the Platonists. In fact, however, as D. P. Walker has pointed out, Zarlino probably had in mind the *spiritus* of Ficino's *De triplici* vita.[56] Only those whose faculties are joined in harmony can appreciate music and enjoy refreshment of that spirit which links the soul and body. Those who lack the proportionate structure of the part of the brain near the ear that judges harmony are deprived of music's healing power:

> Nature has ordered things well in having joined (as the Platonists believe) our body and soul through the spirit. To each [body, spirit, and soul] Nature has provided appropriate remedies when they are weak and infirm. When it is listless and infirm, the body is brought back to health with cures wrought by medicine, and the afflicted and weak spirit, by the aerial spirits and by instrumental and vocal music, which are proportionate remedies for it. As for the soul, locked up in this corporeal prison, it is consoled by means of divine mysteries and sacred theology.[57]

Human harmony resides also in the union of the four elements of the body, "according to the philosophers," who say that the nerves are composed of earth and fire, the bones of water and earth, and the flesh of all four. If this should seem strange, no one would deny that the four humors—black bile, phlegm, blood, and choler—are united in the body through harmony.

Johannes Tinctoris

If celestial harmony had advocates in the fifteen and sixteenth centuries, it also had detractors. Some of them based their disbelief on Aristotle's refutation of this music; others went beyond to raise further objections. Tinctoris gave a prominent place to his rejection of the music of the spheres in the dedication (entitled *Prologus*) of the *Liber de arte contrapuncti* to his employer and patron in Naples, Ferdinand (Ferrante) I, king of Sicily. Why such a refutation should claim prime space in a treatise on counterpoint is not altogether clear. It may have been a lively local issue, since Giovanni Pontano in his *Urania, sive de stellis* had celebrated the planets but conspicuously failed to mention their music.[58]

Tinctoris found nothing but disagreement concerning the pitches the

---

56. D. P. Walker, *Spiritual and Demonic Magic,* p. 28.

57. Zarlino, *Istitutioni,* I, 4, p. 9.

58. See Giuseppe Saitta, *Il pensiero italiano nell'umanesimo e nel rinascimento* (Bologna, 1949) I, 635–36.

planets produced, despite the support celestial harmony had from estimable philosophers such as Plato, Pythagoras, Cicero, Macrobius, Boethius, and Isidor. Aristotle's position, which vigorously rejected the idea that there was any sound, real or potential, in the heavens, seemed to him wiser.[59]

Besides Aristotle himself Tinctoris invokes the authority of "his commentator, together with our more recent philosophers." It is not clear who these are. Seay identifies the commentator as Thomas Aquinas, who does, indeed, side with Aristotle on this question.[60] But it is not likely that Tinctoris would refer to Aquinas, a philosopher in his own right, as a commentator. More likely he referred in this way to Alexander of Aphrodisias or Themistius, both of whom commented on *De caelo*. The commentator is probably not Aquinas also for the reason that only in 1492–93 was Aquinas' commentary copied for Ferrante's library, suggesting that until then it was missing from the collection of books that would have been available to Tinctoris.[61]

Tinctoris does not review Aristotle's objections; he simply reports that the philosopher proved that there was neither actual nor potential sound issuing from the spheres. Aristotle's arguments should be recalled by us, however.[62] The philosopher cites several assumptions of the Pythagoreans: that the heavenly bodies must produce sound because they are so massive and move at high speed; that the speeds of the stars, judged by their distances, are in the ratios of musical consonances and thus produce a concordant sound; that this sound is not audible to men because it has been heard from birth. Aristotle objects that even if one accepts the last argument, loud sounds should leave evidence in other effects, such as splitting stones and other materials, for the noise of objects as large as the stars would be of this magnitude. To this retort Alexander added that if the sounds of these motions were in our ears, we would not hear those made by smaller objects. The critical point for Aristotle was that the stars and planets, not being self-moving, as he showed elsewhere in the treatise,[63] are carried passively and silently in the sweep of the revolving spheres, like the parts of a moving ship, or a ship drifting downstream.

If the commentator Tinctoris had read was Thomas Aquinas, Tinctoris

59. See the passage quoted in ch. 1 from *The Art of Counterpoint*, trans. Albert Seay, pp. 13–14.

60. *In Aristotelis libros de caelo et mundo expositio*, II, 14.

61. According to Tammaro de Marinis, *La biblioteca napoletana dei re d'Aragona* (Milan, 1947–52), I, 63–64, 74–75, n. 29, the manuscript of Aquinas' "Explanatio librorum Aristotelis de coelo et mundo" in Ferrante's library, now Paris, Bibliothèque Nationale, MS lat. 6525, was not copied until then.

62. *De caelo* 2.9.292b.

63. *De caelo* 2.8.

would have known further arguments both pro and contra. For Aquinas introduces the comment of Simplicius, in favor of the Pythagorean position, that the sounds of the celestial bodies is not corruptive of the senses, as excessively loud sound would be, but preservative and vivifying. Simplicius also denied that the Pythagoreans believed people failed to hear the harmony because of habituation; rather it was because their ears were not sensitive to this particular harmony, which Pythagoras himself could hear, just as dogs can smell things that men cannot. Aquinas counters Simplicius' arguments by pointing out that the sun's brightness, although it is vivifying, still corrupts our sight because of excessive light, and similarly the sound of planets would injure the ears. As to the second point, he argues that humans take pleasure in the fragrance of roses and lilies, which animals do not, whereas animals are aware of odors that promise food but not of certain others. But both men and animals recoil from excessive light. Thus there could be no sounds from the movements of celestial bodies unless perceived by men or unless their sense of hearing were ruined by the sounds.

All of these objections to the theory are not detailed in Tinctoris' account, of course. But many of them must have been known to him. It is strange that he did not debate the question in the two works that provided the best opportunity: *Complexus effectuum musices*[64] and *De inventione et usu musicae*.[65]

Who were "the more recent philosophers" unnamed by Tinctoris who denied the existence of a sounding cosmic harmony? One looks immediately at the circle around the Aragonese court in Naples. Giuseppe Saitta[66] has identified a group of philosophers and scientists whose activities centered on the Aragonese court. Giovanni Attaldo taught Aristotelian philosophy at the university and published commentaries upon Aristotle's works. Girolamo Tagliavia promulgated the opinion of Philolaus that the earth revolved around the sun and wrote on the system of the world. Antonio Ferrariis, "il Galateo," demonstrated that one might navigate west to reach the East Indies. Most important of all was Giovanni Pontano, a vigorous opponent of Florentine Neoplatonism. Although he alludes in his poem *Urania, sive de stellis* to mythological figures, such as Saturn and Jupiter, and to the signs of the zodiac, they are for him personifications of natural forces. In the very opening lines he refers to the the stars "slipping silently" (sydera mundo labantur tacito),[67] and nowhere in this or other astronomical

---

64. Albert Seay, ed., *Tinctoris Opera theoretica* II (American Institute of Musicology, 1975), pp. 166–77.

65. Karl Weinmann, ed., in *Johannes Tinctoris und sein unbekannter Traktat "De inventione et usu musicae"* (Tutzing, 1961).

66. *Il pensiero italiano nell'umanesimo e nel Rinascimento*, I, 634.

67. *Urania, sive de stellis*, in *Opera* (Venice, 1513), 1.2.

and astrological works does he broach the subject of the music of the spheres, as if it were unworthy of his attention.

Of the older humanist writers who articulated the case against the harmony of the spheres, the most notable was Coluccio Salutati, but since his unfinished *De laboribus Herculis,* in which he treated this question, was not published, his views may not have been known to Tinctoris. He began the first book, that which is of interest here, between 1383 and 1391, according to the editor, B. L. Ullman.[68] This first book is essentially a defense of poetry, and the subject of the spheres enters into it because, Salutati maintains, the poet intuits within his soul an admirable sweetness of universal harmony. But this exists only in the poet's imagination, not in the movements of the planetary bodies. After much deliberation, he says he arrived at the opinion that there was no probable reason for assigning musical melody, as the Platonists did, to the movement of the heavens.

Nam sonum, qui prorsus	Since sound certainly
exigit aerem per quem	requires air, through which
giris infinitis sese	it unfolds in infinite revolutions
succesive multiplicantibus	successively multiplying themselves,
explicet, cum supra	and since above the
peryferiam ignis impossibile	periphery of fire it is impossible
sit secundum naturam aerem reperiri,	to find air according to nature,
vanum prorsus est celis ascribere	it is surely false to attribute to
et armoniam celestem, sicut illi	the heavens a celestial harmony,
creduntur facere,	or to dream of it, as they [the
somniare.[69]	[Platonists] are thought to do.

Is not the idea of a celestial symphony laughable, he asks.

cum omnes spere rotunde sint,	Since all spheres are round,
si sonum efficiant,	if they produced sound, as those
ut illi velle videntur,	[philosophers] appear to maintain,
a totius mundi	sound would be called forth
circumferentia	from the circumference
excitabitur sonus et	of the whole world, and it would be
supra totam machinam	spread out over the entire machine
universi per inane quoddam,	of the universe, of no use to anyone,
ubi nichil prorsus esse creditur,	as nothing is believed to exist there.
expandetur; imo potius expandi	Nay, indeed, it could not spread
non poterit, cum nichil sit	beyond, because there is nothing
ultra celum quod ad sonus	beyond the sky that could be
impulsum moveri queat,	moved to stimulate sound

---

68. Coluccio Salutati, *De laboribus Herculis,* ed. B. L. Ullman (Zurich, 1951), p. vii. Salutati wrote to a friend in 1405 that he had finished the second book.

69. *De laboribus Herculis,* I, 5, p. 23.

et giros qui	and to unfold the revolutions that
sonum deferunt	propagate sound.[70]

Salutati saw a further difficulty with the theory. If sound were produced at the circumference of a sphere, it would have to be borne toward the center, but this would require a motion that is contrary to the natural motion of sound, which radiates from a center to a circumference, so that the circulations directed toward the center would break against the fluid circulations tending outward, and the sound would never reach the ear. The person receiving the sound appears to be located by Salutati on a surface, the earth, that is covered by the sphere as if by a great dome. The sound produced at the circumference of the dome would have to depart from that "concavity," as Salutati calls it, to descend toward the center, where the listening ear is situated. But the descent is prevented by the outward motion natural to sound. The fact that we hear thunder does not negate the argument, because thunder emanates from a certain region that makes a slit in the spaces of the orbs. That is to say, it does not proceed from the whole circumference in concentric circles inward, but in a lateral direction.

As with arguments against the spheres that we shall encounter later, Salutati departs from a particular conception of the cosmos, then applies principles of mechanics derived from the observation of nature to arrive at a legitimate conclusion. Although the original premise was faulty and the arguments insufficient, the exercise is significant in that a skeptical mind invoked a process of scientific inquiry concerning a natural phenomenon rather than accept as truth an untested metaphysical doctrine.

Francisco de Salinas

The first musical writer who took the trouble to present a refutation of the theory of celestial harmony is Francisco de Salinas. At the outset of his treatise *De musica libri septem* (1577), he declares that he will abandon the conventional division of music into mundana, humana, and instrumentalis to establish a tripartite division that is based on new criteria— whether it moves only the sense, only the intellect, or both. In the category that moves only the sense of hearing belong the songs of birds, which give pleasure but are not subject to harmonic ratio, if by chance harmonic intervals may be found in them. This is irrational and cannot properly be called music.

The second category is that "comprehended under the two [species] of the ancients, mundana and humana, the harmony of which is perceived not with the pleasure of the ears but the contemplation of the intellect."[71] Salinas

---

70. Ibid., I, 9, pp. 40–41.
71. Salinas, *De musica libri septem,* I, 1, p. 1.

would not deny, he says, that there is concord in the disparate movements of the celestial bodies, and particularly in the number 12, which contains the consonances and the whole tone, for this number was called musical (*musikotaton*) by Aristotle. But as to the sound of planetary motion, Salinas emphatically denied its existence:

> We do not believe that celestial motions yield any sounds at all, whether as subject or as efficient cause, as it pleases the physicists. Now aside from the reasons of Aristotle, which we did not wish to translate here, lest we seem to want to teach physics rather than music, it appears certainly probable that the creator of the universal framework would not have made anything superfluous any more than he would have failed to provide the necessities. For such would have been that celestial sound which could not be heard by anyone: not by men, since they give many reasons why it happens that this sound does not reach our ears; and not by the intelligences that move the heavens, since they neither have ears nor need them. For this reason I believe that one must come to the same conclusion concerning celestial music as the music of the elements. Since what is perceived in the combination of the elements and in the seasons depends not on the sense of hearing but on the judgment of reason, it is like that which is found in the parts of the soul in which all the proportions of the consonances are said to reside. Thus the rational faculty holds to the irascible a sesquialter ratio, in which the diapente is shown to be formed, and the irascible to the concupiscible, a sesquitertian, in which the diatessaron is found, resulting in the perfect diapason, in which the soul consists. And, just as in vocal or instrumental music the diapente contains the diatessaron but not the opposite, and the diapason contains them both but is not contained in them, so the faculty of sensation contains the vegetative but is not contained in it, and the rational faculty alone contains the other two but is not contained by them.[72]

Salinas, then, was willing to recognize a harmony in celestial movements, as also in the parts of the soul. But he would not call this music. Their architecture may be shaped by numerical proportions, but this is as far as Salinas would go.

Giovanni Battista Benedetti

A more rigorous refutation of the celestial harmony was undertaken by Giovanni Battista Benedetti. The exact date of his essay is unknown, since the book in which it was published, the *Diversarum speculationum mathematicarum & physicorum liber* of 1585, is a collection of studies undoubtedly compiled over a long period of time. It occurs in a chapter entitled "That the opinion of the Pythagoreans concerning the sound of the celestial bodies

---

72. Ibid., I, 1, p. 2.

was not adopted by Aristotle."[73] The opinion of the Pythagoreans is exploded through the glosses of the philosophers, Benedetti proclaims. The celestial orbs that they maintain they hear sounding are either contiguous or distant from each other. If they are distant, which no one believes, there is a vacuum between them, so that, not touching, they cannot emit a sound. Sound requires that air enter a confined place. If no air or fluid body exists in the ethereal region, the celestial orbs by themselves cannot produce sounds. Experimenting with a fluid body by passing it over another soft body, one will find no sound produced. Also, when a spherical body moves speedily around its own axis, it will not make any sound, since it is not displacing another body. If, on the other hand, the orbs are contiguous, then, because their surfaces are thought to be finely polished and soft, there is no roughness or unevenness to produce a sound when they are rubbed together.

Benedetti fails to find any of the harmonic proportions in the sky. He enumerates the ratios of the consonances, as defined not by the ancients but by modern musicians: 2:1, 3:2, 4:3, 5:4, 6:5, 8:3, and 5:3. The dissonances, which, he says, serve "harmonic modulations," are 9:8, 10:9, 16:15, 25:24, 29:28, and 27:25. Ptolemy, he argues, did not find any of the harmonic intervals in the aspects of the sky.[74] With musical intervals, the diapason can be divided by a harmonic mean into a diapente and diatessaron, and similarly a diapente into a ditone and semiditone, and if a semiditone is subtracted from a diapason, a major hexad remains, whereas if a ditone is subtracted from a diapason, a minor hexad remains. Nothing parallel happens when aspects are subtracted from each other. If a trine is subtracted from a sextile, another sextile remains, and if a quartile aspect is subtracted from the aspect of opposition, another quartile remains.[75] Benedetti admits that there is order in the velocities, magnitudes, distances, and influxes of the celestial bodies, for through the divine providence of God the universe is made perfect, but nothing in these quantities fits the proportions of musical harmony.

Celestial Harmony as Myth and Metaphor

Despite the increasing skepticism about the celestial harmonies, the notion continued to exert its fascination, particularly on poets and dramatists. The

73. *Diversarum speculationum mathematicarum & physicorum liber* (Turin, 1585), ch. 33: "Pytagoreorum opinionem de sonitu corporum coelestium non fuisse ab Aristotele sublatam," pp. 190–91.

74. But for another view, see Jamie Croy Kassler, "Music as a Model in Early Science," *History of Science* 20 (1982):117–20, where Ptolemy is shown to have noted the ratios between the angles as paralleling those of the consonances.

75. Translated into degrees of arc, taking a quartile, or 90 degrees, from the aspect of opposition, 180 degrees, leaves another quartile. Subtracting a sextile (60 degrees) from a trine (120 degrees) leaves a sextile (60 degrees).

most splendid celebration of the idea was the first intermedio of the entertainments of 1589 for the wedding in Florence of Grand Duke Ferdinand
de' Medici and Christine of Lorraine. The verses were written by Giovanni
Bardi, who was partial to Neoplatonic philosophy, and Ottavio Rinuccini.
Rinuccini's chorus of sirens describe how they make the celestial spheres
turn: "Noi, che cantando, le celesti sfere / Dolcemente rotar facciamo intorno" (We, as we sing, make the celestial spheres sweetly revolve). The
classical source is Plato's *Republic,* Book 10, in which Socrates recounts the
myth of Er. Indeed, the description of the entertainment by Bastiano de'
Rossi, tells us—and the surviving scenic designs back him up— that at the
center of the stage was a cloud bearing Necessity and the three Fates.[76]
Around them turned the planets (see Figure 8.5). the spheres in which they
moved as whorls within whorls. On the surface of each whorl was a siren,
"hymning a single sound and note. The eight together form one harmony;
and round about, at equal intervals is another band, of three in number,
each sitting upon her throne: these are the Fates, daughters of Necessity,
who are clothed in white raiment and have crowns of wool upon their
heads, Lachesis and Clotho and Atropos, who accompany with their voices
the harmony of the sirens—Lachesis singing of the past, Clotho of the
present, Atropos of the future."[77] According to Rossi, the Fates invite the
Sirens to climb upwards in the sky and to join Neccesity and the Planets
in song:

Parche	*Fates*
Dolcissime Sirene,	Sweetest Sirens,
Tornate al Cielo, e 'n tanto	return to the heavens, and meanwhile
Facciam, cantando, a gara	let us raise, singing, in contest
Un dolce canto.	a sweet song.
Sirene	*Sirens*
Non mal tanto splendore	Never such splendor
Vide Argo, Cipro, o Delo.	did Argos, Cyprus, or Delos see.
Parche	*Fates*
A voi, regali amanti,	To you, royal lovers,
Cediam noi tutti gran Numi del Cielo.	all we great gods of the heavens yield.

They all then join in praising the wedding couple.[78] This is presented as a
myth, along with others in the succeeding intermedi, all illustrating the

76. Bastiano de' Rossi, *Descrizione dell' apparato e degl' Intermedi fatti per la commedia rappresentata in Firenze nelle nozze de' Serenissimi Don Ferdinando Medici, e Madama Cristina di Loreno,
Gran Duchi di Toscana* (Florence, 1589).

77. Plato *Republic* 617, trans. Jowett.

78. Italian text in *Musique des intermèdes de "La Pellegrina,"* ed. D. P. Walker (Paris, 1963),
p. xxxix.

Figure 8.5.
Necessity and the three Fates, costume design by Bernardo Buontalenti, for the
first intermedio of 1589, Florence, Biblioteca Nazionale Centrale, MS C.B.3.53

power of music: the contest of the Muses and Pierides, the battle between Apollo and the Python, the story of Arion saved by the dolphins, and the granting of music by the Muses to humanity. In associating the harmony of the spheres with these other myths Bardi relegated it to the realm of fiction. As John Hollander characterized the evocations of celestial harmony in seventeenth-century poetry, they became "decorative metaphor and mere turns of wit."[79]

79. John Hollander, *The Untuning of the Sky: Ideas of Music in English Poetry, 1500–1700* (Princeton, 1961), p. 19.

NINE

Gaffurio as a Humanist

f the fifteenth-century writers who specialized in music Franchino Gaffurio was the most assiduous in seeking out classical sources. His *Theorica musice,* based principally on Boethius, presents corroborating or divergent views insofar as other authors were available to him. But Gaffurio worked under one severe limitation: he apparently could barely read Greek. Of the writings in that language only those translated into Latin or Italian, consequently, were accessible to him. There was a good number in the areas of literature and philosophy. But not one of the principal Greek treatises on music had yet been translated at the time of Gaffurio's *Theoricum opus musice discipline* (1480), his first exposition of musica theorica, and not even in the revised and expanded version published in 1492 as *Theorica musice* is there much evidence of his penetration into musical sources of antiquity. As we have already seen, Gaffurio did commission at around this time the translation of the most important of these: the *Harmonics* of Ptolemy, the *De musica* of Aristides Quintilianus, the *Harmonics* of Bryennius, the *Introduction* of Bacchius, and the three anonymous manuals known until recently as Bellermann's anonymous. Meanwhile Giorgio Valla's translation of Euclid's and Cleonides' short treatises came out in 1497,[1] and Carlo Valgulio's translation of pseudo-Plutarch's *De musica* appeared in 1507,[2] though Gaffurio may have seen it already in manuscript.[3]

That Gaffurio knew of the existence of some of these sources already in

1. *Cleonidae harmonicum introductorium* (Venice, 1497).

2. *Charoli Valgulii Prooemium in musicam Plutarchi ad Titum Pyrrhinum* (Brescia, 1507).

3. Gaffurio first mentioned it in *Angelicum ac divinum opus musice* (Milan, 1508), I, 18, fol. D4r. He calls him "Carolo Valgulio Bersano homo doctissimo & experto in tute le discipline." Although Gaffurio did not cite Plutarch in *Theorica* in 1492, he used material from his *De musica,* for example, in I, 1, fol. a1r–v. My attention was drawn to the Plutarch borrowings by Walter Kreyszig, who is preparing an English translation of the *Theorica* and study of sources as a Ph.D. dissertation at Yale University.

1492 is evident from his listing among writings on music in the beginning
of his *Theorica* the following as authors of *copiosa volumina:* Aristoxenus,
Ptolemy, Bryennius, Aristides Quintilianus, and Bacchius.[4] This listing in
the first chapter of Book I, missing in the 1480 version, shows Gaffurio's
increasing awareness of the Greek literature on music, however little of it
he could read. Besides those works he knew survived, there were many
others he knew by reputation and barely mentioned for the sake of
completeness.

How many of the Greek and Roman writings did Gaffurio know firsthand? Of the five authors and the anonymi that he had translated, only
Bacchius appears to be quoted directly in the *Theorica.* Unfortunately we
do not know the date of completion of this translation, apparently done by
Francesco Burana, for it does not survive. The earliest date on any of the
surviving translations is 1494, when the Aristides Quintilianus and the anonymi were completed by Burana.[5] At this time Gaffurio knew Aristoxenus
only through the biased commentary of Boethius, which in turn is derived
from Ptolemy. Likewise, he knew Ptolemy's *Harmonics* only through Boethius and apparently did not realize that the entire Book 5 of Boethius was
a Latin paraphrase and abridgment of part of Ptolemy's Book 1. Neither
Aristides Quintilianus nor Bryennius is cited in the *Theorica,* though their
names are mentioned. Nicomachus and Porphyry, although represented in
manuscripts then available, were never more than names to Gaffurio.

The remaining "authors" on music named by Gaffurio were known to
him only secondhand. Some are musicians whose writings, if there were
any, do not survive: Theodorus Cyreniacus, Xanthus of Athens, Diony-
sodorus, Simmias of Thebes, and Aristo of Athens.[6] Others are authors
who wrote only incidentally about music in works of more general scope
or whose works survive only fragmentarily: Archytas, a mathematician
who may have influenced the author of the *Division of the Canon,*[7] Philolaus,
Eratosthenes, Theophrastus, and Heraclides Ponticus. Most of these must
have been mere names to Gaffurio. On the other hand, he had available
translations of Democritus, Xenophon, Aristotle, Plato, and Themistius.
As for Latin authors, whether classical or medieval, there is no doubt that
Gaffurio read them conscientiously.

In his *Theorica* Gaffurio aimed to embrace the entire corpus of musical

---

4. *Theorica musice,* I, 1, fol. a6r–v.

5. Concerning this and the other translations made for Gaffurio by Burana and Leoniceno,
see ch. 6 above.

6. On these figures see Solon Michaelides, *The Music of Ancient Greece, An Encyclopaedia*
(London, 1978).

7. Books VII–IX of the *Elements of Geometry* are also said to derive from Archytas. See
Edward A. Lippman, *Musical Thought in Ancient Greece* (New York, 1964), p. 153.

theorizing left by the classical Greek authorities. Boethius was his main source, but where he could supplement him, Gaffurio earnestly tried to do so. On a number of points significant for music theory and aesthetics, Gaffurio was able to bring the ancient authors to bear directly on the Boethian doctrine. The most important fresh impulses came from his reading of the works of Plato in Marsilio Ficino's Latin translation, together with Ficino's commentaries on them, the Aristotelian *Problems* in the Latin translation published with d'Abano's commentaries, and the *Paraphrases* of Themistius on the *De anima* of Aristotle in the Latin translation of Ermolao Barbaro.

Whereas in much of the *Theorica* Gaffurio was content to paraphrase or even repeat Boethius verbatim, the almost direct contact with the words of Plato through Ficino inspired him to write his own commentary, in which he at times paraphrased Ficino but more often drew together from diverse dialogues the essence of Plato's ethical doctrine of music. Gaffurio's comentary on musical ethics, for example, occurs in a location parallel to that in Boethius, namely Book I, chapter 1, but it strikes out independently. The passage merits quotation in full:

> Socrates and Plato and also the Pythagoreans, attributing a moral resource to music, ordered by a common law that adolescents and youth, and young women too, be educated in music, not for inciting to desire, through which this discipline becomes cheapened, but for moderating the movements of the soul through rule and reason. Just as not every note is valid for a melody of sounds but only that which makes a good consonance, so also not all motions of the soul but only those that are suited to reason belong to the correct harmony of life.[8] God gave us sound and hearing for this purpose, as Plato in the *Timaeus* is seen to claim, for speech tends and contributes very much toward this purpose. For every use of music was given for the sake of harmony, and harmony, which has motions that are congruent and akin to the wanderings of our soul, was given by the Muses to men who use them with sagacity, not for pleasure devoid of reason, as is now seen to be its usefulness, but so that we may calm through it the dissonant revolutions of the soul and render it a harmony consonant within itself. Rhythm, too, was dedicated to this purpose, so that we might very aptly temper an immoderate character lacking grace in us.[9] Now since the nature of boys is restless and desirous of amusements all the time and on that account does not tolerate severe discipline, Plato himself orders that boys be educated in honest music, the pleasure of which most commonly offers the pathways of virtue. On the other hand, it is occasionally also to be assigned to older men as an honest amusement for the consolation of a laborious life. Those consolations which are valid to amuse this honest

8. Here begins an almost verbatim citation of Plato *Timaeus* 47c–e in Ficino's translation.
9. Here ends the direct quotation from Ficino's translation.

old age are to be studied in youth. For this reason Plato held these same boys
in check by a triple bridle, that is fear, law, and true reason, lest they fall into
the triple impulse of food, drink, and desire of coitus.[10] Thus, with moderate
use from youth of honest pleasures, drawn away from shameful things, they
would gradually be incited to serious studies. He wanted also that they have
leisure for gymnastic games through exercise of the body, as by dance and
wrestling. But dance, whether it imitates the words of the Muse [that is, the
poet], marking her magnificence and freedom, or whether for the sake of good
condition, nimbleness, and form of the body itself as well as its parts and
members, it aptly flexes and bends each and every part so that it fosters a
sufficiently harmonious motion that follows the universal orderliness of dance.[11]

   . . . I agree with Plato that nothing flows so easily into the tender and soft
souls as various tones of song, whose power in either direction is such that it
can hardly be described, for it both excites the lazy and makes the excited
relaxed, and, just as it relaxes souls, it also constricts them.[12] It was of interest
to many cities in Greece to preserve this manner of the antique notes, cities
whose mores were fallen to softness and transformed along with their songs,
or were depraved with sweetness and corruption, as some believed, when their
severity declined because of various vices, and the condition for this mutation
existed in the ears and souls that had been changed. For this reason Plato, that
very wise man of Greece, and by far the most learned, assiduously shunned
this ruin, because he denied that it is possible to change musical laws without
a change of the public laws.[13]

A central passage in the above quotation (delimited by footnotes 8 and
9) is drawn from Ficino's translation of the *Timaeus,* as may be seen in the
comparison below (Gaffurio, left; Ficino, right).

Vocem nanque & eius auditum huius	Vocem quoque auditum que eiusdem
rei gratia nobis deus dedit ut in	rei gratia deos dedisse nobis
Timeo Plato uidetur asserere nam	existimo. Nam
ad hec ipsa sermo pertinet plurimum-	ad haec ipsa sermo pertinet, plurimum-
que conducit. Omnis enim musicae	que conducit, omnisque musicae
uocis usus harmoniae gratia est	uocis usus harmoniae gratia est
tributus. Atque & harmonia quae	tributus. Atqui & harmonia, que
motiones habet animae nostrae	motiones habet animae nostrae
discursionibus	discursionibus
congruas atque cognatas homini	congruas atque cognatas, homini
prudenter musis utenti non ad	prudenter musis utenti non ad
uoluptatem rationis expertem:	uoluptatem rationis expertem,
ut nunc uidetur est utilis: sed	ut nunc uidetur, est utilis: sed

10. Plato *Republic* 439a–e.
11. Plato *Laws* 673.
12. Plato *Republic* 401d–e.
13. Ibid. 424c.

a musis ideo data est: ut per
eam dissonantem circuitum animae
componamus ad concentum
sibi congruum redigamus.
Atque rhythmus ad hoc uidetur
esse tributus ut habitum in nobis
immoderatum gratiaque carentem
aptissime temperemus.[14]

a musis ideo data est, ut per
eam dissonantem circuitum animae
componamus, & ad concentum
sibi congruum redigamus.
Rhythmus quoque ad hoc uidetur
esse tributus, ut habitum in nobis
immoderatum gratiaque carentem
temperemus.[15]

Gaffurio's method of absorbing the ancient writings through direct quotation (without, to be sure, quotation marks) leads to some ambiguities. It is not clear whether Gaffurio's intention was to apply Plato's strictures to the music of his time, or whether, too busy copying, he allowed such an expression as "not for pleasure devoid of reason, as is now seen to be its usefulness," to creep into a statement that, lacking any sign of direct quotation, the reader, mistakenly perhaps, is likely to accept as Gaffurio's own reflection on the music of his time. Such ambiguity is inevitable in a book that is a quilt of quotations. Yet, from all we know of Gaffurio, Plato's puritan attitude fitted his own pious nature.

Another source of misunderstanding is Gaffurio's habit of juxtaposing quotations and paraphrases from various sources. For example, in defending the importance of number in music and in arithmetic, Gaffurio went to the dialogue *Epinomis,* the authorship of which is now in doubt, by way of Ficino's translation and commentary. This Gaffurio paraphrased, preserving key words (Gaffurio, left; Ficino, right):

In cunctis enim rebus Diuus Plato
in Philosopho siue Epinomide numerum ipsum esse necessarium docet:
quod et si pluribus quoque rationibus
monstrari liceat recte nunc hanc
potissima ratione declaratur.
Nanque ceterae artes sublato
numero penitus euanescunt.
utque de nostra facultate sit
sermo. tota ipsa musica motus &
vocum numero indiget.[16]

Ita necesse est omnino numerum
praesupponere. Idemque
necessarium esse,
pluribus etiam rationibus
monstrari licet. Sed recte nunc
ratione hac ostenditur,
quod caeterae artes quas omnes
paulo ante enumerauimus,
sublato numero penitus euanescent.
. . . Nam et tota musica motus et
vocum numero indiget.[17]

In all things, Gaffurio wants to say, Plato taught that it is necessary to start with number, and that if number were removed, all the arts would

14. Gaffurio *Theorica,* I, 1.
15. Ficino trans., 1532 ed., p. 716.
16. Gaffurio, *Theorica,* II, 6.
17. Ficino trans., p. 920.

vanish.[18] The whole art of music depends on the numbering of movement and of notes. After a short commentary on the meaning of this passage, Gaffurio (left) shifts without warning from Plato's words to Ficino's "Argumentum in Epinomidem (right)."

Omnia denique mala esse censuit Plato quae concordi numero & pulchritudine carent: Quae vero consentientibus numeris coaptantur bona.[19]	Mala enim in superioribus nominauit; que concordi numero & pulchritudinem carent. Bona uero quae consentientibus numeris coaptantur.[20]

Gaffurio has here cited Ficino's conclusion as if it were Plato's: "Plato decreed, finally, that all things that lack harmony, number, and beauty are bad; good, on the contrary, are those things that are joined together through numbers that are in common accord."

A resource that Gaffurio did not exploit to full advantage at this time was the translation and commentary on the Aristotelian *Problems* by Pietro d'Abano published in 1475. As we saw in chapter 3, d'Abano transmitted together with his own commentary the translation by Bartolomeo da Messina, handed down from the thirteenth century.[21] Gaffurio already knew the *Problems* when he prepared the *Theoricum opus,* for he cited Problem 19.21 to support his contention that the fourth is tolerated in the higher parts of a contrapuntal texture but not as the lowest interval. The higher sounds, produced by faster and weaker motion, make a more fleeting impression on the ear than the lower notes, which occupy more time and give off more sound: "When the time and slowness is greater, it can make a greater discordance and consequently the dissonance is more greatly perceived, as Aristotle says in his twenty-first problem of music, with which the Conciliator [Pietro d'Abano] concurs in his commentary."[22] This problem, which inquires why out-of-tune notes are more noticeable when singers are in their lower range than in the high, thus permitted Gaffurio to rationalize the equivocal practice of treating the fourth as both a consonance and a dissonance, one of the most difficult usages to square with theory.

18. See *Epinomis* 977d–e, trans. J. Harward (Oxford, 1928), p. 84. The Greek text is published in *Platonis Epinomis Commentariis illustrata,* ed. Franciscus Novotny (Prague, 1960).

19. Gaffurio, *Theorica,* II, 6, fol. d1r.

20. Ficino, Argumentum, p. 917.

21. *Expositio problematum Aristotelis* (Mantua, 1475). Among the books in the library of the Church of the Incoronata in Lodi in 1518 was a copy of the *Problems* of Aristotle. That was the year that Gaffurio donated his library to the church, and the d'Abano commentary must have been in it. See Emilio Motta, "I libri della chiesa dell'Incoronata di Lodi nel 1518," *Il libro e la stampa* 1 (1907):105–12.

22. *Theoricum opus,* V, 8, fols. 112v–113r. This same reason is cited also in *Practica musice,* III, 6, but the passage is omitted in the *Theorica.*

Gaffurio seemed content with this rather feeble rationalization, even though he does go on to say that the fourth needs to be raised from the lowest position in a four-voice texture by only a major or minor third for its dissonance to be "extinguished."

In both the *Theoricum opus* and the *Theorica* Gaffurio cites Problem 19.41 to defend the claim of "Pythagoreans and Platonists" that only multiple and superparticular ratios generate consonances.[23] In this problem the Aristotelian author shows that the double fifth (ninth) or double fourth (seventh) do not form consonances, because they are neither superparticular nor multiple, implying that only these classes of ratios can produce consonances. This problem is brought into a similar discussion in Gaffurio's later work, *De harmonia*.[24]

In the final chapter of the *Theorica* Gaffurio contemplates the wonders of the system of *tropi,* or modes, of the Greeks for expressing diverse words and their meanings. The voice, he says, is apt for moving the souls of men, but even more so is the voice joined by instruments, which can excite, quiet, or expel passions of the soul.

> Thus it happens that the soul may be moved by a double affection, that is, through the excitement of both harmony and words, and that music soothes the human ears with wonderful sweetness derived as nowhere else from such measure, so much order, so much measured sonority. Aristotle, too, discusses this more rigorously in his *Problems concerning Music* and seems also to conclude thus. Again every tone or mode has a top and a bottom, which are drawn to the middle (mese). Indeed, without the mese the melody could not be drawn back alternately to the mode after a change.[25]

The unifying principle of the mode was a wonderful discovery, because the octave contains within itself all the harmonies, and it confines through the modes and tones the many diverse operations that composers utilize in voices and instruments. Gaffurio in this passage seems to refer to Problem 19.20, in which the function of the mese to bring a melody constantly back to a focal point is observed. He may also have had in mind 19.38, which speculates about the reason for the universal enjoyment of rhythm, song, and music in general, concluding that ordered movement is allied to our natures, which thrive on order, and that we are pleased by mixtures of sensations, particularly when extremes are harmonized through some concord. The *Problems* evidently helped Gaffurio to clarify his own thoughts concerning the ethos and functions of the modes.

Of the translations Gaffurio commissioned, the one he must have received

---

23. *Theoricum opus,* IV, 1; *Theorica,* IV, 1, fol. f4v.
24. *De harmonia,* II, 38, fol. 67r.
25. Gaffurio, *Theorica,* V, 8, fol. k4v.

first is that of the *Introduction to the Art of Music* by Bacchius Senior, for he quoted from it quite literally. The date of this translation is unknown and the text of it does not survive, but there is secure evidence that it existed, since it is mentioned both by Gaffurio in the first chapter of *De harmonia* and by Pantaleo Melegulus in his short biographical note at the back of this book.[26] In Book II, chapter 1, of the 1492 book (and missing in the 1480 version) Gaffurio (left below) introduced a long disquisition that derives partly from Bacchius (right below). From this author Gaffurio obtained the division of the elements of music as based partly on nature and partly on usage—"our practice."[27]

Elementorum enim huius musicae rationis quedam naturae insunt quedam usui nostro: Naturae insunt acumina grauitates & diastemata id est interualla ut Baccheus posuit. Vsui autem nostro ipsa pronunciatio & effectio morum circa ipsos sonos.[28]	How does music exist? Partly by nature, partly through our practice. What sort of things by nature? Height and depth of pitch and the intervals. What sort of things through our practice? The rendering of emotion through the use of the pitches.[29]

Gaffurio borrows from Bacchius also the definitions of basic terms, such as tone, "the smallest part of a sung melodic utterance is a tone"; system, "that which is sung melodiously with more than two tones"; *diastema*, "the difference or interval between two tones that are different in acuity or gravity"; diesis, "the smallest of the diastemata or spaces or intervals . . . ; the diesis is the smallest interval that our natural capacity can produce by tension or relaxation"; "the double diesis is a semitone"; "a tone is that by which the diapente is greater than the diatessaron."[30]

Gaffurio also cites Bacchius concerning the number of modes (*modi*) and species of diapason used by the Greeks, which he says was seven.[31] Actually Bacchius stated that some sang only three *tropi:* the Lydian, Phrygian, and

---

26. The statement reads: "Praetereo ueterum musicorum graeca opera: Aristidae quintiliani: Manuelis Briennii: Bacchei senis Introductorium & Ptholomei harmonicon: quae omnia eius cura & impensa a diuersis interpretibus in latinum sunt conuersa." A slightly different version of this is in Lodi, Biblioteca Comunale Laudense, MS XXVIII.A.9.

27. Here I follow Meibom and Ruelle rather than von Jan, who emends *ethopoiia* of the manuscripts to *melopoiia.*

28. Gaffurio, *Theorica,* II, 1, fol. b6v.

29. Bacchius, von Jan ed., 2, trans. Otto Steinmayer, in Bacchius Geron, *Introduction to the Art of Music,* in press.

30. Bacchius *Introduction* 8.

31. Gaffurio, *Theorica* V, 8, fol. k4v.

Dorian. Others sang seven: the Mixolydian, the three just mentioned, and the Hypolydian, Hypophrygian, and Hypodorian.[32]

Gaffurio does not seem to have penetrated far into this treatise at this time. In the *Practica musice* he plumbed it further for definitions: of mutation as the transposition of something similar into a dissimilar location, borrowed from Bacchius' definition of *metabole*,[33] of the sensation of interval not as something audible but rather as something intelligible,[34] and for Aristoxenus' definition of *rhythm* as "a division of time according to each of the things that can be rhythmicized."[35] But he could also give a definition a twist not intended by the original author, as when, on the authority of Bacchius, he defines a *genre* of harmonic music as a "universal phenomenon exhibiting inner diversity and containing species or forms of various musical combinations which we call counterpoint," when what Bacchius called *genre* was "a certain part of harmonics that permits us to recognize the general character of a melody and that contains several diverse forms."[36] Whereas Bacchius was speaking of one of the aspects of the study of harmonics, which could be applied to the composition of melody, Gaffurio interpreted *genre* as a category of polyphonic music. Such misunderstandings were bound to arise when such fundamental terms as *harmonia* could not be isolated from the connotations it bore in Gaffurio's day.

The Greek author whom Gaffurio quoted most extensively in his *Theorica* was Themistius (c. 317–388 A.D.), specifically his *Paraphrases* on the *De anima* of Aristotle. All of Gaffurio's citations can be traced to the translation by Ermolao Barbaro (1454–93) first published in 1481 (Trevisio) and frequently reprinted.[37] Barbaro completed the translation in 1472 at the age of nineteen while reading for a doctorate in letters at the studio of Padua. He later planned to translate all of the works of Aristotle but succeeded in finishing only some of them before he died of the plague in Rome in 1493.

---

32. Bacchius *Introduction* 46.
33. Bacchius *Introduction* 58; Gaffurio, *Practica,* I, 4.
34. Bacchius *Introduction* 72; Gaffurio, *Practica,* III, 1.
35. Bacchius *Introduction* 93; Gaffurio, *Practica,* II, 1.
36. Bacchius *Introduction* 79; Gaffurio, *Practica,* III, 1, trans. Young, p. 123 as: "the principles of harmonious modulation are universal and produce diverse archetypes or ideal models, as well as diverse arrangements of song, which we call counterpoint."
37. The edition I used at Beinecke Rare Book and Manuscript Library at Yale was: *Themistii Peripatetici Lucidissimi, Paraphrasis In Aristotelis Posteriore, & Physica. In libro item de Anima, . . . Hermolao Barbaro Patricio Veneto Interprete* (Venice, 1554), but I usually cite the edition of Paris, 1535, available in the edition by Richard Heinze (Berlin, 1899). This was not the first translation of the *Paraphrases*. William of Moerbeke made one in 1267 for Thomas Aquinas, who used it in his own commentaries on the *De anima*. William's translation has been edited by G. Verbeke: *Themistius Commentaire sur le Traité de l'âme d'Aristote. Traduction de Guillaume de Moerbeke* (Louvain, 1957).

Barbaro aimed to render faithfully the thought of the author, yet in a style
that is truly Latin, elegant, and personal. The translation of Themistius,
according to Kristeller, is the first humanist translation of a Greek commentator on Aristotle.[38]

Gaffurio relied upon Themistius mainly for his penetrating commentary
on Aristotle's theory of sound and hearing.[39] All of the passages citing
Themistius appear first in the 1492 version of the treatise. Gaffurio credits
Themistius at least once in each chapter in which he draws upon him, but
although he quotes him verbatim (or with only a few changes of word
order), he does not employ quotation marks. In this he is consistent, for
quotation marks do not appear anywhere in the treatise, though they were
common enough in publications and manuscripts of the period. In Book II
of the edition of 1492, forty-nine lines of chapter 1, on the definition of
music and its elements, forty-five lines of chapter 2, on sound and the voice,
and four lines of chapter 4, on the formation of consonance, are direct
quotations of Themistius.

Gaffurio showed good judgment in relying so heavily on Themistius'
theory of sound. Through this author's commentaries on Aristotle, supplemented by insights from Nicomachus (through Boethius), Gaffurio
transmits the most enlightened explanation of the nature, production, and
propagation of sound known to the ancient world. This will be shown in
chapter 10 below.

The work of musica theorica that Gaffurio completed after the *Theorica
musice* was the book published in 1518 as *De harmonia musicorum instrumentorum opus*.[40] The publication date is misleading, however, because all of
the surviving manuscripts were completed much earlier. Since in this work
Gaffurio had a chance to utilize the translations of the Greek musical treatises
he had commissioned, it is crucial to determine how much time he had to
absorb these long and complex works while continuing to serve in the
demanding job of maestro di capella at the Duomo of Milan.

Gaffurio speaks in the dedication of the printed edition of keeping "this
somewhat reluctant treatise at home, although it was awaited by all musicians; through a certain inborn modesty the confined work did not dare
to appear in public."[41] But actually he was eager to bring it out, and it
awaited only a patron to subsidize the high cost of printing. The manuscript
copies that survive attest to the difficulty he had in finding sponsorship.
Clement Miller in the introduction to his translation of *De harmonia* has

38. Kristeller, *Studies*, pp. 342–43.
39. *De anima* 2.8.419b–421a.
40. Milan, 1518; facs. ed., Bologna, 1972.
41. Franchinus Gaffurius, *De Harmonia Musicorum Instrumentorum Opus*, introduction and
translation by Clement A. Miller (American Institute of Musicology, 1977), p. 34.

discussed three of these manuscripts, but two others that are relevant to our study were apparently unknown to him. What the manuscripts contribute to the publication history of this book will be detailed in the following annotated chronological list.

1. Lodi, Biblioteca Comunale Laudense, MS XXVIII.A.9. Two inscriptions appear at the end of the manuscript: "Die vero Veneris vigesimoseptimo Mensis Martii hoc opus tradidit Absolutum anno Millesimmo quingentesimo" and "Revisum castigatumque est hoc musicum volumen die duodecimo Martii 1514 ab Auctore in aedibus Divi Marcellini Mediolani." These indicate that Gaffurio finished the work on 27 March 1500, but numerous autograph pasted and marginal insertions as well as the final inscription attest to his continued revision until 12 March 1514. The short biography of the author by Pantaleone Melegulo that is appended to the treatise contains evidence that the dedicatee for whom this beautifully illuminated codex was intended was Bonifacio Simonetta (c. 1441–1502), abbot of the Monastery of San Stefano del Corno. But after the French takeover of the city, he evidently fell out of favor, for on 25 May 1502 Scaramuccia Trivulzio, a relative of the marshall of France who took the city, replaced him. Both the dedication and a portrait of the abbot appear to have been erased in this manuscript. Gaffurio was forced to find another patron.
2. Paris, Bibliothèque Nationale, MS lat. 7208. This was a copy apparently presented or made for Nicolò Leoniceno, translator of Ptolemy's *Harmonics*. It ends with the following words: "Finis. Laus deo: Die Veneris 27° Martij 1500 ego presbiter Franchinus ultimam huic operi manum apposui in Edibus diui Marcellini porte cumane ciuitatis mediolani." (The End. God be praised. On Friday, 27 March 1500, I, Father Franchinus, put my last hand on this work in the edifice [church] of Saint Marcellino at the Porta Cumana of the city of Milan.) This copy, which has not previously been noted in the literature on Gaffurio, is marked at the top of the recto of the first flyleaf: "Dnj Nicolai Leonicenj." It was obviously given to Leoniceno by the author in recognition of the help Leoniceno's translation of Ptolemy had been to him. The binding appears to be the original one, and although this flyleaf is not watermarked, the second flyleaf has the same watermark as the remainder of the pages of the manuscript, a pair of scissors with an arrow, similar but not identical to Briquet 3735, dated 1515, and forms with the back flyleaves a single double folio with that bearing Leoniceno's name. The Paris copy may be one of the earliest made, since the table of contents ends with chapter 6 of Book III, whereas the text that follows has the complete book, as well as all of Book IV.

3.   Lyon, Bibliothèque Municipale, formerly Palais des Arts, MS 47. The inscription at the end shows that it was written by Gaffurio himself: "Die jovis, vigesimo augusti milessimo quingentessimo, ego presbiter Franchinus, hora vigesima tertia ultimam huic exemplo manum posui quod ad exemplari diligenter exscripsi in edibus Divi Marcellini, porte Cumane, civitatis Mediolani." This vellum manuscript, still in its original binding, elegantly illuminated, was offered to Charles Jaufred (Carlo Gioffredo), president of the Parliament of the Dauphiné (Grenoble) and vice-chancellor of the Senate of Milan. The date of dedication is uncertain, but it must be around 1505–06, when three other books published in Milan were dedicated to Jaufred: Alexander Minutianus' edition of Livy, July 1505; Aulus Janus Parrhasius (Aulo Giano Parrasio), an edition of Claudianus, *De raptu Proserpinae cum commentariis,* 12 December 1505; and Johannes Maria Cataneus, an edition of Pliny, *Epistolarum libri x,* 1506. This copy of Gaffurio's treatise is mentioned by Caretta, Cremascoli, and Salamina in a bibliographical listing, but the authors apparently never saw it.[42] Like the Paris manuscript, it is a faithful copy of the first layer of the Lodi manuscript without any of the later additions. But entire chapters are missing. Evidently Jaufred did not accept the responsibility of sponsoring the book, and Gaffurio had to continue his search for a patron.

4.   Naples, Biblioteca Nazionale, MS VIII.D.11. Franchinus Gaforus, *Theorica artis musicae.* This manuscript, undated, is indexed in Kristeller, *Iter italicum,* I, 403, and is described by Miller as a "study codex," the work of two scribes; it omits some of the diagrams.

5.   Vienna, Österreichische Nationalbibliothek, Codex Ser. nov. 12745. This illuminated presentation copy contains a dedication to Johannes Grolier and once belonged to him.[43] It exhibits the following traces of its origins:

> fol. 2 [after table of contents]: "Ego Bernardinus de la rupere   scripsi hunc librum expletum die lune' 19° Aprilis 1507."
>
> fol. 68v: "... Franchinus Gafurius ... p[er]fecit 26° / mensis   Martij 1500 Aetatis sue anno quadragesimonono." Grolier became the French king's treasurer and Intendant of Milan in 1509.[44] The manuscript was apparently first prepared for presentation to another patron, as Unterkircher has shown that there are marks of a different

---

42. Alessandro Caretta, Luigi Cremascoli, and Luigi Salamina, *Franchino Gaffurio* (Lodi, 1951), p. 135.

43. Concerning this manuscript, see Franz Unterkircher, "Eine Handschrift aus dem Besitze Jean Groliers in der Oesterreichischen Nationalbibliothek," *Libri* 1 (1950–51):51–57.

44. Miller trans., introduction, p. 13.

coat of arms under the present one.[45] Grolier must have answered Gaffurio's plea for a subsidy, because the printed edition is also dedicated to him. A presentation copy of the printed book with a manuscript dedication to Grolier by Gaffurio is in Paris, Bibliothèque de l'Arsenal.[46]

This history of delays and variant exemplars reveals that Gaffurio not only had the opportunity but in fact continued to revise the work between 1500 and 1514. In these fourteen years he could have penetrated more deeply into the translations from the Greek, but did he? The revisions tell us that he did not; the insertions that reached the printer but are missing in the Paris manuscript all pertain to modern authors with whom Gaffurio was feuding or to matters that do not touch upon the ancient sources.[47] Gaffurio was content to let the Greek sources rest. There is evidence, indeed, in some autograph glosses on Johannes de Muris that in 1499 he had moved on to investigate medieval music theory.[48]

These circumstances surrounding the publication of Gaffurio's last treatise have considerable bearing on our evaluation of his utilization of the Greek writings on music theory. If the treatise as it stands in the printed edition of 1518 had reflected twenty years or more of assimilation of Greek theory from original sources, our judgment of it would to have to be more severe than if the published treatise remained essentially as it was drafted in 1500, which has been shown to be the case. The 1500 version communicated, as far as the ancient sources were concerned, Gaffurio's definitive statement. Since most of the translations are dated, it may be concluded that Gaffurio had had the Bacchius translation at least eight years, the Aristides Quintilianus and anonymi about six years, the Bryennius a little more than three years, and the Ptolemy barely one year before he completed the draft of the *De harmonia* in 1500.

Although he may have lost interest in the classical authors after 1500, Gaffurio's principal motivation for publishing one more treatise on speculative music after the *Theoricum opus* and the *Theorica musice* was the new insights he received from the translations he had commissioned. For these Gaffurio had gone to two humanists who were learned in both Greek and Latin literature and philosophy, though neither of them had previously been concerned with music.

As we saw in chapter 6, Giovanni Francesco Burana translated the treatises

---

45. Unterkircher, "Eine Handschrift," p. 53.
46. Ibid., p. 51.
47. For an account of these additions, see Miller, trans., introduction, pp. 18–24.
48. *Glossemata quaedam super nonnullas partes theoricae Johannis de Muris,* Milan, Biblioteca Ambrosiana, MS H.165 inf., dated 1 January 1499. See Caretta et al., *Gaffurio,* p. 135.

of Aristides Quintilianus and Manuel Bryennius and the anonymous treatises known as Bellerman's anonymous. He may also have translated the
Bacchius Senior *Introduction*. Gaffurio's own copies of Burana's translations
of the three musical treatises, which he gave to he Church of the Incoronata
of Lodi in 1518, are now in the Biblioteca Capitolare of Verona.[49] The
Aristides translation is dated 1494, and the anonymi 15 April 1494. The
Bryennius is not dated in this manuscript, but a copy in Gaffurio's hand
now in Lodi indicates at the end that Gaffurio finished copying it on 5
January 1497.[50] However, the translation must have been finished at about
the same time as the others, since Gaffurio cites Bryennius in the *Practica
musice* of 1496.

Gaffurio's copy in his own hand[51] of Leoniceno's translation of Ptolemy's
Harmonics is one of the two exemplars that survive, the other being a presentation copy, but not autograph.[52] The translation is preceded by a letter
of dedication, written in Ferrara and dated March 1499, from Leoniceno to
Petro Barotio, bishop of Padua and a close friend of Gaffurio, who apparently had commissioned the translation at Gaffurio's instigation.[53] As we
saw, Leoniceno owned a manuscript copy, now in Paris, of *De harmonia* in
the version finished in 1500. In addition to the notation on the first flyleaf,
"Domini Nicolai Leoniceni" ([property] of Dominus Nicolaus Leonicenus),
there are marks in Greek on the second flyleaf, and on fol. 109r, where
Melegulo mentions the four Greek authors translated for Gaffurio, the four
names are listed in the right margin in Greek letters, probably in Leoniceno's
hand. There are no other marginal notes except those belonging to the
treatise itself. The postils, which mainly agree with those of the printed
edition, appear to be in Gaffurio's hand.

Before proceeding to an analysis of the utilization of the Greek sources
in *De harmonia,* brief mention of their usage in the immediately preceding
work, *Practica musice,* should be made. Clement Miller, in the notes to his
English translation of this treatise and in his study of 1968, has drawn

49. MS CCXL (201); description in F. Alberto Gallo, "Le traduzioni dal Greco per Franchino
Gaffurio," *Acta Musicologica* 35 (1963):172–74; idem, "Musici scriptores graeci," in *Catalogus
translationum et commentariorum: Mediaeval and Renaissance Translations and Commentaries,* ed.
Edward Cranz and Paul O. Kristeller, III (Washington, 1976), 67–68. The list of holdings of
the Incoronata library (see Motta, "I libri," p. 111) names only the Aristides Quintilianus,
probably because it was the first item of a group.

50. Lodi, Biblioteca Comunale Laudense, MS XXVIII.A.8.

51. London, British Library, MS Harl. 3306, fols. 1–46.

52. Rome, Biblioteca Apostolica Vaticana, MS Vat. lat. 4570, fols. 1–58.

53. Gaffurio in *De harmonia,* II, 23, fol. 24v, calls Barotio "vita moribus et doctrina uiri
integerrimi ac mei amantissimi."

attention to Gaffurio's dependence on both ancient and modern sources.[54] Miller has shown that the treatise was drafted over a long period of time and that traces of earlier versions which survive reveal a progressive penetration into the heritage of ancient learning. The book was apparently begun in 1481, and a version of Book I dated 1487 by the scribe cites only four writers: Boethius, Marchettus, Guido, and Isidor.[55] Book I as printed in 1496 cites in addition Bacchius, Martianus Capella, Anselmi,[56] Pietro d'Abano, and Bryennius. Book II must have been finished in an early version by 1492, since it was published that year in an Italian condensation by a pupil of Gaffurio, Francesco Caza, as *Tractato vulgare de canto figurato*.[57] Book IV, on numerical proportions, derives from a work that Gaffurio finished around 1483 and that exists in manuscript in Bologna.[58] Miller has compiled a list of the sources cited in the 1496 publication, and it is a long and impressive one.[59] It includes all of the works translated for Gaffurio except one, the *Harmonics* of Ptolemy, which was apparently not finished until later.

Recourses in the *Practica* to the translations of Aristides, Bacchius, and Bryennius are neither numerous nor important. Gaffurio cites Bacchius, as we saw, for his definition of mutation and Aristoxenus for that of rhythm and the idea that the harmonic principles of melody making are universal.[60] He also draws from Bacchius the nice distinction between the intelligibility and audibility of the interval between two notes, a silent phenomenon that is nevertheless perceived.[61]

Aristides Quintilianus is cited twice in the *Practica*, as a source of information about the Greek poetic feet,[62] and with reference to the division of the whole tone into four enharmonic dieses.[63] These citations are entirely accessory to the arguments at hand.

---

54. Clement A. Miller, ed. and trans., Franchinus Gaffurius, *Practica musicae;* idem, "Gaffurio's *Practica musicae*," *Musica Disciplina* 22 (1968):105–28.

55. Bergamo, Biblioteca Civica, MS E4.37.

56. Giorgio Anselmi, *De musica*, ed. Giuseppe Massera (Florence, 1961).

57. Milan, 1492

58. *Franchini Gafori Laudensis Musices professoris tractatus practicabilium proportionum ad R[everen]dum d[omi]num Coradolum Stangam doctorem Egregium ac S. Antonii Cremon[ensi] preceptorem*, MS A69. See Gaetano Gaspari, *Catalogo della Biblioteca musicale G. B. Martini di Bologna* (Bologna, 1961), I, 216.

59. Gaffurio, *Practica*, Miller trans., p. 110.

60. See above n. 54.

61. Gaffurio, *Practica*, III, 1: "Intervalla vero cum sint quidam taciti transitus a sono ad sonum non sunt audibilia ut Baccheus inquit sed intelligibilia." Bacchius *Introduction* 72.

62. Gaffurio, *Practica*, II, 2; Aristides Quintilianus *De musica* 1.15.

63. Gaffurio, *Practica*, II, 6; Aristides Quintilianus *De musica* 1.7.

On the other hand, Gaffurio used significantly, if not extensively, the anonymi.[64] In an exceptionally restrospective discussion of rhythm and meter, in which Gaffurio recalls the ancient meters and the theories of Diomedes, Augustine, Quintilian, and Bede, he publishes for the first time a table of the Greek temporal signs extracted from one of the tracts. The durations represented by the signs are symbolized as follows:

- ‒ a breve of one tempus
- ≃ a minor long of two tempora
- ∟ a long of three tempora
- ⊔ a long of four tempora
- ω a long of five tempora

Gaffurio further notes that the arsis was represented by placing a dot after the durational sign, while the thesis was marked by the absence of a dot.[65] Gaffurio was to use this knowledge of the ancient rhythms to construct a two-voice melody for a stanza of a fifteen-stanza Sapphic ode by Lancino Curzio, "Musices septemque modos planete," published in De harmonia.[66] Although Gaffurio's publication of the rhythmic signs is not of the order of importance of Galilei's later publication of the pitch signs, it was a step in the direction of lifting the veil of mystery from the practice of Greek music. The two disclosures are worlds apart also in the significance the two authors attached to their revelations. Galilei sought a model for modern music, whereas Gaffurio ends the discussion apologetically, implying that to go into more detail about the methods of applying the ancient time values to melodic composition was a useless exercise, because they were "incongruous and foreign to our customs."[67]

The scope of De harmonia musicorum instrumentorum opus, despite the expression "of musical instruments" in the title, lies squarely in the field of musica theorica. But it enlarges upon this field as defined by the contents of the Theorica musice, which comprehended the curriculum established by Boethius. The De harmonia expands this domain to include both studies of

64. Friedrich Bellermann, Anonymi scriptio de musica Bachii senioris introductio artis musicae (Berlin, 1841); Dietmar Najock, Drei anonyme griechische Traktate über die Musik. Eine kommentierte Neuausgabe des Bellermannschen Anonymus, Göttinger musikwissenschaftliche Arbeiten, II (Kassel, 1972).

65. Gaffurio, Practica, II, 2. Bellermann Anon. I, 1–3; Najock pp. 67–69. The anonymous theorist defines Gaffurio's first sign as worth two tempora. Gaffurio's second sign is not in the edited text.

66. IV, 10, fol. 89r; see transcription in Giuseppe Vecchi's introduction to the facsimile edition (Bologna, 1972), p. ix.

67. Gaffurio, Practica, II, 2; Miller trans., p. 73.

greater relevance to music as practiced by modern musicians and questions of cosmic harmony in relation to the human soul and experience. The act of writing the *Practica musice* and his years as director of a cathedral choir had undoubtedly made Gaffurio more sensitive to problems of music theory that he had been content to gloss over earlier.

If we compare the contents of the *Theorica* and the *De harmonia* we find certain areas of overlap, to be sure. Basic definitions, the system of ratios and their manipulation, the proportions and means, the construction of the Greek gamut, the modes and genera, the intervals, all these are found in both treatises. But the weight given to certain topics differs. In the *Theorica* there is but one chapter on the genera of tetrachords and one on the Greek gamut; in the *De harmonia* most of Book I is devoted to them. Here also Gaffurio proposes a new genus, the *permixtum*. Book II of *De harmonia* deals entirely with matters untouched in the other treatise, the description of the chromatic and enharmonic and the various "shades" of tuning set forth by Archytas, Aristoxenus, and Ptolemy. Book III of *De harmonia,* in addition to a review of the arithmetical, geometrical, and harmonic progressions, contains detailed chapters on these three types of means, and in a separate chapter proposes a new one, the sonorous mean (medietas sonora), which mediates the major and minor sixths and tenths.

Book IV of *De harmonia* deals with the relationships of sounding music to celestial bodies and the effects of music on the senses, body, and mind, and its analogy to the parts of the mind and to other things measured by numbers. Gaffurio's main purpose remains, as in his previous theoretical works, to unite in an orderly way in one place all that is written by various authors in many volumes: " . . . ut studiosorum profectui concinna, compendiosaque brevitate consuluisse dicar; ut quae forent sparsim per Authorum volumina, requirenda in uno opere, convenienti rerum ordine congesta reperiantur."[68] Occasionally, as with the theory of the *medietas sonora,* or of the imperfect consonances, Gaffurio makes an original contribution to the body of speculation handed down by the Greek and Latin authors. But the main source for what is new in the *De harmonia* is the small corpus of newly translated Greek works.

It would be tedious to trace the indebtedness of Gaffurio to the translated treatises on every point. It is more instructive to show how he benefited from them in a number of areas in which *De harmonia* makes a distinctive contribution to the body of theoretical knowledge available at this time. These are in the areas of fundamental definitions, the genera, the shades of tuning, and the modes. The four topics are chosen not only because they

---

68. *Practica,* dedicatory letter.

represent the most positive contributions of the volume, but because in these areas the humanist revival of ancient theory made its greatest impact on musical practice and thought in the sixteenth century.

Gaffurio, like writers before him, tended to adopt the categories of Boethius until gradually he became aware that alternatives existed in the older theoretical literature that perhaps Boethius did not know or simply failed to cite. One of the contributions of Boethius that had proved most lasting was the precision of his distinctions and categories; so it is not surprising that in his earlier treatises Gaffurio followed him. But like other followers of Boethius, he was trapped in the Boethian bias for distinctions that are based on number.

We have seen that in these earlier works Gaffurio supplemented the standard Boethian definitions with others culled from various sources as they became available to him. The intent of these amplifications is not always clear, but they seem inspired more by a desire for completeness than by a critical search for an optimum set of categories. Even in *De harmonia* we seek in vain a critique of theoretical categories. Still, a process of selection was at work, and categories that do not proceed entirely from *ratio* are given attention, if not always favorably. The first chapters of *De harmonia* are rich in categories, many of them unknown to pre-Renaissance Europe, which Gaffurio harvested from the translations of Aristides Quintilianus, Bacchius, and Bryennius, three late interpreters of classical Greek theory.

Already in earlier writings Gaffurio had reported the distinction emanating from Aristoxenus and passed on by Boethius between the continuous and diastematic voice. Now, in his chapter "Concerning Sounds and their Distinctions" (I, 2), he cites a slightly different dichotomy proposed by Aristides, "continuous" and "discrete."[69] The continuous voice is that used by those who read aloud or speak, while the discrete voice is that of singers. Whereas the continuous voice passes over the degrees (*intensiones* and *remissiones*) of pitch quickly, the singing, discrete voice makes these manifest through extension.[70] Bacchius, he notes, calls the continuous voice "pedestrian," while the other he calls "melodizing" (*modulata*) or suitable to melody (*melodiae proprias.*)[71]

For the rest of the chapter Gaffurio paraphrases Bryennius. First he draws from him the comment that sound is never really continuous, because between the percussions of the air there are silences, and it is only the imagination (*phantasia*) that converts these multiple sounds received by the

69. Aristides Quintilianus *De musica* 1.4.

70. Aristides Quintilianus *De musica* 1.4; Gaffurio adds a comment from Bryennius *Harmonics* 1.3, that it is called continuous because it does not seem to the ear to stay in one place.

71. Bacchius *Introduction* 69.

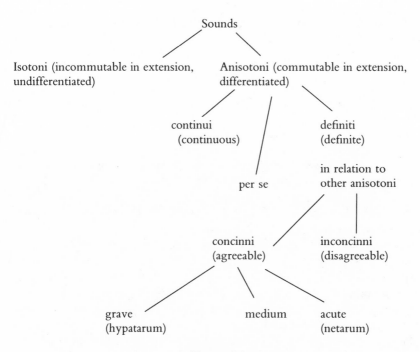

Figure 9.1:
Classification of sounds in Bryennius

ear into a continuous one. He closes the chapter with a description of the classification of sounds by Bryennius, which may be rendered most easily in tabular form (Figure 9.1).

Although Gaffurio, as was his habit, voiced no preference for one or the other system of classification, he was obviously entranced with the completeness of Bryennius' categories and their progression from the undifferentiated to the qualitatively and quantitatively selective. Gaffurio's translator coined the terms "isotoni" and "anisotoni" for their Greek cognates, and Gaffurio did not recognize that these were the same terms that Ptolemy used and that Boethius translated as "unisonae" and "non unisonae." Burana's translation failed to make clear that isotones are monotones, because he translated *tasin* as "extension" rather than "tension." Gaffurio neglects to clarify the terms and seems untroubled by the fact that the category of isotone as he describes it is quite meaningless.[72]

72. Perhaps judiciously Gaffurio omits a level of division Bryennius interposed between *concinni* and grave-medium-acute, namely the threefold division of *concinni* into *consoni*, *unisoni* (or *antiphoni*), and *dissoni*. The translation of Bryennius here may not have been clear, or Gaffurio may have preferred to save these distinctions for the following chapter on intervals.

Chapter 3, "On Various Definitions of Intervals and their Differences,"
opens with a passage from Burana's translation of Aristides Quintilianus,
which is quoted verbatim except for the insertion of Boethius' definition
of musical interval. Aristides recognized two meanings of "interval," "in
general" (*communiter dictum,*) that is, any magnitude determined by fixed
boundaries, and "in particular" (*private,*) that is, the magnitude of tones
circumscribed by two sounds. The next seventy lines of this chapter are
lifted almost verbatim from Burana's translation of Bryennius (1.5). Gaffurio here cites the five criteria by means of which Bryennius distinguishes
intervals from one another: (1) magnitude, (2) consonance or dissonance,
(3) composite or simple, (4) the genus (diatonic, etc.) to which it belongs,
and (5) rational or irrational. The magnitudes recognized by Bryennius go
from disdiapason down to diesis, to which Gaffurio adds the apotome.
Among the consonances, Bryennius recognizes a class of *antiphonae,* that
is, diapason and disdiapason.[73]

Intervals are classed dissonant that are smaller than the trihemitone (minor
third) or that are composed entirely of tones, such as the tritone, tetratone,
pentatone, and the like. Composite intervals are those that are not adjacent,
such as in the diatonic perfect system between hypate hypaton (B) and
lichanos hypaton (d). Incomposite are the adjacent steps in any genus, such
as between hypate hypaton (B) and parhypate hypaton (c) in the diatonic,
or the semiditone in the chromatic.

In explaining the fifth distinction, between rational and irrational, Gaffurio turns from Bryennius to Aristides Quintilianus and Bacchius, and this
with good reason, since Bryennius is sketchy on this point. Aristides, if
too brief, is more explicit. The passage that Gaffurio quotes from Aristides
(without quotation marks, to be sure) defines rational intervals as those
whose ratios we can declare. We call *ratio* an integral and known mutual
relation among numbers. Rational intervals are the diatessaron in the epitrite
ratio, the diapente in the hemiolia, the diapason in the dupla, the diapason-
plus-diapente in the tripla, and the disdiapason in the quadrupla.[74] Gaffurio
skips over Aristides' definition of irrational intervals as those in which no
ratio can be found. He prefers to quote Bacchius, who "is of the opinion
that those whose ratio is difficult to assign are for this reason called irrational." Actually Bacchius speaks of irrational only in reference to the du-

---

73. Here Gaffurio notes that Boethius called this category *aequisonae* and *paraphona,* whereas
the diapente and diatessaron he called *symphoniae.* Two of these terms coincide with the
threefold classification in Ptolemy *Harmonics* 1.7: *homophonoi, symphonoi,* and *emmeleis,* which
Boethius *(De institutione musica* 5.10) rendered "aequisonae," "consonae," and "emmeles."
74. Aristides Quintilianus *De musica* 1.7.

ration of time that is more than two breves but less than a long and "therefore cannot be compared in a ratio, and for this reason is called irrational.[75]

Gaffurio senses the inadequacy of all these definitions and suggests that some intervals are rational according to both nature and art, namely the diatessaron and diapente, the diapason, diapason-plus-diapente, and disdiapason. Others are rational only by art, that is to say, they have a determinate ratio, such as the whole tone of 9:8 proportion, but are not agreeable to the ear and therefore are not rational by nature. Others are produced only by nature in that they are pleasing to the ear, such as the incomposite ditone (the sum of two whole tones) and the incomposite trihemitone (the sum of three semitones), the diapente-plus-tone and the diapente-plus-semitone, but their numerical relations (such as 81:64) cannot be proportionately measured on a string, therefore failing in rationality by art. He admits that it is possible to divide the double-octave system in such a way that the ditone is in the ratio 5:4, the semiditone 6:5, the diapente-plus-tone 5:3, and the diapente-plus-semitone 8:5, and that these can be divided on a string. But they have other disadvantages that exclude them from consideration, he objects. Indeed, in a later place, he shows that 5:4, being superparticular, cannot be divided into two equal tones, as the Pythagorean ditone, 81:64, can.[76] Gaffurio evidently realizes that the acceptance of thirds and sixths as consonances and the possibility of dividing the string to produce them by means of simple ratios blurs the once clear distinction between rational and irrational intervals. He is forced to introduce the double requirement of nature (sense of hearing) and art (ratio), for, while some satisfy the one or other criterion, only the truly "rational" intervals accepted by Aristides satisfy both.

Bryennius is again the source for the determination of the names of the fifteen strings of the perfect system. Gaffurio follows him almost verbatim, except where he occasionally abbreviates Bryennius' elaborate etymologies, notably concerning the terms *mese, trite diezeugmenon,* and those for the steps from nete diezeugmenon to nete hyperbolaion.[77] The division of the monochord for the diatonic tetrachords, which Gaffurio starts from the tetrachord hypaton, is not based on Bryennius, however, and although the numbers for the string lengths agree with those of Boethius, the order of partition of the string differs and may be attributed to Gaffurio himself.[78]

75. Bacchius *Introduction* 95.

76. Gaffurio, *De harmonia,* II, 34.

77. Gaffurio, *De harmonia,* I, 4, fols. 7v–8r; Bryennius *Harmonics* 1.2.

78. There is a sprinkling of further references to Bryennius throughout the *De harmonia:* to Bryennius *Harmonics* 2.2 in Gaffurio II, 16, fol. 38v, and to 3.7 in II, 14, fol. 35v, but they involve small points only.

It was from Ptolemy that Gaffurio derived the revelations that were to
have the most lasting influence on Western music. The tunings that Ptolemy
proposed, one of which was the syntonic diatonic adopted by leading theorists in the sixteenth century, were previously unknown except to those
who read Ptolemy in Greek. Numerous other Greek tunings, or shades, of
the various genera were already familiar through Boethius, whose fifth book
was a translation and condensation of the first book of Ptolemy's *Harmonics*.
Of Boethius' five books this one attracted the least interest through the
Middle Ages and the early Renaissance. Not only is it incomplete—only
the first eighteen and part of the nineteenth of the thirty chapters announced
in the table of contents are extant—but it deals with matters that were of
remote relevance to traditional theory. In the chapters of Ptolemy that
Boethius probably failed to complete, Ptolemy set forth his preferred divisions of the tetrachord in the three genera and gave his reasons for rejecting
the divisons of the Pythagoreans, Archytas, Aristoxenus, and Didymus. In
the extant chapters Boethius transmitted Ptolemy's discussion faithfully,
though occasionally he omitted passages of importance. The chapter headings of the missing portion of Boethius' compendium of Ptolemy may have
led Gaffurio to seek out Ptolemy's book and have it translated. Some of
the headings bore particularly on the new ideas on tuning propagated by
Ramos de Pareja:[79] chapter 21, "How Ptolemy divided the diatessaron into
two parts"; 22, "Which are the dense genera, which the least, and how the
proportions are adapted, and concerning the division of the enharmonic of
Ptolemy"; 26, "The division of the soft diatonic of Ptolemy"; 27, "The
division of the intense diatonic of Ptolemy"; 28, "The division of the toniaic
diatonic of Ptolemy"; and so on.

Gaffurio's chapters 16–20 of Book II of *De harmonia* are dedicated to the
exposition of Ptolemy's theories on the division of the tetrachords through
the various shades. Chapters 18–20 specifically contain the material missing
in Boethius. Besides filling the breach of Boethius' missing chapters, Gaffurio goes also to Ptolemy's Book II, chapter, 13 for the division of the
three genera according to Didymus.

Gaffurio's method in these chapters is to follow Ptolemy's prose consec-
utively through the translation of Leoniceno, but rather than repeat Leoniceno verbatim, rewrite his Latin. Whether he did this rewriting because he
did not like Leoniceno's prose style or whether it was because he expected
Leoniceno to see it is a matter for speculation (Gaffurio sent Leoniceno a
manuscript copy, which, as we have seen, is in Paris). It may have been
some of both. Leoniceno's prose is even more obscure at times than Gaffurio's, although the syntax is simpler and more direct. Occasionally Gaf-

79. Ramos de Pareja, *De musica tractatus* (Bologna, 1482).

furio preferred to copy out the reductions of Ptolemy by Boethius, whose treatise he obviously kept close at hand as he drafted the book.

The following passage (left), on the division of the tetrachord by Aristoxenus, for example, parallels Ptolemy (1.12), but it is obviously taken, though in a truncated form, from Boethius (right):

Aristoxenus autem ut duodecimo primi harmonicae Ptholomeus scribit: quadrifaria tradidit toni diuisionem: diuidit namque tonum in duas partes aequales quas semitonia uocat. Diuidit quandoque in tres aequas partes & eas uocat dieses chromatis mollis. Aliquando autem in quattuor: quas diese enharmonicas dicit.[80]	Hoc igitur diatessaron Aristoxenus per genera tali ratione partitur. Diuidit enim tonum in duas partes atque id semitonium vocat. Dividit in tres, cuius tertiam vocat diesin chromatis mollis. . . . Quoniam enim quarta pars toni diesis enarmonios nuncupari praedicta est.[81]

Gaffurio preserves the thought sequence and most of the syntax of Boethius, but he adds the important information that these are equal divisions.

The following short example illustrates Gaffurio's method of clarifying and glossing Leoniceno's translation of Ptolemy (Gaffurio, left; Leoniceno, right):

Chromaticum sesqualterum genus utrunque interuallorum spissi id est duo grauori tetrachordi interualla facit quartam partem cum octaua unius toni utrunque nouenario describens. Ac reliquum maius & acutissimum unius toni est cum dimidio & quarta toni parte: quod numero.42. pernotatur: ut hic constat.[82]	Sesqualtera uero chromatis, utriunque, duorum interuallorum densi, facit, quartam partem, & octauam, unius toni. Reliquum, unius, cum dimidio, & quartum qualium illorum quidem, utrunque.9. hoc uero 42.[83]
In the chromatic genus hemiolion, he makes each of the intervals of the pycnon, that is, the two lower intervals of the tetrachord, a fourth part plus an eighth part of one tone, assigning 9 to both. And the other larger and higher [he	In the hemiolion of the chromatic he makes each of the two intervals of the pycnon a fourth part plus an eighth part of a tone. The other [he

80. Gaffurio, *De harmonia*, II, 16, fol. 37r.
81. Boethius *De institutione musica* 5.16 (Friedlein ed., p. 365).
82. Gaffurio, *De harmonia*, I, 16, fol. 37v.
83. Ptolemy *Harmonics* 1.12; Leoniceno, fol. 15r.

makes] of one tone and a half plus
a fourth part of a tone, which is
indicated by the number 42, as is
evident here [diagram follows].

makes] of one [tone] plus a half
and a fourth. Thus the former
each are 9, the latter, however, 42.
[Diagram accompanies the statement.]

In this description of the chromatic hemiolion of Aristoxenus, Gaffurio prefers the term "spissum," which was used by Boethius to translate *pycnon,* to Leoniceno's "densum." In the previous discussion Gaffurio (following Ptolemy) had explained that Aristoxenus divided the whole tone into 24 parts. Thus a fourth part, 6, and an eighth part, 3, add up to a value of 9 for each of the lower intervals of the chromatic tetrachord, while the higher interval contains 24 plus 12 plus 6, or 42 parts. Leoniceno's is a perfectly adequate translation of Ptolemy's terse statement, which is accompanied by a clear diagram; Gaffurio's amplification makes some concessions to the modern reader by reminding him of the meaning of pycnon and of the fact that the uppermost interval of the chromatic is always larger than the sum of the two lower intervals.

Gaffurio's chapter on the shades of Aristoxenus (II, 16) presents from Ptolemy 1.12–14 essentially the material that Boethius summarizes in 5.14, 16, and 18. The divisions of the tetrachords, measured in twenty-fourths of a tone, are presented for one type of enharmonic, three chromatics, and two diatonics. Only when Gaffurio comes to enumerate the errors of Aristoxenus does he contribute something not in Boethius, for he reports Ptolemy's criticisms more fully, gathering them together from several chapters. Gaffurio enumerates five errors committed by Aristoxenus.

1. He divides the tone into two equal parts, when 9:8, a superparticular ratio, cannot be so divided. This error is not cited by Ptolemy, who may have thought it specious, since Aristoxenus is not dividing ratios but abstract distances, for the span of 24 units of a pitch scale may be divided at will.

2. He expresses interval differences in simple numbers instead of proportions (Boethius 5.13; Ptolemy 1.13).

3. He presents only two types of chromatic tetrachord, when more should be shown. Moreover the difference between these two—the malakon (soft or flat), and the hemalon (equal)— lies in the lowest interval, namely one-twenty-fourth of a tone, too small to be perceived. Boethius (5.18) reports only the second objection, Ptolemy (1.14) both.

4. Aristoxenus makes the lowest intervals equal in the chromatic tetrachords, whereas the middle interval should always be larger (Ptolemy 1.14; not in Boethius). Gaffurio omits mention of another difficulty (Ptolemy 1.14):the lowest interval of the chromatic should never be as large as that of the diatonic. Aristoxenus assigned twelve parts equally to the lowest interval of the chromatic toniaion, diatonic malakon (soft or flat), and diatonic syntonon (intense or sharp), the difference between the last two hing-

ing on the middle interval, which has six parts in the malakon, eight in the syntonon.

5. The two types of diatonic Aristoxenus presents are too few, for more can be found (Ptolemy 1.14; Boethius 5.18).

Aristoxenus remains, in Gaffurio's book, as in the books of Boethius and Ptolemy, a shadowy figure, talked about but never permitted to speak for himself. Perhaps because Aristoxenus was so maligned by Boethius, Gaffurio was not stimulated to read his work directly, and his treatise is conspicuous by its absence from among those that Gaffurio had translated. To be sure, the *Harmonic Elements* was harder to find in the available codices, but there were several copies that would have been accessible to Gaffurio's translators.[84]

Although Archytas (fl. 400 B.C.) and Didymus (b. 63 B.C.) were centuries apart, Gaffurio combines the discussions of their divisions of the tetrachords into a single chapter (II, 17). Boethius never reached Didymus in his compendium, since Ptolemy postponed discussion of him until his second book. Gaffurio, taking advantage of Leoniceno's complete translation, cleverly inserted a discussion of the tetrachords of Didymus at this point, where they could be compared with the tetrachords of the others. This is the first notice that Didymus received in the Renaissance.

The exposition of the tetrachords of Archytas agrees in substance with that of Boethius (5.18), but, as as in the case of the errors of Aristoxenus, Gaffurio reports Ptolemy's account of the errors more fully. He also interpolates some objections of his own. In brief the divisions of Archytas, as outlined by Ptolemy are:

Diatonic: 9:8   8:7   28:27
Chromatic: 32:27   243:224   28:27
Enharmonic: 5:4   36:35   28:27

Gaffurio details seven objections to these divisions:

1. In the diatonic Archytas made the middle interval larger than the highest, whereas they should be equal, namely 9:8. Gaffurio attributes this objection to Ptolemy 1.13 (recte 14), but it is of his own making, inconsistent with Ptolemy's own preference for two unequal intervals at the top.

2. Another objection invented by Gaffurio is that Archytas made the lowest interval of the diatonic smaller than 256:243, which is the minor semitone. Here he is applying the alien yardstick of the standard Pytha-

---

84. Manuscripts surviving in Italy today from before the sixteenth century are Vat. gr. 191; Venice, Marciana gr. 322; Naples, gr. III.C.2 (G. Valla's manuscript); Bologna, Biblioteca Universitaria, MS 2432.

gorean tuning to a tetrachord division in which the value of the Pythagorean minor semitone has no relevance.

3. In the chromatic neither the ratio of the next-to-the-lowest string to the highest nor to the next-to-the-highest is superparticular, despite Archytas' insistence upon the virtues of this class of proportions (Ptolemy 1.14; Boethius 5.18).

4. The next-to-the-lowest string of the chromatic is only 256:243 lower than the parallel string of the diatonic, whereas it should be lower by more than that. Gaffurio attributes this objection to Ptolemy, but again it is of his own devising.

5. The lowest interval in the chromatic, 28:27, is too small (Ptolemy 1.14; Boethius 5.18). It should be 22:21, says Gaffurio, following Boethius, although Ptolemy does not imply this.

6. The lowest interval of the enharmonic is the same as that of the other genera, although it should be smaller, as is consistent with the nature of this genus.

7. He made the lowest interval, 28:27, much larger than the middle one, 36:35, which is contrary to the nature of the enharmonic.[85] Gaffurio ignores two further objections of Ptolemy: Archytas' divisions fail to conform to the generally known scales, and they do not do justice to the many possibilities that exist for each genus.

Gaffurio is much more faithful to Ptolemy in setting forth the tetrachords of Didymus. He does not consider, to be sure, the context of Ptolemy's remarks in the chapter entitled "The Improvements of the Canon Proposed by the Musician Didymus," which follows a critique of the one-string monochord. Ptolemy explains that Didymus was the first to improve the utilization of the monochord by allowing both sides of a string divided by a movable bridge to be plucked. Gaffurio presents only the section of the chapter that deals with the proportions used in dividing the tetrachord (Ptolemy 2.13.15–32). Didymus, he says, gives divisions only for the greater perfect system, and then only in the diatonic and chromatic, although he recognizes also the enharmonic. The proportions he reports may be outlined as follows:

Chromatic: 6:5   25:24   [16:15]
Diatonic: 9:8   10:9   [16:15]

Ptolemy, Gaffurio reports, condemns Didymus for making the lowest interval in the chromatic larger than the middle one. In the diatonic he should also not have made the highest interval larger than the middle, which is

85. Miller's translation of this remark (II, 17, p. 104) is incorrect in that it has Gaffurio charging that the middle interval is larger.

contrary to the natural simple character of this genus. Didymus sinned, Gaffurio says, in making the lowest interval of the enharmonic equal to the other two, when it should be smaller.

Peccauit insuper: grauissimas in tribus generibus proportiones ae- qualiter disponens: cum in enhar- monico minorem esse opporteat grauissimam tetrachordi proportionem quam in diatonico & chromatico... et adhuc sequentes proportiones, duorum generum, aequales cum minores opporteret, his, quae sunt, in Diatonico.[86]	He sinned, further, in disposing the lowest interval equally in the three genera, because it is essential that in the enharmonic the lowest [interval] of the tetrachord be smaller than in the diatonic and chromatic... and further, the consequent [that is, the lowest] ratios of the two genera [he made] equal, whereas they need to be smaller than those in the diatonic.

Gaffurio confused the issue here by introducing the enharmonic, about which Didymus was silent.[87] Ptolemy is clear on this point; Gaffurio went astray earlier in the chapter, when he (left, below) attributed to Didymus a position concerning the enharmonic that is not warranted by Leoniceno's translation of Ptolemy (right):

Nam accutissimam tetrachordi chordam in enharmonico genere ad eam quae grauissimae uicinior est (puta Hypaten meson ad Parhypaten hypaton) secundum sesquiquartam proportionem ponit.[89]	Nam antecedentus, tetrachordorum ad tertias, ab ipsis, secundum sesquiquartam proportionem, ponit ut utrisque generibus.[88]
Now he placed the highest string of the tetrachord in relation to that which is next to the lowest in the enharmonic genus (that is, Hypate meson to Parhypate hypaton) according to the sesquiquartan ratio.	Now the antecedents [that is the highest strings] of the tetra- chords in relation to the third from these he placed according to the sesquiquartan proportion in both genera.

As Gaffurio correctly stated at the outset, Didymus gave the proportions only for the chromatic and diatonic, so that the 5:4 proportion between the top string and the next-to-the-lowest could apply only to these two genera.

---

86. Gaffurio, *De harmonia* II, 17, fol. 39r.

87. Leoniceno may have sowed the seed for Gaffurio's mistake by making "his, quae sunt" plural, when it was singular in Ptolemy *Harmonics* 1.13 (Düring ed., p. 68, line 31), referring back to *logos* (ratio) in *"logous...isous."*

88. Ptolemy *Harmonics* 2.13; Leoniceno trans., fol. 35r.

89. Gaffurio, *De harmonia,* II, 17, fol. 39r.

Gaffurio had reason to give special attention to chapters 15 and 16 of Book 1, in which Ptolemy presented his own solutions for the divisions of the tetrachords in the three genera. Boethius in the fragment of eleven lines that survives of his last chapter (5.19) gave only the general principles that Ptolemy followed—just enough to excite the reader's curiosity—but not details of the tetrachord divisions. These principles, as summarized by Boethius, are that all the ratios should be superparticular, that the lowest interval should be smaller than any of the others, and that in the dense tetrachords the pycnon should be smaller than the remaining interval, whereas in the diatonic no interval may be as large as the remaining two taken together.[90] To make up for the truncation in Boethius, Gaffurio followed Leoniceno's translation punctiliously, though not literally, interpolating string lengths omitted by Ptolemy and skipping an occasional speculative digression. All of chapters 18, 19, and 20 of Book II of Gaffurio, including most of the diagrams, are thus adapted from Leoniceno's translation.[91] In these three chapters Gaffurio revealed for the first time in print and in a language read by European musicians Ptolemy's own solutions for dividing the tetrachords.[92]

Because of the delay in publication of the De harmonia Gaffurio anticipated these revelations in his Angelicum ac divinum opus musice of 1508. Book I, chapters 14–16, of that work are a compendium in Italian of De harmonia, Book II, chapters 17–20, to which Gaffurio refers the reader for a fuller treatment of the subject.[93] Since the treatment in Angelicum opus is drastically abbreviated, the following discussion will be based on De harmonia.

Ptolemy's tetrachord divisions were for several decades disseminated mainly through Gaffurio's book. Even after a complete translation of the Harmonics was published by Antonio Gogava in 1562, Gaffurio's exposition remained the main source. Therefore it is worth reviewing in detail Gaffurio's exposition of this material.

Without recalling the principles that Boethius had attributed to Ptolemy,

90. Boethius thus reached Ptolemy Harmonics 1.15, Düring ed., p. 33, line 27.

91. Gaffurio omits Ptolemy Harmonics 1.15, Düring ed., p. 33, lines 1–27; p. 36, line 28, to p. 37, line 5; p. 37, lines 12–20; Ptolemy Harmonics 1.16, Düring ed., p. 38, lines 6–17; p. 38, line 29, to p. 39, line 14; p. 40, lines 8–13. The diagrams on fols. 41v and 44v are Gaffurio's (added after 1500); all the other diagrams are from Leoniceno, but Gaffurio inserts the string names for the hypaton tetrachord.

92. Giorgio Valla described these tunings in De expetendis (1501), "De musica," IV, 8–15, but this work was ignored by musicians, and it could not have been known to Gaffurio at the time he wrote these chapters.

93. The woodcut employed to print the diagrams of Ptolemy's enharmonic in Angelicum opus, ch. 14, was reused for De harmonia, II, 28, fol. 40v; other similar parallel diagrams are in Angelicum opus, ch. 15 and De harmonia, II, 18, fol. 41r; and Angelicum opus, ch. 15 and De harmonia, II, 18, fol. 42r.

Enharmonic	276		345		360		368
		5:4		24:23		46:45	
Chromatic malakon	210		252		270		280
(Gaffurio: molle)		6:5		15:14		28:27	
Chromatic syntonon	66 (sic)		77		84		88
(Gaffurio: intentum)		7:6		12:11		22:21	

Figure 9.2:

Dense tetrachord divisions proposed by Ptolemy

Gaffurio launches immediately into an analysis of the division of the tetra-chord. Ptolemy, he says, shows that the ratio 4:3 can be divided into two superparticular ratios only by the following proportions: 5:4 and 16:15; 6:5 and 10:9; and 7:6 and 8:7. For the genera with pycnon the top large interval gets the larger ratios 5:4, 6:5, or 7:6; the two lower intervals taken together are assigned one of the smaller ratios 16:15, 10:9, or 8:7. For this purpose each of the smaller ratios must be divided into superparticular proportions that would be approximately equal. To accomplish this the terms of the ratio, 15 and 16, are tripled, yielding 45 and 48, which are mediated by 46 and 47. The latter is rejected, because it does not form superparticular ratios with both 45 and 48—the boundary numbers. The ratios 48:46 (24:23) and 46:45 are, however, both superparticular. Thus 16:15 may be divided into 24:23 and 46:45, 10:9 by the same method is divided into 15:14 and 28:27, and 8:7 into 12:11 and 22:21. The larger upper intervals are used for the "softer"—we would say flatter— genera, whereas the more intense—we would say sharper—genera will have smaller intervals on top. Thus 5:4 best suits the enharmonic, whereas 6:5 and 7:6 are the basis for the chromatic. The tetrachords shown in Figure 9.2. ensue.[94] Before passing on to the less dense tetrachords, Gaffurio inserts a table that compares graphically the sizes of the intervals of the diatonic, chromatic, and enharmonic "of Py-thagoras" as given by Boethius and the enharmonic and chromatic malakon of Ptolemy, leaving out, inexplicably, the chromatic syntonon.

Gaffurio's chapter 19 attacks the less dense genera, following Leoniceno's translation of Ptolemy 1.15. Since the twofold division 5:4 X 16:15 does not produce a suitable threefold division of 4:3, Ptolemy takes for the higher interval of the twofold division 8:7 and for the lower 7:6. By the method

94. The string lengths given by Gaffurio in De harmonia, II, 18, are taken from Leoniceno's translation of Ptolemy's Harmonics 1.15 and must have been in his manuscript of Ptolemy, though they do not appear in Düring's edition. The highest string of the chromatic syntonon correctly reads 67 in Leoniceno, but 66 is Gaffurio's misreading rather than a misprint, because Gaffurio also gives 66 in Angelicum opus, I, 15.

of triplication used earlier he derives 10:9 and 21:20 by splitting 7:6, and to
this adds 8:7:

Diatonic malakon   63   72   80   84
                        8:7 10:9 21:10

Still following Ptolemy, Gaffurio affirms that if the preceding divisions are
tried on a monochord (*chordotono chordulas*) the ear will find it desires nothing
better. But Ptolemy actually suggested trying them out on an eight-string
kanon, in which the strings were stretched to an equal tension.[95]

Ptolemy describes one further shade, the *homalon*, or "equal," diatonic.
Tripling the terms of the ratio 4:3 to get 12 and 9, he interpolates the numbers
11 and 10, producing the series 12, 11, 10, 9. These permit three almost
equal ratios: 10:9, 11:10, 12:11; and, if the tetrachord is expanded to a fifth
through the ratio 9:8 for the tone of disjunction it may be extended to a
series of four ratios:[96]

Diatonic homalon 8   9   10   11   12
(aequale)   8:9 10:9 11:10 12:11

Gaffurio finally comes to the discussion of the diatonic ditoniaion (Pythagorean tuning), which, according to Ptolemy, is an approximation of
the syntonon. Ptolemy introduces it somewhat apologetically, as a substitute
tuning for the syntonic, because it lacks the superparticular ratios that he
made a requirement at the outset. The name given to this genus by Ptolemy,
ditoniaion, he derives from the fact that it has two consecutive whole tones
at the top. Gaffurio rendered this in Latin "diatonum diatonicum," judiciously emending Leoniceno's "tonium diatonicum." Ptolemy finds this
genus acceptable, because the highest ratio, 9:8, differs only slightly from
the 10:9 of the syntonic, and the lowest ratio, 256:243, though not superparticular, is very close to 16:15, which is. And in both these diatonics the
middle interval is 9:8. Indeed, the difference between the pair of 9:8 intervals
of the ditoniaion and the pair 10:9 X 9:8 of the toniaion is only 81:80, and
the difference betwen 256:243 and 16:15 is minimal, namely 258:256, says
Gaffurio, misreading Leoniceno's 259:256.[97] Two 9:8 intervals joined to-

95. Leoniceno did not render faithfully the phrase τοῦ διὰ πασῶ περιέχοντος ὀκταχόρδον
κανόνος, "an eight-string kanon containing an octave" (Düring ed., p. 37, line 7). Leoniceno
translated it as "diapason continente tetrachordi regula." Throughout the book Ptolemy insisted on using such an eight-string instrument in preference to a monochord.
96. The string lengths given by Gaffurio, *De harmonia,* II, 20, fol. 44r, are not in Leoniceno,
nor is the diagram on fol. 44v, which, furthermore, does not appear in the Paris manuscript.
97. They are both wrong, for 256:243 X 25:26 = 243:240, though expressed as a function
of 256, 259 is closer than 258. Leoniceno, fol. 21r; Gaffurio, *De harmonia,* II, 20, fol. 45r.

gether are also used in place of the 5:4 as the top interval of the enharmonic tetrachord.

Either Gaffurio wished to play down the substitute nature of the genus in Ptolemy's theory or a few lines were dropped by the printer, because mention of the substitution of 10:9 and 256:243 appears in Gaffurio only in reference to the enharmonic. His version (left) may be compared with Leoniceno's (right):

... qua re cum nullis sit profectus effatu dignus propter minimam differenntiam. [Lacuna? ....] Vtebantur quandoque in Enharmonico tetrachordo bis sequioctaua loco sesquiquartae in acutiore interuallo: rursusque minore semitonio loco sesquiquintae decimae in duobus grauissimis tetrachordi interualis.[98]	Propter quod in neutro propositorum generum, constituitur, aliquis effatu dignus profectus, abutentibus ipsis, in intento quidem diatonico, & sexquioctaua, loco, sexquinonam, secundum antecedentem locum: & lemate loco sexquiquintadecimam, secundum sequentem locum. In enharmonio vero, & bis sexquioctaua loco, sexquiquartae secundum antecedentem locum, & lemate rursus, loco sexquiquintadecimam, secundum ambos, sequentes locos.[99]
... for this reason, it is not worthy of mention because of the minimal difference. [Lacuna? ....] They sometimes used in the enharmonic tetrachord the 9:8 twice in place of the 5:4 in the high interval, and, further, the minor semitone in place of the 16:15 in the two bottom slots of the tetrachord.	Because of this in none of the genera proposed is it worthy of mention if by some [the tetrachord] is constructed contrary to usage in the syntonic diatonic with a 9:8 in place of the 10:9 at the top spot, and with the limma in place of the 16:15 in the lowest place. In the enharmonic, however, twice 9:8 [is used] in place of the 5:4 and the limma in both the lower slots in place of the 16:15.

Whether this was a slip or not, Gaffurio was decidedly more positive about the virtues of the ditoniaion than Ptolemy, bolstering its prestige with the authority of Boethius and Guido, who considered it "more natural and better than the others," adding later that "it was established by Pythagoras

---

98. Gaffurio, *De harmonia*, II, 20, fol. 45r.
99. Ptolemy, *Harmonics* 1.16.40; Leoniceno trans., fol. 21r.

and before him celebrated musicians and even posterity as the first and most excellent according to nature and art, being called simply diatonic."[100]

On the other hand, Gaffurio missed no opportunity for disparaging the thirds and sixths that resulted from some of Ptolemy's tunings. In analyzing the implications of Ptolemy's enharmonic tetrachord, which uses a ditone of 5:4, Gaffurio attacks Ramos de Pareja for assigning the ratio 5:4 to the ditone in his monochord division.[101] Similarly, Gaffurio shows the interval produced by the ratio 6:5 in Ptolemy's chromatic malakon to be larger by 81:80 than a tone-plus-semitone, always, of course, in terms of the Pythagorean diatonic. In another chapter (II, 37), Gaffurio shows that the minor sixth in the proportion 8:5 is larger by the same fraction (81:80) than the diapente-plus-semitone. However Gaffurio is beguiled by the possibility of mediating the fifth, 3:2, by a major and minor third "as composers call them," in the proportions 5:4 and 6:5, making the series 4:5:6.[102] In an addendum to the 1500 version of *De harmonia* that appears in the printed edition, Gaffurio presents a diagram entitled "The Dimension of Superpartient Consonances Accommodated through Reason and Sense to Superparticularity According to Ptolemy"[103] (see Figure 9.3).

Here it is shown that such "consonances" as the major third, which normally has a superpartient ratio (81:64), can be converted to superparticularity (5:4). Gaffurio makes the remarkable discovery that if a string is divided into six equal parts, successive portions with respect to the whole or the previous portion will produce the series minor third, major third, fourth, fifth, and octave in the superparticular ratios of Ptolemy's syntonic diatonic, forming the arithmetic progression 6:5:4:3:2:1. His diagram also shows that the major sixth in the ratio 5:3 and the minor sixth in the ratio 8:5 result from this division. The discovery of this phenomenon does not seem to have swayed him, however, from opposing any rival to the Pythagorean monochord.[104]

---

100. *De harmonia*, II, 21, fol. 46r. Giovanni Spataro was to criticize this stand in *Errori de Franchino Gafurio da Lodi* (Bologna, 1521), IV, Error 17, saying that strings were not measured before Pythagoras, nor was this tetrachord adopted by posterity, because, although musical writers followed Boethius in promoting the Pythagorean monochord, "in active practice they held to a different method" (fol. 19v). In V, Error 16, fol. 21v, Spataro states that the syntonic diatonic "produced by Ptolemy, is that which today is practiced in active music."

101. Gaffurio, *De harmonia*, II, 34; Ramos, *Musica Practica*, Pt. III, Sec. 2, ch. 3.

102. Gaffurio, *De harmonia*, II, 35, fol. 62v. In *Practica*, III, 2, Gaffurio admits that in a sixth mediated by a third, the mean pitch must be lowered a small amount by tempering the fourth in the direction of the fifth, and the major third downward toward the minor third.

103. This figure is pasted on p. 89 of the Lodi manuscript and is missing in the Paris and Vienna manuscripts. It occurs on fol. 64v of the 1518 edition.

104. In the *Angelicum opus*, I, 17, fol. D1v, Gaffurio expresses surprise at Ptolemy's recognition of the octave-plus-fourth as a consonance, whereas he fails to recognize the sixths,

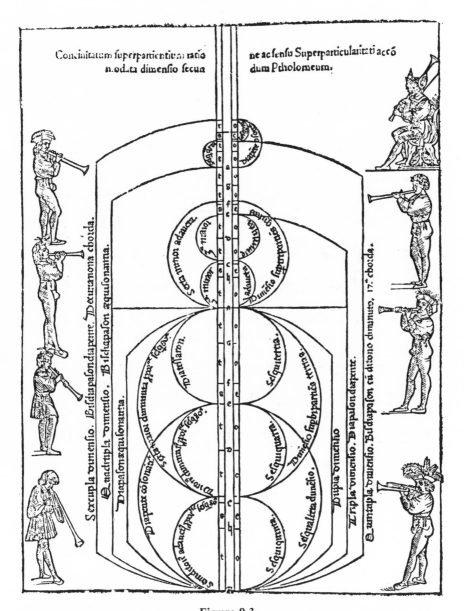

Figure 9.3.
The dimension of superpartient consonances accommodated through reason and
sense to superparticularity, according to Ptolemy, from Gaffurio, *De harmonia*,
1518, II, 37, fol. 64v

Gaffurio's attitude toward Aristoxenus seems to have softened after the first draft of *De harmonia*. In the addendum discussed above he notes that Jacobus Faber published a method of equally dividing a superparticular proportion by geometrically finding the mean proportional between two points on a string, thereby realizing the division of the 9:8 tone into two equal semitones, thought by Boethius to be impossible.[105]

Of the very rich treatise of Aristides Quintilianus, translated for him by Burana, Gaffurio drew mainly theories of a metaphysical or aesthetic nature. The most important exceptions to this statement are definitions of the "continuous" and "discrete" voice (I, 2, fol. 3r), the twofold definition of interval (I, 3, fol. 3v), the definition of rational and irrational intervals (I, 3, fol. 5r), the definition of the chromatic and enharmonic genera as condensations of the diatonic (II, 8, fol. 31r), and the first half of the chapter on the division of the whole tone into four dieses (II, 15, fol. 36v). Gaffurio demonstrated good judgment in extracting particularly passages dealing with philosophical matters, because, of all the Greek writers, Aristides was most concerned with the broader implications of the art of music. In submitting a capsule history of the modes in the first chapter of Book IV, Gaffurio cites Aristides' testimony that the Greeks sometimes called the modes "mores" (Greek *ēthe*) because of their capacity to excite the affections of the soul and body (IV, 12, fol. 83v).

The last chapters of *De harmonia* (IV, 12–20) are inspired by the classical analogies between various elements of music and the Muses, the sexes, the spheres, the numbers, the useful arts, the parts of the soul and body and their functions, the physical elements, the virtues, and the senses. The sources for these speculations are numerous, but prominent among them are Ptolemy and Aristides, both of whom dedicated lengthy and serious discussions to them.

Gaffurio's chapter 13, "That of the Celestial Bodies Some Are Masculine, Some Feminine, Others Mixed," is lifted in its entirety from Aristides Quintilianus.[106] Chapter 17, "That The Parts of the Soul Are Suited to the Intervals," is a juxtaposition of Ptolemy's 3.5 and a section from Aristides.[107] Leoniceno's translation of Ptolemy is reproduced verbatim except for some

---

which are products of the joining of superparticular proportions: 5:4 X 4:3, what "composers call the major sixth," and 6:5 X 4:3, the concord "called by singers minor sixth." Gaffurio disagreed with Ptolemy's classification of the octave-plus-fourth, because the notes of this interval "do not make a smooth concord at all but make a discord together."

105. Jacques Lefèvre d'Etaples, *Musica libris demonstrata quattuor*, (Paris, 1496); (Paris, 1552), III, 35, fols. 29v–30v, cited in Gaffurio, *De harmonia*, II, 37, fol. 65r.

106. *De musica* 3.21.

107. Düring ed., p. 95, line 28, to p. 97, line 27; Aristides Quintilianus *De musica* 3.25.

passages that are summarized. Ptolemy here compares the intellective, sensitive, and habitual parts of the soul to the octave, fifth, and fourth respectively. The three species of diatessaron are compared to the states of the habitual soul: growth, stability, and decay; the four species of diapente to the sensitive soul's sight, hearing, smell, and taste; and the octave's seven species to the parts of the intellect: phantasy, intellect, conception, mind, opinion, reason, and knowledge. An alternate division of the soul into rational, irrational, and concupiscible is similarly related to the consonances and their species.

The most interesting part of this chapter is derived from Aristides and concerns the *furor poeticus*.[108] Here Aristides describes the condition of enthusiasm or inspiration that gives rise to the composition of melody. The soul is oppressed by terrestrial concerns. Having rejected wisdom, it is lost in ignorance and forgetfulness and is at the mercy of the turbulence of the body, replete with terror and consternation. Thus the soul returns to a state not unlike that of its birth; yet because of the soul's great ignorance and oblivion, this condition resembles that of madness. In this state the soul gives forth, it is said, a melody, which is capable of soothing through a certain imitation the irrational part of the soul. Gaffurio reports the passage faithfully, following Burana's translation closely, but in the end he misses the point that melody is the product of this enthusiasm and not solely a cure for it.[109]

108. Aristides Quintilianus *De musica* 3.25; Gaffurio, *De harmonia*, IV, 17, fol. 98r, beginning "Ex Melodiae" and ending "animae et intellectus." Further indebtedness of Gaffurio's Book IV to Aristides may be noted in the following parallel or nearly parallel chapters: IV, 16 = 3.8–9; IV, 18 = 3.18; IV, 19 = 3.13–14.19; IV, 20 = 3.16.

109. Gaffurio, IV, 13, fol. 98r: "Quam quidem ob multam ignorantiam & obliuionem insania refertam: melodia mitigandam esse censuerunt."

TEN

The Ancient *Musica speculativa* and Renaissance Musical Science

peculative music theory at the beginning of the Renaissance, with rare exceptions, was dominated by the Pythagorean, Platonic, and Neoplatonic traditions. As stated earlier (chapter 1), the first ancient music-theoretical source that humanists rediscovered was Boethius, an author identified with these traditions. Though read and respected throughout the Middle Ages, particularly for his *Consolations of Philosophy*, Boethius needed to be repossessed as an authority on ancient music, to be reclaimed from medieval theory. The accretions of the plainchant theorists had to be brushed away, and his image altered from that of a universal musical lawgiver to that of a transmitter of ancient learning. Fifteenth-century humanists could not identify precisely Boethius' sources, but it was clear that he leaned a great deal on Nicomachus and Ptolemy and was against the Aristoxenians. Although there were Aristoxenian elements in both Nicomachus and Ptolemy, and Ptolemy did not always sympathize with the Pythagoreans, Boethius was identified as a Pythagorean.

Pythagoras is usually cited early in a treatise as the inventor of music or the discoverer of the ratios of the consonances. Typically the legend of the blacksmith's shop is recounted. Almost everyone depended upon the embroidered version of the story told by Boethius.[1] The older and fuller accounts of this legend, by Nicomachus and Gaudentius, were not known until the mid-sixteenth century.[2]

As told by Boethius the story goes as follows. By divine will Pythagoras happened to pass a blacksmith's shop, from which he heard diverse sounds as the apprentices were hammering, and these sounds blended in conso-

---

1. *De institutione musica* 1.10–11.
2. For an English translation of the account by Nicomachus, see Flora Rose Levin, "Nicomachus of Gerasa *Manual of Harmonics:* Translation and Commentary" (Ph.D. diss., Columbia University, 1967), pp. 28–32.

nances. Upon observing the smithies and reflecting on what he saw, he theorized that the diversity of pitches was caused by the diversity in strength of those hammering. But on testing the theory by having them exchange hammers, he found that this was not true. He then examined the weights of the hammers and found that one which weighed twice another sounded with it a diapason. Comparing other weights, he found that those in the ratio of 3:2 produced a fifth, and those in the ratio of 4:3 produced a fourth. By this means he determined the ratios of the consonances. After returning home, he made further tests. He attached weights to strings, blew on pipes of various lengths, and filled and partly filled glasses with water and struck them with a copper or iron rod. In all these experiments he found that the same ratios caused the same consonances.

Johannes Gallicus, who relied heavily on Boethius' treatise and referred to it as "that Music, which the so often mentioned Boethius turned into Latin from Greek,"[3] was dubious about Pythagoras' role in this incident. Around a figure of an anvil surrounded by four hammers bearing the numbers 6, 8, 9, and 12, Gallicus writes that it was more likely Jubal who made the discovery of the ratios of the hammers than Pythagoras, as handed down by the Greeks.[4] In the text itself Gallicus represents Jubal addressing the blacksmiths: "Exchange hammers, I pray you, and strike again, for I sense that not a small secret of nature hides either in your arms or in the hammers themselves."[5] After this experiment, Jubal concluded that the weights of the hammers and not the force of the blows determined the pitches.

Gallicus did not give an authority for his ascription of the discovery to Jubal, but Gaffurio, some years later, did. After paraphrasing the account of the story in Boethius, Gaffurio noted that Josephus attributed this investigation to Jubal before the flood, and in the appended figure Jubal is shown overseeing six smithies, five of them swinging hammers weighing 4, 6, 8, 12, and 16 pounds. In accordance with the account by Boethius, three other woodcuts show Pythagoras coaxing the same consonances from bells, water glasses, strings with weights attached, and pipes (see Figure 10.1). These figures illustrate Gaffurio's paraphrase from Boethius.[6]

In both Boethius and Gaffurio, the legend is introduced to show that,

---

3. *Ritus canendi*, I, 4; Coussemaker ed., IV, 304; Seay ed., 11.13: "ea namque musica, quam totiens allegatus Boetius de Graeco vertit in latinum."

4. *Ritus canendi*, I, 10; Coussemaker ed., IV, 310; Seay ed., 21.13: "Tradunt Graeci Pythagoram Hanc inveniisse fabricam./ Sed magis puto consonum/ Opinari dictum Iubal,/ Suum fratrem Tubal Cain/ Frequentasse fabricantem/ Qui ferro patet extitit/ Ac aere malleantium."

5. Ibid., I, 10; Coussemaker ed., IV, 310; Seay ed., 21.7: "Mutate, quaeso malleos ac iterum percutite, non enim parvum aut in vestris brachiis, aut in ipsis malleis latere sentio naturae secretum."

6. Gaffurio, *Theorica musice*, I, 8.

Figure 10.1.
The discovery of the ratios of the consonances by Jubal and Pythagoras, from
Gaffurio, *Theorica musice*, I, 8

given the inadequacy of the hearing when confronted with a multitude of sensations, only the reason coupled with accurate observation and measurement can establish the true relationships of tones. Yet neither author gives evidence of observation or measurement, or reasoning thereon, and neither attempts to demonstrate anything geometrically, mathematically, or by logical induction or deduction. Boethius and Gaffurio simply recount a legend and remain in a narrative mode throughout these chapters. A correspondence between consonances and ratios having been established in this fashion, no further defense appears to them necessary, and this is true also of Nicomachus and Gallicus.

Of the four woodcuts in Gaffurio's figure, only the last represents phenomena that are verifiable. If pipes 4, 6, 8, 9, 12, and 16 units long are alike in other respects, the sequence of intervals that Gaffurio aimed to illustrate, a series comparable to A E a b e a', will result when they are blown. In the other four cases—hammers, bells, glasses partly filled with water, and strings stretched by weights —the intervals will not be the same. With hammers the result is unpredictable, since the pitch emitted depends more on the metal struck than on the hammers. With bells and water glasses the relationships are complex. In the case of weights attached to strings the frequency will vary as the square of the weights. The one medium with which Gaffurio had direct experience, the single stretched string, the division of which would support the series of ratios he wished to demonstrate, is not brought into the account.

Although statements such as Gaffurio's wear some of the trappings of scientific research and demonstration, they are transparent appeals to authority and legend and cannot be considered scientific expositions at all. Hardly indicative of the current state of knowledge of sound, which in all of these authors is quite sophisticated at times, chapters such as these on the hammer story are concessions to a literary convention. Sometimes Gaffurio contrasts different opinions among the ancient authorities, but here too conventional erudition prevails over any impulse to critical choice.

Even in this indiscriminately eclectic, antique-worshipping environment, Valgulio's open-minded defense of both Pythagoreans and Aristoxenians is notable. He was not blind to their differences. The harmonists he recalls, "attribute more authority to the judgment of the ear than to that of reason, like the Aristoxenians do." The canonists "assign the first and most approved grade of judgment to the reason, as the Pythagoreans do, who with respect to genus are also harmonists." Ptolemy held to a middle way and maintained that a musician proceeds correctly "when the judgment of the ears accords with that of the reason."[7]

---

7. Valgulio, *Proemium*, 1530 ed., fol. 247r. See ch. 5 above, for a detailed treatment of his views.

Franchino Gaffurio

Gaffurio similarly contrasts the views of Plato and Nicomachus but is unable to choose one over the other. In a passage that is common to the *Theoricum opus* of 1480 and the *Theorica musice* of 1492, Gaffurio presents Plato's explanation of the mechanics of consonance:

Sit uero auribus ipsa consonantia secundum Platonem hoc modo: quom acutior sonus qui uelocior est grauem praecesserit in aurem celer ingreditur: offensaque extrema eiusdem corporis parte quasi pulsus iterato motu reuertitur: sed iam segnior nec ita celer ut primo impetu emissus aduenit: quo circa acutior ipse sonus nunc grauior rediens sono primum graui uenienti similis occurrit misceturque ei unam efficiens consonantiam.[8]	According to Plato, consonance strikes the ear in this way: the higher of the two sounds, which is speedier, precedes the low sound and enters the ear quickly, and when it has met the innermost part of the ear, it bounces back, as if it were impelled with repeated motion. But now it arrives more slowly, not fast as when emitted by the first impulse. For this reason this higher sound, now returning lower, presents itself as similar to the approaching low sound, and is blended with it, making one consonance

This explanation of consonance was given by Plato in *Timaeus* 80a–b, but Boethius or his source added the clarification of how the faster sound slows down to reach a correspondence with the slower sound, namely, by bouncing back and forth in the innermost part of the ear. Gaffurio in 1480 had no direct access to Plato; so he could not appreciate that he was transmitting a later interpretation along with Plato's views.

Gaffurio now finds in Boethius a competing theory, attributed to Nicomachus.[9] A sound consists of not one impulse but many in quick succession. When a string is tense, it produces frequent and dense pulsations; when it is loose, it produces slow and rare pulsations. If the percussions of the low sounds are commensurate with the percussions of the high sounds, then consonance will result, otherwise not. The words with which Boethius reports Nicomachus' thoughts are repeated almost verbatim by Gaffurio.[10]

In a section of the *Theorica musice* not held over from the 1480 version, Gaffurio went to what was probably the most enlightened source then

8. *Theoricum opus*, II, 3; *Theorica*, II, 4, fol. c5v. This is a paraphrase of Boethius *De institutione musica* 1.30.

9. This is not preserved in Nicomachus' extant works.

10. *Theoricum opus*, II, 3; *Theorica*, II, 4, fol. c5v.

available on the science of sound, the *Paraphrases* of Themistius (c. 317–38 A.D.) on the *De anima* of Aristotle in the Latin translation of Ermolao Barbaro.[11] Themistius now became Gaffurio's main source for the theory of sound and hearing. Themistius had insisted, as d'Abano was later to do, that the air struck by the sounding object was not the same as that which reached the ear. He noted, following Aristotle, that the notions of grave and acute were assigned to sounds by analogy with touch, and elucidated this by saying that the acute voice stabs the air and pungently wounds it, while the grave tone hits bluntly and spreads as it hits. Whereas the acute sound moves the sense a great deal quickly, the grave sound moves it little slowly.[12]

Gaffurio depended on Themistius also to explain the mechanism of hearing. The nature of the ear is akin to that of air in that the ear is congenitally filled with air, which is excited by the air outside and transmits the motion to little sensitized tinders inside a tissue of little breadbaskets (*paniculae*) filled with air. The outside and inside air are continuous, which explains why animals do not hear by their other bodily parts.[13]

Gaffurio made no attempt to reconcile the Aristotelian and Pythagorean-Platonic traditions in his *Theorica musice*. The split became even more intense in Gaffurio's last treatise, *De harmonia,* in which he turned to a wider variety of Greek sources, often eclectic themselves. As he darts from one to another it is nearly impossible to detect any consistent philosophy. Yet when a question touches on some of the fundamental tenets of music theory, he takes a conservative, Boethian position.

Such a question is the tuning of the diatonic scale. Despite the alternatives to the Pythagorean tuning offered by Ptolemy, some of them better suited to current musical practice, Gaffurio never departed from the system sanctioned by Boethian authority. It is characteristic of him to overlook the incompatibility of the ancient theory of intervals with the way composers employed consonances in polyphony. Whereas Boethian theory recognized only the few consonances acceptable by Pythagorean standards, later called "perfect" consonances, musical practice in the fifteenth century required that one of these, the fourth, be treated in most polyphonic situations as a dissonance and that the perfect consonances be mixed and alternated with so-called imperfect consonances, thirds and sixths. In the tuning prescribed by Boethius, the major third was a ditone, 81:64, and the minor third, 32:27, neither too displeasing as a simultaneous concord by itself, but grating

---

11. Themistius *Paraphrases* on Aristotle, *De anima,* Latin trans. Ermolao Barbaro (Paris, 1535), ed. Richard Heinze (Berlin, 1899).

12. Ibid., II, 30, fol. 74.

13. Gaffurio, *Theorica,* II, 2: Themistius, *Paraphrases,* Barbaro trans., II, 28, fol. 72.

when combined together in a three-part chord. One of the tunings described by Ptolemy, indeed the diatonic he most favored, permitted better-tuned thirds on most degrees of the scale, namely those in the ratios 5:4 and 6:5. This was his syntonic diatonic. Yet Gaffurio could not bring himself to accept it.

Ramos de Pareja

The mathematician Bartolomé Ramos de Pareja (c. 1440–after 1491) in 1482 had proposed a similar but not identical tuning purely as a practical strategy.[14] Ramos appears not to have read any of the Greek sources directly, but, like Gallicus and Gaffurio, had studied Boethius closely. He read him, however, more critically than his predecessors. Ramos began the prologue of his book with an encomium of Boethius, paying tribute to the profound arithmetical and philosophical foundations on which the work of Boethius rests and proclaiming that it always has been and always will be greatly prized by the learned. At the same time it always has been and always will be neglected by half-educated musicians, who find it obscure and sterile. This statement may reflect Ramos' own ambivalence toward Boethian theory. He frequently cites its authority for definitions and ancient musical lore; yet, after praising it as subtle, delightful, and useful to theorists, and with only a mild complaint that the monochord division of Boethius is "laborious and difficult for singers to learn,"[15] Ramos proceeds to overturn completely the Pythagorean system. Slily constructing a monochord division that would correct the tuning of the imperfect consonances, he proposes it simply as a method that anyone moderately educated will easily understand. Only toward the end of the book does he make it plain that his imperfect consonances have simpler ratios than those of the Pythagorean system, namely 5:4 and 6:5 for the major and minor thirds, and 5:3 and 8:5 for the major and minor sixths.[16]

According to Ramos' disciple Giovanni Spataro, Ramos arrived at his diatonic division independently of Ptolemy and Didymus,[17] although his system seems to graft the two. The string lengths shown in Figure 10.2, which Ramos does not reveal but were later calculated by John Hothby,

14. *Musica practica* (Bologna, 1482; facs. ed., Bologna, 1969), I, 1, 2; ed. Johannes Wolf in Publikationen der Internationalen Musikgesellschaft, Beihefte, II (Leipzig, 1901), p. 1.

15. Ibid., I, i, 2; Wolf ed., p. 4.

16. Ibid., III, ii, 3; Wolf ed., p. 98.

17. *Errori di Franchino Gafurio da Lodi* (Bologna, 1521), Error 17, fol. 22r: "Io non dico/ o Franchino: che el mio preceptore habia tolto el suo Monochordo da Ptolomeo: perche questo io non el scio di certo: Ma io dico/ che el suo Monochordo predicto non e dissimile da quello de Ptolomeo/ dicto di sopra."

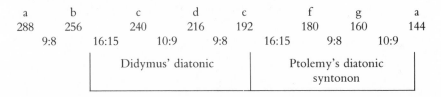

a	b		c	d	c		f	g	a
288	256		240	216	192		180	160	144
	9:8	16:15	10:9	9:8		16:15	9:8	10:9	

Didymus' diatonic	Ptolemy's diatonic syntonon

Figure 10.2:
Ramos de Pareja's monochord division

result from the division of the monochord presented by Ramos.[18] All the thirds on this monochord are just, or pure, that is, 5:4 and 6:5, except B–D (32:27). However, as Hothby pointed out, there are also two poor perfect consonances, the fourth, D–G (27:20), and the fifth, G–D (40:27).[19] Ramos expanded this diatonic system into a fully chromatic scale in a later chapter, but, aside from one more pure third (B♭–D), the thirds are either larger or smaller than just intervals.[20]

Even after Gaffurio discovered that Ramos' innovation was corroborated by Ptolemy, Gaffurio continued to oppose it and attacked Ramos by name in passages he added to his *De harmonia* before publication. He refutes the proposition that a ditone may be in the 5:4 ratio by appeals to authority— Jacques Lefèvre d'Étaples (Jacobus Faber Stapulensis), Boethius, and Porphyry—and by invoking the legendary Pythagoras.

> But a sesquiquartal proportion, since it is superparticular, cannot ever be divided into two equal proportions, as Boethius laid down in the third [chapter] of the first [book] of his Music. So Pythagoras despised all intervals that deviated from the purity of the multiple and superparticular [ratios], omitting in his investigation of consonant and equisonant tones intervals made agreeable sounding by the addition or subtraction of a minimal increment, because a very small error is not evident to the sense of hearing. But Ptolemy does not seem to have agreed with him altogether, for he constituted the incomposite ditonic interval in the enharmonic by subtracting a minimal interval, assigning to [the remaining interval] the proposed superparticular ratio that singers call major third, granted that it is a ditone diminished. We, however, were led to demonstrate [the intervals] with reason, even if the sense does not perceive the

---

18. *Musica practica*, I, i, 2. Ramos translates the points on his string h to p into mese to nete hyperbolaeon and also to letters in the Guidonian gamut, a to a' in his figure of the following chapter.

19. John Hothby, *Excitatio quaedam musicae artis per refutationem*, in Johannes Octobi, *Tres tractatuli contra Bartholomeum Ramum*, ed. Albert Seay (American Institute of Musicology, 1964), p. 25.

20. *Musica practica*, I, ii, 5.

minimal differences, for harmonics, as Porphyry says, hinges on the examination of differences.[21]

Although Gaffurio cites the favorable attitude of Ptolemy toward the sesquiquartal third, he is obviously not swayed from his loyalty to the Boethian-Pythagorean heritage, and his final appeal is to a defender of the rationalist position, Porphyry.

Giovanni Spataro

The defense of Ramos' position was assumed by his pupil, Spataro, choirmaster at San Petronio in Bologna. He was at a considerable disadvantage, for he could not read Latin and had to use an Augustinian friar to translate for him. This also meant that most of the humanist literature was unavailable to him. Spataro nevertheless boldly pointed out errors in Gaffurio's reading of Boethius and other authors. On the point made in the above quotation, Spataro pleads that Ramos should not be blamed for describing the tuning that singers actually use, namely a ditone of 5:4 proportion and not the theoretical one of 81:64. The difference between them, 81:80, is not, as Gaffurio claims, inaudible. Ramos considered it significant and distinctly audible.[22]

Spataro insinuates that Gaffurio admitted the defeat of his own and Pythagoras' theories when he acknowledged that musicians tempered certain intervals by ear, purposely altering consonances from their rational proportions. This *participatio,* as it was called, Spataro argues, means that all intervals besides the octave deviate from the Pythagorean proportions; in other words, the Pythagorean doctrine is unsuited to musical practice, "for if the Pythagorean arrangement followed by you needs the aid of heightening and lowering, such an arrangement in the sole Pythagorean genus cannot suit musical practice. Through this adjustment of the Pythagorean diatonic genus, one passes from this genus to that called by Ptolemy intense diatonic. I say that you *tacite* conclude that the Pythagorean doctrine, as far as practice is concerned, is altogether useless, deceptive, and futile."[23]

---

21. Gaffurio, *De harmonia,* II, 34, fol. 52v. All of this quotation dates from 1500 except the last sentence, which was added before publication in 1518. The subsequent three chapters similarly reject the 6:5, 5:3, and 8:5 ratios for the remaining imperfect consonances.

22. Spataro, *Errori,* Error 22, fol. 21v.

23. Ibid., Error 26, fols. 22v–23r: "perche se la pythagorica institutione (da te seguitata) ha bisogno de aiuto per intensione: et remissione/ tale institutione non potrà conuenire per se al Musico exercitio: in lo solo diatonico genere pythagorico: & perche (per tale adiuuamento) del genere diatonico pythagorico, se passa in quello genere chiamato da Ptolomeo intentum diatonicum genus. Dico che da te (tacite) e concluso/ che la pythagorica doctrina (in quanto a la exercitatione) essere omnino inutile: frustatoria: & uana."

Spataro's case was built entirely on his observation of practice. He was sure that the syntonic diatonic tuning of Ptolemy, "which divides the tetrachord by the ratios 16:15 at the bottom, then 9:8 and 10:9--a monochord produced by Ptolemy—is that practiced in active music today."[24] Spataro's knowledge of Ptolemy evidently came from Gaffurio and Boethius, for like them he made the mistake of attributing a Hypermixolydian octave species to Ptolemy.[25]

Lodovico Fogliano

It was not until Lodovico Fogliano's treatise *Musica theorica* (1529) that the imperfect consonances in just tuning received a logically developed defense. Fogliano was exceptionally well qualified to deal with questions of Greek music theory. He had experience as a singer and composer, and he knew Greek well enough to contemplate the translation of the works of Aristotle into Italian. Pietro Aretino wrote to him: "If you start to render in our vernacular the Greek of Aristotle, you will be the cause of making bigger than men those people who, not understanding the language of others, cannot derive benefit from a gift of nature. Surely you alone are qualified to clarify the obscure with your plain speech, sweetly opening the senses, confused in the clouds of the material. Therefore get on with your honored translation, providing for the enrichment of ambitious intellects."[26]

All that is left of Fogliano's work on Greek authors is a collection of extracts, definitions, and compendia, arranged by subject, in a manuscript headed "Flosculi ex philosophia Aristo. et Auerroijs A ludouico foliano mutinensi excerpti et in hunc vtilissimum ordinem redacti."[27]

Zarlino had a high opinion of Fogliano's work and in response to an inquiry from Gian Vincenzo Pinelli, Giuseppe Moleto prompted Zarlino to report what he knew of him. "I spoke to S. Zerlino on the subject of Foliano. He says that he was neither priest, friar, nor monk, and he never practiced music in public, but that he lived in Venice for a very long time. He was Modenese. He says that for someone who went slowly into musical

24. Ibid., Error 16, fol. 21v: "quale diuide el tetrachordo/ per semitonio sesquintadecimo in graue & per tono sesquioctauo/ & tono sesquinono: & perche tale monochordo (da Ptolomeo producto) e quello/ che in la actiua Musica oggi se exercita."

25. Ibid., Errori 25–26, fols. 36r–37r.

26. Pietro Aretino to Lodovico Fogliano, 30 November 1537, quoted by Girolamo Tiraboschi, *Biblioteca modenese* (Modena, 1781–86), II, 307.

27. Paris, Bibliothèque Nationale, MS lat. 6757, fols. 1–74v. At folio 74v we read: "Expliciunt flosculi doctrina aristo. et auerroijs. Incipiunt quaedam fragmenta diuersarum materiarum." The manuscript ends on fol. 88. Included in the "Flosculi" is material on harmonics, music in education, and the moral effects of music, drawn from Aristotle's *De anima, Politics,* and Averroës' commentaries on the *Metaphysics, Ethics, Posterior Analytics,* and *De anima.*

things, he wrote better than anyone else on the subject."[28] Zarlino's admiration for Fogliano is understandable, since, unlike many of his predecessors, he was not a compiler but sought to investigate questions of music
theory by observation and deduction. Fogliano espoused the method of
Aristotle's *Posterior Analytics* and based his chapters on sound, consonance,
and hearing on his *De anima* and *Physics*.

Fogliano establishes at the outset that the subject of the discipline of music
is sonorous number, namely the number that measures the parts of a string.
For example, if a string is divided into five parts, and a bridge is placed so
that two parts are on one side of it and three on the other, and the two
sides are struck at the same time, we know that the sounds issuing from
them will compare as 3:2. Thus sonorous number is considered the subject
of music. But music, insofar as it consists of sound and this is caused by
motion, is not a mathematical but a natural phenomenon. This places music
as a science in an intermediate position between the mathematical and natural.[29] Fogliano recognizes the existence of both consonance and dissonance
on the grounds that if consonance is perceived, its contrary must also be
perceptible.[30] Before giving his own analysis of the circumstances of consonance and dissonance, Fogliano reviews the position of the Pythagoreans,
who accepted as forming consonance the multiple ratios 2:1, 3:1, and 4:1
and the superparticular 3:2 and 4:3.

Nec plures his posuerunt conso-	They reckoned among the consonances
nantias: ut apparet ex suis quae	no more than these, as it appears
ad nos peruenerunt	from those opinions of his
opinionibus:	[Pythagoras] that have reached us.
Sed haec positio licet maxima	Although this position leans upon
innitatur auctoritate nihilominus	the greatest authority, nevertheless
mihi uidetur falsa: quum	it seems false to me, since it
sensui contradicat: quis enim	contradicts sensation. For who—
nisi sensu	unless he were deprived of the sense
aurium diminutus neget plures	of hearing—would deny that conso-
alias a praedictis quinque: inue-	nances other than the five
niri consonantias? infra enim	established ones could be found?
diapason nonne praeter istas	Are there not found below the octave
inuenitur: Semidytonus:	besides these the semiditone, the

28. Giuseppe Moleto to G. V. Pinelli, 20 January 1580, Milan, Biblioteca Ambrosiana, MS
S.105 sup., fol. 49r: "ho parlato col S. Zerlino in materia del Foliano, egli dice che non era
ne prete, ne frate, ne monaco. et che non esercito la musica in luogo publico, ma che sene é
vissuto à Venetia lunghissimo tempo. Esso modonese, et dice di più che per huomo che andasse
à lentone nelle cose della musica, ha scritto meglio d'ognun' altro intorno à tal cose."

29. *Musica theorica,* I, 1, fol. 1r–v. The notion that harmonics combines physical science
and mathematics is expressed by Aristotle *Physics* 2.2.194a.

30. Ibid., II, 2, fol. 15r.

Dytonus: Hexachordum minus: & Hexachordum maius: similiter supra Diapason: nonne inuenitur Diapason cum semidytono: & Diapason cum dytono: & diapason-diatessaron: Quam posuit Ptholomaeus? necnon diapason cum minori hexachordo: & diapason cum maiori hexachordo: hae autem quas addimus: sunt consonantiae: quae a practicis appellantur Tertia minor: Tertia maior: Sexta minor: Sexta maior: Decima minor: Decima maior: Vndecima: Tertiadecima minor: Tertiadecima maior: quae omnia interualla esse ueras & ualde delectabiles consonantias non potest negari: nisi negato sensu: quod est inconueniens: omnes enim concentuum auctores in suis compo-sitionibus: similiter: Omnes organistae: Omnes cytharoedi: Et omnes naturaliter fine aliqua arte canentes huiusmodi utuntur conso-nantiis: ut scit quilibet in hac facultate mediocriter eruditus.[31]

ditone, the minor hexad, and the major hexad; similarly above the octave, are there not found the diapason-plus-semiditone; the diapason-plus-ditone, the diapason-plus-diatessaron, which Ptolemy included? Are there not also the diapason-plus-minor hexad, and the diapason-plus-major hexad? These, which we yet add, are consonances, and they are called by practicing musicians minor third, major third, minor sixth, major sixth, minor tenth, major tenth, eleventh, minor thirteenth, major thirteenth, all of which intervals, it cannot be denied, are true and very delightful consonances, unless the sense is denied, which is inappropriate. For all authors of part music in their compositions, and, similarly, all organists, all singers to the lute, and in the end all others who make music use consonances of this kind, as anyone moderately learned in this discipline knows.

The experience of the ear and of working musicians and composers have determined that these are all consonances. Indeed, Fogliano defines con-sonance in purely sensory terms: "a mixture of two sounds which are separated with respect to high and low pitch that is pleasing to the ears." Dissonance, on the contrary "is a mixture of two sounds separated with respect to high and low pitch that is displeasing to the ears." Granted that all the intervals mentioned above are consonances, Fogliano proceeds to show that a string may be divided through superparticular proportions other than those accepted by the Pythagoreans and thereby produce consonances. The ditone (5:4) and semiditone (6:5) are two. Moreover there are ratios of the multiple superparticular class that generate consonances: 5:2, or dupla sesquialtera, the diapason-plus-ditone; 10:3, the tripla sesquitertia, the dia-pason-plus-major hexad; 16:5, the tripla sesquiquinta, the diapason-plus-minor hexad. Further, the superpartient genus of ratios generates the fol-lowing consonances: 5:3, the bipartiens tertia, major hexad; 8:5, superbi-

31. Ibid., II, 1, fol. 11v.

partiens quinta, minor hexad. Finally, the multiple superpartient genus of ratio elicits consonances: 8:3, dupla superbipartiens tertia, the diapason-plus-diatessaron; 12:5, the dupla superbipartiens quinta, diapason-plus-semiditone.

Fogliano defends the determination of consonance and dissonance by sense experience through Aristotelian physics, psychology, and logic. First he analyzes the interaction of the sounding body and the air:

Sonum igitur: uniuersaliter generari per expulsionem aeris uiolentiam: ab omnibus concessum est & ratione comprobatum: Aer enim sic expulsus antequam natus sit cedere per naturam: necessario frangitur: unde sic fractus emittit sonum: talem autem uiolentam Aeris expulsionem pluribus modis contingit fieri. Aliquando enim fit ex percussione duorum corporum adinuicem: Quae solida sunt & dura: Aliquando etiam ex concursu unius corporis solidi & firmi ad corpus fluidum: ut quando uirga impetuose mota per aerem generat sonum: aer enim sic scissus uelocissime congregatur: & confluit ex omni parte: uacuum abhorrente natura: unde fit uelocissima quaedam aeris condensatio: quae resistit uirgae percutienti: & talis condensatio fungitur uice corporis solidi.[32]	Sound, therefore, is universally generated by the violent expulsion of air; this is agreed to by all and is corroborated by reason. The air thus expelled, made to give way before it was intended to by nature, is necessarily broken up. Thus fractured, it emits sound. This violent expulsion of air may happen in several ways. Sometimes it is through the striking of two bodies together that are solid and hard. At other times it is through the collision of a solid and firm body with a fluid one as when a switch impetuously swung through the air generates sound. Air thus torn is very quickly compressed and flows together from every direction, since nature abhors a vacuum. Thus a very rapid condensation of air comes about that resists the striking switch, and this condensation is discharged by exchange with the solid body.

Now Fogliano applies Aristotelian logic to distinguish the formal relationships among the elements in the interaction. Three things concur in the generation of sound: that which violently expels the air, the air violently expelled, and the motion of the expulsion. None of these three is formally the cause of sound. The agent expelling the air and the air itself are bodies, species of the genus substance. But sound is an occurrence (*accidens*), not a substance. Sound is also not the motion or the expulsion of the air, because it is a *sensibilis proprium,* an object of a particular sense, not a *sensibilis communis,* an object common to all senses. In *De anima* 2.6 Aristotle makes

32. Ibid., II, 2, fol. 15r.

this distinction: color is a special object of sight, sound of hearing, flavor of taste; movement, rest, number, figure, and magnitude, on the other hand, are objects common to all the senses. Since motion is a "common sensible," whereas sound is a "sensible particular," Fogliano argues, motion of air cannot be sound. Fogliano thus moves away from Aristotle's position, which was that sound was motion, toward the view that it is an effect of motion.[33] Fogliano concludes that sound is a passive or affective quality:

Dico quod sonus est passibilis qualitas proueniens ex motu aeris uiolento ac praecipiti habens esse in aequali mensura cum illo: dicitur autem passibilis qualitas: quoniam: quicquid potens est: immutare sensum est passibilis qualitas: sonus potest immutare sensum: ergo sonus est passibilis qualitas.[34]	I say that sound is a sensible quality arising from a violent and precipitous motion of the air that is commensurate with it. It is said to be a passive quality because whatever is able to alter the sense is a passive quality. Sound is capable of altering the sense; therefore sound is a passive quality.

Sound, then, is a sensible quality arising from the violent motion of the air, is commensurate with it in that it lasts as long as the motion, and has the potential of altering the sense. By altering the sense, Fogliano means that sound acts upon the natural potency of the hearing by producing in it sound's own species. Both sound and hearing being natural potentials, the hearing has definitive cognition of consonance and dissonance.

Freed of the necessity of determining the limits of consonance by numerical definition, Fogliano proposes a new enumeration and classification of consonances. He limits the consonances to seven within the octave, for after the octave they seem to return as if by a cyclical motion, just as numbers do after ten. This happens only with the octave, which, although it has two sounds, strikes the sense as if it were a single sound. All diversity of consonances is limited to the compass of the diapason, so far as the judgment

33. For example, in *De anima* 2.8.420a Aristotle states that: "sound is the movement of what can be moved, in the way that things rebound from a smooth surface when struck against it" (trans. W. S. Hett [Cambridge, Mass., 1967], p. 115). Fogliano may have derived this argument from Albertus Magnus, who in the section *De homine* of Part II of the *Summa*, holds that sound cannot be motion, because motion is an object of the common sense, whereas sound is an object of the hearing only (1498 ed., fol. 120v).

34. *Musica theorica*, II, 2, fol. 15v. Here too Fogliano appears indebted to Albertus Magnus, whose words are similar: "Dicimus ergo quod sonus est qualitas sensibilis perueniens ex fractione motus aeris et ens cum illo. dico autem qualitas sensibilis propter sensum auditus et dico ex fractione motus: quia non quilibet motus aeris facit sonum: sed motus frequens aerem ante quam diuisibilis sit per naturam," *De homine*, 1498 ed., fol. 120v.

of the ear is concerned.[35] The seven consonances, then, are semiditone, ditone, diatessaron, diapente, minor hexad, major hexad, and diapason.

Fogliano limits the perfect consonances to the diapason and diapente. The rest are imperfect, including the diatessaron, which was traditionally a perfect consonance. He proves this by definition:

Probatur sic: eorum quae ab aliqua potentia sub ratione alicuis communis apprehedentur illa sunt perfecta: quae in suo genere uirtutem habent quietandi & complendi appetitum talis potentiae: reliqua uero quibus hoc repugnat: sunt imperfecta.[36]	It is proved this way: of those things which are comprehended by some potential by reason of having something in common, those are perfect which in their genus have the power of quieting and fulfilling the appetite for such a potential. The rest, to which this is opposed, are imperfect.

The diapason, diapente, and bisdiapason are capable of fulfilling the appetite of the auditory sense; hence they are perfect.

Apart from the seven consonances named and their compounds with the octave, all other intervals recognized by musicians are dissonances. These are essential to the progression of the consonances, as in going from the diatessaron to the diapente. Fogliano proposes six dissonances: major tone, minor tone, major semitone, minor semitone, minimal semitone, and comma.[37] In his determination of the ratios of these dissonances Fogliano adopts a system of just intonation. The ratios are 9:8, major tone; 10:9, minor tone; 27:25, major semitone; 16:15, minor semitone; 25:24, minimal semitone; 81:80, comma.

Fogliano applied his empirical methodology to the tuning of the practical musical scale. He proposes dividing the monochord in "a new way, almost according to the sense, and materially (nouo modo quasi secundum sensum: & materialiter)"[38] in contrast to the usual mathematical method. Like Ramos' division, Fogliano's permitted not only pure fifths and fourths, as in the Pythagorean tuning, but also pure major and minor thirds. His diatonic division corresponds to the scale shown in Figure 10.3.

The central tetrachord is identical to Ptolemy's syntonic diatonic, descending 10:9, 9:8, 16:15. However, unlike Ramos', which is laid out on the A octave, Fogliano's is on the C octave, so that there are two identical

---

35. *Musica theorica*, II, 4, fol. 16v: "septem sint consonantiae: quarum maxima est diapason: ad quam tota: quo ad iudicium sensus: terminatur consonantiarum diuersitas."

36. Ibid., II, 5, fol. 17r.

37. Ibid., II, 7, fol. 18r.

38. Ibid., III, 1, fol. 33r.

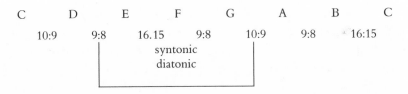

Figure 10.3:
Fogliano's monochord division

tetrachords rising 10:9, 9:8, 16:15, the reverse of Ptolemy's descending pattern. Fogliano was probably aware of these similarities and differences, but he did not name either Ramos or Ptolemy. His choice of the C octave he justifies as *more practicorum*—in the manner of practitioners. But it has important theoretical advantages, because it affords a number of harmonic means to aid in the division of the monochord. The octave c-c′ is divided harmonically with the fifth below and the fourth above, which yields the best-sounding combination of these two intervals (see Figure 10.4). The diapente c-g in turn may be harmonically divided to produce a ditone below and a semiditone above, again offering the best sounding combination of the two thirds. Similarly the diapente f-c′ is divided harmonically by a. The Roman numerals in Figure 10.4 indicate the number of the step in the division. Fogliano further divides the string to obtain a chromatic scale. But in order for each note of the chromatic scale to have a corresponding major and minor third above and below it is necessary to have alternate notes a comma apart, two D's, and two B♭'s. Then the alternate D will be a pure minor third against F, which otherwise would be too small, whereas the normal D will make a perfect fourth with G. Similarly an alternate higher B♭ permits a just minor third with G, whereas the normal B♭ makes a perfect fourth with F. Fogliano admits that having two D's and two B♭'s is an inconvenience in musical practice. Therefore he proposes dividing the spaces between the duplicate notes into two equal parts and at the midpoints placing a compromise D and B♭, which, though not affording precisely just intervals, produce intervals that deviate a mere half comma from purity.[39]

The space that needs to be divided is the comma, 81:80. According to Pythagorean mathematics, this is not possible, as there is no mean proportional between the terms of a superparticular ratio. Fogliano proposes a geometric solution for the required division, relying upon Euclid's construction of Book VI, Proposition 9.[40] Fogliano illustrates the construction in a figure (Figure 10.5). In the figure, AB:BD = 81:80. According to

---

39. Ibid., III, 2, fol. 35v.
40. Cited in ibid., III, 2, fol. 36r.

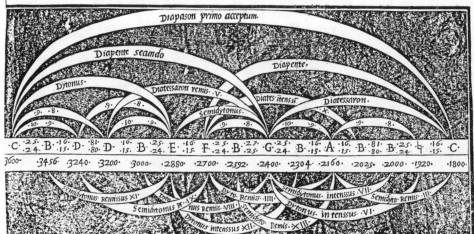

Figure 10.4.
Division of the monochord subject to the ratio of pure numbers, from Fogliano,
Musica theorica, III, 1, fol. 34v

Euclid, if a semicircle is described around the line AD and a perpendicular
to the circumference is drawn from B, BC is the required geometric mean.
Then AB:BC = BC:BD. The string length BC, which cannot be represented by a whole number, will sound the desired intermediate note.

Fogliano was not the first to challenge the impossibility of finding a mean
proportional between the two terms of a superparticular ratio. Those who
preceded him in this had profited, as he had, by the revival of interest in
the *Elements* of Euclid on the part of humanist mathematicians. The medieval
translation by Campano had been published in 1482.[41] In 1496 Jacques
Lefèvre d'Étaples showed how Euclid VI, 9, and VI, 13, could be applied
to find the mean proportional between two string lengths.[42] His object was
to find the geometric mean that would divide the intervals formed by the
fractions 9:8 (whole tone), 4:3 (fourth), 3:2 (fifth), and 2:1 (octave), where
ab:bc = 8:9; ab:bd = 4:3, ae:be = 3:2; and ab:bf = 2:1. A circle is constructed around line abc; similarly around abd, abe, and abf (see Figure
10.6). Then a perpendicular to abc is drawn at b to intersect the circles.
The distance from b to the intersection with the circle is the geometric
mean. So bg is the mean of 9:8, bh of 4:3, bi of 3:2, and bf of 2:1. These

41. *Praeclarissimus liber elementorum in artem geometrie,* trans. Campano of Novara (Augsburg,
1482).

42. *Musica libris demonstrata quatuor* (Paris, 1496), III, 35, fol. g6v. (Paris, 1552 ed., fol. 29v).

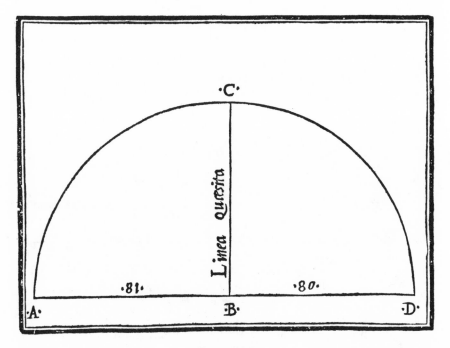

Figure 10.5.
Geometric division of the comma, from Fogliano, *Musica theorica*, III, 2, fol. 36r

lengths are marked on the string bc. The only geometric means of practical interest are those of the whole tone (marking off a mean semitone) and the octave (a tritone).

Lefèvre's demonstration is purely theoretical. Heinrich Schreiber (Grammateus), on the other hand, in 1518 applied the construction to locate a mean-tone between two diatonic steps, for example, the tone between G and A that could serve as both G♯ and A♭.[43]

Erasmus of Höritz, in his unpublished treatise *Musica* of around 1506, showed how the 9:8 tone may be divided by computation and proved the method by Euclidian propositions.[44]

So the revival and spread of Euclid's *Elements* contributed to solving some practical problems that surfaced once theorists began to shed prejudices about numbers. Of those who applied the geometric method, Fogliano was

---

43. *Ayn new kunstlich Buech* (Nuremberg, 1518).

44. Rome, Biblioteca Apostolica Vaticana, MS Reg. lat. 1245, Book VI, Proposition 17, fols. 66r–67r. See Palisca, "The *Musica* of Erasmus of Höritz" in *Aspects of Medieval and Renaissance Music,* ed. Jan LaRue (New York, 1966), p. 640.

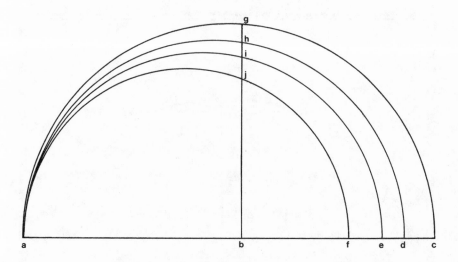

Figure 10.6.
Geometric division of the whole tone, fourth, fifth, and octave, from Lefèvre
d'Étaples, *Musica libris quatuor demonstrata,* III, 35

surely the most aware of the practical implications and the most deliberate
in his methodology and objectives.

Gioseffo Zarlino

Zarlino's relationship to classical sources, to Boethius, and to more contemporary writers is a very complex one. He read very widely and constantly quoted authority. He cited sources when they advanced his argument
and if they were ancient. (The citations are more precise in the 1573 edition
of the *Le Istitutioni harmoniche,* where he gives title, book, and chapter, than
in that of 1558.) Modern authors—as far back as Gaffurio or as recent as
Fogliano and Glarean—he utilized also, sometimes even paraphrased, but
without acknowledgment. Zarlino did not depend on any one school of
thought, nor did he accept any body of theory as a foundation. He constructed a system of his own. How much of it was owed to his teacher and
mentor Adrian Willaert cannot be ascertained, as Willaert left no theoretical
writing. It is probable that he owed more to him in the area of musical
practice than in that of speculative theory.

Zarlino fervently believed in the possibility of a rational explanation for
musical practice and aesthetic preferences. To do something without a reason was the ultimate error. The first two parts (called books in the second
and later editions) of the *Istitutioni* are conceived as a preparation for the

third and fourth, which are practical treatises on counterpoint and the modes. Thus the two speculative books were not intended to have an independent existence, like those of Gaffurio or Boethius, but to serve as a foundation for practice.

Zarlino did not simply accept classical authority, which in any case was full of contradictions. To fulfill the goal he had set for himself he saw that he had to raise every question anew, to doubt every previous solution, to reason out and prove the most obvious principles. If this mode of operation was unimpeachable, his facts, proofs, and solutions often were not. Zarlino was not a Pythagorean, although he was fond of number theories. He cannot be called a Neoplatonist, although Plato's ideas, which he knew through Ficino's translations and commentaries, appealed to him more than did those of the Aristotelians. He had a strong belief in the uniformity, wisdom, and rationality of nature— la Natura—whose secrets he thought he could discover through reason, theology, or by consulting authority, but without further observation or experiment. He was quite consistent in applying Aristotle's categories and dialectics. Of the ancient musical authors, he most admired Ptolemy, whose balancing of reason and sense experience harmonized with his own inclination. Zarlino did not read him thoroughly, however, and he disagreed with some of what he did read. He shows no evidence of having studied Aristoxenus directly in preparation for the Istitutioni. Only in the Sopplimenti musicali (1588) is his influence felt. In the Istitutioni Zarlino used Plutarch, Pliny, and Athenaeus for historical information, and he cited the treatises of Aristides Quintilianus, Cleonides (whom he calls Euclid), and Gaudentius, but there is no evidence in this work of his acquaintance with the Bellermann-Najock anonymi, Nicomachus, or Alypius.[45] In addition he relied on a vast number of general Greek and Latin sources that contain musical, mathematical, humanistic, and philosophical erudition. He had some acquaintance with Greek, as he shows in his book, but it must not have been much, as he requested Antonio Gogava to translate Aristoxenus' Harmonics.

Zarlino was selective in what he took from both the ancient and modern authors. For example, he did not accept the principle that musical intervals are built up from an indivisible unit, like numbers from unity. He attributes to Aristoxenus the theory expressed by Aristotle that the diesis is such a basic unit.[46] He prefers the theory transmitted by Ficino from Plato's Epinomis, that all consonances and intervals begin in the diapason, since 2:1 is

---

45. See the "Index of Classical Passages Cited" in Zarlino, On the Modes, trans. Vered Cohen, ed. Claude V. Palisca (New Haven, 1983), for a sampling of his reading. All of these authors became known to him, however, before he wrote the Soppliplimenti.

46. Metaphysics 10.1.1053a.

the beginning of proportion.[47] Ptolemy's exclusion of all but superparticular ratios from his approved tetrachords in the various genera was unacceptable to Zarlino, even though Boethius seemed to go along with it, because it was an unnecessary limitation that did not advance his purposes.

It is instructive to compare Zarlino with Fogliano, from whom he borrowed a number of concepts and principles. Like Fogliano, Zarlino concluded that the division of the octave sung by contemporary musicians was the one that provided both perfect and imperfect consonances in their simplest ratios. It was based on the species of tetrachord called by Ptolemy the syntonic diatonic, which Fogliano did not identify by either author or name. Fogliano chose it on the grounds of aural experience, and he deemed this sufficient reason, since the ear was the final judge. Zarlino was not confident of the rightness of the ear's choice; rational arguments and authority for the inclusion of intervals within the consonant class had to be found. Thus Fogliano established his classification on the basis of usage and aural preference, whereas Zarlino devised numerical criteria that did not contradict the sense.

Zarlino accepts Fogliano's resolution of the status of musical science as midway between mathematics and natural science. He adds that this is confirmed by Avicenna, who held that music received its principles from natural science and from the science of numbers.[48] Having accepted Fogliano's proposition that the subject of music is the sonorous number, Zarlino (right) quotes, without attribution, his definition of this phenomenon (left):

Numerus sonorus . . . nihil aliud
est: nisi numerus partium sonori
corporis: utputa: chordae: Quae
numeri ac discreti accipiens
rationem: nos certiores reddit
de quantitate soni ab ea
producti.

il Numero sonoro non è altro,
che il numero delle parti d'un
Corpo sonoro, come sarebbe di vna
chorda, la quale pigliando ragione
di quantità discreta, ne fa certi
della quantità del suono da lei
produtto.[49]

Sonorous number is nothing other than the number of the parts of a sounding body, such as a string, which, subjected to an accounting of the discrete quantity, renders us certain [Fogliano: more certain] of the quantity of the sound produced by it.

Zarlino finds this definition incomplete. His objections are semantic and hairsplitting, however, and introduce irrelevant metaphysical considera-

47. *Istitutioni*, II, 48, p. 142. Plato *Epinomis* 991a, Novotny ed., p. 40; Harward trans., p. 107.

48. *Le Istitutioni harmoniche*, I, 20, p. 31.

49. Fogliano, *Musica theorica*, I, 1, fol. 1r; Zarlino, *Istitutioni*, I, 19, p. 29.

tions. He objects to the use of the term *soni,* because vocal tones *(voci),* not sounds, are what the musician considers and those on which he bases what instruments do. He therefore modifies the definition to read:

Numero sonoro è Numero relato alle voci, & a i suoni; il quale si ritroua artificiosamente in vn corpo sonoro, si come in alcuna chorda, la qual riceuendo la ragione di alcun numero nelle sue parti, ne fa certi della quantità del suono produtto da essa, & della quantità delle voci, riferendo, ouero applicando essi suoni ad esse voci.[50]	Sonorous number is number related to vocal and instrumental sounds. It is found artificially in a sounding body, when a string is subjected to an accounting of the number of its arts, for this renders us certain of the quantity of the sound produced by it and, by referring or applying these sounds to vocal tones, the the quantity of the vocal tones.

Fogliano's original definition was better, because it included voices or any other sound source in a more concise formulation. Zarlino's rephrasing is simply an accommodation to his questionable bias for voices as natural, human, and therefore superior and more fundamental than instrumental sounds.

Zarlino evidently was also not satisfied with Fogliano's treatment of the nature of sound and consonance, for he goes back to Aristotle for the generation of sound and develops his own analysis of the causes of consonance. He attributes to Aristotle the principle that the generation of sound requires three things: that which strikes, the object struck, and a medium.[51] He then gives some of the same examples of sound production as Fogliano. So far as consonance is concerned, sounds are the material, numerical proportions the form. However number is not the cause, either proximate or intrinsic, of musical proportions or of consonances. Four things must concur: the goal of the action (playing in harmony), which is to profit and delight; the agent or efficient cause, that is, the musician; the material or material cause, which are the strings; and the form or formal cause, namely proportion. The first two are extrinsic, the last two intrinsic.[52]

Despite the elaborate proof that number cannot be the cause of consonance but only a means for measuring the terms of a proportion, Zarlino conceives a sacred precinct, the *senario*—the set of numbers from one to six—to contain the realm of consonance. His chapter on the virtues of this number is pure numerology. Of the twelve signs of the zodiac, six are always in our hemisphere, the others hidden below the earth. There are six errant bodies in

50. *Istitutioni,* I, 19, p. 29.
51. Ibid., II, 10.
52. Ibid., I, 41.

the sky: Saturn, Jupiter, Mars, Venus, Mercury, and the moon. There are six substantial qualities of the elements: acuity, rarity, movement, and their opposites, obtuseness, density, and stillness. Six circumstances are necessary to existence: size, color, shape, interval, state, and motion. Six are the species of movement: generation, corruption, increase, decrease, alteration, and change of location. According to Plato there are six differences of direction: up, down, ahead, behind, right, and left. Closer to home, the intervals (*voci musicali*) are of six types: unisone, aequisone, consone, emmele, dissone, and ekmele. And the modern modes come in sixes: six authentic, and six plagal! He gives a number of further examples of this ilk[53] before turning to the mathematical and musical properties of the six-part number.[54] Six is the first perfect number, meaning that it is the sum of all the numbers of which it is a multiple, that is, one, two, and three. Any two numbers from one to six yield the ratio of either a simple or composite consonance. (See Figure 10.7.) The two largest perfect consonances are formed from the first three numbers and are divided by harmonic means to produce the next perfect consonances. The diapason, 2:1, in the form 4:2, divided harmonically by 3, yields the diapente, 3:2, and the diatessaron, 4:3. The diapente, 3:2, in the form 6:4, divided by 5, produces the ditone, 5:4, and semiditone, 6:5. The major hexad, 5:3, harmonically divided by 4, yields the diatessaron and ditone. Any of the numbers multiplied by any other will always produce, when juxtaposed with another so generated, a harmonic relation. Further, if the six numbers as they occur in sequence are each squared, the adjacent squares will form the dissonances that separate the consonances, the tones and semitones.

The major hexad, 5:3, is regarded as distinct from the other consonances of the senario for two reasons: it is formed from a superpartient ratio, unlike the others, which are all superparticular in their minimal terms. It is also a composite consonance, made up of a diatessaron and ditone, because in its minimal terms, 5:3, it can be mediated by another number, namely 4. Similarly the minor hexad, 8:5, is mediated by 6, producing a diatessaron and semiditone. Here Zarlino is confronted with a contradictory element, a consonance the terms of whose ratio are not both in the senario. His rationalization for its inclusion is ingenious:

Et benche essa tra le parti del Senario non si troui in atto, si troua nondimeno in potenza: conciosiache dalle parti conte- nute tra esso piglia la sua forma,	Although it is not found in actua- lity among the parts of the senario, it is found in potential, for it takes its form from the parts of which it is a composite,

53. Ibid., I, 14.
54. Ibid., I, 15.

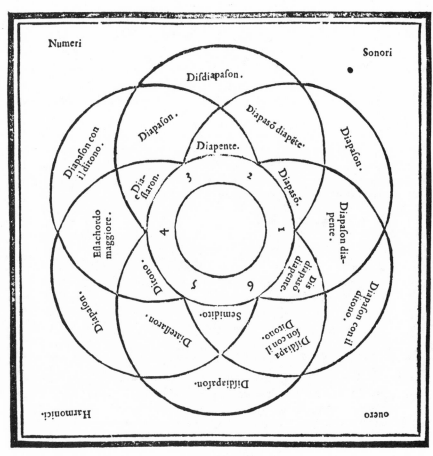

Figure 10.7.
Sonorous or harmonic numbers, from Zarlino, *Istitutioni,* I, 15, p. 25

cioè dalla Diatessaron & dal
Semiditono: perche di queste due
consonanze si compone: la onde
tra'l primo numero Cubo, il
quale è 8. viene ad hauer in
atto la sua forma.[55]

that is, from the diatessaron and
semiditone, because it is composed
of these two consonances.
For within the first cubic number,
8, its form attains actuality.

Zarlino did not in this book extend the realm of consonance to the *ottonario,*
and this with good reason, since it would have admitted the ratios in which
one of the terms is seven, all falling outside the circle of consonances.

55. Ibid., I, 16, p. 27.

Zarlino was too pragmatic a musician to insist on the just consonances for instrumental music. He recognized that it was not possible to tune a chromatic keyboard so that every fifth, fourth, and third was in a ratio of the senario. He was willing to admit compromises in tuning these intervals in instruments, provided vocal music remained pure. His faith in nature demanded that the ideal ratios be operative in the natural medium of voices.

> If it were true that in voices as well as instruments we hear only the consonances and intervals out of their natural ratios, it would result that those which are born of the true harmonic numbers would never reach actuality but would remain always potential. This potential would be futile and frustrated, for every potential that is not put into action is without utility in nature. And yet we see that God and nature never do anything in vain.[56]

For instruments, he thus feels free to devise an "equally tempered diatonic monochord" which is a compromise between the Pythagorean diatonic ditoniaion and Ptolemy's diatonic syntonon. He divides the comma into seven equal parts and subtracts two of these parts from each fifth,[57] resulting in major thirds that are one-seventh comma smaller than 5:4. For dividing a ratio into equal parts, Zarlino gives the same construction as Fogliano but goes beyond the construction to refer to Euclid's proof.[58] He then presents an instrument for finding two mean proportional lines between two given lines that he learned of from Giorgio Valla's *De geometria*.[59]

By relying excessively upon reason and authority, Zarlino laid himself open to attack from those who were bent on testing some of his premises. To counter the attacks that inevitably came, Zarlino explored further the Greek authors on music. We shall, therefore, come back to him after we have considered some theories that rival his.

Francisco de Salinas

The remarkable *De musica libri septem* of Francisco de Salinas (1513–90) belongs more properly to a history of Spanish than Italian humanism. Yet it deserves some discussion here, because Salinas lived in Rome and Naples between 1538 and 1558, years during which he studied the ancient Greek sources and probably drafted parts of his treatise. Blind from an early age, he was trained as a singer and organist. Yearning for a broader education, he exchanged organ lessons for lessons in Latin and later went to the Uni-

---

56. Ibid., II, 45.
57. Ibid., II, 43.
58. Ibid., II, 25; *Elements*, VI, 8.
59. Ibid., II, 25; Giorgio Valla, in *De geometria* IV (*De expetendis*, XIII), 2, fols. u6r–x1r, presents several solutions to this problem, one of which is the mesolabio.

versity of Salamanca, where he studied Greek, philosophy, and the arts. Service with Pedro Gómez Sarmiento, archbishop of Compostella, gave him the opportunity to go to Rome when Sarmiento was made a cardinal by Pope Paul III in 1538. There he became immersed in the study of music theory, for he realized that to be proficient with one's hands, as Vitruvius said of architects, was not sufficient if one sought to acquire real authority. He gives a partial list of the ancient sources he consulted in an autobiographical account in the early pages of his book:

> Those who aided me very greatly in this task, besides Boethius, whom every musician has on his lips, were manuscript books of ancient Greek authors not yet translated into Latin of which I still found a great plenty, above all the three books on harmonics of Claudius Ptolemy in the Vatican Library, to whom I do not know whether astronomy or music owes more, and the very instructive commentaries on them by Porphyry—of which the cardinal of Carpi made me a copy—containing most precious things collected from his reading of the ancients; two books of Nicomachus, whom Boethius follows; also one of Bacchius; three books of Aristides [Quintilianus]; also three of Bryennius, which the cardinal of Burgos of Venice himself attended to transcribing. . . . In this inquiry and investigation I spent more than twenty-three years.[60]

The Porphyry manuscript mentioned must be one of two from Valla's library that had belonged to Cardinal Rodolfo Pio di Carpi, now in Modena, Biblioteca Estense.[61] There were several manuscripts of Ptolemy in the Vatican, and Salinas would have found most of the other treatises he mentioned there also. The two books of Nicomachus may refer to the two books of the *Introduction to Arithmetic* which Boethius practically translated in his *De institutione arithmetica libri duo,* rather than the *Manual of Harmonics,* which is in a single book. Salinas relies on Nicomachus' arithmetic quite heavily in the mathematical sections of the first book. On the other hand, Salinas' list is otherwise an exclusively musical one, and by "two books" Salinas may therefore have meant the two works of Nicomachus—one on music and one on arithmetic—as in the inventory made under Sixtus IV in 1475, which describes item 365 (the present Vat. gr. 198) as "Nicomachi arithmetica et musica."[62] The reference in the quotation to Boethius following Nicomachus could apply to either alternative, since later Salinas refers to Boethius as having "followed Nicomachus in the two books con-

---

60. Francisco Salinas, *De musica libri septem* (Salamanca, 1577; facs. ed. Macario Santiago Kastner, Kassel, 1958), fol. 5r.

61. Numbers 149 and 152 in Puntoni's catalog of that library's Greek manuscripts. "Indice dei codici greci della Biblioteca Estense di Modena," *Studi italiani di filologia classica* 4 (1896):379–536.

62. Robert Devreesse, *Le fonds grec de la Bibliothèque vaticane des origines à Paul V* (Vatican City, 1965) p. 60. It also includes Ptolemy, Porphyry, and Bryennius.

cerning arithmetic, and in the first four concerning music."[63] Salinas' list was not intended to be exhaustive. Plutarch, Euclid, Cleonides, Gaudentius, and Alypius are some of the obvious omissions. Indeed, Salinas cites Plutarch's *De musica,* "Euclid's Isagoge" (the title shows he means Cleonides), and Gaudentius "Introductorium" elsewhere in the book.[64]

From the very title page, where Salinas advertises that he demonstrates the true doctrine of harmonics and rhythmics "according to the judgment of the sense and the reason," he professes his faith in the method of Ptolemy. Critical of both the Aristoxenians and the Pythagoreans, Salinas took a middle road: "In harmonics the judges are the sense and the reason, but not both the same way, because, as Ptolemy asserted, the sense judges concerning the matter and affection, the reason, concerning the form and cause. From these words we can draw the conclusion that, just as matter is completed by form, so sensory judgment is completed by the rational."[65]

Salinas did not disdain modern authors. Although he borrowed a great deal from Fogliano and Zarlino, he hardly mentioned them until he dedicated to each a critical review in a separate chapter of the fourth book.[66] Some of the debts to Fogliano are the theory of sonorous number, the break with the Pythagorean definition of consonance, the espousal of the syntonic diatonic tuning as the basis of modern vocal intonation, and the geometric division of the comma. To Zarlino he owed the theory of the senario, the treatment of the sixths as composite intervals, and the use of the mesolabio, among other doctrines. Salinas was a more perspicacious humanist than Zarlino in that he knew the contents of the ancient treatises more thoroughly and understood them better. But he was less of an antiquarian; he really had little interest in classical civilization as such and was bent on applying to modern music whatever he found useful in the older theories. Zarlino, on the contrary, was deeply interested in classical literature and the lore about Greek music but found little in it that was applicable to an already perfect art.

Their attitudes toward the chromatic and enharmonic genera illustrate the nature of the contrast. Rather than defining these two tetrachords in classical terms as dense in the lower pitches and sparse in the higher, as Zarlino and the older authors did, Salinas followed Nicola Vicentino in

63. Salinas, *De musica,* II, 18, p. 73: "Boethius autem totus Pythagoricus est, & in libris duobus de Arithmetica, & quatuor primis de Musica Nicomachum secutus."

64. Plutarch, in III, 4, p. 109; IV, 25, p. 217; Cleonides and Gaudentius, in II, 9, p. 55.

65. Salinas, *De musica,* I, 3. He devotes IV, 16–21, to a refutation of Pythagorean theories; IV, 22–24, to a critique of Aristoxenian harmonics. These chapters are translated in Arthur Michael Daniels, "The *De musica libri vii* of Francisco de Salinas" (Ph.D. diss., University of Southern California, 1962), pp. 364–94.

66. Salinas, *De musica,* IV, 32–33, trans. in Daniels, "The *De musica,*" pp. 422–36.

making them dense throughout, that is, dividing the entire chromatic tetrachord into semitones and the entire enharmonic tetrachord into dieses.[67]
The inspiration for the revival of the chromatic and enharmonic genera was
surely the example of the Greeks, but neither of these authors modeled his
theory of the genera on the ancient one, which was well known from
Boethius, Gaffurio, and other authors.[68] Vicentino, particularly, is vague
about how the two dense genera were practiced in ancient times. He says
they were put to other uses than the diatonic, which was meant for common
ears in public festivals, the chromatic and enharmonic being addressed to
"purified ears" (*purgate orecchie*) in the private entertainments of gentlemen
and princes, when great men and heroes were praised.[69] Vicentino gives no
source for this, and although in his book he occasionally names ancient
authors—Aristoxenus, Nicomachus, Ptolemy— there is no sign that he had
read any of them. In humanist circles in Ferrara he certainly must have
heard the virtues of the genera extolled, possibly by Francesco Patrizi, but
Vicentino himself was by nature uninclined toward historical scholarship.
Salinas, on the other hand, shows that he read Plutarch, and in Greek, for
he gives in the original language the locus classicus from the speech of
Soterichus on the virtues of the enharmonic and follows it with a translation:

At verò Musici nostri temporis pulcherrimum omnium, maximéque decorum genus, quod veteres propter maiestatem, grauitatém- que ipsius colebant, penitus repudiarunt, adeò vt ne qualis- cunque perceptio curáque sit plerísque Enharmononiorum inter- uallorum. Et tanquam ignauia, atque secordia inuasit eos, vt Diesim Enharmonion, ne speciem quidem omnino cadentium sub sensum praebere putent, eámque de canticis, atque modulaminibus exterminent.[70]	The musicians of our time, however, have repudiated altogether the most beautiful and charming genus, which the ancients, because of its majesty and severity, cultivated, so much so that the majority have no knowledge or concern at all about the enharmonic's inter- vals. So much laziness and sloth overcomes them, that they believe that the enharmonic diesis, of all things falling under the sense, is not perceptible, and they banish it from songs and melodic compositions.

This quotation, however, is not adduced in defense of the enharmonic but
to substantiate its neglect and thereby prove a point against Didymus. In

67. For a detailed study of the different approaches to the genera, see Karol Berger, *Theories
of Chromatic and Enharmonic Music in Late 16th-Century Italy* (Ann Arbor, 1980).
68. Salinas reports the shades of Aristoxenus, Didymus, Ptolemy, and others but only to
show that they were erroneous solutions: *De musica*, IV, 22–29, pp. 212–22.
69. Nicola Vicentino, *L'Antica musica ridotta alla moderna prattica* (Rome, 1555; facs. ed.
Edward E. Lowinsky, Kassel, 1959), I, 4, fol. 10v.
70. Plutarch *De musica* 1145A. Salinas, *De musica*, IV, 25, p. 217.

the chapter in which he introduces the dense genera[71] Salinas calls the enharmonic the best and most adaptable genus, but quite typically he depends
on logical arguments to prove this rather than classical authority.

Salinas was the first modern scholar to distinguish between the tonoi and
octave species and between these and the plainchant modes in a published
book. (Mei preceded him in an unpublished book.) As will be shown in
the next chapter, Salinas' treatment was too brief to give the reader a good
idea of how these systems worked, but he apparently understood their
functions. On the other hand, he obscured some aspects of the theory while
clarifying others. He attributed eight rather than seven tonoi to Ptolemy.
He unjustly charged that Boethius confused the tonoi and modes, when all
he did was to translate *tonos* and *tropos* usually as "modus." Salinas was
right, though, in criticizing Glarean and Gaffurio for having applied to the
modes attributes that belonged to the tonoi.[72] Salinas falls into a similar
error, though, when he associates the ancient harmoniai of Plato with the
modes and then, by dividing six of them through the species of fifths and
fourths, derives twelve.[73]

Salinas admired the work of Fogliano, of whom he says, "he has come
far closer to a true understanding of the science of harmonics than all of
the ancient and more recent [writers]."[74] He makes this statement at the
end of a chapter in which he enumerates what he considers serious errors
on the part of Fogliano. These are not scientific, logical, or scholarly errors
but differences of opinion, and we need not go into them here. There is a
similar chapter on Zarlino, whom he praises as having surpassed all those
who wrote on music before him. The disagreements with Zarlino are also
mainly matters of opinion, and some of the criticisms are founded on
misreadings.[75]

The really significant challenge to the foundations of Fogliano's and Zarlino's speculative theory came from other quarters, from the scientist Giovanni Battista Benedetti and from Zarlino's pupil Vincenzo Galilei, and
preparatory to their work were the findings of Girolamo Fracastoro.

Girolamo Fracastoro

With the work of Girolamo Fracastoro and Giovanni Battista Benedetti
musical science enters a new period of discovery. Up to that time no significant advances had been made over the state of knowledge represented

71. Salinas, *De musica*, III, 2.
72. Ibid., IV, 12–13, pp. 198–201.
73. Ibid., IV, 7–8, pp. 187–91.
74. Ibid., IV, 32, p. 231; Daniels trans., p. 430.
75. Ibid., IV, 33, pp. 231–34.

by Aristotle's *De anima,* the Aristotelian *De audibilibus* and *Problems,* and the commentary of Themistius. Fracastoro and Benedetti, like Fogliano, worked within the Aristotelian tradition, but they were able to correct him and make notable advances.

Fracastoro (1483–1553) studied at the university in Padua, where he pursued literature, mathematics, astronomy, philosophy under Pietro Pomponazzi and Nicolò Leonico Tomeo, and medicine under Girolamo Della Torre and his son Marcantonio. He wrote poetry and practiced medicine and even combined the two in his famous Latin poem *Syphilis sive morbus gallicus* (1530). His *Naugerius, sive de poetica dialogus* (c. 1540) proposes beauty of expression as the distinctive end of poetry and criticizes the theory of imitation. In his scientific work he regarded nature as autonomous, independent of supernatural intervention, a reality that could be studied to reveal its regulating principles. He was contemptuous of astrological and numerological explanations, such as in theories of the critical days of a disease. He sought explanations in immediate causes of concrete events.

His clarification of the action of air waves in the transmission of sound came out of his analysis of contraries in *De sympathia et antipathia rerum liber unus* (Venice, 1546). It is agreed, he says, that material elements tend to return to their natural place. Thus something that is rarefied (*rarefacta*) tends to be condensed (*condensata*), and something condensed tends to be rarefied. Sound, which depends on this principle, requires a dense medium:

Soni quidem, nisi addensetur aer, non sentiuntur, quoniam qualitates, quae sensus mouent, omnes quidem subiectum, in quo per se sunt, densum amant, medium vero, per quod feruntur earum species, non omnes densum volunt, sed quaedam rarum exposcunt, quaedam densius: . . . dico autem densum non per admistionem terrae, sed vi addensatum, quod in aere accidit facto ictu. Inde enim facta prius distractione, tum subita fit addensatio partis post partem, more vndarum, vnde circulationes conflantur, quod non aliud est, quàm successive quaedam aeris addensatio in orbem facta, per quam delata species à	Unless air is compressed, sounds are not heard, because all qualities that move the sense require the substance in which they exist— the medium—to be dense. This medium, through which the qualities' species are made, need not always be dense but sometimes rare, sometimes dense. . . . I say dense not through the admixture of earth, but in the sense of the compression that occurs in the air when it is hit. After a drawing apart and rarefaction has first been made, a condensation immediately follows, part for part, in the manner of a wave, whence the circles are stirred up that are nothing but a successive compression of the air in a circle, through which the species is carried

primo profecta   from where it first set out and is
sensum dimouere potest.[76]   able to move the sense.

The comparison of the sequence of compressions and rarefactions to a wave is significant although not carried far enough. The ancient authors compared the propagation of sound to the circular waves made in a pond when a pebble was thrown into it. Fracastoro goes a step further in saying that the cycle of compression and decompression itself resembles a wave, which, like the circular waves of water, moves in all directions. At the same time he clings to the idea of *species,* that "something audible" carried by the air waves which "moves the sense of hearing," by activating its potential for sound.

In a later chapter Fracastoro applies this model to explain sympathetic vibration:

Unisonum autem aliud unisonum   A unison stirs another unison,
commotat, quoniam, quae similiter   since strings that are stretched
tensae sunt cordae, consimiles   to the same tension are set up to
aeris vndationes & facere, &   make and receive similar waves of
recipere natae sunt, quae vero   the air. Those that are
dissimiliter sunt tensae, non   unequally stretched are not
eisdem circulationibus aptae sunt   apt to be moved by the same circu-
moueri, sed una circulatio aliam   lations; rather one circulation
impedit: ictus enim   impedes the other. The stroke
cordae, motus est compositus è   of a string is composed of
duobus motibus, vno quidem,   two movements, one in which
quo corda pellitur ante,   the string is impelled *ante,*
hoc est versus aeris circu-   that is, toward the circulation
lationes, alio vero, qui retro   of the air; in the other, which is made
fit, corda reducente sese ad   *retro,* the string returns to its
situm proprium: si igitur mota   original position. When, therefore,
vna corda debet & alia moueri,   one string is moved, the other
oportet, vt in secunda talis   must move too. But the second
proportio sit, vt vndationes &   must contain such a proportion [in
circulationes aeris,   relation to the first] that the waves
quae impellunt,   and circulations of the air impelling
& faciunt motum ante, non   and making the motion *ante* do not
impediant motum, qui retro fit   impede the motion that the string
à corda: quam proportionem   makes in return, and this proportion
solum eae cordae habent, quae   only those strings have that
etiam consimilem tensionem habent: have equal tension.
quae vero dissimilem sortitae   Those, however, that are stretched
sunt tensionem, non sese commo-   to an unlike tension do not cause

76. *De sympathia et antipathia rerum liber,* ch. 4.

tant, quoniam dum secundus fit
motus, id est
reditus cordae retro, circulatio secunda illi obuiat, & sese
impediunt: vnde nec motus fit
vllus praeter primam impulsa-
tionem, quae intensibilis est.[77]

each other to move, since as the
second motion is made, that is, the
return of the string *retro,* the
second circulation resists the return
and they impede each other. Therefore
it is not moved beyond the first
impulse, which is inaudible.

Here Fracastoro shows how two strings of equal length stretched to the same tension will be susceptible to each other's vibrations. The impulse or compression given to the air by the first string as it moves from its stationary position will be communicated to the second string. When the first string returns to its position, rarefying the air, the second will also. Were it not in the same tension, the second string would impede the motion of the air produced by the first string, evidently because it takes a longer or shorter time for its rarefaction-condensation cycle. So the second string will cease to move.

Fracastoro does not report any experiment that led to these conclusions, but he describes two analogous observations. When the bell rings in church certain of the statues high above the sanctuary begin to tremble, but others do not. Another experience cited is that of trying to reverse the swing of a pendulum before it has completed its period, which requires a great deal of effort, whereas at the right moment it is easy.

No further progress on sympathetic vibration is known to have been made until Marin Mersenne, citing Fracastoro's explanation, applied it to strings that were not in unison but in simple ratios to each other.[78]

Giovanni Battista Benedetti

In a letter to Piero Vettori of August 1560 from Rome, Girolamo Mei tells of hearing a certain Doctor Benedetti, about thirty to thirty-four years of age, read the natural science, *De coelo,* and *De generatione animalium* of Aristotle, and of regretting that he missed him lecture on the *Physics.* He praises Benedetti highly for his fluency, memory, languages, acumen, and independence of mind. The description fits our Benedetti, and if it was indeed he whom Mei heard, this is the only specific information we have of his teaching in Rome or of his having been there.[79] Benedetti (1530–90) admitted that he had no formal education but studied Euclid's first four

77. Ibid., ch. 11.
78. *Harmonicorum libri* (Paris, 1635), Bk. IV, Proposition 27, pp. 65–68.
79. G. Mei to P. Vettori, 31 August 1560, London, British Library, MS Add. 10,268, fols. 214r–15r.

books with Niccolò Tartaglia, probably in 1546–48. By the age of eighteen he was said to have become a mathematician, philosopher, and musician. From 1558 he was court mathematician to Duke Ottavio Farnese in Parma, and in 1567 he moved to Turin, where he taught mathematics and science at the court of Duke Emanuele Filiberto. In 1553 Benedetti published a theory that bodies of the same material but of different weights would fall through a given medium at the same speed, and not a speed proportional to their weights, as maintained by Aristotle. The demonstration of this in 1554 was plagiarized by Jean Taisnier, another mathematician-musician. Benedetti made numerous other contributions to mathematics and physics.[80] For Benedetti, as for so many of his contemporaries, Aristotle's works were a point of departure, and often the renewed investigation of problems found there led to fresh insights.

In two letters of around 1563 addressed to the composer Cipriano de Rore (1516–65), published in *Diversarum speculationum mathematicarum & physicorum liber* of 1585,[81] he confronted the age-old dilemma of the nature of consonance and its cause. This matter is broached only at the end of the second letter, as if it were an afterthought. For the letters concern theories of intonation. From the standpoint of acoustical theory, however, the remarks constitute an important revelation.

Nec alienum mihi videtur à proposito instituto, speculari modum generationis ipsarum simplicium consonantiarum; qui quidem modus fit ex quadam aequatione percussionum, seu aequali concursu undarum aeris, vel conterminatione earum.[82]	It does not seem foreign to my chosen purpose to speculate on the way the simple consonances are generated. This way is through a certain equalizing of the percussions or through the equal concurrence of air waves, or their cotermination.

There is no doubt, he says, that the unison is the consonance most friendly to the ear, after which comes the diapason, next the diapente, then the others. "Let us see, therefore," he invites the reader, "the order of the concurrence of the termination of percussions or air waves from which sound is generated."[83] Benedetti asks the reader to imagine a stretched string that is divided in half by a movable bridge. If the two halves are each plucked, a unison will be heard.

80. See Stillman Drake, "Benedetti," in *Dictionary of Scientific Biography*, I, 604–09.

81. Turin, 1585, pp. 277–83. The two letters are reprinted in Josef Reiss, "Jo. Bapt. Benedictus, *De intervallis musicis*," *Zeitschrift für Musikwissenschaft* 7 (1924–25):13–20.

82. Benedetti, *Diversarum*, p. 283.

83. Ibid., p. 283: "Videamus igitur ordinem concursus percussionum terminorum, seu vndarum aeris, vnde sonus generatur."

tot percussiones in aere faciet	One part of the string will make
vna partium illius chordae,	as many percussions in the air
quot et altera; ita	as the other. Thus
vt vndae aeris simul eant,	the waves of the air go
et aequaliter concurrant, absque	at the same time and concur equally
intersectione, vel fractione	without their cutting in or
illarum inuicem.[84]	fractioning each other.

Everyone knows, he says, that the longer a string, the more slowly it moves. If a string is divided by a bridge so that two-thirds are on one side and one-third on the other side, and if the two parts are each plucked, the consonance of the octave will be heard. The larger portion of the string will complete one period of vibration (*intervallum tremoris*) during the time it takes the shorter to complete two. If two-fifths of the string are on one side of the bridge and three-fifths on the other, the consonance of the fifth will be generated, the longer portion of the string completing two periods of vibration during the time the lesser portion completes three. Benedetti then arrives at the law which states that the product of the number representing the string length and the number of periods of the longer portion of the string will equal the product of the number representing the string length of the shorter portion and the number of periods of this portion. For example, in the case of the fifth, string length 3 will have 2 periods and the product will be 6; string length 2 will have 3 periods, and the product will also be 6. He proceeds to calculate the products for each of the consonances recognized by Fogliano, which are: diapason 2, diapente 6, diatessaron 12, major sixth 15, ditone 20, semiditone 30, and minor sixth 40. He notes that these numbers agree among themselves with a wonderful reasonableness (*mirabili analogia*).[85]

There are a number of tacit assumptions in this statement: that pitch is caused by periodic vibrations, that air waves transmit sound, and that the frequency of vibration varies inversely with the string length. For Fracastoro waves of air were still a metaphor, and he believed that they began slowly, picked up speed, then slowed down at the end. By contrast, Benedetti assumed that air waves caused sound and that the percussions determining a pitch occurred at a constant frequency. Aristotelian writers implied that frequency varied inversely with string length, giving the ratio of frequencies of the higher to the lower note of the octave as two to one. Benedetti builds on two Aristotelian *Problems*, 19.35 and 19.39, that imply this. In the first of these is stated: "For since *nete* is double *hypate*, as *nete* is two, so *hypate*

84. Ibid., p. 283.

85. For the Latin text and translation into English of this passage, see Palisca, "Scientific Empiricism in Musical Thought," in *Seventeenth Century Science and the Arts*, ed. H. H. Rhys (Princeton, 1961), pp. 106–08.

is one; and as *hypate* is two, *nete* is four; and so on." Since the nete string
is half hypate, either the author was confused, or he was truly referring to
frequency of vibration. That the latter is likely is made probable by 19.39,
which introduces the idea of the concurrence of the terminations of vibrations: "Furthermore, *hypate* happens to have the same conclusions to the
periods in its sounds as *nete*, for the second stroke which *nete* makes upon
the air is *hypate*."[86]

What the Aristotelian problems only imply, Benedetti affirms unequivocally: frequency varies inversely with string length. Whether he observed
the periods of vibration or simply assumed that vibrating strings must
display such periodicity, it is impossible to say. It is unlikely that he succeeded in counting the vibrations. Exactly what is meant by the equalizing
(*equatione*, which can also mean equal distribution) of percussions in unison
strings is not explained. But it must be that the number of percussions of
the air caused by the string per unit of time is the same in both string
segments. Cotermination of percussions is clearer. The end of the compression of the air near one string segment will coincide with the end of the
compression of the air near the other segment every time in a unison, every
second time in an octave, every sixth percussion in a fifth, and so on. Given
the relative number of percussions, it is possible, Benedetti discovers, to
establish the interval of cotermination by multiplying the terms of the
consonance's ratio and to compare this in various consonances. This product
becomes, as it were, an index of consonance. Having created such an index,
Benedetti does not pursue it to any conclusion, although the series of products strongly suggests a hierarchy of consonances. This is reinforced by the
remark that introduces the demonstration:

Nam, nulli dubium est, quin vni-	For there is no doubt that the
sonus sit prima principalis	unison is the first, principal
audituque amicissima,	[consonance] and friendliest
nec non magis	to the hearing, and also quite
propria consonantia; et si	properly a consonance, if
intelligatur, vt	it is thought of as a point
punctus in linea, vel vnitas	is to a line or unity to number.

---

86. The translations are by E. S. Forster in *The Works of Aristotle,* ed. W. D. Ross (Oxford,
1927), VII. Nicomachus also associated higher pitches with higher numbers, but he attributed
these numbers to tension on a string. Flora R. Levin would have us believe that because
Nicomachus' numbers, such as 12 and 6 for the octave, would not yield consonances if applied
to weights suspended from strings— for it would take the ratio of 4 to 1 to produce the
octave—he must have been thinking of rates of vibration. But this is not likely, for Nicomachus
clearly describes the way the weights are hung and couples the numbers with the word *holkōn,*
which Levin translates "pounds." Nicomachus *Manual* 6.7; Levin ed., p. 30; von Jan ed., p.
247, line 13; see also Levin, pp. 158–61.

in numero, quam immediate sequitur diapason, ei simillima, post
hanc verò diapente, caeteráeque.
Videamus igitur ordinem concursus
percussionum terminorum,
seu undarum aeris,
vnde sonus
generatur.[87]

This [unison] the diapason, most
similar to it, directly follows,
then the diapente, and so forth.
Let us see, therefore, the order of
concurrence of the terminations of
percussions of waves of the air
through which sounds are
generated.

It is clear that Benedetti sees no break between the so-called perfect and imperfect consonances. Nor are the sixths in any way inferior to the thirds; indeed the major sixth precedes either of the thirds. The progression from greater to lesser consonance appears to be a continuum rather than a stratification. Had Benedetti carried his investigation into the so-called dissonances, he would have found that the diminished fifth (7:5), with the product of 35, fell between the minor third and the minor sixth.

Benedetti's findings support the claims of just intonation, and therefore Zarlino's theories about tuning, for the consonances in the simple ratios have the most frequent concurrences of vibrations, and Benedetti's scale of consonance could even be interpreted to support the rule of the senario, because, by stopping at the product 30, the problems of the diminished fifth and the nonsenarian minor sixth are sidestepped. Benedetti made no such claim, however, and in the two letters demonstrates, in fact, the opposite, that just intonation is not practicable, whether in instruments or voices. Benedetti was well aware that two eminent music theorists, Fogliano and Zarlino, supported just intonation; he names them both. He also probably knew that his correspondent, de Rore, like Zarlino, was a pupil of Willaert. Yet he, an amateur in music, boldly proceeded to demolish the case for the syntonic diatonic.

Benedetti begins the first letter by telling de Rore that Hector Eusonius is wrong when he says that one can understand the ratios of musical consonances without experiencing them with the senses. Nor can one know the theory of music without being versed in its practice, Benedetti adds. A theorist can no more understand what a diapente is without mastering practice than a pure practitioner can know what a fifth is without adding theory to practice. (Benedetti uses the two sets of terms: diapason, diapente, etc., and octave, fifth, etc., quite deliberately here.) Benedetti himself was obviously trained in both theory and practice, for he mentions in the same letter some motets that he wrote to Latin texts. He enumerates the intervals

87. Benedetti, *Diversarum*, p. 283. D. P. Walker, in *Studies in Musical Science in the Late Renaissance* (London, 1978), p. 31, has contested my claim in "Scientific Empiricism," p. 109, that Benedetti was establishing any kind of hierarchy of consonances.

and their ratios as found in Fogliano's monochord, which, he says, the Modenese author selected from Ptolemy's syntonic diatonic. He then presents seven musical examples (which he promised de Rore he would send) to illustrate the use of these intervals. Among the examples are some excerpts from de Rore's chanson *Hellas comment voules-vous.* The examples demonstrate that there are three sizes of semitones and two of whole tones:

inter diesim, et.b. in	between the b natural and b flat in
superiori, agnosces	the superius, you recognize the
interuallum minimi semitonij	interval of the minimal semitone.
et si ibi sit diesis,	If you take the b natural
tanquam terminus ad quem,	as a *terminus ad quem,*
et.b. tanquam terminus à quo:	and b flat as a *terminus a quo,*
quod autem inter diesim et.b.	then between b natural and b flat
sit semitonium minimum, facilè	there is a minimal semitone. This you
agnosces si subtraxeris	readily admit if you subtract
decimam minorem à maiori, quam	a minor from the major tenth that
facit superius cum inferiori,	the superius makes with the lower
idest cum bassu.[88]	part, that is, the base.

Benedetti does not show the numerical computation. If the major tenth minus the minor tenth equals the minimal semitone, then we have for the ratio of the latter 10:4 / 12:5 = 25:24. A similar analysis shows that in the third example there appears between d and c♯ a major semitone: the seventh (product of the fifth and minor third) minus the major sixth thus equals the major semitone: $3:2 \times 6:5 = 9:5$; 9:5 / 5:3 = 27:25. The fourth example shows the minor semitone: 4:3 / 5:4 = 16:15. By similar means Benedetti illustrates the two sizes of the whole tone. The fifth example shows, in the tenor, a sequence of a minor (10:9) followed by a major (9:8) whole tone; the sixth, in the tenor, two minor whole tones; and the seventh, in the superius part, two major whole tones. Thus Fogliano's monochord assumed three sizes of semitones and two of whole tones. (See Figure 10.8.)

The point of the demonstration is not brought home until the second letter. Here Benedetti declares that if these different sizes of semitones and whole tones are used, as they must be if the consonances are tuned justly, a vocal composition will not end on the same pitch as it began but either higher or lower. Utilizing the same method of calculating the smaller intervals through the addition or subtraction of successive or simultaneous consonances as in the preceding demonstrations, Benedetti now presents two sets of examples. The first (Figure 10.9) consists of a simple diatonic progression in which at each return of the note g′ in the superius, the actual pitch rises a comma. By the end of the example the pitch has risen by four

88. *Diversarum,* p. 278.

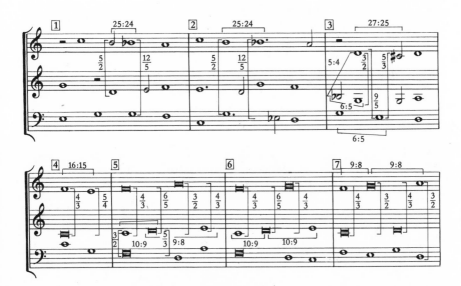

Figure 10.8.
Demonstration of the variety of semitones and whole tones, from Benedetti,
Diversarum, p. 278 (to which have been added the ratios according to Benedetti's
prose)

commas. This is because in each of the four repetitions of the pattern the
upward step g'-a' was a large whole tone, whereas the downward step a'-
g' was a small whole tone. Benedetti's final example (Figure 10.10) shows a
parallel process involving a sharped note, in which the consonances between
the superius and the tenor dictate the size of the semitones, which are always
large (27:25) descending and small (16:15) ascending, thereby realizing a
descent by a comma (81:80) with each statement of the pattern.

This phenomenon, Benedetti remarks, does not occur in organs and

Figure 10.9.
Demonstration of the rise in pitch in a diatonic passage, from Benedetti,
Diversarum, p. 279

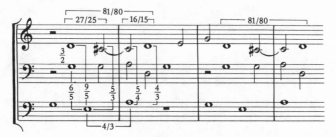

Figure 10.10.
Demonstration of the descent in pitch when a sharp is introduced, from
Benedetti, *Diversarum,* p. 280

harpsichords, because all the consonances besides the diapason or octave
are imperfect, that is, they are less than or greater than their just sizes
(*diminutae, aut superantes a iusto*). The alteration is done, he explains, because
if you take three successive sesquialter proportions, you get a major thirteenth (3:2 × 3:2 × 3:2 = 27:8), as from G to e'. This interval sounds
"hateful" to the ear (*odiosus esset sensui auditus*). When an octave is subtracted
from it, a major sixth that is "unfriendly" (*inimica*) results; this is in the
ratio 13:8, which differs from the just major sixth (5:3) by a comma (81:80).
For this reason "the learned and most excellent Zarlino" distributed parts
of this comma over all the perfect consonances. But because the sense of
hearing cannot distinguish the proper increment by which to raise or lower
each string, Benedetti devised a purely aural tuning procedure for realizing
this distribution of the comma error.

Benedetti began his tuning by making G consonant *grosso modo* with E♭
above it. He then tuned a series of "imperfect" fifths until he got a C,
which he tested with an E♭, a major sixth below. If the sixth was "tolerable,"
he left the fifths alone; otherwise he retuned them until the major sixth was
somewhat large (*aliquantulum excessiva*) but tolerable (*consonet tolerabiliter*).
Modern tuners use the major third for testing the perfect consonances;
Benedetti may have preferred the major sixth, because its number in his
scale, 15, the lowest number among the imperfect consonances, ranks it
higher than the major third, 20. Benedetti continued tuning the fifths slightly
small until he reached a G♯, remaining, however, within a three-octave span
by shifting to a lower octave whenever room was needed to complete the
upward spiral.

Benedetti did not say that his tuning was an equal temperament, but since
his demonstrations show that all semitones and whole tones should be
equalized, this would have been a logical goal. Indeed, his tuning method
is not unlike that proposed by Giovanni Lanfranco in 1533, which J. Murray

Barbour has interpreted as equal temperament.[89] Lanfranco, however, began with F, alternating tempered fifths and fourths, and used a tolerably sharp third rather than a major sixth as a guide for tempering the fifths and fourths. Both Benedetti and Lanfranco went into the sharps only as far as G♯ and into the flats no farther than E♭. In their keyboards G♯ doubled as A♭, and E♭ similarly functioned as D♯. I assume that Benedetti's starting point, E♭, sounded a good tempered fifth against the G♯ that terminated the cycle.

It is striking that in the very letter in which Benedetti demonstrated the coincidence of vibrations in pitches related as simple ratios, he proposed a system in which the consonances deviate from these simple ratios. Whereas Gaffurio and Zarlino expected art somehow to conform to and follow nature, Benedetti realized that this was impossible, that musical practice was not science.

Girolamo Mei and Vincenzo Galilei

No one resolved the conflicting demands of science and art more clear-headedly than Girolamo Mei. It was to Mei that Vincenzo Galilei turned in 1572 when he found glaring contradictions between the ancient and modern authors. Mei had established the reputation of being the best-informed scholar on ancient Greek music, mainly through correspondence with his teacher Piero Vettori. Although a native of Florence, where he was born in 1519, Mei spent most of his mature life elsewhere, from 1546 to 1554 in France, then in Padua, and from 1559 until his death in 1594 in Rome. He had begun his studies of Greek music theory in 1551 while in Lyon, working as tutor and companion to Guglielmo Guadagni, but he had had relatively little time to pursue this subject until ten years later, when he had committed himself to make a thorough study of the sources of ancient Greek music theory, as he reported to Vettori. He describes the surviving sources in a letter of 21 February 1562, to which he appended a list that, unfortunately, is lost, but it must not have been unlike the bibliography he later sent to Galilei.

> The Greek writers that survive of which I have knowledge and who write professionally about this matter, as you will see by a list enclosed in the letter, are eighteen. The oldest of them is Aristoxenus, but we do not have him

89. Lanfranco, *Scintille di musica* (Brescia, 1533), p. 132. See J. Murray Barbour, *Tuning and Temperament* (East Lansing, 1953), pp. 45ff. Mark Lindley, in "Temperaments," *New Grove Dictionary*, XVIII, 662, states that "Lanfranco's keyboard tuning instructions of 1533 are unequivocally for some form of mean-tone." See also Lindley, "Early 16th-Century Keyboard Temperaments," *Musica Disciplina* 28 (1974):129–51, esp. 144–51. Benedetti probably did not know Lanfranco's treatise, since it was an elementary practical tutor rather than a scientific work such as those of Fogliano and Zarlino.

complete. After him, as I understand it, there is Plutarch or Ptolemy, though Plutarch in this matter is of slight importance. But Ptolemy, from what I see, from the standpoint of diligence and intellect I judge to be ahead of all those I have read, twelve in all until today. Of the Latins we have Boethius, marvelous for the most part, and almost, as we say, an ape of Ptolemy. But to want to tell and demonstrate and prove by every path and in many ways every proposition according to his habit is necessarily very long, and for someone whose objective is not entirely this, perhaps tedious. But worst of all is that he is lacking just at the conclusion. Of Ptolemy there is also lacking the end of the third, or last, book I don't know how many chapters, but these do not pertain, so far as one can tell from his words, to things altogether essential to the science [of music]. They were supplemented by the nonsense of a Nicephorus who commented on him. Now, of all these, I have resolved to take as my foundation Ptolemy, for I judge him to be the most complete and most conclusive of all. So I have transcribed a [copy] by my own hand. And to make it a good one I am taking every care possible and I hope to finish it, and being the first to fish in these depths, this will not be a small thing. In Rome there are four exemplars, all of which I can see repeatedly. I utilize the other writers as interpreters. My object is to endeavor to understand the thing first, and, once understood, to resolve, with your advice and that of others, to leave some record for those who would like to see the truth better. At the same time I want to exercise myself and not get entirely rusty.[90]

The list of authors appended to Mei's first letter to Galilei of 8 May 1572 contains nineteen ancient authors, one more than the number in the list sent to Vettori. It reads as follows:

Notice of the writers on music that are still found today whom I have seen
Aristoxenus, two books and a half or a little more, and perhaps half of the
     second book of the Rhythmics
Aristides Quintilianus three books
Alypius with the signs that they used to notate the steps of all the modes
     and the tones in each genus, with I don't know how much missing at
     the end
Anonymous book without name printed under the name of Harmonic
     Introduction of Euclid, also found under the name of Cleoneda or
     Cleomede, one book
Baccheius Senior introduction, one book
Gaudentius introduction, one book
Emanuel Bryennius, three books
Nicomachus "Strazeno" introduction
Plutarch is printed

90. See the letter printed in Palisca, *Girolamo Mei, Letters on Ancient and Modern Music to Vincenzo Galilei and Giovanni Bardi*, pp. 180–82.

Ptolemy, three books
Porphyry on about a book and a half of the music [treatise] of Ptolemy
Psellus introduction. I am told that it is found also printed
Theon, brief compilation, one book
Racendito Josefo, compilation or compendium in one book
Several fragments by diverse authors without name
Ancient Latins
St. Augustine
Boethius
Censorinus
Martianus Capella in the notes of his Philology[91]

The project that Mei described in the letter to Vettori continued to occupy him until 1573, when he completed his principal work on music, *De modis musicis antiquorum,* dedicated to Vettori. Numerous scholars in Florence knew of Mei's studies on music, and it was one of these who recommended him to Galilei.

It was in replying to one of Galilei's questions that Mei formulated his theory of the separation of musical science and musical practice. Evidently Galilei was puzzled as to why the ancients were so concerned about the consonances yet did not use them in singing and playing together; Mei responded:

> The true end of the sciences is altogether different from that of the arts, since the end and proper aim of science is to consider every contingency of its subject and the causes and qualities of these purely for the sake of knowing truth from falsehood, without caring further how the arts will use this knowledge as an instrument or material or for otherwise gaining their ends. . . . The science of music goes about diligently investigating and considering all the qualities and properties of the constitutions, systems, and order of musical tones, whether these are simple qualities or comparative, like the consonances, and this for no other purpose than to come to know the truth itself, the perfect goal of all speculation, and as a by-product the false. It then lets art exploit as it sees fit without any limitation those tones about which science has learned the truth.[92]

Galilei, in his *Dialogo della musica antica et della moderna* of 1581, rephrased this thought. The principal interlocutor, Giovanni Bardi, replies to Piero Strozzi's query as to why the ancients wrote so much about consonances, when they sang only in unison:

> My reply to you is this, that the sciences have a different procedure and different goal for their operations than do the arts. The sciences search for the truth of

91. For bibliographical notes concerning these authors and their works, see Palisca, *Girolamo Mei,* pp. 118–21, nn. 58–77.
92. Mei to V. Galilei, 8 May 1572, in Palisca, *Girolamo Mei,* p. 103.

all the contingencies and properties of their subject, and together with them
their causes, having as a goal the truth of knowledge and nothing more, whereas
the arts have as their aim to operate, something different from understanding.[93]

As late as 17 January 1578 Mei was trying to show Galilei why the imperfect
consonances were not recognized in ancient Greek theory and why, consequently, the Pythagorean tuning was perfectly satisfactory for their purposes. But such historical considerations aside, Mei thought of a better way
to settle the tuning question:

> In the end it is not necessary to adduce these objections (if I am not mistaken)
> to ascertain whether the genus that is sung today is the syntonic or ditonic,
> because the very division of the strings will offer indubitable testimony of it.
> Stretch out over a lute (the larger it is, the more obvious will be what we wish
> to prove to the ear) two strings, either treble [*canti*: g'] or mean [*mezzane*: a],
> or whatever you want to call them, of length and thickness as equal as possible,
> which sound a unison together, and mark underneath them accurately the frets
> according to the distribution of the intervals of each of the two genera—the
> syntonic and ditonic—and then, taking the notes of the tetrachord one by one
> by means of the frets of each string, observe which of the two strings gives
> the notes that correspond to what is sung today. Thus without any further
> doubt the answer will result clear to anyone, even if what I have sometimes
> fancied on my own more as a matter of opinion than judgment is not proved
> true.[94]

Galilei must have proceeded to make this experiment, because that very
year he sent to Zarlino under a pseudonym a discourse, not extant, that
outlined his objections to Zarlino's theories about intonation. Zarlino in
the *proemio* of his *Sopplimenti* speaks of receiving with a letter of 7 June 1578
a "Trattato di Musica," and in the letter the author apologizes for not having
written to him or spoken to him after de Rore left the service of San Marco
in Venice.[95] The author of the treatise, who is obviously Galilei, is quoted
as saying in the letter that he studied counterpoint and other aspects of
theory with Zarlino but profited little from the study. Zarlino claims to
have answered the letter[96] and then received another from his "Discepolo,"
as he calls him, dated 19 July 1578. This time Galilei evidently spoke of
Valgulio's coming to the defense of Aristoxenus (to which Zarlino replied
by quoting a page-long section from Valgulio's discourse).[97] In another
place Zarlino refers again to what must be the same letter, saying that his
disciple sent him "a nice discourse by a gentleman of his who is very

93. *Dialogo,* p. 105.
94. Mei to Galilei, 17 January 1578, in Palisca, *Girolamo Mei,* p. 140.
95. Zarlino, *Sopplimenti musicali,* proemio, pp. 5–6.
96. Ibid., IV, 17, p. 172.
97. Ibid., IV, 17, pp. 173–74.

learned." The gentleman is quoted as saying that "he never found any mention among the ancient writers" of the senario, although "of the Greek authors he carefully read fifteen or sixteen, besides many fragments, and of the Latin authors as many as he could get."[98] The gentleman is obviously Mei. The "nice discourse" must have been taken from a letter of Mei, perhaps that of 17 January 1578, where Mei explains that the ancients did not recognize any consonances except those later called perfect, all of which were determined by multiple or superparticular ratios, but that Ptolemy maintained that the diapason-plus-diatessaron should be added. Ptolemy did not use such simplistic arguments as the senario or similar trivialities, however, Mei added.[99]

These arguments later became the core of the first part of the published *Dialogo*. At the very beginning of this work Galilei reaffirmed his empirical stance in a speech put in the mouth of the interlocutor Piero Strozzi:

> Before your Lordship begins to untie the knot of the proposed questions, I wish in those things which sensation can reach that authority always be set aside (as Aristotle says in the Eighth Book of the *Physics*), and with it the tainted reason that contradicts any perception whatever of truth. For it seems to me that those who for the sake of proving some conclusion of theirs want us to believe them purely on the basis of authority without adducing any further arguments are doing something ridiculous, not to say (with the Philosopher) acting like silly fools. This privilege is not conferred on anyone but the most wise Pythagoras, to whom you referred a moment ago, by his followers.[100]

Toward the end of his career, in an unpublished response to Zarlino's *Sopplimenti* of 1588, Galilei reaffirmed his belief in close observation with the senses as against the acceptance of authority:

gl'huomini che come professori	men who profess
d'un arte o d'una scienza, non	an art or a science do not
sogliono nello scriuerne	in writing about
andarsene presi	it go off half
alla grida come fa il Zarlino.	cocked as does Zarlino.
ma quando trouano uno scrittore	But when they find a writer who
che allega l'autorità d'un altro	cites the authority of another more
piu di lui antico, cerca di uedere	ancient than he, they seek to get
in fonte quella tal cosa; et il	to the bottom of the thing, and
medesimo si fa quando si scriuono	even more when writing
cose udite da gl'amici piu oltre.	about matters heard from friends.
quando anco sono uedute in fonte	When someone has seen to the bottom
le cose di qual sia scrittore,	of the things of any author who

98. Ibid., III, 3, p. 93.
99. Palisca, *Girolamo Mei*, p. 138.
100. *Dialogo*, p. 2.

che tratti pero di quelle cose	treats of matters that
che sono poste al senso; si	are subject to sensation, he
esaminano s'elle sono uere, o no;	examines whether they are true or
et dopo hauere recitato le ope-	not, and after reporting their
nioni loro et conosciuto realmente	opinions and recognizing that
ch'elle non passano per quel uerso	they do not truly pass muster
gli si agiugne il parere suo con	he adds his own opinion with
quella modestia che conuiene.[101]	all due modesty.

Galilei gives several examples of Zarlino's lapses from this method, of which two are of particular interest. One is the case of the ratios of the octave in pipes. Zarlino says that they follow the same rule as strings, namely that a pipe of half the length of another will sound an octave higher than the first.[102] They must be of the same width and thickness also, Galilei objects. Zarlino should have experimented (*esperimentato*) first, which would have been very easy to do. Even though Aristotle makes the same mistake,[103] Zarlino, a musician, is not so easily excused. Similarly Plutarch says that weights attached to strings produce an octave when they are in duple proportion.[104] This is false, Galilei maintains, for they have to be in quadruple proportion.[105]

At what point in his career Galilei developed the laws governing the numerical proportions obtained by measuring the dimensions of different types of sounding bodies—strings, pipes, disks, bells —is not documented. He first revealed some of his findings in the *Discorso intorno all'opere di messer Gioseffo Zarlino da Chioggia* of 1589. At the time he wrote the *Dialogo* he was still unaware of the fact that different ratios could determine the same consonances, depending on whether one measured a length, a surface, a volume, or the tension of a string. In the *Dialogo* his differences with Zarlino on matters of speculative music had revolved mainly around the definition of the tuning currently sung and played. Obviously unaware of Benedetti's critique, Galilei approached the problem in a more conventional manner. Benedetti had analyzed what would happen if punctiliously accurate singers continually adjusted their pitch to each other to maintain at all times the consonances of the simple ratios, both in simultaneous chords and in leaps. It would have been virtually impossible to find four singers capable of doing this; so his findings are true only in an ideal sense. Nevertheless, his analysis shows conclusively that if singers kept to the ideal consonances, their ref-

101. Florence, Biblioteca Nazionale Centrale, MS Galilei 5, fol. 42r.

102. *Sopplimenti musicali*, II, 13, p. 68.

103. *Problems* 19.50.922b–923a.

104. Plutarch, *De anima procreatione in Timeo*, in *Moralia* 1021; Zarlino, *Sopplimenti*, II, 13, p. 68.

105. MS Galilei 5, fol. 113r–v.

erence pitch would be constantly changing, something that Zarlino, had he considered it, would have found totally unacceptable.

Galilei's approach was more static. He pointed that if all the intervals in the gamut of notes normally used were calculated on the basis of the syntonic diatonic as a stationary tuning laid out on a monochord, an excessive number of the perfect and imperfect consonances would be intolerably out of tune. The minor third d–f (32:27), he shows, is not the same as e–g (6:5), nor is the major third a–c♯' (81:64) the same as c'–e' (5:4). The fourth a–d' (27:20) and the fifth d–a (40:27) are out of tune. These are some of the most common of the troublesome consonances. Galilei names many more.[106] The practicing musicians of his day, Galilei's observations showed him, did not adhere to any of the diatonic species described by the ancient authors. They mixed, without knowing it, the intense diatonic of Aristoxenus—an equal temperament—and the tunings Ptolemy called diatonic ditoniaion and diatonic syntonon. The viola d'arco, the lute, and the fretted lyra play the intense diatonic of Aristoxenus, which has equal semitones. The organ, harpsichord, and harp use two unequal semitones. Transverse flutes, cornetti, and similar instruments, in the hands of expert players, adjust to one or another species, depending on the situation, and voices do this also. In composing and singing, the intervals are formed in a tuning somewhere between the diatonic ditoniaion and the diatonic syntonon. Only the octave is found in its true ratio.[107]

Galilei later describes the intense diatonic of Aristoxenus in greater detail. It is one of six distributions proposed by the ancient author, two of which were diatonic, three chromatic, and one enharmonic. Aristoxenus, Galilei explains, divided the diatessaron into sixty "particles" (*particelle*), assigning twelve to the lowest interval of the tetrachord, and twenty-four to each of the higher intervals. Actually Aristoxenus did not divide the diatessaron into sixty parts. He spoke of twelfths of a tone, which was equivalent to dividing the diatessaron into thirty parts. It was Ptolemy who divided the diatessaron into sixty parts in his discussion of Aristoxenus.[108] Galilei had an Italian translation of Gogava's Latin of Aristoxenus, but he must not have looked up this passage.[109] The error does not affect the result, however.

---

106. *Dialogo* pp. 9–19 is mainly given over to calculating the size of these consonances and showing their impracticability. The other intervals, both smaller and larger, are also considered in the preceding or subsequent pages.

107. Ibid., pp. 30–31.

108. *Harmonics* 1.12.

109. The translation is in Florence, Biblioteca Nazionale Centrale, MS Galilei 8. On the basis of watermarks it seems to date from the first half of the 1570's. Approximately the same watermark is on fol. 38r, for example, as on letters of Giorgio Bartoli from 1572 to 1574 in Florence, Biblioteca Riccardiana, MS 2438-bis, vol. III, and his translation of Boethius, Flor-

All the semitones in this sytem are equal and have half as many particles as the whole tones. The result is an equal division, but a purely theoretical one, since Aristoxenus did not propose any arithmetical, geometrical, or other practical means to achieve it. Galilei did not at this time recommend this tuning, except for fretted string instruments, although he became proponent of its more general application years later.

Zarlino's reply to his "discepolo" was erudite, full of elaborate logical and rhetorical constructions, though exceedingly repetitious; it hardly conceded a single point. Zarlino was deeply affected by what Galilei wrote, nevertheless; indeed, he embraced some of his pupil's ideas while appearing to reject them. The cornerstone of Zarlino's defense was the distinction between natural and artificial music making. Voices are natural instruments; all others are artificial. Voices use natural intervals and consonances; instruments must be content with those produced by art. Whatever is produced by nature is superior. Zarlino reaffirms his faith in the syntonic diatonic, but now the justification is not simply numerology, as in the *Istitutioni,* but also philosophic truth.

> The forms of the consonances and other intervals that we use in our times in vocal and natural compositions are not products of art nor inventions of man but primarily of nature itself, collocated and registered among many things and especially among the parts of the perfect number, which is the senario, as I declared in the *Istitutioni,* in which they find their true forms. They are then ordered and rediscovered by art in the species that I call and shall always call natural, named syntonic diatonic by Ptolemy.[110]

Zarlino had to admit the "imperfections" that arose in the syntonic diatonic, but voices, being natural and completely flexible, could steer the harmony to a good consonance when an impure one would result from following the preordained tuning system.[111] The object of musical science is to defend and demonstrate the natural canon or monochord. The proof of this thesis leads Zarlino into a lengthy survey of the quarrels between the Pythagoreans and Aristoxenians. Some of this is of great interest from the point of view of the penetration of humanism into music theory. Zarlino shows that toward the end of his life he read quite extensively in Aristoxenus, Ptolemy, and Porphyry, as well as in other ancient authors. The contents of the *Sopplimenti* substantiates the claim made in the first chapter:

---

ence, Biblioteca Nazionale Centrale, MS Magl. XIX.75, finished in 1579. Bartoli was the copyist of the only existing manuscript of the Mei letters, Biblioteca Apostolica Vaticana, MS Reg. lat. 2021.

110. *Sopplimenti musicali,* I, 1, p. 8.
111. Ibid., IV, 6–7, pp. 141–46.

I have not failed to see and read all those writers, Greek as well as Latin, that I have been able to get my hands on who treat of musical matters, as among the Greeks are Aristoxenus, Euclid [i.e., Cleonides], Nicomachus, Ptolemy, Aristides Quintilianus, Emmanuel Bryennius, Gaudentius the philosopher, Bacchius, Psellus, and Alypius, together with some other writings that are incomplete and by other anonymous authors, although the majority of the exemplars are (I lament over this), partly because of antiquity, partly because of the ignorance of the scribes, imperfect and incorrect. But of the Latins I have not missed seeing and reading many many, some printed, and some handwriten, among them Boethius, the monk Guido of Arezzo, Faber Stopulense [sic], Franchino Gaffurio of Lodi, Lodovico Fogliano of Modena, Glarean, and many others of the best who have written in this discipline, from whom I have learned many things.[112]

Stimulated apparently by reading Valgulio, Zarlino surveyed ancient opinion on the question of whether pitch differences reside in quantities or qualities. The authors he reviews are Archytas, Ptolemy, Aristotle, Theophrastus, Panaetius, Plutarch, and Porphyry, to each of whom he dedicates a separate chapter.[113] In the course of this he interpolates many opinions of his own, so that it is not always easy to pick out those of the ancient authors. He finally decides for the view of Porphyry, that pitch difference is both a quality and a quantity.

Zarlino's *Sopplimenti* is too rich a book to do justice to here. It is an eloquent testimony to the diffusion of ancient learning. Much of the erudition exchanged in letters and esoteric discourses earlier in the century has now become common property. Zarlino does not pass up any opportunity to cite an ancient Greek, Hebrew, or Latin author, quoting him, when he does, in the original language. Some of Zarlino's uses of antiquity are apropos, but much of the time he shows an indifference to the context, and, indeed, a certain contempt for what must have seemed to him the primitive ends and means of ancient music.

Galilei did not delay long in replying in print. The letter of dedication, to Zarlino, of his *Discorso intorno all'opere di . . . Zarlino* (Florence, 1589) is dated the last day of August 1588. Galilei challenged the idea that some intervals are natural, others artificial. To him all musical intervals were equally natural, whether their ratios were within or outside the senario. "The third contained in the 81:64 ratio is as natural as that in the 5:4 ratio. For the seventh to be dissonant in the 9:5 ratio is as natural as for the octave to be consonant in the 2:1 ratio." Sounds produced by instruments are as

---

112. Ibid., I, 1, pp. 7–8. Among the anonymous authors Zarlino probably numbered the Bellermann-Najock anonymi. Compare this list with his reading before the *Istitutioni* of 1558, p. 245, above.

113. Ibid., II, 7–15, pp. 57–74.

natural as those made by voices, for in both cases the material from which the sounds are made is natural.[114] Art is not necessarily inferior to nature. In those things that art can do and nature cannot, art is superior. In those things that nature can do and art cannot, art is inferior. Art and nature are both efficient causes. In making artificial things nature cannot rival art; nor can art rival nature in making natural things. Art, however, can improve on nature. Painting can represent not only natural and artificial things but also anything that it is possible to imagine. It can surpass nature in providing the eye with everything it can desire in the way of excellence of line and color.[115]

In replying to Galilei's inventory of the variety of poor-sounding intervals occurring in the syntonic, Zarlino took refuge, as we saw, in the flexibility of voices and their ability to seek out the best consonances. Galilei was thus forced to point out that if voices departed from the established intervals of the syntonic to seek better sounding consonances, they were no longer following the syntonic. Galilei proceeds to show in a manner perhaps inspired by Benedetti what happens when voices adjust to each other and converge on a just consonance. "We have two parts that sing this interval C–c. Then we make the lower part ascend by a fifth to G, and the upper part by a tone to d, this tone being a whole 9:8. I demonstrate this as follows: between C and G is a fifth, and from the same G to c is a fourth, which will become a fifth every time it is augmented by 9:8, by which the upper part will have risen."[116] This may be represented as in Figure 10.11, example a.

Galilei then goes on to describe a progression by a 9:8 tone in the upper part that would lead to a tenth (an octave plus the 81:64 proportion), an unpleasant "dissonance" (example b). The singers would, therefore, aim for a tone smaller than 9:8. Galilei describes two further progressions (examples c and d) that cause diverse whole tones, but he does not provide the calculations (given in brackets in the example). Moreover there are three sizes of semitones: 16:15 in going from a major third to a fourth, 135:128 from a major third to a tritone, and 25:24 from a major to a minor third. Although this discussion would appear to confirm Zarlino's view, Galilei insists that it does not, since the repetition or alternation of the two sizes of semitones depends on the piece and not on the distribution of the syntonic diatonic. He recognizes, further, the phenomenon pointed out by Benedetti: "According to whether more major or minor [tones] have occurred in the piece, ascending or descending, the singers will find at the end of it to have

114. Galilei, *Discorso*, pp. 92–94.
115. Ibid., p. 78.
116. Ibid., p. 119.

Figure 10.11.
Demonstration of the variety of whole tones, from Galilei, *Discorso,* pp. 119, 122

raised or lowered the steps from the intonation of the beginning."[117] Were
Zarlino willing to accept these facts and abandon his chimerical "natural"
and "artificial," Galilei confesses, he would concede that the genre "that
we sing today agrees more with the very syntonic of Ptolemy than with
any other distribution."[118]

Subjecting Zarlino's theories to a thoughtful review was in itself an important undertaking. (The arrogance of some passages was, to be sure,
regrettable.) But even more significant were some revelations that Galilei
buried in the dense prose—never relieved by a paragraph break—of this
discourse. After spending several pages praising the ancient music theorists
- Pythagoras, Didymus, Ptolemy, and Aristoxenus—Galilei comes to the
account of Pythagoras and the hammers related by Boethius on the basis
of the testimony of Macrobius:

> In this connection I wish to point out two false opinions of which men have
> been persuaded by various writings and which I myself shared until I ascertained
> the truth by means of experiment, the teacher of all things. They believe that
> the weights Pythagoras attached to the strings, better to hear the consonances,
> were the same as those of the hammers from which he first heard them. Now
> that this could not in any way be so, experiment, as I said, demonstrates. For
> if someone wished to hear from two strings of equal length, thickness, and
> quality, the sound of the diapason, it would be necessary for him to suspend
> weights, not in the duple but in the quadruple proportion. The diapente will
> be heard every time that from the same strings are hung weights in the 9:4
> proportion, the diatessaron when in the 16:9 proportion, and the 9:8 tone when
> in the 81:64 proportion. . . . It is not true, therefore (and this is the other fallacy)
> that the consonances cannot be obtained through other genres of ratios than
> the multiple and superparticular.[119]

117. Ibid., p. 121.

118. Ibid, pp. 124–25. D. P. Walker has quite rightly noted this virtual agreement of the
two polemicists and has some interesting reflections on this controversy in *Studies in Musical
Science,* pp. 14–26.

119. *Discorso,* pp. 103–04.

Galilei goes on to say that in pipes (*canne*) the diapason will be obtained "whenever the length and the void (*vacuo*), or shall we say diameter, of the lower pipe is double that of the higher,"[120] the diapente when the two are in the sesquialteral proportion, and the diatessaron when they are in the sesquitertian ratio. Thus, he concludes, the volumes correspond to a cube, weights suspended from strings to a surface, and strings simply stretched to a line. These last remarks are somewhat cryptic, but Galilei later clarified them in an essay entitled "A Particular Discourse Concerning the Diversity of the Ratios of the Octave," of around 1589–90, in which he reported on experiments with strings of different materials, with weights attached to strings, and with coins and pipes. The octave, Galilei concludes, may be obtained through three different ratios: 2:1 in terms of string lengths, which corresponds to linear measurement; 4:1 in terms of weights attached to strings, which is analogous to area or surface measurements; and 8:1 in terms of volumes of concave bodies like organ pipes, which corresponds to cubic measurements.[121]

Galilei was the first to reveal the falsity of the famous story about Pythagoras that had been repeated in almost every book about music. Of the observations Pythagoras was said to have made, only that of the division of the string can have been true. Only in that circumstance would the traditional ratios hold. In pipes, if length alone were measured, these numbers would be approximately correct.[122] Galilei's laws for the correspondence between ratios of consonances and various physical measurements themselves needed to be refined. The behavior of volumes of air is particularly complex, though Galilei's formula is a good approximation.

Galilei's discovery that a variety of ratios could cause consonances, even superpartient proportions such as 9:4 and 16:9, was a fatal blow to numerology in general and the senario in particular. It is true that Vincenzo's son, Galileo, was to restore the traditional numbers by showing that frequencies are the real cause of pitch differences and that they vary inversely with string lengths. We have seen that Benedetti adumbrated this theory but brought forth no experimental proof. Until this new theory of frequencies was firmly

120. Ibid., p. 105.
121. "Discorso particolare intorno alla diversità delle forme del diapason," Florence, Biblioteca Nazionale Centrale, MS Galilei 3, fols. 44r–54v. Further on this essay see Palisca, "Scientific Empiricism in Musical Thought," pp. 129–30. I am planning to publish editions and translations of Galilei's scientific essays in a forthcoming volume of the Yale Music Theory Translation Series called *Documents of the Florentine Camerata*.
122. An anonymous author, probably of the fifteenth century, in Biblioteca Apostolica Vaticana, MS Barb. lat. 283, fols. 37 ff., shows that with pipes one must consider not only length but diameter also. He also makes some observations about cymbals and acoustical properties of various materials, but he maintains that weights attached to strings will give the consonances when in the usual proportions.

established there was no reason to favor the duple ratio for the octave over the quadruple, or 3:2 for the fifth over 9:4.

Perhaps because Galilei was relieved of the tyranny of numbers, he was able to give the first favorable account of the intense diatonic (*diatonico incitato*) of Aristoxenus that is to be found in the theoretical literature. He introduces the discussion in the *Discorso* by saying that he is fulfilling the desire of a number of his Aristoxenian friends. The case is first presented from a modern point of view. If the tone is divided into two unequal semitones, many inconveniences arise: D♯ is not the same as E♭; the semidiapente is larger than the tritone; the major seventh exceeds the diminished octave; D♯ to F is larger than a whole tone; the minor sixth is larger than the augmented fifth; and so on. Turning then to the situation in which Aristoxenus found himself, Galilei imagined that he must have studied every contingency of the two famous distributions then known, that of Pythagoras and that of Didymus, whom Galilei assumed to be older than Aristoxenus. In the system of Pythagoras the tone was divided into two unequal semitones of which the larger was above the smaller; in that of Didymus the reverse was true. In the Pythagorean system the tritone was equal to the semidiapente; in that of Didymus the tritone was larger than the semidiapente. Aristoxenus resolved that there should be only one semitone, the true half of the tone, and thus six tones or twelve semitones in the octave. The remaining intervals were built up from these, so that the minor second contained one semitone, the major second two, the minor third three, and so on. The uniform semitone permitted every interval to be measured exactly, just as one measures weight with the pound of twelve ounces. Galilei then sums up the advantages of this system with these words:

> No demonstrable distribution besides this one can be found among stable steps that is simpler and more perfect and more powerful, whether played or sung, or in which what part of the whole each interval comprises can be comprehended exactly by the sense with as great facility and clarity as could be desired. For the subject of music, which is vocal and instrumental sound, is a continuous and not discrete quantity.[123]

Unlike discrete quantities, which are numbers, continuous quantities can be infinitely divided without running into the difficulties that arise with ratios. One of the benefits of this division is that the tritone and semidiapente, being equal, rise to a new special category of perfect dissonance. Like the perfect consonances, of which there is only one form (rather than major and minor), the tritone-diminished fifth has a single size.[124]

Galilei saw nothing outrageous in Aristoxenus' reasoning, as others had,

123. *Discorso,* p. 113.
124. Ibid., pp. 115–17.

Figure 10.12.
Demonstration of the need for equal temperament, from Galilei, *Discorso intorno all'unisono,* Florence, Biblioteca Nazionale Centrale, MS Galilei 3, fol. 61r
(barlines added)

possibly because as a lutanist he had experienced equal division in tuning his lute, in which accurate quantitative measurement did not enter. The octave in the lute and viol consisted of five whole tones and two semitones. In another of his last essays, the unpublished "Discorso particolare intorno all'unisono" of around 1590, he proposed that equal temperament was a necessary compromise for all instrumental music, not only that of lutes and viols. To prove his point he devised a short musical example that could be played flawlessly only by instruments tuned to the "intense diatonic" of Aristoxenus (Figure 10.12).[125]

Having given this defense of the Aristoxenian system, Galilei could not, however, claim that it is the tuning currently sung, because the ear preferred the fifth, for example, in its sesquialteral form. Experienced singers would always seek the most perfect intervals possible, but it was not feasible to describe or demonstrate with numbers the system that they used in polyphonic music. In an aside he reflects that it is just as difficult to regulate and make proportional through stable canons the movements of the celestial bodies, and with cosmic irony Galilei adds, "and this may be a good part

125. "Discorso particolare intorno all'unisono," Florence, Biblioteca Nazionale Centrale, MS Galilei 3, fols. 55r–61v.

of the congruence that Pythagoras judged there was between the celestial and human harmony," as if to say that what the heavens and human harmony, including polyphonic singing, have in common is a lack of stable proportion. In short, Pythagorean universal harmony is not truly, only wishfully, harmonious.

It is no coincidence that the three men who laid the foundations for modern acoustics, Fracastoro, Benedetti, and Galilei, were all ardent students of ancient learning. Before attempting new solutions, it was reasonable to search first in the ancient writers who were dedicated to investigating the truth of physical phenomena. These ancient writers were mainly in the Aristotelian tradition, and it was there that all three modern investigators found preparatory explorations of the questions they posed. They were able to modify and sometimes overturn the Aristotelian solutions through reflecting upon sense experience, real experiments, and thought experiments. But what they could discover by these efforts was only a beginning. The definitive mathematical and experimental work on these problems was to occupy a host of others in the seventeenth century: Galileo, Beeckman, Francis Bacon, Mersenne, Euler, Christian Huyghens, Kepler, Newton, Stevin, Wallis, and Sauveur, among others.[126]

---

126. See Sigalia Dostrovsky's essay on the history of acoustics in *Geschichte der Musiktheorie,* VI, in press.

ELEVEN

Greek Tonality and Western Modality

othing in Greek music theory so baffled Western students, from the tenth century to the Renaissance, as the system of tonoi and octave species and the so-called harmoniai. The first five hundred years of Western theory of the modes was founded on a misunderstanding of the Greek system. Only in the Renaissance was it recognized, and then only through a slow process, that the modes of plainchant and those of the ancient Greeks were altogether different. Yet the source from which the chain of misunderstandings arose was widely available and, to an open mind, could have yielded all that was necessary to dispel them. This was the *De institutione musica* by Boethius, an author whose name was on everybody's lips but whose music treatise was hardly ever read in its proper context.

Johannes Gallicus

The intensified study of Boethius both in Italy and the north in the fifteenth century, partly inspired by humanism, reopened the question of what the ancient tonalities were. The first Western writer to penetrate some of the unique qualities of the tonoi and appreciate the distance that separated them from the plainchant modes was a participant in this Boethian revival: Johannes Gallicus de Namur, as he is generally known, although his family name was Legrense.[1] He studied at the University of Padua and became a teacher in the school for patricians in Mantua founded by Vittorino da Feltre (1378–1446) under the patronage of Gianfrancesco Gonzaga. It was under Vittorino, Gallicus acknowledged, that he "diligently heard the Music of Boethius; I who earlier considered myself a musician saw that I had not

---

1. That, at least, is what his contemporary John Hothby called him. See Albert Seay, ed., Johannes Gallicus, *Ritus canendi* (Colorado Springs, 1981), p. iii.

attained the true practice of this art."[2] France made him a singer, he admits, but Italy turned him into a grammarian and *musicus* in the Boethian sense, thanks to Vittorino, whom he extols as "imbued generously with both Latin and Greek letters."[3] Gallicus was aware that Boethius had translated a Greek source, for in one place he refers to the book as that "Music" which Boethius translated from the Greek ("ea namque musica, quam totiens allegatus Boetius de Graeco vertit in Latinum").[4] He introduces a chart of the Greek system as he understood it from Boethius with the following . words:

> I wish briefly here to represent [by a diagram] rather than describe [in words], therefore, these eight modes, for it has long been unknown to our singers in general that the gentile philosophers of antiquity judged their songs, chants, and cantilenas not to be in the ecclesiastical tropes, since there was then not yet a church, nor consequently had such modes or tropes yet been discovered. . . . Should not the ancient songs be judged, rather, by the species of diapason and the regular constitutions of steps previously described? For the gentiles did not possess other than the eight tropes or modes or tones before the advent of our Savior, nor any constitution besides that from proslambanomenos to nete hyperbolaeon, including the other intervening strings of the double octave, so that there was no difference among them, unless the varying measure [string length] of the notes and the height and lowness of pitch, as Figure 11.1 shows. This double-octave in whatsoever mode you please has altogether different constitutions, both of octave and octave plus fourth, something our church fathers did not overlook. Therefore, discovering a genre of making melodies to God—not vain or lascivious— they constructed out of the constitutions described above new modes, of which I shall speak in the proper place, not for secular songs but for divine praise.[5]

The legend in the border states:

> These Greek tropes and modes shown, which they also called tones, expressed in Greek letters and made clear by the Latin letters, are rather put together by art than founded in nature: they differ only in location, and in the whole appear alike. In Boethius, however, diverse signs differentiate them, and the measurements [of their string lengths] were dissimilar, I believe, in all. Now our Latin tropes are certainly created by nature totally unlike one another, though arranged in a single system.[6]

By this diagram Gallicus aimed to show that the ancient constitutions all had the same intervallic pattern. It was as if the double octave A–a' were

2. Gallicus, *Ritus canendi*, III, 12; Coussemaker ed., IV, 345a; Seay ed., 78.21.
3. Ibid., Preface; Coussemaker ed., IV, 299a; Seay ed., I, 1.16.
4. Ibid., I, 4; Coussemaker ed. IV, 304; Seay ed. I, 11.13.
5. Ibid., III, 10; Coussemaker ed., IV, 341b–342b; Seay ed., I, 72.6–73.11.
6. Ibid., III, 10; Coussemaker ed., IV, 342; Seay ed., I, 73.12–13.

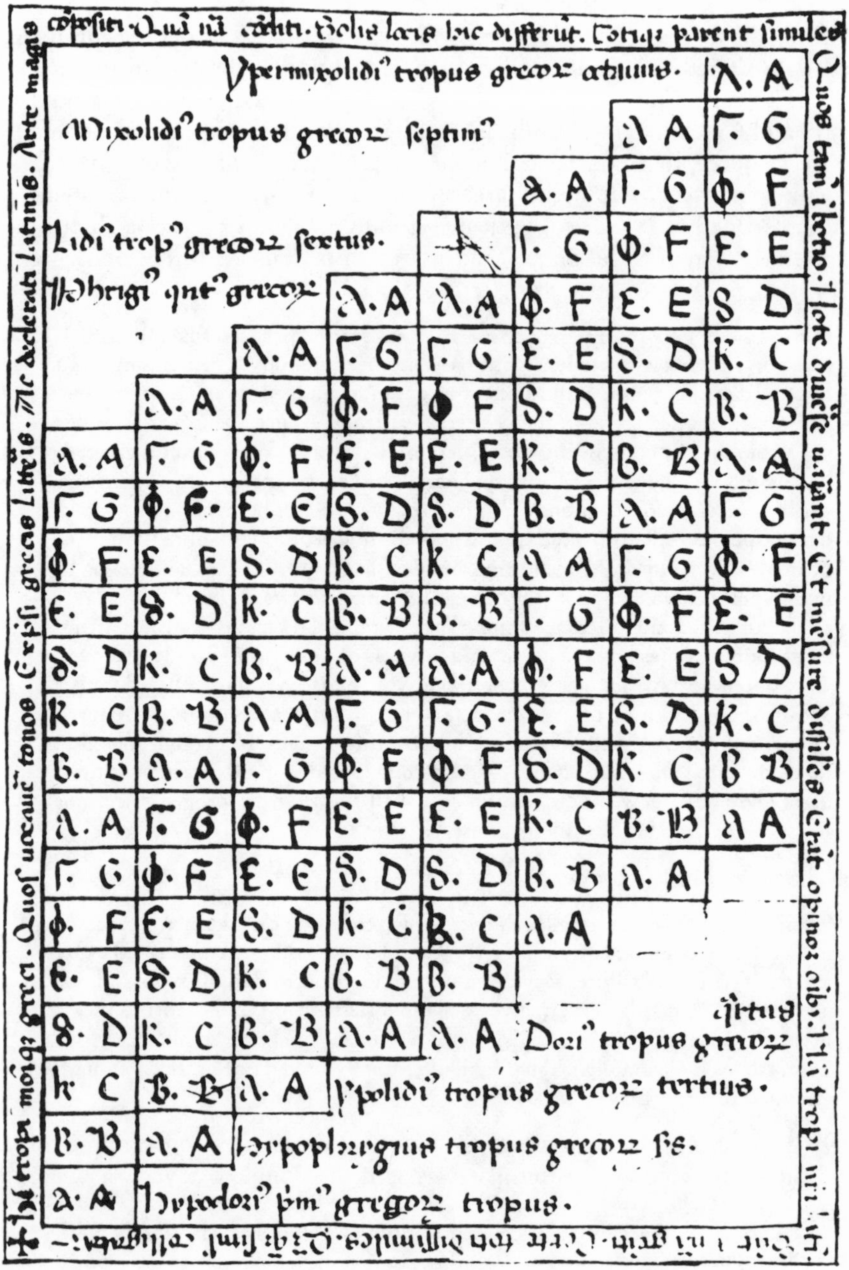

Figure 11.1.
The Greek modes according to Gallicus, from *Ritus canendi,* III, 10, London, British Library, MS Add. 22315, fol. 26. By permission of the British Library.

begun on successive pitches to form the eight tropi, from Hypodorian to Hypermixolydian. In an earlier diagram he showed that each double octave was higher than the preceding one by a tone or semitone, depending on which occurred in the natural series of steps, A, B, C, D, etc.—that is, they were separated from each other as tone, semitone, tone, etc.[7] The Greek letters in the chart, Gallicus explains in the next chapter, can serve, as well as Latin or Hebrew letters, as notational symbols from which to sing melodies. Although Gallicus discusses the octave species in an earlier chapter and notes that the double-octave constitutions are made up by joining such species of consonances, he does not show how the octave species are related to the tonoi, tropoi, or modes.

Erasmus of Höritz

Independently of Gallicus, Erasmus of Höritz arrived at a similar interpretation of the tonal system described by Boethius. Erasmus was a mathematician and had attended and lectured at several universities where Boethius was read carefully, such as Vienna and Cracow. Like Gallicus, he was critical of earlier writers on music, including Boethius himself. Erasmus sought to place music theory on a surer footing by the application of the geometrical theorems of Euclid. His treatise, *Musica,* was completed between around 1504 and 1508 and dedicated to Cardinal Domenico Grimani. The author may have been in the cardinal's circle, but there is no evidence for his whereabouts after he registered at the University of Vienna in 1501. He may have gone to Italy after teaching in Vienna for a while.[8]

Although Erasmus was confused about the chronology of the various systems of modes—the Gregorian, Byzantine, and Greek—he understood that the Greek tonoi, which he called *toni* or *tropi,* were not the basis of the Latin *toni,* as he called them, but reproduced the same order at different levels. His diagram tells us more than his prose. The same Greek signs, those for the Lydian tonos, copied in a very corrupt manner from a perhaps faulty manuscript of Boethius, are assigned to each of the tonoi, perhaps to show that the form and name of the steps were the same and in the same order. The chart is a gross simplification and misrepresentation of Boethius' table of signs, but the general idea of a system of keys to transform a single octave scale is clearly communicated (see Figure 11.2).

---

7. Ibid., III, 9; Coussemaker ed., IV, 341a–b; Seay, I, 70.5–7.

8. Concerning his life and works, see Palisca, "The *Musica* of Erasmus of Höritz," in *Aspects of Medieval & Renaissance Music,* ed. Jan LaRue, pp. 628–48. The presentation copy of *Musica* dedicated to Cardinal Grimani is in the Biblioteca Apostolica Vaticana, MS Reg. lat. 1245.

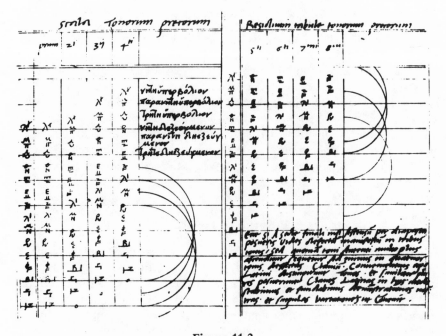

Figure 11.2.
The Greek modes according to Erasmus of Höritz, from Biblioteca Apostolica
Vaticana, MS Reg. lat. 1245, fol. 48r–v

Giorgio Valla

The first humanist who had all the necessary sources for solving the riddle
of the tonoi was another nonmusician, Giorgio Valla. As we have seen, his
collection of Greek manuscripts included the three authors who could have
led him to a good solution: Ptolemy, Cleonides, and Bryennius. Of these
he chose Bryennius as the basis for his treatment of most questions of
harmonics. Valla dedicated two chapters to the tonoi in his *De harmonica,*
a musical treatise within an encyclopedic work *De expetendis et fugiendis rebus
opus,* published in 1501 after his death. The five books on music were already
finished in 1491. In chapters 3 and 4 of Book IV Valla gives a translation
of Bryennius' *Harmonics,* Book 2, chapters 3 and 4, which contain a full
account of the tonoi. Valla follows Bryennius word for word, but the points
he makes are worth recalling, because they were here revealed to nonreaders
of Greek for the first time. Each tonos, Valla states, has its own particular
location with respect to height of pitch. But all tonoi share the same division
of the tetrachord, whether diatonic, chromatic, or enharmonic. Each tonos
consists of two conjunct tetrachords and one *toniaeus* interval. The nete of

the higher tetrachord is the nete of the tonos, whereas the hypate of the lower tetrachord is its hypate. The nete of the lower tetrachord is the hypate of the higher one, and this common step is the mese of the tonos. Beyond the hypate of the lower tetrachord is a toniaeus, or 9:8, interval, leading to the proslambanomenos. Of the eight tonoi, one is highest, another lowest, and the rest lie between these extremes. The same step cannot be the nete of all, but each tonos has its own nete, and likewise for the mese, hypate, and proslambanomenos. The first and lowest of the eight tonoi has its nete at mese, its mese at hypate meson, and its hypate at hypate hypaton. Its proslambanomenos is on proslambanomenos.

Each of the tonoi has a beginning, middle, and end, but only one is complete in that it is possible to sing in the high, low, and middle, and this is the Hypodorian. It is a tetrachord lower than the Dorian tonos and has its nete on mese and its mese on hypate [meson]. Through this [meson] tetrachord, the two unmodulating tonoi can communicate. The second tonos has its nete on paramese, its mese on parhypate meson, its hypate on parhypate hypaton, and its proslambanomenos on hypate hypaton; it is called Hypophrygian. It is a tetrachord lower than the Phrygian.

In this manner Valla, translating Bryennius, describes the system of eight tonoi. A diagram illustrates the description in the manuscripts of the Bryennius treatise, and Valla reproduced the figure in his book (see Figure 11.3). However, either Valla miscopied his Greek source, which was Modena, Biblioteca Estense, MS graecus a.V.7.1 (II.F.8), fol. 19r, or the printer did not follow precisely his layout. If the two diagrams are compared, it is evident that in the Greek source, the labels *hypodorios, hypophrygios,* etc., are centered within each of the bows, or arches, representing the octave spans of each tonos, so that *hypodorios* appears horizontally at the center of that octave span. In Valla's diagram (Figure 11.4). *hypodorius* is lined up with the arch representing the Phrygian tonos, and similarly *hypophrygius* and the subsequent labels are displaced. Although the prose is correct, the diagram is wrong. Either Valla did not understand the exposition he translated, which is not likely, or he was not well served by his draftsman or printer.

There is one error in Valla's Latin text. Where Bryennius states that the Dorian tonos is also called Hypomixolydian, Valla's text has Hypermixolydian. This must be a typographical error, since Valla correctly describes the highest and eighth tonos as Hypermixolydian.

Valla's next chapter (IV, 4; Bryennius 2.4) details the distances between each of the tonoi and each other. The mesai, as the diagram shows, rise tone, tone, semitone, tone, tone, semitone, tone.

Since Bryennius did not relate the species of octave to the tonoi, as Cleonides and Ptolemy had, Valla does not take up this question. However

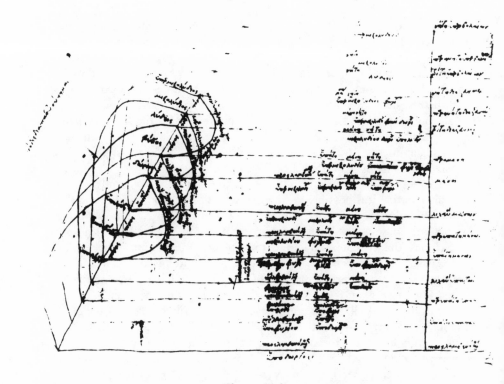

Figure 11.3.
The tonoi according to Bryennius, *Harmonics* 2.3, in Modena, Biblioteca Estense,
MS gr. a.V.7.1, fol. 19r

Bryennius did devote a chapter (3.4) to another kind of species, and Valla translates this in Book V, chapter 4. These are the species of melody (*melōdias eidos*), which Valla translates "modulandi genera." They are also called "echoi" by Bryennius and "sonitus" by Valla. There are eight of them, the first occupying the octave of the Hypermixolydian, and the eighth and last the octave of the Hypodorian. Since neither author gives the interval sequence, it must be assumed that Bryennius had in mind keys rather than modes. This chapter could not have sown anything but confusion in a reader's mind, particularly since Valla says that the *sonitus* are also called *toni* or *tropi*.

Valla's transmission of the theory of the tonoi according to Bryennius must have reinforced in the minds of those who read it the misinterpretations of Boethius already abroad. If proslambanomenos is thought of as A and the Hypodorian as occupying the octave A-a, then the Dorian is d-d' and everything at first glimpse seems in place. The proslambanomenos of the

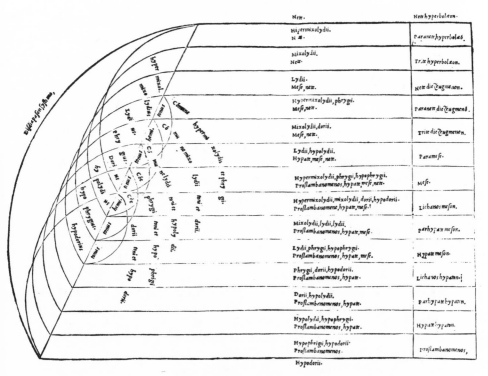

Figure 11.4.
The Greek tonoi according to Valla, *De expetendis,* "De musica," IV, 3

Hypolydian, however, falls on c♯ and that of the Lydian on f♯. But the same thing happens in Boethius if one reads him carefully. Indeed Bryennius and Boethius seem to stem from the same tradition. Valla's book, therefore, was not likely to spur any new reappraisal of the Greek tonal system.

Valla's translation of Cleonides' *Harmonic Introduction* (Venice, 1497), on the other hand, transmitted quite a different system, one unadulterated by Byzantine or medieval conceptions. It has been assumed that this late classical author gave an account of a tonal system set forth in a lost treatise by the great fourth-century musicographer Aristoxenus. Although published before *De expetendis,* Valla's translation of Cleonides was probably finished after it. Valla gives no sign in his encyclopedic work that he had studied Cleonides, and, since there are no annotations by him in the translation, it is impossible to tell whether he understood the implications for an understanding of the tonal system of Cleonides' exposition. However Valla transmits clearly this extremely compressed survey. The tonal system that emerges was explained in chapter 2 and represented in Figure 2.5.

There are clearly two sets of scales whose ethnic designations overlap. Seven of the names—Hypodorian, Hypophrygian, Hypolydian, Dorian, Phrygian, Lydian, and Mixolydian—are applied to a set of interval species described as occupying octaves in the double-octave system from the highest (the Hypodorian) to the lowest (Mixolydian). The three root names, Dorian, Phrygian, and Lydian, are augmented by two more, Ionian and Aeolian, to form composite names with the prefixes "hypo" and "hyper" to designate a set of twelve keys, or transpositions, of the double-octave system. Cleonides does not explain why the nomenclature overlaps, but close study of the two systems would have revealed the link. It is that if the middle octave is carved out of the double-octave system and made to serve as a confined register for melody making, the octave species exhibited by a particular melody will bear the same name as the key or tuning that contains the pitches required for singing or playing it. Thus a melody within this middle range having the configuration of tones and semitones of the Lydian octave species will be in the Lydian tonos. This obviously works only for seven keys, beyond which the names will not agree. Had Valla or anyone else at this time perceived this relationship, it would have explained why Boethius could say that the tonoi arise from the octave species. Neither Valla nor his first readers apparently did so. However the base for such an advance toward unraveling the Greek tonal system was now laid in Valla's translation of Cleonides.

Nicolò Leoniceno

The classic theory of the tonoi has been, at least in our own century, that of Ptolemy. The first Western writer to transmit this theory was Nicolò Leoniceno in his translation of Ptolemy's *Harmonics* prepared for Franchino Gaffurio and finished in 1499. Unfortunately, it was known to very few and had negligible influence on theoretical thought or the historiography of Greek music. Still it is worth considering the intepretation that emerges from the translation.

Leoniceno probably did not see any of Valla's work before embarking on or while engaged in the Ptolemy translation. Each knew of the other's interest in musical treatises, because in a letter of 18 July, probably 1494, Leoniceno replied to one of Valla in which the latter had inquired about a commentary on Ptolemy. Leoniceno reports that Poliziano owned a copy of the treatise of Aristides Quintilianus but not a commentary on Ptolemy. Valla was apparently under the impression that Aristides had completed a commentary on Ptolemy, whereas the author of the commentary he sought was probably Porphyry.[9]

9. Letter no. 15 in Heiberg, "Beiträge zur Geschichte G. Valla's und seiner Bibliothek,"

As we saw in chapter 2, Ptolemy introduced a dual nomenclature for the steps of the double-octave system, one simply naming the strings as if on a fifteen-string kithara, the other assigning functions to each step in a given tonos. The two coincided in the Dorian tonos, which may be thought of as the module being transposed to higher and lower locations or tunings. Leoniceno's translation of Ptolemy's *Harmonics* 2.5 conveys this duality of nomenclature clearly. Why there need to be two sets of names is explained in subsequent chapters.

Ptolemy's next chapter (2.6) begins in a roundabout way to justify the transposition of the functional system from one site to another. There are two kinds of mutation (*transmutatio*), he says. Then, he continues, in the translation of Leoniceno:

Vna quidem, secundum quam, totum modulum, acutiore intentione, percurrimus uel rursus grauiore, seruantes semper, speciei conso- nantaneum [sic]. Secunda uero, secundum quam; non totus permutatur modulus, intentione. Sed pars aliqua, secundum eam, quae, ab initio, consequentiam, propter quod, haec potius diceretur, moduli quam toni, permutatio. Secundum illam enim, non permu- tatur modulus: sed, per totum tonus. Secundum hanc uero modulus quidem, euertitur á propria intentione. Tentio uero, non sicuti tentio: sed tanquam causa moduli. Vnde, illa quidem, non facit, sensibus phantasiam alteritatis, secundum potentiam, á qua, mos moueatur: sed solius secundum acutius vel grauius. Ista uero, ueluti excidere ipsam facit á consueto: et	According to the first we run through the whole melody at a higher pitch, or, again, at a lower one, preserving always the species of consonances. According to the se- cond, on the other hand, not the whole melody is changed in pitch but some part, according to that sequence which obtained at the beginning. Because of this fact, it is better called mutation of melody than of tonos. According to the first the melody is not changed but the tonos entirely so. According to the second the melody is turned away from its proper pitch, but not in the sense of height of pitch but as cause of melody. The first, again, does not make on the senses an impression of change according to function, through which the moral character is stirred, but only with respect to high and low pitch. The second, though, makes this image escape from the usual and

p. 71 (423): "Dixit [Angelus Pollicianus] penes se esse musicam Aristidis, non tamen eiusdem commentationem in musicam Ptholomei."

expectato modulo, quando plu- rimum quidem contrahitur conse- quens: transgreditur uero ab hoc, ad alteram speciem uel secundum, genus: vel secundum, tentionem.[10]	expected melody, when a consequent is strongly brought about. The melody deviates from that expected and goes into another species, whether with respect to genus or pitch [tonos].

Leoniceno gives the impression of having understood that in a change of tonos only the level of pitch at which the melody is sung changes, but that in the second type of mutation the melody runs along as before for a while but then turns in an unexpected new direction, altering the moral character. In the remainder of the chapter Ptolemy gives some examples of the second kind of mutation. The first is of a scale that goes up to mese in a certain tonos, but once there veers into a conjunct tetrachord instead of a tone of disjunction. This amounts to an upward modulation by a fourth, since a conjunction occurs naturally a fourth below at hypate meson. Thus the second type of mutation is really a change of tonos midstream rather than a transposition. His other examples are more complex changes of this second type.

In the next chapter (2.7) Ptolemy shows that, since it is possible to attach a tetrachord by conjunction at mese through mutation or modulation, the synemmenon system is superfluous. Ptolemy is bent on ridding tonal theory of any unnecessary duplication. He asks how far apart one tonos should be from the next, what harmonic relation should exist between tonoi in general, and what should be the maximum distance from the lowest to the highest. When a change of tonos is used just to get a higher pitch, as when changing from one instrument to a higher one or from one voice to a higher one, this is one thing. But there is another purpose to transposition or pure mutation of tonos. Leoniceno has captured the idea in his Latin only dimly, and the justification for it is also rendered darkly:

Sed propterea, ut secundum, unam uocem, idem melos, aliquando quidem, ab acutioribus locis, incipiens: aliquando uero, á gra- uioribus, conuersionem quandam, moris efficiat: quoniam, non am- plius, ad utrosque terminos, moduli coaequantur quae ad uocem pertinent in tonorum permutationi- bus: sed semper, praedesinit, ad	The reason is rather that in the course of one voice the same melody begins sometimes on higher, sometimes on lower steps, and accomplishes a change of moral character. This is because the limits of the melody are not made to corres- pond to those that pertain to the voice in the permutations of the tonoi. But the limit of the voice at one end

10. Ptolemy *Harmonics* 2.6, Leoniceno trans., fols. 27v–28v.

alteram partem uocis, terminus,	always stops sooner than
á termino moduli. Ad	the limit of the melody. At the
contrariam autem partem moduli	opposite end, the limit of the melody
terminus, á modulo uocis:	[is reached] before that of the voice.
itaque, illud, quod aptabatur, ab	Thus that which was adjusted from
initio distantiae vocis,	the beginning of the voice's interval,
partim quidem deficiens, in	in part losing, in part
permutationibus, partim autem,	added to during the permutations,
recipiens, alteritatis phantasiam,	offers the senses of hearing an
praebeat auditibus.[11]	impression of change.

The reason given by Ptolemy for the impression of a change in moral character or ethos is that when a given voice sings a particular melody, such as an octave species, at a higher than normal location, for example, some of the notes of the melody are too high for the voice's range and must be omitted, though they can be regained at the bottom of the voice's range. The changes that the melody thus undergoes affect the impression it makes on the listener's feelings. Leoniceno's expression of this thought is obscure, perhaps because he did not understand it.

In chapters 8, 9, and 10 Ptolemy answers some of the questions he posed earlier—how far apart the highest and lowest tonoi should be, how many tonoi there should be, and how far apart from each other. Chapter 8 proposes that the distance between the highest and lowest tonoi should be within the octave but should not include the octave, because it would duplicate a tonos already existing. Chapter 9 develops a proof for the limitation of the number of tonoi to seven, and chapter 10 defends their conventional order, separated by the distances tone, tone, semitone, tone, tone, semitone, ascending from Hypodorian to Mixolydian. The most significant revelation here is the rejection of the eighth, or Hypermixolydian, tonos, which Boethius and all his followers attributed to Ptolemy. Even Gaffurio, for whom this translation was prepared, continued to attribute an eighth "mode" to Ptolemy. The reason why the number of tonoi should depend on the number of octave species is not clear until chapter 11, which Leoniceno translates as follows:

Quod non oportet, secundum Semi-	That it is not proper to increase
tonium, augere tonos.	the tonoi by semitone.
Cap[ut] XI.	Chapter 11.
Manifestum uero, quod his suppo-	These tonoi having been assumed,
sitis, v[idelicet] nobis, tonis,	by us that is, it is evident, to
eius, quae est in singulis,	be sure, that there is in each a
secundum potentiam, media,	middle note by function, a special

11. Ptolemy *Harmonics* 2.7, Leoniceno trans., fol. 30r.

propria aliqua uox, sit consonantiae diapason, propter esse,
et ipsas, et species aequales,
numero. Assumpta enim diapason,
secundum inter media, quodammodo
loci, constitutionis perfectae,
hoc est, quae sunt, a situ
mediarum, suprema, hypate,
nominata, ad
neten, disiunctarum:
ut uox amicabiliter
reuertat, et uersetur, circa
medias, maxime melodias, raro,
ad extremas exiens, propter
eius, quae est, praeter modum,
remissionis, ut intentionis,
uaehementiam,
et uiolentiam.
media quidem, secundum potentiam,
mixolÿdij, adaptabitur,
loco paranetes
disiunctarum, ut tonus,
primam speciem faciat, in
proposito diapason:
media uero, Lÿdij,
loco tertiae
disiunctarum,
secundum secundam speciem,
media, phrigij loco,
parameses, secundum
tertiam speciem, media
uero dorij
loco mediae
faciens quartam et mediarum
speciem diapasson.[12]

step of the diapason consonance,
because these [tonoi] and the species
are equal in number.
We have adopted the diapason
in the middle with respect to the
locus of the perfect system, that
is, the one from the supreme
—the hypate—of the medians [hypa-
te meson], as named by position, to
the nete of the disjunct [diezeug-
menon], for the voice willingly
returns and revolves around
the middle—rarely sending a melody
out to the extremes because of
the vehemence and force [required]
for those [pitches] that are beyond
the normal in laxity or tension
[lowness or height of pitch].
Thus the middle note by function of
the Mixolydian will be adapted
to the locus of the paranete
of the disjunct, so that
the tonos might produce the first
species in the proposed diapason.
The middle note of the Lydian [will
be adapted] to the locus of the third
of the disjunct [trite diezeugmenon]
in keeping with the second species;
the middle note of the Phrygian, to
the locus of the paramese, in keeping
with the third species, the middle
note of the Dorian, though, to the
locus of the middle note [mese],
producing the fourth and middle
[species] of diapason.

Ptolemy's explanation of how the tonoi and octave species are intertwined is here expressed for the first time in the Latin language. Although Ptolemy does not openly state that the purpose of the tonoi is to produce the seven different octave species within the central octave, this is implied, and Leoniceno's translation, "ut tonus primam speciem faciat in proposito diapason," conveys quite unambiguously the purposive tone of the construction "hin' ho tonos to pròton eidos en tō proskeimenō poiēsē tou dia pasōn" (Düring 65.7–8).

12. Ptolemy *Harmonics* 2.11, Leoniceno trans., fol. 32v.

Franchino Gaffurio

Gaffurio was in a good position to bridge the gap between humanists and musicians with regard to the Greek modes. He was the beneficiary of translations of several major Greek musical authors. He apparently possessed a copy of Gallicus' *Ritus canendi,* for he mentions it in the *Theorica musice.*[13] And he knew Boethius thoroughly. The delay in publication of *De harmonia* after its completion in 1500 gave him plenty of time to absorb the contents of Valla's *De expetendis,* which came out in 1501. He also knew Valla's translation of Cleonides, for he cites it.[14] Despite these advantages, it cannot be said that Gaffurio added materially to the knowledge of the Greek tonal system.

Gaffurio's chart of the Greek tonoi in *Theorica musice* (see Figure 11.5) hints at a derivation from Gallicus' chart.[15] Eight transpositions of the same A-a scale with the names Hypodorian to Hypermixolydian are represented on a grid. Each transposition has the identical letters A to a to indicate that they all have the same intervallic pattern. In introducing the chart Gaffurio explains:

> The philosophers called these seven species of diapason modes from *modulando* or from *moderando,* since they observed that through them every progress of modulation is moderated through certain limits of tension and relaxation. Now the first species of diapason, going from the string proslambanomenos to mese, or from A re to a la mi re, they called Hypodorian. When every step of the Hypodorian undergoes a raising of a whole tone, the second mode, that is, Hypophrygian, results. If all the steps of this Hypophrygian are raised by a semitone, they form the Hypolydian. Raising this system in turn by a tone yields the Dorian.[16]

Gaffurio has here confused octave species, modes, and tonoi. The confusion started in his *Theoricum opus* of 1480, where he spoke of octave species, tropes, *maneries,* constitutions, and modes as interchangeable concepts. He also introduced there the post-Boethian method of dividing the octave into either a fourth below and a fifth above, or the reverse, which he said was the more consonant and perfect division. In both the 1480 and 1492 treatises the chart (Figure 11.5) and the discussion of the modes are part of a chapter entitled "Concerning the species of the diapason consonance," and this chapter follows a similar one on the species of diatessaron and diapente. Gaffurio demonstrates the octave species in the manner of the plainchant

---

13. Fol. a7r, I, 1: "musice facultatis libellum clericis perutilem descripsit." This remark is not in the earlier version, *Theoricum opus,* of 1480.

14. *De harmonia,* II, 16, 23.

15. The identical chart occurs in *Theoricum opus,* 1480, V, 8.

16. *Theorica musice,* V, 8, fol. 3kv.

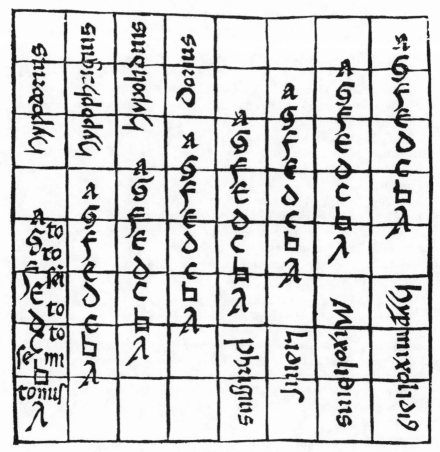

Figure 11.5.
The Greek tonoi according to Gaffurio, *Theorica*, V, 8

theorists. The first species of diapason is made up of the first species of diatessaron, A–d, and the first species of diapente, d–a; the second and third species of diapason are similarly constructed of the second and third species of diatessaron and diapente. But beginning with the fourth species of diapason, d–d', the diapente is below the diatessaron.

In the passage quoted above, which is only in the 1492 version, Gaffurio first says that the philosophers called these seven octave species modes. Then he shows that the first of these species could be transposed successively by tone, semitone, tone, tone, semitone, tone to produce further modes. Thus modes, it would appear, could be both different species and transpositions of a single species. (We shall see that in *De harmonia* Gaffurio eliminated this confusion.)

By introducing "the philosophers" Gaffurio makes a subtle transition from the plainchant theorists to Boethius, who called the transpositions *modi*. However Boethius reported a different scheme of transpositions: tone, tone, semitone, tone, tone, semitone, tone. Gaffurio's departure may have been deliberate, because he justifies it by the Guidonian gamut.

On the other hand Gaffurio may have been misled by the diagram in the edition of Boethius published by Joannes Gregorius de Gregoriis fratres in 1492.[17] Otherwise Gaffurio follows Boethius. He recognizes the functional, or dynamic, nomenclature in that he sees each mode as rising from its proslambanomenos to its mese:

> Thus the proslambanomenos or A re of the Hypodorian is surpassed by the height of a tone by that which is the same of the Hypophrygian. Similarly also the mese or a la mi re of the Hypophrygian exceeds that one which is the same of the Hypodorian by the height of a tone. Thus the intervening steps and the whole order of steps of the Hypophrygian happens to exceed the remaining intervening steps of the entire Hypodorian order by the dimension of a tone. The same order and process occurs in the others.[18]

Gaffurio then makes a cryptic remark that is also derived from Boethius: "It is agreed that these seven modes are deduced according to the seven species of diapason from the same strings and steps, one higher or lower than the other."[19] Boethius did not explain how the modes could be derived from the species, and Gaffurio does not shed any light on this. Having by some process derived seven modes from seven octave species, Gaffurio, again following Boethius, adds an eighth, the Hypermixolydian, which, he says, Ptolemy "put on top" of the rest (*superadnexuit*).[20]

In *De harmonia,* completed eight years later, after Gaffurio had had a chance to consult the translations of Bryennius, Aristides Quintilianus, and Ptolemy, the discussion of the octave species is separated from that of the modes. Indeed, they are in different books. He starts the chapter on the octave species (II, 32) with a citation of Ptolemy, but then proceeds to set them forth in the medieval manner, dividing them into species of fourths

---

17. In the reprint of 1499 that I have seen, the tonoi rise in the diagram as in Gaffurio: tone, semitone, tone, etc., although the text gives the proper sequence of tone, tone, semitone, etc. In the 1499 edition 4.15 is numbered 4.14.

18. Ibid., V, 8, fols. k3v–k4r.

19. Ibid., V, 8, fol. 4kr. Compare this to Boethius *De institutione musica,* 4.15: "Ex diapason igitur consonantiae speciebus existunt, qui appellantur modi, quos eosdem tropos vel tonos nominant. Sunt autem tropi constitutiones in totis vocum ordinibus vel gravitate vel acumine differentes."

20. Boethius *De institutione musica* 4.17; Friedlein ed., 348.3.

and fifths and numbering them as in his two earlier works. This system has no connection with Ptolemy, who numbered them: 1, b-B; 2, c'-c; 3, d'-d; up to 7, a'-a (2.3). The order in Boethius is similar except that he always names the lower note first, thus: 1, B-b; 2, c-c', etc. (4.14).

Inspired by Ptolemy (2.3), probably through Boethius (4.14), on the other hand, is the discussion of the species as terminated by fixed or movable notes (II, 32). This leads Gaffurio to consider placing all of the seven species within the extremes of two fixed notes, proslambanomenos and mese. The different arrangements of tones and semitones requires the division of the octave into a continuous series of semitones, or what Gaffurio calls the *genus permixtum*, a concept he borrowed from Anselmi. (See, for example, the first two species in Figure 11.6). Although Gaffurio expresses the location of the steps of each species in terms of string lengths in the Pythagorean tuning, the scheme of seven octave species may be thought of as the equivalent of the pitches A to a in the modern major keys of C, B♭, A, G, F, E, and D. Just as Ptolemy's tonoi transpose his seven species into the central octave from hypate meson to nete diezeugmenon, so Gaffurio's species transpose his own medieval species into the A-a octave. Gaffurio does not relate either the ancient or modern modes to these transposed species. It is merely an interesting but abstract speculative exercise.

All of Book IV of *De harmonia* is devoted to the modes. Gaffurio draws from a multiplicity of sources concerning their history, ethical effects, and cosmic analogies. This literature is entirely about the ancient tonoi and harmoniai; yet Gaffurio applies it indiscriminately to the plainchant modes, to which the ancient names are assigned (IV, 3–7). Despite the fact that he now had Leoniceno's very adequate translation of Ptolemy, Gaffurio baldly affirms that "Ptolemy, to bring the entire double octave system into accord with the modes, placed on top an eighth mode that would seize upon the highest species of diapason between mese and nete hyperbolaion and that would surpass in pitch the Mixolydian mode by a tone; he called it the Hypermixolydian, as if to say 'above the Mixolydian' " (IV, 9). In only one place does Gaffurio seem to return to the Boethian theory of the modes, which had been the basis of his treatment of the subject in his two earlier works of musica theorica. This is in a chapter entitled "By how great an interval any mode (*tonus*) is lower or higher than another" (IV, 11). Here he makes the statement: "The Hypodorian mode is the lowest of all; it is lower than the Hypophrygian mode in the order of its entire constitution by the interval of a tone." A little later he defines the location of the Hypophrygian in similar terms: "The Hypophrygian mode is higher than the Hypodorian in the entire order of its constitution by the interval of a toniaeic [9:8] step. It is lower than the Hypolydian by the interval of a semitone (not by a tone, as some have laid down)." Gaffurio is deliberately

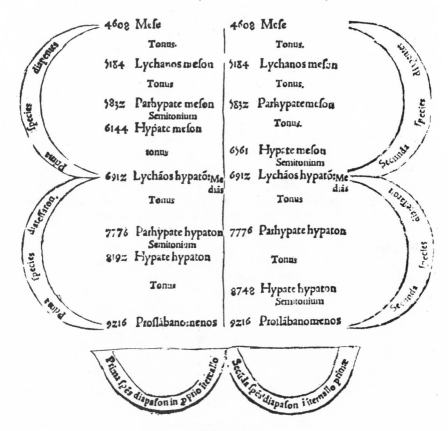

Figure 11.6.
The first two species projected on the octave proslambanomenos to mese, from
Gaffurio, *De harmonia*, II, 32, fol. 57r

departing in the detail of the distances between modes from Boethius and
his sources, yet modeling his discussion on them—that is, instead of Ptolemy's tone, tone, semitone, tone, tone, semitone, Gaffurio prefers, as in
the *Theorica*, the pattern of the natural gamut from A to a: tone, semitone,
tone, tone, semitone, tone, tone. Whether by raising the "entire order of
the constitution" (*totum constitutionis ordinem*) or the "order of the entire
constitution" (*totius constitutionis ordine*) Gaffurio meant to transpose the
entire species of the Hypodorian octave to seven higher levels is open to
question because of the inexactness of his language.

Gaffurio considered the system of eight modes perfect, because it completely filled the double octave. However he notes that Aristoxenus named
in addition to the standard eight five more, namely, the Hypoiastian, Hy-

poaeolian, Iastian, Aeolian, and Hyperiastian. But Bryennius, he reports, considered them useless for an audible harmony of a full and integrated system and suitable only for display of erudition (*Harmonics* 2.4, Jonker ed., 164.3–8). In an addition Gaffurio made after the 1500 redaction of his treatise and before its publication in 1518 (fol. 91r), he points out that Martianus Capella spoke of fifteen modes altogether, a semitone apart from each other. But Gaffurio finds that these more than fill out an octave, which has only twelve equidistant semitones according to Aristoxenus. Also added just before publication was the chart showing this semitonal multiplication of modes (fol. 81v).

Gaffurio's modal theory does not do justice to the sources he possessed. In *Theorica musice* he failed clearly to distinguish between octave species and tonoi, although he seemed to have grasped the difference between the ancient and the modern systems. In *De harmonia* he was evidently too eager to apply ancient erudition to the modern system of modes to show openly that the ancient Greek system was fundamentally different from the modern. It would have made the entire Book IV irrelevant to modern harmonics had he done so. Unfortunately both Glarean and Zarlino trusted Gaffurio and borrowed heavily from him concerning the ethos of the modes, their structure, the octave species, and the ancient nomenclature.

There is another side to the impact of Gaffurio's learning. Mistaken though he was about the ancient modes, he impressed even highly trained and sophisticated readers with the wealth of information about them that he had gathered. Rather little attention had been paid to the modes in treatises of composition or even speculative works. Gaffurio made them central to harmonic theory precisely at the moment when accounts of the marvelous effects of ancient music were daring modern musicians to recapture that power. By appearing to disclose the secrets of the modal system that was reputed to have fabulous powers, Gaffurio stimulated the revival of modal theory and the striving for modal consciousness and purity.

Gioseffo Zarlino

Zarlino had an ambiguous relationship with the Greek "modes," as he called them. Part IV of his four-part *Le Istitutioni harmoniche* develops a theory of modality for modern composition. But the first eight chapters survey the modes and modality in antiquity. For what purpose, one may ask, since Zarlino was convinced that modern composers used the modes "in a manner very different from the ancients" (IV, 10). How many modes there were, in what order they should be named, what intervals separated them, how many steps each had and of what size—things about which the ancient authors differed—did not matter to him, because those modes served different ends and a different kind of music from that currently practiced. Why then spend eight chapters on the ancient modes?

Zarlino did not venture into this thorny subject only to display his erudition, although he was not averse to doing so. I believe he did it to expose the naiveté of Glarean's boast that in his dodecamodal scheme he had reconstructed the ancient Greek system. Just as Zarlino invested nine chapters of Part III in refuting the position of Nicola Vicentino on chromatic and enharmonic music without ever naming him (III, 72–80), so without once dropping Glarean's name Zarlino makes the Swiss humanist's presumption the hidden agenda of these chapters of Part IV.

Zarlino had reason to feel uneasy about Glarean's *Dodekachordon*. Its central thesis obviously appealed to Zarlino, for he adopted it. He could not help finding Glarean's expansion of the traditional eight-mode system to twelve an eminently practical strategy. The literature of both monophonic and polyphonic music abounded with pieces that ended on A or C and exhibited the octave species identified with these notes. Theorists and apologists had gone to great lengths to fit such pieces into an eight-mode configuration, and that rather unsuccessfully. Glarean's proposal, therefore, made good practical sense. Glarean's proof of why there could be no more than twelve modes also convinced Zarlino, for he repeats it (IV, 11). The emphasis on the harmonic and arithmetic divisions of the octave as the essential characteristics of the authentic and plagal modes—concepts peripheral to modal theory before Gaffurio—became central to both Glarean and Zarlino. In numerous details, then, Zarlino copied Glarean's exposition of the twelve-mode system. But Zarlino could not abide Glarean's classicizing rationalizations. Glarean felt bound to legitimize the twelve-mode system by classical examples and concepts, perhaps because he assumed—mistakenly—that the eight-mode system rested on them too. Glarean erected an elaborate historical argument to prove that in naming the four new modes Aeolian, Ionian, Hypoaeolian, and Hypoionian he was restoring some of the neglected Aristoxenian modes. He also scoured Gaffurio's writings and those of Martianus Capella and others for ethical characteristics of the ancient modes that would fit his set of twelve. Zarlino recognized that this was a vain enterprise. Whatever the ancient modes may have been, they surely were not the modes of Glarean.

Zarlino's is the best analysis of the nature of ancient modality that anyone had made until then. It draws upon a wide range of Greek and Roman sources and practically leaves the medieval tradition out of the discussion. He inquires first into the meaning of the word and concept "mode." In ancient usage it did not have the restrictive meaning of a scalar pattern but united a panoply of characteristics within a poetico-musical medium of expression. He concludes: "We can truly say that in ancient times a mode was a certain fixed form of melody, composed with reason and artifice, and contained within a fixed and proportioned order of rhythm and harmony, adapted to the subject matter expressed in the text."[21]

Zarlino shared with Boethius a preference for the term "mode" over "trope," "tone," and "harmonia." "Trope" was not a bad name, Zarlino believed, because it comes from *tropē*, which means turning or mutation, and this, in fact, happens to modes, which are turned from one to another when all the steps of a mode are raised or lowered. As for "tone," Cleonides (whom Zarlino calls Euclid) detailed the multiplicity of its meanings that made it unsatisfactory. Ptolemy, nevertheless, preferred this term and offered the opinion that the tones were so called because the ancient Dorian, Phrygian, and Lydian were a tone apart (*Harmonics* 2.10). Some writers— Plato, Pliny, and Pollux principally—called modes *harmoniai*, because a concinnity of elements made up melos (Zarlino: *melodia*). Indeed Fabius Quintilian defined *harmonia* as "that concordance which is generated by the conjunction of many things dissimilar among themselves."[22]

Zarlino devotes a chapter to the names of the modes and their number (IV, 3). He surveys the views of Plato, Aristoxenus (through Martianus Capella), Cassiodorus, Cleonides, Censorinus, Ptolemy (through Boethius obviously, because Zarlino attributes to him the Hypermixolydian), Pollux, Aristides Quintilianus, Apuleius, and Plutarch. He concludes ruefully that "from the diversity of their ordering, the variety of number, and the difference in names found in all these authors, one cannot draw anything but confusion of mind."[23] In reviewing the affective qualities and ethical effects attributed to the individual modes (IV, 5) Zarlino judiciously confined himself to sources dealing with the ancient modes. The order in which the modes were arranged by various authors is the subject of another chapter (IV, 6). Zarlino gives a most interesting account of the very ancient harmoniai described by Aristides Quintilianus, some containing enharmonic intervals, scales consisting of less or more than an octave, and gapped scales in which the interval between some adjacent notes was greater than a tone. Zarlino quotes the passage in Greek and gives a creditable translation of it, although he suspects that the text is corrupt. When he comes to the modes as set forth by Boethius, he is puzzled by their semblance of being transpositions of a single pattern:

> We shall not be able to find any difference in intervals from one mode to another, for Boethius claims that all the notes of the Hypodorian, as they stand,

21. *Le Istitutioni harmoniche,* IV, 1, in *On the Modes,* trans. Vered Cohen, ed. with an introduction by Claude V. Palisca (New Haven, 1983), p. 10.
22. Ibid., IV, 2; Cohen trans., p. 13, quoting Quintilian *Institutio oratoria* 1.10.12.
23. Ibid., IV, 3; Cohen trans., p. 16.

are moved higher by a whole tone to form the Hypophrygian mode, and that all the notes of this mode are in the same way moved higher by another whole tone in order to produce the notes of the melody of the Hypolydian. Boethius claims that if all these notes are then moved up by a semitone, the Dorian is formed, and so he goes on about the other modes. Under this procedure of obtaining the modes I cannot conceive of any difference between them.[24]

Zarlino finds also another difficulty: the modes of Boethius do not match the modern modes in the intervals between them:

> From the words and examples of Boethius, badly understood, we can understand why modern musicians speaking on this matter have been very much deceived, for they believe that the modern fifth mode is the ancient Lydian, and they make it one whole tone lower than the seventh mode, which they call Mixolydian. They propose that the Lydian is contained within the sixth species of diapason, F to f, and the Mixolydian within the seventh species of diapason, G to g. These, however, are distant from each other by a whole tone, whereas Boethius clearly shows that the ancient Lydian is distant from the Mixolydian by a semitone. He similarly claims that the Dorian is a whole tone away from the Phrygian, something which Ptolemy also claims, and that the Phrygian is another whole tone away from the Lydian.[25]

Thus the moderns contradict what the ancients maintained. Modern musicians, therefore, fall into great error when they call their modes by the Greek names. Zarlino also wondered whether Boethius was reliable: "It might be that in practical matters he was not so knowledgeable."[26]

Zarlino sees clearly that the Boethian modes, which he likens to those of Ptolemy, were not comparable to the modern. They also were of little use to a modern composer, since they afforded no variety of octave species, not to mention the other characteristics of the modern modes that Zarlino stresses in the ensuing chapters. Thus Zarlino's history of modality was an act of liberation from an alien and obsolete system, which could now be set aside in treating the art of polyphonic composition.

Francisco de Salinas

With Salinas and Girolamo Mei, who independently came to similar conclusions based on their reading of some of the same Greek manuscripts in Rome, we come to what might be called the philological phase of our history. Salinas began his studies of Greek music theory the earlier of the

---

24. Ibid., IV, 8; Cohen trans., p. 33.
25. Ibid., IV, 8; Cohen trans., p. 34.
26. Ibid., IV, 8; Cohen trans., p. 35.

two, around 1538, when he accompanied Archbishop Pedro Gómez Sarmiento de Villandrando from his native Spain to Rome.

The *De musica libri septem* of Salinas was not published until 1577, about nineteen years after Salinas returned to Spain. It contained only three brief, though significant, chapters on the tonoi (IV, 11–13). How Salinas, blind from an early age, could have accomplished the research required to write this learned book, in which he cites the ancient treatises by book and chapter, is an object of both mystery and awe. He was fluent in Greek and Latin, but he must have had an equally fluent assistant who could read and write for him; if so, he never mentioned such help. Edward E. Lowinsky has suggested that Kaspar Stocker may have acted in that capacity.[27] Salinas clearly distinguished between a mode, or *harmonia,* and a tonos, or *tonus.* The key to this distinction was Ptolemy's differentiation of two kinds of mutation, or modulation:

> In the second [book] of his *Harmonicorum,* chapter 6, Ptolemy asserts that the difference between mode and "tone" [*tonus*] is very different [from that described by Gaffurio and Glarean]. Concerning this so-called tone, he said, there are two primary kinds of mutation [i.e., modulation]. One is that by means of which we run through a whole melody at a higher or lower tension [that is, pitch] observing the proper interval scheme in the whole species; the other by means of which not the whole melody is changed in tension [pitch level] but part of it, the interval scheme corresponding closely only in the beginning, for which reason this is better called permutation of melody than of tone. For through the permutation of tone the melody is not altered but the tone totally, and through the permutation of melody the harmonia itself is varied. By these words Ptolemy meant, obviously enough, that mutation of mode was one thing, of tone, another.[28]

Ptolemy was here explaining not so much the difference between tonoi and harmoniai, or modes, but two different kinds of mutation. In one a melody was simply transposed to a different key, as we would say; in the other a segment of the melody or scale remained the same, but through a common tone another segment shifted species by changing tonos.

Salinas claimed that none of the modern authors spoke of tonoi, only of modes. In this he was not altogether correct, for, as we have seen, both Gaffurio and Zarlino described them, if not with the insight that Salinas shows in this passage:

---

27. "Gasparus Stoquerus and Francisco de Salinas," *Journal of the American Musicological Society* 16 (1963):241–43.

28. *De musica libri septem* (Salamanca, 1577), IV, 12, p. 198. Most of this chapter is translated, somewhat differently, in Arthur M. Daniels, "The *De musica libri vii* of Francisco de Salinas" (Ph.D. diss., University of Southern California, 1962), pp. 349–53.

Concerning the tones, the moderns have nothing to say, since they do not believe it is pertinent to a vocal composition whether it is sung low or high, for the mutation solely according to tone does not change the affection of the soul. It is otherwise if the mutation is with respect to harmonia: the soul is differently affected when the first mode is changed to the fourth because of the different force of the harmonia. This is not present in the permutation of tone. . . . Those that the moderns call tones, then, are more properly called modes, as the lovers of propriety best observe who call them modes and not tones.[29]

Like his predecessors, Salinas failed to appreciate the link in Ptolemy's theory between the tonoi and octave species. But by emphasizing that in Greek theory there existed both mode—*harmonia*—and tonos, and by showing how mutation could take place with respect to both, he drew attention to the dynamics of melody, raising the lifeless paper schemes to musical actuality.

Girolamo Mei

With Mei we meet the first critical history of the tonal systems of the Greeks. Although he did not publish his findings, the fourth and last book of his *De modis musicis antiquorum* was communicated to a circle of learned men in Florence in 1573, four years before the publication of Salinas' book. Mei began his researches into Greek music around 1550 while in Lyon, but after a year or two he was forced by the pressure of other work to drop the subject until ten years later in Rome, when he was able to devote himself seriously to it. He came to realize, as his predecessors and contemporaries failed to do, that the Greeks had not one tonal system but several, attributable to different periods and authors. He admired the logic of Ptolemy's system of seven tonoi coordinated with seven octave species, of which he set forth a rather special interpretation, but it seemed to Mei to have been too theoretically rational to have been based on actual practice. He could also appreciate the advantages of the system of Aristoxenus and the beautifully symmetrical system of fifteen tonoi of his followers, with its five principal modes, five hypo modes, and five hyper modes, but it also seemed too overrefined to be a product of common practice. Mei surmised that the common system was one of eight modes, as described by Ptolemy (*Harmonics* 2.11) but not approved by him.[30] Mei fully described and diagrammed these schemes in his treatise *De modis* and provided briefer descriptions

---

29. *De musica*, IV, 12, pp. 198–99.
30. The various systems are described in *De modis musicis antiquorum*, Biblioteca Apostolica Vaticana, MS Vat. lat. 5323, Bk. II, pp. 67–99.

without charts in his Italian treatise.[31] He also enclosed in a letter to Giovanni Bardi of 17 January 1578 a set of charts that have not survived.[32]

Of the system of Aristoxenus (Figure 11.7) Mei acknowledges that only an imperfect knowledge survived, though reliable testimony of the number and names of his tonoi and the semitone distances between them existed in Aristides Quintilianus (1.10) and Ptolemy (2.11; *De modis*, p. 68). (He does not name Cleonides in this connection.)

Mei gives a detailed account of Ptolemy's reasons for rejecting the Aristoxenian system (*De modis*, pp. 72–74). He then sets forth the eight-mode system which Ptolemy described with disapprobation. The closeness with which he follows Ptolemy's text may be appreciated by comparing the translations of Ptolemy (left) and Mei (right) juxtaposed below:

For they have simply laid as a foundation the three oldest— the Dorian, Phrygian, and Lydian— thus named from the peoples from which they came or however else one may derive their names— and let them be distant from one another by a whole tone, and for this very reason they called them *tonoi*, that is, tones. Departing from these they proceed through a symphonic interval from the deepest of the three, the Dorian, to that which is a diatessaron higher. This tonos they called Mixolydian because of its proximity to the Lydian. The distance between these two is not a whole tone but the remainder of a diatessaron [limma] after the ditone encompassing the Dorian and Lydian is removed.	Of the three that were the most ancient and first in use, that is the Dorian, Phrygian, and Lydian, they understand them to be exceeded one by another by a toniaeic interval or sesquioctave portion, by which magnitude the diapente exceeds the diatessaron, which I may call a tone, and for this reason modes were called tones by the ancients (for, to be sure, among our musicians something else is meant by this word), undoubtedly because one is established next to the other in height of pitch. From the Dorian, which among these [ancients] was the lowest of the three, by a space of a tone higher is the Phrygian; by the same interval higher is the Lydian. Thus the Dorian is a ditone lower than the Lydian. Since the highest is a diatessaron away from the lowest, the fourth is higher than the Lydian by a limma, which is the remainder of the entire diatessaron, and for the reason that it was closer to it than to the others

31. "Trattato di Musica, fatto dal Signor Hieronimo Mei Gentilhuomo fiorentino." Paris, Bibliothèque Nationale, MS lat. 7209/2, pp. 43–58.

32. The charts sent in the letter are enumerated in a postscript; see Palisca, *Girolamo Mei*, p. 154.

et acuta, atque acutissima, pari numero perficerentur. quod diagramma ipsum indicat.

Aristoxeni modorum ordo, ac nomina.

Hypodorius. omnium gravissimus
Hypoiastius, ac gravior Hypophrygius.
Hypophrygius acutior.
Hypoaeolius, ac gravior Hypolydius.
Hypolydius acutior.
Dorius.
Iastius, ac gravior Phrygius.
Phrygius acutior.
Aeolius, ac gravior Lydius.
Lydius acutior.
Hyperdorius, ac gravior Mixolydius.
Hyperiastius, ac gravior Hypermixo[lydius] Hypermixo lydius
Hyperphrygius, et Hypermixolydius acutior
        Adiecti.
Hyperaeolius.
Hyperlydius. omnium acutissimus.

Hypodorius igitur, modorum omnium gravissimus, constitutio a[b]
ea, quae ... futura erat, apud Aristoxenum integra   Hypermixol.
diapason acumine vincebatur. is tamen, quod iam exposuimus,
et sesquioctauam rationem ac toniaeam in duas aequas
scindi posse non dubitavit, et utrasque Semitonii nomine
appellavit. qui etiam ea de causa et diatessaron sono
consonantiam è quinque Semitoniis, diapente vero è
septem, diapason postremo è duodecim constare existimavit.
quam vero id recte, nihil ad nos. qua vero aduersus
illum dicta sint, nec non quae pro illo dici possent,
meliorem nacti occasionem fortasse non omittemus.

Ionum autem

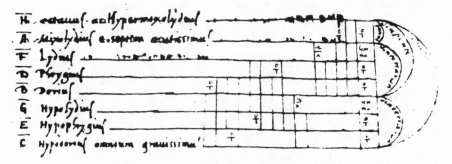

Figure 11.8.
The eight modes described by Ptolemy, from Mei, *De modis,* Biblioteca
Apostolica Vaticana, MS Vat. lat. 5323, p. 77

(being a limma from the Lydian but a
tone away from the others), and thus
being mixed with the Lydian, it was
called Mixolydian.[33]

Mei goes on to paraphrase the remainder of Ptolemy's chapter and to give
a diagram of the eight-mode system that represents more fully than those
in the Greek manuscripts the distances between the various tonoi that are
a diatessaron, diapente, or ditone apart (see Figure 11.8).

Mei now exposes, without any fanfare, for the first time in Western
theoretical writing the error of Boethius, so often repeated after him, that
Ptolemy added an eighth mode. With the help of the chart (Figure 11.8)
Mei (p. 77) perspicaciously shows why Ptolemy rejected the Hypermixolydian as "futile" (*frustrum*) and "plainly superfluous" (*plane superfluus*). According to Mei's accurate report of Ptolemy's arguments, the

---

33. Ptolemy *Harmonics* 2.10; Mei, *De modis,* pp. 74–75: "Trium igitur, qui antiquissimi ac
primi in usu fuerunt Dorius scilicet, Phrygiusque, ac Lydius, toniaeo interuallo, et sesquioctaua
portione, qua uidelicet magnitudine diatessaron consonantiam à diapente superari uiderent, et
quam tonum uocitari possim; etiam à ueteribus (nam apud nostros alia illa nomine ne intelligitur
quidem) non est dubium, unumquemque sibi proximo uel acutiorem, uel remissiorem con-
stituerunt: quasi ea fortasse de causa modos a ueteribus TONOS appellatos fuisse uoluerint.
Horum Dorio, qui apud ipsos extitit omnium grauissimus, sesquioctaua eo toni spatio fuit
Phrygius acutior; hoc uero eadem interualli portione intensior Lydius. Ditono igitur grauior
fuit Dorius quam Lydius. Quibus, ut acutissimus a grauissimo integrae diatessaron spatio
abesset, quartus est adiectus: qui lemmatis, et quod reliquum fuit de tota diatessaron, spatio
esset Lydio acutior. quam cum proprius a Lydio abesset, quam ceteri a sibi proximis (hic enim
lemmate à Lydio, ceteri uero tono a ceteris distabant) quia quasi ea de causa Lydio esset
admixtus, Mixolydiam appellauere."

Hypermixolydian was, first of all, incorrectly named. It was wrong to measure the distance between modes by emmelic (melodic) intervals such as the limma or tone, for the relationship to other modes should always be made in terms of symphonic intervals—the diapente or diatessaron—and the differences of tone and limma are by-products of these, as the chart shows. Thus the relationship of the Dorian and the Hypodorian is a symphonic interval, a diatessaron, but that between Mixolydian and Hypermixolydian is an emmelic interval, a tone. Mei's chart makes plain, moreover, that if the diatessaron and diapente intervals are calculated, BH is shown to be an octave, and the mode [i.e., species] on H would duplicate that on B.

Mei now backtracks to Ptolemy 2.7 to consider the limits that should govern modes. Potentially the number of modes is infinite, as is the number of pitches (*sonitus*). But there are limiting factors in that three things have to be distinguished: the difference in pitch among the modes, the number of such differences, and the boundaries set upon the mode. Or, as Mei otherwise puts it, one must consider the interval between the mode's outer limits, the intervening intervals that comprise it, and the differences among these component intervals. With respect to the first, some believed a mode should be bounded by an octave—that is, it should be an octave scale— others that it should be less than an octave, others that it should be more. Here Mei glosses Ptolemy by means of Aristides Quintilianus, namely his testimony concerning the ancient harmoniai, some of which spanned more, some less than an octave. (This is the same passage that was quoted by Zarlino.) Mei, like Zarlino, has doubts about the accuracy of its transmission:

Nam, tametsi locus ille in omnibus, quos uidi, codicibus mendis omnino quam plurimis scatere non est dubium, liquido tamen ex eius uerbis in primo è tribus, quos de re musica scriptis reliquit, elicitur, constitutiones has, quos modos ac tonos appellamus, non semper integram diapason iuste explere; sed earum nonnullus hac esse minores, alias uero et maiores: Dorium enim (ni mendum in uerbis subest, quod suspicamur) hanc ipsam superare, Iastium uero ab eadem tono, et sesquioctauo ratione deficere, hic idem ratione subducta, expositis

For, although that place in all the codices I saw undoubtedly bubbled with all possible faults, yet in the first of three [books] that he wrote concerning musical matters and that survive from his words there ensues that these constitutions which we call modes do not always fill out an entire diapason but some are smaller than this, others larger.
He attempts to prove that the Dorian (unless there is a fault in the text, which we suspect) exceeds the octave, the Iastian is deficient by the same tone or the sesquioctave ratio, this ratio

que uniuscuiusque interuallis
probare conatus est.[34]

being taken away, after some
intervals were set out.

Mei here refers to two scales spanning more or less than an octave—namely the Dorian, which, Aristides said, consisted of tone, diesis, diesis, ditone, tone, diesis, diesis, and ditone, the total exceeding the octave by a tone; and the Iastian, which he described as comprising diesis, diesis, ditone, trisemitone, and tone, remaining short of an octave by a tone.

This entire gloss of Mei's may not be to the point, however, because, when Mei thought Ptolemy was speaking of the range of a mode (at 2.7, Düring ed., 58.1), he seems to have been concerned with the distance between the lowest and the highest tonoi, for the new theorists, he complains, continually aim at an increase, which leads to the return of the identical harmonic relations. This consideration induces Ptolemy (2.7)—and Mei also, as he continues his commentary—to explain the purpose of the tonoi. They do not exist simply to move a melody higher or lower. Rather they exist for the sake of a change of affection. For when the same melody is begun higher or lower within a given voice, the ethos is altered, because one time the song will reach beyond the limits of the voice at the higher end, another time at the lower end. Mei demonstrates this phenomenon through a diagram that does not have a parallel in Ptolemy's treatise (Figure 11.9).

Mei explains that no voice is granted more than fourteen notes, which may be thought of as hypate hypaton to nete hyperbolaion. The fourteen steps of the voice in its normal location are represented by the scale in the middle of the figure. This range defines the absolute boundaries of the voice's capability, beyond which the singer would have to "summon a remarkable force" (illi uim plane uel ingentem student adhibere). At the bottom of the figure the fourteen-step system is shown starting seven steps lower, so that the melody, marked "cantilena," now goes beyond the low limit of the voice—that is, hypate hypaton—by three steps. In the uppermost scale, the system has been moved up seven steps, and the melody now exceeds the upper limit, nete hypaerbolaion, by three steps. Mei paraphrases Ptolemy:

in eiusmodi tonorum permutatio-
nibus non amplius cum utrisque
cantus terminis quadrare, atque
ad punctum omnino conuenire
perspicue sentiantur:
imo semper altera ex parte

In this kind of permutation of tonoi
the melody no longer squares with
both limits of [the voice],
which are believed clearly not to
agree altogether; rather,
on one end the boundary

34. *De modis*, p. 80. The passage in Aristides Quintilianus *De musica* is at 1.9.

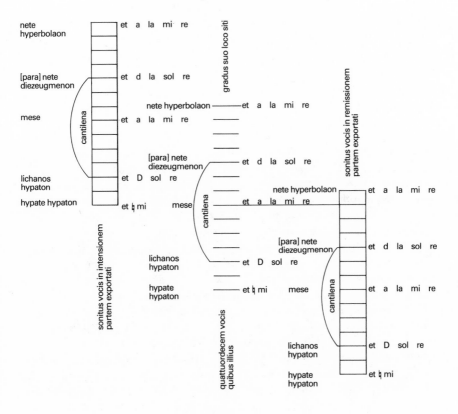

Figure 11.9.
The effect of the transposition of a melody, transcribed from Mei, *De modis,*
Biblioteca Apostolica Vaticana, MS Vat. lat. 5323, p. 83

uocis terminus
praesto magis adesse, quàm
cantus; ex altera uero, atque
illi opposita cantilenae magis,
quam uocis.[35]

of the voice is always nearer at hand
than that of the melody, whereas
on the other, opposite, side
the limit of the melody is reached
sooner than that of the voice.

Thus the limits of the melody do not agree with the range of the voice
as they did when it was situated in the nonpermuted constitution assigned
to it. This change is brought about by the tonoi. When such a change does

35. Mei, *De modis,* pp. 81–82; Ptolemy *Harmonics* 2.7, Düring ed., 58.15–18.

not occur, as in the transposition by an octave, the transposition is to be excluded, because the limits are then as they were in the original constitution.[36]

It should be noted that Mei is not equating his nonpermuted fourteen steps with any absolute thetic system, a virtual standard polychord giving pitches from approximately B to a'. Rather, any one human voice will have its own such standard range, to which by the agency of the tonoi the mutation described in Ptolemy would be applied. All the mutations must take place, however, within the range between the voice's proslambanomenos and nete hyperbolaion: "tota modorum uis intra hos terminos sit locanda; quos cum forma, tum acumine et grauitate, id est loci positu inter se differre nemo dubitari" (the entire range of the modes must be located within these boundaries, which, no one can doubt, differ among each other both in form and height of pitch, that is, in location).[37]

Through this discussion Ptolemy has provided a further reason for the limitation to the octave of the distance from the lowest to the highest tonos. This range may not reach the octave itself but must stop short of it. As there are only seven species of diapason, the number of tonoi must not exceed this number, for beyond that the same species is duplicated, just as after the number 9, the number 1 returns in the form of 10. Mei now enumerates the species of diapason. The first, between hypate hypaton, or mi, and paramese, or mi, Ptolemy assigned to the Mixolydian mode; the second, between parhypate hypaton, or C fa ut, and trite diezeugmenon, or c fa ut, to the Lydian, etc. The seventh and last was assigned to the Hypodorian. Thus the lowest species of diapason is assigned to the highest tonos and mode, the highest species to the lowest, and the median always remains the same. Now Mei digresses from Ptolemy to explicate in his own way the location of a middle step in each species of diapason. The fourth step in each diapason is called the median (*media*). Thus the median of the Mixolydian [species] is hypate meson, or E la mi; of the Lydian parhypate meson, or F fa ut; and so forth. Returning to Ptolemy (2.11), Mei notes that each tonos was assigned a step in the central octave to be its mese. Mei interpreted this placement of the mese in the light of his idea that the fourth step in each species was its mese:

ita tamen, ut paranete diezeugmenon et D la sol re esset, quae uim media Mixolydij omnium acutissimj obtineret: qua in loco ipse modus primam diapason formam, eiectis	Thus paranete diezeugmenon or D la sol re is the note that the median of the Mixolydian, the highest [mode] of all, acquires. At that place this mode produces the first species of diapason, which

36. Mei, *De modis,* p. 84; Ptolemy *Harmonics* 2.8.
37. Mei *De modis,* p. 89.

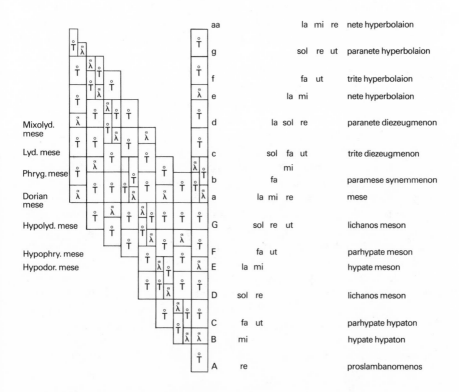

Figure 11.10.
The modal octave species of Ptolemy, from Mei, *De modis,* Biblioteca Apostolica
Vaticana, MS Vat. lat 5323, p. 93

quasi sua e sede reliquis
species sonitibus, quam illi iam
ipse addixerat, conficeret.[38]

attaches itself to the other sounds
which have been, as it were,
driven out from their seat.

This statement is far from lucid, but in the course of a wordy explanation
and a much more communicative diagram—one that has no parallel in
Ptolemy—Mei reveals his unique interpretation of the relation of the modes
to the octave species (see Figure 11.10).

In Figure 11.10 the right-hand bar represents the greater perfect system,
with the whole tones indicated by the abbreviation "To," the semitones by
"lambda-a," for limma, and the tone of disjunction as a split key with fa

38. Ibid., p. 91.

mi in the middle. The steps are named both in terms of the medieval litterae-claves and the Greek string designations. To the left of the perfect-system bar are seven bars representing the seven octave species turned modes. The fourth line from the bottom in each bar represents the mese in that mode, which is labeled at the far left. The highest mode, Mixolydian, is constructed out of the ascending interval species limma, tone, tone, limma, tone, tone, tone, equivalent to the octave hypate hypaton to nete diezeugmenon, or B-b′, with its median note, the fourth from the bottom, situated on paranete diezeugmenon, the step assigned to the Mixolydian as its mese. Similarly the Lydian is built from the second octave species, tone, tone, limma, tone, tone, tone, limma, around the mese on trite diezeugmenon, and so on for the rest. Since Mei recognizes that the tonoi are all formed from the same arrangement of pairs of conjunct tetrachords around a tone of disjunction, he marks this tone of disjunction in each bar as a split key, rising alternately tone limma at the left and limma tone at the right. The Mixolydian shows clearly the pattern of two conjunct tetrachords descending tone, tone, semitone, tone, tone, semitone, below the disjunction, while the Hypodorian exhibits the same conjunct pair above that the disjunction. In the other modes no more than one complete tetrachord falls within the octave span. The tones of disjunction—and, consequently, the tonoi—rise in thirds. Taking the note below the disjunction (mese) as a measure, the sequence of transposed "thetic mesai," if we may call them that (Mei did not!), is B, d, f♯, a, c♯′, e′, g′.

Mei seems to have been misled by the statement in Ptolemy that functional mese (the "dynamic mese" of modern commentators) of the Mixolydian coincides with the locus of the paranete diezeugmenon, and that other notes are similarly assigned the mese function in the other tonoi. If the entire greater perfect system is transposed to accompany the mese, the octave species will be projected on the central span, hypate meson to nete diezeugmenon, and in each octave species the thetic mese will naturally be the fourth note from the bottom.[39] This phenomenon, different from what Mei conceived, may be seen in Figure 2.6 of chapter 2.

In the course of his explanation Mei seizes the opportunity to berate Gaffurio and Glarean for blindly following Boethius in the pursuit of the eighth mode:

Qua in re nostrorum hominum prudentiam saepe requiro, qui octauum hunc a Ptolemaeo modorum numero adiectum tradi-	In this matter I often wonder about the sagacity of our men who transmitted that this eighth was added to the number of modes by

---

39. A more succinct discussion of the ancient modes is found in Mei's "Trattato di musica" in Paris, Bibliothèque Nationale, MS lat. 7209/2, pp. 53–56, trans. in Palisca, *Girolamo Mei*, pp. 50–53.

derunt, Franchini Gafurij
praesertim, uirj sane in hoc
studio exercitatissimj ac longe
doctissimi:
Nam de Glareano minus est meo
quidem iudicio mirandum; is enim
Gafurij authoritate qui se
Ptolemaej scripta legisse
testatus fuerat, facile, cum
ipse ea non legerit,
decipi potuit: Gafurius uero,
qui legit, et Ptolemaej sensum
non est assecutus, et Boethij
uerba, si modo ea legit non osci-
tanter, in suam sententiam inter-
praetatus detorsit: Boethius enim,
cum de Hypermixolydio uerba
faceret, ueritus nimirum, quando
septem tantum esse modos, qui
uidelicet ipsae diapason formae,
affirmasset, atque octauum hunc
postea eorum numero admiscuisset,
ne parum ipse sibi constare
uideretur, rationem se huius
adiectionis paulo posterius alla-
turum est pollicitus, quod uero
cum praestitisset, atque eam diligenter exposuisset, haec ille
statim subiecit: ATQUE
HIC EST OCTAVVS MODVS; QUEM
PTOLEMAEUS SUPERANNEXVIT.
Quae Gafurium in eam sententiam
accepisse uel facile credere
possumus, ut Hypermixolydij
authorem inuentoremque Ptolemaeum
existimasset. Quod non modo
falsum est, sed a Ptolemaei
quoque sententia penitus alienum.[40]

Ptolemy, particularly that of
Franchinus Gafurius, a man certainly
very experienced and altogether
very learned in this discipline.
Less to be wondered at, in my
opinion, is Glareanus. Since he
did not himself read the writings
of Ptolemy, he could
easily be deceived by the authority
of Gafurius, who, it has been
witnessed, read
them, if only sleepily, and did not
pursue the sense of Ptolemy, but,
persuaded by the words of Boethius,
distorted the meaning. As for
Boethius, since he mentioned the
Hypermixolydian, when he affirmed
that there are seven modes, as many
evidently as the species of
diapason, and mixed in with
their number afterwards an eighth,
lest this seem to have been a
trivial thing to him, he promised
to bring forward a reason for this
addition a little later.
This, indeed, he both
fulfilled and
industriously explained.
He submitted it presently: "ATQUE
HIC EST OCTAVUS MODUS; QUEM
PTOLEMAEUS SUPERANNEXUIT."
We can easily believe that
Glareanus accepted Gafurius'
judgment, so that he considered
Ptolemy to be the author and
inventor of the Hypermixolydian.
This is not only false but completely
alien to any opinion of Ptolemy.

Thus was the fiction of Ptolemy's addition of an eighth mode finally put
to rest. Although Mei's work remained unpublished, his interpretations of
the tonoi according to Aristoxenus, his followers, and Ptolemy were pub-

---

40. Mei, *De modis,* pp. 90–91. The references to Boethius are the following: *De institutione
musica* 4.17; Friedlein ed., 343.16–18: "Septem quidem esse praediximus modos, sed nihil
videatur incongruum, quod octavus super adnexus est," and 4.18, 348.2–3: "Atque hic est
octavus modus, quem Ptolomaeus superadnexuit."

lished by Vincenzo Galilei in his *Dialogo* of 1581. Mei had sent charts similar to those he included in his treatise to Giovanni Bardi and Galilei. According to Mei's description of this material, on one page were, to one side the thirteen modes according to Aristoxenus together with those added by his followers, below that the modes according to Boethius, and to the other side the modes according to Ptolemy. These must have been on a large folio and were probably separated from the letters by the time Giorgio Bartoli copied them, for this item is missing from the codex.[41]

Vincenzo Galilei

Galilei presents first the system of Aristoxenus. He took the octave in which the Dorian octave species lies, e to e′, and split it into twelve semitones, not by means of a monochord division but by ear, and assigned each half step to a different mode. The diagram (Figure 11.11) shows the double-octave system at the left, marked A to Aa, and to the right of that thirteen systems, each similarly marked A to Aa, and each a semitone higher than the previous one. The mese is indicated through Mei's device of a split key with b fa in the middle.

The interlocutor Bardi seizes the opportunity of defending the division of the octave into equal semitones. Admitting that in this system of tuning the fourth is too large and the fifth too small to be perfect, he says listeners have grown so accustomed to these tempered intervals that they actually prefer them. However he does not dispose of Ptolemy's arguments against the multiplicity of modes.

Galilei next shows the system of fifteen tonoi of the later Aristoxenians.[42] He then goes on to the system of Boethius, because this is not as artful and as difficult to understand as Ptolemy's, and it fits the description of the eight-tonos system that Ptolemy rejected. Galilei perceptively noticed the discrepancy in the 1492 Venetian edition of Boethius between the intervals separating the tonoi as detailed in the text—tone, tone, semitone, tone, tone, semitone, tone— and their representation in the diagram— tone, semitone, tone, tone, semitone, tone, tone.[43] Galilei adds that he hunted for the editions of Basel and Paris but never found them. However he saw manuscript copies "in various famous libraries."[44] Galilei's own chart is based on the Boethius text and is misleading only in that it singles out in each vertical bar the octave (marked by an arch) that identifies the medieval mode known by the name rather than the octave species proper to the

41. See Palisca, *Girolamo Mei*, p. 154.
42. This chart is in *Dialogo*, p. 57, and is laid out in a format almost identical to that of the thirteen tonoi.
43. Ibid., p. 59.
44. Ibid., p. 60.

Dimoſtratione de' tredici Tuoni, ſecondo la mente d'Ariſtoſſeno.

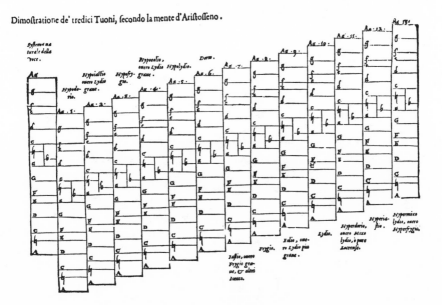

Figure 11.11.
Demonstration of the thirteen tonoi according to the opinion of Aristoxenus,
from Galilei, *Dialogo*, p. 52

tonos. Galilei does not comment on this feature of the diagram (Figure
11.12).

Galilei's explanation and graphic representation of Ptolemy's seven tonoi
follows Mei's thought faithfully up to a point, but the layout may be Galilei's
own. It shows the complete greater perfect system at seven different levels.
The mesai occupy the middle octave, e to e', which coincides with the
fourth species of diapason, belonging to the Dorian tonos. Each other octave
species, whose interval arrangement follows Ptolemy correctly, occupies a
similar place in the other double octave systems, which are built around
the mese according to the normal tetrachordal coupling. The chart (Figure
11.13) shows the systems rising, but the alphabetical letters progress from
D-Dd, C-Cc, etc. to E-Ee. The letters, however, indicate relative pitch—
they are equivalent to the dynamic names—and simply extend the octave
species of each tonos upward and downward. Whereas Mei stressed Ptolemy's confinement of all the transpositions within the thetic double octave,
proslambanomenos to nete hyperbolaion, Galilei's diagram far exceeds this
range both at the lower and higher extremes. The mesai are separated by
tones and semitones, but since they are not Ptolemy's dynamic mesai but
Mei's transposed thetic mesai, they actually progress by thirds. Strozzi in

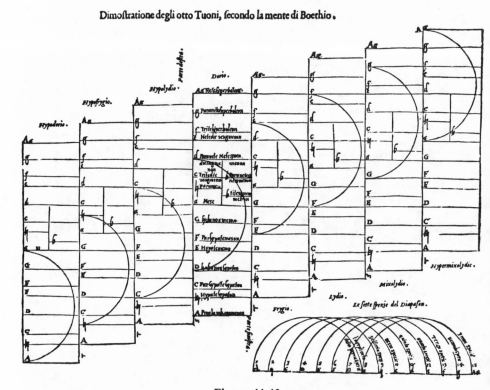

Figure 11.12.
Demonstration of the eight tonoi according to Boethius, from Galilei,
Dialogo, p. 58 (the steps marked A indicate successively pitches analogous
to A, B, C♯, D, E, F, G)

the dialogue notes this discrepancy, saying that "Ptolemy wishes, in addition, that the systems be distant from each other in a continuous order of ditones and semiditones, while you said instead tones and semitones."[45]

The Tonoi and the Waning of Modality

If Glarean's campaign to provide the plainchant modes with a classical pedigree increased their prestige among polyphonic composers, Zarlino's repudiation of this association hastened their downfall. A more deliberate blow at the modal system was Galilei's mockery of it. Encouraged by Mei's views, Galilei in the *Dialogo* condemned modern musical practice for homogenizing modal and tonal differences:

45. Ibid., p. 66. Bardi's reply is translated in Palisca, *Girolamo Mei*, p. 57.

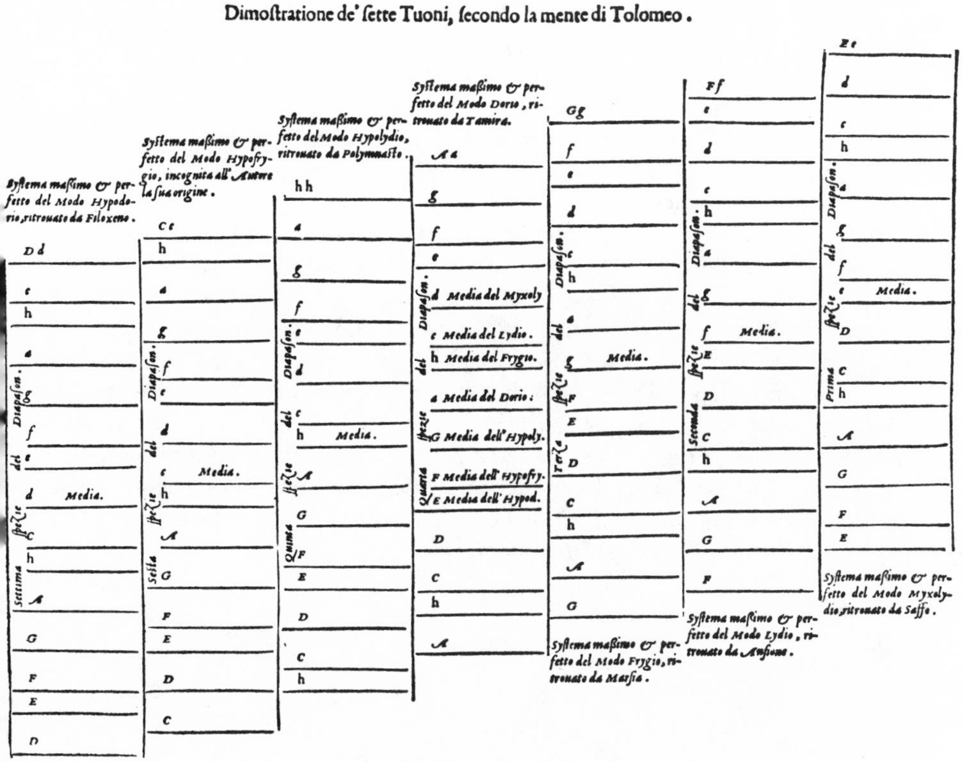

Figure 11.13.
Demonstration of the seven tonoi according to Ptolemy,
from Galilei, *Dialogo,* p. 64

In singing according to this modern practice of figural music (so called from the diversity of notated figures) so many airs together at once, two modes are too many, let alone eight or more. Because any piece performed requires the same quantity and quality of steps with respect to high and low pitch, for all proceed in their parts with the same rhythm with regard to fast or slow movement, since the contrapuntist uses notes of any value and any interval indiscriminately according to his pleasure, giving not a thought in the world to the meaning of the words. In these characteristics reside, as will be proved in the proper place, the diversity and nature of the harmonies and melodies. Thus the modes and the compositions of today come to have the same quality, quantity, and form, and are, as it were, of the same color, flavor, and odor as every other.[46]

46. Galilei, *Dialogo,* p. 78.

In his unpublished counterpoint treatise Galilei was even more vociferous in his repudiation of the modern modes. Here he contended that the modality of a modern piece could only be distinguished through the last note in the bass. Composers were now accustomed to making cadences on any note of a mode. Every little section of a mass, vesper service, or sonnet was in a different mode. Moreover the modes did not influence the pitch of a composition when performed, because "the bass singer has his eye for what tones the piece reaches, and he intones it according to the disposition of his voice, without respecting whether the piece ends on F or on C."[47]

The modern modes had none of the affective qualities of the ancient, so it made no difference what mode a composer chose when setting a text. The practice of making cadences on any degree, the confusion of parts— each moving independently—and the free use of accidentals obliterated any distinct quality of a mode or any modal unity. The force of modern composition resided in the part-writing and harmony, not in modal differences. This disillusionment with the modes was to lead to a number of deliberate experiments in the restoration of the ancient tonoi by Bardi and later by Giovanni Battista Doni and his followers.

Giovanni Bardi

Galilei's *Dialogo* came out in 1582, four years after the letter from Mei bearing the information about the modes. In the meantime Giovanni Bardi (1534–1612) had developed his own interpretation of the system of Ptolemy and had communicated it in a *Discorso* addressed to Giulio Caccini but probably read to an academy, perhaps the informal one that met at his house. Bardi is remembered in the annals of music history chiefly for his leadership of the group that several of his associates referred to as the Camerata, where leaders in science, literature, and the arts gathered to talk and to listen to music. Although the earliest record of a musical gathering at Bardi's is dated 14 January 1573, the sessions must have started earlier.[48] Vincenzo Galilei, who had been Bardi's protégé since the early 1560's, apparently was the musical preceptor of this academy. The circle was deeply affected by the letters Girolamo Mei wrote to Galilei and Bardi between

---

47. *Il primo libro della prattica del contrapunto intorno all'uso delle consonanze*, in *Die Kontrapunkttraktate Vincenzo Galileis*, ed. Frieder Rempp, p. 72.

48. On 14 January 1573 it was recorded in the *Diario* of the Accademia degli Alterati that the regent of the academy, Cosimo Rucellai "sent word through one of his servants that he could not come because he was at the house of Monsignor de' Bardi to make music." See Palisca, "The Alterati of Florence," in *New Looks at Italian Opera*, ed. William W. Austin (Ithaca, 1968), p. 15, and "The 'Camerata Fiorentina': A Reappraisal," *Studi musicali* 1 (1972):205.

1572 and 1578 in response to their questions about ancient Greek music.[49] A document recently discovered by John W. Hill shows that Mei's letters must have figured prominently on the group's agenda during the year 1577. Giovanni Bardi writes on 2 November of that year to Giovanfrancesco di Lodovico Ridolfi:

> Most magnificent Messer Giovanfrancesco, the desire I have of serving you and your amiability give me the courage to ask you to take on a chore. It is this: I would like you to accept the charge to see that the letters which Messer Girolamo Mei (who lives there with you) writes come into the hands of Vincentio Galilei every week. This should be easy for you, because you can have them come weekly with Messer Giovanfrancesco Strozzi, your and my friend, with whom I shall have an understanding, and thus my desire will be fulfilled. I give you this chore, because for two months we have not had the letters promptly as we desire.[50]

Only one letter from 1577 is extant, but many of the thirty "very long" letters that Mei exchanged with Galilei between 1577 and 1582, according to Mei's own count, must have been written that year.[51] One of Mei's letters, of 17 January 1578—this one addressed to Giovanni Bardi directly— in reply to Bardi's of 9 December 1577, bears upon the question of the tonoi of Ptolemy. With it Mei sent charts of the tonoi according to Boethius, Ptolemy, Aristoxenus, and the followers of Aristoxenus.[52]

Although Bardi depended upon both Mei and Galilei for information and interpretations concerning Greek music, he demosntrated in his discourse that he had studied the sources independently and come to his own conclusions. Bardi may have struggled with Ptolemy's text himself. He had a good literary education and read Latin and Greek. He wrote plays, poetry, and music, conceived and directed performances of intermedi and other entertainments, participated in the quarrel between the defenders of Ariosto and Tasso (siding with Ariosto), and kept up with current scientific developments—truly a Renaissance man.

Bardi must have been at work on his *Discorso* in 1577 when he elicited

---

49. The letters that survive are published in Palisca, *Girolamo Mei*, pp. 87–179.

50. Italian text in John Walter Hill, "Oratory Music in Florence, I: *Recitar Cantando*, 1583–1655," *Acta Musicologica* 51 (1979):111, n. 13. Mei lived at the house of Giovanni Francesco Ridolfi from 1574 until he died in 1594.

51. Mei spoke of the thirty letters in writing to Giovan Vincenzo Pinelli on 19 May 1582. The letter is printed in Palisca, *Girolamo Mei*, pp. 183–85.

52. Ibid., pp. 148–54: "As you see, on one side [of the page] are the modes according to Aristoxenus; to his thirteen are added two put into use after him by his followers. There follow below the modes according to Boethius, and on the other side are the modes according to Ptolemy." The folio containing the diagrams was evidently not copied into the Vatican manuscript of the letters by Giorgio Bartoli, perhaps because it was removed by Bardi before the original letter went to Bartoli for copying.

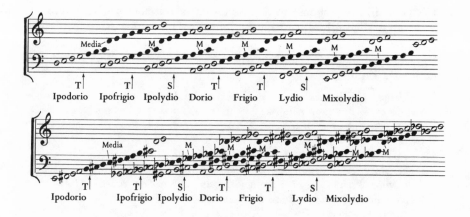

Figure 11.14.
The Ptolemaic tonoi according to Bardi, from *Discorso,* Florence, Biblioteca Marucelliana, MS A287, I, fol. 6r, above, and transposed to their proper pitch level, below

Mei's views on the modes. That he did not depend entirely on Mei's charts and descriptions is attested to by the modifications he made in Mei's interpretation of Ptolemy's theory. Bardi restored the intervallic distances between the tonoi established by Ptolemy. Whereas Mei's and Galilei's mesai rise semitone, tone, tone, tone, semitone, tone, Bardi's rise tone, tone, semitone, tone, tone, semitone, in accordance with Ptolemy's text. However Bardi preserved Mei's idea of building the double octaves around each tonos's octave species according to the standard tetrachord arrangement.[53] If Bardi's chart is translated into modern pitch notation, as in the lower scheme of Figure 11.14, the necessary accidentals indicate from Hypodorian to Mixolydian our keys D, Gb, A, C, E, Ab, Bb.

Bardi sets off the octave species by filling in the note heads. In his chart (upper staves), the tonoi are expressed in natural notes, as if on the white keys of the keyboard. The scheme gives the appearance of a descending

53. The text and diagrams used here are based on the manuscript copy of the essay in Biblioteca Apostolica Vaticana, MS Barb. lat. 3990, fols. 3v–13v. Where noted I have adopted the reading in another copy, Florence, Biblioteca Marucelliana, MS A287, which has corrections by Giovanni Battista Doni and was apparently prepared by him for publication. The latter was the basis for the edition by Antonio Francesco Gori and Giovanni Battista Passeri in G. B. Doni, *Lyra Barberina,* II, *De' trattati di musica di Gio. Batista Doni* (Florence, 1763), pp. 233–48. This edition is full of errors, particularly in the charts. The translation in Strunk, *Source Readings,* pp. 290–301 is based on the Gori-Passeri edition but omits pp. 234–40 and 245–46. My critical edition of this essay, with an English translation, is projected for a volume of the Yale Music Theory Translation Series entitled *Documents in the Florentine Camerata.*

series of scales, but in actuality it is an ascending series. Bardi shows this by changing the clef before each scale; I have rendered it by T or S and an upward arrow. The lower staves of Figure 11.14 give the actual pitches that result, if the appropriate octave species is disposed around each of the "medie" from e for Hypodorian to d' for Mixolydian.

Ptolemy's system was of more than purely theoretical interest to Bardi. He saw in it a model for a modern tonal system. In his *Discorso* Bardi identified the choice of tonality for a composition as one of the critical decisions a composer must make in setting out duly to express the affections of a text. There he stated:

conuiene quando altri	It is good when someone
uol metter in musica madrigale,	wishes to set to music a madrigal,
o, canzone, o, altra poesia	canzone, or other poem
primieramente ben ricordarsi e	first of all to recall and consider
considerare se 'l concetto magni-	whether the subject is magnificent
fico o, lamenteuole sia, se magni-	or plaintive. If it is magnificent,
fico il tuono dorio prenderete	you will take the Dorian tonos,
che in e la mi[54] comincia, et	which begins on e la mi and
ha la sua corda mezana in A la	has its median note on A la
mi re; dando tutta l'aria al	mi re, giving the whole air to
tenore, raggirandoui intorno alla	the tenor, turning around the
corda di mezo quanto più potrete,	middle note as much as you can,
perche come habbiamo detto	because, as we said
altroue le cose grandi,	elsewhere, grand and magnificent
e magnifiche in uoce grata	matters are spoken of in a pleasant
et mezana si parlano. Ma se' l	and median voice. But if the subject
concetto sarà lamenteuole il	should be plaintive, you
tuono mixolydio prenderete	will choose the Mixolydian tonos,
che in B. mi comincia, ed haue	which begins on B mi and has
in E la mi[55] la sua corda mezana	E la mi as its median note,
alla quale intorno più che	around which you will turn as much
potrete u'andrete raggirando,	as you can, giving
dando alla parte del soprano	the principal air to the
l'aria più principale; e così	soprano part. And so
secondo gli altri concetti	you will be guided by
delle parole u'andrete regolando.	the other ideas of the words.
Non ui scordando della natura	You will not forget the nature
del tardo, ueloce, e mezano,	of the slow, fast, and intermediate.

54. The Barberini manuscript, fol. 10r, has "A la mi re," whereas Doni's copy of the discourse, Florence, Biblioteca Marucelliana, MS A287 T. 1, fol. 163r, reads "e la mi," which is correct and has been adopted here.

55. All the sources have "A la mi," which does not exist in the hexachord system, and I have emended it to "E la mi," which is the mese of the Mixolydian octave species in Bardi's chart.

come per essempio douendosi
mettere in musica quella canzone
che comincia Italia mia bench'il
parlar sia 'ndarno, prenderete
il tuono dorio mentouato di sopra
dando l'aria principale al
tenor raggirandoui intorno alla
mezana, addottando il ritmo cioè
la lunga, e la breue che non sia
ne troppo tardo, nè troppo ueloce,
ma che imiti il parlar d'huomo
magnifico e graue.[56]

For example, having to set
to music the song that
begins "Italia mia bench'il
parlar sia 'ndarno," you would choose
the Dorian tonos mentioned above,
giving the principal air to the
tenor, turning around the median,
adopting a rhythm, that is,
the long and short [notes] that
are not too slow nor too fast
but imitate the speaking of a
stately and solemn man.

Clearly, Bardi is not speaking of the church modes, but neither is he speaking of tonoi. His "tuono" could be a translation of *tonos* or the assumption of the most common term in Italian for mode. The ambiguity is not resolved even in the more technical part of the essay. When Bardi describes the tonoi of Ptolemy, the term he uses for them is "tuoni," and for the octave species it is "spetie d'ottaua." The boundary notes and mesai that he names in the above passage belong to the octave species associated with the Dorian and Mixolydian tonoi. Elsewhere in the essay he notes that these species were called "Armonie" (*harmoniai*) by the ancients[57] and he adds in another place that "each species of octave, which we call *tuono,* and the ancients *harmonia,*" was assigned to appropriate verses and instruments. The confusion is compounded when he enumerates the modes by their ethnic names. Then he says that the lowest "species of octave" or "harmonia" was the Hypodorian, a whole tone above that the Hypophrygian, a whole tone higher than that the Hypolydian, a semitone above that the Dorian. Three *harmoniai,* thus, were sung lower and three higher than the Dorian. The confusion is only partly dispelled when Bardi explains that the Mixolydian was the highest tonos but that to this "harmonia" was assigned the lowest octave species, starting on B mi. If Bardi had been consistent in his terminology, he could have made evident that the tonoi were a means for assigning a pitch level to the octave species, or harmoniai, whose interval structure could best be recognized when placed on the steps of the fifteen-note system. But perhaps he did not realize that the conventional location of the octave species, such as B-b for the Mixolydian, was a virtual, not actual, location.

To return now to the quotation, what Bardi refers to as "the octave that begins on E la mi," called Dorian, is that set of intervals that Cleonides and other ancient writers recognized as one of the seven distinctive octave scales, found in the standard fifteen-note system between hypate meson and

56. Barberini MS, fol. 10r–v; Gori-Passeri ed., p. 243.
57. Barberini MS, fol. 6v; Gori-Passeri ed., p. 237.

nete diezeugmenon, our e and e', and by them called Dorian.[58] Bardi locates the median note of this octave species on A la mi re. In so doing he adopts the interpretation of Mei. Ptolemy does assign a functional, or dynamic, mese to each tonos within the e to e' octave, but only the Dorian's is the fourth note from the bottom. The note which is a fourth from the bottom when the Mixolydian octave species is placed in this same central octave is the thetic mese. If then this octave species is transposed to its conventional location, between hypate hypaton and paramese (Bardi's B mi octave), this thetic mese will be the fourth note from the bottom, or E la mi. Actually Bardi regards the B-mi version as the original, and, with Mei, conceives of it as being transposed upward in such a way that the mese assigned to the Mixolydian, d″ (D la sol re), is the fourth from the bottom. However Ptolemy had assigned this note to the dynamic, not the thetic, mese. Bardi glosses over the fact that in the B octave the Mixolydian octave species is expressed in natural notes, whereas in the A octave—where it must be placed to make d' the fourth from the bottom— it must be sung with flatted B and E. Bardi shows elsewhere that he understands this need of *musica ficta,* when he points out that a given instrument could play in only one tonos (he assumes ancient instruments that were not chromatically and enharmonically tuned).

Bardi viewed the octave species as modes, each having a median tone that was a focus for the melody, around which the melody revolved, and each endowed with a moral character. However he was acutely aware of the difference between these ancient modes and the modern plainchant modes, as he shows in this passage:

Diciamo adunque che in	We are saying, then, that in the
tutta la quintadecima sette	entire fifteen-note system there
sono le spetie dell'ottaua,	are seven species of octave,
à ciascuna delli quali gl'anti-	to each of which the ancients
chi un tuono assegnarono da loro	assigned a tonos, by them
armonia nominato i quali tuoni	called harmonia. These tonoi
faceuano le uariation loro, e per	achieved their variety both through
la diuersità della spetie	the difference in the species
dell'ottaua, e per	of octave and the pitch at
cantarsi ne luoghi loro,	which they were sung,
cioè nel graue, o, nel mez-	that is low, intermediate, or
zano, o nell'acuto; onde altre	high. For some
ueniuano cantate, e sonate nelle	were sung and played in the
corde basse della quintadecima,	low notes of the fifteen-note system,
altre nelle mezzane, altre	others in the middle, others in the

58. Cf. Cleonides *Harmonic Introduction* 9; von Jan ed., 197.4–7; 197.14–198.2 trans. in Strunk, *Sources Readings,* pp. 41–42.

nell'acute di essa, come si uedrà
nella dimostratione che faremo
di sette tuoni alla nostra
usanza appropriata. Auuertendo
che non si cantauano i tuoni come
facciamo noi, che sempre
il basso intonando sia Re, o, ut,
o, altra corda, facciamo sempre
la loro intonatione quanto più
possiamo bassa, e così l'armonia non uaria se non quanto
all'ottaua che nel rimanente
sempre i bassi, e tenori, e
l'altre parti cantano ne medesimi
luoghi: i primi toccando le corde
graui, i secondi le mezzane,
ei terzi l'acute. Ma gl'antichi
se intonauano una corda, pogniamo
quella del [D] sol re, che fosse
d'un tuono, ricercauano quell'ottaua secondo quella intonatione
ma se cantauano poi l'ottaua che
fosse la quinta più alta in
A la mi re, andauan cantando per
quella ottaua tutta una quinta
più alta della ragionata.[59]

high notes, as will be seen
in the demonstration that we shall
make of the seven tonoi adapted
to our usage. It should be noted
that the tonoi were not sung the
way we sing the modes, which, when
the bass intones re, ut,
or another note,
pitch the mode as low
as possible, and thus the harmony
does not vary except with respect to
the octave; in the rest of the
piece the basses, tenors, and the
other parts sing in their same
locations. The first hugs to the
low notes, the second to the middle,
the third to the high. But if the ancients intoned a note, let
us say d, which belonged to a tonos,
they sought out the octave [species]
belonging to that pitch,
but if they sang that octave [species]
as if it were a fifth higher at
a, then they went on singing in
that octave, all a fifth higher
than established.

Bardi's explanation is opaque, but he understands the difference between the modern modes and the ancient tonoi coupled with octave species. The modern modes have no pitch identity; they are located by singers to suit their voice ranges. The bass singer pitches his part as low as possible within his range, and the other singers follow suit according to their written parts. A tonos, on the other hand, has a specific pitch location, at which the octave species assigned to it is sung. However, the octave species could be shifted by a specific interval, such as a fifth higher, and sung at that level. Bardi does not say if this would be regarded as a change of tonos. The *Discorso*, regrettably, is not a formal treatise, and one cannot expect ironclad definitions or systematic expositions.

Bardi goes on to consider two other features that individualize the ancient modes—to each species of octave or harmonia was assigned its own proper "verse" (*verso.*) that is, a meter or verse type, such as the heroic, and modes were associated with specific instruments. For example, the Dorian harmonia, because it had a severe and magnificent character, was employed to

59. Barberini MS, fols. 6v–7r; Gori-Passeri ed., p. 237.

sing heroic verse and was given the lyre as an instrument. The Phrygian, which was exciting and furious, received dithyrambic verse and the aulos (*tibia*) as its instrument.[60] Bardi proposed a similar link between ancient modes and modern instruments, since it was customary "besides voices to concert with a large variety of instruments."[61] Of the winds, trombones are best suited to "low and somnolent music," that is, the lower tonoi, whereas cornetti are most apt for high and fast music; and for median and ordinary music, flutes and recorders (*pifferi alemanni*) are most fitting. Viols, harps, and lutes, because they were most like the human voice—being strung with gut strings—are appropriate for the median tonoi, such as the Dorian. This is particularly true of viols, because they have a severe and magnificent quality, whereas harpsichords and citterns— made with metal strings—are more active and more suited to high tonoi.

Within an instrumental family, a large number of differently tuned instruments were needed in ancient times to play the seven modes in the various genera and shades (*spartimenti*). As there were nine diatonics, ten chromatics, and eight enharmonics, the total number of shades was twenty-seven. Each of these could be played in any of seven modes, giving a total of one hundred and eighty-nine possibilities.[62] In modern times, when various types of instruments are mixed in ensembles there is the further problem of the different tuning systems. The viol and the lute, for example, "are tempered" (*temperati sieno*) according to the system of Aristoxenus, whereas harps and the harpsichord (*grauicembalo*) use other systems.

Of the four compositions by Bardi that survive complete or incomplete, one in particular seems to reflect the theories expounded in the *Discorso,* the madrigal "Miseri habitator del ciec'averno" in the fourth of the intermedi for the wedding of Grand Duke Ferdinand of Tuscany and Christine of Lorraine in 1589. The music is set for five voices, and, according to a note in the published partbook for the ninth voice (*nono*), it was accompanied by four trombones, four viols, and one lira.[63] According to the official description of the event by Bastiano de' Rossi, however, the madrigal was sung by a troupe of devils who issued from a trap door below the stage into the set of rocks and caves engulfed by flames. With "a melancholic and plaintive music (the work of our poet) they began, singing over harps, viols, and citterns, to lament" (e con una musica malinconica, e lamentevole [opera del nostro poeta] cominciarono, cantando, sopra arpi, viole, e cetere,

---

60. Barberini MS, fol. 7r; Gori-Passeri ed., p. 238.

61. Barberini MS, fol. 10v; Gori-Passeri ed., p. 243: "hoggi s'usa oltr'alle uoci concertare le musiche con uaria sorte di strumenti."

62. Barberini MS, fol. 6v, has "cento sessanta noue," whereas Gori-Passeri ed., p. 236, has "cento settantanoue," here corrected to 189.

63. Quoted in D. P. Walker, *Musique des intermèdes de "La Pellegrina"* (Paris, 1963), p. xlvii.

à lamentarsi).[64] The instrumentation described by Malvezzi, of four trombones, four viols, and one lira is probably correct.[65]

The poem, by Giovanni Battista Strozzi, addresses the wretched inhabitants of the "blind world of darkness, the kingdom of pain," warning them that nothing more will descend into the underworld but envy and disdain, no more human souls will join the damned already there, for the gates of the cruel prison will close forever—a kind of reverse amnesty or assured absolution in honor of the new duchess. The text is set to music line by line in a manner that contrasts with the method of contemporary madrigalists and that Bardi later described in a letter to the Duke of Ferrara as "according to my usual method, keeping the line intact, and with the expression of the words and the thought" (second'il mio solito col verso intero e con la spressione delle parole e concetto).[66] Each verse, in fact, is given an unbroken line in the canto, while the other four voices follow along homophonically, all coming together at the cadences. In an effort to preserve the longs and shorts of the poetic meter, Bardi freely mixed sets of two and three minims and of two and three semibreves, as reflected in the grouping into four and six quarter notes in my transcription (Figure 11.15).

Analyzed from the point of view of the Gregorian modes, this piece displays some baffling characteristics. The final note in the soprano and bass parts, G, suggests Mode 1 transposed down a fifth. The lines of poetry end harmonically (Basso) and melodically (Canto) on the following degrees of the mode:

line	basso	canto
1	fifth (D)	raised seventh (F♯)
2	fifth (D)	second (A)
3	second (A)	second (A)
4	fourth (C)	first (G)
5	fifth (D)	second (A)
6	second (A)	second (A)
7	first (G)	first (G)

The cadence notes of the bass voice are not incompatible with Mode 1, although there is disproportionate emphasis on the fifth degree, and the

64. Bastiano de' Rossi, *Descrizione dell'apparato e degl'Intermedi fatti per la commedia rappresentata in Firenze nelle nozze de' serenissimi Don Ferdinando Medici e Madama Cristina di Loreno, Gran Duchi di Toscana* (Florence, 1589), pp. 51–52, quoted in Walker, *Musique des intermèdes*, p. xlvii.

65. For a consideration of the instruments called for in the original performance of 1589 and their technical characteristics, see Howard M. Brown, *Sixteenth-Century Instrumentation: The Music for the Florentine Intermedii* (American Institute of Musicology, 1973), especially Appendix VII. D4.

66. Letter to Alfonso II d'Este, 3 October 1595, quoted in Angelo Solerti, *Gli Albori del melodramma* (Milan, 1904; repr. Hildesheim, 1969), I, 47, n. 4.

second degree is somewhat out of character. But more anomalous are the cadences of the top voice, in which the second degree ends four of seven phrases. Moreover, the species of fifth, G-A-Bb-C-D, and species of fourth, D-E-F-G, expected in Modes 1 or 2, are entirely missing in the soprano melody and the other parts as well.

If modal analysis of this madrigal thus proves unsatisfactory, an explanation in terms of Bardi's advice to composers in the *Discorso* is remarkably apropos. From the standpoint of ethos, two possibilities present themselves. Bastiano de' Rossi heard the madrigal as a lament. If this is how the poem is interpreted, the proper tonos, according to Bardi, is the ancient Mixolydian, and the principal part should be given to the soprano. Harpsichord and cornetti would be appropriate instruments. The melody is, indeed, given to the soprano, and it is possible to view the pitch organization as Mixolydian diatonic, to which is added a mixture of the chromatic. Bardi's Mixolydian would have to be transposed a fifth upward, as Bardi indicated was done,[67] to put it in a range suitable for the soprano. Figure 11.16 shows that if the tetrachords are laid out according to the greater perfect system, the segment of it used in this composition falls in the middle of the soprano range, within the two conjunct tetrachords rising e'-a', and a'-d" through bb'. The chromatic version of these tetrachords would add f♯' and b' to this gamut. However c♯', used in two places (mm. 5, 17) in the harmony, and g♯, used once (m. 10), are not accounted for. As these are, technically, ficta notes, introduced to provide smoother cadential progression, this is not a serious drawback to the interpretation of the piece as in antique Mixolydian.

The note to which the soprano melody returns most often is a', the mese of this transposed Mixolydian, which appears at the end of four of the seven lines. It is also the central note of the melody, which has the narrow compass of a fifth, in keeping with Bardi's belief that melodies should be focused and limited to the range of the speaking voice.

The analysis in Mixolydian runs into difficulties, though, with Bardi's prescription for instrumentation. The viols employed in the performance are suited, according to Bardi, to magnificent and grave subjects and to the Dorian, while trombones are fitting to sluggish affections and the lower tonoi. Moreover the text is not really a plaintive one, despite de' Rossi's impression of it; in it a higher authority pronounces a sentence. Its tone is similar to that of Petrarch's canzona "Italia mia," which Bardi would have put in the Dorian. The music is magnificent, if diabolically so, rather than complaining. On these grounds the ancient Dorian is a better candidate than the Mixolydian.

Although the principal part is not given to the tenor, as Bardi advised for the Dorian, it is within a contratenor's range. Interpreting the piece in

67. See the quotation above from Barberini MS, fol. 6v, Gori-Passeri, ed., p. 237.

Figure 11.15.
G. Bardi: "Miseri habitator del ciec'averno"

(Original note-values have been cut in half. Original unbarred in **₵**. Punctuation is the editor's.)

Figure 11.15. *Continued*

Bardi's Dorian requires no transposition, but it is necessary to assume the synemmenon, or lesser perfect, system, in which the two central tetrachords are joined through a common note, mese (Figure 11.17).

Whether one prefers the ancient Dorian or the ancient Mixolydian interpretations, Bardi's madrigal lends itself to these better than it does to a conventional modal explanation. Bardi seems deliberately to have reached for an antique effect, to have aspired, indeed, to the fabled marvelous emotional effects of the ancient modes. The route he took was mapped by the theory of the Greek tonoi and octave species that he learned from Ptolemy

Figure 11.16.
Bardi's Mixolydian tonos, with transposition up a fifth

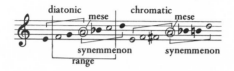

Figure 11.17.
Dorian tonos in the synemmenon system

and Cleonides, both directly and through Valla's translation and Mei's communications.[68]

Giovanni Battista Doni

There was little significant speculation about the Greek tonal system after Bardi and Galilei until the work of Giovanni Battista Doni (1594–1647). Doni credited a letter by Mei that was in circulation with inspiring his studies of Greek music.[69] Doni read the Greek writings in the original language from manuscripts that he found in Rome or that were supplied by his many correspondents. Like Mei and Bardi, Doni was most attracted to Ptolemy among the authors who theorized about the tonoi. Doni knew Mei's treatise *De modis musicis*. Indeed, he had a copy made for him, which is now in Florence.[70] Doni also knew Bardi's discourse addressed to Caccini; a copy of it, partly in Doni's hand, is among his papers at the Biblioteca Marucelliana in Florence.[71] He once planned to publish both these works.

Doni's interpretation of Ptolemy grew out of Mei's and Bardi's. Although Doni studied Ptolemy carefully, he apparently could not dismiss Mei's idea that the octave species constituted seven modes that were transposable to various levels by the tonoi. Doni's tonoi were seven, and they transposed the natural scale successively a tone, tone, semitone, tone, tone, semitone higher. The resulting keys are the same as those of modern interpretations of Ptolemy. But, whereas in the thinking prevailing today only the Dorian octave species was transposed into the other keys, Doni held that the octave species were modes and thus could all be transposed. In his *Compendio del Trattato de' generi e de' modi della musica* (Rome, 1635), he showed by means of a chart how modulation of key and mode would affect two of the modes and tonoi, the Dorian and Phrygian (Figure 11.18).

The Dorian mode has the rising melodic form mi, fa, sol, la, mi, fa sol, la (example 1a). In the second staff (example 2b) Doni shows how it may be transposed to the Phrygian tonos, which is a whole tone higher. The melody has remained the same, the pitch has been elevated by a whole tone,

68. Ercole Bottrigari also based a madrigal on the Greek chromatic genus "Il cantar novo," published in his *Il Melone, discorso armonico* (Ferrara, 1602), pp. 39–46. See the transcription in Ugo Sesini, "Studi sull'umanesimo musicale: Ercole Bottrigari," *Convivium, Rivista di lettere, filosofia e storia* 13 (1941):17–24. It uses the notes of the ancient Dorian chromatic and probably preceded Bardi's experiments by some years.

69. Doni, "Trattato secondo sopra gl'instrumenti di tasti," in *Lyra Barberina*, I, 324.

70. Biblioteca Riccardiana, MS 815.

71. Florence, Biblioteca Marucelliana, MS A287, I, fols. 154r–168v. This copy was the basis of the edition of Bardi's essay in *Lyra Barberina*, II, 233–48, which, however, is full of errors not the fault of Doni.

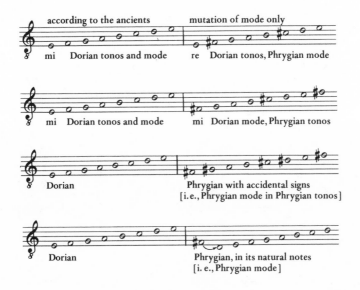

Figure 11.18.
The Ptolemaic modes according to Doni, *Compendio,* 1635, pp. 33–34

or, as we would say, it has been transposed from its natural key to the higher key of two sharps.

On the other hand, if one wished to sing a Phrygian mode in the Dorian tonos, one would remain in the e-e′ octave but use the necessary accidentals to produce the succession characteristic of the Phrygian mode: re, mi, fa, sol, la, mi, fa, sol (example 1b). In going from example 1a to 1b there is a mutation of mode, but the pitch level of the Dorian tonos is maintained. (As we understand Ptolemy today, example 1b represents the octave species produced by the Phrygian tonos in the central octave hypate meson to nete diezeugmenon.) If one wished to sing the Phrygian mode in the Phrygian tonos, one would then sing the same syllables—re, mi, fa, sol, re, mi, fa, sol—starting on F♯ (example 3b), because the Phrygian tonos is a tone higher than the Dorian. The Phrygian melody would not be at its normal Phrygian pitch level.

To bring these ancient tonoi to life, Doni had to surmount two obstacles. One was notational—some of the transpositions required the use of many sharps and double sharps. Doni devised a notation in which all of the music appeared to be in familiar keys, but in fact it was meant to be played on a transposing instrument. The other problem was that of tuning. Doni believed that ancient music employed a system of just intonation. No modern instrument could play all of the keys with equally just tuning. Some keys would be truer than others. To make it possible to play uniformly in all the keys, Doni developed several new instruments, such as the panharmonic lyre (the lyra Barberina), the triharmonic viol, and the triharmonic harpsichord. Examples 4a and b show how the modulation from Dorian tonos and mode to Phrygian tonos and mode would be notated. The initial F♯ would indicate the modulation to the Phrygian tonos; then the Phrygian mode would be written with its natural notes.

Doni sought to interest composers in applying the ancient tonoi, because he felt that the tonal system of his day was lacking in expressive variety. Some of those who experimented with his system were Girolamo Frescobaldi, Ottaviano Castelli, Pietro della Valle, Domenico Mazzocchi, Pietro Heredia, and Gino Capponi. Doni himself wrote some experimental pieces. The most extensive score that survives is by Pietro della Valle, who around 1640 wrote the dialogo (or oratorio) "per la festa della Santissima Purificazione a cinque voci con varietà di cinque tuoni diversi, cioè Dorio, Frigio, Eolio, Lidio et Hipolidio."[72]

72. See Agostino Ziino, "Pietro della Valle e la 'Musica erudita,' nuovi documenti," *Analecta musicologica* 4 (1967):97–111.

TWELVE

A Natural New Alliance of the Arts

 o link music with the verbal arts, with rhetoric as well as poetry, was as characteristic of the Renaissance as it was typical of the Middle Ages to ally music with the mathematical sciences. Although music was a component of the medieval quadrivium, in which it was a companion to arithmetic, geometry, and astronomy, neither poetry nor music had a place in the trivium, which consisted of grammar, rhetoric, and dialectic. The seven liberal arts had to be expanded and redefined to admit either poetry or music as communicative arts. But, then, history and philosophy, it should be recalled, also had no place in the system.

At the threshold of the Renaissance Coluccio Salutati proposed a redefinition of the liberal arts. He distinguished the various verbal arts according to function: philosophy defines, dialectic demonstrates, rhetoric persuades, and grammar narrates and relates. Because simple exposition, the object of grammar, did not fully satisfy the ancients, they conceived of an exquisite kind of narration that went beyond simple and raw grammatical expression. To the coordinated discourse of grammar, therefore, they joined the precision of logic and the ornament of rhetoric. From arithmetic they drew rhythm, from geometry quantity, from music melody, and from astrology proportion, and these they added as ornaments to the arts of the trivium. Out of the amalgam came the art of poetry, the only art worthy of praising the beauty and excellence of the human or of the divine being. Poetry is thus the union of the quadrivium and trivium, a virtual octessential art.

Et quoniam versus est poete
proprium instrumentum, quem
suis partibus, hoc est
pedibus, mensuramus atque compo-
nimus et non omnibus sed certis
numeris alligamus, ex quibus
resultat et queritur musica

Since the proper instrument
of the poet is verse, which
we measure with and compose out
of its parts, that is feet, and
we knit these together not with
any rhythms but with established
ones from which results and is sought

melodia, clarum est poeticam	melody, it is clear that poetic
narrationem ex trivio quadruvio-	narration is composed out of
que componi. . . .	the trivium and quadrivium. . . .
ex omnibus scientiis et libera-	This discipline is assembled from
libus artibus facultas ista	all the liberal sciences and arts
collecta est ac sicut omnige-	and has the fragrance and splendor
num florum manipulus et redolet	of a bouquet of flowers of every
et effulget. Et cum sit ab	species. And since it is a
omnibus, sicut	product of all the arts, as
ostendimus,	we have demonstrated, this art
generata, post omnes artes	is generated after all the arts
et ipsam artem artium,	and even after the art of arts,
philosophiam et theologiam,	philosophy and theology, and
hec ars incipit, et cunctas	presupposes all of them as
utpote preambulas sibique neces-	propadeutic and necessary to its
sarias presupponit, quicquid	existence, capable as it is
dici potest tum suaviter, tum	of narrating anything that may be
ornate, tum subtiliter	within its expressive range with
narratura.[1]	sweetness, ornament and subtlety.

Poetry is to Salutati the queen of the arts, capable of narration and rhetorical persuasion and not a stranger to logic, a beneficiary of the power of number to organize and harmonize its minutest parts. Poetry's great resources, for Salutati, are unity and variety, particularly variety of pitch—gravity and acuity—and of rhythm, mixed in suitable proportion, from which there results a sweet harmony.[2] Although Salutati's seven liberal arts are still scholastically compartmentalized, their union under the banner of poetry looks forward to the fluid mix of the communicative arts in the sixteenth century, when they are united through the principle of imitation propagated by the commentators on Aristotle's *Poetics*. But before that happened some of the fields of learning that were revived or that received new impetus through humanism had to be fitted into some scheme.

We find such a comprehensive system in Angelo Poliziano's *Panepistemon*. He divides the sciences studied in Aristotle's works into three areas: inspired (theology), invented (philosophy), and mixed (divination). Philosophy is subdivided into contemplative (*spectativa*), practical (*actualis*), and rational (*rationalis*). Music is ranked with the mathematical sciences of arithmetic, geometry, and spherics, but architecture, theatre, and ethics are grouped with the practical. Poetics joins the old trivium, to which is added history,

---

1. Coluccio Salutati, *De laboribus Herculis,* I, 3, ed. B. L. Ullman (Zurich, 1951), pp. 18–20. According to Ullman, preface, pp. vii–viii, Book 1 was begun 1383–91 and completed before 1405.

2. Ibid., I, 11; Ullman ed., p. 55.

	Real *(things)*		Rational *(words)*
Contemplative	Practical		Judicial logic
Speculative	Active		Dialectic
Metaphysics			Topics
Physics	Behavioral		Sophistic
Mathematics	Ethics		Hypothetic
Arithmetic	Economics		Rhetoric
Music	Politics		Poetics
Geometry	Craft		History
Astrology	Mechanical arts		Grammar

Figure 12.1:
The liberal arts according to Varchi

all under "rational"—that is, arts that respectively "judge [grammar], narrate [history], demonstrate [dialectic], persuade [rhetoric], and delight [poetry]."[3]

Benedetto Varchi too based his scheme (Figure 12.1) on Aristotle's works but took into account also the *Poetics*.[4] In all of these systems music is represented by theoretical music and not the "fine art" of music, which might be subsumed under poetics but is actually not considered or mentioned. The failure of classical antiquity to recognize the fine arts as intellectual disciplines doomed them to exclusion from these classically inspired schemes.[5]

In view of the lack of recognition of the fine, or creative, arts as a special category in the authors reviewed until now, it is all the more remarkable that Girolamo Mei devised a classification of them based on Aristotle's *Poetics,* a work that had been taken into account in several of the preceding systems. The proposal, unfortunately, was buried in a letter to Piero Vettori of 10 January 1560,[6] as a commentary on *Poetics* 1.4–7.1447a–b. Mei sets forth a scheme of "constructive arts" (*arti fattive*) that includes visual, verbal, and musical media among the imitative arts.

His chart, shown in Figure 12.2, is the clearest and earliest grouping of the imitative arts known to me. They are not the same as the modern "fine arts," for architecture, not being imitative, is left out. But the scheme

3. See the table in Weinberg, *A History of Literary Criticism in the Italian Renaissance*, p. 3.
4. For the Italian terms, see Weinberg, *A History*, pp. 7–8.
5. See P. O. Kristeller, "The Modern System of the Arts: A Study in the History of Aesthetics (I)," *Journal of the History of Ideas* 12 (1951):506.
6. London, British Library, MS Add. 10268, fol. 209. For an English translation of the table, see Palisca, *Girolamo Mei*, p. 45.

Figure 12.2.
The imitative arts according to Mei

embraces all the representational arts.[7] It is interesting that poetry, drama, and other speech arts are united here with dance and music, yet not all as part of poetry. There is also provision for pure instrumental music. Had Mei known more about musical practice, he might not have shrugged off "through harmony only" and "through speech and harmony only" as "not in use," for some instrumental preludes were in free rhythm and could be classified as "harmony only," and plainchant would qualify as "speech and harmony only." It should be noted, however, that as a total system it is not a system of the "fine arts," for constructive arts such as carpentry are included. Only the category of arts "imitative of things" is identifiable with the modern fine arts.

Mei here has gone beyond the text on which he was commenting, as he

7. Compare Mei's system to groupings of imitative, or poetic, arts by other commentators on the *Poetics,* cited by Kristeller in "The Modern System," p. 511, n. 92.

points out to Vettori. Aristotle did not mention in this place painting, sculpture, and other media, only that some imitate through color and form (1.4.1447a). Aristotle did not list them, Mei suggests, because the manner of imitation is not parallel to that of poetry. Sculpture and painting imitate bodies directly and only incidentally actions, whereas those arts allied with poetry imitate actions and only incidentally the person acting. A further difference is that the graphic imitations represent things directly to the sense of sight or touch and only secondarily to the intellect through the imagination, whereas the poetic arts are directed to the intellect and only incidentally to the sense of hearing, as when a poem is recited or listened to, and to the sight, when it is read or staged. Thus the two kinds of arts are as different as the body and soul, Mei concludes, and the philosopher was justified in leaving out the visual arts from his discussion of imitation.[8]

Also inspired by Aristotle's *Poetics* is a proposal by Giulio del Bene to the Accademia degli Alterati for an educational program that would be based on the principle of altering the human personality by imitating nature through the arts.[9] Del Bene distinguishes the liberal arts from the mechanical. Among the first he includes grammar, rhetoric, music, poetics, and dialectic. They have in common the power to alter the mind and soul:

al fine che noi possiamo,
per la gramatica bene et corretta-
mente ragionare, non hauendo
noi questo da natura, per la
retorica persuadere, et tirare la
uolunta delli huomini doue ci pare,
et per la musica imparare ad essere
ordinati, et composti bene nel
animo nostro, et a mouere gli
affetti non meno che si faccia la
retorica et per delettarsi et
solleuarci dalle fatiche
che nelle operationi humane ogni
giorno supportiamo,
et finalmente della poesia che

to the end that we might
through grammar discourse well and
correctly (for we do not have
this [capacity] by nature), through
rhetoric persuade and draw the
will of men wherever we would,
and through music learn to be
well ordered and constituted in
our minds and to move the
affections no less than is done
through rhetoric and for delighting
and uplifting us in the trials
that every day we sustain in human
activities,
and finally through poetry

---

8. London, British Library, MS Add. 10268, fol. 206v.

9. This was in a discourse "Del conuiuio delli Alterati," Florence, Biblioteca Nazionale Centrale, MS Magl. IX.137, fols. 12r–22r. It is attributed there to the academician Il Desioso. It may be dated through the *Diario* of the academy, Florence, Biblioteca Medicea-Laurenziana, MS Ashburnham 558, II, fol. 30r, where the entry for 16 February 1575 reads: "Il Desioso parlò del conuiuio et fece v[n]o discorso sopra l'Alteratione si ducendo alla alteratione delli Alterati." Il Desioso was the academic name of Giulio del Bene. He is identified as such in numerous documents of the academy and in D. Manni, *Memorie della famosa fiorentina accademia degli Alterati* (Florence, 1748), p. 8.

possiamo descriuere et dimostrare	we may describe and exemplify
col imitare lationi delli huomini	by imitating the actions of men
quasi lidea delle uirtu et de	almost the idea of virtue and of
uirtu de gli eccellenti huomini,	that of excellent men,
et id il uerso, il quale è	and through verse, which is
opinione che sia il parlare	thought to be the speech of
delli dei exprimere inoltre	the gods, to express, besides,
concetti et imitare gli affetti	ideas and to imitate the affections
et i costumi altrui, e delettare	and mores of others, and to delight
et giouare l'uno laltro per questa	and profit one another through this
cosi piaceuole et bella arte.[10]	so pleasing and beautiful art.

Of the fine arts Del Bene joins only music to the verbal arts, because he finds it analogous to rhetoric in its capacity to move the affections. Poetry, on the other hand, is seen to *imitate* the affections and to *express* ideas. Music is distinguished also in its conduciveness to ordering the mind and its healing and uplifting qualities. In his discourse Del Bene does not neglect the sciences, pointing out that numbers applied to sensible objects produce music and extolling the benefits of studying geometry, stereometry, and cosmology. He urges the Alterati to be active in all these fields if they want to "alter" their minds for the better: read lectures, compose sonnets, recite orations, write tragedies, canzoni, madrigals, and every other sort of composition, discuss philosophy, and speak extemporaneously on politics, ethics, and poetics. Del Bene's is the broadest possible view of the arts. Especially significant for our discussion is the expansion of the old trivium by joining to it poetry and music and the implication that music is a link between the arts and sciences.

Grammar

Of the arts of the trivium, grammar had the longest association with Western music theory. Guido of Arezzo in 1026–28 in his *Micrologus* (chapter 15) compared the parts of a melody with the parts of a poem. As in verse there are letters, syllables, parts, feet, and lines, in music there are individual tones, groups of tones that make up "syllables," groups of syllables called neumes, and phrases called "distinctions."[11] Johannes dictus Cotto, around 1100, refers to the *distinctiones* of Aelius Donatus (4th century A.D.). Just

10. MS Magl. IX.137, fols. 18v–19r.
11. See the translation of *Micrologus* in *Hucbald, Guido, and John On Music: Three Medieval Treatises*, trans. Warren Babb, ed. Claude V. Palisca (New Haven, 1978), p. 70. For other connections between grammar and music in antiquity and the early Middle Ages, see Edward A. Lippman, "The Place of Music in the System of the Liberal Arts," in *Aspects of Medieval and Renaissance Music*, ed. Jan LaRue (New York, 1966), pp. 545–59.

as in prose there are three kinds of distinctiones, or pauses—namely, colon, comma, and period—so in chant there are pauses, some more, some less final, according to the divisions of the text, and these are marked by endings on the different steps of the mode.[12]

These principles reemerged from time to time in the manuals for improvising and writing organum, for example, in the treatise *Musica enchiriadis*[13] and the Paris treatise.[14] But in the intervening years other considerations, particularly of rhythmic structure, both local and long-range, often based on numerical proportions, took precedence over fidelity to grammatical construction. It was as if music's subordination to mathematics had blocked for a time its natural affiliation with language. With the growing recognition of the natural alliance of music with the verbal arts, it is not surprising that both musical theorists and writers on poetics make demands on the composer that earlier were either ignored or given little priority. One such demand was that composers pay attention to the grammatical structure of the texts they were setting to music.

Composers and theorists turned to grammatical principles again for guidance in laying the syllables, words, and larger grammatical units under the notes. As in the medieval treatises mentioned, grammatical terminology and concepts define the points that articulate the parts of a verse or prose text, and grammar determines the musical pauses and endings and their degrees of finality.

The most thorough application of classical grammar to musical composition was undertaken by Giovanni del Lago in a letter to a certain Fra Seraphin of 26 August 1541.[15] Del Lago published rather little but was greatly revered in Venetian musical circles in the first half of the sixteenth century and was frequently cited as an authority by Pietro Aron, among others. He confided much of his learning to colleagues in lengthy letters. Although the epistolary treatise is a common genre in the Renaissance, it is likely that most of this letter, a virtual treatise on the modes in composition, was drafted well before del Lago had occasion to send it to Fra Seraphin in response to the latter's queries on the subject. A compendium

12. *De musica*, ch. 11; trans. in *Hucbald, Guido, and John on Music*, pp. 116–17; see also Donatus, *Ars grammatica*, "De posituris," in *Grammatici latini*, ed. Henricus Keil, IV (Leipzig, 1864), p. 372.

13. *Musica et Scolica enchiriadis*, ed. Hans Schmid (Munich, 1983).

14. Paris, Bibliothèque Nationale, MS lat. 7202, ed. Ernst L. Waeltner in *Die Lehre vom Organum bis zur Mitte des 11. Jahrhunderts* (Tutzing, 1975), p. 78.

15. Biblioteca Apostolica Vaticana, MS vat. lat. 5318, fols. 2–10. Knud Jeppesen first drew attention to the "wichtige Bemerkungen über das Verhältnis zwischen Wort und Ton" in this letter in "Eine musiktheoretische Korrespondenz des früheren Cinquecento," *Acta Musicologica* 13 (1941):4. Don Harrán has dedicated a full study to this document in "The Theorist Giovanni del Lago: A New View of the Man and His Writings," *Musica Disciplina* 27 (1973):107–51.

of the letter is found in del Lago's only published treatise, *Breve introduttione di musica misurata,* in a chapter entitled "Modo, & osseruatione di comporre qualunche concento."[16] Del Lago's object is to instruct the reader to compose music that is sensitive to the text on several levels: general mood, units of thought or sentences, punctuation, accentuation of words, and length of syllables. In poetic texts he calls attention additionally to the location of long syllables within a line, the place of the caesuras, and scansion.

Del Lago is deeply concerned that a musical composition transmit the formal qualities of a text. To decide where cadences should fall is the heart of the task of setting a prose or poetic text, and this requires that the composer discriminate between various kinds of distinctiones, as the fourth-century grammarian Donatus called them. Del Lago quotes the entire section "De posituris" from his grammatical tract.[17]

Here Donatus points out that there are three levels of punctuation, or *positura: distinctio, subdistinctio,* and *media distinctio,* the first defining an entire sentence or period, the second a colon, the third a comma. Del Lago adds that Venerable Bede translated the Greek *colon* into Latin as "membrum," while the Greek word for comma became "incisio," and for period "clausula" or "circuitus." The place for a musical cadence is where a sentence is complete, but del Lago allows one also at the media distinctio: "A cadence is a certain distinction and rest in music. Or a cadence is a termination of a part of the music, as in the body of a speech the media distinctio and the final distinctio."[18] He advises the composer to make cadences only where a part or member of the oratorical period ends, and "not always in the same place."[19] Musical cadences were thus a means of punctuation, and they could, like periods, colons, and commas, confer a sense of finality or relative finality to an utterance. But a cadence should be avoided when the thought in the text is not complete:

Alcuna uolta fingere di far caden-	Sometimes to feign making a cadence,
tia, & poi nella conclusione di essa	then at its conclusion

16. Giovanni del Lago, *Breve introduttione di musica misurata* (Venice, 1540; facs. ed., Bologna, 1969), p. [39]. Further concerning the relationship of this as well as other letters in the correspondence to the treatise, see Harrán, "The Theorist G. del Lago," pp. 134–42.

17. Donatus, *Ars grammatica,* Keil ed., p. 372, lines 15–23. Del Lago, *Breve introduttione,* p. [42]. In the letter the passage is translated into Italian, fol. 4r; see Harrán, "The Theorist G. del Lago," p. 125, where the two versions are given in parallel columns.

18. MS Vat. lat. 5318, fol. 4r: "La cadentia è una certa distintione, et riposo nel canto. Ouero la cadentia è una terminatione di essa parte del canto, come è nel contesto dell'oratione, la media distintione, et la finale."

19. *Breve Introduttione,* p. [41]: "& auertite di far le cadentie, doue la parte dell'oratione, ouero il membro finisce, & non sempre in un medesimo luoco, perche il luoco proprio delle cadentie e, doue finisce la sententia del contesto delle parole."

cadentia pigliare una consonantia	assume a consonance
non propinqua ad essa cadentia	not nearest to this cadence
per accommodarsi e cosa laudabile.	as a refuge, is praiseworthy.
Et questo s'intende con il soprano,	This is intended for the soprano
o altra parte. Ma bisogna che	or other part. But the tenor
sempre il tenore in questo caso,	in this case
faccia lui la cadentia, ouer distin-	makes the cadence or distinction.
tione. Accio che sia intesa la	This is so that the thought
sententia delle parole cantate.[20]	of the text sung may be heard.

The proviso that one not make the cadence always "in the same place" would be bewildering did it not recall a rule of Tinctoris in his counterpoint treatise:

Septima regula est quod super planum	The seventh rule is: even when singing
cantum etiam canendo duae aut plures	over a plainchant, two cadences must
perfectiones in eodem loco continue	not be made successively on the same
fieri non debent.[21]	place.

The musical example that follows clarifies the meaning of "place," for it shows a counterpoint that makes a cadence three times in succession over the tenor's d. Place—*locus* or *luoco*—therefore, refers to the pitch of the tenor in a cadence. Del Lago wishes that the composer not come back always to the same pitch for his cadences. This advice connects the rules on cadence with the opening of his last chapter, "Modo, & osseruatione di comporre qualunche concento." Here del Lago makes his most interesting observation, that the composer choose a mode according to the subject of the words. And upon the choice of mode depends the choice of cadence tones, as is evident from the opening of del Lago's section on counterpoint:

Circa la cognitione del contra-	Concerning the knowledge of counter-
punto e necessario primieramente	point, it is necessary first
di saper quanti sono i modi ouero	to know how many modes or tones
tuoni, ... & in che modo si	there are ... and in what manner one
compongono, & i loro principii, &	composes in them the beginnings and
le sue distintioni o cadentie, &	their distinctions or cadences, and
doue finiscono cosi regolarmente,	where they end, whether regularly
come irregolarmente.[22]	or irregularly.

The means by which the composer articulates a composition set to a prose or poetic text, del Lago implies, is by choosing within a mode certain pitches in the tenor part—not always the same—according to the distinctions or

---

20. Ibid., p. [39].

21. Johannes Tinctoris, *Liber de arte contrapuncti,* ed. Albert Seay (American Institute of Musicology, 1975), III, 8, p. 154.

22. *Breve Introduttione,* p. [29].

cadences allowed regularly or irregularly within that mode. And the choice of mode depends on the text, as he proclaims in the first sentence of his final chapter.

The text of this opening (right below) is almost identical to the opening of the letter to Fra Seraphin, which in turn is parallel to a passage in a letter of an otherwise unknown writer, Matteo Nardo, to a certain Hieronymo (left). The two texts may be compared:

Quante uolte i dottorj della Musica hanno da componere alcuna Canzone, sogliono prima diligentemente tra si stessi consi- derare, à che fine, et à che proposito quella potissimamente instituiscono, & componeno, cioè quali affetti d'animo con quella cantilena mouer debbano. Et pero se loro intendono, et questo ordinano, cioe con mouer, et accendere li animi, & li spiriti ad ira, pigliano all hora il terzo Tuono, nel quale è il phrygio. spetie del Diapason. Et da quello uogliono la sua cantione dependere stabilirse.[23]	Quante uolte, che i dotti compositori hanno da comporre una cantilena, sogliono prima diligentemente fra se stessi consi- derare a che fine, & a che proposito quella potissimamente instituiscono, & componghino, cioe quali affetti d'animo con' quella cantilena mouere debbino, cioe di qual tuono si deue comporre, perche altri graui, & sedati, alcuni mesti, & gemibundi, di nuouo iracundi, altri impetuosi, cosi anchora le melodie de canti, perche, chi in un modo, & chi in un'altro commuo- uono, uariamente sono distinte da musici.
Whenever doctors of music have to compose a song they are accustomed to ask themselves conscientiously to what end they might be starting and composing it, that is what affections of the soul they ought to arouse with the piece. And if they aim and so arrange it that it move and inflame souls and spirits to anger, they choose then the Third Mode, in which there is the Phrygian species of diapason. And they make the song depend and fix upon it.	Whenever learned composers have to compose a song they are accustomed to ask themselves conscientiously to what end they might be starting and composing it, that is what affections of the soul they ought to arouse with the piece, thus in what mode it should be composed, for some [modes] are severe and sedate, some mournful and lamenting, others angry, or impetuous. So should the melodies of songs be diversely distinctive, some stirring people one way, some another.

This is an early date for such an emphatic assertion of the goal of the composer to move the affections. The critical role assigned to the choice

23. For an almost identical reading as in the treatise in del Lago's letter, see Harrán, "The Theorist G. del Lago," p. 114, where an English translation is also given.

of mode and the humanistic implications of this association of mode and affection also make this a key document in the history of musical humanism. Consequently it is important to determine whether the primary author of this statement was del Lago or Nardo. The watermark on the paper used in the Nardo manuscript suggests for it a date after 1540.[24] The date of the watermark is not so significant, however, because Nardo's letter is a fragmentary copy with neither a greeting nor a signature, and the Valgulio treatise (the preface to the Plutarch translation) that occupies most of the manuscript dates from before 1507. So Nardo's letter may be much older than the watermark.

The language of the two documents may offer a useful clue. Nardo's version shows lapses into Venetian dialect, which are expurgated in both the epistolary and printed versions of the del Lago statement. If Nardo was copying, would he have converted Tuscan to Venetian? He might have done so, particularly if he were a Venetian writing to a compatriot. But it would be more probable for del Lago to aspire to correct Tuscan. The content of the passage favors Nardo's authorship. Whereas Nardo at the point where the two diverge goes on to speak of the choice of mode in terms of the ethical effects of the Greek tonoi, del Lago drops the subject. Thus the opening has more justification in Nardo's letter than in del Lago's treatise. The most persuasive evidence for Nardo's authorship is his attribution to Egnazio of the theory of the modes that he expounds in the ensuing discussion.[25] Nardo praises Egnazio to the skies and says his words are to him as an oracle, and his brilliance illumines "this most splendid city of Venice, the whole universe."[26] Nardo also states that "our Pietro Aron, Fiorentino, worthy of praise without end, that prince of musicians,"[27] observed the character of the modes as he (Nardo) has described them. In view of Nardo's obvious zeal in citing authorities, it seems likely that he would have cited another fellow Venetian, del Lago, if he had borrowed from him. Instead, he gives credit to the humanist Egnazio, a founding member of the Aldine academy, friend of Aldo Manuzio, teacher of his son

24. The watermark closely matches Briquet nos. 3477 (Padua, 1547) and 3480 (Reggio-Emilia, 1545).

25. Giovanni Battista Cipelli from Egna, near Bolzano, who called himself Egnatius or Egnazio, b. 1473 or 1478, d. 1553. This information is from Mario Cosenza, *Biographical and Bibliographical Dictionary of the Italian Humanists, 1300–1800* (2d ed., Boston, 1962–67), II, 1280–84.

26. Biblioteca Apostolica Vaticana, MS Vat. lat. 5385, fol. 57r. Giovanni degli Agostini, "Notizie istoriche spettanti alla vita e agli scritti di Batista Egnazio, sacerdote viniziano," in *Raccolta d'opuscoli scientifici e filogogici,* ed. A. Calogerà (Venice, 1745), pp. 73–90, also speaks of his reputation as "oracolo della città."

27. Biblioteca Apostolica Vaticana, MS Vat. lat. 5385, fol. 59r: "quel nostro senza fine laudabile Pietro Aron fiorentino, prencipe de musicj."

Paolo, and teacher of Erasmus, who praised him in the adage *Festina lente*.[28] It would be interesting from the standpoint of the flow of classical erudition if del Lago could be linked with Egnazio. But the intellectual pedigree that Nardo suggests is equally interesting. Both Nardo and the addressee of the letter, who may have been Hieronymus Bononius Tarvisinus, obviously knew Aron, for he is referred to as "nostro." If not del Lago, certainly Aron was esteemed by and associated with the Aldine intellectual circle. Since Aron did not settle in Venice until 1522 and entered a monastery in Bergamo in 1536, the intervening years must be those during which he enjoyed association with this circle, and they perhaps also circumscribe the period during which Nardo's letter was written.

No writings on music are known by Egnazio, who was born in Venice in 1473 and died there in 1553.[29] He published in the field of Roman history and biography and edited numerous Latin classics for the Aldine press. Even before his appointment to the chair of Latin letters and humanities at the school of San Marco in Venice in 1520, he was a popular teacher, and he continued to win fame until his retirement in 1549. In 1518 he had been a candidate for the Greek chair but could not rival Vettore Fausto in this language and withdrew from the contest. It appears plausible that Nardo, about whom nothing otherwise is known, should look up to him for his knowledge of classical antiquity, including matters musical. Piero Brichi in his funeral oration for Egnazio speaks of his mastery of all seven liberal arts, including music.[30]

Of Nardo nothing is known except that he was from Tossignano and published a biography of Giovanni Battista Prodromia, mayor of Padua, in the dedicatory letter of which, to Stefano Tiepolo, he extolled Egnazio as a model of the union of the liberal and fine arts (*ingenues artes*) and religious studies (*sacrarum studio literarum*).[31] The doctrine of the modes that Nardo transmits confuses the ancient and modern modes. He speaks of the Phry-

28. Concerning his relation to Erasmus see James B. Ross, "Venetian Schools and Teachers Fourteenth to Early Sixteenth Century: A Survey and a Study of Giovanni Battista Egnazio," *Renaissance Quarterly* 29 (1976):539–540 and n. 70. I am indebted to Professor Margaret King for this reference and for searching through other Venetian sources for traces of Egnazio.

29. A short biography and list of works are in Ambroise Firmin-Didot, *Alde Manuce et l'hellénisme à Venise* (Paris, 1875; repr. Brussels, 1966), pp. 449–52. This incorporates a biographical notice from Le Roux de Lincy, *Recherches sur Jean Grolier, sur sa vie, et sur sa bibliothèque* (Paris, 1866), pp. 50–51. See also Martin Lowry, *The World of Aldus Manutius* (Oxford, 1979), *passim*.

30. Piero Brichi, *In Joannis Baptistae Egnatii funere oratio habita Venetiis M. D. LIII.* (Venice, 1553). A copy of this rare edition is in Yale University's Beinecke Rare Book and Manuscript Library, Gr12 Eg68X B76.

31. The biography was printed in Venice in 1550 by Cominus de Tridino: degli Agostini, pp. 59–60.

Aron (1525) *Trattano*, ch. 25	Nardo Letter	Gaffurio (1518) *De harmonia*, IV
I: joy, happiness, merriment	Dorian: grave, sonorous, majestic, fills ear with sweetness	modesty, virile, constancy
II: grave, used by ancients in funerals	Hypodorian:	slowness, slothfulness
III: inflames to anger, animosity	Phrygian: inflames to anger	incietes to anger, war
IV: suited to rest, tranquility	Hypophrygian:	quiet, grave
V: relieves melancholy, troubles	Lydian: pleasing, sweet,	jovial, pleasisi
VI: induces tears, compassion	Hypolydian:	tears, lamenting
VII: mixture of modesty and joviality	Mixolydian:	twofold: exciting and withdrawna
VIII: for merry and happy banquets		

Figure 12.3:
Aron, Nardo, Gaffurio: Modal Ethos

gian as the Third [church] Mode but gives the ethical characteristic of the ancient tonos ("inflames to anger"), which he attributes to its octave species. The Lydian is characterized as pleasing and sweet, fitting to peaceful Lydian people. Of the Dorian he says that it was severe and majestic and filled the ears of hearers with sweetness, and it is here that he credits Egnazio: "This about the Dorian is affirmed by our Doctor Egnatio, whose words are like an oracle to me. I am accustomed to call him a phoenix of the Greeks. From him, as from the sun, this splendid city of Venice, all of Italy, the whole universe is enlightened and illumined."[32]

Nardo's characterizations of the modes may be compared to those of Aron and Gaffurio (see Figure 12.3). It is difficult to see how any composer could be guided by these characterizations, which originally belonged to a set of ancient harmoniai, tonoi, or modes—one is not sure—that were completely different and unrelated to the church modes. The principle that the composer should choose the mode according to the affection of the text is reasonable enough, but on what basis should the choice be made? Surely

32. MS Vat. lat. 5385, fol. 57r: "Questo del Dorio modo afferma el Dottor nostro Egnatio / Le parole del quale à mi sono in luocho de oracolo. El quale io soglio nominare phenice delli Greci. Dal quale, come dal sole, questa amplissima città venetiana, tutta Italia, tutto luniuerso Mundo se illustra, et illumina."

not the affective qualities outlined in the table! Who would compose a stirring martial piece in the church Phrygian, or banish gloom with the sorry tritone-ridden church Lydian? Here is humanism gone awry, a sad legacy of early Renaissance musical scholarship's failure to make necessary distinctions between two totally different tonal systems, the Greek and the Western medieval. Unfortunately Glarean fell into the trap, and most of what he says about the affective qualities of the modes is marked by the same credulity as the characterizations of Aron, Nardo, and Gaffurio.

Zarlino, who cites many of the old ethical characterizations, carefully attributing them to various authorities, seems never to embrace them with any enthusiasm or conviction. Instead he makes one of the few observations in all this literature that is based on musical realities rather than ancient authorities. In the *Istitutioni harmoniche* —not in the book on the modes but in that on counterpoint—he remarks that the Fifth, Sixth, Eighth, Eleventh, and Twelfth Modes are "lively and full of cheer" because the major imperfect consonances are often heard on finals and on the note that divides the octave harmonically or arithmetically (the fifth degree of the authentic modes, the fourth degree of the plagal). In other modes, that is, the First, Second, Third, Fourth, Ninth, and Tenth, when the fifth above the final or mean is divided, the minor third is situated below the major third, and this renders a composition sad, languid, and soft.[33]

Even Zarlino's feeble endorsement of modal ethos was too much for Galilei, who quite clearly saw the futility of the enterprise:

> When Zarlino too would persuade me again of the simplicities which he writes, saying that among our modes one has a quiet nature, another deprecatory, that others are querulous, incited, lascivious, cheerful, somnolent, tranquil, infuriated, and others have yet different natures and characters, and, finally, that the modes as used today by musical practitioners have the same capacities as the ancient modes possessed, I would answer, persuaded by experience, which teaches us the contrary, that these are all tales contrived to confuse loggerheads. If our practice retains a minimal part of these faculties, it does not derive them from the mode or final note or the harmonic and arithmetic divisions but from the way contrapuntists make the parts progress in any of their modes according to what suits them best.[34]

A mode was picked, one suspects, more on the basis of the major-minor distinction expressed for the first time by Zarlino than on the grounds of any conventional assignment of ethos. The availability of certain harmonic

33. III, 10, in *The Art of Counterpoint*, trans. Guy A. Marco and Claude V. Palisca, pp. 21–22.

34. Galilei, *Il primo libro della prattica del contrapunto intorno all'uso delle consonanze*, Florence, MS Galilei I, 99v; Frieder Rempp ed., p. 71.

effects in a given mode or in the modes to which one could modulate from the central one must have played a big part in the choice. Zarlino reminds us that Horace instructs poets not to deal with comic matters in tragic verses; hence, he recommends, if the words denote harshness, hardness, cruelty, and bitterness, the harmony must be similarly hard and harsh.[35] For this purpose a composer should proceed by movements without the semitone, that is, by whole tone and major third, and allow the major sixth to be heard against the lowest part. In another place he notes that the major consonances, particularly in the low part of the texture—and this includes the third and its compounds—can also result in a harsh effect.[36]

Granted that in their enthusiasm for antiquity some of the early sixteenth-century writers fell into the trap of attributing to the plainchant modes ethical traits belonging to the Greek harmoniai, del Lago's and Nardo's confident assertion that composers chose the mode of their compositions according to the affection to be expressed is significant, because it attests to the attention given to matching the text with appropriate music.

Del Lago's strictures concerning the relationship between verbal and musical syntax applied to both prose and poetry. In verse, he admonished the composer to heed, in addition, meter, feet, number of syllables, and whether they are long or short. He should know how to scan it and locate the caesuras and *collisiones,* or elisions. He is told to observe the lengthening of certain syllables in the typical verse lines of Italian poetry: the settenari, ottonari, and endecasillabi. In lines of seven syllables the penultimate is held longer (*si tiene*), in those of eight the third and penultimate, in those of eleven the sixth and penultimate and sometimes the fourth in place of the sixth. The syllables that del Lago asks the composer to prolong in the musical setting are those stressed in reading, and they occur just before a caesura or the end of a line. His rules for their placement would surely have struck a connoisseur of the poetry of the time as oversimplifications, particularly with respect to the hendecasyllabic line, which allowed a variety of stresses. But if his guidelines simply alerted a beginning composer to the phenomenon of accent, they served their purpose. The composer is also cautioned to beware of "barbarisms," that is putting "a short accent on a long syllable" or the reverse:[37]

osseruerete li accenti	observe the grammatical
grammatici, i quali hanno	accents, which have

35. Zarlino, *Istitutioni* IV, 32, in *On the Modes,* trans. Vered Cohen, pp. 94–95.

36. Zarlino, *Istitutioni,* III, 57; Marco and Palisca trans., p. 177.

37. "Barbarism" was a term employed by the Roman grammarians to denote the mispronunciations heard in the speech of non-Romans—Gauls, Africans, etc. See "De barbarismo" in Servius' commentary on Donatus, in *Grammatici latini,* ed. H. Keil, IV, 443.

quantita temporale, cioe	temporal quantity, that is
tempo lungo et breue. Benche	long and short durations, although
sono pochi compositori, che	few composers
osseruano li accenti grammarici [sic]	observe the grammatical accents
nel comporre le notule sopra le	in composing notes over
parole (de indoctis loquor).[38]	words (de indoctis loquor).

Del Lago may have taken the ancient grammarians too literally. They were writing about a Latin diction that actually observed long and short syllables; in setting an Italian text, on the other hand, the longer notes would be set to stressed and not long syllables, and the shorter notes to those unstressed. Del Lago's instructions, despite a certain narrowness, nevertheless reflect a sensitivity to a number of parameters of language that had been neglected by polyphonic composers, particularly in their Latin settings.

Mei on Tonic Accent

It was commonplace in sixteenth-century writings on Italian poetry to speak, as del Lago did, of the quantitative values of syllables, particularly insofar as musical setting was concerned. But were there truly long and short syllables in Italian speech? And if so, what determined length? In their idolization of the classical, were del Lago, Zarlino, and others deceived into imputing quantity to Italian diction? Girolamo Mei examined the question of quantity in his unpublished treatise *Della compositura delle parole* of the early 1540's.[39]

Mei found the temporal and pitch qualities of Tuscan and Greek altogether different. Whereas in Greek and Latin poetry syllables are long or short, in Tuscan such distinctions are not observed. Instead groups of syllables, marked off by acute accents, can be compared in length to each other. Such a comparison often reveals a simple ratio between the two lengths. To be sure, differences of syllable length could be introduced through the kind of delivery practiced by the ancient musicians:

pronunciandosi esso, come fanno	pronouncing it, as the ancient
aperta testimonianzia i musici	musicians openly testify in their

38. Del Lago, *Breve introduttione,* pp. [40]–[41].

39. There are several copies of this treatise. I used that in Florence, Biblioteca Nazionale Centrale, MS Magl. VI.34. Other copies are: Florence, Biblioteca Riccardiana, MS 2598, fols. 149r–255v; Biblioteca Apostolica Vaticana, MS Vat. lat. 6275. Precise dating of this treatise has not been possible so far, but it is probably from the period when Mei was active in the Accademia de' Umidi and its successor academy, the Fiorentina, from 1540 until he left Florence in 1546. The work is not mentioned in Mei's letters to Vettori from France or Rome, which he began to write regularly in February 1546. See Palisca, *Girolamo Mei,* pp. 21–23.

antichi nella diuision' della	classification of the
uoce, in una maniera mezzana	voice, in a manner intermediate
trà il parlar' corrente e' il	between fluent speech and
Canto.[40]	song.

Mei refers here to the Aristoxenian classification of vocal pitch movement into continuous (speech), diastematic (song), and intermediate (poetic recitation).[41] His suggestion that one might adopt a manner of delivery that observes short and long values is prophetic, because it is precisely this that Jacopo Peri proposed to do in his recitative. However, as normally spoken, Tuscan is pronounced with a uniform "continuity and speed of delivery" (*continouanza e' prestezza di corso*), in which each syllable receives approximately the same durational value.

The pitch patterns of Tuscan speech arise from the acute and grave qualities of syllables in individual words. Most words have a single acute accent, but some have more than one or none, so that a word itself may be mostly acute or mostly grave or some of both. This is an important concept in Mei's theory of Tuscan prose and poetry.

Inflection and fluctuation of pitch are natural functions of the speech mechanism:

Imperoche l'acuteza in ciascuna	For height of pitch in each
parola uien generata dal colmo	word is generated by the climax
dell'impeto di quel' fiato, che	of the impulse of the breath that
in una sola intension' uiene	is emitted in a single thrust
spinto fuora nel pronunziar'	when pronouncing
ciascuna di quelle. Il quale	a word. With
con la forza della sua per dir	the force of its—shall we say—
così uniteza, e' uelocità	integrity and velocity together
insieme, fà finalmente quasi	it finally almost stabs
ferirne il sensorio di chi può	the sense of hearing of whoever
udire più in certo modo in un	can hear it in a certain way in one
punto solo. Onde	place only. Consequently
se ne sente il colpo suo somma-	the blow is felt most
mente penetrante, e per opposito	penetratingly and, on the contrary,
non essendo ancor' la forza sua	when its force has not yet
aggiunta al suo colmo, ò uero	reached its climax, or
hauendo trapassatolo, non essendo	having passed it, the breath
il fiato per ciò così unito, ne	is not so united or
si ueloce, e così non potendo il	speedy and thus unable
uigor suo far ferirne il colpo	to strike the sense of hearing

40. Mei, *Della compositura delle parole,* fols. 60v–61r.

41. The only surviving Greek source for the intermediate class is Aristides Quintilianus *De musica* 1.4.

in un luogo, e in certo modo | in a single place and point,
punto solo, ne uien' parimente | as it were. Then the tone of the voice
anche il tuon' della uoce pro- | too becomes less high and less
dotto men acuto, e men' pene- | penetrating,
trante; per il che ne è questo | and for this reason this [tone]
in comparazion' del sommamente | in comparison to that supremely
acuto, quasi, che lo spirito | acute—almost as if the breath
per il suo peso non possa | because of its weight could not
spingerse con pari uelocità, | propel itself with equal speed—
stato chiamato graue. la silla- | is called grave. Therefore the
ba adunque di che le parole son' | syllables of which words
composte, non essendo tutte di | are made up, not being all of
pari grauità, e d'acuteza, non | equivalent low or high pitch,
sono medesimamente ancora di | accordingly are not of equivalent
pari, e simiglianti uirtù: ma | and similar power, but,
secondo che le si trouono in | depending on their location,
esso, ò acute, ò, graue; | whether acute or grave,
hanno seco più, ò meno di quasi | have either more or less force
forza, e uiuacità. E' delle | and liveliness. And of the
parole alcune son' (come è stato | words some (as was stated)
detto) di sillabe tutte acute, | have all acute syllables,
ò tutte graui, ò di parte | or all grave, or partly
acute, e' parte graui.[42] | acute and partly grave.

Thus the force with which the breath is expelled in pronouncing an individual syllable determines whether its pitch is acute or grave. Within a word breath pressure normally reaches a climax where the acute or tonic accent falls, in relation to which the other syllables are grave. This alternation of grave and acute is regularized in poetry. In a line of eleven syllables there is an acute accent on the tenth syllable and in addition either on the fourth or sixth, as in the lines:

Di vaga *fe*ra la vestigia *spar*se (fol. 13r)

or

In cor', cui d'ogni *col*pa scarco *tro*va (fol. 29v)

The final, eleventh syllable receives a grave accent. The other syllables may be either acute or grave. In a seven-syllable line acute accents fall usually on the third and sixth syllables. It is this pattern of grave and acute accents that gives rise to rhythm in Tuscan, a opposed to the rhythm of long and short syllables characteristic of ancient Greek and classical Latin poetry. Thus a line of seven syllables, divided by acute accents on the third and sixth into two similar groups of acute (a) and grave (g) accents—gga / gga—

42. *Della compositura*, fols. 62v–63r.

produces a ratio of 3:3, a proportion of equality, as in the phrase "L'amo*ro*so pen*sie*ro." Or the proportion may be multiple, as in the line "L'immagi*nar' fallace,"* which yields a ratio of 4:2 (ggga / ga). A sesquialter ratio is illustrated in "Di vaga *fe*ra le vestigia *spar*se"— (ggga / ggggga), or 4:6 = 2:3.[43] Because vocal pitch variations are a natural product of the physiology of the human voice under different degrees of stress and relaxation, which cause the vocal mechanism to expel the breath with greater or lesser vigor, producing more frequent or rarer vibrations, Mei was led to develop a theory of natural language based on these fluctuations. In the treatise on prose he argued:

Poiche adunque nel' parlar' si senton' manifestamente e principalmente l'acutezza e grauità della uoce, sue proprie differenze, le quali hanno per lo quasi fonte diuersa qualità di mouimento, di necessità, fà di mestiere che il sensorio, che percosso le dee sentire secondo la uirtù, onde esse hanno origine, quando egli le sente, ne rappresenti alla potenzia, che naturalmente n'è giudice, concetto tutto simigliante. L'acutezza adunque essendo (come apertamente dimosstrono i musici, e' come poco sopra incidentemente s'è detto) generata dalla potenza e uelocita del mouimento, necessariamente non può hauer' uirtù senon' di exprimere e' far' apparir' qualità d'effetto simile e' respondente alla natura di quello, e' interamente diuersa dalla grauità, la cui quasi madre è la lentezza e tardità di lui, e perciò conseguentemente quanto più l'una di queste due uien' soperchiando l'altra nell'udirsi tanto maggiormente è necessario,	Since, therefore, in speech one hears prominently and principally the height and lowness of the voice—its proper differences, which have as their origin diverse qualities of movement— it is necessary that the sense organ, when struck, must hear them according to those qualities in which they originate and which represent concepts altogether resembling these to the faculty that is their natural judge. Height of pitch, therefore, being generated by the force and speed of motion (as musicians visibly demonstrate and as was mentioned in passing a little while ago), of necessity cannot have the power to express and to make felt but qualities of affection similar and corresponding to the nature of that [motion] and entirely different from low pitch, the mother of which is as it were slowness and sluggishness. Consequently as much as one of these [pitch levels] surpasses the other in the sensation of hearing, so much more, of necessity,

43. Mei, *Trattato del verso toscano,* Biblioteca Riccardiana, MS 2597, fols. 52r ff. See the more detailed discussion of this theory in Barbara Russano Hanning, *Of Poetry and Music's Power: Humanism and the Creation of Opera* (Ann Arbor, 1980), pp. 31 ff.

che ui si rappresenti più la	will the power of one be represented
uirtù dell'una, che dell'altra;	than that of the other.
e che là doue le si senton' del	And where one hears a parity
pari n'apparisca mezzane e	[of high and low], an intermediate
temperata disposizione, con cio	and moderate disposition will be
sia che ciascuna simiglianza,	felt, because every resemblance,
quasi destando naturalmente	almost stirring naturally
passioni simili a se, muoua	passions similar to itself, moves
nell'obietto nato al riceuergli	in the object born to receive it
proporzionatamente alla sua uir-	in proportion to its force always
tù sempre affetti simiglianti.[44]	affections that correspond.

Mei here clarified two points that are obscure in the poetic theory of the Renaissance. It was often stated that poetry was a kind of harmony composed of low, high, and intermediate pitches. This was obviously true of Greek and classical Latin poetry, because of the language's grave, acute, and circumflex accents. Mei showed that in Tuscan as well as Greek pitch differences were essential to the construction of a line, even if this factor operated differently in the two languages.

Mei was not alone in his assessment of the quantitative and tonic characteristics of Italian poetry. Vincenzo Maggi in his annotations of Aristotle's *Poetics* considers whether there are poetic feet in the vernacular. This question emerges from his discussion of the passage in Aristotle's *Poetics* (1.4.1447a) in which the philosopher first enumerates the media of poetic imitation, namely, rhythm, language, and harmony. Maggi, in an expansive annotation, attempts to define each of these means. Harmony, he shows, can mean a number of different things, among them the harmony of several voices singing together. He points out that by "harmony" Aristotle did not mean this kind of harmony, in which "many voices oppose each other at once," or in which "low and high voices follow each other in a certain order."[45] Rather, Maggi believed, it is a harmony of short and long syllables:

Nam cùm in carminibus syllabae	For, when in poems syllables are
breues, & longae sint, longae	short and long, the long ones are
quidem tardè, breues uerò	performed slowly, the short ones,
uelociter proferuntur. uelox autem	however, rapidly. Quick motion
motus (ex Boethi sententia libro	(according to the opinion of Boethius

---

44. Mei, *Della compositura*, fols. 61v–62r.

45. Vincenzo Maggi and Bartolomeo Lombardi, *In Aristotelis Librum de poetica communes explanationes* (Venice, 1550), pp. 46–47: "Verum alia est harmonia, quae cùm uoces plures simul refranguntur [recte?: refragantur], efficitur: & haec apertior & harmoniae nomine digna magis uidetur. Alia uerò est, cum graues & acutae uoces ordine se certo consequuntur." In this joint work the *explanationes* which follow the sections (*particulae*) of the text, in the edition and translation of Pazzi, are by Maggi and Lombardi, and the *annotationes* are by Maggi alone.

Musices primo cap. tertio) acutum, tardus uerò grauem efficit sonum. Cùm haec uocum uarietas rectè sit in carminibus ordinata (nam in carmine, rhythmi ratione sequitur harmonia: carminis autem rhythmus certa lege determinatus est) erit ergo & lege carminum harmonia.[46]

in the first book on music, chapter 3) produces a high sound, whereas slow motion produces a low one. When this variety of vocal sounds is properly arranged in poems (for in a poem the rule of rhythm results from harmony; while the rhythm of poetry is determined by a certain law), then the harmony of poems will also [be arranged] by law.

Harmony, in this sense, is a function of rhythm and not of pitch. If, as Aristotle held, harmony in poetry depends on the proportionate arrangement of feet, how could vernacular poetry, which does not observe feet, possess harmony?

Respondeo, pedes quidem ea non habere, quales graecorum, ac latinorum carminum sunt. accentum tamen, tum grauem tum acutum pedibus proportione respondere. nam in pangendis italicis carminibus, praescripta syllabarum quantitate, qualita- teque, simul in oratione iunc- tarum uti necesse est: sicut qui hac de re scripsere, diligentius ostendunt. in scandendis enim carminibus, accentu acuto & graui, loco pedum utimur: cuius sententiae Georgium Trissi- num uirum eruditissimum auctorem fuisse intellexi.[47]

I reply, it certainly does not have feet like those of the Greek and Latin poems. To the proportion of feet, however, corresponds the accent, whether grave or acute. For in writing Italian poems, it is necessary to use a prescribed quantity and quality of syllables, joined together in speech. So declare those who write with care about this matter. In scanning poems, then, we use the acute and grave accent in place of feet. I understood that this was the opinion of Giorgio Trissino, a most learned author.

Benedetto Varchi, writing in *L'Hercolano* in 1570, was also skeptical of the quantitative element in Italian diction:

Il numero, che si ritroua ne' versi, e nelle prose parimente è quello de' Musici, o vero cantori, i quali

The rhythm that is found in verses and in prose also is that of the musicians or singers, who

46. Ibid., p. 47.
47. Giovanni Giorgio Trissino, in his *La Poetica* (Vicenza, 1529; facs. ed., Munich, 1969), fol. xiv r, is less decisive on this point: "sicome i Latini, et i Greci governano i loro poemi per i tempi, noi, come vederemo, sji governiamo per li toni; benche chiunque vorra considerare la lunghezza, e brevità di alcune syllabe, così gravi, come acute, trarà molta utilità di tal cosa, e darà molto ornamento a li suoi poemi."

non tengono conto nè di quantità	do not take into account either the
di sillabe, nè di nouero, o	quantity of syllables, or the number
qualità, o ordine di piedi, e meno	or quality or order of feet, or even
di cesure; ma hora abbreuiando le	of caesuras. But sometimes abbre-
sillabe lunghe, e hora allungando	viating long syllables, at other times
le breui, secondo le leggi, e l'arti-	lengthening the short, according to the
fizio della scienza loro, compongono,	rules and the science of their art,
e cantano con incredibile diletto	they compose and sing with incredible
di sè stessi, e degli ascoltanti,	delight to themselves and to listeners
che non habbiano gli orecchij à	who do not need their ears repaired
rimpedulare, le messe, i motetti, le	the masses, motets, songs, madrigals,
canzoni, i madriali, e l'altre	and other compositions.
composizioni loro.[48]	

The second important clarification contributed by Mei was to explain how the musical voice or instrument could touch, as Capriano was later to put it, "every note of the keyboard of the soul."[49] The very simile of the fingerboard is present in Mei's discussion of the natural expressiveness of the voice:

Nasce questa forza maggior' e'	This major and minor force of
dello spirito dalla uirtù	the spirit is born of the natural
natural' de musicali e' altri	power of musical and other
strumenti che u'interuengono.	instruments that are involved.
i quali nello spignier lo fuora	These in pressing the spirit out
lo uiolentano hor più e' hor'	now with more, now with less
meno, secondo l'arbitrio e'	violence, according to the choice
disegno della uolontà, che	and design of the will that
comanda loro. quasi toccando i	commands them, as if touching
tasti naturali delle corde, o'	natural frets of the strings, or
aprendo i pertugi del flauto.[50]	opening the fingerholes of a flute.

Through the spirit—that is, breath—the musician applies more or less pressure upon the vocal mechanism or instrument, producing high or low tones. Through this natural medium he not only controls the sound of the instrument but, through the vibrating air that eventually reaches the spirit of the listener and plays on his sensibilities, touches the keys, as it were, of the listener's consciousness.[51] In this way the verbal message of the poet is

48. Benedetto Varchi, *L'Hercolano Dialogo . . . nel qual si ragiona generalmente delle lingue, & in particolare della Toscana e della Fiorentina* (Florence, 1570), p. 270.

49. See ch. 13 below.

50. *Del verso toscano*, fol. 3v.

51. The language that Mei uses to describe the mechanics of transmission of energy from the sounding instrument to the hearing is markedly Aristotelian, as Hanning has shown in *Of Poetry*, p. 33, 206, n. 84. Compare Mei's *Del verso toscano*, fol. 2r–v and Aristotle *De anima* 420a.

reinforced by a wordless, direct communication of emotion. Unlike words, which must first penetrate the mind, this message goes directly from the breath of the speaker or singer to the ear, which translates the various rates of motion into higher and lower sounds. But the moving air also affects the spirit directly.[52]

Pietro Bembo

Mei's theory of tonic accent and of the expressivity of pitch levels parallels in some ways Pietro Bembo's theory of gravity and pleasingness set forth in his *Prose della volgar lingua* (1525). There Bembo urged a new sensitivity to the sonic values of poetry, based on an awareness that grew out of his study of Petrarch's earlier drafts of certain poems in the *Canzoniere*. Most often Petrarch's revisions, Bembo discovered, did not change the thought or image as much as the sound of a line. For example, the opening of the first sonnet appears in the published versions as:

Voi, ch'ascoltate in rime sparse il suono
Di quei sospiri ond'io nudriva 'l core

In the draft the second line read: "Di quei sospir, de' quai nutriva il core." Bembo reasoned that the poet first changed "Di quei," because it deprived the following "de' quai" of grace, to "Di ch'io"; at a later stage he restored "Di quei" and chose "ond'io," and "nudriva" for their rounder, more sonorous ring; and "sospiri" was more complete and sweeter than "sospir."[53]

Words differ in their sonic qualities: some are fluent (*sciolti*) and faint (*languide*), others dense (*dense*) and tight (*riserrate*); some are plump (*pingui*), others dry (*aride*), some tender (*morbide*), others rough (*ruvide*); some are sluggish (*tarde*), others swift (*ratte*), and so on. Combinations of words can give a rising effect, such as "Voi ch'ascoltate"; others, such as, "Voi ch'in rime ascolate," have a falling cadence.

Two general qualities give a particular character to a poem or part thereof: gravity (*gravità*) and pleasingness (*piacevolezza*). The category of gravity includes the qualities of modesty, dignity, majesty, magnificence, and grandeur; while pleasingness includes grace, sweetness, charm, smoothness, playfulness, and wit. The rhythm, rhyme, number of syllables, accents, combinations of long and short syllables, the feeling of particular vowels and consonants, as well as the sonorous qualities described above all affect

---

52. There is an echo here of Ficino's *spiritus* theory, developed in his *De triplici vita* (Florence, 1489). See D. P. Walker, "Ficino's Spiritus and Music," *Annales musicologiques* 1 (1953):131–50, or *Spiritual and Demonic Magic from Ficino to Campanella* (London, 1958), pp. 3–11. Mei developed this theory further in his musical writings of the 1570's and 1580's.

53. Bembo, *Prose della volgar lingua,* ed. Mario Marti (Padua, 1967), II, 57.

the gravity and pleasingness of a line of poetry or a sentence of prose.[54] Clearly Bembo's categories have a greater range than those of Mei, although they rely no less on a belief in the inherent expressiveness of sonic linguistic elements.

In 1969 Dean T. Mace put forth the theory that Bembo's way of reading Petrarch started a wave of madrigal writing and stimulated a new manner of setting Petrarch's and his followers' poems to music.[55] He suggested that it replaced the conventional manner of setting verse common in the frottola, ode, and canzona, in which the poem's sound, measure, rhythm, and rhyme were reflected in the music's form rather than in its emotional message. The texture of accompanied melody in these songs, Mace observed, was inadequate to representing the complex web of qualities that Bembo recognized in Petrarchan poetry. Poets and patrons were led to seek out northern composers proficient in the imitative polyphonic idiom, which afforded a greater variety of techniques and sonorous possibilities.

Mace's theory is attractive and plausible, but to document a relationship between Bembo's reading of Petrarch and the earliest polyphonic madrigals is difficult. Although a personal connection between Bembo and Willaert through Venetian cultural circles is probable, such a connection between Bembo and other pioneers of the madrigal, such as the Florentine Bernardo Pisano, is less so.[56] Even without Bembo's guidance musicians could sense the sonic qualities of Petrarch's verse and recognize that its subject matter and tone demanded a more serious and learned approach and a richer technical vocabulary than the frottola composers cared to lavish on lighter verse.

Zarlino, for example, was fully aware of the care poets took to make the sounds of their verses awaken fitting images and feelings. Vergil exemplified, for Zarlino, this attention to musical values. In a chapter praising music's contribution to other disciplines, he says of Vergil:

> He adapts the sonority of the verse with such art that it truly seems that the sound of the words places before the eyes those things of which he speaks, so that where he speaks of love, one sees that he artfully chose smooth, sweet, pleasing sounds supremely welcome to the hearing. Where he needed to speak of warlike subjects, such as describing a naval encounter, a shipwreck, or similar

54. Ibid., II, 63ff.
55. "Pietro Bembo and the Literary Origins of the Italian Madrigal," *The Musical Quarterly* 55 (1969):65–86.
56. For a consideration of the the rivalry of Florence and Venice in the rise of the madrigal, see James Haar, "The Early Madrigal: A Re-appraisal of its Sources and its Character," in *Music in Medieval and Early Modern Europe: Patronage, Sources, and Texts,* ed. Iain Fenlon (Cambridge, 1981), pp. 163–92. See also Howard Mayer Brown, "Words and Music: Willaert, the Chanson and the Madrigal About 1540," in Villa I Tatti, *Florence and Venice: Comparisons and Relations* 2: Cinquecento (Florence, 1980), pp. 217–266.

things, where spilling of blood is involved, ire, disdain, unpleasantness, and every hateful thing, he chose hard, harsh, and displeasing words that terrify the listener.[57]

There is no better example of the exploitation of this richer palette than the madrigal introduced into the discussion by Mace, Willaert's setting of Petrarch's "Aspro core e selvaggio" from *Musica nova* (1559, but probably composed before 1540).[58] (See Figure 12.4.) Mace pointed to the succession of six-three chords and the gravity of movement for the harsh first line as against the simulated triple rhythm and consonant harmony of the setting of the second line, "an exact musical equivalent of the tonal and rhythmic qualities of these verses":[59]

Aspro core e selvaggio, e cruda voglia
In dolce, humile, angelica figura

There are other significant musical devices in this madrigal besides those identified by Mace that parallel the *grave-piacevole* verbal sonorities. Vincenzo Galilei pointed to one of them in his *Fronimo* of 1568. There he speaks of the rule that requires an imperfect consonance to go to the nearest perfect consonance. This may be broken, he says:

> in imitating the words, as the famous Adriano did (among other composers) in the beginning of that learned music he composed for six voices on the sonnet of Petrarch which begins *Aspro core, e seluaggio, & cruda voglia.* There several times, in order to express the subject with grace, he passes not only from a major sixth to a fifth, but from a major third to another by conjunct movement. I shall save for another time to demonstrate the excellence of this musical seasoning.[60]

---

57. Zarlino *Istitutioni harmoniche*, I, 2, p. 5.

58. An early date for this collection was suggested by Armen Carapetyan in "The *Musica Nova* of Adrian Willaert," *Journal of Renaissance and Baroque Music* 1 (1946):200–21. A quantity of additional evidence has strengthened the case since then. See Edward Lowinsky, "A Treatise on Text Underlay by a German Disciple of Francisco de Salinas," in *Festschrift Heinrich Besseler* (Leipzig, 1961), pp. 231–51, for a survey of the literature, to which should be added Helga Meier's introduction to *Fünf Madrigale venezianischer Komponisten um Adrian Willaert,* Das Chorwerk, 105 (Wolfenbüttel, 1969), pp. iii–vi; and Anthony Newcomb, "Editions of Willaert's *Musica Nova:* New Evidence, New Speculations," *Journal of the American Musicological Society* 26 (1973):132–45.

59. Mace, "Pietro Bembo," p. 78.

60. Vincenzo Galilei, *Fronimo dialogo, nel quale si contengono le vere, et necessarie regole del intavolare la musica nel liuto* (Venice, 1568), p. 13: "Patisce secondariamente eccettione ne l'imitatione delle parole, come bene lo manifestò fra gl'altri eccelenti musici in piu luoghi il famoso Adriano, & particolarmente nel principio di quella sua dotta Canzone, che gia compose à sei voci, qual comincia. Aspro core, & seluaggio & cruda voglia, doue passa piu volte, (per esprimere con gratia tal concetto,) non solo dalla Sesta maggiore alla Quinta ma da vna Terza maggior à l'altra col mouimento congiunto, & piacendoui serverò à vn'altra volta il mostrarui

Figure 12.4.

Adrian Willaert, Madrigal: "Aspro core e selvaggio e cruda voglia," prima parte

Figure 12.4. *Continued*

Figure 12.4. *Continued*

Figure 12.4. *Continued*

Figure 12.4. *Continued*

The major sixth to fifth progression of which Galilei speaks is heard four times in the setting of the first line: mm. 3, 5, alto-bass, and mm. 8, 10, canto-tenor. Parallel major thirds occur in mm. 2–3, quinto-bass; and mm. 7–8, sesto-tenor. Zarlino explicitly prohibited parallel major thirds because of the cross relation that they engender: "They produce a bitterness in their

---

maggiormente l'eccelentia di questo condimento della musica." This statement remains intact, if slightly reworded, in the 1584 ed., pp. 13–14, but the end is altered to read "l'eccellenza di questo condimento della Musica d'hoggi, doue concorrono, & venghano cantate in vn'istesso tempo tante arie insieme."

progression, because in the movement of the parts there is missing the interval of the large semitone, in which all the good of music resides. Without this interval every progression of harmony is hard, bitter, and nearly dissonant."[61]

Other devices Willaert used to portray the "hard heart" and to match the harsh sound of the triple consonants of "aspro" are major thirds and their compounds in the harmony and major seconds and major thirds in melodic progressions. As Zarlino said in the passage quoted above, when the semitone is absent in a movement from one interval to the next, the effect is bitter. Indeed, the semitone occurs melodically in the first ten measures only four times. The dominant linear motion consists of major seconds and major thirds. Zarlino wrote of the desirability of these intervals for expressions of harshness and bitterness: "When a composer wishes to express harshness, bitterness, and similar things, he will do best to arrange the parts of the composition so that they proceed with movements that are without the semitone, such as those of the whole tone and ditone."[62] He also advised the use of the interval of the major sixth, which is present in every measure of this passage except mm. 1 and 6: "He should allow the major sixth and major thirteenth, which by nature are somewhat harsh, to be heard above the lowest note of the concentus."[63] Thus in setting the first line Willaert more than matched the effect Petrarch attained with the hard sounding clusters *spr, lv, cr,* and *gl,* and the closed *o* sounds.

The poem's second line: "In dolc'humile angelica figura," by contrast, has a lilting rhythm, liquid consonants, sonorous vowels, and this, of course, to create the impression of the sweet angelic face and form. In the poem the two lines are linked by the rhetorical figure of antithesis. The composer surpassed this by linking them also by a common melodic thread: the first line's E-D-C-E-D becomes D-C-E-D, and its approximate transposition B♭-A-G-B♭-A. By flatting the B every time it occurs in the lower parts, Willaert manages motion by semitone and minor third, which has a sweet, yet sorrowful, effect, as Zarlino explains in the continuation of the passage quoted above: "But when a composer wishes to express effects of grief and sorrow, he should (observing the rules given) use movements which proceed through the semitone, the semiditone, and similar intervals, often using minor sixths or minor thirteenths above the lowest note of the composition, these being by nature sweet and soft, especially when combined in the right way and with discretion and judgment."[64] As major thirds and sixths were

61. Zarlino, *Le Istitutioni harmoniche,* 1558, III, 29; Marco and Palisca trans., p. 62.
62. Zarlino, *Istitutioni,* IV, 32; Cohen trans., p. 95.
63. *Istitutioni,* IV, 32; Cohen trans., p. 95.
64. *Istitutioni,* IV, 32; Cohen trans., p. 95.

prominent before, now minor thirds and sixths are. In the second statement of the second line, mm. 16–21, the canto adopts the flatted version of the melody, affording the sweetening semitone and minor third motion. An even more striking example of antithesis, utilizing similar harmonic resources, is in the seconda parte at m. 106, where "duro cor" is contrasted with "lagrimando."

The textual rhythm, as Mace has observed, is another important factor in the *dolcezza* of the second line. Bembo does not provide any system for scanning. Using Mei's method we may arrive at the following:

Aspro core e sel*v*aggio, e cruda *v*oglia
In dolce, *h*umile, angelica figura

The first line has two acute accents, whereas the second line has two acute accents in the first hemistich alone and another on the penultimate of the line, making it less grave in Mei's sense. The composer made the second line's rhythm less grave by another means. He scanned the line as starting with three iambic feet:

$$\overset{\smile}{\text{In}} \ \overset{-}{\text{dolce,}} \ \overset{-}{\underset{\smile}{\text{humile,}}} \ \overset{-\smile\smile}{\underset{\smile}{\text{angelica}}} \ \overset{\smile-}{\text{figura}}$$

This gave him a triple rhythm in the upper parts, while the bass continued with the *alla breve* duple measure.

There is another expressive resource that received consideration in the sixteenth century which also fits into the grave-piacevole dichotomy: the leaps of the bass or lowest part. Galilei has a disquisition on this in the *Dialogo* of 1581. The bass, Galilei notes (through the interlocutor Bardi), is the part that gives profile and countenance to a multipart composition— "da l'aria (nel cantare in consonanza) alla cantilena."[65] When it leaps up a fifth or down a fourth it gives a sad and subdued effect, whereas when the bass leaps up a fourth or down a fifth, the feeling is happy, excited, virile and natural.

Willaert must have consciously exploited these effects in the madrigal we have been considering. Throughout the first two lines the bass or lowest voice moves consistently by upward leaps of the fifth and downward leaps of the fourth. The beginning of the seconda parte, on the other hand, exhibits frequent leaps of the fourth up and the fifth down, making it more piacevole.

Another technique used by Willaert may not have been inspired by the example of antiquity but it receives a humanistic explanation in Galilei's *Discorso intorno all'uso delle dissonanze*. Here Galilei speaks of the ancient

---

65. *Dialogo*, p. 76.

Greek concept of harmony as an agreement of successive rather than simultaneous events. He suggests that to give a composition a hard and harsh
sound, one may use progressions that are lacking in harmony in this Greek
sense—nonharmonic or poor relations, "senz'Harmonia" or "male rela-
tioni."[66] Willaert uses this effect for the beginning of the last line: "Nè si
freddo voler." The nonharmonic relation between the D major chord and
the following F major chord produces the cross relation, as we call it,
between the upper F♯ and the lower F natural.[67]

This madrigal, then, is a perfect example of "l'imitatione delle parole."
At least so Galilei seemed to believe in 1568. But later he was to turn against
this kind of imitation. In a passage in the *Dialogo* of 1581 that has been
quoted frequently he deplored the word-painting generally practiced in the
madrigal. He introduces the discussion with an affirmation of the importance of what he is about to say: "I come, finally, to treat, as I promised,
the most important and principal part there is in music, and this is the
imitation of the ideas [*concetti*] that are drawn from the words."[68] Galilei's
choice of words is judicious. It is not the words themselves that should be
imitated but the *concetti* behind them.[69] What are these *concetti*? Agnolo Segni
says of them: "Our concetti also are imitations of things outside us; and
nature is that which forms them in the mind [*anima*], which knows how
to imitate them with the voice and the various passions of the soul, not
only in men but in brute beasts also. Names, words, and all discourse
certainly imitates things and concetti."[70] In another place he says that they
are what Aristotle called *dianoias*, hence thoughts, notions.[71] Giulio Cortese
also essayed a definition in *Avertimenti nel poetare* [1591]: "A *concetto* is that
meditation which the spirit makes on some object offered to it about which
it has to write." No one should confuse the subject with the concetto, he
cautions, because they differ, the subject being that about which one speaks,
whereas the concetto is that which the spirit contemplates putting into
words, as, for example, arms, love, beauty, frenzy, and others similar to
them.[72]

The concept bears a close resemblance to Kant's *Vorstellung*, for which

66. *Discorso intorno all'uso delle dissonanze*, Rempp ed., pp. 160–61.

67. See also the example composed by Galilei, transcribed in Palisca, "The 'Camerata
fiorentina': A Reappraisal," *Studi musicali* 1 (1972):229–30.

68. *Dialogo*, p. 88. The section is in Strunk, *Source Readings*, pp. 315–17.

69. Dean Mace acutely observed this in his contribution to the panel "Humanism and Music"
at the international congress in Berkeley, 1977. See the *Report of the Twelfth Congress, Berkeley
1977*, ed. Daniel Heartz and Bonnie Wade (Kassel, 1981), pp. 892–93.

70. *Lezioni intorno alla poesia* [1573], in *Trattati di poetica e retorica del cinquecento*, ed. Bernard
Weinberg (Bari, 1970–74), II, 37.

71. Ibid., II, 34.

72. *Avertimenti nel poetare*, in *Trattati*, ed. Weinberg, IV, 179.

the English "representation" is sometimes used. I have usually rendered it "idea" and occasionally "subject." Galilei understood the term in the manner of Segni and Cortese, and he was sure that it was the concetto and not the word that should be imitated. Contrapuntists are confident, he says, that they have adequately imitated the ideas (*concetti dell'animo*) and the words (*imitato le parole*) of a poem such as the line "Aspro core e selvaggio, e cruda voglia" if "they have made the parts sing many sevenths, fourths, seconds, and major sixths and caused by this means a coarse, bitter, and little pleasing sound."[73]

Willaert's setting of this line has fourths and major sixths but not a single second or seventh; so Galilei either did not recall it accurately or he had in mind another setting.[74] He goes on to criticize those who break into unseemly fast notes at words meaning "to flee" or "to fly," or have the singers suddenly halt at words meaning "to disappear," "to faint," or "to die." To symbolize "alone" composers reduce the music to one part, and for the word "two" or "together," they reduce it to two parts, or they resort to black notes for "dark" and white notes for "light." They imitate drums, trumpets, and other sounds unsuited to voices. The entire battery of so-called madrigalisms is here thrown overboard.

Galilei's about-face was a reaction to his contacts with Mei, whose theory of natural language he now proceeded to expound. Every animal is given a voice as a natural means to communicate with others of its species. The composer should study the qualities of voice—pitch, volume, accents, rapidity, and gestures— used by different categories of people to speak to one another—children, servants, princes, girls, matrons. This is what the ancients did when they sang a poem, choosing a tonos, accents, quantity and quality of sound, and rhythm appropriate to the action and person.

Galilei objects also to the way contrapuntists set verses, whether rhymed or blank verse (*sciolti*), as if they were prose: "Thus they are deprived of their natural faculty and consequently lose their power to operate on the listener those effects that by their nature they could work if simply read and delivered as the qualities of the verses and the poem demand."[75] Galilei wanted composers not only to imitate the essence of the concetto rather than simply its words but to imitate also the sound qualities of the spoken word.

Polyphony, then, although it afforded new resources for the "imitation

73. *Dialogo,* p. 88.

74. Among other settings published before 1581 are those by Girolamo Parabosco (1546), Jehan Gero (1549), Giaches de Wert (1558), and Giachet Berchem (1561). Wert's, which may be seen in his *Opera omnia,* I, 33, may be eliminated as a candidate; although there are parallel fourths and sixths for the first line, there are no seconds or sevenths.

75. *Dialogo,* p. 90.

of the words," also cut the listener off from the poet's form of utterance, the poem's structure, rhymes, rhythms, accents, and intonation, all of which must be rearranged in distributing the words to the various parts.

To return now to Bembo, with whom this discussion began: his ideas were not forgotten later in the century, even if Mei failed to pay his respects to him. Cesare Crispolti in his *Lezione del sonetto* (c. 1592) refers to him by name and also applies to a number of sonnets of Petrarch the distinction grave-piacevole. Interestingly, he ties the poet's care in choosing sonorous values to Aristotle's *Rhetoric* and to the notion of natural language: "Since words conform to the imitation of ideas [*concetti*], as Aristotle teaches in the third of the *Rhetoric,* they must imitate their lowness and loftiness. Since nature gave us speech for no other purpose than to signify with it the ideas [*concetti*] of our mind, and if art discovered verse for this same purpose, it is clear that ideas are the end and consequently the form of discourse [*orazione*] and words and composition, the material and the instrument."[76]

Crispolti substantiates Bembo's theory concerning the effect of vowel and consonant combinations with new evidence. An abundance of vowels falls pleasingly and sweetly on the ears, as in *aura, auro, aureo, fausto, tesauro,* and he illustrates this with Petrarch's stanza that begins: "Erano i capei d'oro l'aura sparsi."[77] Piacevolezza is also enhanced by liquid letters like *l, r, n,* and *m,* as in Vergil's line "Quaecunque lacus late liquidos,"[78] or Petrarch's "E le fere e gl'augei lagnarsi, e l'acque."[79]

Poetic theory in the sixteenth century clarified what share sonic as opposed to discursive components of the art could claim in moving the listener or reader. Collaterally it also explained how the nondiscursive art of music could have even greater power to move the passions. Music had at its disposal several of the elements poetic theorists identified as capable of contributing to this effect, namely, harmony, rhythm, vocal timbre, and structure. These were seen as "instruments" for the imitation of "actions," understood in a broad sense to include affective experience and moral character. Although the possibility of this kind of imitation by instrumental music without any verbal accompaniment was acknowledged, poetic theorists were naturally more concerned with a verbal message as a context for emotion. Among musical writers this led to the concept of "the imitation of the word"—the word as conveyor of already encapsuled action. A word captures not only a meaning addressed to the intellect but also a tone of

76. In *Trattati,* ed. Weinberg, IV, 201.
77. *Canzoniere,* XC.
78. *Aeneid* 4.526.
79. *Canzoniere,* CLXXVI, 10; Crispolti, in *Trattati,* ed. Weinberg, IV, 202–03. Concerning *gravità* he refers the reader to Aristotle *Rhetoric* 3.6, Vincenzo Menni, *Regole della thoscana lingua* (Perugia, 1568), and Bembo's *Prose.*

voice which itself is subject to imitation. Someone could have turned the famous phrase around and said that a word can be "l'imitazione della musica," and Segni implied as much when he suggested that language, harmony, and dance are imitations of each other. So music imitates the musical imitation already present in the word. This is one of the important insights that Bembo and his followers contributed.

Music, the *poetici* tell us also, adds to the delight that must be felt if the message is to be noticed. This function was obvious to everyone and less in need of theoretical justification. Francesco Bonciani in a lecture to the Accademia degli Alterati in 1578 on the more narrow question of the "prosopopea," or fantastic poem, summed up well the place that this sugar coating had in the poet's armory: "Nature gave man of all animals speech so that we may make known to others our varied and diverse ideas and objects of our mind (*concetti dell'animo*) and also to persuade and move other souls to our passions. This is best accomplished if besides arguments and reasons speech contains ornaments and artful manners that render it delightful to listen to with attention."[80] The musical components of poetry are among those ornaments that, as providers of delight, draw and retain the attention of the listener. And the musical setting, it is evident, enhances that delight and acts almost as a lubricant and propellant for both the concetti themselves and the ornaments of speech.

---

80. *Lezione della prosopopea* (1578), in *Trattati*, ed. Weinberg, III, 237.

THIRTEEN

The Poetics of Music

 t was often stated in the Renaissance that in ancient Greece there was an intimate union between poetry and music— that, indeed, the poet and musician-composer were one person.[1] Zarlino, for one, asserted that "The musician was not separate from the poet, nor the poet from the musician, for poets in those times being expert in music and musicians in poetry (as Strabo has it), the one and the other were called by these two names, musician and poet. This is evident from what Plutarch says."[2] After the decline of the ancient world this union of poetry and music dissolved, and the European composer at the beginning of the Renaissance typically was setting either a traditional text or one written by someone else. But this was not universal, and Italy remained a refuge of musical poetizing by the individual creator.

Music as Poetry

In the predawn of the Renaissance Dante bore witness to the practice of some poets to recite— that is, sing—their own creations. Even when the functions of poet and singer were separate, the poem itself united musical and verbal means. Dante esteemed the canzone (*cantio*) above all other poetic

1. D. P. Walker, in "Musical Humanism in the 16th and Early 17th Centuries," *The Music Review* 2 (1941):6–8, surveys a number of authors from the mid-sixteenth century on for whom this belief was central to their program for the reform of modern music.

2. *Istitutioni*, II, 6, p. 67: "Onde il Musico non era separato dal Poeta, ne il Poeta dal Musico: percioche essendo li Poeti de quei tempi periti nella Musica, & li Musici nella Poesia (come vuole Strabone) l'vno & l'altro per vna di queste due voci, Musico, o Poeta erano chiamati. Et questo è manifesto da quello, che dice Plutarco." The remainder of this chapter of Zarlino and those immediately following on the power of music on the passions and its probable causes are heavily dependent on pseudo-Plutarch's treatise, which Zarlino probably knew from the Latin version of Valgulio, though he exploits also other sources, such as Pliny, Horace, Lucian, and other ancient poets and philosophers.

genres, because it contained the total art of singing poetically.[3] Its self-sufficiency put it ahead of the ballata, which required dancers. Since the ballata was superior in form to the sonnet, the canzone surpassed the sonnet also. A canzone, Dante proposed, may be created by its author, and this constitutes an action, as when Vergil said "Arma virumque cano." Or, once composed, it may be recited by its author or by someone else.[4] Dante debated whether what is called a *canzone* is the composition of harmonized words (*fabricatio verborum armonizatorum*) or the melody itself (*ipsa modulatio*). His reply was that the melody was not called *canzone* but sound, tone, note, or melos (*nunquam modulatio dicitur cantio, sed sonus, vel tonus, vel nota, vel melos*). No player of the tibia, organ, or kithara calls his piece a canzone, unless it is joined to a texted canzone. But those who compose "harmonized" words call them *canzoni* and do so even when they are written down without anyone reciting them. It is clear, then, that a canzone is an action accomplished by him who composes harmonized words for a melody.[5]

The entire art of the canzone consists in three things: the partition of the song, the proportionate disposition of the parts, and the number of lines and syllables.[6] The means by which the poem is organized is the stanza, which is a structure of lines and syllables under a determinate melody and a specific disposition (*stantiam esse sub certo cantu et habitudine limitata carminum et sillabarum compagem*).[7] Sometimes a number of stanzas are under a single continuous melody up to the end (*sub una oda continua usque ad ultimum progressive*), without repetition of melody (*sine iteratione modulationis*), whereas in other cases stanzas receive melodic repetition, which may occur both before and after the occurrence of a *diesis*, that is, the passing from one melody to another, or what is called *volta* in the vernacular.[8] Clearly for Dante these poems were musical as well as verbal compositions, and the two aspects could not be separated.[9]

Yet Zarlino's nostalgia, two and a half centuries later, for the antique poet-musician is understandable in the light of the history of Italian secular music in the sixteenth century. The madrigal, with its method of through-

3. *De vulgari eloquentia* 2.3: "tota comprehendatur in cantionibus ars cantandi poetice."
4. Ibid., 2.8.
5. Ibid., 2.8: "Et ideo cantio nichil aliud esse videtur quam actio completa dictantis verba modulationi."
6. Ibid., 2.9: "Tota igitur, scilicet ars cantionis, circa tria videtur consistere: primo circa cantus divisionem, secundo circa partium habitudinem, tertio circa numerum carminum et sillabarum."
7. Ibid., 2.9.
8. Ibid., 2.10.
9. For a technical discussion of the structure of various poetic forms, see Don Harrán, "Verse Types in the Early Madrigal," *Journal of the American Musicological Society* 22 (1969):27–53.

composition, dissolved the repetition schemes inherent in the musical verse types. Madrigal composers either set poetry written in a free idiom or, if it had a "musical" fixed form, they ignored it. In either case the composer felt free to determine the flow of the eventual composition. The musical setting was no longer a vehicle for the poem; it was an independent creation that usurped the poem's message. Zarlino was aware, however, of another tradition of music making that was still alive and clung to the poetry-music nexus. By dissolving that link, he realized, music turned away from the straightest path to the affections of the soul.

La onde vedemo etiandio a i nostri tempi, che la Musica induce in noi varie passioni, nel modo che anticamente faceua: imperoche alle volte si vede, che recitandosi alcuna bella, dotta, & elegante Poesia al suono di alcuno istru-mento, gli ascoltanti sono grande-mente commossi, & incitati a fare diuerse cose, come ridere, pian-gere, ouero altre cose simili. Et di ciò si è veduto la esperien-za dalle belle, dotte & leggiadri compositioni dell'Ariosto, che recitandosi (oltra le altre cose) la pietosa morte di Zerbino, il lagrimeuol lamento della sua Isabella, non meno piangeuano gli ascoltanti mossi da compassione, di quello che faceua Vlisse vdendo cantare Demodoco musico, et poeta eccellentissimo. Di maniera che se bene non si ode, che la Musica al di d'hoggi operi in diuersi soggetti, nel modo che gia operò in Alessandro; questo può essere perche le cagioni sono diuerse, & non simili, come presuppongono costoro: Percioche se per la Musi-ca anticamente erano operati tali effetti, era anco recitata nel modo, che di sopra hò mostrato, & non nel modo, che si vsa al pre-sente, con vna moltitudine di

Even in our times we see that music induces in us various passions in the way that it did in antiquity. For occasionally, it is observed, when some beautiful, learned, and elegant poem is recited by someone to the sound of some instrument, the listeners are greatly stirred and moved to do different things, such as to laugh, weep, or to similar actions. This has been experienced through the beautiful, learned, and graceful compositions of Ariosto: when among other passages, the sad death of Zerbino and the tearful lament of his Isabella are recited, the listeners, moved with compassion, cried no less than did Ulysses hearing the excellent musician and poet Demodocus sing. Thus, if we do not hear that the music of today works on diverse subjects the effects that it did on Alexander, this may be because the causes are different, and not alike, as some [the chromaticists] assume. For, if such effects were wrought by music in antiquity, it was recited as described above and not in the way that is used at present, with a multitude of parts and so

parti, & tanti cantori & istrumenti, che alle volte non si ode altro che vn strepito de voci mesco-
late con diuersi suoni, & vn cantare senza alcun giudicio, &
senza discretione, con vn disconcio
proferir di parole, che non si ode
se non strepito, & romore: onde
la Musica in tal modo essercitata
non può fare in noi effetto alcuno, che sia degno di memoria.
Ma quando la Musica è recitata
con giudicio, & più si accosta
all'vso de gli antichi, cioè
ad vn semplice modo, cantando
al suono della Lira, del Leuto, o
di altri simili istrumenti
alcune materie che habbiano
del Comico, ouer del Tragico, &
altre cose simili con lunghe nar-
rationi; allora si vedeno li suoi
effetti: Percioche veramente pos-
sono mouer poco l'animo quelle
canzoni, nelle quali si
racconti con breue parole
vna materia breue, come si costu-
ma hoggidi in alcune canzonette,
dette Madrigali; le quali benche
molto dilettino, non hanno però
la sopradetta forza. Et che sia
vero, che la Musica più diletti
vniuersalmente quando è semplice,
che quando è fatta con tanto
artificio, & cantata con molte
parti; si può comprender da
questo, che con maggior diletta-
tione si ode cantare alcuno solo
al suono di vn'Organo, della Lira,
del Leuto, o di altri simili
instrumenti, che non si ode molti.
Et se pur molti cantando insieme
muoueno l'animo, non è dubbio,
che vniuersalmente con maggior
piacere si ascoltano quelle
canzoni, le cui parole

many singers and instruments that at
times nothing is heard but a jumbled
din of voices and diverse
instrumental sounds, singing
without taste or
discretion, and an unseemly
pronunciation of words, so that we
hear only a tumult and uproar. Music
practiced in this way cannot have
any effect on us worth
remembering.
But when music is recited with taste,
staying close to the
the usage of the ancients, that is,
to a simple style, singing
to the sound of the lyre, lute,
or other similar instruments
texts
of comic or tragic nature, or
similar subjects, where there are
long narrations, then the effects
are observed. Those songs in which
brief matters are related in
a few words, as is customary
today in certain canzonets
called madrigals, truly
are able to move the soul
but little. Although these
delight us greatly, they do not
have the force alluded to above.
That it is true that music
universally pleases more when it
is simple than when fashioned
with much artifice and sung by many
parts may be understood from
this: that we listen to a solo singer
accompanied by the sound of an
organ, lyre, lute, or similar
instrument with greater pleasure
than to many.
Although many singing together
stir the soul, there is no doubt
that songs in which the singers
pronounce the words together
are generally heard

sono da i cantori insieme pronun- ciate, che le dotte compositioni, nelle quali si odono le parole interrotte da molte parti.[10]	with greater pleasure than the learned compositions in which the words are interrupted by many voices.

It was not so much the divorce of the musician from the poet as of poly-phonic music from the simple style of harmonized song in which the words were plainly intelligible that hindered modern music from having the effect of the ancient. Nevertheless it is obvious that Zarlino considered solo singing to the accompaniment of an instrument a declining art. But this did not dis-turb him very much, because the art displacing it—polyphony—was a higher form of musical composition. His comparison of the accompanied song, particularly the narrative epic, to the madrigal is apt, because the madrigal eclipsed the art of the rhapsodist and singing storyteller. The madrigal, while it realized some of the humanists' ideals, broke a tradition that was still alive in Dante's time and through the fifteenth century.

Nino Pirrotta in a pioneering article in 1966 attacked the question of why Italy did not produce a school of polyphonic composers after the second or third decade of the fifteenth century.[11] After considering some of the political, religious, institutional, and doctrinal factors that discouraged po-lyphony, he focused attention on the humanists, who were little impressed with the technical accomplishment that contemporary counterpoint exhib-ited. Rather they gave the most prominent notice to manifestations of music making that reminded them of practices described in the ancient books— that of the citharodist, rhapsodist, and bard. So the poet Antonio Corna-zano. in his *La Sforziade,* completed in 1459, aims to recreate the flavor of Homeric times as he describes a wedding feast. Into this he introduces the musician Pietro Bono, a singer accompanying himself on an instrument called a kithara (*cetra*) which must have been a lute. Cornazano, comparing him to Apollo and Orpheus, pays tribute to the power of his music over the souls of those present:

Quest'un già puote col percosso nervo
svegliar gli corpi nelle sepolture,
et adolcire ogn'animo protervo;
gli attracti sensi da tucte altre cure
subvertir puote e con sue voci liete
fermar gli fiumi e dar strada a le mure.[12]

10. Zarlino, *Istitutioni,* II, 9, p. 75.
11. Nino Pirrotta, "Music and Cultural Tendencies in 15th-Century Italy," *Journal of the American Musicological Society* 19 (1966):127–61.
12. Quoted in ibid., p. 144.

With the stroke of a few strings he could awaken the dead, sweeten any arrogant soul, distract the senses from the cares of the body, and with joyful tones dam the rivers and pierce a street through a wall. He added to the instrumental sounds words with great animation: "dando col suon vivissime parole," as he sang a variety of romances, of Isotta and Arimini, of the king of Aragon and Lucretia (Alfonse of Aragon and Lucrezia d'Alagno), and other famous lovers.

Pietro Bono was, of course, a real musician, who spent most of his life in the service of the Este in Ferrara, first Borso d'Este, Marchese of Ferrara (1450–71), then Duke Ercole I (1451–1505), and during these years also traveled with members of the Este family to Naples and Hungary.[13] Cornazano represents him as a poet-singer, which he may have been. But even if he was not, there were others who attest to the survival of the species in the fifteenth century. One of the most famous was the Venetian Leonardo Giustiniani (1388–1446), who favored the strambotto as a vehicle for his amatory lyricism.[14]

The most celebrated poet-musician was Serafino de' Ciminelli dall'Aquila (1466–1500), who began his career by memorizing Petrarch's sonnets, canzoni, and trionfi and singing them to his own accompaniment on the lute. He went on to compose and improvise his own poetry. He served Cardinal Ascanio Sforza in Rome from 1484 and also was active in Milan and traveled with members of the Sforza family before eventually entering the service of Cesare Borgia in 1499. Many of his poems were published, but none of his melodies and arrangements have so far been identified in surviving collections.

Also famous for improvised performance of his own poetry was Benedetto Gareth, Il Chariteo (c. 1450–1514), a Spaniard who served the Spanish princes at Naples and in 1495 succeeded Pontano as a secretary of state. A musical setting of the strambotto *Amando e desiando* attributed to him was published in Petrucci's *Frottole libro nono* of 1509.[15] Hearing the Neapolitan Andrea Coscia perform Gareth's strambotti is said to have influenced Serafino's style. Another famous improvisator was Panfilo Sassi (c. 1455–1527). Two settings of his strambotti that may be his own arrangements survive in manuscripts.[16]

As late as 1570, the poet Benedetto Varchi recalls his extreme pleasure on hearing Silvio Antoniano improvise verses to the lira:

13. Lewis Lockwood, "Pietrobono," in *New Grove Dictionary* XIV, 744.

14. See Walter H. Rubsamen, *Literary Sources of Secular Music in Italy (ca. 1500)* (Berkeley, 1943; repr. New York, 1972), pp. 1–2.

15. See ibid., pp. 13ff, and Donna G. Cardamone, "Gareth" in *New Grove Dictionary* VII, 166.

16. See Rubsamen, *Literary Sources,* pp. 18–19, nn. 34, 35.

non udij mai cosa (il quale son pur uecchio, e n'ho udito qualchuna) la quale più mi si facesse sentire adentro, e piu mi paresse merauigliosa, che il cantare in su la lira all'improuiso di M. Siluio Antoniano quando uenne à Firenze coll'Illustriss. & Eccellentissimo Principe di Ferrara Don Alfonso da Este genero del nostro Duca, dal quale fu non solo benignemente conosciuto, ma larghissimamente riconosciuto.[17]	I never heard anything that moved me more inside and seemed more wonderful (and I am old and I have heard a few things) than the singing extemporaneously to the lira of M. Silvio Antoniano, when he came to Florence with the Most Illustrious and Excellent Prince of Ferrara, Don Alfonso d'Este, son-in-law of our Duke, by whom he was not only kindly recognized but most generously compensated.

Many poets, of course, could not project their own verses in this way and had others sing them. Vincenzo Calmeta, Beatrice Sforza's secretary, wrote of the practice as if it were a new vogue: "Another new way has been found, besides the printer, by which the poems, especially those in the vernacular tongue, can be brought to light; for, such a profession being much appreciated in our day, many *citaredi* have arisen, who, taking advantage of the works of a few poets, make such works known in all the courts."[18] The vogue for singing verses may have resulted in part from the zeal of the humanists for reviving the ancient art of the citharedus, particularly after printing had offered a more secure and rapid medium for propagating them. But an even more important reason for the popularity of the singers to the lute and improvisators was the vacuum in native music brought on by the dominance of French and northern secular and sacred music. Pietro Aron listed twelve celebrated Italian singers to the lute as against fifteen native singers "to the book."[19] Although the foreign music had many admirers among rulers and prelates, antipathy to it on the part of numerous humanists is well documented.

The art of musically reciting verses did not die out after the first decades of the sixteenth century, but it was eclipsed by the madrigal, which for both the poet and composer became the musical vehicle of choice. Toward the end of the century there was a revival of musical recitation, as both musicians and poets became disillusioned with the artificiality of the po-

17. Benedetto Varchi, *L'Hercolano* (Florence, 1570), pp. 272–73.
18. Trans. by Pirrotta in "Music and Cultural Tendencies," p. 141, n. 58, from V. Calmeta, *Prose e lettere edite e inedite,* ed. Cecil Grayson, p. 4.
19. *Lucidario in musica* (Venice, 1545), IV, 1, fol. 31v. He lists Conte Lodovico Martinengo, Ognibene da Vinegia, Bartholomeo Tromboncino, Marchetto Mantoano, Ipolito Tromboncino, Bartholomeo Gazza, Marc'Antonio Fontana, Francesco da Faenza, Angioletto da Vinegia, Iacopo da San Secondo, Camilo Michele Vinitiano, and Paolo Milanese.

lyphonic madrigal.[20] The reaction against polyphony found its most eloquent exponents in Bardi's Camerata. Out of it came not only Galilei's critique of the madrigal but also his experiments in monody, which do not survive, and Caccini's monodic airs and madrigals, which put forward a new model for vocal lyricism.

Bardi's leadership gave impetus to this movement in both literary and musical spheres. His partiality to the air emerges clearly in both his literary and musical criticism. In his defense of Ariosto, delivered to the Accademia degli Alterati 24 February 1583,[21] Bardi confessed that one of the qualities that most attracted him to Ariosto's poetry was its musicality, the ease with which it melted into song. Bardi's discourse was in response to Francesco Bonciani, who in a lecture before the Accademia Fiorentina had detailed several faults of artistic level and decorum and shown Ariosto's inferiority to Homer and Vergil.[22] As evidence of Ariosto's lowering himself to common tastes Bonciani had adduced the fact that the stanza which begins "Tu m'hai Ruggier lasciato io te non voglio" was sung to the lute (cetera) by base people. Bardi replied that it was sung by all sorts of people, including noble and wise men, a true indication of the poetry's perfection. All poetry, he said, was made to be sung; indeed if poetry merited greater praise than prose, it was because it contained verse, rhythm, and musical sound. Music, according to Plato, Aristotle, Aristoxenus, Vitruvius, Ptolemy, and Boethius, is defined as verse, rhythm, and pitch. "Those verses are best, therefore, which have the best rhythm, and the best sound, and consequently are the most musical, hence the most singable."[23] Ariosto's verses are so superior in this regard that they attract every kind of person to sing them. Bardi names a host of composers who were enticed by Ariosto's poetry. Giandomenico da Nola, "an excellent musician, wishing to make airy music (musiche ariose) put together almost an entire book, you might say, of stanzas of Ariosto, among which there was specifically that 'Tu m'hai Ruggier lasciato,' and they are sung still in all the musical academies of noblemen in Italy."[24] "Our Messer Vincenzo Galilei," he adds, "having to set to music

20. James Haar considers the relationship between the improvised musical recitation of poetry and the madrigal in "The Early Madrigal: A Re-appraisal of its Sources and its Character," in Music in Medieval and Modern Europe: Patronage, Sources, and Texts, ed. Iain Fenlon (Cambridge, 1981), pp. 163–92.

21. Florence, Biblioteca Nazionale Centrale, MS Magl. VI.168, fols. 50r–75v. Weinberg, in A History, II, 1116, identified this as the lecture delivered on that date using the Diario of the Alterati in Florence, Biblioteca Medicea-Laurenziana, MS Ashburnham 558, II, fol. 37.

22. Bonciani's lecture is known only through Bardi's references to it.

23. Florence, Biblioteca Nazionale Centrale, MS Magl. VI.168, fol. 61v: "adunque que uersi saranno migliori che haranno miglior ritmo e miglior suono e per conseguenza più musicali, onde più cantabili."

24. Ibid., fol. 62r–v: "Giandomenico da Nola musico eccellente uolendo far musiche ariose

in a hurry poetry that would possess an active character, also chose ten stanzas of his, attracted by their sweetness of rhythm and sound."[25]

Bardi distinguished two main types of musical settings of poetry: *musica figurata*, and *ad aria*. The latter in turn he divided into *arie* and *arie musicali*. Among the simple arie there were also some without accompaniment (*accordo*). In making the point that the verses of Pietro Bembo and Petrarch were on everyone's lips, he asked if they deserve to be criticized for this:

meritano donque biasimo questi	Do these excellent men, then,
ecc[elen]ti huomini per esser	deserve blame for being
cantati da tutto il mondo, e	sung by the entire world, both
figuratamente e ad aria,	polyphonically and to airs?
no di uero anzi loda poiche sono	Certainly not; rather praise, for
adoperati per quello, sono	verses were intended for this purpose
stati fatti dall'arte e dalla	by both art and nature.
natura: farò qui un poco	To make here a short digression,
digressione dicendo che l'arie	I say that arias that are
che si cantano non son'altro che	sung are nothing but
musica e composte da huomini	music, whether composed by men
periti in quella scienzia e se	skilled in that science or sung
sono cantate da huomini idioti	by idiots, and this
adiuiene per la loro facilità	arises from their being easy,
nella cui consiste l'eccellentia	in which consists the excellence
della cosa, e di quelle che sono	of the thing. Those that are of
in somma eccellentia	the greatest excellence are used
ciascuno si serue e le adopera	by everyone, and they apply them

---

fece pure si puo dire quasi un libro intero di stanze dell'Ariosto in particolare ui haueua pur quella 'Tu m'hai Ruggier lasciato' i quali si cantarono e ancora cantano per tutte le Accademie musicali da gentilhuomini d'Italia." Bardi goes on to name others who set Ariosto: Cipriano [de Rore], Giaches [de Werth], Orlando [Lassus], Alessandro Striggio, [Francesco?] Rossello, [Stefano?] Rossetto, [Bernardo] Giacomini, and Vincenzo Galilei. Da Nola's *madrigali ariosi* appeared in collections published in Rome by Antonio Barré beginning in 1555: *RISM* 1555[27]: *Primo libro delle muse a cinque voci. Madrigali ariosi di Ant. Barre et altri diversi autori, delle muse,* *RISM* 1562[9], *Il terzo libro delle Muse a quattro voci* (with four by Nola); and also in collections published by G. Scotto in Venice with similar titles, such as *Madrigali Aierosi a quatro voci,* *RISM* 1558[2]. One of the arrangements for solo voice and lute in a manuscript compiled by Galilei, probably for entertaining Bardi's circle, was of a madrigal attributed to Nola, though on a text by Petrarch, *Vivo sol di speranza rimembrando,* in Florence, Biblioteca Nazionale Centrale, MS Landau-Finaly Mus. 2, fols. 5v–6r. The attribution is in the Bottegari lute-song book, Modena, Biblioteca Estense, MS Mus. C.311, fol. 36r, but it appeared as a composition of Lassus in his *Primo libro di madrigali a 4* (Venice, 1560).

25. Florence, Biblioteca Nazionale Centrale, MS Magl. VI.168, fol. 63v: "Il nostro Ms. Vinc.° Galilei douendo hà poco tempo metter' in musica, stanze che hauessero dell'attiuo pur prese anch'egli dieci stanze delle sue tratto dalla dolcezza del ritmo, e del suono che in esse sono."

come dirò tosto.
dico ancora che le nostre arie
sono più secondo la natura che
quelle chiamate musicali, e che
più si appresano alle antiche
tanto celebrate dalli scrittori,
e in particolare quell'arie che
si cantano senza accordo.[26]

in the way I shall describe presently.
I say, then, that our arias
are more according to nature than
those called "musical," and that
they approach more closely those ancient ones so praised by the writers,
and in particular those arias that
are sung without accompaniment.

Bardi speaks here of several types of settings. First is the artfully composed polyphonic setting: *figuratamente*. There is the type of aria for singing poetry, of which he does not cite any examples, but one assumes he means those, like the *aria della Romanesca* or *di Ruggiero*, that take a harmonic accompaniment. This is a formula for singing a particular form of verse, such as capitolo, ottava rima, or sonetto. Then there are the simple arias for singing verses that do not imply any harmonization and are designed for mono-phonic recitation of verses. Finally there is the aria musicale, by which he must mean a melody composed for a particular text. When Bardi speaks of "le nostre arie," he refers to the standard melodic formulas for singing poetry, which he finds to be closer to the melodies sung by the ancient Greeks and Romans.

It is to the singer-composer Giulio Caccini that Bardi addressed his one surviving effort in music criticism around 1578–79, the *Discorso mandato a Giulio Caccini detto Romano, sopra la Musica anticha, e 'l cantar bene*,[27] in which he elaborated this credo. He counseled Caccini as singer and composer to follow certain principles that could be learned from ancient music:

1. The composer and singer must be careful not to spoil the verse by overindulging in musical artifice, such as an excess of contrapuntal ac-tivity.
2. The music, as Plato said, must follow the verse and not be led by it. The words are the soul of music, and the counterpoint the body. Coun-terpoint must take its rule from the text, as the body is governed by the soul. To do otherwise is like seeing a master commanded by a servant on the public square (his words prefigure Monteverdi's definition of the *seconda pratica*): "Would it not appear to you comical if on going to the public square you saw a servant followed by his lord and commanding him, or a child who would give lessons to his father or tutor."[28]

26. Ibid., fol. 63r–v.
27. So it is entitled in Florence, Biblioteca Marucelliana, MS A287, I fol. 3v. Concerning the dating see Palisca, "The 'Camerata fiorentina': A Reappraisal," *Studi musicali* 1 (1972):218.
28. "Hor non ui parebbe egli cosa ridicola s'andando in piazza uedeste 'l seruo del suo Signore esser seguito, e ad esso commandare: o fanciullo al Padre o, pedagogo suo ammaes-tramento dar uolesse." Biblioteca Apostolica Vaticana, MS Barb. lat. 3990, fol. 10r.

3. The length of the syllables of verse must be strictly observed, for in rhythm, as Aristotle said, are images of the affections.

4. A composer must choose a high, intermediate, or low range of the voice and create a melody of few notes out of this segment, revolving around the median tone or mese. He must choose the harmonia or octave species most appropriate to his subject and remain faithful to it.

Bardi's surviving compositions demonstrate that he acted on his own advice. "Lauro, ohime, lauro ingrato," which he contributed to the Ferrarese anthology *Il lauro secco* of 1582,[29] illustrates several of the points. Anthony Newcomb has noted its adherence to the line-by-line principle, the suitability of the topmost voice to pseudo-monodic performance, and the suppression of contrapuntal complexity. The text is made transparently audible by sounding it homorhythmically in all or several of the voices most of the time. Bardi departs from this only for the lines

O pianta insidiosa, in cui si vede
Con fiorita bellezza arida fede.

Here the insinuating growth and flowers of the laurel are depicted through contrapuntal imitation and expansive repetition, still, however, making a cadence at the end of each line and maintaining a songful continuity in the top voice. The soprano line has a compass of a seventh but mostly turns around b♭', on which four of the lines begin. The madrigal begins and ends on G and outlines the species of fifth and fourth of the church Dorian.

More problematic from a modal standpoint is the madrigal "Cantai un tempo" (Figure 13.1) on a text by Pietro Bembo published in Pasquale Trista Bocca da l'Aquila's *Il secondo libro di madrigali a cinque voci*.[30] The subject is plaintive. The poet recalls that he once sang sweetly, but now all pleasures have turned to tears. Unlike those who can restrain their desires, he is at their mercy. How grave his pain is the world will know, as will she who is love's enemy and his too. Harmonically the music is in what we would call G minor, with a modulation in the terza parte to F major.

---

29. *RISM* 1582[5]: *Il lauro secco. Libro primo di madrigali a cinque voci di diversi autori* (Ferrara, 1582). Concerning this anthology see Anthony Newcomb, *The Madrigal at Ferrara, 1579–1597,* (Princeton, 1980) I, 69–80, and about this madrigal in particular, p. 71; an edition of it is in ibid., II, 16–21.

30. *RISM* 1586[20]: Venice, G. Scotto, 1586. This was first published in Palisca, "The Musical Humanism of Giovanni Bardi," in *Poesia e musica nell'estetica del xvi e xvii secolo,* ed. Hagop Meyvalian (Florence, 1979), pp. 61–70. I am indebted to the Centro Studi Rinascimento Musicale and its director, Maestro Annibale Gianuario, for permission to reprint my edition of the madrigal and to rework here portions of the paper delivered at the Center's conference of 3–10 May 1976.

Figure 13.1.
Giovanni Bardi, madrigal: "Cantai un tempo"

Figure 13.1. *Continued*

Figure 13.1. *Continued*

Figure 13.1. *Continued*

Figure 13.1. *Continued*

Figure 13.1. *Continued*

Figure 13.1. *Continued*

Figure 13.1. *Continued*

Figure 13.1. *Continued*

Figure 13.1. *Continued*

Figure 13.1. *Continued*

Cadences		Soprano closes	
1. F		A	
2. B♭		B♭	
3. g		G	
4. A		A	
5. D / g		A	
6. D		F♯	
7. G		G	
8. G		G	
9. F		A	
10. C		G	
11. F		A	
12. D	12. D	A	A
13. F	13. F	A	A
14. G	14. G	G	G

Figure 13.2
Cadences in "Cantai un tempo"

Each line ends with a cadence, and these are on the degrees displayed in
Figure 13.2.

Disregarding repetitions, we have five cadences on G, four on F, three
on D, one on B♭, and one on A. On the other hand, the soprano voice
closes five times on g', seven times on a', once on f♯', and once on b♭'. Its
range is a seventh, from e' to d", the same as that of "Lauro, ohime, lauro."
But the most frequent and prominent note in the melody is a'. Its tonal
system is e' to e" with one flat, and the mese is on the fourth note, a'. This
yields the octave species semitone, tone, tone, semitone, tone, tone, tone,
that of Bardi's ancient Mixolydian, which has been transposed up a fifth
(see Figure 11.14): that is, the mese has been moved from its proper place,
d', to a'. In accordance with Bardi's theory, the plaintive subject calls for
the Greek Mixolydian harmonia, and it should be placed in the soprano.
This Bardi has done.

The composer did not deprive himself of more conventional means of
madrigalistic expression. For the line "Or è ben giunto ogni mia festa a
riva" (Now my every festival has reached shore), Bardi evaded the cadence
prepared at m. 12 so that the line does not reach shore on the first attempt.
He speeded up and used a villanella-style of harmony for "Et ogni mio
piacer" (And my every pleasure), whereas he immediately broadened the
movement for "rivolto in pianto" (turned to weeping). He ended the phrase
with the bass descending a fourth, which Galilei pointed out has a sorrowful

and humble effect ("del mesto e rimesso" are his words).[31] For the line "O fortunato che raffren in tanto" (O happy he who curbs so [his desire]), the rhythm and harmony are again that of the popular song, becoming subdued for the words "che riposato viva" (that in peace he lives).

The terza parte turns immediately to a plaintive mood at the words "Misero che sperava" (Wretched he who hoped, m. 33), with a minor-third harmony followed by a minor sixth, then a descent of a fourth followed by a leap up of a fifth in the bass, effects that Galilei characterized as sorrowful. This series of harmonies is first heard in three voices, then in five. At "A mille che venisser dopo noi" (To thousands who follow us, m. 38), the repetitions of the subject through imitation suggest the multitude of those who follow. For "Or non lo spero" (Now I hope no more, m. 44) the cadence is left hanging. The most dramatic gesture is the setting of "Il mio dolor" with an archaic double-leading-tone cadence (mm. 47–48). The multiplication of syncopations and suspensions for "Di pietade e d'Amor nemica e mia" (Of mercy and love the enemy, and mine too) is another characteristic madrigalistic device.

Throughout Bardi scrupulously followed the rhythms of the text, allowing it to be plainly heard, only occasionally opposing one phrase of text to another. There is much more imitation here than in his other compositions, but it does not draw attention to itself; rather it reinforces the textual exposition. The piece is innocent of the virtuosity that is so characteristic of the age. Yet Bardi is not at all backward for the 1580's in adopting the devices of the avant-garde, and his writing is professional in its polish and sureness of direction. Without violating his ideal of the aria and aria musicale Bardi realized a refined example of musica figurata.

Vincenzo Galilei

It is not surprising to find Bardi's ideas echoed in Galilei's *Dialogo*, published a few years later in 1582, as well as in his later writings. Some of the common ideology may be attributed to the influence of Mei, but the direction that Galilei took as a composer, theorist, and singer to the lute must be credited at least in part to Bardi's consistent championship of the musical recitation of poetry. In one of his last essays, Galilei proposed the simple air for singing poetry as a model for composers to follow. This was the way of nature, for when shepherds and workers in the fields were finished with their labor, they turned to the popular airs, which they sang to the strumming of some instrument. It was also the way of the classic poets who sang to the lyre. The songs of the legendary Olympus were supposed to have

31. Galilei, *Dialogo*, p. 75.

worked wonders with only four strings. This kind of simplicity and limitation of means should be a goal of modern composers.

> Using few notes is natural both in speaking and singing, since the end of one
> and the other is solely the expression of the conceits of the soul by means of
> words, which, when well expressed and understood by the listeners, generate
> in them whatever affections the musician cares to treat through this medium.
> ... And, if someone were to ask me, since it is natural for a man to be able
> to reach with his voice eight or ten notes without straining, whether therefore
> all notes outside of the three or four used by Olympos were to be scorned, I
> would reply in this way. The three or four that Olympos used in one song
> were not apt for expressing all the passions and affections of the soul. The
> three or four notes that a tranquil soul seeks are not the same as those which
> suit the excited spirit, or one who is lamenting, or a lazy and somnolent one.
> For the tranquil soul seeks the middle notes; the querulous the high; and the
> lazy and somnolent the low. Thus, also, the latter will use slow meters; the
> tranquil the intermediate; and the excited the rapid. In this way the musician
> will tend to choose now these and another time others according to the affection
> he wants to represent and impress on the listeners.[32]

Limitation of means, then, demands the selection of the most appropriate
means.

Galilei pointed to a number of the popular airs sung in his own time
which did not extend beyond a compass of six notes, such as "Come
t'haggio lasciato vita mia," "Ti parti cor mio caro," "La brunettina mia,"
"La pastorella si leua per tempo," "L'aria comune della terza rima," the
"Aria della Romanesca" and "della Girometta," and others.[33] The last three
in particular were utilized in the musical recitation of poetry. Caccini's aria,
"Ahi dispietato amor,"[34] for example, is based on the Romanesca aria. The
airs appealed to Galilei also for their expressiveness. The stories of the
marvelous effects that ancient music worked were believable if one considered how the popular airs move people. The effect that the aulos player
made on a Taorminian youth, when Pythagoras ordered the musician to
change from an exciting to a quieting mode, Galilei said, "is understandable
if we compare the excited sound of the Romanesca to the quiet one of the

---

32. *Dubbi intorno a quanto io ho detto dell'uso dell'enharmonio, con la solutione di essi,* Florence,
Biblioteca Nazionale Centrale, MS Galilei 3, fol. 67r–v; Italian text in Rempp, ed., *Die Kon-
trapunkttraktate Vincenzo Galileis,* p. 184; trans. in Palisca, "Galilei and Links Between 'Pseudo-
Monody' and Monody," *Musical Quarterly* 46 (1960):347.

33. For the texts, music, history, and bibliography of these airs, see Palisca, "Galilei and
Links," pp. 348 ff. Concerning the *Girometta,* see also Warren Kirkendale, "Franceschina,
Girometta, and their Companions in a Madrigal 'a diversi linguaggi' by Luca Marenzio and
Orazio Vecchi," *Acta Musicologica* 54 (1972):181–235.

34. *Le nuove musiche (Florence, 1601),* ed. H. Wiley Hitchcock (Madison, 1970), p. 54.

Figure 13.3.
"Unison" contrasted with "consonant" accompaniment, from Galilei, *Dubbi,*
Florence, Biblioteca Nazionale Centrale, MS Galilei 3, fol. 66r

Passemezzo."[35] Galilei recognized in these dance-songs the qualities that so
endeared the characteristic dances to the Baroque composers—a striking
directness in portraying mood and sharp contrasts of affection when they
were juxtaposed.

Bardi's plea to Caccini not to spoil the verse with too much artifice
receives a musician's concrete expression in Galilei's essay. Singing, in its
choice of pitches, "should be different from speech only enough to distinguish it from speaking."[36] This suppression of the artifices of music should
extend to the accompaniment. Galilei had recalled already in the *Dialogo*
Plato's prohibition of consonant accompaniment, or so he interpreted the
passage in *Laws* (812d–e) where a permissible instrumental seconding of the
voice, *proschorda,* is opposed to the unnecessarily elaborate *symphōnos* accompaniment. Galilei saw these two manners—not as we might today, as
on the one hand singing in unison with an instrument, on the other het-
erophonic accompaniment that might include some perfect consonances—
as two kinds of harmonization, one limited to the simplest chordal back-
ground, the other striving for smoothness and independence of lines in the
bass and inner parts, in other words, contrapuntal refinement. He contrasts
two examples (Figure 13.3) which resemble harmonizations of fragments
of popular airs, in a remarkable analysis of their harmonic properties that
closes his essay. Of the first he says that "the three lower parts accord with
the fourth, higher part in such a perfect way that it is as much as can be
legitimately desired through the laws of modern counterpoint."[37] But it can
be further improved: by violating those laws!

> There remains for me only to proclaim what imperfection the modern rules
> of counterpoint bring even to the first "unisono" example of the above-men-
> tioned air, and it is this. Every time that the bass part (in the first example),

35. *Il primo libro della prattica del contrapunto,* Rempp. ed., p. 71.
36. *Dubbi,* fol. 66v, Rempp ed., p. 183.
37. *Dubbi,* fol. 66v, Rempp ed., p. 183.

Figure 13.4.
Galilei's improvement of the "unisono" version, from *Dubbi,* Florence, Biblioteca Nazionale Centrale, MS Galilei 3, fol. 66r.

instead of making a tenth against the soprano in the second minim [the sixth chord] makes an octave, and the contralto at that moment makes with the bass part instead of an octave a fifth, the perfection desired will ensue. What prohibits this is the law of modern contrapuntists which proscribes the use of two octaves, and of two fifths, a law that in this matter is truly against every natural law of singing.[38]

The sequence of chords, as corrected by Galilei, would be as in Figure 13.4. There result pairs of parallel fifths and octaves. The formula for accompaniment is evident: root position chords except for the suspension dissonance at the cadence, no harmonic enrichment that requires going outside the mode (as with the E♭ of the second example), and the bass, renouncing any linear identity, should follow the melody in parallel motion. The ensuing harmony is expectedly not unlike that of the airs for singing poetry, for example, the standard harmonization of the Romanesca (Figure 13.5).

Through the writings and practical experiments of Bardi, Galilei, and their circle the ideal of the union of poetry and music passes from the nostalgic antiquing of the poetic critics into the mainstream of musico-poetic practice. A union is reestablished, if not according to the ancient model of the poet-composer, in the collaboration of poet and composer as

Figure 13.5.
Aria della Romanesca with typical harmonization

38. *Dubbi,* fol. 67v, Rempp ed., p. 184. This edition needs a small correction in this passage: instead of "in qual mestiere," read, with the manuscript, "in quel mentre."

exemplified by Peri and Rinuccini, Caccini and Chiabrera, Monteverdi and
Rinuccini or Guarini.

The Poetics of Imitation

Given the revived ideal of the union of music and poetry, it is not surprising
that poetic theory spilled easily into music theory. Both arts operate in the
temporal realm, with recurrent rhythms, meters, and pauses. Three parameters of sound—pitch, vocal timbre, stress— are common to the two media.
The organization of poetry depends often on musical form. Both arts were
thought to have powerful effects on behavior and emotions, and some
believed that they possessed this capability by virtue of being imitative of
actions and feelings. Others conceived of the act of creation as inspired by
external forces at work during moments of divine madness. Both poetry
and music required the rhetorical exercise of invention, disposition, and
delivery. Finally a primary aim of both poetry and music was pleasure and
delight. Poetic theory, inevitably, was partly about music specifically, but
even more of it dealt with musical aspects of poetry. Most sixteenth century
writers on poetics naturally included statements about music in their theories. Whether they did or not, much of what they said had implications
for music.

Bernard Weinberg in his monumental study of Italian literary theory and
criticism in the Renaissance has shown that a large body of writing arose
from the desire to explicate what Plato, Horace, and Aristotle had written
about the art of poetry, but that effectively it contributed less to a clarification of these authors than to the expression of a contemporary theory of
poetry. Much effort went into reconciling the three authorities, whose
ideologies were not seen as fundamentally opposed.[39] No single text of
Plato could form the basis of poetic theory, but what he said about poetry
in various dialogues was prominently discussed. His banishment of the poets
from the *Republic* (Books 2, 3, and 10) inspired numerous defenses of poetry.
Imitation as a narration—through the assumption of the voice of someone
besides the poet (*Republic*, 394 ff.)—and as an inferior kind of reality (595
ff.) were recurrent ideas in Italian criticism. Perhaps Plato's most important
legacy was the theory of the divine furor, "that the poet produces not by
art but by divine inspiration, that he is moved by the Muses to a state of
frenzy, and that when he speaks it is really the voice of the gods and not
his own that speaks within him."[40]

From Horace's *Ars poetica* the Italian writers drew particularly the dual

---

39. Weinberg, *A History*, particularly pp. 150–55.
40. Weinberg, *A History*, p. 250; Plato *Phaedrus* 245a, 265b; *Ion* 534.

goals of utility and pleasure, *aut prodesse aut delectare*. By utility was understood moral instruction; poetry in this sense taught the art of virtuous living. This instruction was made palatable through beguiling allegories and embellished diction, as well as through imitations of nature that provoked the joy of recognition.

The most important text from the standpoint of penetration into musical thought was Aristotle's *Poetics*. Whereas Horace was read throughout the Middle Ages, and the relevant texts of Plato were made available in the fifteenth century, the treatise of Aristotle was not known directly until Giorgio Valla's translation into Latin was published in 1498. There had been a medieval translation, but it attained no significant circulation.[41] A commentary by Averroës was published in a Latin translation, *Determinatio in poetria Aristotelis,* in Venice in 1481 by Hermannus Alemanus.[42] The Greek text came out in an Aldine edition of 1508, and a parallel text and Latin translation by Alessandro Pazzi in 1536. The earliest commentaries were those of Valla in *De expetendis* and those in public lectures by Bartolomeo Lombardi in 1541 in Padua and by Vincenzo Maggi in Ferrara in 1543, on which notes by Alessandro Sardi survive. Lombardi and Maggi later revised and jointly published their commentaries interspersed with Pazzi's text and translation.[43]

Aristotle's theory of imitation was the single most fruitful resource that poetics offered to musical thought. The philosopher's own breakdown of the categories of artistic imitation according to medium, object, and manner or mode was flexible enough to admit music, and he specifically named music, indeed, even instrumental music, as fitting his theory: "Epic poetry and Tragedy, Comedy also and Dithyrambic poetry, and the music of the flute [*aulētikēs*] and of the lyre [*kitharistikēs*] in most of their forms, are all in their general conception modes of imitation."[44]

In these arts, as opposed to those in which the imitation is made through color or form or the voice, the imitation is made through rhythm, language, or harmony, either singly or combined. Thus in auletic and kitharistic music and in that of the syrinx harmony and rhythm alone are employed, whereas in dancing rhythm is used without harmony. Still, dancing imitates character, emotion, and action through rhythmic movement.[45]

By harmony is meant, of course, not simultaneous consonance, but the ordered relationship of pitches to each other such as is found in melody.

41. *De arte poetica,* trans. William Moerbeke, ed. E. Valgimigli (Bruges-Paris, 1953).
42. See the discussion in Weinberg, *A History,* pp. 352–61.
43. Vincenzo Maggi and Bartolomeo Lombardi, *In Aristotelis Librum de poetica communes explanationes: Madii vero in eundem librum propriae annotationes* (Venice, 1550).
44. *Poetics* 1.2.1447a, trans. S. H. Butcher, p. 7.
45. *Poetics* 1.5.1447a, trans. S. H. Butcher, pp. 8–9.

When Aristotle says that in dancing there is rhythm without harmony, he does not mean to exclude harmony from the music that accompanies dancing but narrows the focus to bodily activity, which is temporally organized and has no need for pitch. Giovan Giorgio Trissino in *La quinta e la sesta divisione della poetica* [c. 1549][46] understands and repeats these distinctions and proposes to discuss only the imitations that are produced by the use of all three means. "But because dancing and singing are also imitations that at times are introduced in the theatre, of which dancing is done with rhythm alone and singing with rhythm and harmony, these things not being pertinent to the poet, we shall otherwise not speak of them and treat only of those that make the imitation with all three of these things, that is, with language, verse, and harmony, such as ballate, canzoni, and mandriali, and comedies and tragedies if they have a chorus, and the like."[47] Trissino adds the clarification that he will, of course, also speak of the imitations that are made by language and rhythm alone, such as heroic poems, the cantos of Dante, and the *Trionfi* of Petrarch.

Despite this disclaimer, Trissino develops Aristotle's ideas on imitation in directions that are musically of interest. Since imitations may be of actions or customs, some take as their subject good, others poor, actions or customs. Thus in dancing, some imitate the better, as when they dance the Gioioso, Lioncello, or Rosina," while others imitate the worse, dancing the Padoana, or Spingardò. Similarly those who sing or play the "Battaglia" imitate the better, but playing the songs "Tocca la canella" or "Torella mo vilan" they imitate the worse.[48] Thus Homer in his hexameters imitated the better, Theocritus the worse. Similarly Dante and Petrarch in their canzoni and sonnets imitated the better, and Burchiello and Berna the worse.

It is significant that Trissino gives examples of imitation in painting (referring to da Vinci, Montagna, and Titian) and in dance and music before he applies the theory to poetry, as if the former were more palpable imitations than poetry. To be sure, it is easier to recognize action in a painting,

---

46. The date is Weinberg's, in *Trattati di poetica e retorica del cinquecento*, II, 653.

47. Weinberg, ed., *Trattati*, II, 11.

48. Fausto Torrefranca quoted this passage in *Il segreto del quattrocento* (Milan, 1939), pp. 35–36, as evidence that polyphonic chansons such as Jannequin's "La bataille de Marignan" and the homophonic four-part villotta existed side by side. He identifies the "Torela mo vilan" as the "Nio" or refrain of a longer dialogue "Da l'orto se ne vien la villanella" (text, p. 250 ff.; music, 437–39). For a history of the song see Claudio Gallico, "Una probabile fonte della canzone 'Torela mo vilan'," *Lares* 27 (1961):15–21, and for polyphonic settings see Gaetano Cesari, "Le origini del madrigale cinquecentesco," *Rivista musicale italiana,* 19 (1912):393. Howard M. Brown, *Instrumental Music Printed Before 1600* (Cambridge, 1965), indexes "Tocca la canella" as a saltarello. This song is found intabulated for the lute in Giovanni Antonio Castellono, *Intavolature de leuto* (Milan, 1536), and Hans Gerle, *Eyn Newes sehr Künstlichs Lautenbuch* (Nuremberg, 1551). See Brown, pp. 55–56, 133–35.

in dance, and in music, in which it is portrayed visually or in performance, than in poetry, which can only narrate action and is normally read in stationary silence. Dance and music are actions that imitate other actions, but when not recited aloud poetry is not an action.

The means by which the various arts imitate is the subject of a chapter in *Della vera poetica* of Giovan Pietro Capriano. As painting imitates with colors and design and sculpture with marble or other material as well as design, so poetry imitates human actions with number, sound, and meaning (*il numero, il suono, e la significazione*).[49] Number arises from the movement of the vocal organs by the breath, which may have shorter or longer durations, producing short and long syllables. From the conjunction of these quantities of syllable lengths arise what the Greeks called "rhythm" in speech, which mainly produced what they called "energy," "an efficacious and vivid expression and representation of something."[50] From the measured composition of these rhythms come the "feet" (*piedi*) of the art of metrics. From the feet, in turn, come about all the various kinds of verse suited to different subjects and "likewise to different musical modes that we moderns call airs (*aeri*), which are like the Phrygian and Lydian among the ancients and today Spanish, French, and others. From these derive the songs, [instrumental] pieces, and dances, which are likewise more severe or more relaxed, according to the variations of numbers."[51] By means of these numbers poets, particularly tragic and comic poets, imitate actions, customs, affections, and movements, sometimes excited, at other times relaxed, temperate, or mixed.

> Similarly this [imitation] is accomplished by excellent musicians in their vocal compositions (*cantilene*) with consonances of the three genera of music which were called by them chromatic (*cromico*), diatonic, and enharmonic, dissimilar in their temperaments (*temperature*), and by those other musicians whom we call instrumental, whether of wind and breath or of strings and percussion (*strepito*), as in the various kinds used among the barbarians and the Moroccans (*Moree*), with numbers that originate and appear to be born in other motions, such as among dancers and acrobats (*saltatori*) and other similar artists (*artefici*).[52]

Some of the same actions can be imitated by painters through colors and design, "but not so vividly."

The second instrument by which the poet imitates is the sound of the human voice, which surpasses all other sounds in sweetness, since it is formed in organs provided by nature and filled with living spirit.

---

49. *Della vera poetica libro uno* (Venice, 1555), in *Trattati,* ed. Weinberg, II, 319–20.
50. Ibid., II, 320.
51. Ibid, II, 320–21.
52. Ibid., II, 321.

From this spirit and from those instruments is born and arises (or so we shall say and perhaps not very differently from the dialecticians) the articulation of the voice, particularly in words, which, when it is fittingly used, almost pierces the soul like an arrow with sweetness and persistent speed and touches every note on its keyboard, as it were, like the hand of a skillful musician who can coax any harmony from a monochord [sic]. From this verbalized voice (voce di parole), if resolved in resonance and in song, issues and pours forth that which is called melody.[53]

Capriano speaks here of the melody of speech, melody that arises from the high, low, and intermediate pitches of the speaking voice, which the Greeks indicated through the acute, grave, and circumflex accents. Through the mixing of these three inflections flows "that harmony and that mellifluous consensus which, when heard or read or delivered by an artful and singular poet or orator, delights us so intensely, all the more when the voice springs from smooth organs. This, the great philosophers said, was the truest harmony."[54] This harmony differs from the liquefied voice of song, and although verse is suited to it, song is not essential to verse. To the two elements number and sound, poetry adds a third, meaningful language, which occupies the remainder of his treatment of the means of imitation.

Benedetto Varchi defines the means of imitation as number (rhythm), harmony, and diction but seems somewhat uncomfortable with the term "imitation," for he introduces it conditionally. When in the dialogue he is asked how he would interpret the action of someone who danced, played, and sang at once, he replies:

Producerebbe numero, harmonia, e dizzione, o vero sermone insieme-mamente, nelle quali tre cose consiste tutta l'imitazione (si può dire) e per conseguenza la poesia; perche potemo imitare, e contraffare i costumi, gl'affetti, o vero passioni, e l'azzioni degli huomini, o col numero solo, come ballando, o col numero, e coll'har-monia, come ballando, e sonando, o col numero, e coll'harmonia, e col sermone, cioè colle parole, come ballando, sonando, e cantando.[55]	He would produce rhythm, harmony, and diction or language together, in which three things consists the whole imitation (one may say) and consequently all poetry. Because we can imitate and counterfeit customs, affections or passions, and actions of men with rhythm alone, as in dancing, or with rhythm and harmony, as in dancing and playing, or with rhythm, harmony, and language, that is words, as in dancing, playing, and singing.

Agnolo Segni, in his Lezioni intorno alla poesia, read to the Accademia Fiorentina in 1573, adopted a more Platonic view of imitation, while re-

53. Ibid., II, 322.
54. Ibid., II, 323–24.
55. Benedetto Varchi, L'Hercolano (Florence, 1570), p. 272.

conciling this with Aristotle's. He widened the application of imitation in poetry, which for both Plato and Aristotle was confined to the poet's speaking in the person of another. He defined it in terms of the instruments used for imitation: "I call instrument of imitation the subject and material in which there is impressed and imitated the form of the exemplar proposed, such as the figures, the statues, the dances, and the sound and singing of musicians, because these also imitate with song."[56] The instruments—and on this Aristotle and Plato agree—are language (*orazione*), music, and dance. Of these only language is essential to poetry. The others were used and still are when poetry is recited, as with popular epics or *favole*.[57] In such recitations language, verse, music, and harmony concur and are enhanced by the reciters' dress, their setting, and ordered movement, called dance. All of these are mimetic. "All these things—language, harmony, dance, and ornament— are imitations one of another, and each accommodates and resembles each other, but all are made similar to a prime [exemplar] and are imitations of it: the life of men, happy or wretched, their actions and morals, and thoughts of the mind."[58]

Poetry is a harmony, in a broader sense, of all of these things: of human morality and life, of language and song and dance. Poetic imitations are fictions and deceptions aimed at the senses. Through them poetry addresses the appetitive part of the soul, which is transformed in conformance with the characters and passions of the sense objects. But the intellect remains steadfast, not bent by sense impressions and not prone to imitate them. Therefore poetry through the imagination addresses the friendlier and more accessible, irrational part of the soul.[59]

Throughout these discussions Capriano and Segni, although they make frequent references to music itself, are concerned with poetry as a total art that embraces musical components. But even when they are not speaking of music directly their theories are applicable to music and inform us of how the mechanisms of imitation operate in the sensory field. However, as far as the specifically auditory field is concerned, much is left unstated. The harmony and rhythm of vernacular poetry is one gray area. Another is pitch accent, which was characteristic of Greek speech and therefore of poetry but is left undefined with respect to Italian verse. Fortunately, as we have seen, another writer on poetics shortly before—Girolamo Mei— went to great pains to explain the functioning of these tonic accents in Italian prose and poetry.

56. Agnolo Segni, *Lezioni intorno alla poesia,* in *Trattati,* ed. Weinberg, III, 26.
57. Ibid., III, 28.
58. Ibid., III, 73.
59. Ibid., III, 77.

The Case Against Mimesis: Francesco Patrizi

The most compelling refutation in the sixteenth century of the mimetic position came from the Platonic philosopher Francesco Patrizi. He had studied with Francesco Robortelli, the first important commentator on Aristotle's *Poetics,* at the University of Padua. Robortelli tried to reconcile Aristotle's theories with Plato's, and Patrizi carried this syncretism forward in his work. In 1578 Patrizi was named by Duke Alfonso II d'Este to a chair of Platonic philosophy created for him at the Studio of Ferrara. In 1592 he was called by Pope Clement VIII to Rome to a similar position. His major work was *Nova de universis philosophia* (1591). Among his other works are a number of translations from Greek, which he studied in Ingolstadt in 1545–46.[60] His monumental history and theory of poetics was only partially published. It consists of seven "decades" or ten-book treatises. *Della Poetica, La deca istoriale* and *Della Poetica, La deca disputata* were both published in Ferrara in 1586. The remaining parts, completed in 1587–88, *La deca ammirabile, La deca plastica, La deca dogmatica universale, La deca sacra,* and *La deca semisacra,* remained in manuscript and have been published together with an annotated and critical edition of the previously printed works by Danilo Aguzzi Barbagli.[61]

Patrizi had a deeper understanding of music theory than most of his colleagues who discoursed on poetics. He was also a keen observer of the musical scene in Ferrara, as he shows by incidental remarks in his writings. For example, in the dedication to Lucrezia d'Este of the *Deca istoriale* he cites some of the distinguished men of medicine (including Nicolò Leoniceno), letters, and music associated with Ferrara. He exalts the house of Este as "regenerator (*rigeneratrice*) of music, for it was regenerated by Guido Monaco in the Abbey of Pomposa, founded by your ancestors, and then developed and refined by Ludovico Fogliani Modanese, taught in its theory and practiced by the Gusquini, the Adriani, and the Cipriani and by so many others, who were first supported here, and finally both the chromatic and enharmonic of D. Nicola Vicentino were first heard in your house."[62] The composers named are, of course, Josquin Desprez, Adrian Willaert, and Cipriano de Rore.

Patrizi's connoisseurship of musical practice is strongly in evidence in his unfinished dialogue *L'amorosa filosofia,* from 1577, dedicated to the singer Tarquinia Molza, who took part in the famous *concerto delle dame* of the

---

60. These include Philiponos' commentary on Aristotle's *Metaphysics* (1583), and Proclus, *Theological and Physical Elements* (1583).

61. Francesco Patrizi, *Della Poetica,* ed. Danilo A. Barbagli (Florence, 1969).

62. *Della Poetica, La deca istoriale,* fol. 3v. Bargagli's edition, I, 4, lacks the words "de' Gusquini," which occur in the 1586 edition.

Ferrara court. He praises her through the interlocutor Carlo Segonio in these words: "No one else could have a singing voice so smooth and round, or such a happy inclination for every kind of *trillo, moto,* and diminution, and be so secure in every difficult composition, or play the lute so angelically or play the bass viol and sing soprano at the same time, or understand counterpoint and the entire art so well."[63]

Patrizi's object in the *Deca disputata* was to demolish the theory of imitation as the basis of the poetic art. In an earlier work he had shown himself a partisan of the theory of poetic furor.[64] And he began the *Deca disputata* with a more thorough review of this theory.[65] The other nine books are primarily a refutation of mimesis, and the ninth analyzes the proposition that "the ancient poems imitated with harmony and rhythm." As Hathaway has shown, Patrizi rejects Aristotle's theory largely on semantic grounds. He seems to accept the idea behind imitation but not the word's literal meaning: "He was intent on eliminating the *word* 'imitation' from the critic's vocabulary even if the idea expressed by the word remained intact."[66]

Not only was Patrizi dissatisfied with the way the word "imitation" was used but with the terms that served to define musical imitation. Both Plato and Aristotle employed the terms *melos* and *harmonia* in often interchangeable and confusing ways. Plato defined *melos* as made up of rhythm, meter, and speech (*Republic* 398c). Aristotle speaks at one time (*Poetics* 1.4.1447a) of poetry as an imitation through rhythm, speech, and harmony, whereas in another place he says it is with rhythm, *melos,* and meter (1.10.1447b). Or again, he defines embellished speech as made up of rhythm, harmony, and melos (6.3.1449b). In these places rhythm never changes name, but speech in the first and second is meter and in the third is a genus. And harmony, which occurs in the first, in the second is called melos, whereas in the third melos is shown to be song. From all these places, therefore, one gathers that melos has three meanings: (1) it comprehends in general song, instrumental sound, and dance; (2) it is harmony; (3) it points to verse or song alone.[67]

Patrizi would have preferred it if "rhythm" always meant movements of the body as in dance and mime, "harmony" consistently referred to instrumental sounds, and "meter" signified verse and speech. Harmony in

---

63. Quoted in Elio Durante and Anna Martellotti, *Cronistoria del concerto delle dame principalissime di Margherita Gonzaga d'Este* (Florence, 1979), p. 132, from Patrizi, *L'amorosa filosofia,* ed. J. C. Nelson (Florence, 1963), p. 13. Patrizi goes on in this vein for several pages.

64. *La città felice* (Venice, 1553). See the discussion in Baxter Hathaway, *The Age of Criticism: The Late Renaissance in Italy* (Ithaca, 1962), pp. 414ff.

65. *Della poetica, La deca disputata,* I, Barbagli ed., I, 7–35.

66. Hathaway, *The Age of Criticism,* p. 17.

67. *Della poetica, La deca disputata,* IX, Barbagli ed., II, 166.

this sense may be either heard alone or accompanied by song. Harmony without song, that is, instrumental music, which Aristotle called "naked music," was considered by Plato to be of no account. He could find no subject in it that was being imitated (*Laws* 669d). Therefore, Patrizi concludes, "the harmonious sound of any instrument whatever not only is not imitation but it does not even resemble any imitation. Consequently, instrumental sound alone without the company of words and rhythm cannot imitate, nor can it be an imitation."[68]

Patrizi finds support for his doubts in Aristotle's *Problems*, "if they are by him," (19.27.919b), in the one that he translates: "Per quale cagione l'udibile solo de' sensibili ha costume?" (Why of things sensed only that heard has [moral] character?). The ancient author had argued that music, even when not accompanied by words, has character, which is absent in colors and odors, because in the movement of rhythms and pitch there is a resemblance to moral characters. But consonance, which lacks motion, has no moral character: "Ma la consonanza non ha costume."[69] Actually the problem supports the opposite of Patrizi's position. For, having assumed that "harmony" means instrumental music, he imagines a modern ensemble, playing in consonance, whereas pseudo-Aristotle meant that consonances, or more specifically those consonances called symphonies, namely fifths and fourths, are static. "Harmony" in this sense has no ethical character. What remains for Patrizi is rhythm, which does give a semblance of action, but rhythm (that is, dance) is an object of the sense of sight, not that of hearing. Thus any possibility of imitation is eliminated from instrumental music.

Patrizi has greater difficulty explaining away the statement in *Politics* 1340a that he translates:

Ne' *meli* vi sono imitamenti	In *mele* there are imitations
di costumi e questo è mani-	of characters, and this is evident,
festo, perciochè tosto la	because even the nature of
natura dell'armonia è diversa,	the harmony is different,
sì che udendole ci dispognia-	so that hearing them we are
mo diversamente, e non nel	affected differently and not in
medesimo modo ci habbiamo	the same way with
verso ciascuna d'esse.[70]	each of them.

Again Patrizi interprets "harmony" as consonant instrumental accompaniment, when Aristotle used the term to mean "mode." This harmony,

---

68. *Della poetica, La deca disputata* IX, Barbagli ed., II, 171.

69. Gerardo Marenghi, ed., Aristotle, *Problemi musicali,* translates this sentence similarly: "L'accordo di più suoni non ha ethos." E. S. Forster, in *The Works of Aristotle,* ed. W. D. Ross, VII, *Problemata* (Oxford, 1927) however, turns the negative into a positive: "for 'symphony' does possess moral character."

70. *Della poetica, La deca disputata,* IX, Barbagli ed., II, 174.

he says, conforms to that of the song, which in turn follows the words, which express sorrow, joy, anger, or other affection. And if the words imitate the affections, so will the harmony. But these words are truly symbols or signs and declarations of the ideas and movements of the soul ("simboli, e segnali, e dichiaramenti de' concetti e de' movimenti dell'animo") and not imitations.

Patrizi insists that even under the best conditions, when song expresses a text and the voice is properly accompanied, there is no imitation:

> The poet singing his poems and his song accompanied by the harmonic sounds (*suoni harmonichi*) of the kithara or lyre or aulos or other such instrument, considered as pure song, realizes an expression of his ideas (*concetti*) but no imitation or resemblance whatever. But when sound and harmony, as that of kitharists and aulos players, is considered of itself, it realizes neither expression nor resemblance, but, as Plato said, confusion, and it is a thing full of rudeness. But when the kitharist or aulete becomes a kitharode or aulode (that is, a singing kitharist or aulete), then he does realize some imitation and resemblance, not of ideas or affections or characters, but of their expressions, that is of sung speech.[71]

Thus the concetti of the poet pass from his imagination through the ears of the listeners to their souls and move in them the same faculties from which they arose in the poet, and they move in them the same affections that the concetti bore, with all the knowledge, fantasies, opinions, and discourses associated with them.[72] Patrizi's explanation bypasses the process of imitation by reducing the communication from poet to listener—for he considers poetry an oral-aural art—to intellectual, emotional, and spiritual faculties addressing each other directly through the medium of sound. Although Patrizi's partiality to the theory of the poetic furor makes him seem conservative, he is in step with the times in appreciating the importance of the arousal of feeling and in seeing this as short-circuiting the cognitive and reconstructive manipulations of the imitative art.

Expressing the Affections

One of the most vehement opponents of the furor poeticus, Lorenzo Giacomini Tebalducci Malespini, was heading for a psychology of artistic creation and communication that also diminished the validity of the mimetic explanation. What the Platonic writers called poetic furor, he maintained, was really "an internal disposition that is often hidden from our knowledge," a natural gift for conjuring up images charged with associations and affections. A combination of *ingegno, giudicio, docilità,* and *memoria* permits

---

71. *Della poetica, La deca disputata,* IX, Barbagli ed., II, 177.
72. *Della poetica, La deca disputata,* IX, Barbagli ed., II, 169.

the poet to enter into an affection through concentrated imagining (*la fissa imaginazione*). In this state the poet composes not artificially and coldly but almost from the heart. For a genuine affection awakens the conceits that will express it and move others to the same affection. What some regard as furor is the poet's capacity to transform himself into one possessed of a certain affection. But after the poet has created in the heat of a simulated affection, he resorts to judgment to correct the offspring of this rapt state, examining it as if it were the work of another.[73] Giacomini did not find this conception of affective expression incompatible with Aristotle's theory of imitation in the tragedy. He wrote an extended commentary on Aristotle's definition: "Tragedy is an imitation of an action . . . through pity and fear affecting the proper catharsis, or purgation, of these emotions."[74] It is entitled "De la purgatione de la tragedia" and was delivered in 1586 at the Alterati Academy.[75] Giacomini understood catharsis as an affection brought about by the representation of a similar affection. In experiencing the passion of the protagonist on stage the spectator is relieved of his own. Giacomini defines an affection as "a spiritual movement or operation of the mind in which it is attracted or repelled by an object it has come to know."[76] People vary in their disposition toward particular affections, depending on the balance and diversity of spirits in their bodies. An abundance of agile and thin spirits disposes a person toward joyous affections, whereas many torpid and impure vapors prepare the way for sorrow and fear. When the soul is in a sad affection, a great quantity of spirits evaporate and rise to the head. The vapors go particularly to the anterior part of the head, stimulating the seat of fantasy. Condensation of these vapors causes the face to contract and tears to flow. This contraction in turn affects the quality of the voice:

> From the same cause arise cries of lamentation, expelled by Nature through a natural instinct without our awareness to remove thus the bad disposition that afflicts the sensitive part of the soul, contracting it and weighting it down and especially the heart, which, full of spirits and heat, suffers most. Therefore the

73. "Del furor poetico: Discorso fatto da L. G. Tebalducci Malespini nel Academia de gli Alterati nel anno 1587," in Giacomini, *Orationi e discorsi* (Florence, 1597), pp. 53–73. What appears to be an earlier version of this is in Florence, Biblioteca Nazionale Centrale, MS Magl. IX.124, no. 21, fols. 168r–186v. See Palisca, "The Alterati of Florence, Pioneers in the Theory of Dramatic Music," in *New Looks at Italian Opera, Essays in Honor of Donald J. Grout*, ed. William W. Austin (Ithaca, 1968; New York, 1976), pp. 9–37.

74. *Poetics*, 6.2.1449b.24–28.

75. Giacomini, *Orationi*, pp. 29–52, reprinted in *Prose fiorentine raccolte dallo Smarrito [Carlo Dati] accademico della Crusca* (Florence, 1716–45), Pt. II, vol. IV (1729), pp. 212–50. See Hathaway, *The Age of Criticism: The Late Renaissance in Italy*, pp. 251–60, for an appreciation of the importance of this essay in the history of the interpretation of tragic purgation.

76. *Orationi*, p. 38: "altro non è affetto che seguitamento o fuga del anima di alcuna cosa appressa da lei, o come convenevole, o come disconvenevole."

heart moves to shake off its pain and expand and liberate itself of anguish. The lungs and other organs of the voice are set in motion and emit shrieks and groans if not impeded by the intellect. In this way the soul, weighted down by sorrow, lightens itself and gives birth to sad conceits and liberates the passionateness that was in it. Having delivered itself of these, the soul remains free and unburdened. So, even if it should want to cry some more, it cannot, because the vapors that filled the head and are the substance of tears have been consumed. They remain scarce until the mind returns to its original disposition because of some internal alteration of the vapors, or through some active qualities, sad imaginings, or an external incident.[77]

Giacomini's mechanical explanation of the purgative process was intended to elucidate Aristotle's definition, but Giacomini applies it also to music, for Aristotle had linked purgation and music in the *Politics,* when he observed that certain melodies cured persons seized with a form of madness as if they had undergone a purgative treatment.[78] Giacomini cites Aristotle's classification of songs into moral, active, and enthusiastic.[79] Aristotle's view that all these kinds of music should be cultivated appealed to Giacomini more than that of Plato, who allowed only ethical music. For ethical music was not capable of effecting purgation, because melodies analogous to the ancient Dorian, an ethical mode, were not suited to this purpose. Most apt to achieve purgation was music like the ancient Phrygian and Mixolydian and the music of the aulos, which was not used in the moral training of youth. "From harmonies that serve to waken the affections, like the Phrygian and Mixolydian, which had the property of making the soul contracted and somewhat saddened, and from purgative songs that are in keeping with these modes, persons who are quickly moved to sorrow, pity and fear, as well as people in general, receive a purgation, alleviation, and relief that not only is not injurious but is delightfully salutary."[80] Music that aroused passion, then, is not to be banished, for it can relieve the listener of real troubled feelings. Only when passions are uncontrolled and misguided, Giacomini argues, are they evil perturbations.

Giacomini reflected an important trend in contemporary music. No longer did the composer seek only to soothe and moderate emotions for ethical ends, but he aimed to move listeners to the strongest passions, perhaps thereby to purge them. The passions could be evoked only through vivid images deeply felt by the composer. Aristotelian though he was, Giacomini was putting forth a theory of expression, like Patrizi, rather than laying on one more commentary on mimesis.

77. Ibid., pp. 39–40. For the Italian text, see Palisca, "The Alterati," p. 26, n. 32.
78. *Politics* 8.7.1342a.
79. Ibid. 8.7.1341b.
80. *Orationi,* p. 42. For the Italian text, see Palisca, "The Alterati," pp. 27, n. 35.

FOURTEEN

Theory of Dramatic Music

n the preface to *Le musiche sopra l'Euridice* (1601) Jacopo Peri asserted that the ancient Greeks and Romans "according to the opinion of many" sang entire tragedies on the stage.[1] In making this assertion, Peri echoed Ottavio Rinuccini, who, in dedicating the play to Maria de' Medici, queen of France, had said: "It has been the opinion of many, most Christian Queen, that the ancient Greeks and Romans sang the entire tragedies on the stage."[2]

Were there truly many who believed that ancient tragedies were sung in their entirety? The idea did have some support among classicists and poetic theorists, but, to judge by sixteenth-century writings that survive, it was an exaggeration to say that there were many. In the circles immediately surrounding Rinuccini and Peri, it may have seemed a majority, because Girolamo Mei had convinced them that the ancient tragedies were sung from start to finish.[3]

Giovanni Giorgio Trissino represented perhaps the conventional view in his *La quinta e la sesta divisione della poetica* of around 1549.[4] He believed that dancing, and singing with the rhythm of dance, were introduced from time

1. Florence: Giorgio Marescotti, 1601; facs. ed. Giuseppe Vecchi, Bologna, 1969. The preface, "A Lettori," is signed 6 February 1600 Florentine style, or 1601.
2. Dedication of *L'Euridice,* Florence, October 1600, reprinted in Angelo Solerti, *Gli albori del melodramma* (Milan, 1904; repr. Hildesheim, 1969), II, 107.
3. Egert Pöhlmann in "Antikenverständnis und Antikenmissverständnis in der Operntheorie der Florentiner Camerata," *Musikforschung* 22 (1969):5–13, examines this opinion together with other "misunderstandings" and "understandings" of ancient literature about music and tragedy. He identifies some of the Greek and Roman sources for the beliefs but does not consider the route of transmission, nor does he allow for the possibility that Zarlino, Galilei, Patrizi, and Bardi—the authors whom he treats —were interpreting rather than "misunderstanding" the sources, however wrong those interpretations may seem today. In the following review of sixteenth-century opinion on this question I shall save Mei's for last.
4. Venice, 1562, fol. 6r.

to time into the theater as auxiliary species of imitation, and that comedies and tragedies, if they had a chorus, also utilized verse and harmony together but without the rhythm of dance. One may gather from this that Trissino recognized three kinds of music in the theater: instrumental music for dancing, dance-songs, and choral chanting. The first two were incidental to the play, the third essential if the play had a chorus. Trissino did not carefully analyze, as others were later to do, Aristotle's statements on the types of poetry occurring in tragedies, because his purpose was really to provide a formula for modern poetry and to justify his own practices, as was true of most of the Italian poetic theorists of the period.

Benedetto Varchi in his *Lezzioni della poetica,* read to the Accademia Fiorentina in 1553–54, did follow closely Aristotle's method of distinguishing the poetic genres according to the means of imitation that they utilized. Dithyrambs and nomoi used rhythm, discourse, and harmony together, whereas the tragedies and comedies employed them separately, that is, sometimes one of these means, sometimes another.[5] What he meant by this emerges in his commentary on Aristotle's definition of tragedy (*Poetics* 6.1449b), which he first translates literally:

La Tragedia è vna imitazione d'alcuna azzione graue, e perfetta, la quale habbia magnitudine, e sia fatta con sermone soaue, operando ciascuna spezie nelle sue parti separatamente, e che non per modo di narrazione, ma mediante la misericordia, e' il terrore induca la purgazione di cotali passioni.[6]	Tragedy is an imitation of some serious and complete action which has magnitude and is made with embellished speech, each species operating in its [the tragedy's] separate parts, that, not in the manner of a narrative but by means of pity and fear, induces purgation of these very passions.

Varchi recognizes that there are obscurities in this definition, and he proceeds to an explication of each phrase. By "sermone soaue" (*hēdusmenō logō*) Aristotle (6.1449b.22) meant speech that is embellished with rhythm, harmony, and melody (*numero, armonia, e melodia*). These three elements are circumscribed by Varchi:

significando per numero, e armonia il verso, e per melodia il canto de i Cori, e la musica, benche alcuni vogliono, che per numero si debba intendere quel modo di saltare con quale gli antichi cosi	By rhythm and harmony is meant verse, and by melody, the song of the choruses and music, although some would have it that by rhythm is meant that manner of leaping that the ancients, whether

5. Varchi, *Lezzioni* (1590), p. 605.
6. Ibid., p. 657.

Greci, come Latini, vsando atti,	Greeks or Romans, using actions,
gesti, e cenni, rappresentauano	gestures, and signs, performed
le tragedie.[7]	their tragedies.

By "ciascuna spezie nelle sue parti separatamente" Aristotle wished to in-dicate that in tragedies rhythm, harmony, and melody were employed not simultaneously but separately— that is, in different parts of the work some-times verse, sometimes song, was heard. But Varchi declines to say more about music or, for that matter, stage properties and machinery (*apparato*), because if a tragedy were not performed (but merely read silently) there would be neither music nor machinery. Varchi implies that music and stage properties are not essential to the genre of poetry called tragedy. By assim-ilating rhythm and harmony into verse, rather than regarding them as components of melos, he effectively excluded music from all parts of the tragedy except the choruses.

Giraldi Cinthio interpreted Aristotle in a similar vein, but by translating the Greek *harmonia* as "melody" rather than regarding it as a harmony of words, that is, verse, he could be more explicit about the combinations of the three elements. In the prologue only speech is used, in the first chorus verse, melody, and rhythm together, in the other choruses only verse and melody.[8] The rest of the tragedy was spoken. Cinthio, with Varchi, re-stricted music to the chorus, but he more distinctively apportioned the several ornaments of speech—verse, melody, and rhythm— to the several parts of the tragedy.[9]

Orazio Toscanella in a handbook on grammar, rhetoric, poetics, history, logic, and related disciplines, published in 1562, on the contrary, leans toward the view that singing pervaded the tragic and comic performances of the Greeks. His book, a primer or aid for teaching and review, capsulates Aristotle's definition of tragedy in outline form. Tragedy, it goes, is

Vna imitatione d'attione uir-	an imitation of a complete,
tuosa perfetta.	honorable action.
Che habbia grandezza, con	That has grandeur, with
parlar soaue, separatamente	embellished speech, separately
in ciascuna sua spetie, nelle	in each of its species, in the
parti di coloro, che uan	parts of those who are

---

7. Ibid., p. 659.

8. Vincenzo Maggi and Bartolomeo Lombardi in their explication of *Poetics* 1.10.1447b, *In Aristotelis Librum de poetica communes explanationes* (Venice, 1550), p. 59, had pointed this out: "siquidem in prologo sermone tantùm, in primo autem ingressu chori rhythmo, harmonia, & metro: in stasimo uerò non est rhythmus."

9. Giraldi Cinthio, *Discorso intorno all comporre delle comedie e delle tragedie,* quoted in Han-ning, *Of Poetry and Music's Power,* p. 16.

negotiando.	involved in the action.

Parlar soaue è quello, che
ha { Numero / Armonia / Dolcezza

Embellished speech is that which
has { Rhythm / Harmony / Sweetness

Conducendo gli AFFETTI non per uia di Narratione, come si fà il poema heroico;

Arousing the AFFECTIONS not by means of Narration, as is done in epic poetry

ma per uia di { Misericordia / Timore[10]

but by means of { Pity / Fear

Toscanella's reading of *Poetics* 6.2–3.1449b is philogically defective and misleading in its omissions but interesting for the place it gives to music. The word *melos* in the definition of "embellished speech" is rendered "dolcezza," but Toscanella seems to understand that song is implied, as is shown in the immediately succeeding outline of the parts of tragedy, each of which is defined: (1) plot (*Fauola*), (2) character (*Costume*), (3) diction (*Elocutione*), (4) subject (*Discorso*), (5) spectacle (*Apparato*), and (6) music (*Musica*). He clarifies what he means by the last:

intende non solamente quello,
che il choro canta tutto
insieme, quanto tutto quel modo,
che fuor del parlare ordinario
usano gl'histrioni recitando
le fauole.[11]

By it is meant not only that
which the chorus sings all
together, but also that manner,
beyond ordinary speech,
that actors use in reciting
plays.

Toscanella leaves no doubt that he believed Aristotle assigned to both the chorus and actors the kind of embellished speech which contains the three elements rhythm, harmony, and song (*rhythmon kai harmonian kai melos*). But in transmitting this conclusion he overlooked the sentence (*Poetics* 6.3.1449.b) which says that the several embellishments of speech are found in separate parts of the play and not all three continuously, and the further clarification that some of these parts are executed in verse alone, others with the aid of song.

Toward the end of the century several authors began to supplement Aristotle's theoretical approach with historical perspective and documentation. Nicolò Rossi in *Discorsi intorno alla tragedia* (1590), bases his account of the history of the tragedy on a wide range of sources: among them the plays themselves, most of which were by now available in Greek editions, pseudo-Plutarch's *De musica,* Plutarch's *Quaestiones conviviales,* Aristo-

10. Orazio Toscanella, *Precetti necesarii et altre cose vtilissime* (Venice, 1562), fol. 82v.
11. Ibid., fols. 82v–83r.

phanes' comedies, Diogenes Laertius' biography of Plato, writings of Pollux and Athenaeus, the lexicon *Suidas,* and a variety of works of Plato and Aristotle, as well as modern commentators, primarily Julius Caesar Scaliger.[12]

Rossi is critical of some of the statements of both the ancient and modern writers, often challenging them on factual grounds. Before Thespis introduced the first actor, the chorus recited the entire tragedy. The genre received rhythm and harmony from the dithyramb and combined them with diction. But tragedy used them separately, "utilizing rhythm and harmony between the acts."[13]

Francesco Patrizi

The most famous partisan of the view that the tragedy was sung in its entirety was Francesco Patrizi.[14] He arrived at this opinion through studying the ancient writings that were most revealing of the practice of musically performing poetry. They convinced him that in antiquity all poetry was sung, that, indeed, it was written in verse to be sung, and moreover, it was almost always accompanied by instruments and often by dance or gestures.[15] In Patrizi's inclusive conception of music, poetry was one of its subdivisions, for he adopted the encyclopedic schemes of the art of music proposed by Aristides Quintilianus and Michael Psellus. The latter, Patrizi reports, divided music into four principal parts: "material," "apergastic," "exangeltic," and "hypocritical."[16] The first, material, had three parts: metric, harmonic, and rhythmic. The second, apergastic, or "productive," was divided into four parts: (1) metrics, which considers letters, syllables, feet, and quantities in verse; (2) harmonics, which considers high and low tones, intervals, ratios, and consonances and dissonances; (3) rhythmics, which considers in terms of temporal durations movement (*phora*), figure or gesture (*schema*), and sign (*dixis*) and (4) "odics" (*odikon*), or the art of perfect *melos.* The third principal part of music, exangeltic, or instrumental, concerned the instruments through which the material and apergastic aspects were made audible and comprehended kitharody, lyrody, and aulody—that

12. *Poetices libri septem* (Leiden, 1561).

13. Nicolò Rossi, *Discorsi intorno alla tragedia* (1590), ch. 1, ed. Weinberg, *Trattati* IV, 65.

14. Leo Schrade called attention to Patrizi's stand in *Tragedy in the Art of Music* (Cambridge, Mass., 1964), p. 153.

15. *Della poetica, La deca istoriale,* Bk. 6: "Del cantare l'antiche poesie," Barbagli ed., I, 309.

16. Patrizi's source for the work attributed to Psellus was probably the edition published by Arsenius in Venice in 1532: *Opus dilucidum in quatuor mathematicas disciplinas.* See Lukas Richter, "Antike Überlieferungen in der byzantinischen Musiktheorie," *Deutsches Jahrbuch der Musikwissenschaft für 1961* 6 (1962):75–115, esp. 95–98; and idem, "Instrumentalbegleitung zur attischen Tragödie," *Das Altertum* 24 (1978):150–59.

is, the arts of singing to each of the three instruments. The fourth principal part, hypocritical, concerned the putting into operation of the other three principal parts—material, apergastic, exangeltic—by means of song, dance, and mime.[17] This scheme is not unlike that of Aristides Quintilianus, to whom Patrizi turns for the division of melopoeia, the art of composing melos. It consisted of five aspects: genus, tonos, system, mode, and moral character. With respect to genus three distinctions were recognized: enharmonic, chromatic, and diatonic; with respect to system: hypatoid, mesoid, and netoid; with respect to tonos: Dorian, Phrygian, Lydian, etc; with respect to mode: nomic, dithyrambic, and tragic; and with respect to moral character: systaltic, median, and diastaltic. To the tragic was assigned the hypatoid system.[18]

It was within this general sphere of the musical arts that Patrizi located tragedy, and consequently he conceived of it as a musical phenomenon. The texts of the plays themselves, being in verse, suggested to him that they were intended for musical performance. But beyond that the evidence was scarce. Patrizi thought there were traces of the singing of the tragedy in several of the Aristotelian *Problems,* which he realized may not have been written by the philosopher himself. He cites four of these, equivalent to our 19.6, 15, 30, 31, and 48, and gives full translations of the last four. Problem 19.6 does not actually support his case, for it asks why recitation of odes with musical accompaniment (*parakatalogē*) has a tragic character. It does not refer specifically to tragedy. The other three do. Problem 48, which he numbers 47, is the key one for this discussion, and he translates it as follows:

Perchè i cori che son nella tragedia non cantano ipodoristi, nè ipofrigisti? O perchè queste armonie minimo hanno il *melos,* di cui massimamente fa uopo al choro. E la ipofrigisti ha costume prattico, però nel *Gerione* lo esodo e l'armarsi fu fatto in questa. E la ipodorista ha del magnanimo e del costante, e per ciò questa armonia di tutte l'altre è convenientissima alla citarodia. E queste cose ambedue al	Why do the choruses in the tragedy not sing Hypodorian nor Hypophrygian? Is it because these harmoniai have the least *melos,* which the chorus uses most of all. And the Hypophrygian has a practical character. Hence in the *Gerion* the exode and the arming was done in that harmonia. The Hypodorian has a magnanimous and constant character, and for this reason this harmonia is the most suitable of all to kitharody. Both these things are

17. *Della poetica, La deca istoriale,* Barbagli ed., I, 311–12.
18. Ibid., I, 326–27.

choro non convengono, e
più proprie sono a quei
che sono in iscena. Perciochè
essi sono imitatori di eroi, e
i duci de gli antichi solo
erano gli eroi, ma i
popoli eran huomini (communi),
de' quali è il choro.
E però conviene a lui il
dolente e quieto costume
e *melos,* perchè sono
cose da huomini (cotali).
E questo hanno l'altre armonie,
de' quali per niente è
l'ipofrigio, perchè è entu-
siastica e bacchica, e per
essa patiamo non so che,
perciochè più sono patetici i
deboli che i potenti, e per
ciò essa è convenevole a'
chori. Ma
per la ipofrigisti e per la
ipodoristi operiamo (e
siamo in azione), il che non
è proprio del choro, perciò
che il choro è un curatore
sfacendato.[19]

unsuited to the chorus and are
more appropriate for those who
are on the stage. Because they
are imitators of heroes, and
only the leaders of the ancients
played the heroes, whereas the
populace was made up of (common)
men, who also formed the chorus.
Consequently to it is suited a
plaintive and quiet character
and *melos,* because these are
things pertaining to (such) men.
The other harmoniai have this
[character], but not at all the
Hypophrygian, because it is
enthusiastic and Bacchic, and
through it we suffer I do not
know what, because the weak are
more subject to pathos than the
strong; therefore this [harmonia]
is suited to the choruses. But
through the Hypophrygian and
Hypodorian we are operative (and
are in action), which is not
appropriate to the chorus, for
the chorus is an idle guardian.

Patrizi explains that in Problem 30 the author had already implied that the actors were on the stage, whereas the chorus was not. The chorus, Patrizi explicates, was in the orchestra. Now, in Problem 48, the Hypodorian mode and kithara accompaniment are attributed to those on stage, namely to the actors, who, consequently, must have sung. Moreover, the Hypodorian and Hypophrygian were active modes, suited to actors taking the parts of heroes. "From this we understand," Patrizi concludes, "that the entire tragedy, made up of actors and chorus, was sung."[20] Application of the term "harmonies" to the Hypodorian and Hypophrygian puzzles Patrizi, because this was no place for instrumental music. As in the *Deca disputata,* the term *harmonia* always suggests instruments to him; yet there is no question of instruments here, he says, but of vocal music, "which is also harmonious and a harmony."[21]

19. Ibid., I, 331–32.
20. Ibid., I, 331–32.
21. Ibid., I, 332.

Another of the *Problems* that distinguishes the music of the actors from that of the chorus is 19.15, which Patrizi cites in support of his view:

Per qual cagione i nomi non si faceano in antistrofi? ma si l'altre ode choriche? O perchè i nomi erano de gli agonisti. I quali, potendo oggimai imitare e durarvi, l'oda si facea lunga di molte spezie, sì come adunque e le parole e i *meli* seguitavano alla imitazione, sempre diversificandosi. Perchè più è necessario imitar col *melo,* che con parole. E però i ditirambi poi, che si feciono imitativi, non più hanno gli antistrofi, e prima l'haveano. La cagione fu perchè per antico i liberi essi medesimi choreavano, e era malagevole opera che molti in agone cantassero perchè in armonia fracantavano *meli,* perchè più facilmente si muta per molte mutazioni ad uno, che a molti, e all'agonista, overo a coloro che conservano il costume. E però più semplici facean i *meli.* Ma l'antistrofo e; semplice, perchè numero è, e con l'uno si misura. E questo stesso è la cagione perchè le cose di scena non sono antistrofi, e quello del choro sono antistrofi, perciochè l'istrione è agonista, ma il choro imita meno.[22]	Why were the nomoi not composed in antistrophes, but other choric odes were? Is it because the nomoi belonged to the actors, who in this day had the capacity to imitate at length; so the ode was made long and of multiple species? Thus both the words and the *mele* followed the imitation, always varying. Because it is more necessary to imitate with *melos* than with words. Therefore the dithyrambs, now made imitative, no longer have antistrophes, which they once had. The reason was that in ancient times freemen themselves were choristers, and it was difficult for many to sing while acting because they sang in harmony *mele,* and it is easier for one to make many mutations than when there are many actors, and easier for an actor or for those who preserve the moral character. Therefore they made the *mele* simple. But the antistrophe is simple, because it is number, and with unity we measure. And this is the very reason why pieces for the stage are not antistrophes but those of the chorus are, because the actor is a participant, but the chorus imitates less.

Patrizi is justified in concluding from this Problem that the imitative songs were assigned to the actors, who could be given long multiform

---

22. Ibid., I, 333–34. I have rendered "agonista" as "actor," or "participant," rather than "contestant," which is the meaning of the Greek word. Patrizi may have wanted to connote "virtuoso" or "soloist," a sort of *Meistersinger.*

pieces, whereas the chorus, made up of many people, had to have simpler antistrophic and therefore repetitive music. However some of the details of the translation are incorrect. "Overo a coloro che conservano il costume" should have been "che a coloro . . . " and the corresponding English translation would become "than for those who preserve moral character." The phrase "perchè numero è, e con l'uno si misura" is meaningless. What the Aristotelian author intended was that the antistrophe has a fixed number of lines and other members, and each subsequent strophe has the same.

Problem 31 Patrizi also finds revealing, and he translates:

Per qual cagione quei circa	Why were those around Phrynis
Frinico (ciò è Frinico) erano	(that is, Phrynis) more than any-
più tosto melopei? O perchè	thing melopoets? Was it because
allora erano molto di più i	at that time there were more
meli ne i metri delle tragedie.	*mele* in the meters of the tragedies.

Patrizi glosses this problem quite eruditely: "Phrynis in the verses of his tragedies, that is in the iambics and anapests, used harmonies, songs, and *mele,* and, in the manner of the melopoets, perhaps strophes and antistrophes. These were then transferred to the choruses, as may be seen in Euripides, and there were not any longer antistrophes in the verses of the actors on stage."[23]

Patrizi also quotes from Claudius Elianus, *Variae historiae* (3.8), who reports that Phrynis was elected captain of Athens because the citizens admired the way he had composed mele suited to pyrrhic and bellicose verses. This is further evidence, then, that Phrynis used melopoeic modes and songs in the tragedies, and this in the active parts rather than the choruses. But Patrizi admits that this custom must have changed, because Aristotle states that some parts of the tragedy are written with verses and others with melos, which Patrizi interprets to mean that "those of the stage are rendered in verses that are recited and not sung, and the choruses are rendered in song."[24] Patrizi was willing to admit that by the time of Aristotle, who lived a century after the last of the great tragedians— namely, Euripides (d. c. 406 B.C.)—the tragic theater had degenerated into a mixture of spoken and sung verse.

The comedy also was sung in antiquity, Patrizi believed. Its name has the root "ode" in it, just as "tragedy" does. If serious and heroic matters were sung, it is credible that laughable and joking matters would be.

Patrizi's final words on the subject are these: "It is clear that the tragedies were sung in performance. Moreover, taking all these testimonies together many things are to be noted. There were teachers who taught how to use

23. Ibid., I, 332.
24. Ibid., I, 333.

the voice, to increase its size, to preserve it, and they were called *phonasci;* that in the theater nomoi were sung; that the tragedies were sung with high and big voice and, as Cicero said, *vox tragoedorum.*"[25] Patrizi's pronouncements about tragedy and comedy were made in the context of a proof that all poetry was sung in ancient times. One of the pieces of evidence he adduced was the "ancient songs" published by Vincenzo Galilei with their Greek notational signs. Patrizi acknowledges the collaboration of Giovanni Bardi in transcribing a few lines with the help of the notational tables of Alypius, which Galilei also published, having obtained them and the songs from Girolamo Mei.[26] Patrizi assumed from the way they were printed in Galilei's book that there were three hymns, although Galilei refers to "quattro antiche cantilene."[27] The copyist of the manuscript from which Mei obtained the songs, Naples, Biblioteca Nazionale, MS graecus III.C.4, overlooked the fact that a new song began at "Kalliopeia sopha."[28]

Patrizi gives the string names for the notational signs accompanying the first line of the first ode, to the Muse, "Aeide mousa moi philē," but for the incipits of two other songs printed by Galilei, the ode to the sun, "Chionoblepharou pater aous," and the ode to Nemesis, "Nemesi pteroesta [sic] biou ropa," Patrizi simply reproduces the Greek notational letters below the text's syllables. Stanislav Tuksar has compared Patrizi's transcriptions of the first of these lines with those of Bottrigari, Bellermann, and Padre Martini.[29] But there are some problems both with Patrizi's proposal for transcription and Tuksar's interpretation of it. Patrizi gives the following equivalents in the Lydian tonos for the Greek notational letters:

25. Ibid., I, 336. The phrase comes from *De oratore* 1.128. Patrizi also quotes in support of his thesis the following places from Suetonius: *Nero* 25.4, 20.1, 20.2, 22.3, and from Quintilian: *Institutio oratoria* 1.10. See *Della poetica, La deca istoriale,* Barbagli ed., I, 335, and Barbagli's notes thereon.

26. *Della poetica, La deca istoriale,* Bk. 6, Barbagli ed., I, 329–330; Vincenzo Galilei, *Dialogo della musica antica et della moderna* (Florence, 1581), p. 97. For the connection with Mei, see Palisca, *Girolamo Mei,* pp. 59–63.

27. Galilei, *Dialogo,* p. 96.

28. See Egert Pöhlmann, *Denkmäler altgriechischer Musik* (Nuremberg, 1970), p. 23. Pöhlmann shows that there are five songs in the group, beginning with the following words: (1) Aeide, (2) Kalliopeia, (3) Euphameitō, (4) Chionoblepharou, (5) Nemesi. Of these, no. 3 is lacking musical signs in the sources, therefore Mei must not have copied it, and it is missing in Galilei. No. 5 in Galilei's edition is lacking the last fourteen lines. The scribe seems to have been aware of the lacuna, because after line 6 is written "leipei," (is wanting).

29. *The Croatian Renaissance Theorists* (Zagreb, 1980), p. 103. I am grateful to Professor Ivo Supičić for calling my attention to this work and sending me a copy. Bottrigari's transcriptions of the hymns, more extensive but still incomplete, are in his *Il Melone,* pp. 10–11. See Sesini, "Studi sull'umanesimo musicale," where they are reproduced.

Figure 14.1.
Hymn to the Muse, Patrizi's solution

sigma = hypate meson—vocal and instrumental
zeta = paranete diezeugmenon—vocal; nete synemmenon—instrumental
phi = lichanos hypaton—vocal

Galilei, however, supplies only the vocal notation; indeed none of the sources
gives the instrumental notation for this ode. Moreover, Patrizi misread the
tables of Alypius as given in Galilei's publication. Zeta in the vocal notation
is paramese; it is paranete diezeugmenon in the instrumental notation. To
determine an approximate pitch level and therefore the most appropriate
modern pitches for transcription, one should follow Bardi's diagram of the
system, which places the Lydian tonos between A and a' with four sharps.[30]
Patrizi's reading would then be as shown in Figure 14.1.

If in this example the value for zeta is corrected, from paranete diezeugmenon to paramese, which changes f ' to d ', the phrase is then identical
to modern transcriptions of it (and also that given by Tuksar) expect that
Patrizi's is placed a semitone lower.[31] The important point that Patrizi
wanted to make with these musically notated odes was that, if they were
sung, other melic, lyric, and epic poems could also have been sung, each
in one of the seven or eight "tropes." Patrizi's citation of the Greek odes
raises the question of a possible influence on him of the ideas of the group
around Giovanni Bardi and the Camerata's mentor on matters of Greek
music, Girolamo Mei.

Girolamo Mei

Mei traversed some of the same territory in his writings and letters of the
1570's and 1580's as Patrizi did later in his *Deca istoriale*. Much of Mei's
work was made available to Bardi and his circle. They possessed more than
thirty letters that Mei claimed in 1582 to have written to Galilei just in the
previous five years.[32] They may not have known Mei's principal treatise,

30. See above, p. 320.
31. See Pöhlmann, *Denkmäler*, p. 15, no. 1.
32. Palisca, *Girolamo Mei*, p. 12.

De modis musicis antiquorum, the fourth book of which had been sent to Piero Vettori in Florence with permission to circulate it among his friends (but not copy it).[33] On the other hand, an unfinished Italian treatise, which begins "Come potesse tanto la musica," may have been available to them.[34] In a letter to Galilei in 1581, probably of September, Mei informed him that he had completed the section on rhythmics. This section, like Patrizi's treatment of the subject, is based on Aristides Quintilianus.[35]

Although a number of problems concerning the choral music of the tragedy came up in the extant correspondence, the question of the singing of the solo roles did not. However, Mei apparently supplied an Italian translation of the entire Problem 48 with the letter datable September 1581. Comparison of this translation with Patrizi's shows no dependence on Patrizi's part. Mei's quite drastic emendations of the text have no parallel in Patrizi.[36] Mei emended all references to Hypodorian to read Dorian, and in all but one case he emended Hypophrygian to Phrygian. He explained in a letter to Vettori in 1574[37] that Hypodorian and Hypophrygian could not stand, because these two tonoi were not known in Aristotle's time, and besides, Aristotle in *Politics* 8.8-9.1342a-b described the Dorian and Phrygian in terms here used for the two "hypo" tonoi. Some modern editors have made a similar emendation, notably Ruelle, Knoellinger, and Klek.[38] In one place Mei changed Hypophrygian to read Lydian, because the mode is described as furious and Bacchic. Most editors have emended this place to read Phrygian. Mei saw that the text of this problem was faulty and contradicted not only Aristotle's views but those of other ancient writers, whereas Patrizi accepted the reading of the editions or manuscripts uncritically, and this despite the fact that Galilei paraphrased Mei's interpretation in his *Dialogo.*[39] It is likely, then, that Patrizi arrived at his belief in the musical performance of the tragedy and of poetry quite independently.

Of the "many" to whom Rinuccini and Peri referred as believing in the musical performance of the tragedy, Mei must figure prominently. He had

33. Mei sent it to Vettori in 1573. See ibid., p. 31.

34. A fragment from it, in the hand of Giorgio Bartoli, is in the collection of Mei-Galilei letters in Biblioteca Apostolica Vaticana, MS Vat. lat. 2021, fols. 27r–31v. See Palisca, *Girolamo Mei,* pp. 83–84. There is no evidence, however, that Galilei or Bardi requested or received a more complete copy of it, and no copies exist in Florentine libraries. Some of the material may have been covered in the more than twenty letters from Mei to Galilei that do not survive.

35. Ibid., p. 178.

36. See the text of Mei's translation in ibid., 178–79. Galilei cites Mei's emended text in *Dialogo,* p. 145.

37. Mei to Vettori, 28 February 1574, London, British Library, MS Add. 10,268, fols. 322r–323r.

38. *Aristotelis quae feruntur problemata physica* (Leipzig, 1922).

39. P. 145.

expressed this conviction in several of his writings. The earliest was the completed but unpublished treatise *De modis musicis antiquorum*. In Book IV, which Mei sent to Pietro Vettori in 1573, he elaborates upon Aristotle's consideration of the means of imitation in poetry, though he does not identify the text he is commenting upon. One genre of poetry, the epic, was content to imitate with verses alone, but even this was sometimes sung to the lyre and thus received melody. But other genres utilized all the means of poetry—namely verse, melody, and rhythm:

Dithyrambici semper et melicj,	The dithyrambic and melic poets,
quum choros instituerent,	since they wrote choral poems
omnibus que (uti dicitur) nume-	and made melody complete and
ris absolutum melos conficerent,	finished by all types of number
uersu, numero, et harmonia	(as it was called), made
perpetuo uterentur.	constant use of verse, rhythm,
Tragoedi uero et ueteres	and melody. The tragic poets,
comoedi (nouorum enim non	though, and the old comedians
eadem fuit ratio) et	(the new comedy was not the same
satyri in ea sola	in nature) and the writers of
suj operis	satyr plays [used melody and rhythm]
parte, quae	only in that part of the work
chori, qui multitudinem	assigned to the chorus that
ipsam repraesentabat,	represented the crowd, the
tribuebantur, id que quum	chorus, that is, when it was not
chorus ipse non staret; in	stationary. In the remaining parts,
reliquis uero ipso tantum uersu	however, they used only verse
et harmonia: quemadmodum	and melody. How this happened
et in ijs euenisse suspicarj	we may also conjecture
possumus, qui elegos ad Tibiam	from the example of those who sang
canerent, quum chorum non	elegiac verses to the aulos,
haberent.[40]	since they did not have a chorus.

Three types of musical setting result from this analysis. The active chorus in the tragedy and old comedy sang with melody and rhythm (that is, the rhythm of dance). The stationary chorus used melody but not the rhythm of dance. The actors likewise sang without rhythm but were accompanied by the aulos. Mei believed that the aulos played continually during the performance, except during choruses. He refers to this practice in a passage in which he gives examples of what may have been meant by poetic imitation through both harmony and verse:

Ita uero nunc harmonia est	This is how "harmony" is to be
accipienda, ut humanae uocis	assumed: it is to be understood as

40. Biblioteca Apostolica Vaticana, MS Vat. lat. 5323, IV, 18.

cantus cum tibiae uel lyrae
aut citharae uel alius
isticesmodi instrumenti
cantu coniunctus intelligatur.
Melicorum poetarum
permulta sane
genera extiterunt, qui omnes
tum ab instrumentorum diuersi-
tate tum à suo poemate appelarj

the singing of the human voice
joined by the playing of the
tibia and lyre or kithara or another
instrument of this kind.
Very many kinds of melic poets
existed, all of whom, to be sure,
were accustomed to be
called, sometimes by the variety of
instruments, sometimes by their verse.

consueuerunt. in citharoedos
enim et auloedos
primum sunt dispertitj; quod
hi ad citharam aut lyram, ad
Tibiam istj, quam *aulon*
graeci dicunt, suo poemata
canere instituerunt. Hic uero
illud non est omittendum Tragoe-
dos et Comoedos perpetuo Tibijs
usos fuisse: quod etiam et de
Satyris, ni fallor, est existi-
mandum. Fuerit namque Satyri
apud ueteres graecos medium quod-
dam poematis genus inter
Comoediam et Tragoediam.[41]

They first spread
among those who
sang to the kithara and to the
aulos; these began to sing their own
poems, some to the kithara or lyre,
some to the tibia, which the Greeks
called *aulos.* Here should not be
omitted the fact that tragic and comic
actors used tibiae constantly,
which is considered true also even
of the satire, if I am not mistaken.
For the genre of satire among the
Greeks was a genre of poetry
somewhat intermediate between
comedy and tragedy.

Although Mei does not identify it as such, this is a commentary on Aristotle, *Poetics* 6.2–3.1449b. Mei endeavors to explain what is meant by "embellished speech," and particularly the ornament of "harmony." But by assigning to the actors in this statement the continuous accompaniment of the aulos, and by saying in the previous passage quoted that the actors had both verse and melody, he seems to be contradicting Aristotle, who said that some parts of the tragedy were rendered by verse alone.

Mei clarified but did not alter his views on the music of the tragedy and comedy in his Italian treatise, on which he was still working in 1581. There again he sought to distinguish the musical means used in the different genres of poetry:

il Canto e' il suono, la battuta
del Rythmo, e il uerso tutti insieme
seruiuano comunemente ne
Dithyrambi, ne Nomi, e' in somma
in quelle tutte canzoni, ch'essi

Song, instrumental sound, the beat
of rhythm, and verse, all together
served generally in dithyrambs and
nomoi and, in sum, in all those
songs that they called "odes," in

41. Ibid., IV, 18.

chiamauan' ode, e' altramente,
come quelli, che per questi tutti
aiuti hauesser' ogni perfezzione,
di che essi potesser' esser'
capaci, canti perciò perfetti;
e' di più nella Tragedia; e'
medesimamente nella commedia
insino a tanto che l'hebbe Choro;
e' nella satyra, che appresso i
greci era una forma tale di
poema quasi mescolato di queste
due. Vero è che non parimente
in queste tutte. Perche la Tragedia, e' quella tal' commedia
e' la satyra non se ne ualeuan'
congiuntamente sempre per tutto,
come auueniua nell'ode. concio-
siachè nel recitarsi i perso-
naggi di questi poemi non con-
correua la battuta del Rythmo
per la danza, per non ui hauer'
questa allhora luogo (come è cre-
dibile) conueniente; ma solamente
in quella sola parte del choro,
che non era stabile. doue nella
Dithyrambica, e' nella Nomica
concorreuan' tutti sempre
insieme.[42]

other words in those
which through all these aids
acquired every perfection
of which they were capable,
becoming thereby perfect songs.
In the tragedy, and
likewise the comedy,
insofar as they had the chorus,
and in the satyr-play, which among
Greeks was a form of
poem that was a mixture of the two,
it cannot be said that this is true
all the time. For the tragedy and
that type of comedy and the satire
did not take advantage always of
all [the means] jointly as did
the ode. For the
rhythmic beat of dance did not
accompany the reciting of the
personages of these poems,
this not properly
belonging (as is credible),
but only
in that part of the chorus
that was not stationary. In the
dithyrambic and nomic poetry, on the
other hand, all of these means
always concurred.

Again, the active chorus is given all the resources of verse, song, and dance rhythm. The reciters of the character parts and the stationary chorus, however, have only song and free rhythm, without a recurring regular beat. As for the kind of singing practiced in the chorus, Mei elaborates also upon this:

cantandosi però sempre da qual
si uoglia moltitudine di cantanti
insieme una aria sola di canto,
senza hauerui altra mescolanza
di contrappunto ò uarietà di
uoci consonanti fuor' che della
sola diapason. e' questa si per
la sua unione, come per la
necessità de' cantanti. i

Whenever a multitude of singers,
however many, sang together,
they sang only a single melody,
without mixing in any
counterpoint or diversity of
consonant parts except at
the octave. It was used
both because of its united sound
and the need of the singers,

42. Paris, Bibliothèque Nationale, MS lat. 7209², p. 98.

quali molte uolte essendo ò per	who often, being by virtue of
l'età ò per altro accidente	age or other circumstance
diuersi d'organo di uoce	different in their vocal organs,
non poteuan' tutti seruirsi del	could not use
medesimo luogo di tuono. la	the same pitch location. The
qual' aria ueniua secondata	melody was seconded
dallo strumento uno ò più,	by an instrument or more than one,
ò fusse di fiato, ò fusse di	whether wind or
corde, ò d'ammendue insieme.	string, or both together.
col sonar' ne primi tempi le	In the earliest times this playing
medesime corde appunto che	consisted of the very same notes
cantauan' le uoci senza alcuna	that the voices sang without any
diuersità da quelle. e' come essi	difference from them, or, as they
diceuano *proschorda,*	called it, *proschorda.*
e' ne conseguenti,	Later, in ensuing times,
poi che l'ambizzion'	the ambition of the instru-
de gli artefici, abbandonata in	mentalists, who, having abandoned
tutto la riuerenza di quella	all reverence for that
semplice e' costumata antichità,	simple and familiar tradition,
e' datasi tutta preda à fauori	and falling prey to the favors
de Theatri, s'arrischiò à	of the audiences, risked,
pigliar campo rispondendo	in order to gain the field, answering
all'aria della uoce naturale	the melody of the natural voice
con accordi di consonanze, e'	with chords of consonant notes, or,
come dà lor' si diceua	as they called it,
symphōnōs.[43]	*symphōnōs.*

The chorus always sang in unison or in octaves and was similarly accompanied in unison or octaves until the players of instruments began to cater
to the crowd and departed from this simple style to indulge in exhibitionist
sallies that Plato criticized when he introduced the two terms *proschorda* and
symphōnos.[44]

Mei went into the form of the choral ode in response to a question from
Galilei as to the meaning of "antistrophe." Mei explained that sections of
a choral ode corresponded with each other with respect to verse, melody,
and rhythm, like the stanzas of a modern canzone. The ode was divided
into three parts: strophe, antistrophe, and epode. The strophe and antistrophe were of equal number and "quality" of lines, whereas the epode was
different, but if the strophe and antistrophe were repeated, the further epodes
were modeled on the first. The names of these parts of the ode came from

43. Ibid., pp. 100–101.
44. *Laws* 7.821d–e. In his letter of 8 May 1572 to Galilei (Palisca, *Girolamo Mei,* pp. 112–
13), Mei speculates about the transition from the instrumental practice of shadowing the voices
to that of leading the way and introducing different rhythms, diminutions, and *passaggi.*

the fact that they were sung while dancing in a circle. The strophe was danced by beginning in a right-handed direction, then moving to the left, then returning to the right. The antistrophe went in the opposite directions, whereas the epode was sung standing still. With time the strict observance of the form was loosened, first in the nomoi, then in the dithyrambs, because as the poems became imitative it was not possible to conform to the repetition, which prevented the poets "from suitably expressing actions and ideas (concetti) as new verses, full of affections for the most part contrary to the first, came up." Mei does not specifically relate this antistrophic form to the tragic chorus, but it is obviously relevant.[45]

Mei's description of the music of the solo roles in the Italian treatise is also consistent with his earlier statements:

Ne' personaggi poi della Tragedia e' della Commedia e' della satyra si seruiuano solamente del uerso e' dell'harmonia così di uoce come di strumento, ualendosi in questo caso de' Pifferi soli, come di quelli, che fusser' accommodati à soprastar' con la quasi gagliardia del lor' suono ogni tumulto de gli spettatori. doue (e' questo spezzialmente appresso i latini) il suono dello strumento à recitanti soleua nel pronunziare seruir' in certo modo di guida, si della battuta del Rythmo, come dell'aria della uoce; quasi sostinendola e' facendola co' suoi modi e' forme, essendo seguitato da lei, quasi la strada innanzi. e' non come auueniua ne' chori tutti tanto di questi poemi quanto de gli altri, ne' quali il suono haueua più tosto luogo di compagnia che d'altro; andando con essi à suo piacer' consonando.[46]	For the actors' parts of the tragedy, the comedy, and the satyr-play they employed only verse and melody, whether in the voice or instrument, relying in this case upon pipes alone, in that they were suited to surpass with the vigor of their sound all the uproar of the spectators. The sound of the instruments, especially among the Romans, used to serve the actors as a kind of guide to their delivery, whether for the beat of the rhythm, or the melody of the voice; almost sustaining it and paving the way with its modes and forms, since the voice followed it. This was not like what happened in the choruses, whether of these poems or of others, in which the instruments had the function of keeping the chorus company more than anything else, going along with it, making consonances at will.

Unfortunately Mei tended not to cite references unless two or more

45. Letter, Mei to Galilei, c. September 1581, in Palisca, Girolamo Mei, pp. 167–69.
46. Ibid., p. 101.

authors disagreed. His statements concerning the music of the tragedy represent not so much documented facts as conclusions based on wide reading of many disparate sources. They were syntheses and reconstructions. One may assume that he knew most of the founts that are cited by modern authors who have defended the pervasive role of music in the tragedy. The most controversial question is surely the nature of the declamation of the solo roles. Aristotle in his *Poetics* says little specifically about the musical performance of actors. In 12.1.1452b.18, he mentions stage songs (*apo tēs skēnēs*) peculiar to certain plays, and the kommoi, or joint lamentations of chorus and actors. The places in the *Problems* identified by Patrizi were undoubtedly known also to Mei. Numerous references in plays of Aristophanes and in the scholia to them to musical performance in the tragedies had surely not escaped his attention. To proceed from these and other scattered references to the belief that actors declaimed continuously to the sound of the aulos or that the entire tragedy was sung was nevertheless a bold leap of the imagination.

Modern scholarship has tended to vindicate, in part at least, the view, for long unpopular, that music had a large part in the performance of the classical tragedies. A recent study by Mario Pintacuda presents a sympathetic, yet critical, review of the evidence for the musical side of the Greek tragedy.[47] He sets out to determine which of the parts of the tragedies were spoken, which were declaimed with the accompaniment of the aulos (*parakataloghē*), and which were sung. He finds that the meter is the best guide to making these distinctions. The iambic tetrameter was intended for simple spoken recitation. Lyric verses, intended for singing, were of varied rhythm and unequal length. Between these two categories fall those lines declaimed with the accompaniment of the aulos. Ottavio Tiby imagines the transition between speech and accompanied declamation as follows: "When the action unfolds in tranquility, the characters say their iambic trimeters with hardly any emotion. The aulos begins its melodies, upon which the declamation of iambics and anapests is modeled. As the lyric flight and the pathetic impulse become more intense, the rhythms more varied and lively, the chorus and the performers burst into song."[48]

In the most ancient tragedies the first choral entry, the *parodos*, in anapests, was sung while the chorus made its procession into the orchestra. Once in

---

47. Mario Pintacuda, *La musica nella tragedia greca* (Cefalù, 1978). See also Giovanni Comotti, *La musica nella cultura greca e romana,* in Società Italiana di Musicologia, *Storia della musica,* I, 1, pp. 34–35. The most thorough investigation of the question is Lukas Richter, "Musikalische Aspekte der attischen Tragödienchöre," *Beiträge zur Musikwissenschaft* 14 (1972):247–98. Also see his "Instrumentalbegleitung zur attischen Tragödienchöre," *Das Altertum* 24 (1978):150–59.

48. *La Musica in Grecia e a Roma* (Florence, 1942), p. 110, quoted in Pintacuda, *La musica nella tragedia greca,* p. 26.

place it sang its first ode accompanied by dancing. From here on the chorus had three stasimons, separated by four episodes. The episodes contained the active parts of the drama. But the chorus could interact with the actors in kommoi, as in the grand kommos in *Choephoroe* ("The Libation Bearers") of Aeschylus, lines 305–476, in which Orestes, the Chorus, and Electra alternate strophes and antistrophes.[49] Aristotle called the kommos "a joint lamentation of Chorus and actors."[50] Finally there were the sung monodies and dialogues divided between two or three persons. These solo numbers were a late development, and there is only one in Aeschylus (*Prometheus*, lines 574–612) and two in Sophocles (*Electra*, lines 86–120, and *Oedipus at Colonus*, lines 237–53), while there are seventeen in twelve tragedies of Euripides.[51]

This is how modern scholarship circumscribes the role of music in the Greek tragedy. Mei and Patrizi went well beyond. Who can say that they went utterly beyond the pale? As D. B. Monro reminds us, "Several indications combine to make it probable that singing and speaking were not so widely separated from each other in Greek as in modern languages with which we are most familiar. Music and grammar, he points out, share numerous key words, such as *tonos,* which means both "accent" and "pitch" or "key," and *oxys* and *barys,* which mean "acute" and "grave", respectively, and also "high" and "low." A long syllable is equal to two short, and a syllable may have two accents. So a word becomes like a musical phrase.[52] Whether Mei and Patrizi were right about the Greek theater may depend on where we draw the line between speech and song and on whether we draw it at all.

So far as the Roman stage is concerned also, our two authors find some support in modern commentaries. William Beare in his study of the Roman theater has marshaled impressive evidence for his conclusion that "the greater part of most Latin plays was declaimed to musical accompaniment."[53] "It is generally agreed," he states, "that the passages in iambic senarii were meant for utterance without accompaniment, and that all the other metres were meant to be accompanied by the pipes." Plautus expected the tibia player to accompany all meters except the iambic senarii. The letters *C* (for *canticum*) and *DV* (*diverbium*) which appear in the scripts were probably an indication of whether the scene was accompanied or not.[54]

49. See the schematic outline in Pintacuda, *La musica nella tragedia,* pp. 115–16.

50. *Poetics* 12.1452b.24–25, trans. S. H. Butcher, p. 43.

51. Pintacuda, *La musica nella tragedia,* p. 29.

52. D. B. Monro, *The Modes of Ancient Greek Music* (Oxford, 1894), p. 113.

53. *The Roman Stage,* 3d ed. (New York, 1963), p. 168.

54. See also Comotti, *La musica,* pp. 51–53; Günter Wille, *Musica romana: Die Bedeutung der Musik im Leben der Römer* (Amsterdam, 1967), pp. 158–78.

Jacopo Peri

Jacopo Peri, who was neither a literary man nor a humanist but a singer and composer, drew upon a number of the findings and ideas of the humanists to forge a new style of vocal music. In the preface to the published score of his *Euridice,* after stating, as quoted at the head of the present chapter, that it was the opinion of many that the ancient Greeks and Romans sang their entire tragedies, he proceeded to justify his strange new style of setting the actors' parts. Peri's indebtedness to humanist predecessors for the ideology behind this innovation is revealed by an analysis of key passages of this apology.[55]

Peri acknowledges that his object was to imitate in song a speaking voice, realizing a heightened speech like that of the ancient tragedies:

Onde veduto, che si trattava di poesia Dramatica, e che però si doueua imitar col canto chi parla (e senza dubbio non si parlò mai cantando) stimai, che gli antichi Greci, e Romani (iquali secondo l'openione di molti cantauano su le Scene le Tragedie intere) vsassero vn'armonia, che auanzando quella del parlare ordinario, scendesse tanto dalla melodia del cantare, che pigliasse forma di cosa mezzana.[56]	Seeing that dramatic poetry was concerned and that therefore one ought to imitate with song someone speaking (and without doubt people never spoke singing), I decided that the ancient Greeks and Romans (who according to the opinion of many sang entire tragedies on the stage) employed a melody that, elevated beyond ordinary speech, descended so much from the melody of song that it assumed an intermediate form.

Peri did not identify any of "the many" who believed that the entire tragedies were sung in antiquity. He may not even have known who some of them were. But it is likely that the immediate source of the idea was the circle around Bardi and that the ultimate source was Girolamo Mei. Peri himself may not have attended the musicales and discussions at Bardi's house, since he was a rival of Bardi's protégé Giulio Caccini, but he would have been in touch with the ideas circulating there through Ottavio Rinuccini and Vincenzo Galilei, who were patronized by Peri's sponsor and collaborator Jacopo Corsi. The latter also held musicales and discussions at his house, attended by Florentine literary, scientific, and musical leaders, and, indeed, was the sponsor of the production of *Euridice* put on for the

---

55. The preface is reprinted in Angelo Solerti, *Le origini del melodramma* (Turin, 1903), pp. 45–49, and is translated in full in Strunk, *Source Readings,* pp. 373–76, where it differs in some small details from the translation given here.

56. Peri, *Le musiche sopra l'Euridice* (Florence, 1600; repr. Bologna, 1969), fol. a1r.

wedding of King Henry IV of France and Maria de' Medici and first performed on 6 October 1600.

Peri elaborates upon the nature of the melody that was intermediate between speech and song in the next passage from the preface:

E per cio tralasciata qualunque
altra maniera di canto vdita fin
quì, mi diedi tutto a ricercare
l'imitazione, che si debbe a questi
Poemi; e considerai, che quella
sorte di voce, che dagli Antichi al
cantare fu assegnata, la quale
essi chiamauano Diastematica (quasi
trattenuta, e sospesa)
potesse in parte affretarsi,
e prender temperato corso tra
i mouimenti del canto sospesi, e
lenti, e quegli della fauella
spediti, e veloci, & accomodarsi al
proposito mio (come l'accomodauano
anch'essi, leggendo
le Poesie, & i versi
Eroici) auuicinandosi all'altra del
ragionare, la quale continuata
appellauano; Il che i nostri
moderni (benchè forse ad altro
fine) hanno ancor fatto nelle
musiche loro.[57]

For this reason, putting aside
every other manner of singing heard
up to now, I dedicated myself wholly
to searching out the imitation that
is owed to these poems. And I
reflected that the sort of voice
assigned by the ancients to song,
which they called diastematic (as
if to say sustained and suspended)
could at times be hurried,
and take a moderate course between
the slow, sustained movements
of song and the fluent and rapid ones
of speech, and thus suit
my purpose (just as the
ancients, too, adapted the voice
to reading poetry and
heroic verses), approaching that
other [voice] of conversation,
which they called continuous
and which our moderns (though
perhaps for another purpose) also
used in their music.

The distinction between diastematic and continuous cited here is direct evidence of the reading on the part of Peri or his mentors of the ancient authors, if not Aristoxenus, who seems to have originated the classification, at least Boethius, who reported it. Boethius mentioned also a third type of voice, which, he said, was recognized by Albinus: "We read a heroic poem neither in a continuous flow as in prose nor in the sustained and more sluggish manner of voice as in song."[58] Those who read this passage in Boethius may not have realized that the intermediate style had earlier been described by Aristides Quintilianus.[59]

While remaining true to the intervallic nature of music, in which discrete pitches are sustained, however lengthily or briefly, Peri sought to imitate

57. Ibid., fol. a1r.
58. Boethius *De institutione musica* 1.12; Friedlein ed., p. 199: "His, et Albinus autumat, additur tertia differentia, quae medias voces possit includere, cum scilicet heroum poema legimus neque continuo cursu, ut prosam, neque suspenso segniorique modo vocis, ut canticum."
59. *De musica* 1.4.

the more rapid and less pitch-conscious inflections of speech, in which the voice slides over a range of pitches without stopping on any of them. It is significant that he recognized this creative effort as an act of imitation, not in the sense of an emulation of the ancients, which it is also, but of imitation of natural speech. Music, like poetry, was an imitation of action, as Aristotle taught.

To realize this imitation Peri had to strike out in a direction different from the ancients, for the speech he was bent on imitating was Italian speech. The literary theorists had shown that Italian poetry was accentual rather than quantitative, that it was organized through pitch inflection rather than metrical time units. Peri now perceptively points out another quality of Italian speech, one not marked by the literary theorists. Certain vowels in a sentence are sustained, while the speaker rushes through many others. Thus Italian speech is a mixture of the sustained diastematic motion of the voice and the continuous. The proportion between sustained and gliding syllables and the rapidity of delivery varied with a speaker's state of mind and affection:

Conobbi parimente nel nostro par-lare alcune voci, intonarsi in guisa, che vi si puo fondare armonia, e nel corso della fauella passarsi per altre molte, che non s'intuonano, finchè si ritorni ad altra capace di mouimento di nuoua consonanza; & hauuto riguardo a que' modi, & a quegli accenti, che nel dolerci, nel rallegrarci, & in somiglianti cose ci seruono, feci muouere il Basso al tempo di quegli, hor piu, hor meno, secondo gli affetti.[60]	I recognized likewise that in our speech certain sounds are intoned in such a way that a harmony can be built upon them, and in the course of speaking we pass through many that are not so intoned, until we reach another that permits a movement to a new consonance. Keeping in mind those manners and accents that serve us in our grief and joy and similar states, I made the bass move in time with these, faster or slower according to the affections.

Although Peri does not ally his principle of sustained vowels with the accentual interpretation of Mei and other literary theorists, in practice he observes the accents that convention dictated for eleven- or seven-syllable lines. For example, in the passage in the speech of the messenger, Dafne, who announces to Orfeo the sudden death of Euridice, the accents may be identified as follows (marked by a italics):

Ma la *bel*-la Eu-ri-*di*-ce
1   2 3   4   5 6 7

60. Ibid., fol. a1r.

Mo-uea dan-zan-do il *piè* sul ver-de *pra*-to
1   2   3   4   5 6 7 8   9 10 11
Quand'ahi *ria* sor-te a-*cer*-ba
1   2 3 4   5 6 7
An-gue *cru*-do, e spie-*ta*-to
1 2 3   4 5   6 7
Che ge-la-to gia-*cea* tra fio-ri e *l'er*-ba
1   2 3 4 5 6 7 8   9 10 11

Recalling that in the seven-syllable line the accents are usually on the third and sixth syllables, whereas in the eleven-syllable line they are on the fourth or sixth and tenth, we find that Peri has observed all of these accents by lengthening the duration of the sung note relative to surrounding note values (see Figure 14.2). The rate of delivery passes from an eighth-note per non-accented syllable in normative passages to a sixteenth-note per syllable in excited moments, such as mm. 5 and 6. Peri has in this manner imitated the Italian reciter of poetry, not some antiquarian quantitative model of classical prosody.[61] Peri's most original contribution to the synthesis of spoken recitation is described in the words that immediately follow in his preface:

e lo tenni fermo tra	I held [the bass] fixed through
le false, e tra le buone	both dissonances and
proporzioni, finchè	consonances until the
scorrendo per varie note	the voice of the speaker, having
la voce di chi ragiona, arriuasse a	run through various notes, arrived
quello che nel parlare ordinario	at a syllable that, being intoned
intonandosi, apre la via a nuouo	in ordinary speech, opened the
concento; E questo non solo,	way to a new harmony. I did this
perchè il corso del ragionare	not only so that the flow of the
non ferisse l'orecchio	speech would not offend the ear
(quasi intoppando negli incontri	(almost stumbling upon the
delle ripercosse corde, dalle	repeated notes with more frequent
consonanze piu spesse,) ò non	consonant chords), but also so that
paresse in vn certo modo ballare al	the voice would not seem to dance to
moto del Basso, e principalmente	the movement of the bass, particularly
nelle cose, ò meste, ò graui, richie-	in sad or severe subjects, granted
dendo per natura l'altre piu liete,	that other more joyful subjects would
piu spessi mouimenti:	require more frequent movements.
Ma ancora, perchè l'vso delle	Moreover, the use of dissonances
false, ò scemasse, ò ricoprisse	lessened or masked
quel vantaggio, che ci s'aggiugne	the advantage gained
dalla necessità dell'intonare	from the necessity of intoning
ogni nota, di che per cio fare	every note, which perhaps for

61. For a more detailed analysis of this example, see Palisca, "Peri and the Theory of Recitative," in *Studies in Music* 15 (1981):51–61.

Figure 14.2.
From Peri, *L'Euridice* (Florence, 1601), p. 15

poteuan forse hauer manco
bisogno l'antiche Musiche.
E però, (sìcome io non
ardirei affermare questo essere
il canto nelle Greche, e nelle
Romane fauole vsato),
così ho creduto esser quello, che
solo possa donarcisi dalla nostra

this purpose was less needed
in ancient music.
Thus (though I would not
venture to assert that this was
the singing style used by the Greeks
and Romans in their plays),
I believed it was the only style
that our music could yield that

solo possa donarcisi dalla nostra	that our music could yield that
Musica, per accomodarsi alla nostra	would be suited to our
fauella.[62]	speech.

A note set to one of the syllables intoned in speech is accompanied by a bass note and chord that is consonant with it. This bass note and chord remain fixed while the voice moves on through the syllables that are not sustained. Repetition of the chord under each such passing note is avoided so as not to produce the clashes that would "offend the ear." Likewise the bass does not move to form a new harmony under each syllable, because this would cause the voice "to dance to the movement of the bass." Rather the bass and harmony change only when the singer reaches a new sustained syllable, which then is accompanied by a consonant bass and harmony. The syllables that are not intoned may get either consonances or dissonances, since they do not have to obey any rules of harmony. The frequency of meeting of the voice with the consonances built upon the bass varies according to the affection. In moments of joy a speaker intones or sustains syllables more often, which a composer imitates by changing the notes of the bass more frequently to meet the freshly intoned syllables. Speaking excitedly or beset by sorrow, the voice intones fewer syllables, leading the composer to move the bass more slowly.

By this means Peri realized an imitation of heightened speech, the "parlare soave" of the Aristotelian commentators. The voice is not hindered by contrapuntal obligation to other parts. So it is free to declaim the text according to speechlike accents and durations, hurrying and hesitating in imitation of the character and passion. Passing notes between intoned, chordally accompanied, pitches simulate the continuous motion of the voice of speech, for the mixture of consonances and dissonances masks the diastematic nature of the singing. An almost random mixture of consonances and dissonances among the nonintoned syllables diverts the mind from constantly anticipating resolution of dissonance into sweet concordance. The listener's attention is thus directed to the message of the text, as it would be in hearing ordinary speech.

Peri's new style of *recitar cantando* was born of the meeting of creative intuition and humanist learning. If we believe his words, it was the fruit of a search for a manner of singing, like that of the ancient tragedy, which was neither speech nor song but something in between. Peri in the passages of the preface analyzed here concentrated on setting the active parts of the play, those which in ancient times, according to the theories of Mei and Patrizi, would have been sung with melody and verse but without the rhythm of dance. Of the task of setting lyrical moments, interpolated songs,

62. Peri, *L'Euridice,* fol. a1r.

and choruses, both danced and reflective, he did not speak. For here he followed conventions that were already established in theatrical music.[63] Some of these conventions betray earlier waves of humanist influence. However, the three categories of theatrical music recognized by Mei and Patrizi were not realized in a single work before Peri's score. The reflective choruses are set in madrigal style; although they are regular in musical meter, they lack the rhythm of dance, in conformance with the views of the literary theorists; these are equivalent to the ancient stasimons. The active choruses, parallel to the antistrophic choruses of old, exhibit the rhythm of dance and are composed in a conventional manner rather than in imitation of speech. Finally, there is a category of chorus which was new, and which Peri must have subsumed under the speechlike idiom he described: one vocal line sung either by a member of a group or by the entire group in unison and composed in the recitational style. Sometimes it is answered by a polyvoice chorus, like the ancient *kommoi* in which the chorus had a dialogue with an actor. An example would be the lamenting unison chorus "Cruda morte," which is answered by a five-part chorus in canzonet style, "Sospirate."[64] An example of a reflective chorus is "Poi che gl'eterni imperi."[65] There are several examples of dance-choruses, the most elaborate of which is the final chorus, "Biond'arcier." *L'Euridice*, then, embodies a conscious striving for a return to an ancient manner of singing, inspired by the revival of interest in ancient theater and in the theory of dramatic poetry.

63. See Nino Pirrotta and Elena Povoledo, *Li due Orfei, da Poliziano a Monteverdi* (Rome, 1969; rev. trans. as *Music and Theatre from Poliziano to Monteverdi,* by Karen Eales, Cambridge, 1982); and Wolfgang Osthoff, *Theatergesang und darstellende Musik in der italienischen Renaissance* (Tutzing, 1969).

64. 1600 ed., pp. 19–20; pp. 76–77 in Howard M. Brown ed. (Recent Researches in the Music of the Baroque Era, vols. 36 and 37; Madison, 1981).

65. 1600 ed., pp. 39–40; Brown ed., pp. 140ff.

Works Cited

Abano, Pietro d'. *Expositio problematum Aristotelis (cum textu, latine)*. Mantua: Paulus Johannis de Puzpach, 1475.

Agostini, Giovanni degli. "Notizie istoriche spettanti alla vita e agli scritti di Batista Egnazio, sacerdote viniziano." In *Raccolta d'opuscoli scientifici e filologici*, edited by A. Calogerà, XXXIII, 1–191. Venice: Simone Occhi, 1745.

Albertus Magnus. *De caelo et mundo*. In *Opera omnia*, V, 1. Albertus Magnus Institute of Cologne, 1951–78.

Alexanderson, Bengt. *Textual Remarks on Ptolemy's Harmonica and Porphyry's Commentary*. Studia graeca et latina Gothoburgensia, 27. Göteborg, 1969.

Alvisi, Edoardo. *Cesare Borgia, Duca di Romagna, Notizie e documenti*. Imola, 1878.

Ambros, August Wilhelm. *Geschichte der Musik im Zeitalter der Renaissance bis zu Palestrina*. Geschichte der Musik, III. Breslau, 1868.

[Anonymi of Bellermann]. Edited by Friedrich Bellermann in *Anonymi scriptio de musica Bachii senioris introductio artis musicae*. Berlin, 1841. Edited by Dietmar Najock in *Drei anonyme griechische Traktate über die Musik: eine kommentierte Neuausgabe des Bellermannschen Anonymus*. Göttinger musikwissenschaftliche Arbeiten, 2. Kassel, 1972. Translated by Giovanni Francesco Burana. Verona, Biblioteca Capitolare, MS CCXL (201), fols. 37v–44v.

Anselmi, Giorgio. *De musica*. Edited by Giuseppe Massera. Florence, 1961.

Aristides Quintilianus. *De musica libri tres*. Edited by R. P. Winnington-Ingram. Leipzig, 1963. *Musica e graeco in latinum conversa*. Translated by Giovanni Francesco Burana. Verona, Biblioteca capitolare, MS CCXL (201), fols. 1r–25v, dated 15 April 1494. *On Music In Three Books*. Translation, with introduction, commentary, and annotations by Thomas J. Mathiesen. New Haven, 1983.

Aristotle. *[De audibilibus.] Dell'oggetto dell'udito overo delle cose udibili, libbro frammentato di Aristotile*. Translated into Italian by Ercole Bottrigari. Bologna, Biblioteca Universitaria, MS lat. 345 (326), no. 6, dated 14 January 1606. Translated by Francesco Patrizi as *De iis, quae sub auditu cadunt sive de audibilibus Aristotelis libri fragmentum*. Bologna, Biblioteca Universitaria, MS lat. 345 (326), no. 5. Translated by W. S. Hett in *Minor Works*. Cambridge, Mass. 1936. *See also* Gogava.

———. *On the Soul*. Translated by W. S. Hett. Cambridge, Mass., 1967.

435

———. *Poetics*. Translated by William of Moerbeke as *De arte poetica,* edited by E. Valgimigli. Bruges-Paris, 1953. Translated by Giorgio Valla as *Ars poetica.* Venice: Simon Papiens dictus Bevilaqua, 1498. *See also* Butcher.

———. *Problemata.* Translated by [Bartolomeo da Messina] in Pietro d'Abano, *Expositio problematum Aristotelis (cum textu latine).* Mantua: Paulus de Puzbach, 1475. Translated by [Bartolomeo da Messina] and Theodore Gaza in *Problemata Ar[istotelis] cum duplici translatione, antiqua et noua T. Gaze: cum expositione Petri Aponi.* Venice: Bonetus Locatellus, 1501. Translated by Theodore Gaza in *Aristotelis Philosophi Problematum particula prima.* Rome: Johannes Reynhardt, 1475. Idem, *Traductio noua problematum Aristotelis.* Mantua: Iohannes Vurster & Iohannes Baumeister, 1475(?). Edited by Charles-Émile Ruelle, Hermann Knoellinger, and Joseph Klek in *Aristotelis quae feruntur problemata physica.* Leipzig, 1922. Edited and translated by Gerardo Marenghi. Florence, [1957]. Section 11 also edited by Gerardo Marenghi as *Problemi di fonazione e di acustica.* Naples, 1963. Translated by E. S. Forster in *The Works of Aristotle,* edited by W. D. Ross, VII. Oxford, 1927. Translated by W. S. Hett. Cambridge, Mass., 1936–37. Section 19 translated into Italian by Lorenzo Giacomini. Florence, Biblioteca Riccardiana, MS 1612, fols. 86r–100r.

Aristoxenus. *Elementa harmonica.* Edited and translated by Henry S. Macran in *The Harmonics of Aristoxenus.* Oxford, 1902. Edited and translated by Rosetta da Rios. Rome, 1954. *See also* Gogava, Meurs.

Aron, Pietro. *Lucidario in musica.* Venice: Girolamo Scotto, 1545.

———. *Thoscanello in musica.* Venice: Bernardino and Matheo de Vitali, July 1523.

———. *Trattato della natura et cognitione di tutti gli tuoni di canto figurato.* Venice: Bernardino de Vitali, 4 August 1525.

Athenaeus of Naucratis. *Deipnosophistae.* Edited by Marcus Musurus. Venice: Aldo Manuzio, 1514. Translated by Noël dei Conti. Venice: Andrea Arrivabene, 1556. Translated by Charles Burton Gulick. London, 1941.

Averroës. *Determinatio in poetria Aristotelis.* Translated by Hermannus Alemanus. Venice, 1481. Edited by Lorenzo Minio-Paluello, in Aristoteles Latinus, no. 33. Leiden, 1968.

Bacchius Senior. *Introductio artis musicae.* Edited by Friedrich Bellermann in *Anonymi scriptio de musica Bachii senioris introductio artis musicae.* Berlin, 1841. Translated by Otto Steinmayer as *Introduction to the Art of Music.* In press.

Barbaro, Daniello. *I dieci libri dell'architettura di M. Vitruvio tradotti e commentati.* Venice: Francesco de' Franceschi Senese and Giovanni Chrieger Alemanno, 1567.

Barbour, J. Murray. *Tuning and Temperament.* East Lansing, 1953.

Bardi, Giovanni. *Discorso mandato a Giulio Caccini detto Romano, sopra la Musica anticha, e 'l cantar bene.* In G. B. Doni, *Lyra Barberina,* (Florence, 1763), II, 233–248; Biblioteca Apostolica Vaticana, MS Barberinus lat. 3990, fols. 4r–13v; Florence, Biblioteca Marucelliana, MS A287, I, fols. 3v–13v.

———. "In difesa dell'Ariosto." Florence, Biblioteca Nazionale Centrale, MS Magliabecchiana VI.168.

Baron, Hans. *The Crisis of the Early Italian Renaissance.* Princeton, 1955; rev. ed., 1966.

Bartoli, Giorgio. *Degli elementi del parlar toscano.* Florence: Giunti, 1584.

Beare, William. *The Roman Stage*. 3rd ed. New York, 1963.

Becker, Heinz. *Zur Entwicklungsgeschichte der antiken und mittelalterlichen Rohrblattinstrumente*. Hamburg, 1966.

Bembo, Pietro. *Prose . . . della volgar lingua*. Venice: G. Tacuino, 1525. Edited by Mario Marti. Padua, 1967.

Bene, Giulio del. *Del conuiuio delli Alterati*. Florence, Biblioteca Nazionale Centrale, MS Magliabecchiana IX.137, fols. 12r–22r.

Benedetti, Giovanni Battista. *Diversarum speculationum mathematicarum & physicorum liber*. Turin: Successors of Nicola Bevilaqua, 1585.

Berger, Karol. *Theories of Chromatic and Enharmonic Music in Late 16th-Century Italy*. Ann Arbor, 1980.

Bernstein, Lawrence F. "Notes on the Origin of the Parisian Chanson." *Journal of Musicology* (1982):275–326.

Bertola, Maria. *I due primi registri di prestito della Biblioteca Apostolica Vaticana*. Vatican City, 1942.

Besseler, Heinrich. "Das Renaissanceproblem in der Musik." *Archiv für Musikwissenschaft* 22 (1966):1–10.

——. *Die Musik des Mittelalters und der Renaissance*. Potsdam, 1931.

——. "Renaissance." In *Die Musik in Geschichte und Gegenwart*. Vol. 11, pp. 224–80. Kassel, 1963. Translated by M. D. Herter Norton in *Renaissance and Baroque Music*, pp. 3–80. New York, 1967.

Boethius, Anicius Manlius Severinus. *De arithmetica libri ii. De musica libri v. De geometria libri ii*. Basel: H. Petri, 1546.

——. *De institutione arithmetica libri duo. De institutione musica libri quinque. Accedit Geometria*. Edited by Gottfred Friedlein. Leipzig, 1867.

——. *[De institutione musica.]* Translated by Ercole Bottrigari as *I cinque libri di musica*. Bologna, Biblioteca Universitaria, MS lat. 345 (326), dated 1597. Translated by Giorgio Bartoli as *La Musica di Boethio*. Florence, Biblioteca Nazionale Centrale, MS Magliabecchiana XIX.75, dated 17 March 1579.

——. *Opera*. Venice: Giovanni e Gregorio de Gregori, 18 August 1492.

Bottrigari, Ercole. *Il Melone, discorso armonico*. Ferrara: Vittorio Baldini, 1602.

Bouwsma, William J. *The Culture of Renaissance Humanism*. American Historical Association, pamphlet no. 401. The American Historical Association, 1973.

Bower, Calvin. "Boethius and Nicomachus: An Essay Concerning the Sources of *De institutione musica*." *Vivarium* 16 (1978):1–45.

Brichi, Piero. *In Joannis Baptistae Egnatii funere oratio habita MDLIII*. Venice (?), 1553 (?).

Brown, Howard M. *Instrumental Music Printed Before 1600*. Cambridge, Mass., 1965.

——. *Music in the Renaissance*. Englewood Cliffs, 1976.

——. *Sixteenth-Century Instrumentation: The Music for the Florentine Intermedii*. Musicological Studies and Documents 30. American Institute of Musicology, 1973.

——. "Words and Music: Willaert, the Chanson and the Madrigal About 1540." In Villa I Tatti, *Florence and Venice: Comparisons and Relations* 2: Cinquecento. Florence, 1980.

Bryennius, Manuel. *The Harmonics*. Edited with translation, notes, introduction, and index of words by G. H. Jonker. Groningen, 1970. Translated by Antonio de Albertis as *De musica libri tres . . . e graeco in latinum sermonem conversi.* Vienna, Österreichische Nationalbibliothek, MS 10,437. Translated by Giovanni Francesco Burana. Verona, Biblioteca capitolare, MS CCXL (201), fols. 48r–119r.

Burckhardt, Jacob. *Die Kultur der Renaissance in Italien.* Basel, 1860.

Burdach, Konrad. *Von Mittelalter zur Reformation.* 11 vols. Leipzig, 1893–1937.

Burzio, Nicola. *Florum libellus.* Edited by Giuseppe Massera. Florence, 1975.

——. *Musices opusculum.* Bologna: Ugo Ruggeri, 1487.

Butcher, S. H. *Aristotle's Theory of Poetry and Fine Art,* with a critical text and translation of the *Poetics* and a prefatory essay entitled "Aristotelian Literary Criticism" by John Gassner. 4th ed. New York, 1951.

Bylebyl, Jerome J. "Leoniceno." In *Dictionary of Scientific Biography,* edited by Charles C. Gillespie, VIII, 284–50. New York, 1973.

Caccini, Giulio. *Le nuove musiche.* Florence: I Marescotti, 1601. Edited by H. Wiley Hitchcock. Madison, 1970.

Campagnac, E. T., and K. Forbes. *Sadoleto on Education.* London, 1916.

Carapetyan, Armen. "The *Musica Nova* of Adrian Willaert," *Journal of Renaissance and Baroque Music* 1 (1946):200–21.

Cardamone, Donna G. "Gareth." In *New Grove Dictionary of Music and Musicians,* VII, 166.

Caretta, Alessandro, Luigi Cremascoli, and Luigi Salamina. *Franchino Gaffurio.* Lodi, 1951.

Cassiodorus. *Istitutiones humanarum litterarum.* Book 2, chapter 5 translated by Helen Dill Goode and Gertrude C. Drake. Colorado College Music Press Translations, 12. Colorado Springs, 1980.

Caza, Francesco. *Tractato vulgare de canto figurato.* Milan: G. P. de Lomazzo, 5 June 1492.

Cesari, Gaetano. "L'Origini del madrigale cinquecentesco." *Rivista musicale italiana* 19 (1912):1–34, 380–427.

Cesis, F. Calori. *Pico della Mirandola.* Mirandola, 1897.

Chadwick, Henry. *Boethius: The Consolations of Music, Logic, Theology, and Philosophy.* New York, 1981.

Cicero. *De Re Publica.* Translated by Clinton Walker Keyes. Cambrdige, Mass., 1951.

Cleonides. *Harmonicum introductorium.* Translated by Giorgio Valla. Venice: Simon Papiens dictus Bevilaqua, 1497. *See also* Solomon.

Comotti, Giovanni. *La musica nella cultura greca e romana.* Società Italiana di Musicologia, Storia della musica, I, 1. Turin, 1979.

Cosenza, Mario. *Biographical and Bibliographical Dictionary of the Italian Humanists, 1300–1800.* 2d ed. Boston, 1962–67.

Crocker, Richard L. "Pythagorean Mathematics and Music." *The Journal of Aesthetics and Art Criticism* 22 (1963):189–98; 325–35.

D'Accone, Frank. "The Florentine Fra Mauros, A Dynasty of Musical Friars." *Musica Disciplina* 33 (1979):77–137.

Daniels, Arthur Michael. "The *De musica libri vii* of Francisco de Salinas." Ph.D. dissertation, University of Southern California, 1962.

Dante Alighieri. *De vulgari eloquentia*. Edited by Bruno Panvini. Palermo, 1968.

Devreese, Robert. *Le fonds grec de la Bibliothèque vaticane des origines à Paul V*. Vatican City, 1965.

Diller, Aubrey. "Three Scribes Working for Bessarion: Trivizias, Callistus, Hermonymus." *Italia medioevalia e umanistica* 10 (1967):403–06.

Dionisotti, Carlo. "Aldo Manuzio umanista." *Lettere italiane* 12 (1960):375–400.

Donatus, Aelius. *Ars grammatica*. Edited by Henricus Keil in *Grammatici latini*, IV. Leipzig, 1864.

Doni, Giovanni Battista. *Compendio del Trattato de' generi e de' modi della musica*. Rome: Andrea Fei, 1635.

——. *Lyra Barberina*. Edited by Antonio Francesco Gori and Giovanni Battista Passeri. 2 vols. Florence, 1763.

Dostrovsky, Segalia, et al. *Geschichte der Musiktheorie*, VI. Darmstadt, in press.

Drake, Stillman. "Benedetti." In *Dictionary of Scientific Biography*, edited by Charles C. Gillespie, I, 604–09. New York, 1970–80.

Durante, Elio, and Anna Martellotti. *Cronisteria del concerto delle dame principalissime di Margherita Gonzaga d'Este*. Florence, 1979.

Düring, Ingemar, ed. *Die Harmonielehre des Klaudios Ptolemaios*. Göteborgs Högskolas Årsskrift, 36, no. 1. Göteborg, 1930.

——. *Porphyrios Kommentar zur Harmonielehre des Ptolemaios*. Göteborgs Högskolas Årsskrift, 38, no. 2. Göteborg, 1932.

Düring, Ingemar, trans. *Ptolemaios und Porphyrios über die Musik*. Göteborgs Högskolas Årsskrift, 40, no. 1. Göteborg, 1934.

Erasmus of Höritz. *Musica*. Biblioteca Apostolica Vaticana, MS Reginensis lat. 1245.

Euclid. *Praeclarissimus liber elementorum in artem geometrie*. Translated by Giovanni Campano da Novara. Augsburg: Erhard Ratdolt, 1482. Translated by Bartolomeo Zamberti as *Euclides Megarensis philosophi platonici mathematicarum disciplinarum janitoris . . . Elementorum libros xiii cum expositione Theonis*. Venice: Tacuinus, 1505.

Faxolis, Florentius de. *Liber musices*. Milan, Biblioteca Trivulziana, MS 2146.

Fellerer, Karl Gustav. "Zur Erforschung der antiken Musik im 16.–18. Jahrhundert." *Jahrbuch der Musibibliothek Peters für 1935*, 43 (1936):84–95.

Ferguson, W. K. "The Reinterpretation of the Renaissance." In *Facets of the Renaissance*, pp. 1–18. New York, 1959. Reprinted in Ferguson, *Renaissance Studies*, pp. 17–29. New York, 1963.

——. *The Renaissance in Historical Thought, Five Centuries of Interpretation*. Boston, 1948.

Ferrari, Sante. *I tempi, la vita, le dottrine di Pietro d'Abano*. Genoa, 1900.

Ficino, Marsilio. *Opera*. Basel: Officina of Heinrich Petri, 1576. Facsimile edition introduced by Paul Oskar Kristeller and Mario Sancipriano. Turin, 1959.

Fogliano, Lodovico. *Musica theorica*. Venice: G. A. e fratelli de Sabio, 1529. Facsimile edited by Giuseppe Massera. Bologna, 1970.

Forin, Elda Martellozzo, ed. *Acta graduum academicorum ab anno 1501 ad annum 1525*. Padua, 1969.

Fracastoro, Girolamo. *De sympathia et antipathia rerum liber unus*. Venice: Successors of L. Giunta, 1546.

——. *Naugerius, sive De poetica dialogus.* In *Opera omnia,* fols. 153r–64v. Venice: Giunta, 1555.

Gaffurio, Franchino. *Angelicum ac divinum opus musice.* Milan: Gottardo Ponzio, 1508. Facsimile, Bologna, 1971.

——. *Apologia . . . adversus Ioannem Spatarium & complices musicos bononienses.* Turin: Agostino da Vicomercato, 20 April 1520. Facsimile, New York, 1979.

——. *De harmonia musicorum instrumentorum opus.* Milan: Gotardus Pontanus Calcographus, 27 November 1518. Facsimile edited by Giuseppe Vecchi. Bologna, 1972. Translated with an introduction by Clement A. Miller. Musicological Studies and Documents 33. American Institute of Musicology, 1977.

——. *Glossemata quaedam super nonnullas partes theoricae Johannis de Muris.* Milan, Biblioteca Ambrosiana, MS H.165 inf., dated 1 January 1499. Edited by F. Alberto Gallo in "Lo studio della 'musica speculativa' di Johannes de Muris in Polonia e in Italia." *Pagine* 3 (1979):45–58.

——. *Practica musice.* Milan: Guillermus Signerre, 1496. Translated and transcribed by Clement A. Miller. Musicological Studies and Documents 20. American Institute of Musicology, 1968. Translated and edited with musical transcriptions by Irwin Young. Madison, 1969.

——. *Theorica musice.* Milan: Filippo Mantegazza, 1492. Facsimile edited by Gaetano Cesari. Rome, 1934.

——. *Theoricum opus musice discipline.* Naples: Francesco di Dino, 8 October 1480.

——. *Tractatus practicabilium proportionum.* Bologna, Civico Museo Bibliografico Musicale, MS A69.

Galilei, Vincenzo. *Dialogo della musica antica et della moderna.* Florence: G. Marescotti, 1581.

——. *Discorso intorno all'opere di Gioseffo Zarlino da Chioggia.* Florence: G. Marescotti, 1589.

——. *Discorso intorno all'uso dell'enharmonio, et di chi fusse autore del cromatico.* Edited by Frieder Rempp in *Die Kontrapunkttraktate Vincenzo Galileis,* pp. 163–80. Cologne, 1980.

——. *Discorso intorno all'uso delle dissonanze.* Edited by Frieder Rempp in *Die Kontrapunkttraktate Vincenzo Galileis,* pp. 77–161.

——. *Discorso particolare intorno alla diversita delle forme del diapason.* Florence, Biblioteca Nazionale Centrale, MS Galilei 3, fols. 44r–54v.

——. *Discorso particolare intorno all'unisono.* Florence, Biblioteca Nazionale Centrale. MS Galilei 3, fols. 55r–61v.

——. *Dubbi intorno a quanto io ho detto dell'uso dell'enharmonio, con la solutione di essi.* MS Galilei 3, fols. 62r–68r. Edited by Frieder Rempp in *Die Kontrapunkttraktate Vincenzo Galileis,* pp. 181–84.

——. *Fronimo dialogo, nel quale si contengono le vere, et necessarie regole del intavolare la musica nel liuto.* Venice: Girolamo Scotto, 1568.

——. *Il primo libro della prattica del contrapunto intorno all'uso delle consonanze.* Florence, Biblioteca Nazionale Centrale, MS Galilei 1, fols. 148r–96v. Edited by Frieder Rempp in *Die Kontrapunkttraktate Vincenzo Galileis,* pp. 7–76.

Gallico, Claudio. "Una probabile fonte della canzone 'Torela mo vilan'." *Lares* 27 (1961):15–21.

Gallo, F. Alberto. "Le traduzioni dal Greco per Franchino Gaffurio." *Acta Musicologica* 35 (1963):172–74.

——. "Musici scriptores graeci." In *Catalogus translationum et commentariorum: Mediaeval and Renaissance Translations and Commentaries,* edited by F. Edward Cranz and Paul O. Kristeller, III. Washington, 1976.

Gallo, F. Alberto, and G. Mantese. "Nuove notizie sulla famiglia e sull'opera di Nicolo Leoniceno." *Archivio veneto* 72 (1963):5–22.

Garin, Eugenio. *Der italienische Humanismus.* Bern, 1947.

——. *L'Umanesimo italiano: Filosofia e vita civile nel Rinascimento.* Bari, 1952.

Gaspari, Gaetano. *Catalogo della Biblioteca musicale G. B. Martini di Bologna,* I. Bologna, 1890. Reprint. Bologna, 1961.

——. *Musici e musicisti a Bologna, Ricerche, Documenti e Memorie riguardanti la storia dell'arte musicale in Bologna.* Bologna, 1969.

Gaudentius. Translated by Giovanni Battista Augio (?) as *Gaudentij Philosophi Harmonica introductio.* Milan, Bibioteca Ambrosiana, MS P.133 sup., fols. 1r–8r.

Geanakoplos, Deno J. *Interaction of the "Sibling" Byzantine and Western Cultures in the Middle Ages and Italian Renaissance (300–1600).* New Haven, 1976.

Gerbert, Martin, ed. *Scriptores ecclesiastici de musica sacra potissimum.* St. Blasien, 1784. Reprint. Milan, 1931.

Giacomini Tebalducci Malespini, Lorenzo. "De la purgatione de la tragedia. Discorso fatto nel Academia degli Alterati 1587." In *Orationi e Discorsi,* pp. 29–52. Reprinted in *Prose fiorentine raccolte dallo Smarrito [Carlo Dati] accademico della Crusca,* IV, 212–50. Florence, 1729.

——. "Del furor poetico" [1587]. In *Orationi e Discorsi,* pp. 53–73.

——. *Orationi e discorsi.* Florence, 1597.

Glarean, Heinrich. *Dodekachordon.* Basel: Heinrich Petri, September 1547. Translated, transcribed, and edited by Clement A. Miller. Musicological Studies and Documents 6. 2 vols. American Institute of Musicology, 1965.

Gogava, Antonio, trans. *Aristoxeni . . . Harmonicorum elementorum libri iii. . . . Cl. Ptolemaei Harmonicorum . . . lib. iii. Aristoteli de objecto auditus.* Venice: V. Valgrisio, 1562.

Gottschalk, H. B. "The De audibilibus and Peritatetic Acoustics," *Hermes* 96 (1968):435–60.

Guido of Arezzo. *Micrologus.* In *Hucbald, Guido, and John On Music: Three Medieval Treatises.* Translated by Warren Babb, edited, with introductions, by Claude V. Palisca, pp. 47–83. New Haven, 1978.

Haar, James. "The Early Madrigal: A Re-appraisal of its Sources and Character." In *Music in Medieval and Early Modern Europe: Patronage, Sources, and Texts,* edited by Iain Fenlon, pp. 163–92. Cambridge, 1981.

——. "The Frontispiece of Gafori's *Practica musicae* (1496)." *Renaissance Quarterly* 27 (1974):7–22.

——. "*Musica mundana:* Variations on a Pythagorean Theme." Ph.D. dissertation, Harvard University, 1960.

Handschin, Jacques. "Anselmi's Treatise on Music Annotated by Gafori." *Musica Disciplina* 2 (1948):123–41.

——. "Ein mittelalterlichen Beitrag zur Lehre von Sphärenharmonie." *Zeitschrift für Musikwissenschaft* 9 (1927):193–208.

Hanning, Barbara Russano. *Of Poetry and Music's Power: Humanism and the Creation of Opera.* Ann Arbor, 1980.

Harrán, Don. "The Theorist Giovanni del Lago: A New View of the Man and His Writings." *Musica Disciplina* 27 (1973):107–51.

——. "Verse Types in the Early Madrigal." *Journal of the American Musicological Society* 22 (1969):27–53.

——. "Vicentino and His Rules of Text Underlay." *The Musical Quarterly* 59 (1973):620–32.

Hathaway, Baxter. *The Age of Criticism: The Late Renaissance in Italy.* Ithaca, 1962.

Heiberg, Johann Ludwig. "Beiträge zur Geschichte Georg Valla's und seiner Bibliothek." *Zentralblatt für Bibliothekswesen* 16 (1896):353–481.

Heninger, Simeon K., Jr. *Touches of Sweet Harmony: Pythagorean Cosmology and Renaissance Poetics.* San Marino, California, 1974.

Heyden, Sebald. *De arte canendi.* Nuremberg, 1540. Translated by Clement Miller. Musicological Studies and Documents, 26. American Institute of Musicology, 1972.

Hill, John Walter. "Oratory Music in Florence, I: *Recitar Cantando,* 1583–1655." *Acta Musicologica* 51 (1979):108–36.

Hollander, John. *The Untuning of the Sky: Ideas of Music in English Poetry, 1500–1700.* Princeton, 1961.

Hothby, John. *Excitatio quaedam musicae artis per refutationem.* In *Tres tractatuli contra Bartholomeum Ramum.* Edited by Albert Seay. Corpus Scriptorum de Musica, 10. Rome, 1964.

Jan, Karl von. *Musici scriptores graeci.* Leipzig, 1895; Reprint. Hildesheim, 1962.

Jeppesen, Knud. "Eine musiktheoretische Korrespondenz des früheren Cinquecento." *Acta Musicologica* 13 (1941):3–39.

Kämper, Dietrich. *Studien zur instrumentalen Ensemblemusik des 16. Jahrhunderts in Italien.* Rome, 1970. Translated as *La musica strumentale nel Rinascimento.* Rome, 1976.

Kassler, Jamie Croy. "Music as a Model in Early Science." *History of Science* 20 (1982):103–39.

Kibre, Paul. *The Library of Pico della Mirandola.* New York, 1936.

Kinkeldey, Otto. "Franchino Gafori and Marsilio Ficino." *Harvard Library Bulletin* 1 (1947):379–82.

Kirkendale, Warren. "Franceschina, Girometta, and their Companions in a Madrigal à diversi linguaggi' by Luca Marenzio and Orazio Vecchi." *Acta Musicologica* 54 (1972):181–235.

Kristeller, Paul Oskar. *Iter Italicum.* 2 vols. London, 1965–67.

——. "The Modern System of the Arts: A Study in the History of Aesthetics (I)." *Journal of the History of Ideas* 12 (1951):496–527.

——. "Music and Learning in the Early Italian Renaissance." *Journal of Renaissance and Baroque Music* 1 (1947):255–74.

——. *Renaissance Thought.* New York, 1961.

——. *Studies in Renaissance Thought and Letters.* Rome, 1956.

——. *Supplementum Ficinianum.* Florence, 1937.

Labowsky, Lotte. *Bessarion's Library and the Biblioteca Marciana: Six Early Inventories.* Rome, 1979.

Lago, Giovanni del. *Breve introduttione di musica misurata.* Venice: Ottaviano Scotto, 1540. Facsimile. Bologna, 1969.

Lanfranco, Giovanni Maria. *Scintille di musica.* Brescia: Lodovico Britannico, 1533.

Lefèvre d'Étaples, Jacques. *Musica libris demonstrata quattuor.* Paris: Johann Higman and Wolfgang Hopyl, 22 July 1496; Guillaume Cavellat, 1552.

Legrense, Johannes Gallicus. "Ritus canendi vetustissimus et novus." In *Scriptorum de musica medii aevi,* edited by Charles-Edmond-Henri de Coussemaker, IV, 298–421. Paris, 1876. Reprint. Hildesheim, 1963. Edited by Albert Seay. Colorado Springs, 1981.

Le Roux de Lincy. *Recherches sur Jean Grolier, sur la vie, et sur sa bibliothèque.* Paris, 1866.

Levin, Flora Rose. "Nicomachus of Gerasa, *Manual of Harmonics:* Translation and Commentary." Ph.D. dissertation, Columbia University, 1967.

Liddell, H. G., and Robert Scott. *A Greek-English Lexikon.* 9th ed., revised by H. Stuart Jones. Oxford, 1925–40.

Lindley, Mark. "Early 16th-Century Keyboard Temperaments." *Musica Disciplina* 28 (1974):129–51.

——. "Temperaments." In *New Grove Dictionary of Music and Musicians,* XVIII, 660–74.

Lippman, Edward A. *Musical Thought in Ancient Greece.* New York, 1964.

——. "The Place of Music in the System of Liberal Arts." In *Aspects of Medieval and Renaissance Music,* edited by Jan LaRue, pp. 545–59. New York, 1966.

Lockwood, Lewis. "Jean Mouton and Jean Michel: New Evidence on French Music and Musicians in Italy, 1505–1520." *Journal of the American Musicological Society* 32 (1979):191–246.

——. "Pietrobono." In *New Grove Dictionary of Music and Musicians,* XIV, 744.

——. "Willaert." In *New Grove Dictionary of Music and Musicians,* XX, 421.

Lockwood, Lewis, ed., translator. *Palestrina, Pope Marcellus Mass.* New York, 1975.

Lowinsky, Edward E. "Gasparus Stoquerus and Francisco de Salinas." *Journal of the American Musicological Society* 16 (1963):241–43.

——. "Humanism in the Music of the Renaissance." In *Medieval and Renaissance Studies,* edited by Frank Tirro, pp. 87–220. Durham, North Carolina, 1982.

——. "Music in the Culture of the Renaissance." *Journal of the History of Ideas* 15 (1954):509–53.

——. "Music of the Renaissance as Viewed by Renaissance Musicians. " In *The Renaissance Image of Man and the World,* edited by Bernard O'Kelly, pp. 129–77. Columbus, Ohio, 1966.

——. "A Treatise on Text Underlay by a German Disciple of Francisco de Salinas." *Festschrift Heinrich Besseler,* pp. 231–51. Leipzig, 1961.

Lowry, Martin. *The World of Aldus Manutius: Business and Scholarship in Renaissance Venice.* Oxford, 1979.

Mace, Dean T. "Humanism and Music: Remarks." In *International Musicological Society, Report of the Twelfth Congress, Berkeley 1977*, edited by Daniel Heartz and Bonnie Wade, pp. 892–93. Kassel, 1981.

———. "Pietro Bembo and the Literary Origins of the Italian Madrigal." *The Musical Quarterly* 55 (1969):65–86.

Macrobius. *Commentary on the Dream of Scipio*. Translated by William H. Stahl. 2 vols. New York, 1952.

Maggi, Vincenzo, and Bartolomeo Lombardi. *In Aristotelis Librum de poetica communes explanationes*. Venice: Vincenzo Valgrisio, 1550.

Maniates, Maria Rika. *Mannerism in Italian Music and Culture, 1530–1630*. Chapel Hill, 1979.

Manni, Domenico M. *Memorie della fiorentina famosa accademia degli Alterati*. Florence, 1748.

Manuzio, Aldo. *De quesitis per epistolam*. Venice, 1576.

Marenghi, Gerardo. "Un capitolo dell'Aristotele medievale: Bartolomeo da Messina traduttore dei *Problemata physica*." *Aevum: Rassegna di scienze storiche, linguistiche, filologiche* 35 (1962):268–83.

Marinis, Tammaro de. *La biblioteca napoletana dei re d'Aragona*. Milan, 1947–52.

Massera, Giuseppe. *Severino Boezio e la scienza armonica tra l'antichità e il medio evo*. Parma, 1976.

Mathiesen, Thomas J. "Humanism and Music: Response." In *International Musicological Society, Report of the Twelfth Congress, Berkeley, 1977*, edited by Daniel Heartz and Bonnie Wade, pp. 879–80. Kassel, 1981.

———. "Problems of Terminology in Ancient Greek Theory: 'ΑΡΜΟΝΙΑ.'" In *Festival Essays for Pauline Alderman: A Musicological Tribute*, edited by Burton L. Kanon, pp. 3–17. Provo, Utah, 1976.

Mauro, Fra, da Firenze. *Utriusque musices epitome (Dell'una et l'altra musica)*. Edited by Frank A. D'Accone. Corpus Scriptorum de Musica, 32. American Institute of Musicology, 1984.

Mei, Girolamo. *De modis musicis antiquorum*. Biblioteca Apostolica Vaticana, MS Vat. lat. 5323.

———. [Della compositura delle parole]. Florence, Biblioteca Nazionale Centrale, MS Magliabecchiana VI.34.

———. [Trattato del verso toscano]. Florence, Biblioteca Riccardiana, MS 2597.

———. [Trattato di musica]. Paris, Bibliothèque Nationale, MS lat. 7209/2.

Meibom, Marcus. *Antiquae musicae auctores septem*. Amsterdam, 1652.

Meier, Helga. *Fünf Madrigale venezianischer Komponisten um Adrian Willaert*. Das Chorwerk, 105. Wolfenbüttel, 1969.

Menni, Vincenzo. *Regole della thoscana lingua*. Perugia, 1568.

Mersenne, Marin. *Harmonicorum libri*. Paris: Guillaume de Baudry, 1635.

Meurs, Johann von. *Aristoxenus, Nicomachus, Alypius, auctores musices antiquissimi, hactenus non editi*. Leiden: L. Elzevir, 1616. Edited by J. Lamius in Meursius, *Opera omnia*. Florence, 1741–63.

Meyer-Baer, Kathi. *Music of the Spheres and the Dance of Death*. Princeton, 1970.

Michaelides, Solon. *The Music of Ancient Greece, An Encyclopaedia*. London, 1978.

Michelet, Jules. *Histoire de France.* Paris, 1855.

Miller, Clement A. "Gaffurio's *Practica musicae:* Origin and Contents." *Musica Disciplina* 22 (1968):105–28.

Mittarelli, Giovanni Benedetto. *Bibliotheca codicum manuscriptorum Monasterii S. Michaelis Venetiarum prope Murianum.* Venice, 1779.

Monro, D. B. *The Modes of Ancient Greek Music.* Oxford, 1894.

Monteverdi, Giulio Cesare. "Dichiaratione della Lettera Stampata nel Quinto Libro de suoi Madrigali (1607)." In *Claudio Monteverdi,* edited by G. Francesco Malipiero, pp. 72–85. Milan, 1929. Translated by Oliver Strunk, in *Source Readings in Music History,* pp. 405–15.

Motta, Emilio. "I libri della Chiesa dell'Incoronata di Lodi nel 1518." *Il libro e la stampa* 1 (1907):105–12.

Müller, Karl. *Fragmenta historicorum graecorum,* II. Paris, 1848.

Müntz, Eugène, and Paul Fabre. *La bibliothèque du Vaticane au xve siècle.* Paris, 1887. Reprint. Amsterdam, 1970.

Musica et scolica enchiriadis, una cum aliquibus tractatulis tradiunctis recensio nova post Gerbertinam altera ad finem omnium codicum manuscriptorum. Edited by Hans Schmid. Bayerische Akademie der Wissenschaften: Veröffentlichen der musikhistorischen Kommission, 3. Munich: Verlag der Bayerischen Akademie der Wissenschaften, 1981.

Narcini, Deborah. "Pietro d'Abano's *Expositio problematum Aristotelis,* Book 19." Paper read at Yale Renaissance Studies Seminar, 1978.

Nares, R. *A Catalogue of the Harleian MSS in the British Museum.* London, 1808.

New Grove Dictionary of Music and Musicians. Edited by Stanley Sadie. 20 vols. London, 1980.

Newcomb, Anthony. "Editions of Willaert's *Musica Nova:* New Evidence, New Speculations," *Journal of the American Musicological Society* 26 (1973):132–45.

———. *The Madrigal at Ferrara, 1579–1597.* Princeton, 1980.

Nicomachus. *Introduction to Arithmetic.* Translated by Martin Luther D'Onge. New York, 1926.

Nolhac, Pierre de. *La bibliothèque de Fulvio Orsini.* Paris, 1887.

Omont, Charles. "Inventaire des manuscrits grecs et latins donnés à Saint-Marc de Venise par le cardinal Bessarion (1468)." *Revue des bibliothèques* 4 (1896):129–187.

Osthoff, Wolfgang. *Theatergesang und darstellende Musik in der italienischen Renaissance.* Tutzing, 1969.

Ott, Johannes. *Missae tredecim.* Nuremberg, 1539.

Palisca, Claude V. "The Alterati of Florence, Pioneers in the Theory of Dramatic Music." In *New Looks at Italian Opera, Essays in Honor of Donald G. Grout,* edited by William Austin, pp. 9–38. Ithaca, 1968.

———. "The 'Camerata Fiorentina': A Reappraisal." *Studi musicali* 1 (1972):203–36.

———. *Girolamo Mei: Letters on Ancient and Modern Music to Vincenzo Galilei and Giovanni Bardi.* Musicological Studies and Documents, 3. American Institute of Musicology, 1960; 2d ed. 1977.

———. "The *Musica* of Erasmus of Höritz." In *Aspects of Medieval and Renaissance Music,* edited by Jan LaRue, pp. 628–48. New York, 1966.

——. "The Musical Humanism of Giovanni Bardi." In *Poesia e musica nell'estetica del xvi e xvii secolo,* edited by Hagop Meyvalian, pp. 45–72. Florence, 1979.

——. "Peri and the Theory of Recitative." *Studies in Music* 15 (1981):51–61.

——. "Scientific Empiricism in Musical Thought." In *Seventeenth Century Science and the Arts,* edited by H. H. Rhys, pp. 91–137. Princeton, 1961.

——. "Theory, theorists." In *New Grove Dictionary of Music and Musicians,* XVIII, 741–62.

——. "Vincenzo Galilei and Some Links between 'Pseudo-Monody' and Monody." *The Musical Quarterly* 46 (1960):344–60.

Panzer, Georg W. F. *Annales typographici ab artis inventae origine ad annum MD.* Nuremberg, 1793–97.

Patrizi, Francesco. *L'amorosa filosofia.* Edited by J. C. Nelson. Florence, 1979.

——. *La città felice.* Venice, 1553.

——. *Della poetica.* Ferrara: V. Baldini, 1586. Edited by Danielo Aguzzi Barbagli. 3 vols. Florence, 1969–71.

Peri, Jacopo. *Le musiche sopra l'Euridice.* Florence: Giorgio Marescotti, 1601. Facsimile edited by Giuseppe Vecchi. Bologna, 1969. Edited by Howard M. Brown as *Euridice, An Opera in One Act, Five Scenes.* Recent Researches in the Music of the Baroque Era, 36 and 37. Madison, 1981.

Pietzsch, Gerhard. *Die Klassifikation der Musik von Boetius bis Ugolino von Orvieto.* Halle, 1929.

Pintacuda, Mario. *La musica nella tragedia greca.* Cefalù, 1978.

Pirrotta, Nino. "Music and Cultural Tendencies in 15th-Century Italy." *Journal of the American Musicological Society* 19 (1966):127–61.

——. "Novelty and Renewal in Italy: 1300–1600." In *Studien zur Tradition in der Musik,* edited by H. H. Eggebrecht and Max Lütolf, pp. 49–63. Munich, 1973.

Pirrotta, Nino and Elena Povoledo. *Li due Orfei, da Poliziano a Monteverdi.* Rome, 1969. Translated by Karen Eales as *Music and Theatre from Poliziano to Monteverdi.* Cambridge, 1982.

Pizzani, Ubaldo. "Studi sulle fonti del 'De Institutione Musica' di Boezio." *Sacris eruditi* 16 (1965):5–164.

Plato. *The Epinomis.* Translated by J. Harward. Oxford, 1928. *Epinomis Commentariis illustrata.* Edited by Franciscus Novotny. Prague, 1960.

——. *Opera latina.* Translated by Marsilio Ficino. Venice: Bernardinus de Choris de Cremona and Simon de Luere for Andrea Torresano d'Asola, 13 August 1491.

Plutarch. *De anima procreatione in Timeo.* Translated by Harold Cherniss in *Plutarch's Moralia in Seventeen Volumes,* XIII, 1, pp. 132–345. Cambridge, Mass., 1976.

——. *De musica.* Edited and translated by Benedict Einarson and Phillip H. De Lacy in *Plutarch's Moralia in Fifteen Volumes,* XIV, 344–468. Cambridge, Mass., 1967. Edited by François Lasserre in *Plutarque, De la musique.* Olten, 1954. *See also* Valgulio, *Prooemium.*

Pöhlmann, Egert. "Antikenverständnis und Antikenmissverständnis in der Operntheorie der Florentiner Camerata." *Die Musikforschung* 22 (1969):5–13.

——. *Denkmäler altgriechischer Musik.* Nuremberg, 1970.

Powers, Harold. "Mode." In *New Grove Dictionary of Music and Musicians,* XII, 397.

Psellus, Michael. *Opus dilucidum in quatuor mathematicas disciplinas*. Venice: S. Sabio, 1532.

Ptolemy, Claudius. *[Harmonics]*. Translated by Nicolò Leoniceno. Biblioteca Apostolica Vaticana, MS Vat. lat. 4570; MS Vat. lat. 3744, fols. 1–64; London, British Library, MS Harl. 3306, fols. 1–46. Edited and translated by John Wallis as *Harmonicorum libri tres*. Oxford, 1682. See also Düring.

Puntoni, V. "Indice dei codici greci della Biblioteca Estense di Modena." *Studi italiani di filologia classica* 4 (1896):379–536.

Ramos de Pareja, Bartolomé. *Musica practica*. Bologna: Baltasar de Hiriberia, 11 May 1482. Edited by Johannes Wolf. Publikationen der internationalen Musikgesellschaft, 2. Leipzig, 1901.

Reese, Gustave. *Music in the Renaissance*. New York, 1954.

Reiss, Josef. "Jo. Bapt. Benedictus, *De intervallis musicis*." *Zeitschrift für Musikwissenschaft* 7 (1924–25):13–20.

Rempp, Frieder. *Die Kontrapunkttraktate Vincenzo Galileis*. Cologne, 1980.

Reynolds, L. D., and N. G. Wilson. *Scribes & Scholars, A Guide to the Transmission of Greek and Latin Literature*. 2d. ed. London, 1974.

Richter, Lukas. "Antike Überlieferungen in der byzantinischen Musiktheorie." *Deutsches Jahrbuch der Musikwissenschaft für 1961* 6 (1962):75–115.

———. "Instrumentalbegleitung zur attischen Tragödie," *Das Altertum* 24 (1978):150–59.

———. "Musikalische Aspekte der attischen Tragödienchöre." *Beiträge zur Musikwissenschaft* 14 (1972):247–98.

Ridolfi, Roberto. "La biblioteca del cardinale Nicolo Ridolfi." *La Bibliofilia* 31 (1929):173–93.

Riemann, Hugo. *Das Zeitalter der Renaissance (bis 1600)*. Handbuch der Musikgeschichte, II, 1. Leipzig, 1907.

Rose, Paul Lawrence. *The Italian Renaissance of Mathematics*. Geneva, 1975.

Ross, James B. "Venetian Schools and Teachers Fourteenth to Early Sixteenth Century: A Survey and a Study of Giovanni Battista Egnazio." *Renaissance Quarterly* 29 (1976):521–66.

Rossi, Bastiano de'. *Descrizione dell'apparato e degl'Intermedi fatti per la commedia rappresentata in Firenze nelle nozze de' serenissimi Don Ferdinando Medici e Madama Cristina di Loreno, Gran Duchi di Toscana*. Florence: Anton Padouani, 1589.

Rossi, Nicolò. *Discorsi intorno alla tragedia*. Vicenza: Giorgio Greco, 1590.

Rubsamen, Walter H. *Literary Sources of Secular Music in Italy (ca. 1500)*. Berkeley, 1943. Reprint. New York, 1972.

Ruelle, Charles-Émile, translator. *Alypius et Gaudence, Bacchius l'ancien*. Paris, 1895.

Rutherford, William G., ed. *Scholia Aristophanica*. London, 1896–1905.

Sabatier, Paul. *La vie de Saint François d'Assise*. Paris, 1893.

Sabbadini, Remigio. *Le scoperte dei codici latini e greci ne' secoli xiv e xv*. 2 vols. Florence, 1905–14.

Sachs, Klaus-Jürgen. "Counterpoint." In *New Grove Dictionary of Music and Musicians*, IV, 833–45.

———. *Der Contrapunctus im 14. und 15. Jahrhundert: Untersuchungen zum Terminus, zur Lehre und zu den Quellen*. Wiesbaden, 1974.

Sadoleto, Jacopo. *De pueris recte instituendis.* Venice: Ioannes et fratres de Sabio, 1533; Basel: Thomas Platter, 1538.

Saitta, Giuseppe. *Il pensiero italiano nell'umanesimo e nel rinascimento.* 2 vols. Bologna, 1949.

Salinas, Francisco de. *De musica libri septem.* Salamanca, 1577. Edited by Macario Santiago Kastner. Kassel, 1958.

Salutati, Coluccio. *De laboribus Herculis.* Edited by Berthold L. Ullman. Zurich, 1951.

Scaliger, Julius Caesar. *Poetices libri septem.* Leiden: Antonius Vincentius, 1561.

Schmid, Hans, ed. *Musica et Scolica enchiriadis.* Munich, 1983.

Schrade, Leo. "Renaissance: the Historical Conception of an Epoch." In *Kongress-Bericht der Internationale Gesellschaft für Musikwissenschaft, Utrecht 1952,* pp. 19–32. Amsterdam, 1953.

———. *Tragedy in the Art of Music.* Cambridge, Mass., 1964.

Schreiber, Heinrich (Henricus Grammateus). *Ayn new kunstlich Buech.* Nuremberg: Stüchs, 1518.

Seay, Albert. "The 'Liber Musices' of Florentius de Faxolis." In *Musik und Geschichte—Music and History, Leo Schrade zum sechszigsten Geburtstag,* pp. 71–95. Cologne, 1963.

———. "Ugolino of Orvieto." In *New Grove Dictionary of Music and Musicians,* XIX, 320.

Seligsohn, Rudolph. *Die Übersetzung der ps.-aristotelischen Problemata durch Bartholomaeus von Messina, Text und Textkritik.* Berlin, 1934.

Sesini, Ugo. "Studi sull'umanesimo musicale: Ercole Bottrigari." *Convivium, Rivista di lettere, filosofia e storia* 13 (1941):1–25.

Solerti, Angelo. *Gli Albori del melodramma.* Milan, 1904. Reprint. Hildesheim, 1969.

———. *Le Origini del melodramma.* Turin, 1903.

Solomon, Jon D. "Cleonides *Eisagoge harmonike:* A Critical Edition, Translation, and Commentary." Ph.D. dissertation, University of North Carolina, 1980.

———. "Vaticanus gr. 2338 and the Eisagoge Harmonike." *Philologus* 127 (1983):247–53.

Spataro, Giovanni. *Errori de Franchino Gafurio da Lodi.* Bologna: Benedetto di Ettore Faelli, 12 January 1521.

Stabile. Giorgio. "Burana." In *Dizionario biografico degli Italiani,* IV, 386–89.

Stahl, William H. *Martianus Capella and the Seven Liberal Arts.* 2 vols. New York, 1971.

Strunk, Oliver. *Source Readings in Music History.* New York, 1950.

Surian, Elvidio. "Bologna." In *New Grove Dictionary of Music and Musicians,* III, 1–9.

Tateo, Francesco. *I centri culturali dell'umanesimo.* Bari, 1971.

Themistius. [*Paraphrases* on the *De anima* of Aristotle]. Translated by William of Moerbeke, edited by G. Verbeke as *Commentaire sur le Traité de l'âme d'Aristote.* Corpus latinum commentariorum in Aristotelem graecorum, 1. Louvain, 1957. Translated by Ermolao Barbaro as *Paraphraseos de anima libri tres.* Paris: P. Calvarin, 1535. Edited by Richard Heinze. Berlin, 1899. Translated by Ermolao Barbaro as *Paraphrasis in Aristotelem.* Treviso: Bartolomeo Confaloneri and Morello Gerardino, 15 February 1481. Translated by Ermolao Barbaro as *Paraphrasis in Aristotelis posteriore, & physica. In libro item de anima.* . . . Venice: Girolamo Scotto, 1554.

Thode, Henry. *Franz von Assisi und die Kunst der Renaissance.* Berlin, 1885.

Thomas Aquinas. *In Aristotelis libros de caelo et mundo . . . expositio.* Edited by Raymundus M. Spiazzi. Turin, 1952.

Thorndike, Lynn. *A History of Magic and Experimental Science.* New York, 1923–58.

———. "Peter of Abano: A Medieval Scientist." *Annual Report of the American Historical Association, Year 1919,* 1:315–26.

———. "Peter of Abano and Another Commentary on the Problems of Aristotle." *Bulletin of the History of Medicine* 29 (1955):517–23.

Tiby, Ottavio. *La Musica in Grecia e a Roma.* Florence, 1942.

Tinctoris, Johannes. *Liber de arte contrapuncti.* In *Opera theoretica,* edited by Albert Seay, II, 11–157. Corpus Scriptorum de Musica, 22. American Institute of Musicology, 1975. Translated by Albert Seay as *The Art of Counterpoint.* Musicological Studies and Documents, 5. American Institute of Musicology, 1961.

———. *Complexus effectuum musices.* In *Opera theoretica,* edited by Albert Seay, II, 159–77. Corpus Scriptorum de Musica, 22. American Institute of Musicology, 1975.

———. *De inventione et usu musicae.* Edited by Karl Weinmann in *Johannes Tinctoris und sein unbekannter Traktat "De inventione et usu musicae."* Tutzing, 1961.

———. *Terminorum musicae diffinitorium.* Edited by Armand Machabey. Paris, 1951.

Tiraboschi, Girolamo. *Biblioteca modenese.* Modena, 1781–86.

Torrefranca, Fausto. *Il segreto del quattrocento.* Milan, 1939.

Toscanella, Orazio. *Precetti necessarii, et altre cose utilissime.* Venice: Avanzo, 1562.

Traversari, Ambrogio. *Epistolae et orationes.* Edited by Lorenz Mehus. Florence, 1759.

———. *Hodoeporicon.* Edited by Alessandro Dini-Traversari in *Ambrogio Traversari e i suoi tempi.* Florence, 1912.

Trissino, Giovanni Giorgio. *La Poetica.* Parts I to IV: Vicenza: T. Ianiculo, 1529; parts V and VI: Venice: Andrea Arrivabene, 1562.

Troeltsch, Ernst. "Renaissance und Reformation." *Historische Zeitschrift* 90 (1913):519–56.

Tuksar, Stanislav. *The Croatian Renaissance Theorists.* Zagreb, 1980.

Ugolino of Orvieto. *Declaratio musicae disciplinae.* Edited by Albert Seay. Corpus Scriptorum de Musica, 7. Rome, 1959.

Ullman, Berthold L., and Philip A. Stadter. *The Public Library of Renaissance Florence: Niccolo Niccoli, Cosimo de' Medici, and the Library of San Marco.* Padua, 1972.

Unterkircher, Franz. "Eine Handschrift aus dem Besitze Jean Groliers in der Oesterreichischen Nationalbibliothek." *Libri* 1 (1950–51):51–57.

Valgulio, Carlo. *Libellus, quo demonstratur Statutum Brixianorum de sumptibus funerum . . . eiusdem contra vituperatorem Musicae.* Brescia: Giovanni Antonio de Gandino detto de Caeguli, 1509.

———. *Prooemium in musicam Plutarchi ad Titum Pyrrhinum.* [Includes translation of

Plutarch *De musica.*] Brescia: Giovanni Antonio de Gandino detto de Caeguli, 1507. Also in *Plutarchi Chaeronei . . . Opuscula (quae quidem extant) omnia.* Basel: Officina Andreas Cratandri, September 1530. Leiden: S. Gryphius, 1549. Anonymous Italian translation of *Prooemium* in Biblioteca Apostolica Vaticana, MS Vat. lat. 5385, fols. 50–56. Anonymous Italian translation of *Proeemium* and Valgulio-Plutarch in Florence, Biblioteca Nazionale Centrale, MS Galilei 7.

———. *Cleomedis de contemplatione orbium excelsorum disputatio.* Brescia: Angelo Britannico, 1497.

Valla, Giorgio. *De expetendis et fugiendis rebus opus.* Venice: Aldo Romano, 1501.

Varchi, Benedetto. *L'Hercolano Dialogo . . . nel qual si ragiona generalmente delle lingue, & in particolare della Toscana e della Fiorentina.* Florence: Giunti, 1570.

———. *Lezzioni della poetica.* Florence: Giunti, 1590.

Vecchi, Giuseppe. "Medicina e Musica, Voci e Strumenti nel 'Conciliator' (1303) da Pietro d'Abano." *Quadrivium* 8 (1967):5–22.

Vettori, Piero. *Commentarii in primum librum Aristotelis de arte poetarum.* Florence: Successors of Bernardo Giunti, 1573.

Vicentino, Nicola. *L'Antica musica ridotta alla moderna prattica.* Rome: A. Barre, 1555. Facsimile edited by Edward E. Lowinsky. Kassel, 1959.

Vitaliani, Domenico. *Della vita e delle opere di Nicolò Leoniceno Vicentino.* Verona, 1892.

Voigt, Georg. *Die Wiederbelegung des classischen Alterthums.* Berlin, 1893.

Waeltner, Ernst L., ed. *Die Lehre vom Organum bis zur Mitte des 11. Jahrhunderts.* Tutzing, 1975.

Walker, D. P. "Ficino's Spiritus and Music." *Annales musicologiques* 1 (1953):131–50.

———. "Musical Humanism in the 16th and Early 17th Centuries." *The Music Review* 2 (1941):1–13, 111–21, 220–27, 288–308; 3 (1942):55–71. *Der musikalische Humanismus.* Kassel, 1949.

———. *Musique des intermèdes de "La Pellegrina."* Paris, 1963.

———. *Spiritual and Demonic Magic from Ficino to Campanella.* London, 1958.

———. *Studies in Musical Science in the Late Renaissance.* London, 1978.

Weinberg, Bernard. *A History of Literary Criticism in the Italian Renaissance.* Chicago, 1961.

———. "Nuove attribuzioni di manoscritti di critica letteraria del cinquecento." *Rinascimento* 3 (1952):245–59.

Weinberg, Bernard, ed. *Trattati di poetica e retorica del cinquecento.* 4 vols. Bari, 1970–74.

Wille, Günter. *Musica romana: die Bedeutung der Musik im Leben der Romer.* Amsterdam, 1967.

Zarlino, Gioseffo. *Dimostrationi harmoniche.* Venice: Francesco dei Franceschi Senese, 1571. Reprint. Ridgewood, New Jersey, 1966.

———. *Le Istitutioni harmoniche.* Venice, 1558. Reprint. New York, 1965. Part III translated by Guy A. Marco and Claude V. Palisca as *The Art of Counterpoint.* New Haven, 1968; New York, 1976, 1983. Part IV translated by Vered Cohen as *On the Modes.* Edited, with an introduction, by Claude V. Palisca. New Haven, 1983.

——. *Sopplimenti musicali*. Venice: Francesco de' Franceschi Sanese, 1588. Reprint. Ridgewood, New Jersey, 1966.

Ziino, Agostino. "Pietro della Valle e la 'Musica erudita,' nuovi documenti." *Analecta musicologica* 4 (1967):97–111.

Index